Environmental, Social and Governance (ESG) Laws, Regulations and Practices in the Digital Era

Environmental, Social and Governance (ESG) Laws, Regulations and Practices in the Digital Era

Peter Yeoh

Wolters Kluwer

Published by:
Kluwer Law International B.V.
PO Box 316
2400 AH Alphen aan den Rijn
The Netherlands
E-mail: international-sales@wolterskluwer.com
Website: www.wolterskluwer.com/en/solutions/kluwerlawinternational

Sold and distributed by:
Wolters Kluwer Legal & Regulatory U.S.
7201 McKinney Circle
Frederick, MD 21704
United States of America
E-mail: customer.service@wolterskluwer.com

ISBN 978-94-035-4175-4

e-Book: ISBN 978-94-035-4180-8
web-PDF: ISBN 978-94-035-4181-5

About the Author

Peter Yeoh has been involved with the School of Law, Social Sciences and Communications, University of Wolverhampton, UK, as Researcher and Lecturer in Corporate and Financial Services Law for more than a decade. He teaches at the undergraduate and postgraduate levels. He has published more than fifty UK-/US-based peer-review journal papers in corporate and financial services law, including four book chapters, and various books pertaining to emerging technology governance and regulations, as well as presenting more than twenty peer-review conference papers in the UK and other EU Member States. He is a regular paper reviewer of various law journals, and also a contributing associate editor in corporate governance (CG) of a UK-based business law journal. He worked previously at senior levels in the business world for more than two decades. He has multiple degrees in Economics, Marketing, Management and Law; a Master's in Business Administration (MBA) and Financial Services Law (L.L.M.); a PG teaching certificate; and a Doctorate (Ph.D.) in Financial Services Law. He currently mentors tech start ups, and social entrepreneurship ventures. He has also been an Honorary Research Fellow at the University of Wolverhampton.

Table of Contents

Preface

Attention on modern CG practices has grown considerably since the 1970s largely because of scandalous failures of various large corporations across the world, but more notably in the United States (US), United Kingdom (UK), the European Union (EU), and also in Asia, the home of many newly emerging regional multinationals (MNCs). Corporations have been the most popular entity of choice because of its limited liability provisions. The notion and practice of the separation of ownership and management are the essential hallmarks of corporations, as they grew bigger and bigger to be mega multinationals. The CG phenomenon gravitated toward big corporations in the capital and financial markets across the world, as small and medium enterprises (SMEs) tend to operate in more different forms, from sole proprietorships to partnerships because of costs and other considerations. Although of late, SMEs have been gaining more attention from policymakers because of their employment effects and other contributions, media offline and online coverage still primarily focused on the big corporations. However, increasing attention is now given also to emerging tech start-ups because of their big potentials for transformation into big corporations as they scale their business across borders, as demonstrated in several notable examples of tech unicorns in both advanced and developing economies.

Considerations for SMEs have upped the status of the "S" element in Environmental, Social and Governance (ESG), and rightly so for social inclusion enthusiasts. Conversely, harmful impacts on the environment such as generated by multinationals in oil and resource extraction businesses across the world have upped the "E" element in ESG. Before the current ESG surge, and before the imposing of nonfinancial ESG reporting obligations for listed companies in the major bourses of the world, these were part of the traditional CG reporting practices. To avoid ambiguity and confusion, this book would treat the CG lexicon as the equivalent of the present ESG lexicon. After all, CG hitherto included environmental ("E") and social ("S") issues too, but though not with the degree of focus that ESG now enjoys since it was introduced to the world in 2015 through the UN Principles of Responsible Investments (PRIs). Traditional CG practices and reporting have included environmental and social matters when companies choose to engage and report on corporate social responsibility (CSR) activities, while those companies cheered for engaging with such activities have been identified in designated indices, like the FTSE4Good back then in 2001. The acceleration and more concentrated attention given to ESG practices and disclosures are for the most part driven by the COVID-19 pandemic. This high-profiles diversity and worksite health safety considerations, and the phenomenal impacts of climate change that destroyed massively properties and many innocent lives.

Inevitably, when big numbers of companies make fatal mistakes resulting from reckless corporate actions, they attract both attention and public condemnation, and ergo, upping the "G" element in the ESG paradigm. The contagion impact they heaved on national economies gets quickly radiated across national borders, more often leading to serious financial crisis. Even when not of this serious scale, distortions or malignments of corporate activities could still hemorrhage hitherto healthy businesses and industries. This helps to explain why rules and regulations continue to evolve to keep down the levels or numbers of corporate miscreants. A lot has been researched and written upon on this corporate theme, including a lot on guidance and advice for those corporate captains and boards seeking insights on how best to avoid these kinds of harmful corporate mishaps.

Yet, despite the outpourings of many helpful insights from theories to practices from across the world, but more so from Western economies, continuous lessons are being sought for more effective antidotes to deal with these sorts of issues. Effective solutions have not been that easy to design, as shown by the continuous evolutions of rules, regulations and more reforms, but this does not necessarily imply that these have all been wasteful. Though not perfect, these reforms and rebooted advice have their usefulness, limited though they could have been in some persistent areas. The quests for answers therefore soldier on.

Corporate reckless actions or misdirection has been, still are, and would continue to be human-directed activities. As such, they would be subjected to human foibles and failings, but these days, also subjected to waves of political and technological transformations, changes in the capital and financial markets, and systemic events flowing from excessive financialization, as exemplified in the 2007-2009 global financial crisis (GFC), and in the ongoing COVID-19 pandemic, where many businesses have been destroyed by massive market evaporation impacts, and where issues like health and safety in work environments together with diversity and inclusion issues loom large. Getting more serious and more attention from policymakers along with the business community is the ravaging impacts of climate change on the environment and vast disruptions to the business landscape. These have taken stakeholder capitalism (SC) operationalized as ESG to new levels across major economies of the world, including leadership roles for the US, EU and the UK. Discussions on CG going forward without taking into account the ESG approach would therefore be incomplete, even though the "G" element in the tripartite ESG framework is for many still relatively more important.

Human behaviors have been, still are, and would continue to be almost impossible puzzles to solve. What could be better achieved would be to prioritize and resolving on those challenges, such as ESG in the digital era, that are likely to matter over the next decade. This book is written for this mission. It would not dare to pretend to offer all the answers against corporate shortfalls and misdeeds. Instead, it focuses on those ESG challenges that would impact businesses in the coming years, more so in the US, EU, and the UK. These respective economies taken together are likely to continue exerting dominating influence across the world.

This book would therefore engage with unresolved CG issues dragged out by the current COVID-19 pandemic, as well as various other envisaged corporate challenges, when more and more businesses are digitalized. It prioritizes discussions on ESG laws, regulations, and practices in the US, EU, and the UK, with material relevant comments of other major economies elsewhere. ESG practices, and in particular ESG strategies, are given some attention because of their growing importance.

Acknowledgments

ESG treated in general as the equivalent of the conventional CG lexicon is generally viewed in the legal community as their turf, while the business community equally thinks the same. Both could be equally right in the sense that the phenomenon is usually taught and researched in law and business schools; and, equally not so right in the sense that other disciplines from politics, sociology, culture, and economics do give some attention too to the subject matter as CG practices impact the lives and livelihoods of most institutions and individuals.

Given early appreciation of this, I had for the most part of my working life, from business to academia tried to gather insights from all these major disciplines, as well as from corporate managers, corporate boards, policymakers, and various financial gatekeepers that devote some attention to ESG. I believe I learn and continue to learn various aspects of the ESG process from these various distinguished parties, apart from my own research initiatives. I hope to have absorbed the right messages and signals about the benefits of good ESG practices that I now wish to share with others across the world. Of course, I would also draw attention to the consequences of bad ESG practices that had degenerated into seminal corporate scandals that bothered policymakers and regulators considerably. Of late too, the hitherto conventional CG law and practices seemed to be tilting toward SC and operationalized as Environment, Social and Governance (ESG), especially since the onset of the COVID-19 pandemic, and dramatic effects of climate change on the planet. Various business acquaintances and colleagues have advised me that this would be the likely trend for CG practices going forward, with balanced considerations of the environment (E) and the social (S) elements, rather than as secondary to the governance or "G" element, and that I should dedicate some good attention to this and the digital economy context. I thank all those giving me guidance and direction when writing this book.

Finally, I like to thank all my immediate family members for providing me with various support. Without their care and attention, I might not be able to complete the book in good time. I also thank members of the academic community in the UK, the EU,

US, Australia, and elsewhere for discussing various ESG issues with me over the years. Their participation in these helped to shape my thinking on ESG matters from time to time, and from a global perspective. I thank them all for their kindness and generosity.

Peter Yeoh
October 2021.

CHAPTER 1
Overview

As the world enters the Industrial Revolution, the modern corporation has already come into play through the Joint Stock Companies Act 1844 as a response to the hugely difficult days of the South Sea Bubble. The statute provides at the time all the basic essentials to keep businesses away from unsavory practices. This paved the administrative way for corporations to have a separate legal unified entity, from which the rights and duties of all investors and managers could be directed. This was further ensured by the Limited Liability Act of 1855 that limited investors' liabilities to the size of their investments in the corporation, irrespective of the corporations' fates. The uncomplicated registration procedures and limited liability of investors eventually codified in the Joint Stock Companies Act 1856 maintained these fundamental characteristics through to the present-day corporate legislation, namely, the Companies Act 2006 (CA 2006) in the UK.[1]

Over in the US, most US corporations choose to incorporate their presence in Delaware. This US state provides a modern and nationally recognized corporation statute and well-developed case laws that facilitated business planning. These have been strengthened by the highly respected Court of Chancery that has been more than capable of dealing with company law issues as they arise, an efficient user-friendly Secretary of States' Office, and a legislature that prioritizes on company law issues so as to keep Delaware's business laws contemporary.[2] Presently, especially in the US and the UK, SC operationalized as ESG sparked fresh debates in the legislatures and in the corporate corridors as the rebooted approach for CG practices going forward. This book will begin with a brief historical sketch on the evolution of corporate governance (CG) in the US and the UK leading toward ESG in the digital era. The ESG principles and practices in both these jurisdictions are followed widely across the world, especially in the new settings. Their dominance in this area could be attributed to the overwhelming size and stretch of their capital markets, as well as the global influence of their banking and financial systems, inclusive of the use of Fourth Industrial Revolution (FIR) enabling technologies. Some good attention is given to ESG laws and practices in the EU too, as EU is seen to be relatively quicker in the framing of ESG policies and

1. R. Tomasic. 2013. "Company law modernisation and corporate governance in the United Kingdom". *Victoria University Law and Justice Journal*, Vol. 1 (1): 43-61.
2. L.S. Black. 2007. *Why corporations choose Delaware*. Dover: Delaware.

laws in Europe. The more salient aspects of ESG from the historical perspective will be taken up in Chapter 2, following this.

1.01 ESG METAMORPHISM

Foremost, the traditional CG lexicon includes also the environment (E), and social (S) elements, though with relatively less attention than the present tripartite ESG framework that puts equivalent status to the "E" and "S" elements with the "G" element as SC appears to be coming into the forefront, especially since the onset of the COVID-19 pandemic in early 2020. By way of example, UK's CA 2006 though largely viewed as showing a shareholder primacy approach also tasked companies to give due regard to the "E" and "S" elements, and this has courted some controversies over its intended underlying corporate philosophy. This has been further complicated by UK's latest CG Code that insists on companies following it to include key "E" and "S" elements in their reporting. To simplify matters and to avoid this sea of ambiguity, this book uses the CG and ESG lexicons as equivalent, but with the caveat that these are treated differently in other quarters because of the ongoing philosophical contest between the shareholder primacy and stakeholder-orientation. This book will thus begin in Chapter 2 with a brief historical sketch on the evolution of CG toward ESG in the US and the UK. The hitherto CG principles and practices in both these jurisdictions are followed widely across the world.

Under the US federal law system, the limited liability provision was only recognized in California in 1931. However, relatively earlier, New York enacted a corporate statute in 1811, New Jersey in 1816, and Delaware in 1883, while early general incorporation laws enabling corporations to form without a charter from legislatures were found in New Jersey in 1896,[3] and Delaware in 1899.[4] Delaware persisted as the leading corporate state from 1920 onward, as it was generally seen as the state best able to reduce agency costs to the best interests of shareholders. Most companies in the US prior to the late 19th century were incorporated by special state legislations. Companies seeking the benefits of monopolistic structures though sought special legislative incorporations, but in 1819, the US Supreme Court treated corporate charters inviolable and not subject to arbitrary amendments or withdrawals by state legislatures.[5]

CG formally emerged in the US in the 1970s, but became well entrenched by the end of the 1990s. Further developments from the policymaking and regulatory fronts accelerated in the aftermath of the dotcom or internet bubble in 2000 through the Sarbanes Oxley of 2002 (SOX). The 2007-2008 GFC provided further CG directions and

3. D. Arner. 2007. "Development of the American Law of Corporations to 1832". *SMU Law Review*, Vol. 55 (1): 23-57.
4. C. Alva. 1990. "Delaware and the market for corporate charters: History and agency". *Delaware Journal of Corporate Law*, Vol. 15: 885-920; L.S. Black Jr. 2007. "Why corporations choose Delaware?". *Delaware Department of State Division of Corporations*, https://corpfiles.delaware.gov/pdfs/whycorporations_english.pdf, accessed July 21, 2020.
5. *Trustee of Dartmouth College v. Woodward, 17 U.S. (4 Wheat) 518 (1819).*

guidance for corporations through the Dodd-Frank Act of 2010 (DFA). Relentless pressures from social activists and others, a spate of high-profile corporate scandals, and the renewed push by the World Economic Forum (WEF) led by its CEO Klaus Schwab recently have reignited the interests of leading corporations in the US toward SC that Nobel Laurette Milton Friedman featured earlier in the 1970s. SC involves corporations seeking long-term value creation through taking into consideration the interests of their main stakeholders, inclusive of the community. The Business Roundtable (BRT), a forum for CEOs of leading US companies, led the charge by advocating for businesses to extend from the primacy to the stakeholder approach (SA) in 2019 through the release of its Statement on the Purpose of a Corporation. Subsequently, SC became operationalized as ESG in recent years. The ESG path though is not necessarily smooth, as businesses are not all in entire consensus, with advocates on both sides hotly debating on both sides of the divide.

Over in the UK, CG was formally introduced by the Cadbury Committee (CC) in the early 1980s in response to the Bank of Credit and Commerce International (BCCI), Maxwell, and other high-profile scandals. ESG received a boost in 2001, when the FTSE4Good Index series was launched. ESG matters have since evolved with extensive reliance on hard laws found in CA 2006, and soft law best practices via the country's CG Code supervised in general by the Financial Reporting Council (FRC). The UK Code has embraced ESG principles and practices. These are seen in the Code's Provisions on Remuneration, Workforce Engagement, and Board Diversity and Effectiveness. The FRC, owing to various corporate scandals linked to bad CG practices, would soon be replaced by an agency dedicated to the administration of ESG matters.

The historical journeys of corporate laws both in the US and the UK, as briefly sketched, could help to define the early contours of CG. Initially, this was primarily dictated by behaviors of companies with regards to the applicable statutes. This was eventually expanded to include rules and regulations governing corporate actions in the business arenas,[6] as well as those applicable in the capital and financial markets.[7] These also brought with them the expectations of corporate performance. CG since then has been generally perceived to be about performance and conformance of business corporations.[8]

Unsurprisingly, CG has largely evolved through the legal perspective, and hence CG definitions tend to go in this direction, and in particular on the legal aspects of direction and control of corporations. However, as the phenomenon evolved in the business domain, it attracted the interests of financial institutions, employees, customers, suppliers, local communities, policymakers and regulators. Inevitably competing definitions evolved too, as each tried to look at the phenomenon from its perspectives.

6. G. Siedel, et al. 2013. *Government regulation and the legal environment of business.* Washington, DC: Saylor Foundation.
7. G.G. Castellano. 2012. "Towards a general framework for a common definition of "securities": Financial markets regulation in multilingual contexts". *Uniform Law Review*, Vol. 17 (3): 449-481.
8. C. Cornforth & N. Chambers. 2010. "The role of corporate governance and boards in organizational performance" in K. Walshe, G. Harvey & P. Jas (eds.). *Connecting knowledge and performance in public services: From knowing to doing.* Cambridge: Cambridge University Press.

Chapter 2 covers these, as well as discussions on why CG and now ESG matters,[9] the good and not so good aspects of the corporate form,[10] internal versus external guard rails[11] for decent corporate behaviors, and now importantly, the growing enthusiasms for ESG. The chapter sets the contextual background against which to explain the different views on ESG taken on by different disciplines in the academic community and by the different market participants. These matters are explored further in Chapter 3.

1.02 COMPETING ESG PERSPECTIVES

While there has been growing consensus on why CG matters, different prisms have been used to examine the CG phenomenon. Chapter 3 covers discussions on the main competing perspectives of CG. These extend from agency[12] and contractual[13] theories to transaction cost[14] theory, stewardship[15] theory, and enlightened shareholder[16] theory. The main CG approaches[17] now in play in the corporate world, together with some serious conversations on the primary shareholder value versus stakeholders' agendas,[18] would also be addressed in this chapter.

Globalization, financialization, and digitalization of business operations have contributed to the cross-border dimensions of ESG practices. This largely means the transplanting of the US and UK models of CG practices into many other economies of the world. The degree of impact and influence of this is also covered in this chapter. Noting the different kinds of capitalism and consequential different kinds of capitalization structures going on in different parts of the world, Chapter 4 discusses the implications of these financial structures for ESG practices in the US and the UK, as well as some brief comments on the impacts of these to other capital markets elsewhere in the world.

---

9. D. Larcker & B. Tayan. *Corporate governance matters: A closer look at organizational choices and their consequences.* London: Pearson Education.
10. T.L. Hazen. 1979. "The decision to incorporate". *Nebraska Law Review*, Vol. 58: 627-643.
11. N. O'Sullivan & S. Diacon. 2002. "Internal and external governance mechanisms". *Corporate Governance: An International Review*, Vol. 7 (4): 363-373.
12. J.G. Vargas-Hernandez & M.E.T. Cruz. 2018. "Corporate governance and agency theory: Megacable case". *Corporate Governance and Sustainability Review*, Vol. 2 (1): 59-69.
13. H.N. Butler. 1989. "The contractual theory of corporation". *George Mason University of Law Review*, Vol. 11: 99-123.
14. J.A. Saravia & S. Saravia-Matus. 2016. "Corporate governance and transaction cost economics: A study of the equity governance structure". *Corporate Board: Role, Duties and Composition*, Vol. 12 (1): 33-44.
15. S.E. De Falco & A. Renzi. 2007. "Agency theory, stewardship theory and residual right: Logics and interpretative models". *Tourism & Management Studies*, Vol. 1 (3): 27-41.
16. E. Pichet. 2011. "Enlightened shareholder theory: Whose interests should be served by the supporters of corporate governance". *Corporate Ownership & Control*, Vol. 8 (2): 354-362.
17. C.E. Gordon. 2016. *Behavioural approaches to corporate governance.* Abingdon: Routledge J.R. Copland. 2018. "New approaches to corporate governance-Why the shareholder wealth maximization norm make sense". *OECD Paper 12/04/18*, https://www.oecd.org/naec/James_R_Copland_NAEC.pdf, accessed July 21, 2020.
18. F. Brandt & K. Georgiou. 2016. "Shareholders vs stakeholders' capitalism". *Comparative Corporate Governance and Financial Regulation*, Vol. 10 (2016): 4-75.

1.03 ESG AND CORPORATE OWNERSHIP PATTERNS

Guided by insights from Chapters 2 and 3, Chapter 4 analyzes the implications of corporate ownership structures[19] for ESG. ESG practices could be impacted by corporate ownership structures, and potentially also cultural, political, and economic-socio-legal factors.[20] Foremost, concentrated and dispersed ownership structures could have varying implications for ESG practices, especially pertaining to the right to control a business corporation that could provide the controlling party with various private financial and nonfinancial benefits.[21]

Legal systems, like the Anglo-Saxon common law, the European civil law system, or other mixes of customary and faith-based systems influenced the kind of ownership and control structures, whether insider or outsider[22] that in turn shaped the nature of CG in different jurisdictions. Also, of some significance, are the roles played by corporate groups operating in the form of pyramidal entities,[23] family-controlled entities[24] making use of pyramidal structures for various reasons, or state-controlled business entities, commonly referred to as government-linked corporations[25] that are popular in some big emerging economies, and even some advanced economies.

Of late, socialist tendencies are seen in China's crackdowns on China-based global digitalized platform businesses for not giving enough attention to inequality and fair competition matters, while India, the other major Asian economy, continues to follow the US approach where relatively greater emphasis is given to growth aspirations. However, the COVID-19 pandemic and the climate change phenomenon have accelerated US, UK and EU companies to accelerate fresh ESG initiatives in bigger ways for both traditional and digital platform companies. Therefore, another fast-emerging phenomenon that is expected to impact CG practices in both advanced and emerging economies is the onsetting of the digital economy. Chapter 5 following this will therefore identify and offer a preliminary assessment of the impact of digitalization on ESG practices.

---

19. A. A-N. Abdallah & A. Ismail. 2017. "Corporate governance practices, ownership structure, and corporate performance in the GCC countries". *Journal of International Financial Markets Institutions and Money*, Vol. 46 (2017): 98-115.
20. M. Maher & T. Andersson. 1999. CG: *Effects on firm performance and economic growth*. Paris: OECD; D. Prochazka. 2017. "The impact of ownership and other corporate characteristics on performance of V4 companies". *Journal of International Studies*, Vol. 10 (2): 204-218.
21. Prochazka 2017, *supra* note [20].
22. Maher & Andersson 1999, *supra* note [20].
23. S.A. Bank & B.R. Cheffins. 2010. "The corporate pyramid fable". *ECGI Law Working Paper No. 146/2010*: 1-65.
24. J. Piesse, I. Filatotchev & Y-C, Lien. 2007. "CG in family-controlled firms in Taiwan". *International Review of Economics*, Vol. 54 (1): 176-193.
25. C.J. Milhaupt & M. Pargendler. 2017. "Governance challenges of listed state-owned enterprise around the world". *ECGI Law Working Paper No. 352/2017: 1-60.*

1.04 ESG PRACTICES IN DIGITALIZED BUSINESSES

Historical legacies as well as the above-alluded to factors contributed to the shaping of ESG practices in many economies, including those in the US, UK, and the EU. ESG practices evolved, as influenced by these said factors, but more so by big corporate scandals[26] that exposed major flaws in corporate behaviors. Financial gatekeepers,[27] like global development agencies,[28] global credit rating agencies (CRAs),[29] capital market regulators,[30] institutional shareholders,[31] and private equity firms[32] draw attention to major ESG deficiencies now fast unfolding in the digital era. Much of present-day ESG weaknesses are exposed by whistleblowers and like-minded activists.[33] Private-led entities have also emerged as ESG rating agencies, but these have been shrouded with various kinds of controversies.

All these are discussed in Chapter 5, with particular focus on digitalized businesses in this virus pandemic era. This is because various rules and regulations introduced, especially in the US and UK, to help save lives and livelihoods are likely to impact the manners businesses are managed and controlled going forward. These rules and regulatory measures could be temporary, but others could be of longer term. Examples of these include state financial assistance in various forms, business-friendly bankruptcy laws, as well as new measures to curb excesses of those digitalized businesses using the might of their technological and financial powers. Thus, both hard and soft laws are now being deployed to deal with corporate scandals and present financial pressures, but these too have been used in the past. As such, Chapter 6 following this will review what has been done in the past and why these regulatory approaches have been unable to perform to expectations, thereby prompting further regulatory reform initiatives not only in the US and the UK but also in the EU that has also been bothered by various ESG practices deficiencies.

26. T. Kuhn & K.L. Ashcraft. 2003. "Corporate scandal and the theory of the firm formulating the contributions of organizational communication studies". *Management Communication Quarterly*, Vol. 17 (91): 20-57.
27. Y. Fuchita & R.E. Litan. 2006. *Financial gatekeepers: Can they protect investors*. Washington, DC: Brookings Institution Press.
28. IMF. 2017. "The IMF and good governance". https://www.imf.org > files > factsheets, accessed July 21, 2021.
29. C. Bourne. 2012. "Rating agencies as a CG mechanism: Power and trust reduction in debt capital markets". In R. Tench, W. Sun & B. Jones (eds.). *Corporate social responsibility: A challenging concept (critical studies on corporate responsibility, governance and sustainability, Vol. 4)*. Bingley: Emerald Group Publishing.
30. F. Haque, T.G. Arun & C. Kirkpatrick. 2008. "CG and capital markets: A conceptual framework". *Corporate Ownership and Control*, Vol. 5 (2): 1-14.
31. M. Faccio & A.M. Lasfer. 2001. "Institutional shareholders and CG: The case of UK pension funds". *Center for Research on Pensions and Welfare Policies Working Paper 11/01: 1-41.*
32. E. De Fontenay. 2014. "Private equity firms as gatekeepers". *Review of Banking & Financial Law*, Vol. 33 (2014): 116-189.
33. H. Lam & M. Harcourt. 2019. "Whistle-blowing in the digital era: Motives, issues and recommendations". *New Technology, Work and Employment*, Vol. 34 (2): 174-190.

1.05 ESG SCANDALS: HARD AND SOFT LAW RESPONSES

This chapter looks at ESG scandals in the US and the UK that prompted various regulatory reform initiatives. Some attention is also given to EU on these matters. The chapter would also draw some attention on why these reform initiatives have been generally effective in some respects, but not in some key aspects. Importantly, the chapter would seek out reasons as to why particular ESG failings continue to recur, despite the implementation of various regulatory reforms. Further, businesses on their own would be unlikely able to ascertain properly as to the quality of their ESG practices, unless they benchmark against national standards such as the UK CG Code and UK Wates Principles (WP), or the Business Roundtable (BRT) Principles in the US; or against available international best practices offered by respectable economic and business development forums, like the G20/OECD and the International Organization of Securities Commissions (IOSCO). These are covered in Chapter 7.

1.06 GLOBAL AND NATIONAL ESG BEST PRACTICES

Most CG Codes or best practices presently are mostly framed as CG codes, but which in reality have included environmental and social considerations in their updated versions. As such, CG and ESG are used interchangeably here. As mentioned above, private sector response to serious flaws exposed in corporate scandals usually emerged as further improvements to existing forms of best practices ESG codes. These are obviously self-regulatory approaches designed to deter the launching of relatively stiffer responses from either lawmakers or regulators.[34] These global[35] and national CG codes[36] could be enforced by private law mechanisms,[37] but these have drawn various reactions. The general disappointments over the feasibility of Codes of Conduct as mechanisms for sound ESG practices[38] have instead led to more state interventions.[39] The challenges posed by these issues are thus discussed in Chapter 6. The kind of ESG approach employed by businesses is dictated by who holds the sway in corporate direction and control. The matter is not simple, as the power for this is contested

34. P. Di Betta & C. Amenta. 2004. "Incentives in CG: The role of self-regulation". *Symphonya Emerging Issues in Management January 2004 Paper.*
35. J. Veldman. 2017. "Self-regulation in international CG codes". In J. du Plessis & C. Low (eds.). *Corporate governance codes for the 21st century.* Cham: Springer.
36. N. Haskovec. 2012. "Codes of CG: A review". *Millstein Center for CG and Performance Paper June 2012,* https://millstein.law.columbia.edu/sites/default/files/content/docs/Codes%20 of%, accessed July 21, 2020.
37. E. Berglof & S. Claessens. 2006. *Enforcement and good CG in developing countries and transition economies.* Oxford: OUP.
38. E. Mujih. 2018. "CG reform and corporate failure in the UK", *London Metropolitan University Paper Presented at the International Conference on Corporate Social Responsibility at the Social Responsibility Research Network in Bangalore, India September 2018,* http://repository.londonmet.ac.uk/5837/1/Art-CorpGov-II_5-May-2020.pdf, accessed July 21, 2020.
39. Department for Business, Energy & Industrial Strategy (DBEIS). 2017. "CG reform: The government response to the green paper consultation". *DBEIS Paper August 2017.* https://assets.publishing.service.gov.uk/government/uploads/system/uploads/attachment, accessed July 21, 2020.

between directors, corporate executives, shareholders, and increasingly even other stakeholders as the business landscape goes through bouts of turbulence, such as now brought about by digitalization and the COVID-19 pandemic. These power tussles and their implications for ESG practices are discussed in Chapter 8.

1.07 DELINEATION OF POWERS IN CORPORATIONS

The matter of delineation of powers in corporations is thus addressed in Chapter 8. The division of powers in modern corporations, especially in dispersed ownership structures, such as found in Anglo-Saxon economies, led to the concentration of powers in the hands of corporate managers. This would require not only the control of these powers but also the design of incentive structures to align the interests of the principals or shareholders to the agents as represented by directors and corporate executives. With this development, the company becomes a separate legal entity, differentiated from its shareholders or the owners of the shares, and directors who become the corporate managers. For the most parts and in practice, operating business decisions are made by the board of directors, while the constitutional decisions pertaining to the rules of administration and the relationships between shareholders, directors, and other corporate constituents are made by the shareholders, as the equity owners of the company.

Some discussions are made for the important aspects of directors' duties, including board diversity and board remunerations that have surfaced increasingly as contentious issues in the business world. When rights extended by the company's constitution are perceived to have been breached, like self-interested transactions by controllers and so on, various shareholders' remedies could be tapped upon. Then, there could be the no less important matter of internal governance of not sufficient monitoring of the behaviors of corporate managers. Accordingly, it had been suggested that the takeover mechanism could become an important governance mechanism whereby shareholders could replace underperforming or opportunistic managers. Thus, the governance role of takeovers will also be discussed in this chapter.

External governance impacts particularly how businesses access various forms of capital from various kinds of capital markets. Coverage of governance in capital and financial market institutions could fill in the gaps posed by the limits of corporate laws. Indeed, it has been strongly proposed that the quality of company law essentially would decide whether securities markets arise, whether ownership could separate from control, and whether the modern company could prosper. The US, the UK, and the EU legal structures have been quite decent, and shareholders are generally well protected. However, ownership had still been unable to separate from control in many instances, because managerial agency costs had been particularly high, while corporate laws had also not burrowed into the firm to weed out those managerial agency costs that flow from mediocre business decisions.[40] It appeared that judicial doctrine and legal inquiry especially from the US perspective addressed self-dealing, but not bad

40. M.J. Roe. 2002. "Corporate law's limits". *Journal of Legal Studies*, Vol. 31 (2): 233-271.

business judgment. The consequential business judgment rule (BJR), where the courts would not second-guess managerial mistakes, extended the full range of agency costs, like overinvestment, overexpansion, or reluctance to take on profitable but uncomfortable risks beyond direct legal inquiry.[41]

This could mean that managers could lose for shareholders as much, or even more, than they could pilfer from them, as law directly controls only the second costs, not the first.[42] This could further suggest that where the risk of managerial error varied widely across nations, or from company-to-company, ownership structure would vary widely, even when traditional company laws tightly protect shareholders everywhere.[43] The roles played by securities laws,[44] global CRAs,[45] institutional shareholders,[46] and whistleblowers[47] in the context of this are accordingly discussed in this chapter. The way companies respond or benchmark against national and global best practices are generally decided upon by the board, but it is not free from second look by shareholders, especially institutional and activist shareholders as shown in more recent cases.

Since the dawn of the separation of ownership and power in modern corporation, shareholders as principals have in general entrusted the management and direction of companies to directors operating as their agents. The history of business corporations has shown the tensions between them as businesses take on many critical decisions that at times caused the two to take divergent views. How the directors get around this, and how shareholders take remedial actions when things go awry are discussed in this chapter. As this book is about the theory and practice of ESG, it would be in order and helpful to have insights on key moments in ESG practices that triggered the wider interests of the public, but in particular those of policymakers and regulators. The latter generally needs to show to their public constituents that they are doing what they proclaim to do in general, meaning the protection of consumer welfare and the containments of corporate excesses. As such, various high-profile ESG scandals in the US and the UK are examined in closer details in Chapter 9 through case analysis to ascertain where and how ESG practices in these cases have gone awry.

1.08 ESG CONTROVERSIES: SELECTED US AND UK CASES

Guided by observations of ESG practices in the US and the UK, this chapter has selected for analysis three categories of businesses that are likely to be of interest to the legal community: other CG practitioners, like banks and financial institutions and business

41. Roe 2002, *supra* note [40].
42. Roe 2002, *supra* note [40].
43. Roe 2002, *supra* note [40].
44. A.C. Pritchard. 2018. "CG, capital markets, and securities law". In J.N. Gordon & W-G Ringe (eds.). *The Oxford handbook of corporate law and governance.* Oxford: OUP.
45. A.B. Matthies. 2013. "Empirical research on corporate credit-ratings: A literature review". *SFB 649 Discussion Paper No. 2013-003: 1-25.*
46. K.H. Chung & H. Zhang. 2009. "CG and institutional ownership". *Journal of Financial and Quantitative Analysis*, Vol. 46 (1): 247-273.
47. T.V. Eaton & M.D. Akers. 2007. "Whistleblowing and good governance". *The CPA Journal*, Vol. 77 (6): 66-71.

corporations; other stakeholders like employees, business customers, and suppliers; as well as policymakers and regulators. These cover those engaged in conventional businesses, such as Coca-Cola, Walmart, and Canon in the US, and Carillon and Thomas Cook in the UK. Attention is also provided for banks and financial institutions, such as Goldman Sachs (GS) and Wells Fargo (WF) in the US, and the Royal Bank of Scotland (RBS) and Greensill Capital (GC) in the UK. The special focus on financial services is because of the wider systemic risk they posed to the wider economy, as exemplified in the 2007-2009 GFC.

Not to be left out are the digitalized businesses engaged with the enabling technologies provided by the FIR, as they are the future business forms going forward. Included in the analysis are Uber and Robinhood in the US and Funding Circle (FC) and Deliveroo in the UK. These and other tech companies have been praised for their contributions to social inclusion, but of late have also been criticized for not doing enough with regards to employee welfare. The insights derived from the analysis on the theories and practices governing ESG thus far provide ESG signposts or future ESG issues that are likely to require attention from corporations, directors, other stakeholders, as well as policymakers and regulators. The identified themes for future attention are discussed in Chapter 10.

1.09 CURRENT AND EMERGING ESG THEMES

The book thus far covered internal and external governance addressing concerns over their capacities to help ensure good corporate behaviors. The 2020 ongoing COVID-19 global pandemic pummeled the world economy impacting both developing and advanced economies. It also teased out the hitherto hidden flaws of corporate systems and behaviors that remained not wholesomely resolved, as well as newly emerging contentious issues. These matters sewn together to provide the signposts or ESG themes going forward are discussed in this chapter. Decisions would need to be taken to resolve the ongoing debate between short versus long-term value;[48] uncertainty and sustainability challenges;[49] workplace and workforce transformation;[50] socioeconomic-political pressures for diversity, equity, and inclusions;[51] moving the

48. K. Tang & C. Greenwald. 2016. "Long-termism versus short-termism: Time for the pendulum shift?", *S&P Global Paper April 2016*, https://www.pionline.com/assets/docs/CO105897627.PDF, accessed July 21, 2020.
49. I. Gregurec, M.T. Furjan & K. Tomicic-Pupek. "The impact of COVID-19 on sustainable business models in SMEs". *Sustainability*, Vol. 13 (2021): 1098-1121; S. Agrogiannis & I. Kinias. 2018. "Sustainability dilemmas: Risk and uncertainty in supply chain management". *Journal of Business Theory and Practice*, Vol. 6 (2): 95-117.
50. A. de Lucas Ancillo, M.T. del Val Nunez & S.G. Gavrila. 2020. "Workplace change within the COVID-19 context: A grounded theory approach". *Economic Research*, https://doi.org/10.1080/1331677X.2020.1862689, accessed March 25, 2021.
51. K.M. Kniffin, et al. 2020. "COVID-19 and the workplace: Implications, issues, and insight for future research and action". *Harvard Business School Working Paper 20-127*, https://www.hbs.edu/ris/Publication%20Files/20-127_6164cbfd-37a2-489e-, accessed March 25, 2021.

ESG Agenda[52] forward more quickly; and rebooting or reorienting risk management[53] in both the financial and nonfinancial sectors. These themes are explored in further detail in this chapter. Insights flowing from this chapter and all the other earlier eight chapters are meant to say something about the theory and practice of ESG particularly in the US, the UK, and the EU. These will be highlighted in Chapter 11, the concluding chapter for the book.

1.10 CONCLUSIONS

Insights on key internal and external CG issues in the past and now and trends in the future have been fleshed out in this book. Chapter 11, the concluding chapter for the book, would use insights from these to draw out salient ESG matters, which shareholders, boards, policymakers and regulators might wish to reflect further on for their future actions. Importantly, the book argues that the purpose of business is to make profits and grow by addressing efficiently socioeconomic challenges confronting society, and doing this within procedures and rules decided by the community. Businesses can achieve this mission effectively with the board providing the necessary leadership and oversight role while engaging proactively where needed with regulators and other stakeholders whenever society pressures for reforms.

In turn, primary shareholders should entrust the management and governing aspects of businesses to the board, and intervene only when board leadership and oversight functions are lacking through available sources of legal remedies and/or the market for corporate control. Corporate gatekeepers would just need to play out their entrusted functions steadfastly and consistently without getting into bouts of inattentiveness. Regulators would need to be mindful of their mandates of overseeing the functions of corporate gatekeepers and conducts of businesses and directors reinforced by timely and consistent enforcements. Policymakers might do better than merely playing to the gallery, and instead make fair and balanced decisions as to the appropriateness of shareholder primacy, enlightened shareholder, or stakeholder models of business governance. This way, board leadership and board oversight can have better odds in helping to deliver the desired societal outcomes, and not getting preoccupied or distracted by other agendas. Hopefully, what this book says about ESG are the relevant matters for delving into by ESG law practitioners, policymakers and academicians.

52. A.S. Matsuo. 2021. "Evolving focus on ESG post-COVID-19", https://advisory.kpmg.us/articles/2020/evolving-focus-post-covid-19.html, accessed March 25, 2021.
53. World Economic Forum (WEF). 2020. "Challenges and opportunities in the post-COVID-19 world", http://www3.weforum.org/docs/WEF_Challenges_and_Opportunities_Post_COVID_19.pdf, accessed March 25, 2021.

CHAPTER 2

ESG Metamorphism

CG has been appropriately referred to as the direction and control of corporations. This take continues to evolve as businesses transform and scale across borders. Its early modern form to its current ESG version has been a journey of ups and downs. ESG guidance has been hailed as the potential savior of good corporate conduct when framed or reframed in response to scandalous business conduct, and criticized as flawed, when seen incapable of halting the tide of corporate misdeeds.ESG, as being now generally understood, talks of the environment ("E") as comprising matters, like energy and water consumption, climate change, and greenhouse gas (GHG) emissions; "S" as comprising matters, like data privacy, worksite health safety, human rights, employee diversity, inequality, supply chain management, and charity contributions; and "G" as comprising matters, like executive compensation, political donations, board diversity, risk management, cybersecurity, corporate purpose (CP), and stakeholder agenda. Previously, the traditional CG paradigm accounted for various "E" and "S" elements too, depending on the nature of the business and the issues different companies face in the business environment, meaning the width of CG practices varied from company to company. However, the ESG paradigm as is now generally understood appears to suggest that the stakeholder philosophy underpinning it is different, as the "E" and "S" elements are put under the same pedestal as the "G" element, but to what extent this is backed up by laws could be a different matter, and could vary between different jurisdictions.For ease of analysis and comparison with previous CG practices, as alluded to earlier, CG, ESG, CSR, sustainability is used interchangeably in this book, but making distinctions of their nuances, where appropriate. In fact, the FTSE4Good indices, incorporating the "E" and "S" elements, have been deployed since 2001 under the traditional CG paradigm, while CSR has been practiced and reported upon voluntarily when companies elect to parade this credential for marketing and related reasons. The UN's sustainable development goals (SDGs) launched in 2015 included calls for businesses and others to incorporate the "E" and "S" elements to help ensure sustainability in the economy. Earlier, John Elkington authored in March 2007 "Partnership from Cannibals with Forks: The Triple Bottom Line of 21st Century Business" in *Environment Quality Management* that those effective long-term partnerships would be crucial during the sustainability transition, some forged between the public and private sectors, others between companies, and yet others between companies and groups campaigning for a wide range of triple-bottom-line objectives, meaning profits, people and planet.

The 2005 Freshfield report mentioned that it was arguably part of the fiduciary duty of investment companies to integrate ESG factors into their investment decision-making process, while UK's Law Commission in 2014 equally mentioned that pension trustees and others are not prevented by law from taking into consideration ESG factors when making investment decisions. The investment community has been bombarded by green and eco labeling, including socially responsible investment (SRI), sustainable financing, sustainability, ethical financing and so on, but a survey of some 350 global investment professionals in 2008 found that the bulk of professionals in the investment community opted the use of ESG when referring to such information. The UN-led Principles for Responsible Investment (PRI), the UN Environment Programme Financing Initiative (UNEPFI), and the UN Global Compact in their September 2015 "Fiduciary Duty in 21st Century" joint report advocated that the failure to incorporate long-term investment value drivers, like the ESG factors, could constitute a failure of fiduciary duty. Despite Milton Friedman's 1960-1970s contention that the integration of ESG considerations into financial practice would negatively impact financial performance, there were increasing signals from the academic community and the industry pointing to more evidence supporting the relationship between consideration of ESG matters and positive financial performance. This together with signals from the legal community on relevancy of fiduciary duty to this, including the broader recognition of the necessity of sustainability of investments in the long term, suggests that ESG factors are now becoming the in-thing in the investment world, much mora of a pragmatic initiative than rhetoric.

ESG began in its traditional form in the UK, the US and the EU before journeying to elsewhere in the world. This will ergo provide the contextual background for the identification of the more mainstream definitions of ESG, including the working definition used in this book. Why ESG matters in economies would then be highlighted. The advantages and disadvantages of the corporate form that underpinned the ESG phenomenon will also be touched upon. From here, discussions would follow through with some main comparative insights on internal versus external aspects of the ESG paradigm.

2.01 BRIEF HISTORICAL SKETCH

ESG's modern features began to surface with regularity in the UK as the 1990s got underway. The CC, or the Committee on the Financial Aspects of CG, has been argued to be the main source of inspiration for the rise of the phenomenon in the UK. ESG though could have attracted major attention in the 1970s in the UK, as it did then in the US then. That said, back in the 1990s, the UK would have ensured the rise of the ESG phenomenon in the early 1990s, even with the absence of the CC.[54]

54. B.R. Cheffins. 2015. "The rise of CG in the UK: When and why". *Paper Delivered in UCL Law Faculty's Current Legal Problems Lecture Series April 2015*, https://core.ac.uk/download/pdf/35280113.pdf, accessed July 21, 2020.

ESG, then known as CG in its narrow confine, made the maiden scene with regularity in the US in the 1970s, as a species of managerial revolution,[55] but this was not so much the case in the UK. In fact, the US witnessed the triumphs of managerial capitalism in the 1950s and 1960s with full-time professional managers fully in charge, lording over key sectors of the US economy, with scandals of the kind seen these days, as the exception rather than the rule, as senior corporate executives then hesitated for the most part from exploiting personal advantage of their positions as corporate assets' stewards, thereby putting internal governance off the business radar, and leaving the phrase ESG largely a rarely used lexicon. The challenges posed by the complexities of sprawly corporate empires together with the significant rise of bribery and related corporate misbehaviors in the 1970s culminated with illicit payments in the Penn Central debacle. Pen Central then had to undertake to create board-level audit committee and appointments of additional nonexecutive directors (NEDs) to settle Securities Exchange Commission (SEC) charges. The company also had to abide by the New York Stock Exchange (NYSE) listing rules, requiring its audit committee to comprise mainly NEDs. All these developments in effect brought CG as it was then known to the forefront of the corporate landscape. This soon expanded the narrower view of CG to the expanded version that covers CSR activities, albeit with no mandatory disclosure requirements.

These were quickly followed by two bills in 1980 proposing the mandating of major governance roles for NEDs to motivate corporations to operate in more democratic and accountable manners.[56] The academic and legal communities offered some theoretical foundations for CG when advocating imposition on these directors a host of other responsibilities, besides recommending that local communities be provided with the opportunity to vote on corporate activities that were deemed harmful.[57] The American Law Institute (ALI) together with the American Bar Association (ABA) and the NYSE cosponsored a conference dedicated to CG issues that was followed by extensive media coverage soon after.

These above developments in the US appeared to bypass the UK corporate landscape,[58] even with an impressive book contribution,[59] as the CG phrase was not drawn upon at all by the main media, until the late 1980s to early 1990s.[60] This could be puzzling, considering that the US and the UK shared the outsider ownership and control features, with large listed entities, commonly lacking a core shareholder capable of imposing inside influence, as well as the common feature of managerial

55. A.D. Chandler. 1977. *The visible hand: The managerial revolution in American business*. Boston: Belknap Press. 484.
56. These were the *Protection of Shareholders' Rights Act, S. 2567, 96th Congress, 2d Sess., 126 Congressional Record*, and the *Corporate Democracy Act of 1980, HR 7010, 96th Congress, 2d Sess.*
57. R. Nader, M. Green & J. Seligman. 1976. *Taming the giant corporation*. New York: WW Norton & Co.
58. H. Yong. 1976. "The lessons of a Prime Minister". *Sunday Times 24/10/76: 41*; B. Barker, 1980. "Foreword" in K. Midgley (ed.) *Management accountability and CG*. London: Macmillan.
59. R.I. Tricker. 1984. *CG*. London: Gower.
60. B.R. Cheffins. 2013. "The history of CG". In M. Wright, D. Siegel, K. Keasey & I. Filatotchev (eds.). *The Oxford Handbook of CG*. Oxford: OUP.

agency costs generated by self-serving managers unconstrained by apathetic shareholders that provided a major potential governance risk. This was in contrast to those elsewhere, where the main CG concern was that dominant shareholders could exploit outside investors.[61] Hence, despite sharing equivalent CG priorities with the US, the UK did not experience the kind of CG surge until the early 1990s, or two decades later than the US. This also could not be due to the presence of sizeable family block holders in the UK, as the US style of diffuse share ownership was also a feature in the UK by the 1970s or even earlier.[62]

The early greater presence of institutional shareholders did not catalyze the early arrival of the CG notion, as would have been thought.[63] However, the idea that market forces were fostering managerial accountability did appear to play a role in helping to explain why CG did not embed in the UK before the 1990s. More so was the process in the capital markets that encompassed the scrutiny to which listed shares were subjected to, as well as the risk of takeover threats.[64] Corporate managers' fear of takeover threats and risks of being dismissed had a meaningful incentive to manage corporations well to keep share prices sufficiently high to deter unwelcome or hostile takeover bids. This implied that this phenomenon together with internal CG mechanisms, like board monitoring, shareholder activism and incentivized executive remunerations, helped to motivate management to align with shareholder interests to sidelined debates on CG.[65] The late 1970s did not see much mergers and acquisitions (M&A) activities in the UK. The 1980s in contrast saw hyper M&A activities, and that could have triggered the onset of takeover risks for corporate managers,[66] but this came with the caveat that the UK was too reliant on takeovers as a remedy for poor corporate management.[67]

The feature of US conversations pertaining to CG was also argued to be absent in the UK, despite the equivalent Penn Central-style debacle, in the 1971 collapse of Rolls Royce. This corporate embarrassment was marked by the lack of managerial accountability, despite danger signals to the main board that unfortunately was saddled by the trappings of pride, arrogance, misjudgment and blind optimism.[68] The sort of commotions that the Penn Central debacle got because of securities regulations never took root

61. Cheffins 2013, *supra* note [60].
62. J. Foreman-Peck & L. Hannah. 2011. "Extreme divorce: The managerial revolution in UK companies before 1914". *Economic History Review*, Vol. 65 (2011): 1217.
63. D. Kynaston. 2001. *The city of London, vol. IV: A club no more, 1945-2000*. London: Pimlico.
64. Committee to Review the Functioning of Financial Institutions. 1977. *Evidence on the financing of trade and industry, vol. 3*. London: HMSO. 91.
65. K.J. Hopt. 2013. "Comparative CG: The state of the art and international regulation". In M.F. Andreas & K.J. Hopt (eds.). *Comparative CG: A functional and international analysis*. Cambridge: Cambridge University Press; P. Stiles. 2014. "Corporate governance" in P.C. Flood & Y. Freeney (eds.). *Wiley encyclopedia of management: Vol. 11-Organisational behavior*. New Jersey: Wiley.
66. B. Chiplin & M. Wright. 1987. *The logic of mergers: The competitive market in corporate control in theory and practice*. London: Institute of Economic Affairs (IEA).
67. T. Jenkinson & C. Mayer. 1992. "The assessment: CG and corporate control". *Oxford Review of Economic Policy*, Vol. 8 (3): 1-3.
68. P. Wilsher. 1973. "Where was Whitehall when Rolls' light went out?". *Sunday Times 05/08/1973:50*.

in the UK, then despite the paying of sizeable illicit commissions in the 1970s, such as exemplified in the Racal group.[69]

Corporate trends in the 1980s setting the entrenchment of CG in US company landscape in the 1990s were also prevalent in the UK. Indeed, trends pertaining to public-listed corporations and their executives were present in both jurisdictions as the 20th century closed, such that the UK became readied for CG to advance to the limelight, even with the absence of the CC's contribution. US securities' regulations had wider disclosure obligations, but the UK also at the time did not have the equivalent of the SEC that was skilled at leveraging disclosure rules for spotlighting CG.[70] The SEC took actions against the culprits, besides pushing forth a voluntary disclosure initiative whereupon corporations could report questionable payments without offering details. Some 350 corporations responded, and that contributed to the enhanced reputation of the SEC as a regulator,[71] and to bringing CG on the official agenda through its orchestrated board-related settlements, with corporations' admitting to questionable payments.

The industrial democracy debates also helped to distract CG from the corporate landscape before the 1990s. The UK when it joined the European Economic Community (EEC) in 1973 was obliged to implement the EEC's draft Fifth Directive, which, if adopted, would have required it to promulgate mandatory rules pertaining to the internal structure and decision-making processes of listed companies, including the provision for a two-tier board made up of a managing organ and a supervisory organ comprising NEDs and employee representation. This differed substantially from the unitary board standard in the UK that was also without a tradition of employee director or heavy representation of NEDs. This tilted massive attention to the analysis of board structures precluded attention to CG developments in the US at the time.[72] The EEC proposal to provide for employee participation in the board structure when implemented fully could fully transform the prevailing legal relationship between shareholders and the board, as well as between the board and corporate managers.[73] This would have enraged the UK business community of a new industrial revolution and a jolt to class balance.[74] Timing was therefore out of kilt. Intense conversation over employee representation on boards and industrial democracy was happening simultaneously, at a time when CG was emerging strongly in the US.[75]

69. Economist. 1977. "It's official". *Economist 12/11/77: 78.*
70. A. Johnston. 1973. "The city can look after itself". *Sunday Times 06/05/73: 63.*
71. M.C. Jensen. 1975. "SEC to continue action against business payoffs". *New York Times, 18/06/75: 74.*
72. C. Schmitthoff. 1976. "Company structure and employee participation in the EEC-The British attitude". *International Comparative Law Quarter*, Vol. 25 (1976): 611-614; M. Routh. 1973. "Directors see no benefit in two-tier-boards". *Financial Times 18/04/73: 38.*
73. D.D. Prentice. 1978. "Employee participation in corporate government-A critique of the Bullock report". *Can Bar Review*, Vol. 56 (1978): 277-285.
74. B.D. Nossiter. 1977. "British business is enraged by promise of worker power". *Washington Post 27/01/77: A20;* J. Elliott. 1977. "A jolt to class balance". *Financial Times 27/01/77: 18.*
75. R.I. Tricker. 1978. *A study of the non-executive director and of the audit committee.* London: Tolley.

Attention on CG changed drastically in the UK, as the 1990s unfolded. Theoretical arguments on the state of governance in the UK, especially pertaining to board structures, caught enhanced attention in 1990.[76] This accelerated throughout the 1990s.[77] The work of the CC helped to catalyze the renewed interest in CG, but which in any case would still have risen to prominence in the UK in the 1990s, even without its presence.[78] No matter, the Cadbury launched in May 1991 jointly by the London Stock Exchange (LSE) the FRC, key members of the accountancy profession, and representation from the Confederation of British Industry drew attention to the erosion of confidence in the standard of disclosures in published corporate accounts and the ability of auditors to meet expectations of users of financial statements.[79] As it was, the CC was also mandated to take into consideration wider CG matters, including the responsibilities of executive and NEDs.[80]

The CC in December 1992 issued its final version of its Code of Best Practice and supporting report providing the rationale for its recommendations.[81] This was quickly followed by the LSE launching its "comply or explain" obligation in its listing rules.[82] Critics argued that the guidance was too vague, did not go far enough, and that improvements would be incremental, given that adherence to the guidelines was not required by law. The 1995 review of the Cadbury report, together with the Greenbury report on executive pay, maintained real progress in raising governance standards in the UK,[83] while Sir Ronald Hampel's review of the 1995 Greenbury report on executive pay mentioned that it was generally accepted that implementation of the code's provisions had led to higher standards of governance.[84] The 1998 Hampel Report further stressed that Cadbury provided metrics against which CG in other markets could be measured,[85] and as the 1990s drew to a close, the Cadbury Code became the world leader on CG matters.[86]

Still, it has been argued that the CC did not in and of itself generated a galvanizing impact.[87] Difficult economic conditions in the UK then had been unmasking managerial weaknesses the booming times of the 1980s had shielded, like the steep rise in executive pay, when profits were falling drastically. This reinforced the notion that not enough was done to hold top executives to account in big UK corporations.[88]

76. S. Holberton. 1990. "Where the power lies". *Financial Times 04/07/90*: 10; S. Holberton. 1990. "Why the ideal board is so elusive". *Financial Times 04/07/90: 4*; R. Waters. 1990. "Minister backs calls to reform board structure". *Financial Time 08/12/90: 11.*
77. L. Vincent. 1992. "Hard nut in the boardrooms". *Observer 06/12/92:36.*
78. Cheffins 2013, *supra* note [60].
79. L.F. Spira & J. Slinn. 2012. *The Cadbury Committee: A history*. Oxford: OUP.
80. S. Holberton. 1991. "DTI will back in-depth review of companies". *Financial Times 31/05/91: 7.*
81. D. Norberg & T. McNulty. 2013. "Creating better boards through codification: Possibilities and limitations in UK CG". *Business History*, Vol. 55 (2013): 348-362.
82. LSE. 1993. "Listing rules". Paragraph 12.43 (j).
83. Committee on the Financial Aspects of CG. 1995. *Compliance with the Code of Best Practice.* London: Gee; Greenbury Committee. 1995. *Directors' remuneration: Report of a study group chaired by Sir Richard Greenbury*. London: Gee.
84. Committee on CG (Chaired by Ronald Hampel). 1998. Report. London: Gee.
85. Committee on CG 1998, *supra* note [84].
86. G. Vinten. 1998. "CG: A UK/USA comparison". *Credit Control*, Vol. 19 (6): 18-19.
87. Cheffins 2013, *supra* note [60].
88. L. Buckingham. 1992. "Greed still the boardroom creed". *Guardian 02/05/92: 38.*

Further, a series of corporate scandals happening contemporaneously with the work of the CC gave the latter unanticipated attention. This CC itself acknowledged this in its final report saying that had its Code been in existence in the past, a number of these reported scandals would have received good attention earlier.[89] This included the downfall of Polly Peck International, when efforts to restructure the board to deal with the high-profile chairman, CEO and dominant shareholder failed. This led to the biggest fraud in corporate history at the time.[90] The following year, 1991, had been described as the unprecedented year for scandals. The BCCI was shut down amidst revelations of minimal boardroom oversight of its business, plagued by rampant fraud, deceit, and corruption.[91] Public-listed Maxwell Communications Corporation (MCC) and Mirror Group Newspapers (MGN) both led and dominated by Robert Maxwell went belly-up due to improper diversion of pension funds, deployment of an illegal share price support scheme, and lack of proper oversight from NEDs.[92]

The work of the CC became very timely, as these scandals brought good attention to board responsibility and composition. These were themes in sync with mainstream CG, and auditing and accounting at the time.[93] While the CC's work could tantamount to a pivotal episode in the UK's CG history, it has been counterargued that wider forces were at play, to suggest that CG would probably rise to prominence, without its contributions.[94] Here, a look at the US context would be illuminating.

The 1970s interest in CG in the US highlighted US corporations as political structures to be governed. They were nevertheless potentially a poor fit, in a decade where the market doctrine was triumphant and suspicions of government growing. This was further worsened with Ronald Reagan coming into power that took CG reform off the legislative radar. The ALI leant toward the law and economics perspective and retreated from proposals to endorse mandatory rules pertaining to board structure.[95] The takeover fever that radiated across the US in the 1980s contributed to CG's resilience. The shift away from the politically flavored 1970 version of CG matched up well with the market-oriented framework of the 1980s while the takeover fever reoriented CG around shareholders.[96] Perceptions about the balance of power between management and shareholders were as such tilted toward shareholders' favor, and perceptions of CG also evolved in turn. Institutional shareholders generally objected to corporate defensive tactics in the 1980s, as this would provide them with the opportunity to dispose of their shares when responding to premium-priced takeover

89. Committee on the Financial Aspects of CG. 1992. *Report, Committee on the Financial aspects of CG*. London: Gee.
90. G. David. 1990. "Polly peck: From 2 billion to zero". *Sunday Times 28/10/90: 2.*
91. J. Beaty & S.C. Gwynne. 2004. *The outlaw bank: A wild ride into the secret heart of BCCI.* Washington, DC: Ramjac Inc.
92. J. Preston. 2020. *Fall: The mystery of Robert Maxwell.* London: Penguin Random House.
93. A. Brummer. 1992. "Cracking the secret code that helps to shield investors". *Guardian 28/05/92: 10.*
94. Cheffins 2013, *supra* note [60].
95. B.R. Cheffins. 2015. "The CG movement, banks and the financial crisis". *Theological Inquiries in Law*, Vol. 16 (2015): 1.
96. K.J. Hopt. 2013. "Comparative CG: The state of the art and international regulation". In A.M. Fleckner & K.J. Hopt (eds.). *Comparative CG: A functional and international analysis*. Cambridge: Cambridge University Press.

offers, but which brought clashes when listed corporations then began using poison pills and equivalent takeover defense mechanisms to ward off hostile takeover bids.

The pushback by institutional shareholders against takeover defenses in the US in the 1980s was never replicated in the UK, despite equivalent takeover fever pitch in the UK.[97] This was because UK's City Code on Takeovers and Mergers introduced in the late 1960s by the Bank of England (BOE), the LSE and big London firms precluded listed corporations from engaging with frustrating actions without shareholder consent upon the materialization of takeover offers. Besides, UK corporate law and capital market regulations also discouraged them from mounting takeover defenses, before a bid is in sight. This meant that US-style takeover defense mechanisms could not provide the fodder in the UK for any kind of catalysts about shareholders' rights, or more generally about CG.[98]

The takeover wave retreated in 1990, when a nascent recession, and a debt market chill, then hit hostile offers, particularly hard. This took with it the disciplinary effects of takeovers. However, it brought bringing increasing attention to director rules, shareholder activism, and connected internal governance systems for keeping managers in check, as well as a surge in the use of stock options. The dismissals of several high-profile CEOs also suggested that US boards were becoming more alert, while the increasing trend toward pay-to-performance sensitivity of CEO remuneration also paved the way for a substantial and controversial hike in aggregate levels of managerial compensation during the 1990s.[99]

By the 1990s, key thrusts of the post–World War II managerialist era subsided, such that corporate leaders of listed corporations began not only having wide opportunities but also with greater risks for failures, and which potentially meant that CG should logically enjoy higher prominence particularly in the context of deregulation in full swing in the 1980s. Management, in the face of significant foreign competition, and withering union power, enjoyed wider discretions, when responding to technological transformation, and intensified competition, through downsizing and outsourcing. Unlike the previous decades, financialization of the economy accelerated,[100] giving a wide range of options for financing existing operations, new acquisitions and expansion plans, and importantly more competition from new entrants. These transformed the notion of the competent manager to the imperial chief executive or charismatic leader, implying that under the new conditions, CEOs could do more to shape corporate performance, than hitherto.[101]

This had phenomenal implications for CG, as having the best possible leader in charge, logically ascended in priority. It, together with compensation packages,

97. B. Chiplin & M. Wright. 1987. *The logic of mergers: The competitive market in corporate control in theory and practice.* London: Institute of Economic Affairs.
98. Cheffins 2013, *supra* note [60].
99. Cheffins 2013, *supra* note [60].
100. T.I. Palley. 2007. "Financialization: What it is and why it matters". Levy Economics Institute of Bard College Working Paper No. 525, https://www.econstor.eu/bitstream/10419/31686/1/571722628, accessed July 21, 2020.
101. R. Khurana. 2002. Searching for a corporate savior: The irrational quest for charismatic CEOs. Princeton: Princeton University Press.

provided corporate executives with robust incentives to manage effectively. Increasing focus on linking managerial pay packages to performance and board-led dismissals of CEOs at several high-profile US-listed corporations in the early 1990s suggested that there indeed was a telling governance response to a corporate landscape laced with market and regulatory trends.[102] On the other hand, this did not necessarily imply that CG was operating well, as shown by the steep rise in complicated executive pays in the 1990s, together with bad corporate behaviors, as exemplified in Enron,[103] World-Com,[104] and others[105] in the early 2000s. The tougher regulatory response through the Sarbanes-Oxley Act of 2002 (SOX)[106] and increased board and media alertness led to an apparent new postrevolutionary flow of power in corporate America, with CEOs relatively less risk adventurous, and more beholden to their boards.[107] The process was also seemingly replicated in the financial services sector, owing in part to tougher regulations introduced after the 2008 GFC, via the DFA of 2010,[108] as well as through a new breed of relatively more conventional less swashbuckling bank leaders.[109] This remained the norm for corporate America, but not for too long though, as the increasingly digitalized global and US economy brought with them further contentious CG matters.

Equivalent trends were also observed in the UK CG scene in the 1990s to support the contention that CG would likely ascend into prominence, even in the absence of the CC's contributions. In 1990, the year before the CC came into play, the UK was impacted by an unprecedented series of corporate scandals. Pertaining to the wave of takeovers in the 1980s in the US, there were significant parallels in the UK, as both jurisdictions saw the retreat of hostile takeover bids, thereby taking away the limelight they enjoyed in the 1980s while CG matters witnessed increasing ascendancies.[110] The marginalization of takeovers as a governance instrument generated in the UK a potential managerial accountability gap that other mechanisms like board-level oversight and shareholder activism could potentially address.[111]

It did not really matter that M&A activity rebounded in the mid-1990s in the UK, as these were strategic for building market shares, or for exploiting economies of scale, and not the financial value creation style of displacing underperforming managers of

102. D. Jenter & F. Kanaan. "CEO turnover and relative performance evaluation". *The Journal of Finance*, Vol. 70 (5): 2155-2184.
103. B. McLean & P. Elkind. 2004. *The smartest guys in the room: The amazing rise and scandalous fall of Enron*. London: Portfolio Trade.
104. Knowledge Wharton. 2002. "What went wrong at WorldCom?". *Knowledge Wharton 03/07/02*, https://knowledge.wharton.upenn.edu/article/what-went-wrong-at-worldcom/, accessed July 21, 2020.
105. H. van Driel. 2018. "Financial fraud, scandals and regulation: A conceptual framework and literature review". *Business History*, Vol. 61 (8): 1259-1299.
106. S. Wagner & L. Dittmar. 2006. "The unexpected benefits of Sarbanes-Oxley". *Harvard Business Review April* 2006, https://hbr.org/2006/04/the-unexpected-benefits-of-sarbanes-oxley, accessed July 21, 2020.
107. A. Murray. 2007. "After the revolt". *Wall Street Journal 12/08/13: C1.*
108. The Dodd-Frank Wall Street Reform and Consumer Protection Act of 2010 (Dodd-Frank Act).
109. M. Colchester. 2013. "Today's bank chiefs can spin a yawn". *Wall Street Journal* 12/08/13: C1.
110. Economist. 1994. "Watching the boss". *Economist 29/01/94: 7, 13.*
111. H. McRae. 1991. "The changing mood of shareholders". *Independent 03/12/91:23.*

the 1980s.[112] UK corporate health in the 1990s hence differed substantially from those in the 1950s and 1960s. This was dubbed as the golden era for UK businesses because of buoyant trading conditions and macroeconomic stability.[113] Like the situation in the US in the 1950s and 1960s, senior executives of UK corporations executed their duties faithfully or sufficiently to avoid scandals. But the 1980s witnessed takeover raiders, as national heroes liberating corporations from their overmanned bureaucracies.[114] With or without Cadbury, the situation in the UK was not far off from those in the US, where the upgrading of CG represented a sensible counterreaction to the evaporation of the organization man. Faced with powerful dominant CEOs, the UK and the US at the time became perturbed by CG challenges.[115] The 1970s, as such, was called the decade of the established corporatists; the 1980s the decade of the self-made autocrats; and the 1990s emerging as the decade of low-key but highly professional technocrats.[116] It was no mere coincidence that both the UK and the US faced transformation of organization man to corporate buccaneers. This ascended CG as the sensible response, as both jurisdictions witnessed parallel changes and challenges to their corporate lifestyles.[117]

Improving access to capital in the UK, as it similarly did in the US in the 1980s and early 1990s, demonstrated, for example, how the Maxwell and other scandals generated various CG implications, like board structures and financial reporting obligations. Consequentially, conversations on governance intensified, while executives were monitored more closely, with institutional shareholder more willing in the early 1990s to respond with appropriate initiatives publicly in corporations where they hold shares, including the using of NEDs to dismiss CEOs of high-profile listed corporations. Checks imposed on executives were not robust enough to erase worries about managerial accountability, such that in the absence of Enron-style of corporate excesses, there were still newsworthy illustrations of shareholder activism and recurrent executive pay packages controversies to keep CG issues in the limelight. Still, changes to the managerial function in the early 1990s helped to sustain CG as an integral feature of the listed company domain thereafter. This was a point flashed out by the imprudent behaviors of various leading banks prior to the 2008 GFC.[118] Thus, the underlying trends in the US and their parallels in the UK would likely have lifted CG into prominence, irrespective of the contributions of Cadbury which though played a catalytic role. These trends in the US and the UK in the 1990s are considered unlikely to be replicated globally.[119]

As for the rest of the world, an OECD CG advisory group had opined that by the late 1990s, CG and by extension ESG had emerged as a theme of immense international

112. W. Kay. 1995. "Takeover fever is back". *Independent on Sunday 29/01/95: Business, 3.*
113. A. Dignam & M. Galanis. 2009. *The globalization of CG.* Farnham: Ashgate.
114. A. Sampson. 1995. *Company man: The rise and fall of corporate life.* New York: Harper Collins.
115. L. Buckingham. 1992. "Swashbucklers put to the sword". *Guardian 12/12/92: 38.*
116. M. Lynn & R. Olins. 1993. "The gold-collar workers". *Sunday Times 22/08/93: Business, 3.*
117. V. Treves & J. Ukropina. 1992. "Powerful push from the ranks". *Times 02/06/92: 27.*
118. D. Walker. 2009. *A review of CG in UK banks and other financial industry entities: Final recommendations.* London: Walker Review Secretariat.
119. Cheffins 2013, *supra* note [60].

interest and concern.[120] Still, this OECD report conceded that CG arrangements differed across borders, depending on various circumstances and factors. For instance, managerial accountability has been the top priority in the US and the UK as separation of ownership and control has been the standard in listed corporations. Elsewhere, dominant shareholders[121] prevailed, with the risk of potential exploitation of outside investors linked to this kind of ownership structure, thereby making this high on their governance agenda. Corporate laws in the US and UK in contrast though have provisions for minority shareholders' remedies. This difference, however, has not held back ESG developments resembling those in the US and the UK. This is mainly because corporations in a wide range of economies had been seeking capital to compete in an increasingly competitive global market needed to be responsive to investors' concerns across the world, but more so from the leading US and UK global capital markets. This meant paying attention and adhering to their ESG norms, and in particular the best practice Cadbury CG Code that has been regularly updated. This helped to explain how and why the CG Plus CSR or ESG approach had been replicated or adapted in many other economies across the world.

Meanwhile, the EU, US and the UK continued to dominate trends in ESG developments well into the 2020s, as their capital markets continue to lead the world in size and reputations. This was despite occasional knocks on the quality of CG practices in these three respective economies over these last two decades. A decade after the DFA of 2010 and a series of upgrades to UK's CG Code, corporate scandals unmasking bad and illicit corporate misbehaviors in the US[122] and the UK[123] demonstrated that there were still flaws needing remedial attention. While many businesses had been badly maligned by the COVID-19 pandemic, governments across the world have responded with various macroeconomic adjustments.

Lawmakers and regulators too have responded appropriately in the corporate legal environment to provide various insulation measures against those with misguided intents.[124] Calls for paying adequate attention to ESG matters have during the COVID-19 also escalated. This prompted answers as to how[125] or more simplified

120. Business Sector Advisory Group on CG. 1998. *CG: Improving competitiveness and access to capital in global markets.* Paris: OECD.
121. J. Dahya, O. Dimitrov & J.J. McConnell. 2017. "Dominant shareholders, corporate boards and corporate value: A cross-country analysis". *Journal of Financial Economics*. Vol. 87 (1): 73-100.
122. R. Cole, S. Johan & D. Schweizer. 2021. "Corporate failures: Declines, collapses, and scandals". *Journal of Corporate Finance,* Vol. 67 (2021): C. Florio, G. Gotti & R. Stacchezzini. 2021. "New Challenges in reporting on CG". *Journal of Management and Governance,* Vol. 25 (2021): 1-5.
123. I.F. Awolowo, N. Garrow, M. Clark & D. Chan. 2018. "Accounting scandals: Beyond CG". *Journal of Modern Accounting and Auditing,* Vol. 14 (8): 399-407; M. Kyere & M. Ausloos. 2020. CG and firm's financial performance in the United Kingdom". *International Journal of Finance & Economics,* https://doi.org/10.1002/ijfe.1883, accessed March 25, 2021.
124. United Nations Office on Drugs and Crime (UNODC). 2020. "COVID-19 vaccines and corruption risks: Preventing corruption in the manufacture, allocation and distribution of vaccines", https://www.unodc.org/documents/corruption/COVID-19/Policy_paper_on_COVID-19_vaccines_and_corruption_risks.pdf, accessed March 25, 2021.
125. M. Miller. 2021. "SEC on ESG risk disclosure-Moving from "if" to "how"". *JD Supra 26/03/21,* https://www.jdsupra.con/legalnews/sec-0n-esg, accessed March 27, 2021.

approaches[126] for dealing with various ESG concerns that had surfaced pronouncedly, and not just mere why. Increasingly because of seemingly nonstop digital disruptions, CEOs and corporate boards also needed to measure success in digital-type metrics. These accelerating transformations in the corporate landscape signaled the need for CG practices to adapt to these changes. The subsequent chapters would deal with these various challenges.

Beyond the US and UK space, the EU has also been busy addressing contemporary ESG issues, but even more comprehensively and steadfastly. In 2018, the European Commission (EC) paved the way for the design of a sustainable finance framework so as to promote the flow of private finance toward sustainable economic activities, as well as to facilitate the transition to a carbon-neutral economy by 2050. Toward this end, the EU adopted its Taxonomy Regulation on 18 June 2020, whereby its Taxonomy provided a common categorization of economic activities substantially contributing to environmental objectives, as guided by science-based criteria. The EU further instituted a comprehensive disclosure regime for both financial and nonfinancial entities to provide investors with the information needed to make informed sustainable investment decisions. These included the introduction of the Sustainable Finance Disclosure Regulation (SFDR) that became effective since March 2021; the Corporate Sustainability Reporting Directive (CSRD) as proposed by the EC in April 2021; as well as the adoption of the Sustainability Preferences by the EC in April 2021. The EU has also provided a broad toolbox for market participants, companies and financial intermediaries to design sustainable investment solutions so as to deter greenwashing practices. To this end and more, the EU Climate Benchmarks Regulation became applicable since April 2020. The EC has on 6 July 2021 also proposed the Standard for European green bonds.

The above regulatory initiatives aside, new actions contemplated by the EU included the following:

(a) Financing the transition of the real economy toward sustainability. These efforts include supporting the financing of designated economic activities to curtail greenhouse carbon emissions, extension of the EU Taxonomy framework for recognition of transition initiatives and inclusion of further activities, and the extension of sustainable finance standards and labels that support financing the transition to sustainability, as well as other phased transition initiatives.
(b) Driving toward a more inclusive finance framework. These efforts include empowering retail investors and SMEs to access sustainable finance opportunities, using digital technologies to leverage the opportunities for sustainable finance, managing climate and environmental risks through increasing insurance coverage, reporting on social taxonomy, and the designing of green budgeting and risk-sharing mechanisms.

126. M. Eltobgy & J. Gullot. 2021. "Yes, ESG is complicated. Together, we can simplify it". World Economic Forum (WEF) 26/03/21, https://www.weforum.com/agenda/2021/03/yes-esg-is, accessed March 27, 2021.

(c) Improving the financial sector's resilience and contribution to sustainability. These efforts include working on financing reporting standards to sufficiently reflect sustainability risks, ensuring that ESG emergent risks are systematically captured by credit ratings and rating outlooks with enhanced transparencies, integrating sustainability risks in the risk management systems of banks and the prudential framework for insurers, and monitoring and responding to potential systemic risks arising from sustainability challenges so as to achieve long-term financial stability.

(d) Promoting global initiatives and collaborations. These efforts include clarifying the fiduciary duties and stewardship rules of investors to show financial services' contributions to EU Green Deal targets, improving the availability, integrity and transparency of ESG market research and ratings, evaluating supervisory powers to address greenwashing, developing a robust monitoring framework for measuring progress made by EU financial services, promoting collaborations in international forums, expanding the work of the International Platform on Sustainable Finance to cover emerging topics and governance, and supporting low and middle-income economies in their transition initiatives.

As the EU drives the above ESG initiatives, China, the world number two economy, is drawing global attention with its surprising tighter regulatory reins on China-based global digital platforms. The US, EU, the UK and others have been wrestling with finding the appropriate way to deal with these behemoths in their own respective economies as these platforms continue to pose regulatory challenges in terms of market dominance and alleged abusive use of users' personal data. Despite the vast economic success of its homegrown global digital platforms, China regulators tighten their grips on them with tighter regulatory rules to curb their anticompetitive stance. These had the immediate impact of vastly damaging the market capitalizations of these platforms and also blocking the growth paths of those seeking funding in Western capital markets. This and the use of other rules to dissuade the exploitative use of users' personal data at the regulatory level suggest the importance the country placed on the "S" element of ESG. As for the "E" and "G" elements of ESG, China and its businesses still have a long way to go. Interestingly, Subodh Mishra's July 26, 2021, Harvard Law School paper, "Stewardship Excellence: ESG Engagement in 2021" suggests that the investing community in the US/UK/Canada axis, governance, diversity and equality joins climate as the most commonly identified important themes for engagement, whereas for those in continental Europe and Australia, human rights and labor rights considerations join climate as the more important themes. All now in general are surging toward ESG in earnest.

Meanwhile, the former UK colony, Hong Kong, now a part of China, still preserved many of its inherited UK common law traditions. When it comes to ESG laws and traditions, Hong Kong has been largely replicating the UK approach on many matters in its banking and capital markets. This partly helped to explain its success as one of the leading bourses in Asia. The Stock Exchange of Hong Kong requires issuers to publish ESG reports under its ESG guide. This covers four interlinked areas, namely board-level engagement, materiality evaluations, ensuring that each and every of the required disclosure are addressed, and the use of the option to "explain." This is a provision for which "comply and explain" is required.

2.02 DEFINING ESG

The OECD defined CG as involving a set of relationships between a company's management, its board, its shareholders and other stakeholders.[127] The definition guided OECD's Principles of CG.[128] It implies that CG would involve the management of relationships between corporate management, its board, shareholders, and other stakeholders by improving the legal, regulatory and institution framework for CG as measured by efficiency, stability, and sustainability metrics. This is a comprehensive and demanding kind of ask for corporations and boards, but still doable, albeit with the help and use of many resources which some corporations might find difficulties in mustering. The OECD's 2020 *ESG Investing: Practices, Progress and Challenges* monograph defines ESG investing as an approach that seeks to incorporate ESG factors into asset allocation and risk decisions so as to generate sustainable, long-term financial returns. The OECD paper argues that the rapid rise of ESG investing is due to the recognition that its returns are not inferior to traditional financial investments, that societal values toward ESG issues could likely impact corporate performance, and that there is a growing momentum for companies and financial institutions to migrate from short-term perspectives of risks and returns so as to better reflect longer-term sustainability in investment performance.

The IMF, another multilateral developmental institution, viewed governance in its widest term to refer to the various institutions, mechanisms, and established practices through which economies exercised governmental authorities, discharged responsibilities, and managed their public resources, including processes at the country level, as well as institutional arrangements.[129] The IMF further viewed governance as a neutral term, depicting a framework incorporating the institutions, mechanisms, and practices by which an economy exercised governmental authority and managed its public resources, but not its outcomes. It also clarified that international organizations tend to advance various definitions tilted toward their mandates. The OECD, for example, considered governance as the use of political authority and the exercise of control in a society pertaining to the management of its resources for social and economic development, while the Asian Development Bank (ADB) treated governance as the manner in which powers were exercised in the management of a nation's economic and social resources for development.[130]

Apart from the functioning capability of the public sector, governance from the perspective of the ADB, the IMF and the OECD also encompassed the rules and

127. OECD. 2015. G20/OECD principles of CG. Paris: OECD.
128. OECD 2015, *supra* note [127].
129. IMF. 2017. *The role of the fund in governance issues*. Washington, DC: IMF.
130. Asian Development Bank (ADB). 1999. *Governance: Sound development management*. Manila: ADB.

institutions that generate the framework for the undertaking of both public and private businesses, including accountability for economic and financial performance, and regulatory frameworks pertaining to companies, corporations, and partnerships. In this sense, governance is about the institutional environment wherein citizens interacted among themselves and with government entities or officials.[131] Essentially, because of their mandates, the OECD, IMF, and ADB focused on the macro dimensions of governance as these are linked to national developments, with some attention though given to the regulatory frameworks governing good governance extending from the public to the private sector, and in this sense occasional references to CG at the enterprise level.

The IMF and ADB though would pay particular attention to governance practices in the banking and finance sector, while the OECD to all businesses, but especially to big global corporations like multinationals (MNCs), as demonstrated by their design of the Base Erosion Profit Shifting (BEPS) Framework[132] now guiding financial reporting practices or obligations of MNCs. The IMF in its 2019 Global Financial Stability Report defines sustainable finance as the incorporation of large tracts of ESG principles as these might have material impact on corporate performance to give rise to financial stability risks through exposures of banks and insurers and large losses from climate change. The IMF further argues that the integration of ESG factors into a company's business model, as prompted by regulators, a company's own interest, or by investors, might assist in mitigating these risks. Investors' interests in ESG factors continue to rise, despite the absence of consistent evidence of the superior performance of sustainable finance. Further, ESG-related disclosures remained fragmented and sparse, attributed in part to associated costs, the often-voluntary nature of disclosure, and the lack of standardization. The IMF accordingly further argues that policymakers have a role to play in developing standards, promoting disclosure and transparency, and the advancing of integration of sustainability considerations into business and investment decisions. Of late, the IMF through the 2021 September issue of its Finance & Development quarterly publication draws attention to the dramatic impacts of climate change, and what and how governments and businesses might have to do to mitigate such impacts.

The IOSCO, comprising a grouping of capital market regulators and others, is the global governance standard setter for the securities sector.[133] It develops, implements and promotes adherence to internationally recognized standards for securities regulations, and works intensively with the G20 and the Financial Stability Board (FSB). The IOSCO basically endorsed the CG definition provided by the OECD. It also stressed that CG would provide the structure to which the objectives or strategy of the company would be set, the means of achieving those objectives, and how performance monitoring would be determined.[134] Responding to its own mandate, the IOSCO's objectives

131. ADB 1999, *supra* note [130].
132. EY. 2021. "OECD releases new transparency framework for Action 5 for 2021 through 2025", *EY 26/02/21*, https://www.ey.com/en_gl/tax-alerts/oecd-releases-new-transparency-framework, accessed March 30, 2021.
133. IOSCO. 2021. *International Organization of Securities Commissions*. Madrid: IOSCO.
134. IOSCO. 2012. *Changing perspectives in CG*. Madrid: IOSCO.

included investor protection; fair, efficient and transparent markets; and reduction of systemic risk. To this end, IOSCO principles included attention to conflicts of interest and misalignment of incentives that should be avoided, eliminated, disclosed or otherwise managed; and for market intermediaries to establish internal compliance and ensure proper risk management.[135] The IOSCO reinforced these with what it viewed as the elements of CG. These included the roles for boards, shareholders, and financial institutions, and with focus on those matters substantially involved in the financial and capital markets (now read to include ESG matters).[136]

IOSCO's April 2020 report on Sustainable Finance and the Role of Securities Regulators and IOSCO suggested three recurring themes. These refer to multiple and diverse sustainability frameworks and standards, including on sustainability-related disclosure; the lack of common definitions of sustainable activities; and greenwashing and other challenges to investor protection. The IOSCO highlighted that the various existing frameworks could be complementary and mutually supportive, and that the most commonly referenced sustainability-related frameworks, principles, and guidance include those from the global reporting initiative (GRI), the sustainability standards board (SASB), the taskforce on climate-related financial disclosures (TCFD), and the SDGs. It also noted that the momentum is heading toward a more structured approach to corporate reporting on sustainability-related issues.

The IOSCO's June 2021 Final Report on Sustainability-Related Issuer Disclosures draws attention to several most prominent global initiatives and their progress to date. These include those from the International Financial Reporting Standard (IFRS) Foundation Trustees, the Alliance of Sustainability Reporting Organisations, the recommendations of the TCFD, and the report from the WEF. These highlighted the absence of a generally accepted international framework for the reporting of the material aspects of ESG, and other considerations for long-term value creation that are in contrast with the well-established standards for reporting and verifying financial performance. The WEF International Business Council (IBC) responded with an agreed common set of measures and metrics on principles of governance, planet, people and prosperity, on which their members have committed to reporting. From a jurisdictional perspective, the IOSCO found that the EU has the most advanced progress on sustainability reporting.

EU's Non-Financial Reporting Directive (NFRD) that became effective in 2018 requires large companies to disclose certain information on the manner they operate and manage social and environmental challenges. The EC followed through on April 21, 2021, with a proposal that extends the scope to all large companies and oil companies listed on regulated markets. This requires the audit or assurance of reported information, and introduces more detailed reporting requirements and a requirement to report according to mandatory EU sustainability reporting standards. The proposal also requires companies to digitally "tag" the reported information, so as to align with other pieces of EU legislation on sustainability. The EC's 2019 Guidelines on reporting

135. IOSCO 2012, *supra* note [134].
136. IOSCO 2012, *supra* note [134].

climate-related information and 2017 Non-Binding Guidelines on Non-Financial Reporting distinguish financial materiality and environmental/social materiality. Financial materiality is defined with reference to the impact of sustainability-related matters on the development, performance and position of the reporting company that is relevant for determination of the enterprise value and material to investors and other participants in the capital markets, or sometimes referred to as the "outside-in" approach. Environmental and social materiality, in contrast, refers to the external impact of the company's activities, and that sustainability-related information should be reported where needed for better understanding of the external impacts of the company on the environment, or sometimes referred to as the "inside-out" perspective. Reporting on both dimensions is commonly understood as applying a double materiality prism. There could though be considerable overlap in reporting under the two lenses. However, the dynamic nature of materiality also implies that the relationship between these two lenses would continue to evolve.

IOSCO's engagement with stakeholders in its two roundtable sessions suggests that many market participants, including issuers, are waiting for regulators to help drive clarity, consistency and quality of sustainability reporting across jurisdictions. There is recognition that there may be limitations to private sector initiatives, particularly where these may be more regional or focused on designated topics, and which might lead to fragmentation and inconsistency in reporting. Drawing from these insights, the IOSCO on February 24, 2021, announced three priority areas wherein improvements could be made in the system for sustainability disclosures that could align with IOSCO's objectives. These refer to the encouraging of globally consistent standards, the promoting of comparable metrics and narratives, and the coordinating of approaches to achieve international consistency of sustainability-related disclosures with focus on enterprise value creation.

The IOSCO following this announced three key elements of its vision to deliver the priorities for improvements. These refer to the establishment of an International Sustainability Standards Board (ISSB) with a strong governance foundation; advancing on existing sustainability-related reporting frameworks to set investor-oriented standards focused on enterprise value, beginning with climate change; and encouraging a "building-blocks" approach via a coordinated mechanism. There was strong support for the key elements of the IOSCO vision from the Roundtable participants who were also supportive of the Prototype developed by the Alliance as a starting point for ISSB's "climate-first" reporting standard.

In turn, the EC also articulated its support for global initiatives by the G20, the G7, and FSB and others to develop a baseline of global sustainability reporting standards, and in particular cited the IFRS Foundation's ISSB initiative. The IOSCO's earlier January 2019 Statement on Disclosure of ESG matters by Issuers had stressed that ESG matters, though sometimes tagged as nonfinancial may have a material impact on issuers' business operation, as well as risks and returns for investors and their investment and voting decisions. In this regard, the IOSCO further emphasized that there should be full, accurate and timely disclosure of financial results, risk and other information that is material to investors' decisions.

The academic and research community had also provided their inputs, and given the lack of consensus on the ESG paradigm, various definitions had arisen over the years, depending on the sentiments of the period.[137] Earlier definitions intertwined corporate finance and ESG, arguing that equity and debt could be deemed as alternative structures of governance, with the latter leading to rules-based structures, and the former to discretionary ones.[138] Others tweaked this to argue that ESG has been about the manners wherein suppliers of finance to companies assure themselves of getting returns on their investments, thereby premising this on the agency theory of the firm.[139] From a narrower prism, CG had been viewed as a system of legal and real control of companies extending to systems of accountability of those in control.[140] In this sense, ESG pertains to the structures and processes for the direction and control of corporations, and ergo pertained to the relationships among management, board of directors, shareholders and other stakeholders.[141] The CC took this equivalent position defining ESG or rather CG, as the system by which companies are directed and controlled.[142] The idea was for good ESG practices to contribute to sustainable economic development by enhancing the performance of corporations, increasing access to external capital and boosting confidence in the market leading to stability.[143]

ESG has been further defined as the checks and balances impacting those who run companies.[144] It had also been referred to as an umbrella term that incorporated particular issues arising from interactions among senior management, shareholders, boards of directors, and other corporate stakeholders.[145] These kinds of definitions provided no signals on the tensions in the CG process. Others made timid reference to this, by saying that CG would deal with the appropriate board structures, processes, and values to cope with the rapidly changing demands of both shareholders and stakeholders in and around their corporations.[146]

Drawing attention to the macro and micro dimensions of ESG is deliberate, as it had been argued that effective systems of CG would have two requirements, one micro and the other macro.[147] ESG at the micro level would need to ensure that the company as a productive enterprise would operate in pursuit of its objectives. The conventional US/UK approach would treat the company as a mechanism to promote the well-being of its owner/shareholders, such that good governance is a way of ensuring that

137. J. Farrar. 2001. *CG in Australia and New Zealand*. Oxford: OUP.
138. O.E. Williamson. 1996. *The mechanisms of governance*. New York: OUP.
139. A. Schleifer & R. Vishny. 1997. "A survey of CG". *Journal of Finance*, Vol. 52 (1997): 737-782.
140. Farrar 2001, *supra* note [137].
141. PwC. 2021. "CG". https://www.pwc.com/gx/en/about/global-regulatory-affairs/corporate-governance.html#: ~ :text = Corporate%20governance%20refers%20to%20the, accessed March 28, 2121.
142. A. Cadbury. 1992. *Report of the committee on the financial aspects of CG: The code of best practice*. London: Gee Publishing.
143. PwC 2021, *supra* note [141].
144. R.E. Wright. 2014. *Corporation nation*. Philadelphia: University of Pennsylvania Press.
145. B. Tricker. 2001. *Pocket director*. New York: Viva Books.
146. B. Garratt. 2003. *Thin on top*. London: Nicholas Brealey Publishing.
147. K. Keasey, S. Thompson & M. Wright. 2005. "Introduction". In K. Keasey, S. Thompson & M. Wright (eds.). *CG: Accountability, enterprise and international comparisons*. Chichester: John Wiley & Sons Ltd.

decisions would be taken and implemented in pursuit of shareholder value. Consequentially, this would involve undertakings that reconcile the need to protect the downside risk to shareholders, meaning the accountability of managers, as well as encouraging managers to take risks to enhance shareholder value, meaning the encouraging of managers to act entrepreneurially. Where the corporation's purpose is modified to accommodate the interests of other stakeholders, like those promoted by the wider ESG paradigm, the objective would have changed, but the need for mechanisms to advance this objective might have not.[148] Prominent UK-based academicians, Jill Solomon and Aris Solomon, as far back as 2004, have succinctly put CG (or ESG) as the system of checks and balances, both internal and external to corporations, that ensures that they discharge their accountability to all their stakeholders and act in a socially responsible way in all domains of their business activity. Their take could have helped to shape the enlightened shareholder approach defined in UK's CA 2006, where directors' drive toward company success would also need to give due consideration to ESG factors for the company's long-term well-being.

ESG, at the macro dimension, has evolved to more effectively promote the allocation of a nation's savings to its most productive use.[149] Hence, in the financing of corporate activity via equity or debt, savings would be channeled into productive undertakings, the returns of which would eventually determine national prosperity. Corporate failures in the 1990s and 2000s, or even earlier, would serve to remind that where failures at the corporate level had been adequately serious or widespread, misallocation of funds would occur in the short term, and systemic damaging consequences for longer-term investments where confidence is damaged.[150] Indeed, for developing and emerging economies, a major challenge has been to design governance systems that would engender sufficient trust to enable private savers to supply domestic entrepreneurs with their funds.[151]

In sum, ESG had because of the many diverse perspectives become one of those heavily and perhaps even overused business lexicon, contributed in part by bad things happening to businesses all over the world. Thus, as mentioned earlier, there would be those treating ESG as being primarily about legal structures; for others about business controls, and the checks and balances on how the different corporate organs and people undertake their work; and yet for others, ESG is a broader notion incorporating the entire manner businesses are led and managed.[152]

A persuasive case has now been made that effective ESG is founded on five interrelated pillars, where each has to be in place and running well for good governance

148. K. Keasey & M. Wright. 1993. "Issues in corporate accountability and governance". *Accounting and Business Research*, Vol. 23 (1993): 291-303.
149. A. Greenspan. 2003. *Speech Delivered at the Conference on Bank Structure and Competition*, Chicago 08/05/03.
150. B. Holmstrom & S. Kaplan. 2003. "The state of US CG: What's right and what's wrong?". *Journal of Applied Corporate Finance*, Vol. 15 (3): 8-20.
151. A. Shleifer. 1997. "Government in transition". *European Economic Review*, Vol. 41 (1997): 385-410.
152. PwC. 2015. "CG in the boardroom: A practical perspective". *A PwC Point-of-View Paper June 2015*, https://www.pwc.com/ee/et/publications/pub/corporate-governance, accessed July 28, 2020.

to deliver. These pillars comprise leadership strategy and culture (tone, conduct, chairman & CEO, decision-making, strategy formulation, reserved matters and delegation, board meetings, and relationships with management); structure and performance oversight (board composition (BC) and commitment, appointment succession and reelection, board committees, board evaluation, induction and training, management information and advice, entity governance, and auditor relationships); risks (risk appetite, risk and control culture, major risks and going concerns, risk management framework, risk and control monitoring, policy framework, and effectiveness evaluation); management information and controls (compensations and benefits schemes, performance-linked remunerations, incentive schemes, remuneration balance, risk-adjusted rewards, balanced scorecard, and nonfinancial performance); and transparency and reporting (stakeholder engagements, stewardship code, annual general meetings (AGMs), financial and nonfinancial reporting, and regulators).[153]

The ongoing COVID-19 pandemic demonstrated that trust in corporations is crucial. Also, where stakeholders' scrutiny goes wider and more intense, it becomes more important than ever for corporations to act in accordance with their core purpose and principles so as to protect reputation and trust. ESG is ergo an essential mechanism, where boards could ensure that the actions of their personnel would align to the corporation's purpose and principles, and where corporate goals and values would be translated into the decision-making process and actions.[154]

Viable ESG could be compacted into three distinctive themes.[155] Foremost, effective ESG would be grounded in a clear view of what matters most to the corporation, the comprehensive range of risks confronting the corporation, and how these risks relate to the business and its strategic priorities. Second, good CG would begin and would end with the board that is responsible for mapping out a clear CP, demonstrating the right values, and ensuring that these are being implemented. Third, the litmus test for good CG, especially when crisis hits, would be when behaviors and decisions respond to moments that matter.

Recent research suggests that ESG analysis had thus far been largely one-sided, where the focus had been on internal accountability mechanisms, namely, boards and shareholders that have both been becoming more effective since ESG became prominent since the 1970s.[156] There are now concerns about whether the positiveness of the process would continue. Simultaneously, arguments have been raised that it would be timely to expand the analysis of ESG. This could involve drawing attention to three external accountability mechanisms that could operate as effective constraints on managerial discretion, namely, governmental regulation of corporate activities; competitive pressures from rival corporations; and organized labor. The common thread running through these three external mechanisms is that each of these represents a constituent of the theory of countervailing power developed in the 1950s pertaining to

153. PwC 2015, *supra* note [152].
154. PwC 2015, *supra* note [152].
155. PwC 2015, *supra* note [152].
156. B.R. Cheffins. 2019. "CG and countervailing power". *ECGI Working Paper Series in Law No. 448/2019 April 2019.*

corporations at a time when external accountability mechanisms contributed more than internal mechanisms to keeping management in alignment.[157] The foci were on constraints pertinent to corporate behaviors in general, rather than to corporate executives in particular. Still, the sources of countervailing power raised then could still be relevant for management, as well as corporations.[158]

For the traditional CG landscape, the 1950s and 1960s represented an era of loyalty to the corporation, not only with corporate scandals hardly surfacing but also with neither boards nor shareholders playing active roles in fostering managerial accountability. Boards and shareholders dominated CG conversations, with proposed answers to concerns about managerial accountability commonly being channeled through adjustments to these twin internal governance mechanisms. Indeed, boards and shareholders had become a governance afterthought during the glory days of managerial capitalism, and where restraint was the norm for corporate captains. The governance-linked paradox of 1950s and 1960s managerial accountability appeared resolved by the idea of countervailing powers that at the time focused on the corporation than management, as it had been assumed that executives would seek to promote growth so as to increase their personal powers and influence, rather than exploit the discretion accessible to them in a narrowly personal way.[159] Still, the disciplines which unions and government regulation imposed on public corporations and their executives during the middle decades of the 20th century contributed to helping explain why managerial wrongdoing was uncommon.

The above told a tale of ESG, as it evolved as governance plus CSR format, or in its newer stakeholder model that Klaus Schwab, the CEO of WEF, first wrote in 1971, and now operationalized as ESG. Back then, Schwab had argued that the shareholder capitalism in the West and state capitalism in the East that had enabled unprecedented advances in wealth had also led to historical inequality, and the degradation of the environment. He further argued that the world could not continue with economic systems driven by short-term profit maximization, avoidance of tax and regulation, or the externalizing of environmental harm. Accordingly, he proposed a third way, known as SC where companies seek long-term value creation instead of short-term profits, where governments cooperate to create the greatest possible prosperity for their people, and where the civil society and international organizations complete the stakeholder dialogue, thereby helping to balance the interests of profits, people, and the planet. He updated this in his 2021 book, *Stakeholder Capitalism*.

The ESG lexicon, as drawn from the stakeholder paradigm, has since then been repackaged to the world sometime in 2005 by the investing community riding on the hot heels of the SRI that received worldwide attention through the GRI. Rather than as a single framework on its own, ESG as the world knows it today has been the outcome of a series of connected actions of the business community that accelerated subsequent to Milton Friedman's advocation in 1970 that the social responsibility of business is to

157. J.K. Galbraith. 1993. *American capitalism: The concept of countervailing power*. Abingdon: Routledge.
158. J.K. Galbraith. 2007. *The new industrial state*. Princeton: Princeton University Press.
159. Galbraith 2007, *supra* note [158].

increase its profits, whereas others argued, for CP beyond profit maximization or the shareholder primacy perspective. Further momentum was provided by the Domini 400 Social Index in 1990, the first of its type that tracked sustainable investment. A decade later in 2000, the UN introduced the Global Compact Initiative (GCI) supported today by more than 14,054 corporate signatories across more than 162 national economies providing more than 83,974 public reports on ESG matters.

The global financial community was galvanized into action by GCI's endorsing global financial institutions "Who Cares Wins" 2004 report that ESG factors impact long-term shareholder value. This was followed by the founding of the UN PRI in 2005 partly in response to growing perceptions among investment professionals that ESG factors could be deemed material enough and by increasing acceptance among investment professionals that the appropriate evaluation of these could be necessary in fulfilling the fiduciary duties of investment managers. The Asset Management Group a year later found conclusive evidence that ESG factors impact shareholder value in both the short and long term, that the effect of ESG factors on share value could be valued and quantified, and that key ESG factors have varying importance between different economic sectors. The 2009 Mercer Report in turn highlighted the need to develop comparable reliable standards so as to mainstream the integration of ESG factors into the investment process. The earlier 2004 GCI report had claimed that the manner ESG matters are managed in the globalized, interconnected and competitive world represented the pivotal part of the company's overall management quality needed to compete successfully. Those companies performing more effectively on these issues could uplift shareholder value through effective risk management, being more alert to regulatory actions, and in tapping ESG opportunities in emerging markets. Such matters are also likely to have powerful impact on reputation and brands that are now important components of corporate valuation.

Thus, ESG concerns are viewed in general to be nonfinancial or intangible factors accounted for in enterprise valuation. Though widely seen in academic and professional literature, it has no universally accepted definitions. ESG has been variously viewed in the context of competitive strategy, sustainability, SRI, intangible measures, CSR, investment methodologies, and risks dimensions. This raises the risks of improper analysis and inconsistent calibrations. Vincent Whitlock in January 2015 responded to this need in his "Environmental Social Governance Management" article in the *International Journal of Business Information Systems* that ESG activities or processes are connected with an enterprise's relationship with its ecological landscape, its coexistence and interactions with human organisms and its corporate system of internal control and procedures to direct and control the business affairs of the enterprise so as to address the interests of primary and secondary stakeholders.

This definition cleverly adds the environmental and social considerations into the already widely followed 1990 Cadbury's "direction and control" definition for CG to become ESG as we know it today. It is necessary though to differentiate this with CSR that is sometimes equated with it. Howard Bowen in his 1953 *Social Responsibilities of the Businessman* seminal book described CSR as an enterprise's initiative to fulfill its socially responsible commitments, from an enterprise self-regulated perspective. ESG as mentioned earlier is used as a set of criteria for evaluating enterprise value by the investment community. As such, CSR seeks to make an enterprise accountable for its activities, whereas ESG criteria make such business initiatives measurable. In recent years, CSR has been more viewed as a marketing tool showing the symbolic gestures of an enterprise, whereas ESG is increasingly seen as triple-bottom-line (profit, people, and planet) business metric employed by socially conscious investors to identify and measure an enterprise's sustainability and societal impact.

ESG factors considerations gradually rebranded the substance of CSR and SRI. Thus, the "doing good while doing well" strategy has been in part substituted by business risk considerations and investment opportunities associated with ESG matters. The UN answered the call for elaborating ESG metrics since 2009. Eventually through collaborations with various international business entities, including the World Federation of Exchanges, a model guidance, inclusive of key performance indicators, was released in 2015, that in turn were updated in 2018.

The British Academy (BA) draws on CP as the basis for ESG, citing Oxford University's Professor Colin Mayer definition that CP pertains to finding solutions to the problems of people and planet, not profiting from creating problems for either. The BA further advocated that the key to inducing companies to a purpose-led orientation is ensuring that companies and board directors are held accountable through a supportive legal, regulatory, governance and reporting framework, combined with more effective implementation of CPs.

The swing toward greater ESG application is now driven by the investing community, employees and consumers together demanding transparent purpose-led business practices that match with their own value or priorities. Kevin Spellman & David Nicholas highlighted in their "ESG Matters" 2019 article in *ISS Governance* that some 93% of the world's largest enterprises in terms of revenues have publicly disclosed their ESG performance, while 31 S&P 500 companies cited ESG on earnings calls, thereby confirming the widespread use of ESG across the world.

As ESG matters to good corporate citizenry, business corporations are tasked to take leadership role by implementing ESG principles and policies, and to provide information and reports on related performance in more consistent and standardized formats, particularly in the annual reports of companies. To assist in this endeavor and to facilitate communications between investors, and other market participants, the Sustainability Accounting and Standards Board (SASB) was launched in 2011 to promote the standardization of sustainability accounting and measurements across some seventy-seven industries. Accordingly, five standard-setting entities, namely the carbon disclosure project (CDP), the carbon disclosure standards board (CDSB), the GRI, the international integrated reporting council (IIRC), and the sustainability accounting standards board (SASB) in December 2020 unveiled a template for climate-related financial disclosure standard demonstrating how their shared vision and concepts could be applied to climate-elated disclosures, including contents and metrics consolidated into a single practical guide. In turn, the Paris Agreement sprung into higher global prominence in 2015 at the UN Framework Convention through further boosting of the SDGs.

The COVID-19 pandemic surfacing in early 2020 impacted the operations of many businesses in the US, the EU, the UK and elsewhere. Importantly, diversity and inclusion, worker health and safety at worksites, and climate change environmental damage issues came into enhanced prominence in corporate corridors. This even led leading institutional investors like the IMF, Blackrock, and others to advocate for sustained corporate attention and actions on ESG issues going forward, as these matter to corporate performance and resilience. This helps to explain why close to USD 2 trillion are invested in ESG sustainability-focused funds, as reported on April 30, 2021, by Pippa Stevens in Consumer News and Business Channel (CNBC). Market signals here suggest that when companies perform well by ESG metrics, they have the likelihood of doing well from a financial angle too.

2.03 INTERNAL VERSUS EXTERNAL ESG

Insights from the 1950s and 1960s demonstrated why it is useful analytically then (and even now) to perceive CG or ESG in terms of external, as well as internal accountability mechanisms. The market for capital control; market disciplines; auditors; CRAs; the media; competition from rivals; unions; and governmental regulation is a good and growing list of external accountability mechanisms.[160] For big public corporations in the 1950s and 1960s with enviable levels of profits were flushed with cash resources mainly because of their market power and the then buoyant economy,[161] but in other contexts, capital markets could be a powerful restraint on managerial discretions. Historical evidence aside, it has been pointed out that internal accountability mechanisms of both boards and shareholders had become substantially more robust since the middle decades of the 20th century. It had been further contended that there could be few obvious structural initiatives left to strengthen monitoring capabilities. Pertaining to shareholders, hedge funds had emerged since 2000 as a meaningful source of public corporation discipline, but it had been lamented that hedge fund activism could have peaked,[162] while the business models of index trackers would suggest that it would be unlikely for them to be exercising substantial control over corporate executives soon enough.[163] Guided by these foreseeable trends, it could be timely for external mechanisms to be on par with internal mechanisms when analyzing ESG.

Both the internal and external aspects of ESG would require good attention.[164] The more obvious range of controls for corporations would flow from its internal mechanisms that would track the progress and activities of the corporation and would

160. N.M. Brennan & J.F. Atkins. 2008. "CG, accountability and mechanisms of accountability: An overview". *Accounting Auditing & Accountability Journal*, Vol. 21 (7): 885-906.
161. M.S. Mizruchi. 2013. *The fracturing of the American corporate elite*. Boston: Harvard University Press.
162. Insightia. 2021. "The activist investing annual review: The eight annual reviews of trends in shareholder activism". https://www.activistinsight.com/research/Insightia_AIAR2021.pdf, accessed March 28, 2021; A. Brav, W. Jiang & H. Kim. 2015. "Recent advances in research on hedge fund activism: Value creation and identification". *Annual Review of Financial Economics*, Vol. 7 (1): 579-595.
163. Cheffins 2013, *supra* note [60].
164. A. Naciri. 2010. *Internal and external aspects of CG*. Abingdon: Routledge; I. Filatchev & C. Nakajima. 2010. "Internal and external CG: An interface between an organization and its environment". *British Journal of Management*, Vol. 21 (3): 591-606.

induce remedial actions when seeing material deviations from organizational goals and objectives.[165] These internal mechanisms would serve the internal objectives of the corporation and its internal stakeholders, extending from employees to managers, and owners. These objectives extend from ensuring smooth operations, clear reporting lines, to performance measurement systems. The internal aspects of ESG further include oversight of management, independent internal audits, structuring of boards of directors into spans of responsibilities, and segregations of control and policy development.[166] The internal aspects of ESG have increased board responsibility and accountability to the health and safety considerations for employees, and risk management of climate change effects.

The external dimension could either be market-oriented, or assumed the form of credit ranking, and/or social requirements.[167] These external mechanisms would be controlled by those external to the corporation serving the objectives of regulators, governments, trade unions, CRAs, and financial institutions.[168] Such objectives would include adequacy of debt management and legal compliance. External mechanisms are frequently imposed on corporations by external stakeholders in the shape of regulatory guidelines or kinds of union contracts. Industry associations too could suggest guidelines for best practices, but businesses could opt to adhere to these, or simply ignore them.[169] Where corporations opt to follow these guidelines, they would report the status and compliance of external ESG mechanisms to the stakeholders involved. As mentioned earlier,[170] external accountability mechanisms have been gaining traction, while there have also been continuous improvements in the internal aspects over the years. Since the ascendance or high-profiling of ESG metrics by the investing community in 2005 as alluded to earlier, several ESG rating agencies have emerged focusing on the ratings of ESG activities in companies along the lines of the CRAs. Thus far, unlike the previous experiences of the CRAs, there have been no loud calls for the services of a supervisory body that the CRAs had since the 2007 to 2008 GFC been subject to. This though does not necessarily imply that the quality and consistency of these ratings have not drawn criticisms.

Both internal and external CG accountability mechanisms would rely a lot on ESG disclosures as found in nonfinancial reporting. The external factors would comprise country-specific legislations and scandals, and internal factors like financial performance, size, and culture. Part of the wider literature on corporate financial reporting includes using simple proxies for ESG mechanisms. Examples include BC characteristics for analyzing the impact on financial reporting quality and corporate valuation. The determinants and consequences of ESG reporting could be interlinked, but many quantitative explorations failed to account for these links and their multiple impacts

165. J. Davoren. 2021. "Three types of CG mechanisms". https://smallbusiness.chron.com/three-types-corporate-governance-mechanisms-66711.html, accessed March 28, 2021.
166. Davoren 2021, *supra* note [165].
167. Davoren 2021, *supra* note [165].
168. Davoren 2021, *supra* note [165].
169. Davoren 2021, *supra* note [165].
170. Cheffins 2013, *supra* note [60].

sufficiently. Poor financial performance, for instance, could be a determinant and consequence of the underlying governance that ESG reporting sought to capture.

The likely links between the external determinants (like social/cultural, stakeholder pressures, media interest, and scandals) and internal determinants (like business size, industry positions, stakeholder relations, corporate performance, impression management, managerial incentives, and culture); formal mechanisms (like strategy monitoring, performance and risk analysis as measured by board characteristics, board independence, board committee composition, and responsible corporate citizenship and accountability, as measured by stakeholder inclusivity); informal mechanisms (like ethical culture and effective control systems); and external consequences (like corporate performance, ESG indices, legitimacy & reputation); and internal consequences (like decision-making capability) of strong or weak ESG would be often linked.[171] These have thus been compacted into a useful framework for corporate guidance.

Both the internal and external ESG mechanisms are subject to independent audit.[172] The audited financial statements and the accompanying auditor's report could assist investors, employees, shareholders and regulators in determining the financial performance of the corporations. These audited statements could provide a wide but limited view of the corporation's internal working mechanisms, and some insights on future prospects. Those had been the expectations over many decades, but continuous weaknesses and flaws of independent audit reports even after serious interventions from SOX 2002 and DFA 2010 in the US and extended corporate reporting obligations from the CA 2006, as well as CG Codes in the UK had begun to cast doubts on the quality and integrity of auditing reports.[173] The UK has in fact now begun consulting again on how to improve the efficacy and reliability of the accounting and auditing industry.[174]

2.04 WHY ESG MATTERS

To recapitulate, for the mainstream Anglo-American shareholder primacy model, CG essentially deals with the protection of shareholder interest that involves the use of rules or laws necessitating managers or agents to operate in the best interests of

171. C. de Villiers & R. Dimes. 2021. "Determinants, mechanisms, and consequences of CG reporting: A research framework". *Journal of Management and Governance*, Vol. 25 (2021): 7-26.
172. Davoren 2021, *supra* note [165].
173. I.D. Gow & S. Kells. 2018. *The big four: The curious past and perilous future of the global accounting monopoly*. Melbourne: La Trobe University Press; C. Shore & S. Wright. 2018. "How the Big 4 got big: Audit culture and the metamorphosis of international accountancy firms". *Critique of Anthropology*, Vol. 38 (1): 1-22.
174. Department for Business, Energy & Industrial Strategy (DBEIS). 2021. "Restoring trust in audit and CG: Proposals on reforms". *DBEIS 18/03/21*, https://www.gov.uk/government/consultations/restoring-trust-in-audit-and-corporate-governance-proposals-on-reforms, accessed March 28, 2021; DBEIS. 2021. "Restoring trust in audit and CG: Consultation on the government's proposals". DBEIS March 2021, https://assets.publishing.service.gov.uk/government/uploads/system/uploads/attachment_data/file/970673/restoring-trust-in-audit-and-corporate-governance-command-paper.pdf, accessed March 28, 2021.

shareholders. It entails various mechanisms that enable shareholders to exercise voting powers to insist that those in operating power of the enterprise honor their interest.[175] Corporate laws operate to resolve explicit managerial incompetence and conflicts of interest within boards and management. Other than in seminal cases exemplified by Enron and WorldCom, ESG clearly had never been an issue for full owner cum manager of corporations, or even for majority shareholder groups that enjoyed the power to hire and dismiss managers. The protection for minority interest though is a different matter. ESG becomes an issue for minority shareholders in corporations controlled by managers, as being dispersed and disparate, they are not able to collaborate conveniently as a collective group to protect their agenda. Dispersed ownership patterns are mostly associated with US and UK corporations, while concentrated ownership patterns are associated with companies in emerging and developing economies or in free market economies with strong elements of socialisms, such as found in various Eastern European economies.

Governance though differs from management. Governance seeks to ensure that the firm is being well run and being guided in the direction of the corporate objective, while management pertains to the helming of the firm to fulfill operational and financial objectives. The board of directors oversee CG, but this would be rarely observed in organizational charts that conventionally show a management hierarchy, with the CEO or managing director at the top heading the organizational pyramid, and various managerial levels functioning through the concept of delegation of authority and responsibility for management functions downwards while insisting on accountability upwards. The board responsible for governance in effect did not have a hierarchical structure, as every director generally enjoys equivalent duties and powers. In unitary boards such as those typically found in the Anglo-Saxon ESG model, members of management might have a position on the board; their roles as board members differ from their role as a member of management. A director's primary task is to direct the corporation toward its objective by overseeing the management process and managers.

However, managerialism with management wielded dominant powers in corporations in much of the 1980s-1990s. The practical responsibility for running and helming the corporation together was largely in the hands of corporate management. They dominated in the running and direction of the corporation culminating in a less effective board of directors who were largely incapable of fulfilling their responsibilities in overseeing the undertaking of the business of the enterprise and in protecting the interests of shareholders and other stakeholders.[176] This has been attributed to the dependence of the board on management. In turn, board independence had been

175. K.E. Scott. 2002. "Agency costs and CG". *The New Palgrave Dictionary of Economics and the Law*. London: Palgrave Macmillan.

176. C.L. Adam. 2004. "Power plays: A longitudinal examination of CEO/BDO power circulation and its impact on organisational performance". Florida State University Doctoral Thesis.

compromised by conformity and domination of management in the board, informational social influence, influence of inside directors on outside directors, and information dependence of the board on management.[177]

It has been further contended that management enjoyed considerable powers over the appointment of outside board members such that they ensured the appointment of compliant directors that essentially rubber-stamped management policies. In turn, the general passive behaviors of board members because of lack of adequate insights into corporate affairs compared to management worsened board ability to monitor managerial conflicts. Indeed, managerialism's focus on informational dependence of the board, routines for selecting board members, directors' characteristics and social and time constraints of board members highlighted the impediments of these to the ability of board to monitor management effectively. This prompted the countering of this trend through the design of various structural rules that could dilute managerial influences, like the giving of board nomination powers to institutional investors' association.[178] This helped to explain the reason for ESG codes calling for the appointment of independent NEDs.[179]

This aside, there has also been the need to curtail the domineering influence of management over shareholders arising from the dualism principle, where the CEO was also the board's chairman.[180] This helped to explain the huge controversies generated by this duality function in US and UK capital markets. Based on agency theory, separating the chair and CEO role would increase the board's independence from management leading to better monitoring and oversight, but in contrast the stewardship or administrative theory argues that the benefits were not so clear-cut, and that having clear and unambiguous authority concentrated in one individual is essential to effective management, as unity of command creates clear lines of authority, to which management and the board could respond more effectively, besides providing an important signal to stakeholders as to who would be accountable.[181] Unfortunately, the academic literature on this controversial phenomenon is for the most part unsettled.[182] Given this dilemma, one study suggests that policymaking and shareholder guidelines focusing primarily on role separation might omit the dimension of effective board leadership, and as such the focus instead should be on the effectiveness of the prospective or incumbent chair of the board.[183] Where there is no appropriate individual on the board to fill the role, the board could be better off relying on a unified structure, instead of forcibly putting themselves into a separate structure.

177. L.L. Dallas. 1996. "The relational board: Three theories of corporate board of directors". *The Journal of Corporation Law*, Vol. 22 (1996): 1-25.
178. Dallas 1996, *supra* note [177].
179. S. Bhagat & B. Black. 1999. "The uncertain relationship between board composition and firm performance". *Business Lawyer*, Vol. 54 (1999): 921-963.
180. M. Tonello, R. Leblanc & K. Pick. 2011. "Separation of Chair and CEO roles". *Harvard Law School Forum on CG 01/09/11*, https://corpgov.law.harvard.edu/2011/09/01/separation-of-chair-and-ceo-roles, accessed August 22, 2020.
181. Tonello, Leblanc & Pick 2011, *supra* note [180].
182. Tonello, Leblanc & Pick 2011, *supra* note [180].
183. Tonello, Leblanc & Pick 2011, *supra* note [180].

Despite the continuous flurries of corporate scandals in the US, UK, EU and elsewhere,[184] there have been more corporations not materially dented by these because of guidance from various ESG guidance and best practices.[185] Markets have demonstrated that good CG would lead to superior outcomes for corporations and stakeholders, and that investors would do best by avoiding corporations with the most questionable ESG practices. This would help to explain why investors in both advanced and developing markets have historically placed ESG premiums on corporations with low ESG-related risks and CG discounts on corporations with poor governance.[186] Policies and practices like opaque or limited disclosures, unqualified boards, limited shareholder rights, poor executive compensation packages, and other governance red flags are observed by investors and factored into their analysis. These would be the main reasons as to why ESG matters more so now as shown by the impacts of the COVID-19 pandemic and climate change.

ESG drivers would extend from stakeholder oversight and performance expectations; urgent and critical need to manage volatility, uncertainty, complexity, and ambiguity (VUCA);[187] accelerating global risks; decelerating cost of governance, risk and compliance (GRC); ESG codes and regulations; and the need for locked-in investments. Previously, the foci were on legal structures and internal business controls as the primary core of ESG, but elements like the management of external risks, getting the appropriate tone from the top corporate hierarchy, and the embedding of a culture of ethical values and behaviors have ascended into equal or more important in the governing of business nowadays.[188] Indeed, the most effective drivers would be those focusing on the mission of doing the right thing, than those imposed on corporations, as a consequence of regulation. The business case for investing in quality governance could be seen in the benefits flowing from good ESG practices. These comprised enhanced performance and decision-making, strategic competitive advantage, enhanced stakeholder trust and confidence, cost efficiency and better returns on investments, the boosting and sustaining of market value and reputation, enhanced enterprise resilience, and improved compliance and transparency.[189]

ESG, while essentially an issue for corporations and their shareholders, also merits good attention from governments and multilateral developmental entities, like the OECD or the World Bank. Five reasons have been identified for this.[190] Foremost,

184. G. Szalay. 2019. "The impact of the lack of transparency on CG: A practical example". *Corporate Law & Governance Review*, Vol. 1 (2): 21-28.
185. M. Kyere & M. Ausloos. 2020. "CG and firms financial performance in the United Kingdom". *International Journal of Finance & Economics*. https://doi.org/10.1002/ijfe.1883, accessed March 28, 2021.
186. Chartered Financial Institute (CFA). 2018. "The CG of listed companies: A manual for investors". https://www.cfainstitute.org/-/media/documents/article/position-paper, accessed March 28, 2021.
187. W. Bennis & B. Nanus. 1987. Leaders: *The strategies for taking charge*. New York: Harper & Row.
188. PwC 2015, *supra* note [152].
189. PwC 2015, *supra* note [152].
190. S. Nestor. 2001. "International efforts to improve CG: Why and how?". https://www.oecd.org/corporate/ca/corporategovernanceprinciples/1932028.pdf, accessed March 28, 2021.

the institution of the limited company might not have arisen in the absence of explicit backing of public policy and legislative action.[191] Second, over the last two decades, the level of state assets transferred to private owners through privatizations amounted to about USD 1.3-1.4 trillion.[192] Such enormous transfers of new ownerships and control structures could saddle corporate elites with tougher challenges than state ownership arrangements. This would also imply new relationships with labor, and a fundamental shift in future employment generation to the private sector, as well as new modes of financing, essentially meaning a switch from debt to equity. This correspondingly would further imply that ESG could directly impact all these areas, and why governments would be monitoring closely how decisions are made and implemented in the private corporate sector.

Third, the privatization process had brought with it the phenomenal growth of equity markets because of the accelerating process of disintermediation in the financial markets that shifted savings from banking to equity and bond markets.[193] This would imply that with an increasing proportion of the population becoming residual claimants of the corporate sector, policymakers would pay close attention as to how these savings have been applied and allocated by corporations. Also, as seen in past events, ESG issues could turn into a systemic instability matter in the capital and financial markets because of the potential risk of herd behavior in difficult market conditions.

Fourth, the spectacular growth of financial institutions as equity owners in private corporations has also propelled equity market growth.[194] Around hundred large nonbank financial institutions, mostly pension funds and insurance companies, accounted for around 20% of the top twenty more liquid markets in the world. Such global shareholders represent fiduciaries of millions of people. Generally, they would take a long-term posture of investment, as early exit would not often be an option for them, and most of their holdings follow stock market indexes. Therefore, further to being a crucial element of financial stability, better ESG has increasingly become a factor in the welfare of aging societies that have come to rely more on savings and pension funds.

Finally, international capital flows, including illicit financial flows, had leapt by more than twenty times. These are mostly private, or some 85% of total capital flows, compared to some 20% in the 1980s, with most directed toward equity.[195] The 1997 Asian Financial Crisis (AFC) showed that those economies with the lowest ESG standards, especially in terms of protection of minority shareholders, were also those experiencing the largest exchange rate depreciation and stock market capitalization compression. This puts ESG in the radar of those needing to deal with international financial stability, as well as catalyzing the drafting of the OECD Principles that could ensure quality governance.

191. Nestor 2001, *supra* note [190].
192. Nestor 2001, *supra* note [190].
193. Nestor 2001, *supra* note [190].
194. Nestor 2001, *supra* note [190].
195. Nestor 2001, *supra* note [190].

The different traditional CG and ESG viewpoints highlighted in this chapter suggest similarly the different theories underpinning each of these diverse thinking on ESG. The next chapter will dive deeper into these differences and their implications for ESG practices and thinking now and into the future.

CHAPTER 3

Competing ESG Perspectives

Until the formal introduction of ESG metrics in 2015, as alluded to earlier, the "E" and the "S" factors were not separately identified as such, and were deliberated under the governance "G" umbrella. It is not that environmental and social issues had never been under corporate radars, but merely not high-profiled as is now, given the different landscapes that businesses in recent years have to navigate through. Moreover, before this, CSR was more used than when accounting for environmental and social impacts implications for companies. Four perspectives could be broadly identified in the hitherto narrower ESG domain.[196] These being the classic principal-agent or finance perspective; the myopic market perspective; the abuse of executive power perspective; and the stakeholder standpoint that is now strongly engaging the attention of policymakers, regulators, and boards of directors. Other points of view emanating from transaction cost economics, stewardship theory, and enlightened shareholder theory would also be discussed in this chapter. The resurging ESG perspective flowing from the health and social impacts of the COVID-19 pandemic and climate change effects though are given relatively more attention here.

3.01 AGENCY AND CONTRACTUAL THEORIES

The legal-economics prism views the firm or corporation as nexus of contracts between the board and shareholders in a principal-agent relationship, voluntarily entered into without compulsion.[197] The contractual paradigm[198] provides the premise for efficiency. This approach has been supported further by other research inputs, suggesting that the company tantamounted to a legal fiction, serving as a series of contracting relations between production factors, and therefore has no power or authority any

196. K. Keasey, S. Thompson & M. Wright. 2005. "Introduction". In K. Keasey, S. Thompson & M. Wright (eds.). *CG: Accountability, enterprise and international comparisons*. Chichester: John Wiley & Sons Ltd.
197. R.H. Coase. 1937. "The nature of the firm". *Economica*, Vol. 4 (16): 386-405.
198. A.A. Alchian & H. Demsetz. 1972. "Production, information costs, and economic organization". *The American Economic Review*, Vol. 62 (5): 777-795.

different from conventional market contracting between two parties.[199] Shareholders, as residual claimants, function as monitors disciplining the collaborating parties to deter responsibility avoidance. Hence, the interactions between managers and shareholders constituted an agency relationship, where the risk of responsibility avoidance would provide the incentive for management to manage their own behaviors.[200]

The contractual paradigm,[201] underpinned by the idea that the company with no real existence or set boundaries, represented the aggregate of market contracts between different parties seeking to maximize their own interests by executing transactions with unknown factors in the exchange price. Pinning to the company's total parts, the paradigm diluted the significance of managerial power. Also, for others sharing similar thinking on the matter, but taking the institutionalist's approach,[202] the company represented not only the aggregate of transactions among maximizing parties but also a hierarchical governance structure, where the parties could be untrustworthy or opportunistic. Rather than leaving this to a nexus of contracts to resolve the issues, such risks would be addressed through the governance structures and processes. The contractual managerial and institutional approach both support the market process and would discourage state interventions.

Extending from the contractual theory, the agency relationship in corporations is viewed as the contractual relationship between the principals or shareholders who contributed the capital to the corporation, and the agent as represented by the CEO and the management team manning the corporation. This separation of ownership and control approach has persisted largely because of the unlikelihood of a singular party having both the managerial skillsets and the financial capital to run and nurture business corporations. However, the approach is not without constraints. Where uncertainty and incomplete information prevail, these could give rise to the agency issues of moral hazard. This is the scenario where people or agents do not suffer from the outcomes of reckless actions, and consequently because of this are ever more prepared to take greater or more risks.[203] This also extends to the issue of adverse selection,[204] where the principal could be uncertain of an agent's ability to perform owing to the agent's self-seeking motives.

Managers and shareholders tend to hold different world views toward risk. Managers might not act in the best interest of shareholders, especially when they

199. F.H. Easterbrook & D.R. Fischel. 1991. *The economic structure of corporate law*. Cambridge, Massachusetts: Harvard University Press; O. Hart. 1989. "An economist's perspective on the theory of the firm". *Columbia Law Review*, Vol. 89 (7): 1757-1774; M.C. Jensen & W. Meckling. 1976. "The theory of the firm: Managerial behavior, agency costs, and ownership structure". *Journal of Financial Economics*, Vol. 3 (1976): 305-360.
200. M.C. Jensen & W.H. Meckling. 1976. "Theory of the firm: Managerial behavior, agency costs and ownership structure". *Journal of Financial Economics*, Vol. 3 (4): 305-360.
201. H.N. Butler. 1989. "The contractual theory of the corporation". *George Mason University Law Review*, Vol. 11 (4): 99-123.
202. A. Styhre. 2020. *The institutional theory of the firm*. Abingdon: Routledge.
203. Cambridge Dictionary. 2020. "Moral hazard". https://dictionary.cambridge.org/dictionary/english/moral-hazard, accessed July 23, 2020; W. Kenton. 2020. "Moral hazard". *Investopedia 23/07/20*. https://www.investopedia.com/terms/m/moralhazard.asp, accessed July 25, 2020.
204. J. Dobson. "Moral hazard, adverse selection and reputation: A synthesis". *Managerial Finance*, Vol. 19 (6): 2-8.

possess a wider range of social and economic needs, like pay maximization, security, or status for reputation boosting agendas. By comparison, shareholders tend to focus mainly only on maximizing returns on investments,[205] although of late, because of the ESG mantra, there are early signs of stronger passions for these kinds of agendas. The management or agent could also focus on quick short-run returns, but with high risks, while the principals or shareholders would be comfortable only with the longer-term orientation,[206] especially in recent years. Where the opportunistic behavior is assumed in the agency theory, this could further distance the gap between managers and the shareholders owing to information asymmetry, with managers having the edge over shareholders in terms of having relatively better insights into corporate affairs.[207] Where there are little or ineffective restraints on their activities, managers could be self-motivated to expand on the asset base and boosting turnover with the sacrifice of profitability, and ergo maximization of shareholders' returns through scale to enjoy higher compensation packages, but which could also trigger higher risk levels.

Conflicts of interest challenges would go beyond those between controlling shareholders and managers in the context of agency cost of equity, as alluded to earlier.[208] This could well extend to those between external minority shareholders and controlling shareholders,[209] or between debt holders and shareholders.[210] These agency costs could be broken down into monitoring costs, or costs borne by shareholders for measuring, tracking and control of the actions of managers; the bonding costs of establishing and complying with the instruments of guaranteeing that agents would compensate principals where they behave contrary to the interests of the principals; and residual costs that could arise because the cost to overcome the agency matter would exceed the benefits obtained from doing so.[211]

The principal-agent perspective joined by the finance perspective[212] would therefore view governance arrangements, including the organ of NEDs, shareholding rights, and so on, as mechanisms that finance suppliers need, so as to safeguard their interests in a world of imperfectly verifiable actions. The finance perspective in

205. R. Cole, S. Johan & D. Schweizer. 2021. "Corporate failures: Declines, collapses, and scandals". *Journal of Corporate Finance*, Vol. 67 (2021): 1-11; R. Morris. 2018. *Early warning indicators of corporate failure*. Abingdon: Routledge; M.C. Jensen. 1994. "Self-interest, altruism, incentives, and agency theory". *Journal of Applied Corporate Finance*, Vol. 7 (1994): 40-45.
206. M.F. Brauer. 2013. "The effects of short-term and long-term oriented managerial behaviour on medium-term financial performance: Longitudinal evidence from Europe". *Journal of Business Economics and Management*, Vol. 14 (2): 386-402.
207. A. Suryani, M. Mufidah & K. Pirzada. 2018. "Analysis of opportunistic behaviour of management to company performance". *Polish Journal of Management Studies*, Vol. 18 (1): 379-388; R.L. Watts & J.l. Zimmerman. 1986. *Positive accounting theory*. New Jersey: Prentice Hall.
208. J.S. Ang, R.A. Cole & J.W. Kin. 2000. "Agency costs and ownership structure". *The Journal of Finance*, Vol. 4 (1): 81-106; M.C. Jensen. 1986. "Agency costs of free cash flow, corporate finance and takeover". *The American Economic Review*, Vol. 76 (2): 323-329.
209. Y-H, Lin. 2017. "Controlling controlling-minority shareholders: CG and leveraged corporate control". *Columbia Business Law Review*, Vol. 2 (2017): 453-510; R. La Porta, et al. 2000. "Investor protection and CG". *Journal of Financial Economics*, Vol. 58 (2000): 3-27.
210. Jensen & Meckling 1976, *supra* note [200].
211. Q. lei, B-X, Lin & M. Wei. 2013. "Types of agency cost, CG and liquidity". *Journal of Accounting and Public Policy*, Vol. 32 (3): 147-172; Jensen & Meckling 1976, *supra* note [200].
212. Jensen & Meckling 1976, *supra* note [200].

particular examines the situation of a 100% owner-manager looking at the option of selling equity interest to outsiders. As the initial sole owner's shareholdings get diluted, the incentive to generate further wealth gets weakened. In the absence of any controls on the owner-manager's anticipated post-float behavior, the issue price of outside equity would drop to reflect the corresponding threat to shareholder wealth.

Hence, with full anticipation of the impact of the manager-shareholder relationship, the total *ex ante* cost would fall on the would-be issuer of the outside equity, meaning the owner-manager. This would induce a corresponding incentive to have mechanisms to control and track managerial behavior, meaning the setting up of governance arrangements. Given this line of thinking, an efficient capital market would induce effective governance arrangements, minus the need for external interventions. Thus, those advocating the principal-agent perspective would tend to view unrestricted capital and managerial labor markets,[213] as the most effective restraints on executive malperformance. Taking this position, well-functioning capital markets tend to be able to resolve both the micro-level governance problem and the macro-level objective of efficient funds allocation by directing funds to those managers appearing to provide the best risk-return formulations.

The agency theory in sum would involve the seeking of suitable governance mechanisms between principals and agents to ensure the efficient alignment of their respective interests so as to minimize agency costs. The board, shareholder activism, capital markets, and takeover markets represent some of the monitoring mechanisms to control agency costs matters. This perspective has been generally held to be a critique of the public corporation by the major researchers behind the theory of the firm. This has now been treated by current research as a misinterpretation, and that the view, as articulated earlier, was supportive of the cause of public corporations. This is attributed to high agency costs working to depress share prices, that would in turn work against the interests of corporations, as well as outside investors. This thereby gives those in charge correspondingly a market-driven incentive to reduce agency costs.[214]

Shareholders' interest could also be protected by aligning manager's pay packages to business performance. This approach might not work for all corporations, as seen from the evidence of various corporate failures even with massive corporate law reforms over the last two decades, or even now.[215] On this count, there would be those who would perceive the capital market as fundamentally flawed and myopic in its attention for short-term returns where private contracts between corporate owners and funds' suppliers would not yield effective governance; and where the myopic capital

213. E. Fama. 1980. "Agency problems and the theory of the firm". *Journal of Political Economy*, Vol. 88 (1980): 288-307.
214. B.R. Cheffins. 2020. "What Jensen and Meckling really said about the public company". In E. Pollman & R. Thompson (eds.). *Research handbook on corporate purpose and personhood*. Cheltenham: Edward Elgar.
215. R. Cole, S. Johan & D. Schweizer. 2021. "Corporate failures: Declines, collapses, and scandals". *Journal of Corporate Finance*, Vol. 67 (2021): 1-11.

market motivated managers to underinvest in long-term projects.[216] Many longer-term investments were crowded out when higher capital costs were applied to them than strictly justifiable economically. Supporters of this myopic market position did not necessarily question the shareholder value maximization approach, but merely arguing that in its presence, there would likely be systemic distortions of investments in the economy to the harm of long-run growth.

3.02 TRANSACTION COST ECONOMICS THEORY

Linked to the agency paradigm is the transaction cost theory (TCT), where different organizational or institutional arrangements would be said to be in play primarily for the purpose of facilitating or reducing costs of transactions.[217] Whereas the agency theory treats the firm as a nexus of contracts, as it was not possible to have a contract perfectly aligning the interests of principal and agent in a corporate control scenario, the transaction cost paradigm[218] treats the firm as governance structure. This theory in essence suggests that conducting transactions would be costly and that different modes of organizing transactions within a market or a firm would involve different costs.[219] As such, the theory argues that a comparative examination of the related transactions costs or their indicants of these alternative modes would show how a particular transaction should be carried out.[220]

Both the transaction and agency cost theories argue that costs could arise in terms of time and resource for parties to assess information about the contracting environment and the corporation. This includes that too of opportunisms, where managers would seek to act opportunistically so as to mislead or distort the other party. Thus, the opportunism phenomenon would give rise to pre- and post-transaction costs[221] in the form of monitoring behavior and ensuring that the other party did not act opportunistically.[222] Transaction cost analysis could therefore offer efficiency-based guidelines to ascertain which governance structure would be apt for which kinds of routines, and would accordingly endeavor to align a governance structure with transactions needed for the undertaking of the routine.

---

216. W.A. Sahlman & H.H. Stevenson. 1985. "Capital market myopia". *Journal of Business Venturing*, Vol. 1 (1): 7-30.
217. O.E. Williamson. 1985. *The economic institutions of capitalism*. New York: Free Press; R.H. Coase. 1937. "The nature of the firm". *Economica*, Vol. 4 (16): 386-405.
218. A. Rindfleisch. 2019. "Transaction cost theory: Past, present and future". *Academy of Management Science Review*, Vol. 10 (5).
219. Coase 1937, *supra* note [197].
220. Williamson 1985, *supra* note [217].
221. P.G. Klein & H.A. Shelanski. 1996. "Transaction cost economics in practice: Applications and evidence". *Journal of Market-Focused Management*, Vol. 1 (1996): 281-300.
222. V. Grover & M.K. Malhotra. 2003. "Transaction cost framework in operations and supply chain management research: Theory and measurement". *Journal of Operations Management*, Vol. 21 (4): 457-473.

3.03 STEWARDSHIP THEORY

Thus far, the agency paradigm demonstrated that opportunistic agents' actions could be restrained by alert monitoring, and the support of incentive schemes weaved around extrinsic rewards, like money and promotions, or around disincentives, like sanctions and disciplinary measures. There could, however, be intrinsic incentives targeted at achievements and altruism, as well as the commitment to meaningful work. Such intrinsic incentives are not usually quantifiable, like self-actualization, affiliations, and growth opportunities. This approach treats the agents as responsible stewards motivated by the desire to do good for the corporation. It further views them as trusted managers with the capacity to balance competing shareholders' and stakeholders' agendas, thereby helping to make decisions in the best interest of all. Stewards would therefore safeguard and maximize shareholders' welfare via business performance, as by accomplishing this, their own utility functions would be also maximized in the process too.[223]

The UK's FRC provided support for the stewardship paradigm through its Stewardship Code.[224] The FRC defined stewardship as the responsible allocation, management and oversight of capital to generate long-term value for beneficiaries leading to sustainable benefits for the economy, the environment, and society. The UK Stewardship Code 2020 (UKSC) is applicable to asset owners like pension schemes, insurers, foundations, endowments, local government pension pools and sovereign wealth funds; assets managers managing assets on behalf of UK clients or investing in UK assets; and service providers like investment consultants, proxy advisors, data and research providers supporting asset owners and asset managers exercising their stewardship responsibilities. The Code comprises twelve apply and explain principles for asset managers and asset owners and a separate set of six principles for service providers. There are four main sections in the Code, namely Purpose and Governance; Investment Approach; Engagement; and the Exercising of Rights and Responsibilities.

The Code focuses on reporting stewardship activities and outcomes. Code signatories would need to show how they have practiced stewardship during the reporting period to fulfil their policies and objectives. Activities would identify actions incurred by the reporting entities during the reporting period to fulfil the "principles," whereas "outcomes" would explain the result of actions taken during the reporting period. The use of case studies for these purposes is encouraged. Effective outcome reporting is clear about the progress made against objectives and also identifies future initiatives where appropriate. Fair reporting would also identify areas where objectives have not been fulfilled and lessons learned. The FRC has also provided a review of early

223. M. Waldkirch & M. Nordqvist. 2016. "Finding benevolence in family firm: The case of stewardship theory". In F. Kellermanns & F. Hoy (eds.). *The Routledge companion to family business*. New York: Routledge; J.H. Davis, F.D. Schoorman & L. Donaldson. 1997. "Toward a stewardship theory of management". *The Academy of Management Review*, Vol. 22 (1): 20-47.
224. Financial Reporting Council (FRC). 2020. "UK Stewardship Code". https://www.frc.org.uk/investors/uk-stewardship-code, accessed July 28, 2020.

reporting for general guidance.[225] FRC's early review showed good examples and case studies evidencing stewardship activity. Reporting, however, would need to improve by reflecting on the effectiveness of approach, demonstrating continuous improvement and disclosing outcomes. Further, statements would need to be supported with specific evidence from the reporting period, and that reporting would need to address all asset classes and geographies.

3.04 STAKEHOLDER THEORY

As mentioned earlier, US managers before the 1980s acted more as stewards, rather than agents of corporations focusing on ensuring the growth and stability of corporations by balancing the claims of key stakeholders, like employees, the local community and shareholders.[226] The 1980s saw in contrast a culture of hostile takeovers and shareholder militancy where shareholders' needs became paramount.[227] The 1990s saw CG in the US and the UK as the mechanism for fostering shareholder wealth, where the market is deemed as the optimal mechanism for the efficient allocation of resources,[228] where the labor markets are seen as perfectly efficient, where shareholders are viewed as carrying the greater risk thereby making their contributions to capital relatively more important than the contributions of human capital, and ergo it is their returns that had to be maximized.[229]

The Anglo-American shareholder primacy model then in play saw shareholders wielding considerable power over corporate manages via CG mechanisms indirectly, hiring and firing them and forming their pay packages. In the era of the nexus of financial contracts between agents and owners, CG is seen as a principal-agent problem where in the absence of proper incentives, managers could avoid fulfilling their formal duties to potentially engage in reckless organizational growth strategies.[230] To curb the incidence of potential conflicts of interest between management and shareholders, pay packages became linked to performance directly and indirectly with share price, while hostile takeovers emerged as a device to discipline managers. The control of corporations would thus be the market.[231]

225. FRC. 2020. "The UK Stewardship Code: Review of early reporting". *FRC September 2020.* https://www.frc.org.uk/getattachment/975354b4-6056-43e7-aa1f-c76693e1c686/The-UK-Stewardship-Code-Review-of-Early-Reporting.pdf, accessed March 28, 2021.
226. P. Osterman. 2001. *Securing prosperity: The American labor market: How it has changed and what to do about*. Princeton, NJ: Princeton University Press.
227. B. Holmstrom & S.N. Kaplan. 2001. "CG and merger activity in the US: Making sense of the 1980s and 1990s". *Journal of Economic Perspectives*, Vol. 15 (2): 121-144.
228. F. Allen & M. Zhao. 2007. "The CG model of Japan: Shareholders are not rulers". *PKU Business Review*, Vol. 36 (2007): 98-102.
229. B.D. Merino, A.G. Mayper & T.D. Tolleson. 2010. "Neoliberalism, deregulation and Sarbanes-Oxley: The legitimation of a failed CG model". *Accounting, Auditing & Accountability Journal*, Vol. 23 (6): 774-792.
230. E.F. Fama and M.C. Jensen. 1983. "Separation of ownership and control". *Journal of Law and Economics*, Vol. 26 (2): 301-325; E.F. Fama & M.C. Jensen. 1983. "Agency problems and residual claims". *Journal of Law and Economics*, Vol. 26 (2): 327-349.
231. Merino, Mayper & Tolleson. 2010, *supra* note [229].

However, in the light of the 2008 GFC, the validity of the modern financial marketplace as the underlying basis for CG became challenged increasingly.[232] More so, when short-termism orientation led to long-term sacrificing of value creation, a far cry from the market theory of the invisible hand maximizing economic output.[233] There were also growing evidence that short-term investor expectations had become one of the more pressing ethical challenges confronting the business community, where managers are pressured into achieving quarterly earnings by all manners possible,[234] and ergo needed public legitimacy, and where transparency could offer a control mechanism for all stakeholders.

Despite the growing calls for greater pluralism in corporate goal formulation, the legitimacy of the rights of non-shareholder stakeholders in the US/UK CG model then is a matter with insufficient focus.[235]

Then the notion of sustainability became a major societal concern, arising from the growing awareness of the degree of environmental damage inflicted by business activities of the firm. Fear over finite natural resources began to take root[236] to galvanize a more stakeholder-oriented stance, despite the hegemony of the shareholder-centric paradigm. Here, organizational sustainability is understood to mean the ongoing viability of the corporation pertaining to the fulfillment of its responsibilities to its key stakeholders, whom are defined as any group or individual capable of impacting or being impacted by the accomplishments of the corporation's objectives.[237] Most stakeholder advocates though followed a more firm-centered approach, where primary stakeholders, like suppliers, customers, employees, and community members are seen as those whose continued participation in a corporation's business would be crucial for its survival.[238]

There are also those who advocated the instrumental and normative perspectives of organizational stakeholders. The instrumental perspective focuses on the financial value of stakeholders to the firm, where stakeholders are viewed as parties that had to be managed so as to maximize financial returns. It further suggests that a corporation using this approach has the ulterior motive of ensuring that stakeholders controlling crucial resources work to promote rather than damage the firm's commercial success, and where relationships with those stakeholders deemed unprofitable would be

232. Y. Chahed & H.E. Muller. 2008. "Executive pay: Where is the stick?". *Transfer*, Vol. 14 (1): 158-160.
233. S. Goshal. 2005. "Bad management theories are destroying good management practices". *Academy of Management Learning & Education*, Vol. 4 (2005): 75-91; J. Graham, C. Harvey & S. Rajagopal. 2005. "The economic implications of corporate financial reporting". *Journal of Accounting and Economics*, Vol. 40 (1): 3-73.
234. J.M. Wellum. 2007. "Long-term stewardship and our capital markets". *Management Decision*, Vol. 45 (9): 1387-1396.
235. S. Ayuso & A. Argandona. 2007. "Responsible CG: Towards a stakeholder board of directors?". *Working Paper No. 701 IESE Business School, Barcelona.*
236. R. Isaksson & U. Steimle. 2009. "What does GRI-reporting tell us about corporate sustainability?". *The TQM Journal*, Vol. 21 (2): 168-181.
237. R.E. Freeman. 1984. *Strategic management: A stakeholder approach*. Boston: Pitman.
238. M. Clarkson. 1995. "A stakeholder framework for analyzing and evaluating corporate social performance". *Academy of Management Review*, Vol. 20 (1995): 92-117.

disregarded.[239] The normative approach, in contrast, maintains that a stakeholder-orientation should be pursued on grounds that a corporation had an intrinsic responsibility to stakeholders as its actions would impact them.

Then the idea of CSR emerged, advocating that corporations being part of the wider society had a duty of care to others beyond their legal obligations.[240] The main concern for CSR is the creation of value for stakeholders and to fulfill responsibilities to them.[241] CSR nevertheless emerged as a self-regulatory initiative that became vulnerable to ad hoc CSR implementations, especially when profits are at risk.[242] CSR whitewashing or impression management became concerns, as some corporations deployed these to deflect attention away from wider non-CSR behavior, implying that doing well commercially by doing good in society is applicable only when it is financially logical.[243] CSR is largely self-regulatory where a company unilaterally evaluates its own CSR performance. In some jurisdictions, and for some businesses, CSR evolved into a co-regulatory stance. This gave rise to wider notions of corporate accountability that enables stakeholders to hold the firm to account for its CSR performance. However, for this to work, the firm has to be governed via a formal structure reflecting stakeholder groups on corporate boards, or board diversity.[244]

The momentum toward board diversity has been gaining traction,[245] but more could be achieved when the conceptual differences between the shareholder and stakeholder perspective in terms of governance structure, governance process, performance metrics are being adequately resolved. This is not necessarily easy, given the general preponderance of the Anglo-Saxon shareholder primacy approach, until of late with the resurgence of ESG in its more modern format. A pressing issue has been the need to prioritize which key stakeholders to include in corporate boards, given the need also of keeping board size manageable. One suggestion categorizes stakeholders into consubstantial, contractual, or contextual stakeholders.[246] Consubstantial stakeholders are those crucial to a firm's business survival, like shareholders and investors,

239. O.H.M. Yau, et al. 2007. "Developing a scale of stakeholder orientation". *European Journal of Marketing*, Vol. 41 (11): 1306-1327.
240. N.M. Brennan & J. Solomon. 2008. "CG, accountability and mechanisms of accountability: An overview". *Accounting, Auditing & Accountability Journal*, Vol. 21 (7): 885-906.
241. R.E. Freeman & S.R. Velamuri. 2006. "A new approach to CSR: Company stakeholder responsibility". In A. Kakabadse & M. Morsing (eds.). *Corporate social responsibility: Reconciling aspiration with application*. Houndmills: Palgrave Macmillan.
242. A.B. Carroll & A.K. Buchholtz. 2009. *Business & society: Ethics and stakeholder management*. Mason: Cengage Learning.
243. G. Coronado & W. Fallon. 2010. "Giving with one hand: On the mining sector's treatment of indigenous stakeholders in the name of CSR". *International Journal of Sociology and Social Policy*, Vol. 30 (11): 666-682.
244. B. Banerjee. 2007. *CSR: The good, the bad, and the ugly*. Georgetown: Edward Elgar; P. Prasad & M. Elmes. 2005. "In the name of the practical: Unearthing the hegemony of pragmatics in the discourse of environmental management". *Journal of Management Studies*, Vol. 42 (4): 845-867.
245. R. Goyal. "Improving CG with functional diversity on FTSE 350 boards: Directors' perspective". *Journal of Capital Market Studies*, Vol. 3 (2): 113-135.
246. M. Rodriguez-Frenandez, A.I. Gaspar-Gonzalez & E.M. Sanchez-Teba. 2020. "Sustainable social responsibility through stakeholder's engagement". *Corporate Social Responsibility and Environmental Management*, Vol. 27 (96): 2425-2436.

strategic partners or employees, and hence to be prioritized for representation on corporate boards. Contractual stakeholders, like financial institutions, suppliers, subcontractors, and customers tend to have some form of contractual arrangements with the firm, but might not be too concerned with its long-term survival. Contextual stakeholders are from social and natural systems in which the firm operates, like local communities, societies, and national economies, and these could get to be very complicated, multifarious, and even messy.[247] As such, while more corporations would be paying attention to the orientation toward the SA, even more solutions are being sought as to how best to do this, without distracting materially the primary agenda of the corporation. Effective CG though would require effective negotiations, coordination, cooperation, and conflict resolution to distribute the composite gains among multiple parties of interest.[248]

3.05 ENLIGHTENED SHAREHOLDER THEORY

The Cadbury CG Code that emerged in 1990 specified that CG would involve the implementation of a corporate system, by means of which a corporation would be directed and controlled. The Enlighted Shareholder Theory (EST) varied this perspective with the notion of a system comprising all of the internal mechanisms enabling shareholders to be informed of the proper functioning of their corporation, controlling it via their AGMs, and by the powers they delegate to the board of directors while ensuring corporate strategy complied with existing laws in the long-term interest of the firm. For this new theoretical framework, the first or primary obligation of the board of directors is to defend the firm's long-term social interests, at all times and places.[249] Despite a well-defined objective, CG could offer directors wider margins for interpretation and a central role not only in this disciplinary space but also, and above all, in the sphere of strategy formulation.

A further practical outcome of the EST pertains to the composition of the board of directors that would need to be carefully appointed. The board would need to be competent in corporate law and accounting; possess perfect insights into a firm's organization, operations, and sector; and able to evaluate the risks of a firm's activity for itself, and for its stakeholders. What would be novel would be the insights that a board would require about corporate culture and behavioral biases, including practices like board of directors' meetings outside of the presence of executives that could, for instance, reduce biases like submission to authority.[250] The framework would also impact the prescriptions for determining a board's composition. To defend a firm's long-term interests, the board would need different kinds of expertise, besides being capable of integrating and understanding a company's culture.[251] Thus, the main

247. Coronado & Fallon 2010, *supra* note [243].
248. Ayuso & Argandona 2007, *supra* note [235].
249. E. Pichet. 2011. "Enlightened shareholder theory: Whose interests should be served by the supporters of CG?". *Corporate Ownership & Control*, Vol. 8 (2): 354-362.
250. Pichet 2011, *supra* note [249].
251. Pichet 2011, *supra* note [249].

problem of governance would appear to relate to the legitimacy of actors, and especially the role of board members who are the key actors in governance matters.

Questions persist as to whom do the board members work for; to whom they should be accountable; and who would be the main beneficiaries of their governance.[252] It has been demonstrated that at this level, stakeholders would not be the main target, while shareholders would benefit at times, but not always. In reality, it would be the long-term interest of the firm that must be the aim of CG and the incessant concern of board members, and ergo the foundation offered by the Enlightened Shareholder paradigm.[253] This paradigm is premised on shareholder reasoning, but integrating useful elements from stakeholder theories,[254] as well as recent contributions from cognitive theory.[255] The latter argues for the need to expand the financial vision of governance so as to consider the quality of the relationship between managers and investors and the potential to enhance the efficiency of the firm to identify and build opportunities for growth. The cognitive approach in a wider perspective leads to the studying of governance systems in terms of their influence on the different dimensions of cognitive processes of value creation.[256]

The enlightened shareholder value (ESV) approach provided by section 172(1) of UK's CA 2006, while seen as a significant new development in UK law approach, is argued to be little different from the shareholder value approach.[257] At first glance, the objective of companies as set out in section 172(1) would appear to have moved the UK a significant distance from the shareholder value principle toward the SA. On closer examination, however, this might not be the case. The legislation did not appear to have really changed the law, as provided that directors' actions were taken ultimately to foster shareholder benefits, it was not going to be impugned, even if the directors in their decision-making process took into account the interests of other constituents.

Shareholder value over the years had been criticized, mainly because it is said to lack precision, as it fails to offer an avenue for balancing the conflicting interests of different stakeholders, while stakeholders have no way of enforcing any failure on the part of directors to take into account appropriately constituency interests. There appears to be a lack of precision in mapping out how ESV is to operate. Also, stakeholders have no right of enforcement where section 172(1) is breached. Apart from the legal problems of having no right to launch legal proceedings, a stakeholder would also have the practical problems of establishing the arguments that his/her

252. Pichet 2011, *supra* note [249].
253. M. Jensen. 2001. "Value maximization, stakeholder theory and the corporate objective function". *Journal of Applied Corporate Finance,* Vol. 14 (3): 8-21.
254. J. Donaldson. 1992. *Business ethics: A European casebook.* Cambridge, Massachusetts: Academic Press Limited; R.E. Freeman. 1984. *Strategic planning: A stakeholder approach.* Boston: Pitman Publishing; R.E. Freeman & D.L. Reed. 1983. "Stockholders and stakeholders: A new perspective on CG". *California Management Review,* Vol. 25 (2): 88-106.
255. G. Nassreddine & J. Anis. 2012. "A cognitive approach to CG: A visualization tests of mental models with the cognitive mapping technique". *Journal of Defense Resources Management,* Vol. 3 (1): 65-82.
256. Nassreddine & Anis 2012, *supra* note [255].
257. A. Keay. 2007. "Tackling the issue of the corporate objective: An analysis of the UK's 'enlightened shareholder value approach'". *Sydney Law Review,* Vol. 29 (2007): 577-612.

interests are not accounted for by directors and that his/her interests should have prevailed.[258]

Much fanfare is made during the evolution of the ESV of the suggestion that there would be the intention of creating something that would make the decision-making of directors more enlightened to take into account a wider range of interests. The review of prior consultation papers of the Company Law Review Steering Group (CLRSG) noted that having regard for the interests as set out in section 172(1) would not be based on fairness, but on efficiency and seeing shareholders get more overall.[259] There would likely be few occasions when any breach against the interests of non-shareholders being enforced, as the ESV would not be making directors accountable to them, and as such, the ESV could not be treated as an example of a shareholder value jurisdiction moving toward the continental European approach where corporate objectives are concerned. In reality, it would be more likely that the Anglo-American approach advocating shareholder value remains quite strong.[260]

Indeed, the best that stakeholder advocates could hope for would be that section 172 would drive the way toward a change in corporate law that would actively account for stakeholder interests.[261] Until material changes come by, the real significance of section 171 for now does not seem to favor those taking a stakeholder view of the provision.[262] Equally, the provision, as it stands, could also likely raise concerns for those adhering to the shareholder primacy perspective. For it could be argued that the discretion given to directors in their consideration of interests of groups, other than shareholders, could disrupt the traditional emphasis placed on the maximization of shareholder wealth.[263] This could also provide opportunities for directors to advance their own interests on the grounds that they have to have due regard for the interest of others. Indeed, shareholder value advocates could claim that the UK position would be even more of a concern than those in many parts of the US, where directors are merely permitted to consider non-shareholder interests, whereas UK directors are required to have due regard to non-shareholder interests.[264]

Where such is the position, the UK provision might end up pleasing no parties. Future developments in the UK might follow the direction taken in Australia, a

258. S. Kiarie. 2006. "At crossroads: Shareholder value, stakeholder value and enlightened shareholder value—Which road should the UK take?". *International Company and Commercial Law Review*, Vol. 17 (2006): 329-342.
259. The Company Law Review Steering Group (CLRSG). 1999. "Modern company law for a competitive economy: The strategic framework". 36-37. https://www.berr.gov.uk/files/file23279.pdf, accessed September 29, 2020; S. Bambridge. 2003. "Director primacy: The means and ends of CG". *Northwestern University Law Review*, Vol. 97 (2003): 547-563.
260. C. Williams & J. Conley. 2009. "An emerging third way? The erosion of the Anglo-American shareholder value construct". *University of Carolina Legal Studies Research Paper No. 04-09.* Contrary to the conjecture made here.
261. J.D. Springer. 1999. "Corporate constituency statutes: Hollow hope and false fears". *Annual Survey of American Law*, Vol. 85 (1999): 104-105.
262. Keay 2007, *supra* note [257].
263. K. Hale. 2003. "Corporate law and stakeholders: Moving beyond stakeholder statutes". *Arizona Law Review*, Vol. 45 (2003): 823-840. Here, Hale has argued that as directors are generally not obliged to consider non-shareholder interests, this should not necessarily lead to a disruption of the shareholder value approach.
264. Keay 2007, *supra* note [257].

jurisdiction with equivalent corporate law system and value in many instances. Here, the Australian Corporations and Markets Advisory Committee (CMAC) followed the Australian Parliamentary Joint Committee on Corporations and Financial Services in rejecting the UK approach. In their views, requiring or permitting directors to have regard to certain matters or the interests of certain classes of stakeholders could be counterproductive, as there could be a real danger that such a provision would blur rather than clarify the purpose that directors are to serve. By so doing, it could make directors less accountable to shareholders without significantly enhancing the rights of other parties.[265]

Arising from the impact of the 2007 GFC, there appears to be a confluence of market and regulatory changes that have provided investors greater influence in the future direction of CG practices. Leading institutional investors have begun to deploy their powers to advance stakeholder-oriented approaches to accountability, risk management, and governance to challenge traditional understandings of corporate accountability. ESV would represent such an alternative vision and one that would offer theoretical and normative advantages over the shareholder wealth maximization norm.[266] It would also offer principled responses to many of the concerns surrounding shareholder empowerment and rising shareholder activism.

UK's CA 2006, and regulatory initiatives at state and federal levels in the US for improving disclosures of corporate risk management policies, clarified standards for corporate nonfinancial reporting. This is helping to make institutional investor activism more transparent to fund beneficiaries, and the discouraging of short-termism across the financial services industry. Such developments could well move corporations more quickly in the ESV direction. However, whether regulatory changes would lend support or not, investor-driven ESV suggests that the practice of CG had already moved beyond the shareholder-stakeholder divide. It would appear that the agenda for future CG reform is the focus on how best to optimize the contributions of stakeholders, shareholders, and corporate boards to firm success in light of this reality. As to how this balance would eventually be set for public corporations would remain to be seen. However, where the ascendancy of shareholder primacy is of any guide, emerging market-driven norms like ESV could eventually shape the rules of the game for corporations as much more than positive legal rules.[267]

3.06 SHAREHOLDER PRIMACY VERSUS STAKEHOLDER DEBATE

The shareholder primacy theory is argued to be the sensible proposition for the function of businesses, meaning that the social responsibility of business is to increase its profits for shareholders within the laws of a private property free economy, and

265. Corporations and Markets Advisory Committee (CMAC). 2006. "The social responsibility of corporations". https://www.cmac.gov.au/camac/camac.nsf/byHeadline/PDFFinal+Reports+2006/Sfile/CSR_Report.pdf, accessed July 29, 2020.
266. V.H. Ho. 2010. "Enlightened shareholder value: CG beyond the shareholder-stakeholder divide". *The Journal of Corporation Law*, Vol. 36 (2010): 59-112.
267. Ho 2010, *supra* note [266].

leaving the other social functions of society to be served by governments or other social entities.[268] As such, other stakeholders or constituencies' interests would be best served by state regulatory apparatus, and not through CG mechanisms. This is to avoid undermining private property, agency duty, and value-creating capacities of businesses that a SA could bring. In the shareholder primacy paradigm, corporations could be held accountable to their shareholders via effective internal monitoring like disclosure obligation, shareholder voting rights, or oversight by NEDs; and via external mechanisms like the market for corporate control.

On the other hand, stakeholder advocates would claim that the contribution of corporations to societies is not confined to individual wealth creation, but more on whether corporations could assist society achieve a relatively enhanced sense of community values by respecting individual dignity and the promotion of overall welfare.[269] As such, corporations have been bestowed with limited liability charters for commercial purpose, and more importantly, as a social entity for general community support. The corporation is thus a collective rather than an individual identity, with managers functioning as guardians of all corporate stakeholders' agendas.

The choice between the shareholder primacy versus the SA could not be answered by financial yardsticks, as the relative returns between the two approaches were found not to be significantly different, and hence inconclusive.[270] Corporate debacles, such as those found in the pre-SOX years, could not be seen as justification of the superiority of the stakeholder-orientation over the shareholder primacy orientation. Rather, the saga tells more of misinterpretations of both approaches, where both approaches also take into account the matters of board oversights and balances, authority and power abuse, board roles, effectiveness of executive directors and NEDs, and other governance mechanisms.[271] Responding to this corporate dilemma, US boards and managers have been advised to speak of their corporate objective as the maximizing of their companies' contribution to the economy, or more simply the maximizing of their companies' values rather than maximizing shareholder value; getting board approval for management to operate freely under either approach for the foreseeable future; and ensuring the clarity in organizational communications, no matter the choice of approach, so as to provide a firm grounding upon which operational decisions could then be made.[272]

The practical difficulties posed by implementation of the SA included the problems in identifying the different categories of stakeholders and their respective relative importance to the company, and the corresponding difficulties of identifying the nature and extent of directors' responsibility for each. This could lead to directors

268. M. Friedman. 2007. "The social responsibility of business is to increase its profits". In W.C. Zimmerli, M. Hlozinger & K. Richter (eds.). *Corporate Ethics and Corporate Governance*. Berlin: Springer.
269. D.P. Sullivan & D.E. Conlon. 1997. "Crisis and transition in CG paradigms: The role of the Chancery Court of Delaware". *Law & Society Review*, Vol. 31 (4): 713-763.
270. M. Omran, A. Peter & P. John. 2002. "Shareholder versus stakeholders: Corporate mission statements and investor returns". *Business Ethics: A European Review*, Vol. 11 (4): 318-326.
271. H.J. Smith. 2003. "The shareholders versus stakeholders' debate". *MIT Sloan Management Review*, Vol. 44 (4): 85-90.
272. Smith 2003, *supra* note [271].

being accountable to no particular constituency and hence no party, as there might not be a clear metric for evaluation of performance, and clearly a recipe neither for corporate success nor for effective governance.[273] Indeed, it is for these formidable challenges that the ESV approach has been mooted, as discussed earlier, to bridge the gap between the two paradigms. The ESV approach would thus give considerations to stakeholder agendas, but would also simultaneously specify long-term enterprise value maximization as the corporate objective. This would solve problems flowing from the multiple objectives underpinning the traditional stakeholder paradigm by giving management a distinct and clear avenue for making the trade-offs among corporate stakeholders.[274]

The shareholder primacy approach, for long, and the financial philosophy behind the global dominance of the Anglo-American style of CG have had serious beatings linked to corporate scandals in the Dotcom bubble of 2000,[275] the 2007 GFC,[276] and some serious CG failures of tech corporations[277] in the now highly digitalized global economy. Yet, the approach still dominated capital market across most parts of the world. Nonetheless, questions are now raised as to its viability and efficiency in the midst of the ongoing 2020 COVID-19 pandemic, and serious climate change impacts. The BRT had earlier in 2019 changed the purpose of business corporations from the shareholder primacy approach to the SA.[278] The much hyped Roundtable Statement declared the commitments of global US corporations to deliver value to all their constituencies, for their own future success, for their communities, and for their country. The Business Roundtable edict stimulated chin-stroking debates among academics,[279] policymakers,[280] and practitioners,[281] as to whether anything would actually change in the manner business corporations operate.

273. R. Hampel. 1998. *Committee on CG: Final report*. London: Gee & Co Ltd.
274. R. Williams. 2012. "Enlightened shareholder value in UK company law". *UNSW Law Journal*, Vol. 35 (1): 360-377; M.C. Jensen. 2001. "Value maximization, stakeholder theory and the corporate objective function". *Journal of Applied Corporate Finance*, Vol. 14 (3): 8-21.
275. G.T. Goodnight & S.E. Green Jr. 2010. "Rhetoric, risks and markets: The Dot-Com Bubble". *Quarterly Journal of Speech*, Vol. 96 (2): 115-140; A. Kraay & J. Ventura. 2005. *The Dot-Com Bubble, the Bush deficit deficits, and the U.S. current account*. Chicago: University of Chicago Press.
276. P. Yeoh. 2010. "Causes of the global financial crisis: Learning from the competing insights". *International Journal of Disclosure and Governance*, Vol. 7 (1): 42-69.
277. M. Fenwick, J.A. McCahery & E.P.M. Vermeulen. 2019. "The end of 'corporate' governance: Hello 'platform' governance". *European Business Organization Law Review*, Vol. 20 (2019): 171-199.
278. M. Kline. 2020. "Why the debate over stakeholder value versus shareholder value is all wrong: The Business Roundtable's new statement on the purpose of corporations is a much-needed update". *Inc. 26/08/19*, https://www.inc.com/maureen-kline/why-debate-over-stakeholder-value-vs-shareholder-value-is-all-wrong.html, accessed December 23, 2020.
279. L.A. Bebchuk & R. Tallarita. 2020. "Was the Business Roundtable Statement (BRS) on corporate purpose mostly for show-(1) Evidence from lack of board approval". *Harvard Law School Forum on CG 12/08/20*, https://corpgov.law.harvard.edu/2020/08/12/was-the-business-roundtable-statement, accessed August 15, 2020.
280. E. Warren. 2020. "Elizabeth Warren: Business Roundtable declaration 'was just an empty publicity stunt'". *Fast Company 29/09/20*, https://www.fastcompany.com/90557370/elizabeth-warren, accessed September 30, 2020.

Skeptics frowned upon this as no more than window dressing.[282] In an empirical study, out of the 1,173 companies signing the BRT and responding to the survey, 47 indicated that the decision is approved by the CEO, and not by the board; only 1 confirmed that the decision is made by the board; and some 98% of the respondents have had no approvals from the board, when making their commitments to the BRT.[283] The most plausible explanation for the CEOs not seeking board approval for committing their respective companies to the BRS has to do with the manner CEOs viewed the content of the BRS. It would appear that the CEOs did not regard the BRT as a commitment to make major changes in how their companies treat stakeholders, and thus in the absence of a major shift, they assume that there is no need for a formal board approval. The BRT therefore likely reflects an affirmation that corporate past practices have been consistent with its principles, rather than an expectation that the company would make major changes in its future treatment of stakeholders.

The BRT merely reflects the CEOs' positive assessment of how their companies have been treating stakeholders thus far, and importantly the CEOs expectation that the BRT would not lead to substantial changes in how stakeholders would be treated.[284] Indeed, recent reports and commentaries have shown that many industries had been quietly sunsetting the positive things they have been doing for workers' welfares and the local communities during the onset of COVID-19 since June 2020.[285] Further evidence of this orientation could be seen from business groups' criticisms of Biden's corporate tax hikes to fund his infrastructural plan, as the hike would result in getting US corporate tax rate to what it was before its significant reduction made by the previous administration. Instead, businesses advocated for the user-pay approach.[286] Most CEOs would probably continue to answer investors' concerns of financial returns, and importantly preoccupied with share prices that linked to their pay packages. This is something close to what many corporations have been doing when leveraging on the use of special purpose acquisition company (SPAC)[287] to get yet to be profitable

281. L. Fink. 2019. "Larry Fink's letter to CEOs: Profit and purpose". https://www.blackrock.com/americas-offshore/en/2019-larry-fink-ceo-letter, accessed January 11, 2020. Blackrock's CEO expressed commitment to a long-term approach prioritizing on ESG thrusts.
282. Bebchuk & Tallarita. 2020; L.A. Bebechuk & R. Tallarita. 2020. "The illusory promise of stakeholder governance". *Cornell Law Review*, Vol. 16 (2020): 91-178.
283. Bebchuk & Tallarita 2020, *supra* note [282].
284. Bebchuk & Tallarita 2020, *supra* note [282].
285. E. Stewart. 2020. "Corporate America was here for you on coronavirus until about June: Big employers are quietly rolling back pandemic-related perks and benefits". *Vox 24/07/20*, https://www.vox.com/covid-19-coronavirus-economy-recession-stock-market/2020/7/24/21334368/pandemic, accessed September 30, 2020.
286. Business Roundtable (BRT). 2021. "BRT calls for bipartisan infrastructure legislation, will oppose corporate tax increases". BRT 30/03/21, https://www.businessroundtable.org/business-roundtable-calls-for-bipartisan-infrastructure, accesses 01/04/21; Mashayekhi. 2021. "Business groups balk at Biden's corporate tax hikes to pay for infrastructural plan". *Fortune 01/04/21*, https://fortune.com/2021/03/31/biden-infrastructure-plan-corporate, accessed April 2, 2021.
287. Y. Li. 2021. "SPACs break 2020 record in just 3 months, but the red-hot industry faces challenges ahead". *CNBC 19/03/21*, https://www.cnbc.com/2021/03/19/spacs-break-2020-record, accessed March 20, 2021.

businesses listed through a backdoor route,[288] and conveniently forgetting the abusive use and excessive risk of SPAC in the 2000 Enron debacle.[289]

However, it has been counterargued that large corporations had understood for some time the importance of creating value for all stakeholders apart from their investors, and that the BRT merely updated the executives' outward-facing communications to support a direction that is both underway and unstoppable. The BRT demonstrated a recognition of two phenomena. The first has to do with the business case for creating stakeholder value that has already been proven, as without creating value for a variety of stakeholders, and without mitigating the risks linked with subtracting value from stakeholders, a corporation cannot deliver profits to shareholders anyway, at least not over the medium to long-term. Creating value for stakeholders when managed strategically would not take away from enhancing profits for shareholders, it adds to it, and is part of good management, not a zero-sum trade-off. Second, the US economy has been suffering from short-termism, that is, investors squeezing profits out of companies within shorter time spans. Corporations pressured to deliver greater and greater profit margins to their financial owners in the space of a quarter or less might not be making the investments and strategic directional decisions that would enable them to thrive in the longer term.[290] Others would argue that the signs for serious corporate transformation have already been seeded by the impact of COVID-19 on business corporations, especially with regard to corporate sustainability.[291]

It has now been argued that many forces are pushing and pulling corporations in new directions in 2020, where so many of society's problems have rolled past the front doors of government agencies and onto the door steps of corporations to solve. These role-reversals that took root in 2020 would represent a new permanent corporate direction catalyzed by the massive impact of COVID-19. Hitherto, there were various stakeholders seeking attention from corporations for various remedial actions, but since COVID-19, the momentum of this role has been accelerating, as everything impacting society has persisted in getting louder, requiring corporate leaders to be seriously attentive to matters of great interest to various stakeholders. This further required corporate leaders to navigate all the different stakeholders to do the right thing by picking on the social and environmental issues that matter most, or risk standing for everything, but in effect standing for nothing.[292]

288. P. Eavis & L. Hirsch. 2021. "After failed IPO, WeWork will go public through a merger: The money-losing office space plans to merge with a blank-check company backed by big Wall Street investors". *The New York Times 26/03/21*, https://www.nytimes.com/2021/03/26/business/WeWork-Spac-ipo.html, accessed March 27, 2021.
289. S.L. Schwartz. 2002. "Enron and the use and abuse of special purpose entities in corporate structures". *University of Cincinnati Law Review*, Vol. 70 (2002): 1309-1318.
290. Kline 2020, *supra* note [278].
291. A. Bryant. 2020. "The stakeholder-shareholder debate is over: The role of corporations in society shifted permanently in 2020". *Strategy & Business 22/12/20*, https://www.strategy-business.com/blog/The-stakeholder-shareholder-debate-is-over?gko=90678, accessed December 23, 2020.
292. Bryant 2021, *supra* note [291].

3.07 ESG PERSPECTIVE

Sustainable investing, responsible investing, and ESG are broad lexicons referring to the embedding of ESG factors into investors' decision-making. Typically, investors assess ESG considerations drawing on nonfinancial data on environmental impact, like energy consumptions; social impact, like employee diversity; and governance attributes, like board compensations. Responsible investors would in general avoid or curb involvements with investments with greater ESG risks or seek to influence businesses to render them more ESG-friendly so as to generate more positive societal outcomes. ESG investing is presently gaining grounds in overall capital market investments. Though not easy to estimate, the Global Sustainable Investment Alliance in 2019 highlighted more than USD 30 trillion globally managed assets under responsible investment metrics in 2018, with more pervasive ESG investing in Europe. The US though is fast catching up, as reflected by the US SIF Foundation's estimate of some USD 12 trillion in assets under management (AUM) using ESG strategies. Pedro Matos' 2020 monograph *ESG and Responsible Institutional Investing Around the World* questions the reliability of these various estimates and whether ESG investing is another Wall Street fad, or that the investment world is at an inflection point representing a structural shift in the manner investors allocate resources.

With ESG still evolving, ESG implementation according to Matos has not been defined consistently. Morningstar reported in 2019 that active management in the asset management space is encountering fierce competitive pressure from index investing, but that ESG strategies are gaining grounds when it comes to new funds being launched. There are, however, growing concerns over potential greenwashing or rainbow washing, or the false or exaggerated view pertaining to how well aligned investments are with sustainability goals. From the structural perspective, ESG considerations are driven by societal change, like the transferring of wealth from baby boomers to the millennial generation with preference for allocating wealth in more sustainable ways. These are also pushed by the increased regulation subsequent to the 2007-2008 GFC, as exemplified by prudential regulation impacting asset owners, stewardship codes for investment managers, and corporate disclosure rules framed by policymakers and the capital and financial markets. Many investment managers are said to commit to UN's Principles for Responsible Investment (PRI), but the extent of actual actions is unclear, as a lot of them do not precisely disclose how ESG considerations are taken into account. As for the wider investing community, there are understandably no clear consensus as to whether ESG considerations drive enterprise value or curb enterprise risk in the longer term. They are struggling as to whether they could execute effectively the "doing good doing well" combo.

ESG evaluates a company's aggregate awareness of social and environmental factors. It may be applied for various designated purposes. ESG commenced as the endgame of measuring elements linked to sustainability and societal impact of companies for the overall aim of gauging risk, but has now emerged as a major force driving business strategy. ESG evolved as an UN-inspired CSR initiative some two decades ago into a global force with more than USD 30 trillion in AUM in 2018 according to an article penned by Michael Holder in Green Biz on April 8, 2019.

Morningstar's 2019 article "The Evolving Approaches to Regulating ESG Investing" reported 253 investment funds switching to the ESG focus in 2020, with some 87% rebranding in the process. Some USD 17.67 billion surged into ESG-linked products, representing an increase of some 525% over 2015, while the fourth-quarter of 2020 alone accounted for USD 120 billion as new money.

Socially responsible investing (SRI) therefore came to the financial space in the 1970s, 1980s, and 1990s as responses to various social and environmental shortfalls. The Investment Foundation Forum (IFF) reported in 2010 that SRI funds expanded from some USD 12 billion in 1995 to some USD 179 billion in 2005. These funds also advocated and shifted their investment and marketing strategies incorporating the "G" in ESG into their approach, thereby injecting sound governance to their social agenda and rebranding SRI as ESG, as well as embedding moral and financial factors claiming that SRI funds could be both morally and financially superior to other funds with lower risks and higher returns, according to Michael Knoll in his February 2002 "Ethical Screening in Modern Financial Markets: The Conflicting Claims Underlying Socially Responsible Investment" article in the *Business Lawyer*. The incorporation of these factors especially from the 1990s on brought theoretical and empirical credibility supporting the SRI claims, especially in the context of the rise and dramatic falls of Enron and WorldCom primarily because of faulty governance practices.

The SRI investing approach therefore rode on the back of CSR as employed in the UN signaling to institutional investors the comprehensiveness of due diligence and the notion of materiality, or the relevancy of corporate strategies and actions for investors' informed decision-making. This logically advanced to ESG, the extended iteration and definition of what nonfinancial concerns to include as being material or relevant for evaluation of businesses performance, or as metrics for informed investment decision-making. The 2004 UN-led dialogue engaged with finding ways to integrate ESG as an investment tool for the capital markets of the world. This culminated in two reports that suggested that the incorporation of ESG factors into investment decision-making is a viable and prudent mechanism that would generate positive outcomes for both companies and society, and ergo makes good business sense for financial valuation. Insights from these said reports provided the impetus for the launching of the Principles for Responsible Investment (PRI) in the NYSE in 2006. The PRI on June 14, 2021, boasts signatories of more than four thousand holding some USD 100 trillion in AUM, and this remarkable success has been attributed to the slick move in getting first the support of pension funds and asset owners to make ESG a market requirement. The ESG investing framework was further boosted by the colossal financial damage inflicted by the 2007-2008 GFC that induced the search for more effective risk measurements mechanism, with more advocating that the incorporation of ESG factors as the way forward.

Hitherto, the how aspect of SRI was pursued through various approaches. These included the use of positive selection where investors get to select a defined set of ESG factors or via the best-in-class high-performing ESG compliant entities; the use of activism where strategic voting is used to support particular causes; the use of constructive shareholder engagement by investment funds monitoring the ESG performance of their portfolios; large institutional investors interacting with the top echelon of companies to ensure advancement; the use of negative or exclusion criteria where particular sectors of cohort of companies are rejected based on prior identified ESG factors, and finally through ESG integration whereby ESG risks and opportunities are included in conventional financial evaluation of enterprise value. ESG integration has now become popularly used by the investing community. To avoid ambiguity, ESG investing motivated by offering a benefit to a third party for moral or ethical reasons is identified as collateral benefits ESG, whereas ESG investing undertaken to improve risk-adjusted returns is identified as risk-return ESG. This was clarified by Grim and Berkowitz in their 2018 Vanguard Research article "ESG, SRI, and Impact Investing." Schanzenbach & Sikoff have argued in their 2020 article "The Law and Economics of ESG Investing by a Trustee" in the *Stanford Law Review* that this clarification is meaningful, in the light of trust fiduciary law's emphasis on motive.

Indeed, ESG integration is premised on the notion that where ESG is material, this would drive investment decision-making. In this connection, the EC is said to be exploring the use of double materiality, taking into account what is material to a company, like the value of its natural resource reserves; and what is material to for the planet at large, like the cutting down of carbon emissions. Moody's 2021 Global ESG Outlook Report has advocated that the expanding plethora of sustainability standards and disclosure requirements via the financial and corporate systems could subject financial flows to enhanced scrutiny and oversight. This is envisaged to have mounting influence on investment decisions at all levels, extending from consumers to asset managers and financial institutions.

The present issue though is the absence of transparency in how ESG rating agencies compile their ESG scores, something also encountered previously by the CRAs before the 2010 DFA reforms. The issue is about disclosures of data and methods used, and assurance of consistent quality. This has accordingly made it harder for investors to compare ESG scores, even harder for them to understand the methodology behind the compilation of the scores. This led Tariq Fancy, a former Chief Investment Officer at Blackrock, the largest asset manager in the world with USD 8.7 trillion AUM, claiming in his March 16, 2021 article, "Financial World Greenwashing the Public with Deadly Distraction in Sustainable Investing Practices" in *USA Today*, that what he had previously messaged to the world that pursuing good was also good for the bottom line was largely aspirational. For him, now and in truth sustainable investing waters down to little more than marketing hype, public relations spin, and disingenuous promises from the investing community.

Tariq argued further that across the industry, existing mutual funds have been cynically rebranded as "green," with no distinctive change to the fund itself, or its underlying strategies, while in other instances, ESG products contain irresponsible companies, like petroleum majors, and other large polluters, like fast fashion manufacturing. Some portfolio managers are also said to have been mining ESG data to bet against responsible companies for short selling, while risk managers have been focusing on protecting their investment portfolios from potential damages done by a worsening climate, rather than helping prevent that damage from happening in the first place. Thus, it appears that claiming to be environmentally responsible is a profitable undertaking, as reflected in 2020 with ESG mutual funds and exchange-traded funds

(ETFs) doubling, and cheers for those with good bottom line by doing nothing that compromises profits, as making real changes in the environment are unlikely to yield the equivalent returns. The US SEC is though not idling by. It announced in early March 2021 the formation of a Climate and ESG Taskforce to proactively identify ESG-related misconducts, like inaccurate or incomplete disclosures by funds and companies. This unprecedented initiative appears to suggest that there could be abuses gone unnoticed or addressed.

In practice, ESG data is qualitative, nonfinancial and not easily and readily quantifiable in monetary terms. This is because the ESG intangibles are particularly subjective and difficult to calibrate and even less easy to verify. Tariq's earlier comments and those from the research community suggest the absence of explicit standards and transparent monitoring and mainly functioning for the main purpose of greenwashing and other corporate public relations agenda while taking attention away from real initiatives to help improve the environment and lives and livelihoods of the community. A major issue has to do with disclosure. In ESG general practice, a company under study provides its own data and disclosures that have been seldom externally verified. This lack of ESG universal standards and regulations typically implies that the measurement of such data is generally inherently subjective. Some efforts though have been made to offer universally accepted standards for the measurement of ESG, such as exemplified by the International Organisation for Standardisation (ISO). Investment consultancies, like Probus-Sigma, have also designed approaches for calibrating the ratings for an ESG-based rating index premised on ISO standards and externally verified. The formalization of the acceptability of such standards as the means for calibrating and verifying EG disclosures is nevertheless not yet universal.

The "G" of ESG, however, has a relatively longer history of regulation as seen in the Combined Code on CG that came about in 1992 in response to big governance notable failures at Maxwell Group of Companies, Polly Peck, BCCI, and others. Later known as UK CG Code, this has since 1992 been regularly updated and even replicated for use in many parts of the world. These regular updating exercises have transformed the Code befitting ESG as the world knows it today. EU's 2014 NFRD requires large European companies to disclose nonfinancial and diversity data, including providing information on how they run and manage social and environmental challenges. The idea is to assist policymakers, investors, consumers and other stakeholders to assess the nonfinancial performance of reporting companies. Major capital markets provide ESG relevant rating indexes, such as the FTSE4Good Index, the MSCI ESG Indices, the Bloomberg ESG data, the Down Jones Sustainability Index, the Global ESG benchmark for real estate assets (GRESB) benchmarks, and so on. The credibility of these various induces in general lack clarity, consistency, and reliability, thereby undermining their general reliability. The EU has responded with rules and measures to address the threat from greenwashing. As such, under EU ESG reporting, companies have to present data from financial and nonfinancial sources demonstrating they comply with the standards of agencies, like the SASB, the GRI, or the TCFD.

Kenneth Pucker, a former Chief Operating Officer (CCO) of Timberland in his 2021 *HBR* article "Overselling Sustainability Reporting" responded to over two decades of progressive thinking that a more sustainable form of capitalism would emerge, when companies regularly measured and reported on their ESG performance. He acknowledged that while such reporting has become more widespread, and some companies benefiting from this, environmental damage, and some inequality, is still growing. Sustainability reporting and sustainability investing are saddled with various problems, like nonstandard metrics, inadequate auditing, unreliable ESG ratings, and more. He is of the view that real progress requires not just better measurement and reporting practices but also needed changes in regulations, investment incentives, and mindsets. He cited British economist Paul Collier's view that market alone would not resolve worsening social and environmental challenges. This is because capitalism underpinning it do not work on autopilot. Periodically, capitalism in its 250-year history faltered, and when that happened, it was up to public policy to get it back on track via public policy, and collaborative initiatives from private citizens, firms, and families. Also, eventually, companies exist within a wider system. Executives and investors have benefited by leaning on shareholder primacy, but this has left future generations with increasing bills to pay. Such overdue invoices include environmental degradation, biodiversity loss, income inequality, and climate change. Moving forward, stability and enhancing economic welfare need the advocation for structural changes to facilitate attention beyond quarterly financial numbers.

Leape, Zou, Loadwick, Nutfall, Stone and Simpson have responded to ESG's ambiguity, complexity, and overlapping challenges in their November 2020 *McKinsey Quarterly* article "More Than a Mission Statement" through advocation for a more effective framing of Purpose, ESG, and the 6Ps of Portfolio Strategy and Products, People and Culture, Processes and Systems, Performance Metrics, and Positions and Communications. The idea is to compare the breath of ESG with the uniqueness of the purpose. ESG incorporates society's wide menu of expectations about the purpose or role of business. There is a plethora of ESG options, requirements, and variations, extending from community service to inclusivity, transparency in reporting, waste management, and more. On the other hand, Purpose helps companies to prioritize all the things they could or must do in ESG. It directs businesses toward the niches they seek to win, as opposed to niches they need to participate, or where businesses could meet the societal ceiling, but for want of time and resources could go no further, at least for now.

Upon identifying which ESG initiatives are their "musts" or "priorities," businesses need to embed these within their companies, and this is where the 5Ps can help as a practical checklist. Take governance, the "G" in ESG. Effective governance would strengthen a company's bond with its people and culture through, for instance, employee safety and nondiscriminatory hiring and promotion; through enforcing principles and standards pertaining to portfolio strategy and products, like product-safety guidelines and the impacts of these products on society and the planet; through helping processes and systems working to best effect by ensuring that suppliers are accountable; and through assuring that performance metrics and positions and communications are true and transparent. In the US context, good governance could also provide the momentum for companies to form or reconstitute as public-benefit corporations, or seek B-Corp certification. Indeed, as business leaders seek to embed purpose throughout their companies, ESG would feel less like a cost of doing business and more like a source of competitive strength. This results from business purpose being authentic and infused throughout the organization, and not forced or tacked on.

For now, according to Denise Young in a June 2021 *S&B* article "How Environmental, Social, and Governance Reporting Grew Up," ESG is employed as a risk management tool. Its potential is hampered by a lack of common standards, leaving it being exploited for greenwashing purpose. The ESG is not effectively designed to deliver a sustainable economy, even though many investors and other market participants hold this expectation. There are, however, hopeful signs that there is some forward momentum toward achieving a globally accepted framework for sustainability reporting. A core gathering of leading global standard-setting entities have rallied behind the WEF-led endorsement of the IFRS Foundation's work in this space, and together with other initiatives could help to usher in the needed transformation for ESG.

Then, there is the no small matter of the regulatory environment. A lot of ESG or CSR reporting in the US is voluntary and ergo left to their discretions. Christensen, Hail and Leuz in their 2019 ECGI article "Adoption of CSR and Sustainability Reporting Standards" suggests substantial variation in CSR disclosures reflecting the diversity in enterprise's business activities, and that renders objective comparative analysis of companies' CSR practices not easy. With regards to regulators designing and enforcing of reporting standards, the authors found that increasing the quantity and quality of the CSR information could generate gains to the capital markets in terms of greater liquidity, lower capital cost, and more efficient asset allocations. However, they also found that corporate disclosures attract proprietary and litigation costs, and that mandatory CSR reporting would encounter implementation issues in terms of the CSR standard-setting process, the materiality of CSR disclosures, use of boilerplate language as avoidance tools, as well as difficulties in enforcement. They theorized that a fusion of private assurance with public enforcement could most likely succeed.

The OECD 2017 article, "Investment Governance and the Integration of Environmental, Social, and Governance Factors," with regards to investor stewardship codes instructs institutional investors on their responsibilities in integrating ESG factors in the monitoring of their investments. Such codes as initially launched in the UK in 2010 in response to perceived reckless risk-taking among financial firms are typically voluntary or on a comply or explain basis. The Code provides incentives for institutional owners to curb excessive risk-taking, by requiring them to monitor their investee companies, have clear voting policy, and publicly disclosing their stewardship and voting proxies. Those initiated by the UK FRC are binding, while those issued by industry entities like the Canadian Coalition for Good Governance are frequently voluntary. There are concerns that Codes could be superficial, with companies signing up merely to tick the box, but not to actually doing stewardship as intended, as highlighted by the 2015 FRC report "Developments in Corporate Governance and Stewardship 2014" that too many signatories fail to follow through on their commitments to the Code.

Matos alluded to earlier explained that at the global level, different jurisdictions are proceeding at different paces on ESG regulation. The EU appears to be at the head of the pack with its far-reaching regulatory agenda backed by strong political support for transition to a low-carbon economy, while the US has just resurged its commitments through firm initiatives from the new Biden administration in 2020. The EC's 2018 "Sustainable Finance" report set out EU's policy initiatives targeted at reorienting private capital toward sustainable projects so as to comply with its 2030 commitments to the Paris Agreement. The package of initiatives included a taxonomy for classifying sustainability activities, standards and labels for green financial products, and the developing of sustainability benchmarks. Others included obligations for institutional investors to disclose how they integrate ESG considerations into their investment process and engaging with investors about their ESG priorities.

The US regulatory environment stalled by five years of Trump administration could be on the move again with the Biden administration returning the country's commitment to the Paris Agreement. However, the regulatory environment pertaining to pension plans reflects the country's present partisan divide, with active discussions on whether fiduciary duties of loyalty and prudence could include the incorporation of ESG factors. The general standards for fiduciary duties require institutional investors to invest their beneficiaries' funds prudently and in the best interest of their clientele. Thus, whether to integrate ESG metrics into this duty would depend on the materiality of these factors' impact on portfolio performance and the duty of care consideration, as well as the well-being of beneficiaries so as to be consistent with the duty of loyalty. The US Department of Labor (DOL) in its 2018 Bulletin "Clarifying Issues Regarding Proxy Voting, Shareholder Engagement, and Economically Targeted Investments" allowed the use of ESG criteria in the fiduciary's investment framework during the Obama administration in 2015, but in 2018 under the Trump administration, the DOL reaffirmed that fiduciaries have to avoid too readily treating ESG matters as being economically relevant, and that under the Employee Retirement Income Security Act of 1974 (ERISA), ERISA fiduciaries have to always put first the economic interest of the plan in providing retirement benefits.

The SEC Investor Advisory Committee in May 2020 approved recommendations urging the Commission to commence updating reporting requirements for issuers to include material, decision-useful ESG factors. The ESG Subcommittee of the SEC Asset Management Advisory Committee (AMAC) in December 2020 issued a preliminary recommendation that the Commission would require the adoption of standards, by which corporate issuers disclose material ESG risks. The SEC Acting Chair Allision Herren Lee in March 15, 2021, directed SEC staff to evaluate SEC's disclosure rules to facilitate disclosures of complete, comparable, and reliable information on climate change. Public input is being sought on the Commission's disclosure rules and guidance as they apply to climate change disclosures requirements in Regulation S-K and Regulation S-X, as well as potential new Commission disclosure requirements that the Commission might adopt in its disclosure rules. On March 4, 2021, the SEC announced the formation of a Climate and ESG Task Force in the Division of Enforcement. On July 7, 2021, the SEC AMAC issued various recommendations regarding issuer disclosure of material ESG matters.

The SEC has been advised by the AMAC to foster meaningful, consistent and comparable disclosure by encouraging issuers to adopt a framework for disclosing material ESG matter and to provide an explanation where no disclosure framework is adopted. The AMAC further recommends that the SEC accelerates its study of third-party ESG disclosure frameworks for the disclosure of material ESG matters and to acquire relevant subject matter expertise to evaluate how frameworks could play a more authoritative role in the near future. Additionally, the SEC is advised to suggest best practices to enhance ESG investment product disclosure, including alignment with the terminology developed by the Investment Company Institute (ICI) ESG Working Group, and incorporating a clear description of each product's strategy and investment priorities, as well as description of nonfinancial objectives, like environmental impact or adherence to religious requirements. These recommendations were subsequently adopted by the SEC.

Gary Gensler the newly appointed SEC Chairman on May 13, 2021, announced a regulatory framework focusing on disclosure of climate investing risks and human capital disclosures. He highlighted investor interest in such information, stressing that an explicit set of disclosure rules would also benefit issuers and help them deliver precisely the kind of information their investors seek.

Other members of the SEC though like Commissioner Hester Peirce on April 12, 2021, criticized this initiative arguing that the objective materiality standard for investor disclosure together with the SEC's 2010 climate guidance already provides an explicit framework and that advocates for a new ESG framework would be overlooking the difficulty in implementing a prescriptive ESG framework. Peirce further argued that while she agreed that there should be accountability for the deficiencies and concerns raised by SEC's Risk Alert, she does not share the view that ESG products, offerings and disclosure pose problems would be needing a new ESG regulatory framework. Instead, she further contended that the existing general principles upon which the SEC operates are adequate and that with regards to issues of climate risks and other ESG considerations, the SEC should continue to insist on accuracy and cohesiveness between advisers' claims and practices, not to evaluate whether any particular strategy is feasible, but to ensure that investors know what they are getting. She doubted whether investors are best guided by requiring companies to adhere to a designated menu of policies and procedures for ESG factors, in contrast to existing general principles requiring that the internal policies of a company be suitably framed to that company's particular investment strategy, whatever this could be.

Importantly, on April 30, 2021, Peirce pointed out that the US Supreme Court has provided an objective test over what disclosures about ESG considerations are material, that is whether there is a substantial likelihood that a reasonable investor could consider information when making financial decisions about the company. She drew further attention to the difficulties involved when designing objective standards for the potential issues and concerns linked to ESG and climate disclosures and doubts SEC's competence in formulating a successful objective framework. She asserted that an asset manager's job is to inform investors on the what and the how of their activities, and disagreed with the notion of the SEC taking on the task of seeking nonfinancial information for investors simply because of a demand for this. Commissioner Lee counterargued that existing disclosure requirements do not contain clear climate or ESG-linked clauses, where such types of information are often disclosed only unsystematically and only when linked to other information already revealed. She further lamented that not all information that is material is required to be disclosed, adding that there is sufficient evidence demonstrating how executives, lawyers, and other professionals could generate flawed determinations on the materiality issue. Despite these ongoing debates within the SEC itself, John Scottie's May 2021 article "SEC Chair: New Climate Risk and ESG Regulatory Framework a Top Priority" in *JD Supra* cautioned issuers to be mindful of SEC Chair Gensler's unequivocal statements that a new regulatory framework for climate risks and other ESG disclosures would be a top priority for the SEC moving forward.

Katz & McIntosh in their May 2021 article "SEC Regulation of ESG Disclosures" in the Harvard Law School Forum opined that while the SEC has traditionally required disclosure of financially material information, new leaders at the helm are clearly considering requiring reporting of ESG-related information whether or not it is financially material. The SEC disclosure framework is driven by the reporting of information that is financially material to investors, not necessarily information that might be important at the societal level. The authors noted that ESG factors are important to society and merit full consideration and resolution, but via a process of democratic accountability. They further asserted that while the SEC could and should take incremental initiatives to improve issuer disclosure of material ESG information, and while it has the capacity to facilitate public engagement on these important themes, as an agency it would be better served by preserving its credibility as a nonpartisan regulator. The policy decisions that have to be made in the immediate years pertaining to ESG and corporate America are of crucial importance and has far-reaching implications for fundamental issues of law and governance. It is unlikely that the eventual outcome would satisfy all stakeholders, but it is even far more important that the decision-making process be seen as legitimate, by both the regulated and the regulators.

The US and the EU aside, in the aftermath of Brexit, the UK has chosen not to follow the EU's Regulation on Sustainability-Related Disclosures in the Financial Services Sector (SFDR) or the Taxonomy Regulation, and instead electing to set up its own domestic green taxonomy and ESG disclosure regime. Thomas Reilly in his March 2021 article "ESG and the UK" in Global Policy Watch explained that UK's legislative decision has to be understood in the context of UK's broader "Global Britain" strategy. This in turn is marked by a determination to migrate from its hitherto EU-centric policies toward a more deliberate beneficial wider international approach, exemplified by its current efforts to join various regional economic blocs to give the country greater economic opportunities. This strategic policy choice is reflected in its other tactical decision to follow instead the standard set by the FSB's Task Force for Climate-Related Disclosures (TCFD). By becoming the first jurisdiction in the world to mandate the TCFD's standards, the UK strategically sets a high bar to attract financial services companies from across the world seeking to show off their green and broader ESG credentials under an exemplary global standard. Also, with UK's prioritization for COP26, it has been inspired to treat ESG reporting as the chance to support the country's green economy agenda and credential.

The UK shares with the US their relatively slower pace toward ESG regulations, as well as not having an overarching legislation, but a hotchpotch of substantive domestic ESG-related and EU-inspired laws and regulations. As alluded to earlier, the country's primary disclosure regulations are located in CA 2006, the Updated UK CG and Stewardship Codes, Listings Rules in the LSE, as well as the Disclosure Guidance and Transparency Rules (DTRs). Following the recommendations of the TCFD, UK's Chancellor Rishi Sunak's statement to the Parliament on November 9, 2020, signals its intention to introduce mandatory reporting of climate-related financial information across its economy by 2025, and with significant portions of mandatory requirements in action by 2023. A full roadmap for setting up these disclosure requirements was released on the same day.

Since 2018, various designated listed companies have been under the obligation to incorporate nonfinancial reporting in their annual reports, but the regulatory impact of the fresh initiatives is envisaged to apply to a wider range of companies (listed commercial enterprises, UK-registered companies, banks and building societies, UK-authorized asset managers, Financial Conduct Authority (FCA)-regulated life insurers and pension funds, and occupational pension funds) along different timelines. Arising from a new listing rule, companies with premium listing in the LSE are required to provide on a comply or explain basis, disclosing on or after January 1, 2021, on how they managed climate-related risks and opportunities. As the nature and scope of ESG and ESG-linked regulations in the country continue to evolve strongly, these signal to companies to be mindful of their potential increased ESG reporting obligations. Clearly, it also means that UK companies would lose the gains from harmonizing with EU regulations. The present UK government in taking the country out of the EU has set its eyes on the much wider global frontier by aligning its ESG rules with international ESG standards already being pursued by vibrant economies, like Switzerland, New Zealand, and potentially, the US. It is also likely that the UK would find the way to converge with key aspects of EU ESG regulations.

All in all, the ESG perspective provides another level of due diligence benefiting both primary and secondary stakeholders. In particular, ESG standards help to sift out unsustainable companies with outdated business practices, besides helping to minimize risk for investors as they seek out businesses with greater probability of succeeding in the longer term. Regardless of ESG being treated as an investment philosophy or corporate core value, it is now surging as a competitive tool for many companies seeking to succeed as builders of profits, society, and a sustainable environment.

3.08 ESG IN DIGITALIZED BUSINESSES

The confluence of geopolitical-tensions, digitalization, and the ongoing virus pandemic have emitted signals that CG practices would be at the crossroad, with one foot in the past for traditional businesses and one foot in the new for businesses at the forefront of digitalization. Particularly noticeable phenomena arising from these turbulent times are the humongous disruptions going on in the supply chain world. The onset of trade wars, COVID-19 business disruptions, and digitalization disruptions are causing massive havocs to the input and output dynamics of businesses. These days, almost all businesses are impacted by digitalization in one way or another. The virus pandemic hugely benefited businesses at the forefront of businesses at the marketing end, but they too have to deal with massive disruptions to their supply chains. Others saw their markets melting almost completely, while yet more others are able to withstand these newly emerging challenges with feasible contingency plans.

Governments in the US, EU and the UK introduced new rules and regulations to assist those particularly badly impacted. These are exemplified by new laws providing various forms of financial help for impacted and eligible businesses, including new insolvency laws to give space and time for those badly impacted to regain their pre-pandemic business health. Some of these new regulations could be sunset once the crisis is over, but others could be of longer-term duration. How these would impact CG practices going forward would be addressed in greater details in Chapter 5.

3.09 CONVERGING TREND IN ESG PRACTICES

Western-inspired governance principles, whether of the Anglo-Saxon shareholder primacy strain or of Continental Europe's stakeholder ESG strain, are believed to have been transplanted in varying degrees in various economies, with the former taking hold in many former British colonies, and the latter in the social economies of Eastern Europe and some large Asian economies, like Japan and China. Where the laws and regulations underpinning ESG practices had been perceived to have been transplanted from particular sources, this would suggest considerable legal borrowing or legal harmonization. This would point to ESG laws and regulations converging as they developed.[293] Social-economic structures and ultimately cultural convergence would tend to follow thereafter, as laws, regulations, and institutions converged. Already, the corporate mode has been achieving a high degree of uniformity,[294] especially as global capital markets get to be more linked or integrated.

The main reason for the likely converging trend had been the general view that managers should act for the interests of shareholders and stakeholders in the longer term. Convergence protagonists nevertheless might have overlooked the immense practical difficulties of inserting or adapting particular sets of laws and regulations efficiently and uniformly by nations or institutions. It does not need much reminding that the manners wherein companies sought financing, the corporate ownership structure relied upon, economic structures, legal system, socio-cultural-religious systems in isolation or together would exert considerable impact on the choice of the governance system in particular jurisdictions.

Such convergence of ESG practices usually referred to the perceived shift from the closed to the open governance regime with early evidence suggesting some degree of

293. C. Kerr. 1990. *Industrialism and industrial man*. Cambridge, Mass: Harvard University Press.
294. H. Hansmann & R. Kraakman. 2012. "Reflections in the end of history for corporate law". In A.A. Rasheed & T. Yoshikawa (eds.). *The convergence of CG*. London: Palgrave Macmillan; H. Hansmann & R. Kraakman. 2001. "The end of history for corporate law". *Georgetown Law Journal*, Vol. 89 (2001): 439-472.

tilting toward the Anglo-Saxon approach.[295] This would appear to give support to the earlier assertion that corporate law and practice had been converging toward the standard shareholder value maximization model because alternative models like the managerial-oriented or labor-oriented models had failed. Also, globalization and increasing interconnectivity of product and capital markets show that only the more competitive CG practices could survive.[296] The standard shareholder-oriented (SSM) model appears to be more adaptable to all ownership structures, as long as they, as a class, enjoy identical claims on company cash flows. Though the SSM model as implemented had a managerialist bias, it would nonetheless prevail as the dominant CG regimes because of the lack of stronger viable alternatives.[297]

Others argued against this trend on grounds that ESG practices developed in various economies due to their particular cultures.[298] or political history.[299] These have prevailed without significant convergence. Convergence could occur in form, meaning increasing similarity of legal framework and institutions. Or convergence could occur in function, meaning that different economies might have different rules and institutions, but they could still perform the same functions of ensuring fair disclosures and accountability by managers.[300] Functional convergence, viewed as decentralized market-driven changes at the enterprise level of ESG practices, had been seen to be easier, than form convergence, and ergo the reason for their more frequent occurrences. Subsequent research insights suggest that ESG has been trending toward hybridization with selective adoption of and careful adaptation of governance practices in individual countries. There were though significant signs that cross-listing and the spread of more crossing-borders businesses have facilitated the process of governance harmonization.[301]

Legal transplant in general then would encounter three main difficulties when it comes to implementation.[302] There is first the path dependence theory, where the persistence of historical patterns could derail the implementation exercise.[303] Second,

---

295. D. Wojcik. 2005. "Convergence in CG: Empirical evidence from Europe: 2000-2003". *Jesus College Oxford University Working Paper.*
296. Hansmann & Kraakman 2001, *supra* note [294].
297. Hansmann & Kraakman 2012, *supra* note [294].
298. A. Licht. 2001. "The mother of all path dependences towards a cross cultural theory of CG systems". *Delaware Journal of Corporate Law,* Vol. 26 (2001): 147-209.
299. M. Roe. 2003. *Political determinants of CG: Political context corporate impact.* Oxford/New York: OUP.
300. R. Gilson. 2006. "Controlling shareholders and CG: Complicating the comparative taxonomy". *Harvard Law Review,* Vol. 119 (6): 1641-1679; R. Gilson. 2000. "Globalizing CG: Convergence of form or function". *Columbia Law School Center for Law and Economic Studies Working Paper No. 174*; R. La Porta, F. Lopez-de-Silanez & A. Schleifer. 1999. "Corporate ownership around the world". *Journal of Finance,* Vol. 54 (2): 471-520.
301. A.A. Rasheed & T. Yoshikawa (eds.). 2012. *The convergence of CG: Promise and prospects.* Basingstoke: Palgrave Macmillan; B. Clift. 2007. "French CG in the new global economy: Mechanisms of change and hybridization within models of capitalism". *Political Studies,* Vol. 55 (3): 546-567.
302. Wojcik 2005, *supra* note [295].
303. Y. Pavlova. 2013. "Legal transplants in Chinese criminal law: The dilution of due process across national boundaries". *Legal Studies Honors Thesis University of California Berkley*; G. Ferris. 2012. "The path-dependent problem of exporting the rule of law". *The Round Table,* Vol. 101 (04): 363-374; L.A. Bebchuk & M.J. Roe. 2004. "A theory of path dependence in corporate

the incomplete law theory suggests that both statutory and case laws might be unsafe to specify all relevant contingencies. The history of financial regulations supports this contention too. This is because it is almost impossible for the host jurisdiction's judiciary to understand the borrowed laws in the same way as the source economy, because of path dependence.[304] Third, there are also the problems posed by the "Olson" problem. This refers to those elites with vested political and other interests who make the implementation process unduly difficult.[305]

US and European experiences dominated the transfer of laws across national and cultural boundaries. This is generally referred to as legal transplantation or the transfer of laws and institutional structures across geopolitical or cultural borders. A legal transplant is a body of law or legal rule borrowed from a law or rule already in play in another economy, usually a more successful economy, rather than developed by the domestic legal community. The act or process of borrowing is relatively simple, but the rationale behind the process was and still continues to be very complex matters and challenging to explain. Questions continue to be raised relating to whom to borrow from and under what circumstances.[306] Legal transplantation could be imposed, or voluntarily adopted. It could involve entire systems or single legal principles, like corporate and securities laws, and integration of different cultures.[307]

Legal transplantation occurs because it is a quick and cheap way of borrowing from a generally respectable source already using it successfully, indicating thus a form of practical utility motivation. It could also be a kind of political motivation subsequent to colonization. When borrowing from respectable sources, such as ESG rules and regulations from the US or the UK, this could be a form of symbolic motivation. Or, in some other cases, it could just be mere borrowing out of convenience, or related purposes.[308] This is not often necessarily wholesale, but in massive proportions, as exemplified by the case of English common law in Commonwealth jurisdictions.[309] Whatever the motivations, and the list could be expanded, these have significant implications for its success or failures in host economies.[310]

ownership and governance". In J.N. Gordon & M.J. Roe (eds.). *Convergence and persistence in CG*. Cambridge/New York: Cambridge University Press.

304. K. Pistor & C. Xu. 2002. "Law enforcement under incomplete law: Theory and evidence from financial market regulation". Discussion Paper No. TE/02/442 The Suntory Centre December 2002.
305. L.A. Bebchuk & Z. Neeman. 2010. "Investor protection and interest group politics". *Review of Financial Studies*, Vol. 23 (3): 1089-1119.
306. A. Watson. 1996. "Aspects of reception of law". *American Journal of Comparative Law*, Vol. 44 (1996): 335-351.
307. J. Gillespie. 2006. *Transplanting commercial law reform: Developing "a rule of law" in Vietnam*. Ashgate: Aldershot.
308. G. Ajani. 2007. "Transplants, legal borrowing and reception". In D. Clark (ed.). *Encyclopedia of law and society: American and global perspectives*. Thousand Oaks: Sage; Watson 1996, *supra* note [306].
309. G. Anthony. 2002.*UK public law and European law*. Oxford: Hart.
310. C.J. Milhaupt & K. Pistor. 2008. *Law and capitalism: What corporate cries reveal about legal systems and economic development around the world*. Chicago: University of Chicago Press; H. Kanda & C.J. Milhaupt. 2003. "Re-examining legal transplants: The director's fiduciary duty in Japanese corporate law". *American Journal of Comparative Law*, Vol. 51 (2003): 887-902.

There are serious disagreements among those arguing that legal transplantation is impossible, because it is culture specific;[311] those arguing that domestic constitutional structures and interest group coalitions make successful transplantation rare;[312] and those arguing that it could be socially feasible.[313] Yet, others viewed it as a form of market for legal culture determining which rules could be imported from abroad, and where the most efficient legal doctrine survives or gets replicated effectively across the world.[314] The notion of legal transplant has now been generally embraced across the world.[315] This is probably accelerated by the 2000 Enron debacle, the 2007-2008 GFC, the subsequent 2012 European banking crisis in Europe, and the globalization process that has enhanced interconnectivity across the world.[316]

The 2007-2008 GFC and the subsequent 2012 European banking crisis raised further doubts and questions about the shareholder value maximization approach. Similarities in formal laws and financial regulations as a consequence of transplantation of corporate laws have been unable to translate into similar trends in financial development. In turn, this has been attributed to the interactions between formal and informal models of governance.[317] This aside, emerging and developing economies in particular are marked by the dominance of family businesses and state-owned enterprises (SOEs) pushing diverse and different corporate objectives. Given this context, the impacts of political connections on corporate performance justify attention, as studies have suggested that developed political connections are linked to improvements in corporate performance, while inherited political connections are associated with a decline in corporate performance.[318]

At this juncture, it might be worthwhile to take a step back and acknowledge that there could be no endpoint of the traditional governance model. There could be no optimally efficient Anglo-American model, just as there would unlikely be no optimally efficient ESG models elsewhere.[319] ESG would need to adjust to ever-changing circumstances. Specific combinations of ESG might work at certain points in time, but change would inevitably be needed again. The convergence protagonists rode on the status and power of the Washington Consensus in the 1980s, where the IMF and the World

311. C. Brants. 2010. "Legal culture and legal transplants". *Electronic Journal of Comparative Law*, Vol. 14 (3): 1-72; W.E. Daniel. 2003. "CG in Indonesian listed companies: A problem of legal transplant". *Bond Law Review*, Vol. 15 (1): 345-375; L. Legrand. 2001. "What legal transplants?". IN D. Nelson & J. Feest (eds.). *Adapting legal cultures*. Oxford: Hart.
312. G. Edwards. 2007. "Legal transplants and economics: The world bank and third world economies in the 1980s: A case study of Jamaica, the Republic of Kenya, and the Philippines". *European Journal of Law Reform*, Vol. 9 (2): 243-284; O. Kahn-Freund. 1974. "On uses and misuses of comparative law". *The Modern Law Review*, Vol. 37 (1): 1-27.
313. J.W. Cairns. 2013. "Watson, Walton, and the history of legal transplants". *Georgia Journal of International & Comparative Law*, Vol. 9 (1): 637-696; Watson 1996, *supra* note [306].
314. Milhaupt & Pistor 2008, *supra* note [310]; R. Dragneva. 2007. *Investor protection in the CIS: Legal reform*. Leiden: Martinus Nijhoff Publishers.
315. Cairns 2013, *supra* note [313].
316. Milhaupt & Pistor 2008, *supra* note [314].
317. Armour. 2009.
318. J. Cao. 2008. "The nature of political connections and firm value". *International Finance Review*, Vol. 9 (1): 461-494.
319. D.W. Puchniak. 2007. "The Japanization of American CG? Evidence of the never-ending history for corporate law". *Asia-Pacific Law & Policy Journal*, Vol. 9 (1): 7-70.

Bank pushed through conditioned financial aids to recessionary and transitional economies in Eastern Europe, and later to Asian economies in the 1997 AFC. While the Anglo-Saxon traditional ESG models have been vigorously promoted by academicians and other advocates across the world, ESG practices in the US and in the UK too are metamorphosing. Shareholder primacy and hostile takeovers have been deployed to much-needed corporate restructuring in the 1980s. Directors are in turn supported by discretionary powers to rebuild the restructured companies and are insulated from hostile takeovers as they go about the process. Bank monitoring is also applied to reduce agency costs throughout the period.

As a consequence, the US traditional governance approach in particular transformed a lot from the 1980s to the 1990s. ESG practices in other economies also metamorphosed. For example, the Japanese main bank model which resisted change throughout much of the 1990s has been adapted in recent years to respond to the new circumstances and toward its own approach, and not necessarily following the US model. Another case in point pertains to the implementation of the US/UK inspired independent directors' system. In China that demonstrated no significant progress.[320] Large shareholders and concentrated shareholding structures have complicated stricter monitoring requirements, like majority representation of independent directors, compulsory committee structure requirements, and stricter nominating rules. This has been made worse by the lack of qualified candidates to fill independent director positions and a two-tiered board structure. These differences have therefore been shaped by local forces affecting the adoption and implementation of the system. These developments have also led to the argument that there is no particular benefit in evaluating the gap between broadly defined ESG models that were also constantly evolving in unpredictable ways themselves. Hence, it has been further argued that it would make better sense to focus on how each country's system of governance successfully adapted to changing times.[321]

The above developments would imply less emphasis on the traditional governance convergence theory, and more analysis toward better understanding of the persistency of cross-nation diversity in traditional CG practices. The approach alluded to earlier[322] have argued that investors' rights would depend on the legal rules of the jurisdictions where the securities are issued. Such laws and quality of their enforcements would determine how well these would be protected. Such differences flow from differences in their legal origins. These help to explain why in the 1980s to 1990s, common law countries like the US, UK, Australia offers relatively better protection rights, than those in civil law jurisdictions. These earlier insights are seriously dented by various corporate scandals that unfolded in Enron and Enron-type cases in 2000 and 2007-2008 in these jurisdictions. In the US and the UK, these have to do with the abusive use of off-balance sheet mechanisms and SPACs in nonfinancial services in

320. Y. Jie. 2007. "Formal convergence and substantial divergence? Evidence from adoption of the independent system in China". *Asia-Pacific Law & Policy Journal*, Vol. 9 (1): 71-104.
321. Puchniak 2007, *supra* note [319].
322. R. La Porta, F. Lopez-de-Silanez & A. Schleifer. 2002. "Investor protection and corporate valuation". *Journal of Finance*, Vol. 3 (2002): 1147-1170.

2000 and banking services in 2007-2008. While, for Australia, hitherto the paragon of virtue in governance, serious misconducts in the banking, superannuation and financial services industry in Australia from 2005 to 2009 were unmasked only in 2019, some ten years later.[323]

There have been considerable corporate law reforms subsequent to these various crises in the US, UK and the EU. Massive overhauls of corporate law and EsG practices were enacted in the 2000 SOX and 2010 Dodd-Frank legislations in the US. These though appear to encounter difficulties in containing the occasional outbursts of corporate scandals, particularly in banking services well into recent years.[324] These have also now been complicated by the questionable business practices of tech and digitalized corporations[325] in the now unfolding digital economy. The UK saw a massive sea-change in CA 2006, regular updating of its CG Code, as well as special niche regulations to do with enhanced disclosures of pay packages and so on. These too have failed in varying degrees to curb corporate misconducts appearing on various occasions,[326] as well as serious weaknesses in the accounting and auditing industry that weakened their role as gatekeepers.[327] Such developments are now expected to see considerable law reforms. Still, ESG practices in both the US and UK are watched closely across the world as they continue to dominate the global capital and securities markets.

The above developments aside, the political variable continues to be used to help explain the differences in governance across the world,[328] while others[329] also claim that cultural norms linked to ethnicity, customs, beliefs, shared values, and religions could have contributed to these differences. Further research continues to demonstrate that while legal origins remain an important variable in explaining the diversity of investor protection across different jurisdictions, the cultural and political dimensions remain equally important in providing enhanced understanding as to why variations in governance practices and business purpose persist.[330] despite global efforts in formulating a global approach, such as exemplified by the OECD governance principles.[331]

323. *Royal Commission into Misconduct in the Banking, Superannuation and Financial Services Industry Final Report February 1, 2019.* https://www.royalcommission.gov.au/sites/default/files/2019-02/fsrc-volume-1-final-report.pdf, accessed February 8, 2019.
324. I. H-Y. Chiu & M. McKee. 2015. *The law on CG in banks.* Northampton: Edward Elgar.
325. E. Segal. 2021. "How companies are trying to discourage and detect misconduct by executives". *Forbes 09/02/21,* https://www.forbes.com/sites/edwardsegal/2021/02/09/how-companies-are, accessed February 10, 2021.
326. C. de Villiers & R. Dimes. 2020. "Determinants, mechanisms and consequences of CG reporting: A research framework". *Journal of Management and Governance,* Vol. 25 (2020): 7-26.
327. Department for Business, Energy & Industrial Strategy (DBEIS). 2021. *Restoring trust in audit and CG.* London: DBEIS.
328. M. Roe. 2003. *Political determinants of CG: Political context corporate impact.* Oxford/OUP.
329. A. Licht, C. Goldschmidt & S. Schwartz. 2003. "Cultural rules: The foundations of the rule of law and other norms of governance". *William Davidson Institute Working Paper No: 605 August 2003.*
330. M. Matoussi. 2008. "International CG and finance: Legal, cultural and political explanations". *Paper Delivered at the Equity and Economic Development ERF 15th Annual Conference, 23-25 November 2008, Marriot Cairo Hotel, Cairo.*
331. OECD. 2021. *Recommendations of the Council on principles of CG.* Paris: OECD.

Often, the use of traditional ESG codes, particularly those flowing from the UK and OECD, has been followed closely across the world as a good mechanism for fostering the convergence of ESG practices. Suggestions have been made that these governance codes exerted impacts on the structure and functioning of the board of directors.[332] helped to reduce the agency cost of managerial entrenchment and enhanced board oversight[333] while also positively impacting share prices.[334] Second, traditional governance, inclusive of both internal and external environments and other issues, could also impact the degree of convergence. Third, traditional governance institutions, extending from higher-order to lower-order institutions, could operate in diverse configurations.[335] One way of identifying the degree of convergence or otherwise would involve examining the drivers and impediments of traditional governance at the national or enterprise levels,[336] including looking for evidence of the direction of its convergence.[337]

In the context of the diversity in the worldwide diffusion of codes of good governance,[338] the initiatives of multilateral development agencies like the World Bank, the IMF and the OECD could be seen as promoting a direction toward a more general global model.[339] Other external forces driving toward the confluence of CG practices would include globalization, market liberalization, powerful institutional investors, like Blackrock, and best practices from multinationals.[340] The Anglo-American model of nonbinding governance codes would appear to be the dominant source of diffusion across national economies,[341] probably because of the vastness of the former British empire now appearing in the form of the Commonwealth of Nations. Still, other forces like institutional embeddedness, cultural attributes, and politics could impede this movement toward convergence, and instead breed hybrid forms of practices.[342] The Anglo-American code version of comply or explain has not been interpreted similarly in, for instance, the Netherlands and Germany,[343] while capital

332. C. Alves & V. Mendez. 2004. "CG policy and company performance: The Portuguese cases". *CG: An International Review,* Vol. 12 (3): 290-301.
333. E. Dedman. 2002. "The Cadbury Committee recommendations on CG-A review of compliance and performance impacts". *International Journal of Management Review,* Vol. 4 (4): 335-352.
334. A. Chizema. 2008. "Institutions and voluntary compliance: The disclosure of individual executive compensation in Germany". *CG: An International Review,* Vol. 16 (4): 347-362.
335. I. Haxhi. 2015. "Comparative CG". In A. Sorge, N. Noordenhaven & C. Coen (eds.) *Comparative International Management.* London: Routledge; I. Haxhi & R.V. Aguilera. 2014. "CG through code". In C. Cooper (ed.). *Wiley encyclopaedia of management 3rd edition, Vol. 6 international management.* New Jersey/Oxford: Wiley-Blackwell.
336. T. Yoshikawa & A.A. Rasheed. 2009. "Convergence of CG: Critical Review and future directions". *CG: An International Review,* Vol. 17 (3): 388-404.
337. I. Haxhi & R.V. Aguilera. 2011. "Are codes fostering convergence in CG? An institutional perspective". In A.A. Rasheed & T. Yoshikawa (eds.). *Convergence of CG: Promises and prospects.* New York: Palgrave.
338. I. Haxhi & H. van EES. 2010. "Examining diversity in the worldwide diffusion of codes of good governance". *Journal of International Business Studies,* Vol. 41 (4): 710-726.
339. Haxhi & Aguilera 2011, *supra* note [337].
340. S.A. Reid. 2003. "The internationalization of CG codes of conduct". *Business Law Review,* Vol. 24 (10): 233-238.
341. Haxhi & van EES 2010, *supra* note [338].
342. Haxhi & van EES 2010, *supra* note [338]; Yoshikawa & Rasheed 2009, *supra* note [336].
343. Haxhi & Aguilera 2011, *supra* note [337]; Yoshikawa & Rasheed 2009, *supra* note [336].

markets across the world are cherry-picking those that aligned with their agendas, and in this sense, governance codes have not been necessarily boosting convergence all the way.

Rather than focusing on governance mechanisms convergence, it would be relatively more beneficial at least for those in developing economies to look toward the use of regulatory dualism,[344] so as to capture the quicker and easier embrace of relevant best practices. This approach would not impose a comprehensive reform for those elites and other groups with vested interests, but could enable others to tap into the market. With this, those benefiting from the existing frameworks would not have much incentive to resist or fight the reforming regime. This approach would thus offer both existing and new enterprises a choice between two or more alternative rules governing a particular issue within a comprehensive scheme of regulation.

Thus, as globalization persists and interconnectivity continues, the search for global governance standards also carries on.[345] As alluded to earlier, the process of legal transplant could, depending on the particular circumstance in the host economies, become one where there could be substantive convergence to the borrowed rules and regulations from the source of origin, be it the outsider or insider governance regime; or a kind of failure with these rules largely ignored or resisted by local participants. These borrowed rules and regulations could also survive through a form of regulatory dualism where eventually the most effective law would triumph.

As for the many economies in Europe, Asia, or Latin America, marked by distinct differences in the way the three dominant governance regimes took root, they could continue to be subjected to the influence of international ESG best practices pressures, as well as the dictates of local politics, culture and other impediments. The world was caught off-guard, when the COVID-19 pandemic hit almost all economies in 2020 bringing with it massive disruptions for economies and businesses in all parts of the world, including those in the US, EU, and the UK. These accelerated the digitalization of businesses owing to the need to rely more on work from home (WFH) for health safety considerations, as well as for other efficiency reasons. Simultaneously, shortly before and into the COVID-19 pandemic years, many parts of the world were hit by forest fires and massive flooding of epic and unprecedented proportions setting the stage for climate change panaceas. The EU leads the charge with its European green bond standard, corporate disclosure of climate-related information, EU climate benchmarks and ESG disclosures, sustainability-related disclosures in financial services, and contributing to the building up of an international platform on sustainable finance to up the flow of private capital into environmentally sustainable investments. The US, under Biden's administration, called for climate change mitigation, and the UK is expected to go in an equivalent direction. Businesses are now learning and adjusting

344. M.T. Kawakami. 2010. "Diffusion of regulatory dualism: Making legal transplants feasible and its impact on legal convergence". *Tilburg International Business Law LLM Thesis 06/05/2010*; R. Gilson. 2000. "Globalizing CG: Convergence of form or function". *Columbia Law School Center for Law and Economic Studies Working Paper No. 174.*

345. A. Dignam & M. Galanis. 2013. *The globalization of CG*. Farnham: Ashgate; M. Moore. 2013. *CG in the shadow of the state*. Oxford: Hart; T. Clarke & D. Branson (eds.) 2012. *The Sage handbook of CG*. London: Sage.

the impacts of these on their narrower governance practices that are now increasingly driven by more modern ESG practices in most major capital markets, including those in the US, UK, EU, and major parts of Asia.

Meanwhile, as the world continues to engage in the pros and cons of the three dominant governance models of shareholder primacy, stakeholder, and ESV, ownership structures would also continue to influence the choice of governance approach going forward, especially in the context of the turbulence highlighted here. These new demands for more funding could lead to various changes in ESG responses. Those flushed with cash surpluses, arising from being at the forefront of digitalization, such as those becoming more dominant in their business spheres, could be watched closely in the capital markets on the way they reward their CEOs and directors. Those relying more on external funding from the capital or financial markets to stay afloat might have to deal with new demands from capital suppliers that might impact their ESG approach moving forward. These and more would be taken up first in Chapter 4, as capitalization structures in the form of either more equity or more debts, or more of both could lead to some impacts on traditional governance practices, now popularly tagged as ESG practices, and therefore the choice of ESG approach going forward.

CHAPTER 4
Governance and Corporate Ownership Patterns

Socioeconomic-legal-politico-cultural factors could shape ESG systems and practices in national economies, including, of course, ownership patterns. Varying ownership patterns in different economies of the world could generate different sets of challenges to the governance of corporations, as corporate ownership and control in practice have been seldom completely separated. This implies that diverse or concentrated ownership patterns would impact the concept and practice of corporate direction and control. How these are played out in traditional governance practices of family-controlled, state-controlled, and market-controlled enterprises will be discussed in this chapter, including the impact of capitalization structures on ESG practices. These are already demonstrated in the actions of global institutional investors, like Blackrock and others with their ongoing efforts to rebuild from post-COVID-19 and work toward protecting the environment, inequality and diversity matters, as well as health and safety at worksites.

4.01 BOARD-OWNER RELATIONSHIP AND CORPORATE OWNERSHIP PATTERNS

Board in general exists primarily because of the legal rule that corporations are legal entities detached from the people who owned them or the shareholders as principals, and those agents as managers who run them. This structure prevails to protect owners from unlimited liability while providing managers with various discretionary powers. Still, despite the requirements to act on behalf of the artificial corporation, boards in general always derived their authority to act from the owners or shareholders. This accountability claim is weakened when boards fail to acknowledge that they have the obligations, not the mere authority to direct.[346] As representatives or agents of the

346. J. Carver & C. Carver. 2002. *Corporate boards that create value: Governing company performance from the boardroom.* New Jersey: John Wiley & Sons.

owners, the board have the obligations to carry out the owners' rightful prerogatives.[347] Boards need to be authoritative in their role, lest owners are deprived of their voice.

General observations of ownership structures and patterns indicate several options in play. While there could be varying kinds of ownership structures and pattern for performing the functions of business, there have been particular structures and patterns viewed from a governance prism. The more commonly observed pattern seen from this perspective is the widely distributed ownership mode, with no party enjoying dominant shareholding position. It has been proven, as far back as the 1930s, that as shareholdings get to be widely dispersed, the pertinence of the promoter-owner gets overwhelmed.[348] Conventional agency problems are normally associated with such corporations, as no shareholders appear to demonstrate the interest in advancing governance of the enterprise. Each and every shareholder has assumed to their later regrets that there are other shareholders who were doing that. This came to be far from the case, as seen in occurrences of corporate scandals at recurring intervals. Largely free from pressures of shareholders and the wider public, there were early warnings of the risk of ascendance of management control and unchecked corporate power that could spell potentially serious consequences for both business and the wider society.

These concerns are not without solid illustrations, such as shown by the more seminal governance failure cases from the 1960s well into current years, where corporations appear to be acting largely on their own without decent considerations for the welfare of the other stakeholders. These are reflected a lot by the less trustworthy aspects of the operations of some notable multisided platforms.[349] Nevertheless, these corporations still encounter pressures in particular from institutional shareholders, and the capital market in general that managers did not face some four decades ago. However, for those in the US, EU and the UK, given the relative decreasing roles of banks in serving as gatekeepers of business corporations, corporate managers now enjoy a relative greater degree of autonomy than their predecessors.[350] These matters pertaining to the direction of corporate power and control deserve even more attention in governance paradigms and practices.

On the other hand, there could be dominant shareholders with large block ownership. These could be promoters and their families, institutions like investment banks, venture capital funds, private equity, mutual funds, hedge funds, or insurance entities. Over the years, these institutions have grown in importance, holding higher

347. P. Wallace & J. Zinkin. 2005. *Mastering business in Asia: CG*. New Delhi: Wiley.
348. M.S. Mizruchi. 2004. "Berle and Means revisited: The governance and power of large U.S. corporations". *Theory & Society*, Vol. 33 (2004): 579-614; A.A. Berle & G.C. Means. 1932. *The modern corporation and private property*. New York: Harcourt, Brace & World.
349. J. Mattila & T. Seppala. 2018. "Distributed governance in multi-sided platforms: A conceptual framework from case: Bitcoin". In A. Smedlund, A. Lindblom & L. Mitronen. *Collaborative value creation in the platform economy*. Translation Systems Sciences, Vol. 11. Singapore: Springer.
350. Mizruchi 2004, *supra* note [348].

levels of shareholdings.[351] In particular, the burgeoning index fund industry is dominated by just three large US asset managers, namely, Blackrock, Vanguard and State Street. These three are collectively fast becoming the new dominant owners of most US-listed corporations and those in other economies too. Still, the extremely broad ownerships in thousands of enterprises imply that these Big Three did not have firm-specific interest, but instead industry or economy-wide interests. However, as index investors, they too view risky enterprise behaviors or very short-term impact strategies that could negatively impact the portfolios of their retail investors. Owing to this, and other considerations, they professed to be champions of long-termism, but this though has not been consistently reflected in their voting behaviors. Nevertheless, owing to their enormous size and broad corporate ownership, the Big Three performed an almost public-utility role in the US and UK. This could mean that in the immediate years, the public, regulators, and investors of the Big Three might advocate for a voting behavior that would be more in line with their declared long-term or patient governance strategies.[352] It is interesting to note here that institutional shareholders have also been able to contribute to enhancing sustainable firm performance and constructing governance mechanisms also in stakeholder-oriented system.[353]

At times, as was the case with the UK in the early 1960s, the state would incorporate companies to drive and carry out the implementation of certain businesses or industries, such as exemplified by the use of quango-like structures where the government would hold substantial or majority stakes in corporations. These though had been reduced considerably through privatization and other state divestment strategies in the Thatcher years of the 1980s because of the need to curb the dismal performances of these state-led enterprises.[354] On the other hand, other economies, including some advanced economies in the Asia and Pacific belt, have witnessed positive contributions to their national economies from state-led or public-private joint-ownership enterprises.[355] They have been especially important in sectors that had weak economic pressures, and in sectors like mining and natural resources that are usually saddled by serious governance challenges.[356] Their sheer scale and their poor performance in some of these economies highlighted the importance of reforms. Reform advocates observed that there has not been a single path to reform, as approaches differ, depending on institutions, history and political preferences. Nevertheless, the advocates argue that there were common elements of a reform agenda, including the importance of hard budget constraints, financial accounting transparency, competitive market structures, and regulatory frameworks that would protect the

351. J. Fichtner. 2019. "The rise of institutional investors". In P. Mader, D. Mertens & N. van der Zwan (eds.). *International handbook of financialization*. Abingdon: Routledge.
352. Fichtner 2019, *supra* note [351].
353. H. Sakawa & N. Watanabel. 2020. "Institutional ownership and firm performance under stakeholder-oriented CG". *Sustainability*, Vol. 12 (2020): 1021-1041.
354. C. Bolick. 1995. "Thatcher's revolution: Deregulation and political transformation". *The Yale Journal on Regulation*, Vol. 12 (1995): 527-548.
355. E. Ginting & K. Naqvi. 2020. *Reforms, opportunities and challenges for state-owned enterprises*. Metro Manila: Asian Development Bank.
356. Ginting & Naqvi 2020, *supra* note [355].

public interest.[357] It might well be that privatization would be the preferred approach, but this would be effective only where the necessary requisites have been in place.[358]

Owing to the consideration that many developing economies and even some advanced economies are having some dominating presence of SOEs, the OECD has provided governance guidelines for them, as it did for private enterprises earlier. The OECD takes the position that the major challenge has been the search for a balance between the state's responsibility for actively exercising its ownership functions, like the nomination and election of the board, while simultaneously refraining from imposing undue political interference in the management of the corporation.[359] The other important challenge involves ensuring a level playing field in markets where private sector companies could compete with SOEs, and that governments did not distort competition in the manner they applied their regulatory or supervisory powers. The approach of China's federal regulators toward Fintechs in the early 2000s compared to their present approach is a good illustration of what could change.

The OECD guidelines basically suggest that the state should exercise its ownership functions through a centralized ownership entity, or effectively coordinated entities, that should act independently and in accordance with a publicly disclosed ownership policy. They further recommend the strict separation of the state's ownership and regulatory functions. When implemented well, these recommended reforms would help to ensure that state ownership is exercised in a professional and accountable way, and that the state could well play a positive role in improving governance across all sectors of the national economy leading to healthier, more competitive, and transparent enterprises.[360] It ought to be clear that SOEs need the requisite authority, competencies and objectivity to execute their function of strategic guidance and monitoring of management, and hence acting with integrity and being held accountable for their actions.

This further means that SOEs' boards need to be assigned an explicit mandate and ultimate responsibility for enterprise performance. SOEs' boards also need to be executing their functions of monitoring management and providing strategic guidance together with the authority to appoint and dismiss CEOs. Additionally, they need to be structured such that they could exercise objective and independent judgment, such as exemplified by the separation of the chair from the CEO, besides subjecting the board themselves to annual appraisals of their performance. SOEs in Singapore have generally performed creditably for some time and have won accolades from distinguished business scholars, like Professor Michael Porter at Harvard Business School.

Family-owned enterprises (FOEs) are also dominating the business scene in absolute terms globally, including those in the US, EU and the UK.[361] FOEs have been

357. Ginting & Naqvi 2020, *supra* note [355].
358. J. Cooper. "Privatization and deregulation". In *Margaret Thatcher and Ronald Reagan*. London: Palgrave Macmillan.
359. OECD. 2015. *OECD guidelines on CG of state-owned enterprises*, 2015 edition. Paris: OECD.
360. OECD 2015, *supra* note [359].
361. V.K. Patel, T. Pieper & H.F. Joseph Jr. 2012. "The global family business: Challenges and drivers from cross-border growth". *Business Horizon*, Vol. 55 (3): 231-239.

generally recognized for their contributions to GDP and employment.[362] In their initial or formative years, family members themselves have been able to direct and manage their firms, as there are usually relatively less governance issues arising from agency problems at this phase, largely because ownership and control rested within the same family unit.[363] The merging of ownership with management negated any issue of trust and the necessity of monitoring management's activities. However, where a family-owned large dominant holding is also part of management, the interests of minority shareholders might get sidelined, as managers had tended to safeguard the interests of the family and not those of shareholders in general. While FOEs in their formative years could be run as closed private affairs, this becomes untenable when they grow in scope and scale, as family members might not have the full range of expertise and experience to manage different functions, or might face the lack of sufficient family members to manage the different functions.[364] However, appointees to such FOEs tend to be advisory in nature, or are commonly there for incorporation purposes.

Research findings suggest that the greater the evaluation of board performance, the better is enterprise performance in relation to competitors.[365] Global trends appear to converge in a single-board approach. When this, or other well-followed models, becomes a key prerequisite for enterprises entering the international financial markets, family enterprises would still need to avoid overlooking the features that are fundamental to family businesses governance. While FOEs have a goal to attain pertaining to board role and composition, a transition process toward best practices adjusted to individual enterprise culture has to occur. This transition phase would depend substantially on individual enterprise maturity, in terms of life cycle, and in terms of enterprise experience with boards of directors. Research further suggests that boards of directors have enriched corporate management by including nonfamily professional board members. This has helped in increasing transparency and increased confidence in corporate management for family members who are not actively participating in the family business.

Also, a board comprising nonfamily and family board members has led to a balance of skills and experiences, thereby injecting dynamisms into the operations of the enterprise. Further research findings show that contributions from both kinds of directors complemented each other. This is because family board members have

362. PwC 2021. "From trust to impact: Why family businesses need to act now to ensure their legacy tomorrow". https://www.pwc.com/gx/en/family-business-services/family-business-survey, accessed March 30, 2021; M.H. Rahman, R. Sanguino & A. Barroso. 2017. "Impact of family business on economic development: A study of Spain's family-owned supermarkets". *Journal of Business and Management Sciences*, Vol. 5 (4): 129-138.
363. OECD. 2009. "Governance challenges for family-owned businesses". In *Practical guide to CG*. Paris: OECD.
364. OECD 2009, *supra* note [363].
365. E.R. Brenes, K. Madrigal & B. Requena. 2011. "CG and family business performance". *Journal of Business Research*, Vol. 64 (2011): 280-285.

knowledge and experience of their business, while nonfamily board members inject into the enterprise an objective vision and a professional point of view.[366]

Generally, FOEs opt either for family or business councils, but not both.[367] This is because families needing to activate their family protocol quickly due to conflict to put in motion their managerial succession mechanism have found hesitations from business councils in implementing this, as business councils' functionality comprises conflict resolution. Additionally, families have not yet considered protocols addressing family wealth management because families manage dividends usually on an individual basis. However, families that have not undergone conflict found the family council even more functional as a way to socialize and communicate with each other. Nevertheless, family governance appears more relevant for larger families where large numbers of them do not take active part in the family business.

A major challenge to the design, implementation, and maintenance of good governance practices has to do with conflicts of interest that basically afflict most forms of ownership patterns, where some of these are general in nature, and others more conventional to the kind of ownership structure. Conflicts of interest observed of a general nature include directors having pecuniary interest beyond compensation; independent directors coming from legal firms providing counseling services to the enterprise; CEO appointments of former classmates or colleagues; company auditor doubling up as independent director in affiliated companies in a group structure; and directors following a narrow scope agenda reflecting the agenda of the sponsoring shareholders, instead of the entire shareholders as a group, as mandated by law.[368]

The top four tiers of conflicts of interest include actual or potential conflict between a board member and the enterprise having to do with salaries and perks, misappropriation of enterprise assets, self-dealing, appropriation of corporate opportunities, insider dealings, and board work negligence; conflicts arising when a board member's duty of loyalty to the enterprise or stakeholders is compromised, such as when particular board members exercised influence over others through compensation, favors, relationships, or psychological manipulation; conflicts emerging where the interests of stakeholder groups have not been appropriately balanced or harmonized needing actions in contemplative proactive ways; and conflicts involving those between an enterprise and society when the enterprise acted in its own interests at the wider expense of society that would require conscientious directors to differentiate good from bad and for the board to act as stewards for safeguarding long-term responsible value creation for the common good of the community.[369]

366. J. Baron & R. Lachenauer. 2021. "Build a family business that lasts". *Harvard Business Review January-February 2021*. https://hbr.org/2021/01/build-a-family-business, accessed March 25, 2021; Brenes et al. 2011, *supra* note [365].
367. Brenes, Madrigal & Requena. 2011, *supra* note [365].
368. A.J. Felo. 2001. "Ethics programs, board involvement, and potential conflicts of interest in CG", *Journal of Business Ethics*, Vol. 32 (2001): 205-218.
369. D. Cossin & A.H. Lu. 2021. "The four tiers of conflict of interest faced by board directors", https://www.imd.org/research-knowledge/articles/the-four-tiers, accessed March 11, 2021.

Conflicts of interest commonly associated in SOEs include interference by politicians and bureaucrats pushing through their private agendas.[370] The checking of political intrusion would require visible and steadfast commitments at the higher levels of government, as well as vigilance on the part of SOE directors and executives, the media, and the society at large to ensure that formal governance arrangements are operating effectively.[371] Conflicts could arise where institutions holding sizeable stakes are also having a variety of financial interests.[372] Thus, individuals investing in enterprise equity via mutual funds could be exposed to agency conflicts of interest of corporate managers, as well as agency conflicts of investment managers. Cross directorships by professional managers in these and linked outfits could add to the problems. Financial conglomerates have been alleged to have been involved in using their lending and consulting powers in influencing their customers to use services provided by members and affiliates in their group thereby contributing to the problem of conflicts of interest, as particularly exemplified in the fund management industry.[373]

Conflicts of interest commonly associated with FOEs could arise when separating ownership from management becomes difficult, or when listed FOEs transacted with entities linked to family members. Three topical themes have been identified, namely, causes for the conflicts in FOEs;[374] effects of conflicts in FOEs;[375] and management of conflicts in FOEs.[376] Conflicts of interest is still a central issue for this kind of enterprise because of the familial relations that could cause conflicts to escalate much more easily to rapidly shift to the personal level where particular conflict dynamics and logic could emerge with the potential to destroy economic, as well as meta-economic values, and to endanger the enterprise and family.[377]

4.02 SHAREHOLDING STRUCTURES RATIONALE AND CONTROL IMPLICATIONS

The two main patterns of corporate ownership structures, namely dispersed versus concentrated ownerships, have over the years generated controversies as to which particular mode dominated their presence in capital markets. Earlier pioneering

370. S.C.Y. Wong. 2018. *The state of governance at state-owned enterprises.* Washington, DC: IFC; J. Radon & J. Thaler. 2009. "Resolving conflicts of interest in state-owned enterprises". *International Social Science Journal,* Vol. 57 (s1): 11-20.
371. Wong 2021, *supra* note [370].
372. A. Dasgupta, V. Fos & Z. Sautner. 2020. "Institutional investors and CG". *ECGI Working Paper Series in Finance NO. 700/2020 September 2020.*
373. R.C. Smith & I. Walter. 2006. *Governing the modern corporation: Capital markets, corporate control, and economic performance.* New York: OUP.
374. K.A. Eddleston, R.F. Otondo & F.W. Kellermanns. 2008. "Conflict participative decision making, and generational ownership dispersion: A multilevel analysis". *Journal of Small Business Management,* Vol. 46 (3); 456-484.
375. F.W. Kellermanns & K.A. Eddleston. 2007. "A family perspective on when conflict benefits family firm performance". *Journal of Business Research,* Vol. 60 (10): 1048-1057.
376. J. Yan & R. Sorensen. 2004. "The influence of Confucian ideology on conflict in Chinese family business". *International Journal of Cross-Cultural Management,* Vol. 4 (1): 5-17.
377. F. Hermann, et al. 2011. "Conflicts in family firms: State of the art and perspectives for future research". *Journal of Family Business Management,* Vol. 1 (2): 130-153.

insights suggest the prevalence of dispersed ownership in the US that culminated in the notion of separation of management and ownership, and ergo, control.[378] It has been observed that, as corporations grow in scale, their appetites for more financial support from the capital market escalate enormously in general.

Solutions come in the form of increasing response actions from large numbers of dispersed group of shareholders largely without connections or affiliations. The emerging dispersed ownership structure is argued to be mainly the outcome of laws and regulations governing financial intermediaries designed for political and ideological reasons. This contributes to a control gap that has been filled mainly by directors and managers out of practical necessity. This initial observation has been challenged by alternative observations that give evidential support that instead of dispersed ownership as claimed, concentrated ownership in the US has been the characteristic.[379] This has been equally observed at the global level too,[380] which in turn has been the outcome of varying law quality,[381] varying levels of property rights protection,[382] and differing enforcement prowess of national legal institutions.[383] It has been further contended that controls are laid mainly in financial intermediaries in the shape of formal business cooperation, or informally via interlocking shareholdings and directorates.[384] This has since been further borne out by further evidential support.[385]

Still, the argument that the global capital markets have been moving to the Anglo-Saxon model of governance marked by dispersed ownership lingers on.[386] This is despite more evidence to the contrary that national governance laws have been thriving with company law and governance codes that continue to reflect cultural heritage, public policy choices, and prevailing ideological and political principles of the states enacting them, as well as the growing importance of the stakeholder model, the impact of transnational regulation on national corporate laws, and the acceptance of a public role for corporate law in some jurisdictions.[387]

---

378. A.A. Berle & G. Means. 1932. *The modern corporation and private property*. Commerce Clearing House: New York.
379. A. Shleifer & R. Vishny. 1986. "Large shareholders and corporate control". *Journal of Political Economy*, Vol. 94 (1986): 737-782; M. Zeitlin. 1989. *The large corporation and contemporary classes*. New Jersey: Rutgers University Press.
380. S. Claessens, S. Djankov & L.H.P. Lang. 2000. "The separation of ownership and control in East Asian corporations". *Journal of Financial Economics*, Vol. 58 (2000): 81-112; R. La Porta, et al. 1999. "Corporate ownership around the world". *Journal of Finance*, Vol. 54 (1999): 471-519.
381. La Porta et al. 1999, *supra* note [380].
382. C.J. Milhaupt. 1998. "Property rights in firms". *Virginia Law Review*, Vol. 84 (6): 1145-1194.
383. K. Pistor, et al. 2002. "The evolution of corporate law: A cross-country comparison". *University of Pennsylvania Journal of International Economic Law*, Vol. 23 (4): 791-871.
384. J. Scott. 1997. *Corporate business and capitalist classes*. Oxford: OUP.
385. K. Ojah & C. van der Hoven. 2019. "Shareholders and institutional investment". In F.N. Ngwu, O.K. Osuji, C. Ogbechie & D. Williamson (eds.). *Enhancing board effectiveness: Institutional, regulatory and functional perspectives for developing and emerging markets*. Abingdon: Routledge.
386. H. Hansmann & R. Kraakman. 2001. "The end of history of corporate law". *Georgetown Law Journal*, Vol. 89 (2): 439.
387. M. Welsh, et al. 2014. *Australian Journal of Corporate Law*, Vol. 29 (2014): 148-168.

The inception of the corporate form as advocated earlier has led to the separation of ownership and control thesis.[388] where capital suppliers or the shareholders are not synonymous to those deciding on the deployment of these financial inputs. The distinction implies that the role linked with ownership becomes largely nominal. This means the right to receive revenues in exchange for investing in corporations, in contrast to effective ownership or the ability to control the destiny of corporate assets[389] or the destiny of corporations, has been sought because of access to financial and nonfinancial benefits flowing from the control of decision-making in corporations. Corporate control has been of no issue for those with complete share ownership or majority-shareholdings, as commonly witnessed in various FOEs and SOEs. The issue would arise in those holding minority shareholdings, together with those depending on the use of management control mechanisms that could be challenged by particular groups of powerful shareholders, like the increasing dominance by institutional financial intermediaries. This latter category has been relying on formal shareholders' remedies for minorities,[390] and through access to influential networks.[391]

The agency theory, alluded to earlier, where the corporation has been described as a nexus of contracts populated by diverse groups of production factor suppliers, whose behaviors are shaped by ownership costs, like monitoring; risk-bearing; and collective decision-making. These in combination could be large, where the owners have originated from very dispersed groups.[392] This implies that in an enterprise with dispersed shareholding structures, no shareholder has sufficient incentive to monitor management effectively, as the gains for any single shareholder have been too meagre to cover monitoring and related transaction costs. These costs are considerably reduced when managements are also controlling majority shareholders, as typically found in various FOEs and SOEs, but not where shareholdings are largely dispersed groups. Hybrid solutions, where shareholders share ownership with management for this dilemma might be feasible, but as discussed earlier, conflicts could arise between the management and the shareholding groups, culminating with the imposition of the objectives of the more dominating group.

The controversies generated by the relative superiority of dispersed shareholding governance system over the concentrated shareholding system appear to linger. This could be attributed to the powerful showings of the latter in global capital markets context, as well as their strengths and continuing resilience. It has been argued that

388. J. Lotto. 2012. "The effect of separating ownership from control on corporate leverage". *Business Management Review*, Vol. 16 (2012): 1-17.
389. A.M. Pacces. 2008. *Featuring control power: Corporate law and economic revisited*. Rotterdam: Rotterdam Institute of Law and Economics; P. Gourevitch & J.J. Shinn. 2006. "Political power and corporate control: The new global politics of CG". *Foreign Affairs (Council on Foreign Relations)*, Vol. 85 (1): 1-1.
390. J.H. Farrar & L.J. Boulle. 2001. "Minority shareholder remedies-Shifting dispute resolution paradigms", *Bond Law Review*, Vol. 13 (2): 1-32.
391. L. Marques, J.A. Ribeiro & R.W. Scapens. 2011. "The use of management control mechanisms by public organizations with a network coordinating role". *Management Accounting Research*, Vol. 22 (4): 269-191.
392. B.L. Connelly, et al. 2010. "Ownership as a form of CG". *Journal of Management Studies*, Vol. 47 (8): 1561-1589.

their different approaches have been driven by different contextual backgrounds. In Asia, Latin America, and much of Europe, the aims have not been about achieving and retaining control. These have been accomplished through concentrated ownership and reliance on family or bank finance that determined the shareholder context. It has also been attributed to boards with aligned incentives, where the boards have been dependent on the same outcomes as the controlling shareholders; limited disclosure and insufficient minority protection; and illiquid capital markets with restricted takeover activities and an underdeveloped new issue market.

The US and UK models of governance, in contrast, are market based and market driven. In theory and in practice for most occasions, dispersed shareholdings and sophisticated investors examine stock fundamentals. The Anglo-Saxon model of governance carves out a very different shareholder environment, where shareholders enjoy equal rights and minority shareholders are expected to enjoy some form of protection. To accomplish these, the board has somewhat different roles and structures. NEDs tend to be in the majority, while the incentives of board members have not been necessarily closely aligned with the interests of the absent owners represented by all holders of non-preferential shares.[393] Consequentially, transparency and accountability are of big importance, and shareholders in principle are envisaged to be treated equally, and are also entitled to enjoy access to substantial information coming from mandated disclosures obligations. More importantly, the Anglo-Saxon model assumes liquid markets with all that this entails, such as in terms of active hostile or friendly takeovers, as well as a wealth of private equity options and offerings, including initial public offerings (IPOs). In general, reforming the institutional context, like government reform, regulatory arrangements, and the local exchanges, is as equally important as reforming corporate behaviors.[394] Failures in this domain could generate market premiums that would impact how investors view their investment options across countries.

The continuing debate between the concentrated shareholding governance approach and the dispersed shareholding model appeared to suggest that both had strengths and weaknesses of their own, such that both continue to be represented in the major capital markets of the world. For now, it would seem that the US and UK models of governance are still relatively more popular and dominant.[395]

4.03 INTERNAL VERSUS ESG SYSTEMS

The US and UK models of governance are also viewed as the outsider system of control,[396] in contrast to the insider system.[397] The insider system is exemplified by the

393. P. Coombes & M. Watson. 2001. "Corporate reform in the developing world". *The McKinsey Quarterly*, Vol. 4 (2001): 89.
394. Coombes & Watson 2001, *supra* note [393].
395. R. Bozec & M. Dia. 2015. "Governance practices and firm performance: Does shareholders' proximity to management matter?" *International Journal of Disclosure and Governance*, Vol. 12 (3): 185-209.
396. M. Maher & T. Andersson. 1999. *CG: Effects on firm performance and economic growth*. Paris: OECD.

approaches adopted in Japan, where the banks of industrial groups are their major shareholders; in China and France where the state plays influencing roles; in South Korea, where the "chaebols," or family groups represent the interest of the dominant shareholders; and in various Eurasian economies where mass privatization with favorable conditions for employees created prerequisites for this model of governance.

The outsider model (OM) focused on market regulation where active markets exist for corporate control through hostile takeovers, in particular. Here is where shareholders tend to have transitory interests in an enterprise, where there is notable absence of close relationships between them and management, and where the primacy of shareholders rights over those of other organizational groups is held.[398] In contrast, the insider model (IO) prioritized stakeholder control, where shareholders tend to have enduring interests in an enterprise, where shareholders hold positions in boards or other senior managerial positions, where the relationships between management and shareholders are stable and close, where there is little semblance of a market for corporate control, and where there is existence of formal rights for employees in influencing managerial decisions.[399]

Employee role in traditional governance practices has been important, as reflected in widespread use of governance guidelines and codes of conduct, and in some multinational board guidelines with emphasis that shareholders' value would never be maximized in the absence of stable cooperation between employees and management.[400] The EU has been promoting the CSR idea since 2001 in its Green Paper "Promoting a European Framework for CSR," where CSR is treated as a concept whereby enterprises integrate social and environmental concerns in their business operation and in their engagements with stakeholders voluntarily, and where within businesses, CSR refers to quality employment, lifelong learning, consultation and participation of workers, equal opportunities, and where social dialogue is viewed as a powerful instrument for resolving employment-related issues. Employees' participations are undertaken through collective bargaining, information and consultation procedures. These further extend to financial participation, whether via equity sharing or profit sharing, or via codetermination with employees' representation on boards and works council. Employee stock options are widely employed in the US and UK for the compensation of senior management employees in particular, used to a lesser degree in the EU, in mass privatization exercises in Eastern European and Asian economies, and with priorities for senior management in multinationals. However, CSR focuses largely on introspection or self-evaluation of an enterprise's social and environmental missions, usually voluntary in nature, and in recent years have operated more as promotional or marketing tool for companies. This helps to explain why external ESG ratings have come to being relied upon, more and more, as independent assessment of an enterprise's ESG or ESG-related activities, despite various flaws.

---

397. Maher & Andersson 1999, *supra* note [396].
398. Maher & Andersson 1999, *supra* note [396].
399. Maher & Andersson 1999, *supra* note [396].
400. Maher & Andersson 1999, *supra* note [396].

Sustainability and the wider notion of social responsibility have implied a change in the spirit of governance that promotes the de facto convergence between different ESG systems operating across the world. Substantial ESG convergence would suggest that different economies might have different corporate ownership structures, rules, and institutions, but the corporate boards might still be able to perform common goals, with focus on equivalent key performance indicators, like ensuring fair disclosures or accountability.[401] It has been observed that enterprises have performed more effectively pertaining to the triple bottom line. This has increased shareholder value and contributed simultaneously to the sustainable development of societies wherein they operated.[402]Indeed, research has confirmed the contribution of sustainability in the process of ESG convergence, and in light of this encouraged policymakers to translate sustainable best practices into laws and recommendations so as to strengthen the mutual influence between formal and substantial convergence.[403]This then also helps to explain the resurgence of ESG laws and practices across the world.

4.04 CAPITALIZATION, FINANCIAL STRUCTURES AND ESG

Capitalization or financial structures of corporations have ESG implications, more so now, as the investing community increasingly leaned on the use of ESG metrics and reliance on ESG corporate ratings. US and UK corporations rely relatively more on the capital markets for their funding requirements, while many Eurasian economies rely relatively more on bank borrowings. Consequentially, US and UK corporations are subjected to takeover threats that keep corporate managers in line with shareholder interests, whereas businesses relying more on bank borrowings have bank and labor representatives on their boards following the stakeholder model tradition. Research suggests that when both creditors and shareholders interact to actively monitor the manager, *ex post* to floating debt, active shareholders might unilaterally shirk their monitoring duties to shift the burden of costly monitoring to debt claimants,[404] but this view is far from over.

Board members are fiduciary responsible to shareholders for the governance of the enterprise. In quoted enterprises, their shares have been exchanged or transacted between investors through a process enabled by financial intermediaries in the capital markets. Capital market institutions include venture capital and private equity entities, financial institutions and commercial banks, investment banks, brokers and financial advisors, and stock exchanges. Mutual funds, pensions funds, foreign institutional investors, the accounting community, regulatory agencies, CRAs, together with a framework of laws designed for formations of corporate entities, corporate management practices, board structures, and board and CEO compensation practices all play

401. D.M. Salvioni & F. Gennari. 2016. "CG, ownership and sustainability". *Corporate Ownership & Control*, Vol. 13 (2): 606-614.
402. Salvioni & Gennari 2016, *supra* note [401].
403. D.M. Salvioni, F. Gennari & L. Bosetti. 2016. "Sustainability and convergence: The future of CG systems". *Sustainability*, Vol. 8 (2016): 1203-1227.
404. N. Rajan. 2012. "Capital structure implications for CG". *PhD Thesis University of California Berkley Fall 2012.*

their respective roles in nurturing and ensuring the healthy functioning of capital markets for the good of investors' protection, and consequently sustainable economic growth.

Financial intermediaries are thus involved in helping enterprises to raise funds or to deploy their funds in the capital markets, and with some doubling up as financial gatekeepers as they continuously gather and relay information regularly and consistently to facilitate fair and efficient execution of financial engagements.[405] The intermediaries and investors constitute the external wings impacting ESG practices which are vital in the maintenance of healthy capital markets. As mentioned earlier, institutional investors have grown into prominence over the years, especially in the US and the UK capital markets. Increasing active involvements of institutional investors in these markets, and by investment bankers and regulators in markets relying relatively more on banking finance, have helped to ensure that appropriate queries are raised in relevant occasions to avoid wide variations from a desired set of practice. These financial intermediaries in recent years have been promoting and supporting ESG practices, notably seen in May 2021 when ExxonMobil lost board seats to a small ESG-inclined hedge fund.

It has been generally observed that the perceived dispersed shareholding thesis advanced initially for the US and UK capital markets imply the separation of ownership and control. The agency paradigm discussed earlier focused on the contractual nature of enterprises and the potential for a range of internal governance mechanisms to reconcile the interests of shareholders and managers of listed enterprises. The paradigm, nonetheless, has conceded that on some occasions, internal governance has not been sufficient in monitoring the behaviors of corporate managers. This has led to the reliance on takeovers, constituting a vital external governance mechanism whereby underperforming or excessively opportunistic manager could be replaced.[406] Hostile takeover bids generally signal that the target's assets have not been maximized for shareholders' benefits, and in particular internal governance has been ineffective. The governance role of takeovers is premised on the rationale that the capital markets represent objective evaluations of managerial performance. In general, corporations become attractive targets in the market for capital control when the opportunity to generate new value through the redeployment of assets or the replacement of existing managers becomes real.[407]

405. M. Avcin & H. Balcioglu. 2017. "CG: A model of modern CG framework for the better governance of companies" in D. Crowther & S. Seifi (eds.) *Modern organisational governance (Developments in CG and responsibility, Vol. 12)*. Bingley: Emerald; R.C. Smith & I. Walter. 2006. *Governing the modern corporation: Capital markets, corporate control, and economic performance*. New York: OUP.
406. M.C. Jensen. 1986. "The takeover controversy: Analysis and evidence". *Midland Corporate Finance Journal*, Vol. 4 (1986): 6-42.
407. H.G. Manne. 1965. "Mergers and market for capital control". *Journal of Political Economy*, Vol. 73 (1986): 110-120.

4.05 THE MARKET FOR CORPORATE CONTROL

Throughout the last few decades, in the US and UK capital markets, there have been waves of takeovers, marked by their own dominant characteristics giving support to the governance role of takeovers. Central to this argument is the faith that takeovers are sought to correct for ineffective enterprise performance and is relied upon mainly to reconcile the interests of shareholders and managers by improving the performances of target enterprises.[408] Two approaches have emerged to enhance the understanding of enterprise performance surrounding takeover activities.[409] Event studies analysis argues that a suitable measure of performance is where shareholders are the ultimate holders of the right to organizational control, and thus they need to be the focal point of any deliberations surrounding it.[410] This approach further claims that the relevant metric is obtained by analyzing share market data to ascertain the economic impact of takeovers by focusing on abnormal stock price gyrations at particular points during the takeover process, and hence the importance of specific dates, like the announcement date, or the outcome date.

The other approach relies on conventional accounting measures, like returns on assets, sales, and capital employed. This is based on the suggestion that changes in stock prices merely reflect shareholders' expectations. These expectations are argued to be compromised by an asymmetry of information between managers and outsiders,[411] or that stock price movements surrounding takeover activities merely reflect shareholders' anticipation of wealth transfers from existing bondholders.[412]

Research on balance did not offer consistent support for the contention that takeover targets demonstrate inferior pre-bid performance, compared to nontargets.[413] Additionally, when takeover targets are differentiated between hostile and friendly bids, no consistent performance differences have been observed. It would appear that on the face of it, the absence of pre-bid underperforming market and accounting-based metrics would reflect takeovers having a poor governance function. But subsequent research demonstrating higher rates of CEO turnovers in takeover targets showing weak pre-bid performance has provided some support for takeovers having a governance role. This has raised important questions pertaining to the classification of hostility. The bulk of research studying pre-bid performance has focused on completed bids, while significant numbers of takeover bids have been unsuccessful, with many

408. R.M. Cyert, et al. 2002. "CG, takeovers and top-management compensation: Theory and evidence". *Management Science,* Vol. 48 (4): 453-469.
409. R. Michal. 2017. "The impact of takeovers on the acquiring firms in the pharmaceutical market". *Journal of Competitiveness,* Vol. 9 (1): 89-102.
410. M.C. Jensen. 1984. "Takeover: Folklore and science". *Harvard Business Review,* Vol. 62 (1984): 109-121.
411. R. Morck, A. Shleifer & R. Vishny. 1989. "Characteristics of targets of hostile and friendly takeovers". In A.J. Auerbach (ed.). *Corporate takeovers: Causes and consequences.* Chicago: University of Chicago Press.
412. A. Shleifer & R. Vishny. 1988. "Value maximisation and the acquisition process". *Journal of Economic Perspective,* Vol. 2 (1988): 7-20.
413. N. O'Sullivan & P. Wong. 2005. "The governance role of takeovers". In K. Keasey, S. Thompson & M. Wright (eds.). *CG: Accountability, enterprise and international comparisons.* Chichester: John Wiley & Sons. Ltd.

arising from the inability of bidders to overcome managerial resistance.[414] Markets appear to react positively to some bids, but negatively to others. This implies that once takeover occurs, actions are taken to correct the weak performance. This then raises questions as to the applicability of hostile/friendly taxonomy when seeking to distinguish takeovers driven by governance objectives.

Significant numbers of takeovers launched have not been completed. Resistance by target management has been important brakes to these. Research suggests that such resistance could be in the interests of either shareholders or managers, while further research would be needed for developing insights on how governance characteristics impact managers' reactions to bids.[415] Some research has drawn attention to the role of board independence in influencing target reaction to bids. Those boards with higher representation of NEDs appear to resist takeover bids more, culminating in greater bid premiums for shareholders. It would appear that the most significant influence on target company reaction to takeovers has been the ownership of managers, where significant managerial ownership could generate dilemmas for managers in the context of takeovers. This is because managers would resist protecting their job interest, but takeovers could be perceived by them to be at the expense of their ownership interests. On balance, research insights have been consistent with the increased probability of hostility when managerial ownership is low, and a positive association between managerial ownership and friendly bids, as well as, bid success.

Where takeovers have been driven by governance objectives, it would be helpful to evaluate the impact of takeovers on shareholders' wealth in both the target and bidding enterprises.[416] The impact on target shareholders' wealth is usually observed through short-term event studies, as measured by the bid's impact on the target's share price. Abundant evidence for this shows takeovers generating very significant wealth gains for target shareholders. The magnitudes of shareholders' gains are usually influenced by particular bid characteristics. Takeovers financed by cash and takeovers which are resisted particularly in the presence of more independent boards appear to generate higher returns for target shareholders. The impact though of takeover bids on the bidding companies' wealth has been less clear, and generally inconclusive.

Examinations of the impact of particular bid characteristics demonstrate that the announcement impacts of cash-finance bids and bids resisted by management might be more positive.[417] Examinations of the relative size of bidder and target corporations show some evidence that larger bids generate more positive returns, while there has also been some evidence that acquiring targets in linked businesses exert positive impacts on bidder returns. A majority of studies on the post-bid performance of bidders show that bids have a negative impact on the long-run performance of bidders. Findings from these have shown that corporate efficiency did deteriorate in the subsequent years after acquisitions, while more current studies show increased

414. G.W. Schwert. 2000. "Hostility in takeovers: In the eyes of the beholder?". *Journal of Finance*, Vol. LV6 (2000): 2599-2640.
415. O'Sullivan & Wong 2005, *supra* note [413].
416. O'Sullivan & Wong 2005, *supra* note [413].
417. O'Sullivan & Wong 2005, *supra* note [413].

productivity, more efficient use of labor, and no evidence of significant job losses. Hostile takeovers though generally have been accompanied by significant divestment of assets, but less has been known about the employment impact of such divestments.

Consistent findings of takeover research suggest the increased probability of managerial turnover following successful takeover bids.[418] The rates of management turnover have been significantly higher than either prior rates of turnover in targets or turnover levels in nontargets. A growing stream of research suggests that post-acquisition turnover is influenced by the target's pre-acquisition performance. Other research suggests that the acquisition-turnover relationships might have transformed during the 1990s when businesses have been seeking alternative governance mechanisms, like greater board independence, block holder activism, and incentive-based pay packages to ensure managers aligned with shareholders' agenda. Despite the scarcity of research on the governance implications of abandoned bids, research work undertaken suggests that failed bids disclosed important information that commonly culminated in prolonged positive revaluations of the target by investors. Also, successful defense of takeovers by management did not necessarily ensure management's own employment. Examinations of management post-bid have shown that the rate of management turnover in failed targets appears to exceed what could be envisaged in no-targets prior to the bid. These few findings available for abandoned bids have provided some support to the governance role of such bids.[419]

Thus, the market for corporate control, as illustrated here, refers to the market for acquisitions and mergers where there is competition for control rights. In the market for corporate control paradigm, the conduct of takeover by corporations in that market and the accompanying threat of takeovers has shown that external control mechanisms could reduce agency costs. The contrary perspective has argued that the market for capital control could not resolve principal-agent problems, and that as such, M&A are manifestations of acts of agency that could worsen contradictions between management and shareholders. It has been generally held that the US and UK corporate stock rights have been highly decentralized, and that shareholders have limited influence over corporate operations and management. This has helped to explain why the market for corporate control has been quite dynamic and its functions could be effectively deployed. However, in economies like Japan and Germany, and those in Southeast Asia where family holdings dominate, the market for corporate control has been relatively less dynamic, as share rights are largely more concentrated.[420] There are likely to be advantages and disadvantages of hostile takeovers as the external mechanism of governance. Hostile takeovers appear to provide several advantages to protect shareholders when internal controls have been ineffective. Simultaneously though they do have several disadvantages, like the risks of overpaying for takeover activities,

418. O'Sullivan & Wong 2005, *supra* note [413].
419. O'Sullivan & Wong 2005, *supra* note [413].
420. C. Mayer. 1996. "CG: Competition and performance". *OECD Economic Studies*, Vol. 27 (1996): 7-34.

and risks of poison pills in the form of divestment of assets deemed vital to the acquirer.[421]

4.06 THE IMPACT OF COVID-19 ON THE MARKET FOR CORPORATE CONTROL

The 2020 COVID-19 pandemic has contributed to the collapse of many industries and businesses because of the sudden and inevitable collapse of markets through no faults of many corporate boards, as market demand for their products and services simply evaporated. Those businesses impacted more, like those in the travel, tourist and hospitality domains, suddenly became soft targets for takeover contemplators, even though many of them are household brand names in their respective industries. One such case in the UK came with the decision from the UK Takeover Panel (UKTP) that COVID-19 and UK lockdown are insufficient grounds to trigger standard material adverse conditions (MAC).[422] As has been common of such conditions in UK Takeover offers, these have been worded in very general terms, with the intention that they would have a very wide scope of potential application, but there is though no specific mention of COVID-19 conditions. The Offeror in the case has earlier sought a ruling from the UTP to authorize it to lapse the offer on the grounds that it should be entitled to trigger certain of the standard MAC provided in the scheme document because of the impact on the offeree of the COVID-19 pandemic and related UK governmental measures.[423]

The UKTP when announcing its decision has not provided significant details for refusing the application, but instead allowed the offeror to apply to the Hearings Committee of the UKTP for a review of its decision. This has not been taken up by the offeror, and as such the UKTP's decision stands. In the absence of substantive reasoning behind the UKTP decision, it would appear to conform to precedent.[424] Further, UKTP's Practice Statement No. 5 (as amended) guidance has stated that in the case of general conditions, such as the MAC, compliance to the Rule 13.5(a) requirement would depend on the offeror showing that the pertinent circumstances are of very considerable significance thereby stabbing at the heart of the transaction's purpose. The UKTP has ruled that, while the standard required for invoking such a condition is high, the test did not require the offerors to show frustration with the offer.[425]

The UKTP has further indicated that when considering this matter, its practice is to take into account all pertinent factors, such as whether the pertinent condition has

421. D. Ali & B. Mansur. 2020. "Hostile takeovers as an external mechanism of CG: Advantages and disadvantages". *Economic and Management Research Journal*, Vol. 13 (3): 99-111.
422. UTP. 2020. "Offer by Brigadier Acquisition Company Limited ("Brigadier") for Moss Bros Group PLC ("Moss Bros")". *UTP 19/05/20*, https://www.thetakeoverpanel.org.uk/publication, accessed November 10, 2020.
423. Rule 13.5(a) of the City Code on Takeovers and Mergers.
424. UTP. 2001. "The Takeover Panel: Offer by WPP Group PLC ("WPP") for Tempus Group PLC ("TEMPUS")". *UTP 06/11/01*, https://www.thetakeoverpanel.org.uk/wp-content/uploads/2008, accessed November 10, 2020.
425. UTP 2020, *supra* note [422].

been the subject of negotiation with the offeree, whether the condition has been expressly presented to the offeree shareholders' attention in the offer document, or announcement with clear account of the circumstances that gave rise to the right to invoke it, and whether the condition has been included to take into consideration the particular circumstances of the offeree.[426] The UKTP could have taken into consideration the specific reference to the potentially significant impact of COVID-19 on the offeree's business and share price performance, the absence of any specific reference to COVID-19 in the conditions, the timing of the intention of the offeror to make the offer that came after national lockdown commenced in Italy, as well as the consideration that the measures implemented by the UK government have not been specific to the offeree.[427]

It is also notable that the bidder has sought to rely on various general boilerplate conditions to its offer. There is always the scope for specific conditions to be negotiated into an offer, and a bidder could be in stronger turf, when seeking to invoke this kind of condition, provided conditions articulated in Practice Statement 5 have been adhered to, including drawing to the attention of target shareholders, clear account of the circumstances that could give rise to the bidder's right to invoke it.[428] Bidders might also need to be conscious of important conditions falling outside the scope of the materiality test, as provided in the Takeover Code.[429] A bidder might need approval from its own shareholders to proceed with its offer for various reasons, such as to approve the transaction itself as consequence of regulatory obligations in its own jurisdiction, or to issue securities in connection with the offer. Where such conditions are included, and in circumstances where the offer has become materially less attractive to the bidder because of deterioration of the target's businesses, and so on, such that it is no longer in its interest to proceed, the bidder would be generally free to recommend that its shareholders vote against the relevant resolutions and invoke the condition to lapse the bid.

Obviously, any conditions, not subjected to the usual materiality threshold, could introduce the element of optionality for the bidder in terms of its ability to lapse its offer, commonly known in the market as backdoor MAC.[430] Hence, the scope and inclusion of such conditions would consistently depend on the relative bargaining powers of the respective parties and the background to the offer, including as to whether it falls into the category of distressed or forced M&A. The scope of any such conditions in the current climate would be a special area of focus for target companies because of their potential impact on deal certainty. In the case of distressed M&A, the target's business could be threatened by insolvency risk raising real concerns for the

426. UTP 2020, *supra* note [422].
427. T. Wozniak, I. Wright & M. Lewis. 2020. "UK Takeover Panel: COVID-19 and UK lockdown insufficient to trigger MAC conditions". *JD Supra 01/06/20*, https://www.jdsupra.com/legalnews/uk-takeover, accessed November 10, 2020.
428. P. Whitlock, et al. 2020. "COVID-19: What might mean for public M&A in the UK?". *Norton Rose Fulbright July 2020*, https://www.nortonrosefulbright.com/en/knowledge/publications/17507804/, accessed November 10, 2020.
429. Whitlock et al. 2020, *supra* note [428].
430. Whitlock et al. 2020, *supra* note [428].

bidder. In actual insolvency of a target company during the offer period, a bidder would be released from its obligation to proceed with the offer, but the more difficult matter for bidders would arise, where the positions of the target business deteriorated significantly, but fell short of actual insolvency. In these situations, a bidder might wish to take action to mitigate the risk of insolvency and protect the deal, by way of providing financing or through other ancillary transactions. Where this is proposed, the restrictions on frustrating action and offer related agreements in Rules 21 of the Takeover Code would likely be involved. Nevertheless, in those circumstances where the very existence of the target is under threat, it is envisaged that the UKTP would apply a pragmatic approach to potentially dispense with full compliance with the requirements of Rule 21.[431]

On June 25, 2020, the Corporate Insolvency and Governance Act (CIG Act)[432] came into force. This legislation introduced fundamental changes to the country's company and insolvency laws. It not only provided temporary assistance to companies and their directors during the COVID-19 crisis but also bolstered the UK's restructuring tool kit on a permanent basis. These combined together represent the most significant change to English insolvency law in nearly two decades. The permanent reforms include the following:[433]

(1) A new restructuring procedure or Restructuring Plan based primarily on the existing procedure for Schemes of Arrangement, but with additional discretion for the Court to allow dissenting classes of creditors to be bound, as long as one class of creditors approves the plan.
(2) *Ipso Facto* clauses which allow for the termination of an agreement on grounds that a party has entered into an insolvency process are now unenforceable in a wide range of supplier contracts.
(3) A pre-insolvency, stand-alone moratorium for businesses in financial distress, with designated carve-outs.

The temporary measures seek to provide support and flexibility to companies encountering financial difficulties because of the economic impact of the corona pandemic. Such measures were applicable until September 30, 2020, with retrospective effect to March 1, 2020, or March 26, 2020, in respect of governance rules, and included the following:[434]

(1) Suspension of wrongful trading rules.
(2) Suspension of the use of statutory demands as a basis for a winding up petition and issuance of winding up petitions where a business could show the cause was the financial impact of COVID-19.

431. Whitlock et al. 2020, *supra* note [428].
432. "Corporate Insolvency and Governance Act 2020". https://www.legislation.gov.uk/ukpga/2020/12/pdfs/ukpga_20200012_en.pdf, accessed November 10, 2020.
433. I. Jack, E.L. Menzies & S. DE Souza. 2021. "The Corporate Insolvency and Governance Act 2020: Changes to UK Insolvency Laws". *The National Law Review*, Vol. XI (103): 1-9.
434. Jack et al. 2021, *supra* note [433].

(3) Flexibility on requirements pertaining to the holding of shareholders' meetings and extension of time to make certain filings at Companies House.

Market reactions to both permanent and temporary changes have been generally positive.[435] However, three aspects of the legislation would fundamentally impact how funding for UK corporations would be structured and documented. A crucial feature of the new law is the moratorium on enforcement. This could last for twenty business days, but could be extended for up to a year, subject to certain conditions. One criterion for extension is that specified debts incurred before the moratorium, and which fall due before, or during the moratorium, must have been repaid. Where the borrower goes into liquidation, administration or other restructuring within twelve weeks after the end of the moratorium, that specified debt, which has fallen due, would get super-priority over all other creditors, other than those holding fixed charges. Thus, the new legislation is envisaged to impact the structuring of financing for business enterprises in the UK in perhaps three awkward ways:[436]

(1) First, attention is drawn to the feature that a moratorium can offer super-priority to revolving loans, but not term loans. The new insolvency provision appears to prefer revolving over term loans in most circumstances. It would also motivate revolving lenders to make replacement loans during the moratorium, so as to get super-priority in the resulting administration or liquidation and ensure that they would not be subordinated to other creditors that could get super-priority.
(2) Second, the new insolvency law would treat borrowers and guarantors differently.[437] It would motivate revolving loans to be made to the most creditworthy entities in a group of companies, rather than being made to finance companies or special purpose vehicles with guarantees.
(3) Third, the new insolvency law would treat some bonds differently from loans, and hence encourage financing to UK corporations to be structured as loans, rather than as bonds.[438]

The new legislation is criticized for being rushed through in Parliament, but the government has indicated that it might later adjust the super-priority and moratorium arrangements where they proved to be not working well through secondary legislation. It is though more likely to require some insolvencies with adverse publicity before the government makes those adjustments.

On the wider implications, COVID-19 generated unprecedented challenges for businesses in all economic sectors, including market upheavals and volatile share

435. Jack et al. 2021, *supra* note [433].
436. B. Johnston. 2020. "Strange effects of the UK's new insolvency law". *Morgan Lewis & Bockius 29/06/20*, https://www.lexology.com/library/detail.aspx?g=29cec1a0-5c67, accessed November 10, 2020.
437. Johnston 2020, *supra* note [436].
438. Johnston 2020, *supra* note [436].

prices. Considerable barriers to deals have emerged, particularly with the de-prioritization of M&A owing to operational inward focus on both sides of deals, absence of clear roadmaps as to when business performance would turnaround, valuation dislocations, absence of available acquisition financing, hostile target management teams, and logical difficulties for conducting face-to-face meetings. Despite these formidable challenges, there has been a growing momentum toward greater M&A readiness, since the second half of 2020, because of rising valuation opportunities, private equity and financial sponsors needing to deploy their capital, the attraction of first mover advantage, and challenges in accessing liquidity.

Market participants might need to be conscious that COVID-19 concerns have evoked a widespread trend globally toward more protectionism and a readiness by domestic authorities to intervene in M&A transactions which would have national interest or security concerns and to protect businesses vulnerable to bids especially from overseas bidders.[439]As is indeed the case, the UK has tabled changes to the Enterprise Act 2002 to expand the circumstances wherein the government would be empowered to review foreign takeovers of UK businesses.[440] These proposed rules would allow the government to intervene in foreign takeovers of businesses that are directly involved in the COVID-19 response.

In the meantime, the UKTP has begun consultation for its proposed new rules.[441] The Takeover Code has been designed to ensure that shareholders are treated fairly, are not denied opportunities to decide on the merits of a takeover, and are afforded equivalent treatment by an offeror. This would therefore provide an orderly framework, within which takeovers could be conducted.[442] UKTP's proposed recommendations seek to simplify the offer timetable to accommodate regulatory approval processes that have become more complex, to remove the historical distinction between the treatment of UK and EC competition conditions, and to make changes to the existing Code timetable with respect to contractual takeover offers in particular.[443]

The UKTP's Code Committee in its consultation paper proposed various amendments to the City Code on Takeovers and Mergers (Code) which when adopted would lead to major departures from existing rules. The primary objectives of the proposed changes are to:[444]

439. J. Modrall, S.H. Reisinger & A.Y. Mahfoud. 2020. "Global rules on foreign direct investment: Summary of regulations in light of COVID-19". *Norton Rose Fulbright 12/05/20*, https://www.nortonrosefulbright.com/en-us/knowledge/publications/cb7bbd10/global-rules, accessed November 10, 2020.
440. M. Israel & K. Kelliher. 2020. "UK ushers in new foreign takeover restrictions for Coronavirus-critical businesses and national security activities". *White & Case 22/06/20*, https://www.whitecase.com/publications/alert/uk-ushers-new-foreign-takeover-restrictions-coronavirus-critical, accessed November 10, 2020.
441. UTP. 2020. "Public consultation by the Code Committee". *UTP 27/10/20*, https://www.thetakeoverpanel.org.uk/wp-content/uploads/2020/10/PCP, accessed November 10, 2020.
442. UTP. 2016, 12th edition. *The Takeover Code*. London: UTP.
443. UTP 2020, *supra* note [441].
444. L.N. Ferera, et al. 2020. "UK Takeover Panel's Code Committee proposes changes to treatment of offer conditions and offer timetable". *Jones Day White Paper November 2020*. https://www.jonesday.com/en/insights/2020/11/uk-takeover-panels-code, accessed December 21, 2020.

(1) simplify the offer timetable and amend it to accommodate regulatory approval processes that are currently more complicated and of longer duration than was the case when the existing timetable was initially structured;
(2) remove the historical differentiation between the treatment of UK and EC competition conditions and all other conditions pertaining to official authorizations and regulatory clearances; and
(3) make other changes to the existing Code timetable, in particular, for contractual takeover offers.

The rationale behind the proposals is to provide consistent treatment for all regulatory conditions, and to make material significance requirement applicable to Competition and Markets Authority (CMA) and EC regulatory conditions. The key changes proposed comprise the following:[445]

(1) Offer conditions pertaining to the CMA or the EC not commencing a Phase 2 competition review to be subject to the "material significance" requirement before they could be revoked, meaning those conditions will be treated consistently with conditions relating to other regulatory approvals and authorizations.
(2) The abolition of requirement for offers to contain a term that they will lapse if there is a CMA or EC Phase 2 competition review before a given date.
(3) The introduction of a single "unconditional date" for the compliance of all offer conditions to contractual takeover offers. This would be set at the 60th day after posting the initial offer document, subject to acceleration or extension.
(4) The acceptance condition for contractual takeover offers to be the final condition to be satisfied and to be capable of compliance only after all other conditions have been satisfied or waived.
(5) Having withdrawal rights available for offeree company shareholders from the outset of a conditional takeover offer until it becomes or is declared wholly unconditional.

The UKTP has on March 31, 2021, published its response statement (RS) outlining changes to the Takeover Code pertaining to the conditions to an offer, especially those pertaining to the regulatory/merger control clearance and to the offer timetable.[446] The RS confirms that the Panel will adopt the amendments proposed in its Public Consultation Paper (PCP) 2020/1 published by the Panel on October 27, 2020, subject to minor modifications. The rule changes would go into force on July 5, 2021, and would be applicable to all firm offers that are announced in accordance with Rule 2.7 of the Code on or after July 5, 2021, other than when to do so would give the

445. Ferera et al. 2020, *supra* note [444].
446. UTP. 2021. "Conditions to offers and the offer timetable: Response statement by the Code Committee". *UTP Statement RS 2020/1 31 March 2021*, https://www.thetakeoverpanel.org.uk/wp-content/uploads/2021/03/RS-2020_1-FINAL-31-March-2021.pdf, accessed April 7, 2021.

amendments retroactive effect. Firm offers announced prior to that date (or in competition with an offer announced prior to that date) would continue to be subjected to the existing rules. As alluded to earlier, the key changes to the Code are as follows:[447]

(1) Conditions pertaining to clearance by the CMA and EC. The Takeover Code will no longer differentiate between CMA/EC conditions and other merger control clearance conditions. A bidder will only be able to invoke a condition to an offer pertaining to merger control clearance in the UK and the EU if the circumstances on which it is seeking to rely on are material in the context of the offer, as is already the case for merger control conditions in jurisdictions outside the UK/EU.
(2) There would be various changes to the offer timetable, including a requirement that all conditions to an offer must be satisfied by Day 60, instead of Day 81, but there will be greater ability to freeze the offer timetable if there is an outstanding official authorization or regulatory clearance.
(3) A contractual offer will have a long-stop date. This is a date whereupon a bidder can seek to lapse an offer where not all the conditions are satisfied.
(4) Panel Practice Statement No. 5 will be updated to provide further guidance on the factors that would be taken into consideration when deciding whether a bidder should be able to invoke a condition, especially where the condition relates to an official authorization or regulatory clearance.

Similar to the overhauling of the rules in 2011, there would be no transition period. This implies that there would be a period of time whereupon it is possible that some offers would be progressing under the existing regime, while others would be subject to the new rules. The changes are far reaching and would likely have a considerable impact on market practices. The amendments are generally logical, in particular the consistent approach to regulatory conditions. Some market practice familiarization would be helpful though, especially with regards to the use of acceleration statements, but more so because the existing timetable for takeovers has largely been unamended for some time.

The implications of corporate financial structures for the governance process, especially on the role of the market for corporate control as a market disciplining device, have been discussed in depth in this chapter. This provides the context for which to discuss in depth their impacts on tech businesses at the forefront of digitalization, where M&A are becoming generally active and attracting controversies. This is accordingly taken up in Chapter 5.

Finally, this chapter attached a lot of importance to the "G" element in the ESG paradigm, but it also alerts attention to the new institutional investors' drive to incorporate ESG factors in their investment decision-making process, regardless of

447. M. Bardell, A. Kirkby & R. Moore. 2021. "Public M&A-Takeover Code changes relating to conditions to an offer and the offer timetable". *Herbert Smith Freehills 6 April 2021*. https://hsfnotes.com/corporate/2021/04/06/public-ma-takeover-code-changes-relating-to-conditions-to-an-offer-and-the-offer-timetable/, accessed April 8, 2021.

concentrated or dispersed ownership patterns. At the global level, the FSB, the IOSCO, the IMF, the OECD, and others are helping global institutional investors' drive toward enhanced ESG practices and disclosures obligations.

CHAPTER 5
ESG in Digitalized Businesses

As China ascended in economic terms, lifting millions out of poverty, besides accomplishing globally respected technological innovations in business and in the frontiers of space, it attracted global attention. In recent times, it is becoming clearer that this was less about poverty eradication for the good of mankind, but more about business and technological tensions between China and other superpowers, but in particular the US that sees its economic and political might being challenged by not only China but also Russia. These have spilled into the business landscape, as the US and its close allies accused China for competing unfairly through state subsidies for businesses, insufficient or token curbs on intellectual property rights infringements, uncompetitive home market practices, human rights infringement linked to labor in business, and so on, while the angst against Russia revolves around interference into the US election system, as well as the providing of safe harbors for cybercriminals heaving havocs to businesses and other public spaces in the US.

The rising geopolitical tensions between the US, China and Russia until the change of US administration also included tensions between US and even EU, its close ally when it comes to trade. US MNCs have been dominating the global digital economy, leading to accusations of unfair dominance across the world, while China's MNCs are being condemned for unfair business practices. The onsetting of the 2020 COVID-19 pandemic accelerated further the rising gap between freer trade and economic nationalism, leading to serious and massive disruptions in the global supply chain for business. As businesses continue in their digitalization journeys, they are increasingly finding challenges to their business practices, inclusive of those with ESG implications. This chapter, as such, will examine in depth the ESG challenges for those businesses at the forefront of digitalization.

5.01 IMPACT OF GEOPOLITICAL TENSIONS, DIGITALIZATION AND THE VIRUS PANDEMIC: THE CULTURAL CLASH AND BOARDS AT CROSSROADS

The convergence of the escalation of geopolitical tensions especially between economic superpowers, accelerating digitalization of business systems, and the massive disruptive effects of the COVID-19 pandemic has generated huge and pervasive pressures for many businesses. Business entry into the digital era, already formidable on its own with its huge demand for the right technological skills as well as the capital needed, is further impeded by market and supply chain challenges. Consequentially, business systems and management processes and structures too begin to come under severe pressures. These could either be good or bad for some and not others.

The virus pandemic prompting economic lockdowns in the US, EU, UK and elsewhere brought massive disruptions at the marketing and business inputs fronts. Those needing physical interactions, such as those in hospitality and personal grooming businesses, suffered massively as customers were unable to check in for their services, while those that could be undertaken online, like online-gaming, online finance, and so on, were bombarded by huge surge in demand for their services and had to scale up further. There were those in-between offering hybrid delivery services. The degree of market and/or supply chain disruptions therefore varies, depending on the degree of business digitalization required in different business types or business models. Obviously, businesses respond by varying or adjusting their business models or business processes and systems.

Board leadership and oversight of the direction and control of digitalized businesses in view of this has to adjust to take care of a model that requires the use of automation, AI, the internet of things, digital platform technology, and these days blockchain technology for some others. No longer can board and board members function by focusing attention only on the more conventional aspects of management processes from business planning, business implementation, and business controls. They need to get more familiar with the impact of how FIR enabling technologies disrupt businesses in terms of scale, speed, and complexity. They need to collaborate with internal and external experts. Other than those directors in tech start-ups, most other directors even as they lead at the forefront of the digitalization space tend to be a mix of those with strong ICT skills and those barely coping, besides having to link up with tech-savvy executives down the line.

General observations have it that there is a management cultural distance gap, where significant numbers of directors grew from the earlier management era confined to objectives and controls, whereas others in the digitalized business focus relatively more on data management and control and the laws that go with them. Also, unlike traditional forms of businesses that tend to follow more hierarchical structures, digitalized businesses tend to follow more decentralized forms of management structures that also rely more on automation and lesser discretionary decision-making options because of the push for greater speed. This gives rise to more haste more risk challenges. This is why, US, EU and UK regulators are looking into the accountability of board and management on the cybersecurity risks in their companies in the new digital era.

Digitalized businesses could likely benefit relatively more when both executives and NEDs are able to bridge or find ways to close the cultural gaps between the two different groups, as mentioned here. Corporate culture is the outcome of how a company works and operates, and comprises the collective experiences of employees, what they believe in, and what they value. Leadership, purpose, and how work could implement a vision are also parts of corporate culture. Professor Ethan Bernstein of Harvard Business School sees culture as the glue that either keeps a company doing things well or keeping it doing things poorly.[448] Digital culture on the other hand is a set of seven attributes:[449]

(1) Innovativeness, or the prevalence of behaviors that support risk-taking, disruptive thinking, and the exploring of new or novel ideas.
(2) Leveraging on use of data and analytics to improving the decision-making process.
(3) Collaboration, or the designing of cross-functional departmental teams toward the optimization of corporate skills and competencies.
(4) Open culture, or the extent of partnerships with external networks like third-party vendors, start-ups or customers.
(5) Digital-first mindsets where digital solutions are the default way forward.
(6) Agility and flexibility meaning the speed and dynamism of decision-making and the ability of the enterprise to adapt to changing demands and technologies unfolding in volatile, uncertain, complex and ambiguous (VUCA) times.
(7) Customer centricity involving the use of digital solutions to expand the customer base, transform the customer experience, and co-creation of new products.

In short, digital success needs a digital culture, or else the old-world organization could doom a company's reinvention for the new world. Great working places are unlikely to be mere lush benefits or worksites with great lunches, but a fortress of stunning colleagues built on self-driven and high-performing individuals.[450] Positive digital culture helping to bridge the technology-business divide forms an important part of the digital transformation process to deliver value. There are seven key lessons on how digital transformation can deliver value:[451]

448. J. Buvat, et al. 2017. "The digital culture challenge: Closing the employee-leadership gap". https://www.capgemini.com/wp, accessed March 25, 2021.
449. Buvat et al. 2017, *supra* note [448].
450. J. Bughin. 2017. "Digital success requires a digital culture". *McKinsey 3 May 2017*. https://www.mckinsey.com/business-functions/strategy-and-corporate-finance/our-insights, accessed March 19, 2021.
451. McKinsey. 2021. "Seven key lessons on how technology transformations can deliver value". *McKinsey March 2021*. https://www.mckinsey.com/business-functions/mckinsey-digital/our-insights/seven-lessons-on-how-technology-transformations-can-deliver-value, accessed April 10, 2021.

(1) Technology investments are creating significant business value.
(2) Human-focused makeovers make the most value.
(3) Talent is the key to successful digital transformations, not easy to execute, but valuable to pursue.
(4) The talent challenge has clear implications for talent-sourcing strategies that are relying more on external providers.
(5) Increasing reliance on multiple initiatives that are at times running parallel.
(6) Wider usages of advanced technologies could generate outsize value in digital transformation.
(7) Bridging the business-technology divide is pivotal to high business performance. This explains why successful players tend to monitor the transformation process using business-oriented metrics, like user satisfaction, time-to-market, or financial impacts.

Rapid digitalization though brings with it various ESG implications. Directors need to be prepared to deal with them as they unfold.

5.02 IMPACT OF RAPID DIGITALIZATION ON ESG PRACTICES

In contrast to growth that has to do with short-term returns and capital expansion with less interest on longer-term impacts, rapid digitalization is a long-term strategy taking into account how businesses invest in innovation and sustainability, and ergo value creation. Directors are generally aware that value creation in the current context stretches beyond immediate decisions on dividends and investment strategies for adherence to a durable and sustainable business model. Its dual mission of building a strong enterprise and a strong stock continues to be challenging in today's global CUVA landscape. It is about staying ahead of opportunities and risks.[452] Businesses, including entrenched global leaders, could be pulled under at any one time, by digital or blockchain technology, AI, or virtual reality.

Leading global institutional investors and private equities, like Vanguard, State Street Global Investors and Black Rock, have in recent years been urging directors to take more active roles in transforming their enterprises into corporations valuable to their customers, investors, the local communities, as well as the overall marketplace. More directly, these primary stakeholders are urging directors to adopt governance practices that support long-term, sustainable value creation.[453] These practices have evolved to now include mandatory sustainability reports for listed entities in some capital markets and in proxy statement in the US that goes beyond check-box compliance statements to more disclosures of an enterprise's strategy, performance, compensation and culture.

452. H.J. Gregory. 2017. "Governing through disruption: A boardroom guide for 2018". https://www.sidley.com/-/media/publications, accessed November 10, 2020.
453. Boardroom Resources. 2018. "The proxy statement: 4 best practices for the 2018 season". https://boardroomresources/, accessed November 10, 2020.

Directors besides making important decisions in M&A, market expansions, manpower management, supply chain management, and innovativeness are likely to be building on the stewardship or caretaker approach from which they traditionally view such decisions through the private equity framework because of the opportunities, threats, and risks posed by CUVA.[454] More than ever, directors leading progressive enterprises are making decisions through the value-seeking lens of investors combined with the cautionary prism of a steward. Appropriate corporate leadership, for example, at Apple, Microsoft, and Amazon has steered their hither billion-dollar enterprises into trillion-dollar market capital enterprises,[455] while enterprises with ineffectual guidance have moved in the opposite direction.[456]

The above companies' forward-looking boards, and equivalent others, like Tesla, have shifted from cautious stewardship style to innovative business leaderships. Those able to move in this positive direction have not been held back by decades of traditional legacies, but instead have been agile enough in their business processes to respond effectively to the challenging but doable demands of value creation. Directors contemplating the decisive battle between being laggards and being innovative leaders have turned to increasingly proven models. Managing disruptions in the digital era is not altogether novel, as the ideas were already in play some five years earlier from the late renowned Harvard Business School Professor Clayton Christenson when he cautioned businesses to rise to the challenges posed by business disruptors and by business/ technological systems disruptions.[457]

One good example of dynamic digital-resilient business approach suggests a two-prong model.[458] First, this involves focusing on operational engagement that in particular implements fresh tactics for collaboration, shaping board structures, especially board committees for the value creation mission, while using technology to keep in pace with what goes on inside and outside the enterprise. Second, this would involve an introspection of the existing board behavior profile, to assess the degree of change in the profile needed in order to shift toward a value creation corporate culture. It is vital to bear in mind constantly that value-focused boards are not built instantaneously, but develop over time via incremental changes to business.[459] Powerful ideas are unlikely to be enough, as the transformations are likely to require a series of regular

454. A. Gains & A. Schmitz. 2020. "Is your portfolio company's value creation plan still on track?". *Bain & Company 14/10/20.* https://www.bain.com/insights/is-your-portfolio-companys-value-creation-plan, accessed November 10, 2020.
455. R. Viastelica & D. Bass. 2021. "Microsoft rises to join Apple in exclusive $2 trillion dollar club". *Bloomberg 23 June 2021.* https://www.bloomberg.com/news/articles/2021-06-22/microsoft-rallies, accessed March 25, 2021.
456. Y. Malenkov, et al. 2021. *Journal of Open Innovation: Technology, Market and Complexity,* Vol. 7 (2021): 108-128.
457. C. Christensen & J. Euchner. 2020. "Managing disruption: An interview with Clayton Christensen". *Research-Technology Management,* Vol. 63 (3): 49-54.
458. B. Stafford & D. Schindlinger. 2019. *Governance in the digital age: A guide for the modern corporate board director.* New jersey: Wiley.
459. L.A. Hill & G. Davis. 2017. "Boards: Innovation is your responsibility too". *Harvard Business Review November-December 2017.* https://hbr.org/2017/11/the-boards-new-innovation-imperative, November 10, 2020.

brainstorming sessions on several good and bad ideas to sift out that most likely to work for a particular enterprise.

5.03 LEADING AND MANAGING CORPORATIONS IN THE ESG ERA

The six areas where board roles, responsibilities, and processes are evolving have been identified as value creation, resilience, risk management, strategy, sustainability, and personal accountability. Board behavioral profiles or governance personality traits too could transform over time in response to emerging specific situations. These are respectively further explained below:[460]

(1) Value Creation. Directors are keeping themselves more closely in touch with change to be better equipped to talk about and to respond to new developments and trends. Many are turning to fresh perspectives from different industries and with expertise in emerging digital technologies, like blockchain, AI, and data analytics. Directors from all backgrounds are educating themselves via tactics, like site tours, customer visits, and listening to experts in emerging tech sectors. They are also strengthening how they work together as a whole. This means going beyond PowerPoint presentations with open and ongoing discussions enriched by thought-provoking questions. Digital era collaborations further include making time for big questions and long-term thinking about innovation. Some boards are installing committees dedicated to value creation, with the ultimate goal of achieving richer, deeper conversations for sharper, faster decision-making. In the end, it is important for directors to appreciate the appropriateness of setting the right tone and standards from the top, establish a growth plan through the CEO, and led by a board that is fresh and refreshed to effectively execute an innovation strategy that involves things outside the confines of the enterprise.

(2) Maintaining resilience. The capacity to generate value, manage risk, and guide an enterprise into CUVA times requires exceptional skills in communicating and linking the dots, supported by strong and appropriate governance processes, and an atmosphere of trust. These variables working in concert provide the crucial competitive differentiator of resilience. Board resilience is best shown by what happens in its absence. Examples of these would include frauds costing money and tainted reputation, offending behaviors going unnoticed owing to lack of board oversight, unacknowledged due to conflicts of interest, and unaddressed because of poor decision-making and governance structures. Other examples would include serious breach of customer information when directors do not have the right information at the right time, besides lacking the confidence and candor to engage with the threat in a direct, informed, and timely way. The board's strengths in dealing with

460. Stafford & Schindlinger 2019, *supra* note [458].

these difficult challenges would include lining up the expertise and perspectives they are likely to need by developing formal and informal matrices of desired skills and proactively networking through new channels, like alumni groups and reputable financiers. Some boards are also enabling more timely decision-making by streamlining management reports to bring the most salient information to the fore. This could simply involve asking the directors what they want to see or know, or the use of online tools to facilitate document exchange, scheduling, and searching. It has been argued that the most important tool for board resilience is intangible candor, meaning the capacity to challenge one another, or at time to agree to disagree. This would imply that security, anonymity, and trust are pivotal for a resilient board.

(3) Managing risk. Headlines like state-of-the-art malware attack exposing millions of customer accounts, series of sexual misconduct allegations against senior management or board members, or regulatory violations entailing damaging lawsuits and stock devaluations have upped the ante for boards in risk management. When directors neither know about impeding crisis nor act upon it in a timely and informed way, such ignorance and failure to act may cause both financial losses and serious dents to corporate reputation. With limited time span, it is important to know what the problem is, or could be, and not worry too much about their origins. To have insights on mission-critical areas like cybersecurity, and equivalent insights of this nature, some boards are educating directors on the latest threats and training them on practices, like secure digital communications. By keeping closer communications with management, boards are driving the information-gathering process, as regular reports on threats and security measures are tapped upon. Or boards could also be deploying technology to render such information timely and swiftly digestible. They are also allocating time for risk discussions in board agendas. In some companies, boards are forming dedicated committees for risk, empowered with the mission to dig deep into the details on the full board's behalf. Such a committee could meet up with experts about security benchmarking and evaluations, emerging threats, new technologies, and more. Some boards even go so far as to engage in scenario testing of a communication system hack, or sensitive email leaks in order to try out their own cyber risk response action plans. The board's idea is to make the enterprise better, not the directors happy. This means the need to be fair, to be candid, and to let directors understand what have been done, where the enterprise still faces risk, and why this still exists, and what could be done about it.

(4) Shaping strategy. It is necessary to understand that business vision represents only one important part of enterprise success. The other equally important dimension is about effective execution of the vision by mastering the tactical decisions, or the execution of enterprise strategy. Global business consultant has reported that some 70% of board time is spent on quarterly reports, audit review, budgets and compliance, instead of prioritizing time for matters

critical to the future direction and health of the enterprise.[461] Boards are now rectifying the flaw by encouraging directors in self-guided learning to stay abreast of macrotrends in their industries, and from unexpected sources. These could extend from industry reports, to competitors earnings call, to events within and external to an enterprise's core business. Technology has also been helping directors to get the info they require, when they need them, such as offered by several types of reliable info dashboards in the marketplace. It is envisaged that a decade or so from now, the world could see boards having real-time data and know-how to read and interpret this. This would imply the potential need for a robust cloud strategy, IT architecture that maps to business demands, and the right talents, from both employees and freelancers.[462]

(5) Operating responsibly and sustainably. For most listed companies these days, good corporate citizenship is *sine qua non* with business imperative. Investment houses like Blackrock, JP Morgan and Vanguard have initiated factoring ESG metrics into investment decisions, designing ESG-focused indices and funds, and stressing the vitalness of ESG in communications to corporate leaders. The benefits of ESG are real, and their neglect could spell bad financial and other consequences. Over the last decade, signatories to the UN Principles for Responsible Investment (PRI) who integrate ESG into their analysis of investment decisions have reported assets increasing from USD 6 trillion to USD 60 trillion. Many companies are now deploying resources like State Street's ESG investing solutions tools, and online Knowledge Hub by the TCFD to evaluate their carbon footprint, including effectiveness in areas like diversity and responsible labor practices. Board members are also being roped in to serve as information-gatherers and ambassadors. ESG standards and metrics continue to evolve, making it strategically sensible to think bigger than itself in manners that also address stakeholders and profitability concerns. Relevant ESG matters for reflections include assessing whether a board's ESG commitment is structural or cultural, what are investors' most pressing ESG concerns, how the board have been responding, and how a company is making positive impacts in the community.

(6) Raising and enforcing personal accountability. These refer to having good corporate behavior and doing the right thing in the face of risks from increased scrutiny and consequences for management's role in data breaches, discrimination, sexual harassments and other disturbing issues. Enhanced levels of board accountability together with stakeholder monitoring made directors more proactive in monitoring the business ecosystem, as well as interacting with key stakeholders more often. Corporate management boards are also deploying dashboard, scorecards, and key performance indicators

461. McKinsey & Company. 2016. "Board perspective: A collection of McKinsey insights focusing on boards of directors". *McKinsey & Company August 2016.* https://www.mckinsey.com/~/media/mckinsey/featured%20insights/leadership/, accessed November 10, 2020.
462. McKinsey & Company 2016, *supra* note [461].

(KPIs) to track progress and effectiveness, with the acknowledgement that metrics and models would transform in line with the evolving business environment. Meaningful actions include the suggestion for more accountability, more information flowing to directors in more timely and transparent manner, and the spotlighting of trust, high-quality relationships and candor, and with dissent, and less group think.

(7) Emerging board profiles. Board behavioral experts, like Diligence, have identified four board behavioral profiles, namely, foundational, structural, catalyst, and futuristic. Boards with foundational profiles often seen in start-ups when keeping in pace with changes in the business and technology environment tend to change their profiles over time, depending on circumstances, like when catalysts traits emerged for a board, subsequent to a crisis, or during a transformation. A catalyst board is more likely to have a separate chairperson and CEO, rather than having one individual serving both roles. It also tends to focus on collaboration, ushering in a wider diversity of perspectives, and with directors making their own insights and opinions to management, instead of merely following the strategic direction set by management. A structural board, on the other hand, spends a great deal of their time examining compliance reports and general data protection regulation (GDPR), or the equivalent data rules in play. A futuristic board leans substantially on AI in shaping the future of corporate direction.[463] No profile should be inherently good or bad, as particular profiles could be more common during certain times in a board's evolution to offer certain strengths and benefits.

Guided by insights from research and interactions with directors in industries around the world, a board thinking of achieving better outcomes in sustainable value creation could start by keeping pace with macro trends, narrowing focus to what counts, asking provocative questions, measuring progress, and leading by example. Particular areas, like risk management, corporate citizenship, and the ability to inform strategy with well-timed insights, would always link up to value creation, no matter the geographical space, the industry focus, or corporate size and reach. In turn, the key takeaways for value creation would include the following:[464]

(1) The key to value creation and resilience is board diversity. The tapping of new perspectives leads to richer, deeper conversations and sharper decision-making.
(2) Expanding board insights outside of the boardroom, by making visits to other businesses, working with experts and encouraging colleagues to ask searching questions.

463. M. Hilb. 2020. "Towards artificial governance? The role of artificial intelligence in shaping the future of corporate governance". *Journal of Management and Governance*, Vol. 24 (2020): 851-870.
464. Stafford & Schindlinger 2019, *supra* note [458].

(3) Getting better acquainted and comfortable with technology, by not relegating tech to a single committee or taskforce, that leaves much of the board out of decisions that might well have broad impacts on the business.
(4) Learning how the corporation might need to react to create and maintain value by interacting with customers and employees.
(5) Reflecting on the company's board profile traits, and why and how it might need to shift for greater value creation; and
(6) Above all, building value through right practices and people.

The ongoing impact of the COVID-19 pandemic on the business ecosystem appears to drive pressure on the shareholder-centric model toward perhaps a richer model of governance that puts the health and resilience of the company at the forefront. The pandemic has made it clear that society relies on well-governed companies to cater to most of its important needs, and that companies operate primarily to maximize returns to shareholders. Boards, as such, are increasingly under pressure not only to focus solely on returns to shareholders but also to cater to a full range of factors that enable companies to create value over time. This though is unlikely to diminish boards' accountability to shareholders, but does imply changes in the nature and scope of that accountability. Indeed, the confluence of the three major factors of geopolitical tensions, environmental calamities of huge proportions, and the pandemic have combined to challenge the core premises of the agency model of governance in at least three ways that bear significant implications for boards. These new realities are identified as follows:[465]

(1) More structured attention to stakeholders. The disruptive forces as highlighted have demonstrated the limitations of the shareholder primacy cornerstone of the agency model of governance, by drawing urgent attention to the importance of each and every stakeholder group to a company's ability to function. The crisis has largely validated the rationale of interdependence behind the Business Roundtable's 2019 statement on CP. Here, 181 CEOs of multinationals pledged commitments to each of the five stakeholder groups of customers, employees, suppliers, communities and shareholders, and reverse its previous endorsement of shareholder primacy. As companies evolved, there could be times when employee welfare comes first, times when customer interests come first, times when public need is more important, and times when the interests of shareholders should be of prime concern. As demonstrated in the present crisis, much depends on the nature of interests at stake, and the circumstances of the company. This tells why it would be important for directors to have a shared understanding of the company's purpose and strategy, including a framework designating the company's stakeholders and responsibilities to each. While many companies claimed

465. L.S. Paine. 2020. "COVID-19 is rewriting the rules of corporate governance". *Harvard Business Review 6 October 2020.* https://hbr.org/2020/10/covid-19-is-rewriting-the-rules-of, accessed November 10, 2020.

commitments to all their primary stakeholders, few though have a structured process for overseeing those commitments, or for monitoring the company's performance for the non-shareholder stakeholders. Even when they do, these matters might not be regularly discussed in boardrooms, similar in the way that performance for shareholders is regularly discussed or reviewed. Stakeholder concerns could come into strategy or M&A decisions, but these tend to be somewhat ad hoc, or by exception, instead of being a routine part of the analyses that boards received. In the face of current and ongoing socioeconomic pressures, boards are likely to encounter increasing calls to incorporate stakeholder perspectives, especially those of employee into their oversight and decision processes.

(2) More attention to how business and society intersect. For close to a decade, calls have been made growingly for businesses to help resolve systemic concerns, like increasing income and wealth inequality, environmental degradation, climate change, racial and ethnic discrimination, declining health and education, rising corruption, deteriorating public institutions, and increasing risks of pandemics. Many companies have found ingenuous ways to resolve many of these problems; others have looked the other way, or treat these as matters outside the legitimate boundaries of businesses, as boards and management are fiduciaries of shareholders. The pandemic supports the contention that these are legitimate areas of business concerns, and in fact are sources of both opportunities and risks that forward-looking boards would have to deal with. Similar to market forces, these societal forces could profoundly impact the business and its landscape. Boards are growing increasingly accustomed to the recognition that the company's risk management and oversight systems need to incorporate risks arising from this massive scale of societal problems. This further implies the need to ensuring that the company's strategic planning and resource allocation processes take these problems into considerations to further ensure that at the very least they do not aggravate the magnitude of their harms, but better still, ameliorate them. Following the disruptive impacts of the pandemic on lives and livelihoods, boards are likely to face enhanced expectations from institutional investors, governments, and the general public for greater attention to societal problems, and to take a more active posture in dealing with them. Boards would more and more be expected to oversee the business and society interface. Rather than being the exception, robust oversight over sustainability, corporate responsibility, corporate citizenship, all integrated under the ESG label, would become the rule.

(3) More attention to BC. The earlier Milton Friedman model on agency treats directors' identities and personal traits as mainly irrelevant for their roles. While female representation in corporate boards has increased from 9% in 2009 to some 19% in 2019 in the US (and close to 30% in the UK), racial and ethnic disparities persist, despite changing ethnic compositions. Increasing digitization in businesses together with the complexity of the pandemic impact has drawn attention to the need for boards to comprise individuals

with diverse perspectives and skillsets as being crucial for boards performing their jobs more effectively. Boards of diverse ethnic, social, and work experiences and skillsets backgrounds are now viewed as likely to be able to monitor and manage better the company's relationships with its key stakeholders, in formulating strategy, in overseeing risk, in reviewing societal engagements, in evaluating pay practices, in overseeing management's diversity and inclusion initiatives.

In view of the envisaged developments in the business landscape, the immediate years ahead, and drawing on discussions with corporate leaders across the world, it has been argued since 2011[466] that companies need to stop seeing themselves as bystanders, and instead design innovative business strategies that address the disruptors, produce sustainable growth, and help strengthen institutions at the community, national, and international levels. The problems of social inequality, global trade strife, and environmental degradation as such were brought up more than a decade ago. These issues though still persist. Renewed calls are now made for businesses to help rebuild public confidence in the market system distressed by the kind of problems seen in the wake of the COVID-19 pandemic, and having the ability to function in a way that generates inclusive and sustainable prosperity.[467]

The emergence of the digital economy and increasing digitalization of businesses have thus spawned the so-called new era in governance practices. This has also promoted responses from the legal community. Drawing from relevant insights distilled from businesses, one such initiative has come out with the following ideas and arguments:[468]

(1) Politics and market forces are argued to be as important as corporate law in shaping how governance has evolved. This aside, some legal developments could be treated as evolutionary in nature, like the common law tradition, and others seen as revolutionary, like SOX and the *Smith v. van Gorkom*[469] case. An important market development came in the early to mid-1990s, when institutional ownerships of public equities surpassed those of home ownership, and accompanied by the rise of proxy advisory services. Given this contextual development, it has been argued that corporations are to be governed for the benefit of shareholders, but that the directors and officers

466. J.L. Bower, H.B. Leonard & L.S. Pine. 2011. *Capitalism at risk: Rethinking the role of business*. Boston: Harvard Business Press.
467. J.L. Bower, H.M. Leonard & L.S. Pine. 2021. *Capitalism at risk, Updated and Expanded: How business can lead*. Boston: Harvard Business Press.
468. T.A. Cole. 2020. "CEO leadership and the board". *The Corporate Board March/April 2020*; T.A. Cole. 2019. *CEO leadership: Navigating the new era in corporate governance*. Chicago: University of Chicago Press.
469. *Smith v. Van Gorkom-488 A.2d 858 (Del. 1985)*. Here the court held that the business judgment rule (BJR) is a presumption that in making a business decision, the directors of a corporation acted on an informed basis, in good faith and in the honest belief that the action taken was in the best interest of the company. This means that the party challenging a board decision as unformed must rebut the presumptions that its business judgment was an unformed one.

have wide latitude to take actions that are beneficial to non-shareholder stakeholders, as long as there is some reasonable nexus to long-term shareholder value. Also, duties are owed to all of a corporation's constituencies, but that duties to non-shareholder stakeholders are derived from very specific laws, regulations and contractual provisions, while generalized fiduciary duties are appropriately owed only to shareholders.

(2) Governance is defined mainly in terms of decision-making authority. However, when management-centric evolved into board-centric decision-making in the 1980s over the bigger issues of strategy, succession, compensation, risk oversight and material transactions, risk could arise when some boards inappropriately cross the line into deliberations best delegated to management teams. However, where the line should be demarcated would vary from company to company, and is a function of various factors. Thus, when seeking to assemble and operate an effective board, it is important to be mindful of standards of conduct, standards of judicial review, director accountability and the suite of protections against director financial exposures.

(3) With regards to activism and the threat of shareholder-centricity, it is useful to recognize different kinds of activists that partake in governance, CSR and finance, as well as their tools. An important observation is the synergistic relationship between governance and financial activists. Various arguments are raised against providing shareholders with authority over decision-making beyond that provided by statute. In most situations, shareholders have no fiduciary duties to their fellow shareholders and could act in their own unrestrained self-interest. They could force decisions, but not to stay around to face the consequences. They are also not necessarily fully informed, or are experts in issues they are advocating.

(4) There are critical differences between leadership and management. There are risks that boards crossing the line, together with pressures from financial activists, could impede the ability of CEOs to lead and to focus on the long-term. To address this challenge, CEOs and boards are urged to have a common understanding of the purpose of governance, the requirements and appropriate limits of board-centricity, and how to be better prepared for shareholder activism. In this respect, it is helpful for CEOs to develop an effective partnership with their nonexecutive chairs or lead independent directors. General observations of CEOs routines suggest that they spend considerable amount of their time dealing with governance issues, and that they do not always find that to be time well spent in the context of advancing the business of the enterprise.

The business ecosystem, as highlighted earlier, has since the onsetting COVID-19 in early 2020 generated serious economic and health issues in all economies. These have reenergized previous earlier calls for more attention on ESG issues, but this time with law reforming implications.

5.04 THE REINVIGORATED ESG MANTRA FOR BUSINESS

A pivotal outcome of the difficult operating circumstance for business corporations has been the confluence of seismic events like enhanced levels of geopolitical tensions and their impacts on the global business landscape, the sagging performances of economies and businesses because of the COVID-19 pandemic, and a series of calamitic environmental disasters across both advanced and emerging economies. These have together collectively pressured businesses for the appropriate response, not least in their corporate behaviors. For some time now, various businesses have flirted with the ESG motto mostly on voluntary basis, and as part of good corporate strategy, but the combined impacts of these three main forces over the last one year or so have catalyzed second deeper looks from policymakers and regulators into the using of formal rules to make ESG more meaningful and effective.

This reinvigorated call for adoption of ESG as a vital component of business resilience has reached feverish pitch, suggesting clearly and unequivocally that corporate practices need to incorporate these without further hesitation, and with stronger commitments.[470] Diligent's 2021 White Paper "Modern Governance in Australia in 2021: Four Priorities for Boards, Management & Governance Professionals" argues that for boards, management, and governance professionals to truly thrive, they need to prioritize on digitization, oversight of key nonfinancial risks, board effectiveness, and putting ESG at center stage. Thus, to stay ahead of competition, Diligent advocates in its September 2021 White Paper "Winning the ESG Race" that companies should deploy a collective approach to climate change to take care of the environment, create worksites that reflect their communities to take care of the social side of enterprise, and its boards driving accountability and transparency to take care of its governance process. This is because boards play a pivotal function in linking ESG with strategy and culture to strengthen alignment and motivate better performance.

As businesses strived to put one leg in the past, and the other into the future, it is necessary to assess whether previous soft and hard laws have contributed sufficiently to enrich and ensure good corporate practices, as advocated in the ESG philosophy. Major corporate law reforms undertaken in previous years to deal with the past major financial crisis would next be examined in further details in the next chapter. This one leg into the past together with one leg into the future approach is undertaken to generate a more balanced view, as to what works in exemplary ESG practices, and what do not, as shown in those cases linked with dismal outcomes.

470. M. O'Leary & W. Valdmanis. 2021. "An ESG reckoning is coming". *Harvard Business Review 04 March 2021*. https://hbr.org/2021/03/an-esg-reckoning-is-coming, accessed March 25, 2021.

CHAPTER 6
ESG Scandals: A Review of Hard and Soft Laws Responses

The hardiness of financial and corporate crises that loomed large since the 1930s, or earlier, is becoming better known these days, but the extent of real lessons being learnt by policymakers, corporations and individuals remained, and would remain insufficiently or unsatisfactorily answered. This could be attributed to the complexity of human behaviors and traits when it comes to finance and profit-hunting. This continues to perplex the analytical capacities of researchers and well-intentioned practitioners. This chapter would look very briefly into how financial and corporate crises metamorphosed over the years, how policymakers and regulators try to respond with more and more arsenals or legal mechanisms designed or redesigned to curb these economic welfare harmful practices, how and why ESG scandals in particular appear to persist, despite new enacted laws and widely claimed sharper regulations. Importantly, how and why despite the strong presence of internal and external ESG mechanisms designed to curb reckless corporate behaviors, these have been largely found to be inadequate in meeting public expectations. Though these seminal cases highlighted mostly the "G" in ESG because of its serious failings, the social "S" element is also seen in the form of sexual harassment incidences, as well as in diversity and inequality cases in some of these, while the "E" environmental aspects are seen, the climate change impacts in the form of huge forest fires and massive floods that destroy properties, lives and livelihoods.

6.01 ESG FAILINGS AND SCANDALS

Corporate scandals or bad business management practices in many instances helped to spawn financial crises that at times became contagion and crossing borders to inflict financial pains or hardships to linked economies. Many of these financial mishaps have been stories of human greed and irrationality in abundance that led to the calls for greater regulatory scrutiny by the academic, business, and regulatory communities.[471]

The contributions from the ESG paradigm helped to add some clarity to the mysteries of manias, panics, crashes and reforms claiming the mantra of "never letting it happened again," but over the years, still consistently happening again.[472] As would be soon gleaned from subsequent pages of this chapter, irrationality and greed together time and again trumped over more sober professional calculations to invite further investigations for better answers, and each time, thus far, coming up short. This chapter would not pretend to have the capacity to produce the sought answers, and has only the limited ambition of raising more awareness of the importance of exercising self-restraint when it comes to the matter of wealth aggrandizement. Indeed, good ESG practices, if only embedded earlier in some of these errant companies, could have prevented their happenings.

6.02 US ESG SCANDALS AND REGULATORY RESPONSES

There were initially no national laws governing the flow of financial information to investors in the capital market in the US. The "never letting it happen again" mantra probably took root in a big way in the 1929 stock market crash in the US that attributed part of the blame to insufficient and badly presented financial information to investors. The Securities Act of 1933 (SA 1933) mandated financial disclosure requirements for IPOs, while the Securities Exchange Act of 1934 (SEA 1934) listed disclosure requirements for those corporations already listed, including those traded in the over-the-counter (OTC) market. These and other federal securities and financial regulations superseded concurrent state laws. The SEA was set up under SEA 1934 to administer these securities regulations.

The SEC, an independent federal agency, relied on the Federal Accounting Standards Board (FASB) to develop Generally Accepted Accounting Practices (GAAP) that provided guidance on financial reporting best practices to US corporations. The SEC, despite this, occasionally intervened when it found the private sector practices not moving in the desired direction, or moving unusually slowly. Since the 1970s, the SEC focused on disclosures, rather than measurement matters. The SEC's policy target has been the protection of individual investors, as well as the safeguarding of the securities trading system.

The SEC has been perturbed by various creative accounting practices in the capital markets that had the effects of distorting profit and loss statements, or the

471. J.C. Crisanto, J. Ehrentraud & M. Fabian. 2021. "Big techs in finance: Regulatory approaches and policy options". *Bank for International Settlements (BIS) Financial Stability Institute (FSI) Briefs No. 12 March 2021*. https://www.bis.org/fsi/fsibriefs12.pdf, accessed March 25, 2021; J. Cohen, et al. 2010. "Corporate fraud and managers' behavior: Evidence from the press". *Journal of Business Ethics*, Vol. 95 (2010): 271-315.
472. N.R. Augustine. 1995. "Managing the crisis you tried to prevent". *Harvard Business Review November-December 1995*, https://hbr.org/1995/11/managing-the-crisis-you-tried-to-prevent, accessed November 10, 2020.

understating of debts.[473] It had responded with a four-point plan to address these matters. These involved improving the accounting framework; enhancing the statutory audit for listed corporations; strengthening the audit committee process; and pursuing work culture changes within the professional, financial, business, and regulatory authorities. The SEC's stringent views of these various problems are reflected in its various enforcement actions.[474] To help improve the quality of external audit, the Public Oversight Board Panel on Audit Effectiveness issued numerous guidelines.[475] While the Treadway Committee recommended a much stronger and independent audit committee, the Blue-Ribbon Committee made other recommendations on their nature and functions.[476] SEC's message to the corporate and financial communities appeared initially to induce some positive effects. These though appeared inadequate to altogether eliminate creative accounting practices, as perpetrators were motivated by stronger countervailing forces and pressures. Enron and other subsequent related financial scandals that unfolded from 2000 onward give credence to this view, and more, as these led to the enactment of the 2002 Sarbanes-Oxley Act (SOX).

The SOX sought to improve the reliability of public corporation's financial reporting, as well as restoring investor confidence in the wake of more high-profile cases of corporate crime, that unfolded unceasingly then. Its main thrust is to make corporate financial reporting irregularities punishable for those directly and indirectly involved in the activity. The then President called the legislation the most far-reaching reforms of US business practices since the time of Franklin Roosevelt. SOX was then enacted to never let bad financial practices of the kind observed to ever happen again.

The SOX established sweeping auditing and financial regulations for listed corporations. The legislation was enacted to help protect shareholders, employees and the public from accounting irregularities or fraudulent financial reporting practices. Senior corporate officers, accountants and auditors became accountable to the new set of rules. These new legal provisions were amendments and additions to several laws enforced by the SEC, including the SEA of 1934 and the Investment Advisors Act of 1940. The SEC was empowered to enforce SOX. The legislation focused on increasing criminal punishment, accounting regulation, new protections, and corporate responsibility. Though SOX focused on listed corporations, some provisions were applicable to private enterprise and nonprofit entities. SOX also established penalties for noncom pliance with its various provisions. Compliance with the legislation pertained to financial disclosures and governance.

SOX is arranged into eleven sections, or titles, but two sections, namely section 302 and section 404 deserved particular attention.[477] Section 302 refers to corporate

473. A. Levitt. "The numbers game". *Speech in New York City University Center for Law and Business 28/09/98*, https://www.sec.gov/news/speeches/spch220.txt, accessed November 10, 2020.
474. SEC Enforcement Cases 01/09/999, https://www.sec.gov, accessed November 10, 2020.
475. Public Oversight Board (POB). 2000. "Audit Effectiveness Releases Exposure Draft". POB 06/06/20.
476. M. Young. 2002. *Accounting irregularities and financial fraud: A CG.* Oxford: Harcourt.
477. B. Lutkevich. 2021. "Sarbanes-Oxley Act". https://searchcio.techtarget.com/definition/Sarbanes-Oxley-Act#:~:text=The%20Sarbanes%2DOxley%20, accessed March 25, 2021.

responsibility for financial reports. This requires chief executive officers (CEOs) and chief financial officers (CFOs) to review all financial reports and that the reports are "fairly presented" and do not contain misrepresentations. The CEO and CFOs will be responsible too for corporate internal accounting controls. Section 404 deals with management assessment of internal controls. This requires corporations to publish details about their internal accounting controls and their procedures for financial reporting as part of their annual financial returns. The section further requires corporate executives to personally certify the accuracy of their corporate financial statements making them also individually liable where the SEC finds violations. The Whistleblower Protection Act under SOX provides protection for whistleblowers, whereby employees and contractors reporting fraud and/or testifying about fraud to the Department of Labor will be protected against retaliation, including dismissal and discrimination.[478]

Other key provisions include mandated disclosures in periodic reports of transactions that are off-balance sheet, but impacting financial health; near-ubiquitous prohibitions of personal loans from a corporation to executives; establishment of fines and terms of imprisonment for tampering or destroying documents in investigations events or court actions; and requirements for legal advisors representing corporations before the SEC to report security violations to CEOs.[479] New legal requirements are also provided for corporate auditing practices, such as requiring public corporations to appoint independent auditors to review their accounting practices and defining their rules of engagement for corporate audit committees and external auditors.[480] There are also rules for separation of duties whereby a number of non-audit duties are prohibited and where corporate auditors could not engage in during audits, so as to guard against fraudulent practices and conflicts of interest.[481] SOX has also led to the creation of the Public Company Accounting Oversight Board (PCAOB) that sets standards and rules for audit reports. Under PCAOB, all accounting firms that audit public corporations are required to register with it.[482] The PCAOB investigates and enforces compliance of registered accounting firms.

Following SOX, the then New York State Attorney carried out a series of high-profile cases against CEOs, outside directors, auditors and financial advisors.[483] The bulk of the cases were settled out-of-court with heavy fines, but a few individual perpetrators were sent to jail for the willful distortion and manipulation of financial reporting. These aside, settlements have also been reached between the ten largest investment banks in the US and the SEC and the New York Attorney General. This 2002 Global Legal Settlement Scheme involves a fine of USD 1.4 billion on the accused

478. P. Yeoh. 2014. "Whistleblowing: Motivations, corporate self-regulation, and the law". *International Journal of Law and Management*, Vol. 56 (6): 459-474.
479. Lutkevich 2021, *supra* note [477].
480. Lutkevich 2021, *supra* note [477].
481. Lutkevich 2021, *supra* note [477].
482. Lutkevich 2021, *supra* note [477].
483. J.O'Brien. 2005. "Redesigning financial regulation: Eliot Spitzer, State-Federal relations and the battle for corporate control". In J. O'Brine (ed.). *Governing the corporation: Regulation and CG in an age of scandal and global markets.* West Sussex: Wiley.

financial institutions, with further undertakings by them to improve the quality of financial information. The latter requires these financial institutions to make their analysts' recommendations public, and to contract with at least three independent research firms to provide research to their brokerage customers over a five-year period.[484]

The above enforcement actions are clearly a direct response to problems posed by conflicts of interest in corporate affairs. Some of these settlements apply deferred prosecution agreements (DPAs), whereby the enforcement agencies would suspend prosecutions in exchange for specific undertakings by defendants. This is exemplified by the fine imposed on KPMG for its alleged role in the designing of sham tax shelters for their customers. Apart from payment of a hefty fine, KPMG had to undertake to be on good professional behavior for one year, and be further subjected to a mandatory review of its professional conduct by an independent consulting firm.[485] This generated a climate of financial reporting compliance fear in the capital market, even though it has the good intention of promoting greater professionalism and ethical behaviors. This nevertheless is rudely disrupted by the management share options backdating scandals that unfolded in late 2006, despite the provisions for such disclosures in SOX.[486] Unfortunately, this incident did not effectively alert enforcement authorities to other errant corporate misconducts that have been brewing then, and which came to a head in 2007 that contributed to the spawning of the 2007-2008 GFC.[487]

There have been abundant writings and research on the causes for GFC from various competing perspectives. Subprime mortgages catalyzed the GFC, but the crisis appears to be the combined outcome of adverse macroeconomic conditions, loose regulatory oversights, and bad governance practices. Nevertheless, errant and reckless corporate conducts are the common theme running through these different perspectives.[488]Thus, it had been contended that flawed governance practices in both the public and private sectors were largely responsible for the financial catastrophe; and that the tendencies to blame it all on US corporations have been overplayed, as bad governance practices have always been a global phenomenon.[489] It has been further argued that little would be achieved where bad corporate behaviors not effectively addressed are allowed to persist in a business as usual manner, upon the economy recovering. The aim should not focus on rhetoric to calm public angst, but instead lay the foundation for a more serious and robust system of governance practices with foci on the vital elements of transparency, accountability and prompt remedial disciplinary actions. Those culpable of unlawful actions must be sanctioned fast, while those

484. F.S. Mishkin. 2006. *The economics of money, banking and financial markets*. Boston: Pearson.
485. J.K. Robinson & P.E. Urofsky. 2005. "Deferred prosecutions and independent monitor". *International Journal of Disclosure and Governance*, Vol. 2 (4): 325-347; US Department of Justice (DOJ). 2005. "Re: KPMG-Deferred Prosecution Agreement".
486. T. Bawden. 2006. "American economy under threat from notes on a scandal". *The Times 09/12/06: 66*. The article stressed the seriousness of the problem where some 160 corporations came under SEC investigations, with more being expected.
487. H. Davies. 2010. *The financial crisis: Who is to blame*. Cambridge: Polity Press.
488. P. Yeoh. 2010. "Causes of the global financial crisis". *International Journal of Disclosure and Governance*, Vol. 7 (1): 42-69.
489. Yeoh 2010, *supra* note [488].

negligent too must answer for their actions or inactions, and only then will governance practices be accorded the respect they deserved.[490]

The huge catastrophe in the US led to a massive legislative response in the shape of the 2010 DFA. This legislation is also enacted so as not to let such financial crisis of contagion scale to ever happen again. This rhetoric has also been used at the time of launching of SOX 2002, SA 1933, and SEA 1934. The DFA incorporated investor protection measures, executive compensation, CRA regulation, securitization retention requirements, regulatory enforcements and remedies, private fund adviser regulation, OTC derivative regulation, and systemic risk mitigation regulation to ensure financial stability.[491] These legislative and regulatory initiatives were embarked upon in response to deficiencies in SOX, and risk problems that unfolded in the run-up to the 2007-2008 GFC.

The DFA along with other regulatory mechanisms a decade after their implementation contributed to rebuilding the banking sector's strength and resilience via more demanding capital and liquidity buffer requirements, including rigorous stress tests of the largest banks.[492] However, disruptions surfaced in the financial markets in March 2020, as the COVID-19 pandemic spread. This threatened to render an already sharp contraction in economic activity even worse. This also demonstrates that the work of protecting financial stability, and that of ensuring the flow of much-needed credit and other critical services in good and bad times, has been far from complete.[493] Particularly, much work remains for nonbank finance, especially the channeling of credit through markets. Further, it has become increasingly evident that interest rate could be at historically low levels for at an extended period, and such low interest rates could induce risk-taking in markets, thereby contributing to the potential for instability that might adversely impact economic activity and employment. This potential for new threats underpins the inherent challenge for regulation, meaning it has to be dynamic and have an ongoing evaluation process, and not becoming mere periodic changes.[494]

As it is, the emergence of the pandemic led to panic in financial markets. This had to be restrained by massive and unprecedented interventions by central banks and governments globally, led by the US. Benefiting from some of the effects of earlier reforms, the banking sector remained resilient and able to cater to the extraordinary demands for credit created, when the interruptions of economic activity caused by the pandemic seriously diminish cash flows.[495] The nonbank sector though showed significant fragility and market dysfunction that prompted central bank and government interventions. It is now claimed that regulatory gaps and changes in market structure and behavior, as driven by new regulations, new technologies, and new

490. Yeoh 2010, *supra* note [488].
491. D.S. Huntington, et al. 2010. "Summary of Dodd-Frank Regulation legislation". *Harvard Law School Forum on CG 07/07/10*, https://corpgov.law.harvard.edu/2010/07/07/summary-of-dodd-frank, accessed November 10, 2020.
492. G. Hubbard, et al. 2021. *Task Force on Financial Stability Report June 2021*. https://www.brookings.edu/wp-content/uploads/2021/06/financial-stability_slides.pdf, accessed June 3, 2021.
493. Hubbard et al. 2021, *supra* note [492].
494. Hubbard et al. 2021, *supra* note [492].
495. Hubbard et al. 2021, *supra* note [492].

market entrants, have the combined effects of extending or prolonging risks.[496] Various suggestions accordingly are made to resolve these weaknesses, besides enhancing the ability of the existing regulatory structure to dynamically identify and address new risks to financial stability in the ever-evolving financial space. The Task Force on Financial Stability (TFFS) formed in 2019 explains that financial stability is when the financial system reliably supplies credit intermediation and other financial services needed for the real economy to continue to grow at a sustainable rate.[497] While micro prudential regulation examines the safety and soundness of individual institutions, it does not take into account risks to the overall financial system, which macroprudential regulation does. Instability could originate from excessive leverage, maturity and liquidity mismatches, interconnection among institutions and markets, correlated exposures, perverse regulatory incentives, and unintended consequences.[498]

The TFFS Report 2021 examines beyond banks into US treasury market liquidity, open-end mutual funds, housing finance, derivatives clearinghouses, insurance companies, and regulatory structure and processes:[499]

(1) COVID-19 shows again that during periods of stress, the market for the world's safest and most liquid security signals bouts of illiquidity, leading to fire sales to threaten the flow of credit to the entire economy. It is claimed that it is imprudent to depend on the Federal Reserve to intervene with huge Treasury purchases. The TFFS recommends adjusting regulatory requirements to enhance supply of market liquidity provided by banks and dealers; reducing demand for liquidity at times of stress; creating new Fed standing repo facility; and considering central clearing of Treasuries and Treasury repo.

(2) Open-end mutual funds. Money market and some bond funds provide daily redemption for investors, but much of their portfolios are longer term or securities that could only be sold with significant price concessions. During stressful times, some investors rush to be the first to withdraw funds. This could lead to large sales of Treasuries by the mutual funds, and possibly including fire sales of private assets. In turn, this could disrupt credit markets with adverse outcomes for the wider economy. To deal with these problems, recommendations are made for adopting swing pricing and/or redemption fees, and eliminating connection between liquidity buffers and rates in prime money market funds. As for other open-end funds, swing pricing should be required where sensible.

(3) Housing Finance. Major problems arise when aggregate demand spillover from overindebted households, when nonbank servicers fail causing disruption to credit supply, and when there is disruption in the mortgage securities market causing spillovers to other asset classes. Key recommendations

496. Hubbard et al. 2021, *supra* note [492].
497. Hubbard et al. 2021, *supra* note [492].
498. Hubbard et al. 2021, *supra* note [492].
499. Hubbard et al. 2021, *supra* note [492].

include imposing residual income cap for owner-occupied properties and loan to value caps on investor properties and cash-out refinancing; streamlining refinancing and forbearance during national emergencies, strengthening mortgage modification toolkit; creating central liquidity facility for government-backed mortgage securities; and making the Federal Housing Finance Agency (FHFA) the prudential regulatory entity for nonbank servicers, and requiring it to account for systemic risk in overseeing Fannie, Freddie and the Federal Home Loan Bank System (FHLB).

(4) Insurance Companies. Major problems could arise from the growth of variable annuities with minimum-return guarantees and the use of shadow reinsurance entities with fewer capital requirements that under stress could lead to fire sales and reduced appetite for corporate bonds; as well as from inadequate reporting that hides some risks. Key recommendations include strengthening the Federal Insurance Office, mandating standardized stress tests of insurers and state guaranty funds, and mandating more transparency on liabilities, and shadow insurance.

(5) Clearinghouses for derivatives (CCPs). Major problems arise when CCPs concentrate operational and credit risk. Derivative CCPs are for-profit that could create misalignment of interests with clearing members. Some actions taken by CCPs could push losses onto members that might trigger fire sales, disrupt markets, and expose end users to unanticipated losses. Such problems could spread across CCPs and across borders. Major recommendations include expanding the scope of Fed oversight of CCPs; improving through-the-cycle margining and collateral practices; strengthening stress testing standards, oversight and transparency; and aligning interests of CCPs and members.

(6) Regulatory structure and process. Major problems arise from inconsistent attention to financial stability across the members of the Financial Stability Oversight Council (FSOC); too little accountability for identifying financial stability risks in advance with follow-up actions; and insufficiently comprehensive financial data. Major recommendations include providing each agency with explicit financial stability mandate and establishing internal financial stability offices; focusing accountability by making the Secretary of Treasury the sole author of the FSOC annual report with comments from agencies, apart from revising its format to improve usefulness; creating new under-secretary of Treasury for financial stability; and turning the Office of Financial Research (OFR) into a new Comptroller for Data and Resilience.

(7) It is claimed that the regulatory design and process reforms as recommended would not insulate against all possible future risks, but they would shore up the biggest weaknesses in the current system and make new threats of the same magnitude less likely. It is further urged that even when most of the recommendations are adopted and implemented, that periodic independent reviews be undertaken of how the system is fairing, given the continued evolution of the financial system, and especially in the light of emerging risks from climate change and cyberattacks.

Apart from serious deficiencies in the core "G" element of CSG, several disturbing "S" and "E" issues emerged from the aftermath of the 2010 DFA leading into the 2020 COVID-19 pandemic year and beyond. Policymakers, regulators, businesses and social activists appeared to be reaching mainstream consensus over these two rising matters perceived to be material to the resiliency and sustainability of business corporations. Earlier, because of the general neglect of SMEs and the relatively greater attention paid to the recoveries of big manufacturing companies and banks, this turned into an inequality issue.

The Obama administration responded with the Jumpstart Our Business Startups (JOBS) Act of 2012. The legislation loosens regulation instituted by the SEC on small businesses through the lowering of costly reporting and disclosure requirements for companies with less than USD 1 billion in revenue. This comes together with the permitting of advertising of securities offerings, as well as greater access to crowdfunding, besides significantly expanding the number of companies that could offer shares via "Regulation A" without going through SEC registration. In short, the JOBS Act is designed to make it easier for start-ups to raise capital while simultaneously allowing retail investors to invest in start-ups. The JOBS Act therefore comes with the benefit of decreased regulation, easier access to smaller investors, easier matching up of small businesses seeking funds for growth with small investors looking for better returns via digital technology.

The powerful "#MeToo" and "Black Lives Matter" movements brought into prominence inequality and human rights issues, while diversity matters loomed large in tech companies and multinationals with the gross underrepresentation of women and other minorities, as well as various aspects of employee welfare that surfaced in the COVID-19 pandemic. This "S" component of ESG simultaneously coalesced with massive property and loss of lives calamities wrought by colossal scale forest fires and floods, the "E" component. The onslaught of these factors pressured businesses to be mindful of these concerns and to act with appropriate ESG remedies and solutions to regain resiliency and sustainability. The SEC's newly appointed Chairman has boldly signaled that ESG disclosure regulation would be the central focus of his time in office. The SEC has traditionally mandated disclosure of financially material information, but the new leadership at its helm seems to be pushing for mandatory reporting of ESG-linked information regardless of its financial materiality. Given the pushbacks from other SEC board members and the need for the SEC remain as a nonpartisan regulator, market participants, and in particular, the investing community and consumers await anxiously the future direction of mandatory ESG disclosures in the US.

6.03 UK ESG SCANDALS AND REGULATORY RESPONSES

There are several memorable cases demonstrating the fatal "G" or governance failures that in turn prompted regulatory responses. This started with the corporate adventures and later misadventures of Robert Maxwell in the publishing businesses in the late 1960s and the decade that followed. Maxwell was the then bitter rival of Rupert Murdock, the current owner of the global media giant News Corporation. Maxwell misappropriated funds from companies under his control, and was kept unchecked through the dominance of the boards of companies under his leadership.[500] Not only did internal governance flopped in terms of financial reporting irregularities but also external governance mechanisms, and in particular the lapses and failures of statutory auditors as perpetuated by the then Big Five auditing firms. The financial scandals perpetuated by the Maxwell Group and others prompted the CC to recommend and help launch the CG Code of Best Practice[501] for corporations in the UK. The initiation of the Code did not close the lid of further corporate failings. Those then were not borne of market demand collapse beyond management control, such as the current COVID-19 pandemic, but arising from bad corporate conduct, as exhibited by the likes of Polly Peck[502] and BCCI.[503]

When the Dot.Com corporate bubble broke out in the US in 2000, US policymakers responded with SOX. The UK instead took the position that its Code of Best Practice together with its perceived relatively more effective principles-based regulations as monitored and enforced through a unitary structure led by the Financial Services Authority (FSA) could inoculate it from governance problems of the kind witnessed in the US then. Thus, instead of doing a British version of the SOX, the UK approached the matter through a process of consultation with the private sector. This led to a series of targeted measures, not many needing the force of statutes in order to achieve a higher quality of financial reporting and independent audit reviews.

Where the Companies Audit, Investigations and Community Enterprise Act 2004 (CAICEA) is concerned, it expanded beyond its original focus on auditing. Part 1 of the CAICEA places additional responsibilities on existing approved professional bodies to ensure that auditing of public companies is independently undertaken. The FRC is empowered to set audit standards and enforce and oversee approved accountancy bodies. Funding for the FRC is provided by contributions from members of the LSE, the professional community, and the government. Section 18 of the CAICEA provides that those institutions assigned tasks by the FRC would be insulated from particular liabilities, suggesting that liability only existed for misfeasance and acts incompatible with public rights.[504]

Section 3 of the CAICEA in effect enables the Secretary of State to set up a professional Oversight Board of accountability to regulate auditors. Section 4 empowers the Secretary of State to delegate further functions to this new body. In pursuance of the matter of auditor independence, section 7 requires the mandatory disclosure of other services extended by auditors. Under section 8, auditors are now empowered to draw upon a wider group of personnel than before to provide them with information and explanation that they need. It is also now a criminal offense to knowingly provide or recklessly provide auditors with misleading, inaccurate, or deceptive information. Directors' Reports are now required to state that directors are unaware of material

500. T. Bower. 1996. *Maxwell: the final verdict*. London: HarperCollins.
501. Cadbury Report. 1992. Report of the Committee on the financial aspects of CG. London: Gee.
502. D. Barchard. 1992. Asil Nadir: *The rise and fall of Polly Peck*. London: Victor Gollancz.
503. J.R. Adams & D. Frantz. 1993. *A full services bank: How BCCI stole billions around the world*. London: Simon Schuster.
504. E. Smerdon. 2004. *A practice guide to CG*. London: Thomson.

information not disclosed to statutory auditors. Directors would also be liable to imprisonment or fine, or both, where they fail to take reasonable actions to prevent the release of public information, deemed to be false, or of a reckless nature. The ought-to-know test would now be applicable to this. Section 214 of the Insolvency Act (IA) of 1986 has already codified this, while this is also adhered to by common law decisions.

Pertaining to defective accounts, the Financial Reporting Review Panel (FRRP) has been empowered to apply for court approval to amend unreliable accounts, seek information from the Inland Revenue, and insist on the disclosure of information relevant to its tasks. Those failing to accede to FRRP's request would be deemed to have acted in bad faith, or in contempt of court. The Secretary of State has also been empowered to select an institution to issue new standards for a new form of formal operating report, referred to then as the Operating and Financial Review (OFR). The OFR as introduced earlier was subsequently withdrawn in the face of strong protests from the business community who preferred the less stringent "Business Review" requirement.[505] The powers of the Department of Trade and Industry (DTI) investigators and Inspectors are considerably enhanced under the CAICEA to improve their capacity to access information. Whistleblowers are provided with immunity protection so as to assist the push for quality financial information.

The above and other developments paved the way for the enactment of the CA 2006, despite considerable delays in Parliament over various contentious matters. The legislation seeks to provide a comprehensive code of company law to replace almost all the provisions in CA 1985, CA 1989, and CA 2004. The section on FSA Transparency Rules and the new statutory basis of damages for false and misleading statements in financial reports have been brought into force on January 20, 2007, but whether this provision could have been harnessed for enforcement actions have been questioned in subsequent later cases, where several of these have been alleged to be located in several annual corporate reports that gatekeepers failed to give the attention that they deserved.[506] The empowerment of the Takeover Panel became operative on April 6, 2006. This helps to maintain the 1968 City Code that prohibits defensive measures once a takeover has become imminent. This though is still viewed in some quarters as a self-regulatory instrument that continues to reflect the identity and interests of its drafters.[507]

In its entirety, the CA 2006 implies more codified obligations for directors and enhanced powers for regulators and auditors and other gatekeepers to ensure better compliance to financial reporting obligations. Importantly, the CA ushers in the Enlightened Shareholder Value Model (ESVM) of governance that appears to differ from the hitherto conventional Shareholder Primacy and Stakeholders models that have been discussed earlier. Critics of the ESVM have though consistently argued that

505. P. Yeoh. 2010. "Narrative reporting: The UK experience". *International Journal of Law and Management*, Vol. 52 (3): 211-231.
506. G. Kirkpatrick. 2009. *The CG lessons from the financial crisis*. Paris: OECD.
507. A. Johnston. 2007. "Takeover regulation: Historical and theoretical perspective on the City Code". *The Cambridge Law Journal*, Vol. 66 (2): 422-460.

section 172 of CA 2006 makes it difficult for the courts to enforce the section pragmatically. It had been further contended that despite the laudable statutory reconceptualization, section 172 only injected little improvement on the conventional common law shareholder primacy, and with enforcement constraints, as its greatest shortcoming.[508]

Other than the above, the Fraud Act 2006 has been widened. The legislation has also integrated the offense of fraud now to include fraud by false representation, fraud by failing to disclose, and fraud by abuse of position. There would probably be significant implications flowing from the questionable use of off-balance sheet instruments in some corporate financial activities. As these said provisions have transformed such misdemeanors into dishonesty-based offenses, various complex civil law matters could arise in the future. UK companies have also been impacted in varying degrees by directives flowing through from the EU. Examples of these include the European Community 4th Directive that standardized key features of the form and contents of financial reporting; the Transparency Directive that insists on more explicit disclosures of major financial terms; and the 2002 IFRS requiring its compliance by 2005. The CA 2006 has empowered the FSA to implement any EU directive on governance applicable to listed corporations. The legislation refers to CG as the manner wherein directors conduct themselves, as well as the relationship between shareholders and boards of directors.

Aside from these developments with regard to hard laws, ESG practices in the UK before the onset of the 2007 GFC have been guided by the governance code as monitored and supervised by the private sector-led FRC. In its 2007 review, the FRC found that the Code continued to have a broadly beneficial impact, and is seen as having contributed to higher overall standards of governance among listed corporations and professional entities. The FRC, as such, focused its efforts on improving the practical application of the Code, as it considers this to be of greater benefit, than a major overhaul of the Code's content that already enjoys broad support. In view of these findings, the FRC consulted on removing provision A.4.3 on individuals chairing more than one FTSE 100 company, and amending provision C.3.1 for listed companies outside the FTSE 350 to allow the company chairman to be a member of, but not chair the audit committee provided he/she is viewed as independent on appointment.[509]

508. C.C. Ajibo. 2014 "A critique of enlightened shareholder value: Revisiting the shareholder primacy theory." *Birkbeck Law Review*, Vol. 2 (1): 1-58; "A director of a company must act in the way he considers, in good faith, would be more likely to promote the success of the company for the benefit of its members as a whole, and in doing so to have regard (amongst other matters to (a) the likely consequences of any decision in the long term, (b) the interests of the company's employees, (c) the need to foster the company's business relationships with suppliers, customers and others, (d) the impact of the company's operations on the community and the environment, (e) the desirability of the company maintaining a reputation of high standards of business conduct, and (f) the need to act fairly as between members of the company." *Section 172 (a)-(f) CA 2006.*

509. FRC. 2007. "2007 review of the Combined Code: Consultation on proposed changes to the Code". *FRC December 2007*, https://www.frc.org.uk/getattachment/012a7f92-86f1-4ffd-935d, accessed November 10, 2020.

These have been taken into account in the revised Combined Code on CG on June 27, 2008.[510]

The law reforms and the updates of the self-regulatory Combined Code on CG are expected to curb corporate misconducts in financial services and nonfinancial services businesses. The run and subsequent collapse of Northern Rock once again reminds policymakers and regulators of the unsustainability of the never letting sizeable corporate scandals to recur rhetoric, in both the US and the UK. As the bigger and more contagious impacts have been on financial services, it is unsurprising to observe the acceleration of governance reforms for financial services in the UK.[511] Many of these reforms have also been recommended for inclusions in the Combined Code, and for which the FRC subsequently sought consultation.

Insights from the fumbles and panics of US financial regulatory authorities when facing the sudden big impacts of the 2007 GFC stimulated the UK into quickly enacting the Banking Act 2009 (BA 2009) to strengthen its statutory framework for financial stability and depositor protection. BA 2009 provides for a special resolution regime (SRR). This empowers the BOE, the Prudential Regulation Authority (PRA), the FCA, and the Treasury with the use of various instruments to protect financial stability in banks, building societies, investment firms, banking group companies and central counterparties that are failing while also protecting depositors, client assets, taxpayers, and the broader economy.[512] The SRR includes three Stabilization Options, through which the assets and liabilities of a bank, and its share capital and other securities that it has issued, might be transferred, in whole or in part, to other commercial organizations or regulatory organizations. It also provides for two new insolvency procedures for banks.[513] The legislation confers fairly radical powers to the UK authorities. Deployment of the legislation draws attention to the value of some guidance being developed to help a bank or building society that is confronted with a scenario on how best to work out its positions with the regulator, and eventually with the BOE and the Treasury.

The UK early intervention approach drawing on the powers of the FSA to intervene in a failing bank and BOE's stabilization powers have been compared with discretionary Canadian and the rules-based US system.[514] It has been contended that the parameters surrounding the challenges of early intervention require identification so as to enable the regulator and the regulated to appreciate what to do and what to envisage, where situations arise.[515] This implies that while the actions might not be different to the actions taken where a bank is shut, this decision when taken is before that fatal moment has been reached, and strengthened by the confidence the regulator

510. PwC. 2008. "Best practice: CG reporting". *PwC December 2008.* https://www.pwc.com/gx/en/corporate-reporting/archive/publications/assets/, accessed November 10, 2020.
511. T. Sarkar, S. Jay & G. Manley. 2010. "An analysis of the Walker Review of CG in U.K. banks and other financial institutions". *The Banking Law Journal,* Vol. 127 (3), 242-250.
512. A. McKnight. 2015. "The Banking Act 2009". *Law and Financial Markets Review,* Vol. 3 (4): 325-332.
513. McKnight 2015, *supra* note [512].
514. D. Singh. 2010. "The UK Banking Act 2009, pre-insolvency and early intervention: Policy and practice". *University of Warwick Legal Studies Research Paper No. 2010-27.*
515. Singh 2010, *supra* note [514].

has that the bank could turn around its affairs. For such decisions, the time period would be relative, but the situations surrounding the decisions and outcomes could be structured. Early intervention practice would need to focus considerably on market conditions to guide and foretell the kinds of institutions that might face problems. It should avoid stressing simply on capital levels, but wider matters, including, for instance, around mismanagement that could be probable contribution to poor capital or liquidity levels. More analysis could be made to ascertain whether the institutions have been managing their risks ineffectively. Where such matters seemed endemic, then it would be fair to deduce that further attention be provided to the bank. It would further imply that the regulator would require enhanced information of the strategy that the bank has employed and the implications of this to its financial sustainability.

Insights on what transpired in Northern Rock and RBS[516] suggest that, in general, regulators have provided little attention to these matters, which would have forewarned in many instances, including the relatively high risk-taking appetites of these respective banks. As such, some type of impact evaluation of key decisions would be a useful starting point for ascertaining the implications of decisions turning bad. It would appear that the timing of decisions to prevent a failing bank from collapsing for lack of intervention would be deemed effective where the supervision preceding it has acted sufficiently. As a bank could fail because of bad governance practices despite regulators' actions, it would be useful and necessary for authorities to have a transparent set of guidelines, whether in the shape of the discretion or rules-based approaches.[517] The timing issue is highly pertinent when employing an early intervention model, irrespective of the approach taken, as its effectiveness would depend on its use and timing, but not necessarily the shape it would assume.

As more UK banks became seriously impacted by the 2007-2008 GFC, further reforms were made in the banking sector, including the Financial Services (Banking Reform) Act 2013 (BRA 2013). The BRA 2013 provides the outline for the implementation of various recommendations of the Independent Commission on Banking (ICB). This was a committee set up by the government in June 2010 to make recommendations for reforming UK banking services. The recommendations include a plan to ensure that in the future, catastrophic losses in the investment banking of large banking entities would not harm the viability of its high street banking operations. The answer to the problem involves ring-fencing retail bank services from wholesale and investment banking services. However, the initiative to make banking safer for the retail clientele and the taxpayer would involve banks bearing the additional costs, raising the suggestion that a regulatory regime premised on the notion of whistleblowers and economic incentives as found in the 2010 DFA would be a more viable alternative.[518] Research also highlighted further alternatives. These extend from

516. F. Mor. 2018. "Bank rescues of 2007-09: Outcomes and cost". *House of Commons Research Briefing 08/10/18.* https://commonslibrary.parliament.uk/research-briefings/sn05748/#: ~ :text = From%20September%202007%20to%20December, accessed November 10, 2020.
517. Singh 2010, *supra* note [514].
518. M.S. Korotana. 2016. "The Financial Services (Banking Reform) Act 2013: Smart regulatory regime". *Statute Law Review,* Vol. 37 (2016): 195-211.

diversification, performance and risk management, and banking stability and efficiency to the more popular idea of higher capital adequacy requirements[519]that regulators in the US and Europe appear to prefer.

For the UK, its financial services regulatory environment has metamorphosed dramatically over the past two decades, starting with the restructuring of the banking and financial services sector where the FSA becomes no longer the one-stop regulator. The new twin-peak approach has the BOE taking more control over the country's financial stability, and with the FCA and the Prudential Regulatory Authority (PRA) sharing regulatory and supervisory powers over other activities. This tripartite arrangement includes participation from the Treasury. Enhanced attention is extended to banking regulation, especially subsequent to the financial crisis where it was found that where the wholesale banking system was in trouble, taxpayers and the entire economy faced huge financial burdens. As it was, the aim of the BRA 2013 is to safeguard consumers' welfares and to maintain stability in the financial system, along with the ultimate goal of making the banking system safer.

The push for further banking regulations though might need to take into consideration that these actions could cause more harm than good to the banking sector, as it would increase moral hazard due to the decline in market discipline and banks' anticipation of bailouts, while further contentions have been raised that systematic regulation policies could contribute to a collective moral hazard problem, as they enable banks to access cheaper capital so as to increase their borrowings and reduce their liquidity.[520] From this perspective, bigger banks or too big to fail (TBTF) banks would be more strongly motivated than smaller banks to undertake risky strategies owing to the safety net provided by the state.

Additionally, many of the market failures could culminate in moral hazard problems as the risk-taking party would not bear all the associated costs of their activities, but gained all of the associated benefits. In fact, the Turner Review Report 2009 had highlighted that such moral hazards could infect the entire financial market, forcing many of their participants to assume excessive levels of risks.[521] It has been pointed out that one of the main reasons for the recurring debate on this issue has been the failures of many regulatory agencies in preventing bank crises or bank collapses in several economies.[522] Market failures have also contributed to different financial markets deviating from their standard functions. Some examples of these include information deficiencies in both securitization markets and the market of home loans; non-competitiveness of markets; and the presence of regulatory interventions, like the use of depositor protection schemes and bank bailouts.[523] There is also good evidence

519. P. Chalermchatichien, et al. 2014. "The effects of the ownership concentration on capital adequacy, liquidity and capital stability". *Journal of Financial Services Research*, Vol. 45 (2014): 219-240.
520. E. Fahri & J. Tirole. 2012. "Collective moral hazard, maturity mismatch, and systemic bailouts". *American Economic Review*, Vol. 102 (2012): 60-93.
521. The Turner Review. 2009. *A regulatory response to the global banking crises, March*. London: Financial Services Authority.
522. A. Bush. 2009. *Banking regulation and globalization*. Oxford: OUP.
523. The Turner Review 2009, *supra* note [521].

of excessive risk-taking by financial institutions that contributed to the financial crisis.[524]

Banking regulation could take the form of precise rules, but this is often inaccurate where such rules did not actually reflect risks faced by the banks, leading to either inadequate capital buffers that risk bank failures or too much unnecessary capital that would impose excessive costs on the banks.[525] Basel II provides a list of best practices for regulation and supervision banks so as to improve stability of the system, risk management practices, and market disciplines through enhanced risk-based capital and disclosure requirements. This includes enhanced attention provided to the capital adequacy requirement covered in Pillar 1 of Basel II that seeks to provide tools to enable banks to hold less risky portfolios when managing the risk-taking behaviors of banks.[526] In the case of the UK, the BRA 2013 seeks to contain the risk taken by banks. Positive market reactions on bank shares suggest that the market accepted this, while the negative impact on the shares of insurance companies demonstrates that insurance companies are perceived to have taken on some additional risks as a consequence of the legislation.[527]

When more exposures of serious flaws in ESG practices in the sector mounted, this eventually led to further banking law reforms in the UK.[528] The SRR Code of Practice regime introduced through sections 5 and 6 of the BA 2009 supports the legal framework of the SRR, and offers guidance as to how and in what situations the authorities could apply the special resolution mechanisms.[529] Section 1 of the Code deals with banks, building societies, investment firms and banking group companies, commonly referred to as banking institutions, while section 2 deals with central counterparties. Following the implementation of the Bank Recovery and Resolution Directive (BBRD) and changes in the regulatory architecture, together with the creation of the FCA and PRA, the Code has been updated. The present update reflects changes flowing from the UK's exit from the EU emerging in the form of the Bank Recovery and Resolution (Amendment) (EU Exit) Regulations 2020. The Code's current version is applicable to the use of the SRR subsequent to the end of the transition period defined as December 31, 2020, by the EU Withdrawal Agreement Act 2020. The Treasury issues the present Code having consulted the FCA, PRA, the BOE and Financial Services Compensation Scheme (FSCS) in accordance with section 6 of BA 2009.

524. A. Wilmarth. 2011. "The Dodd-Frank Act: A flawed and inadequate response to the too-big-to-fail problems". *Oregon Law Review*, Vol. 89 (2011): 951-1057.
525. G.E. Chortareas, C. Giordone & A. Ventuori. 2013. "Financial freedom and bank efficiency: Evidence from the European Union". *Journal of Banking and Finance*, Vol. 37 (2013): 1223-1231.
526. Z-Y. Zhang, J.Wu & Q-F. Liu. 2008. "Impact of capital adequacy regulation on risk-taking behaviours of banking". *Systems Engineering Theory & Practice Online*, Vol. 28 (2008): 183-189.
527. T.V. Parise & V. Shenai. 2018. "The value effect of financial reform on U.K. banks and insurance companies". *International Journal of Financial Studies*, Vol. 6 (3): 81-109.
528. HM Treasury. 2020. "Banking Act 2009: Special resolution regime code of practice". HM Treasury Presentation to Parliament pursuant to sections 5 and 6 of the Banking Act 2009 31 December 2020, https://assets.publishing.service.gov.uk/government/uploads/, accessed January 11, 2021.
529. HM Treasury 2020, *supra* note [528].

The SRR as set out in Parts 1 to 3 of the BA 2009 is applicable to banking institutions in situations where their failure has become highly probable. It comprises five stabilization options, namely, transfer to a private sector purchaser; transfer to a bridge entity; the asset management vehicle tool; the bail-in tool; and transfer to temporary public sector ownership. It further includes the bank (or building society) insolvency procedures that facilitate the FSCS in providing prompt payout to depositors or transfer of their account to another institution; and the bank administration procedure for use where there has been a partial transfer of business from a failing institution.[530] Guidance is also provided on the application of the Investment Bank Special Administration Regulations 2011 (SAR). Authorities and firms may use the SAR regime to enable the quick distribution of the clients' assets to the firm's clients, as well as distributing firm funds among creditors and others with claims. The special resolution mechanisms could be employed by authorities to resolve a failing banking institution. The temporary public ownership powers would not extend to banking group companies, other than holding companies. The bank insolvency procedures are applicable to banks and building societies, while the bank administration procedures are applicable to banks, building societies and investment firms.

Via section 5 of the BA 2009, the Code sets out guidance on the following:[531]

(1) The mandatory write-down and conversion of capital instruments and relevant internal liabilities.
(2) How the special resolution objectives are to be understood and achieved.
(3) The choice between different resolution options.
(4) The information to be provided as part of any consultation between the authorities and the giving of advice between one authority and another.
(5) How to determine whether Condition 2 in section 7 of the legislation is met. This condition stipulates that before a banking institution could be placed into the SRR, the BOE must have determined that it is not reasonably probable that action would be taken by or in respect of the institutions that would mean it was no longer failing or likely to fail.
(6) How to determine whether the test for the use of stabilization powers in section 7 is satisfied. Which is how the BOE would determine the public interest test for the use of the private sector purchaser, bridge bank, bail-in and asset management vehicle stabilization options.
(7) The management and control of asset management vehicles.
(8) Sections 63 & 66 or BA 2009 pertaining to general continuity obligations, that is, the continuity of provision of service and facilities where the transfer powers are used.
(9) Compensation that might be payable, as a consequence of the use of the SRR.
(10) BA 2009's sections 12 & 13 will require the inclusion in the Code particular matters relating to the governance of bridge banks and temporary public

530. Hm Treasury 2020, *supra* note [528].
531. HM Treasury 2020, *supra* note [528].

ownership. These describe the legal powers under the legislation, including the legal constraints on the authorities. The authorities are legally obliged to have regard to the Code under section 5(4) of Ba 2009.

(11) The Treasury considers that a primary purpose of the Code is to provide a clear guide, for banking institutions and the financial markets as to how the authorities seek to achieve the special resolution objectives and how the SRR powers might be applied in practice. As such, other than describing the legal powers, the Code also outlines the authorities' policy approach to using these powers. The authorities must have regard to the statements of policy intention under section 5(4) of the legislation, when exercising SRR powers. This implies that the statements of policy intention would offer greater insights into how the authorities would expect to act so as to achieve the special resolution objectives.

The "G" of ESG practices in banking and financial services deserves particular attention, as it has the inherent capacity to be contagion and to disrupt entire national economies, as well as much of the world economy. This could be seen in the different magnitude impact between the 2000 Dotcom debacle and the 2007-2008 GFC. Though the former involved extensive abusive and manipulative use of off-balance sheet instruments by large business enterprises to fool the world leading to extensive business corporation bankruptcies, authorities have been able to quell the risks of financial contagion through quick and well-coordinated actions by policymakers and regulators, including the enactment of SOX 2002 that puts heavy responsibilities on CEOs and corporate boards and which comes with heavy sanctions. The 2007-2008 GFC, in contrast, involved the manipulative applications of off-balance sheet instruments on a much larger and wider scale by mega global banks and financial services that downed the entire US economy through its contagion effect, and very quickly many other big economies, such as the UK and the EU. It had to be contained by vast financial and tough financial regulatory measures, as well as introduction of the more comprehensive DFA 2010 that incorporates stern investors protection measures, and equally strict governance measures for banks and corporations in general.

The above disturbing narrations confirm again why governance practices in banks and financial services merit special focus, even though the related issues to governance in the banking industry did not differ essentially from the issues related to the governance of any business corporation. It is important also to bear in mind the pivotal roles played by the banking industry in national and international economies, and their stricter regulations by comparison to other business enterprises. From the governance perspective, banks offer several particular features that might impact agency issues.[532] They are by nature inherently highly leveraged enterprises, meaning having very high debt to equity ratios in their balance sheets, with an important portion of these debts comprising highly liquid demand deposits. As their assets are generally

532. D. Heremans. 2006. "CG issues for banks. A financial stability perspective". *K.U. Leuven Department of Economics Working Paper*, https://core.ac.uk/download/pdf/6978897.pdf, accessed November 10, 2020.

illiquid, the corresponding maturity mismatch generates substantial risks for their debt holders.

Banks further differ from other business enterprises in the nature of their products and services and their claimholders.[533] Bank products are of a fiduciary nature and bank balance sheets are notoriously opaque to investors. As these financial or structured products get increasingly complex, as they did, at the onset of the GFC, the quality of the loan portfolio could become harder to evaluate. This tends to aggravate information asymmetry problems, making it harder to monitor the management behaviors of banks, especially when small depositors are not good with this. Banks, as such, rely critically on depositor confidence in contrast to nonfinancial companies where debtholders are institutional shareholders that have generally more incentives, expertise and powers in monitoring. Besides, banks present systemic externalities raising unique concerns for bank solvency and financial stability.[534] The threats to the stability of the financial system depend on the occurrence of negative disturbances and the presence of negative externalities, such that economic shocks are inherently systemwide.

Conventional systemic risks often originate from banking problems. Banks are exposed to different shocks, facing as they do, different kinds of liquidity, credit, market and operating risks.[535] Its operating system itself contains powerful propagation mechanisms that could amplify small initial shocks, being much more interconnected than is the situation for the other sectors of the economy. Though conventional contagion mechanisms of runs by depositors on banks in trouble are generally no longer applicable in a world where depositors benefit from deposit insurance (Northern Rock case, being the unique exception[536]), these domino impacts are more likely to happen at the wholesale level, especially through the interbank market. Enhanced reliance on interbank financing might lower the likelihood of individual bank failures. This though could increase the likelihood of total collapse, where real economic activity could be seriously disrupted as money production is at the center of the banking system. Hence, the wider macroeconomic distortions in banks distress situations helped to explain the special concern for banking and financial stability.[537]

When banks efficiently mobilize and allocate funds, this lowers capital cost to business enterprises, boost capital formation and stimulates productivity growth, while weak governance of banks reverberates throughout the economy with negative ramification for economic development.[538] Also, banking operations' activities are masked in relatively greater complexity and greater opaqueness that increased information asymmetry and reduced stakeholders' capacity to monitor the actions of bank

533. Heremans 2006, *supra* note [532].
534. Heremans 2006, *supra* note [532].
535. Heremans 2006, *supra* note [532].
536. D.T. Llewellyn. 2009. *The failure of Northern Rock: A multi-dimensional case study*. Louveciennes: The European Money and Finance Forum (SUERF).
537. D. Heremans. 2003. "Systemic risks and prudential policy. What role for the EU?". *Review of Business and Economic Literature,* Vol. 0 (3): 417-442.
538. R. Levine. 2013. "The CG of banks: A concise discussion of concepts and evidence". *World Bank Policy Research Working Papers 21/06/13*, https://doi.org/10.1596/1813-9450-3404, accessed November 10, 2020.

CEOs and bank managers, and all this despite them operating in a relatively highly regulated environment than that faced by other business corporations in general.[539]

These attributes of greater opaqueness in banks combined with greater government regulations than other industries weaken many conventional governance mechanisms, like the reliance on the effectiveness of internal control systems, audit committees and reliance on global auditors with seemingly stellar reputations. Yet, time and again flaws in their governance practices have been exposed in various banking scandals,[540] the largest of which centered around the GFC.[541] This suggests the importance of strengthening the ability and incentives of private investors to exert governance over banks, instead of relying excessively on government regulators.[542]

The governance element is thus a necessary complement to regulatory and supervisory intervention, and as such, should be approached from both the perspective of profitability and the perspective of financial stability.[543] Compared to nonfinancial enterprises, debt governance distortion might arise especially in banks, owing to their vulnerability to excessive risk-taking. It raises the need to examine how different governance arrangements that are applicable to nonfinancial corporations would impact the incentives and the powers of parties involved in the banking firms in relation to excessive risk-taking. This suggests that the usual criticisms on the predominant block holders' model for banks should be further qualified. While they apply to controlling ownership with complex structures, like pyramids, straightforward controlling ownership by nondiversified shareholders might, however, provide an important governance mechanism. This could also help to explain the predominance of family ownership in the banking sector. Also, the analysis of risk attitudes of the parties involved in the banking firm would introduce a new prudentially relevant definition of independence for directors. This would have important implications for the appropriate composition of the board of directors for banks, a matter that needs to be approached more systematically.

It has been argued that the governance mechanisms in banks have changed subsequent to the 2007-2008 GFC,[544] not least from newly imposed rules for banks in the US by the DFA 2010 alluded to earlier, and other rules from the SEC and other US federal authorities; and from BA 2009 for banks in the UK together with amendments from time to time, as discussed earlier. Findings from empirical studies suggest that Anglo-American banks following the common law system and the shareholder primacy model have been able to maintain their high level of governance effectiveness subsequent to the crisis, while continental European banks following the civil law system stakeholder model increased their effectiveness after the crisis. These included

539. Levine 2013, *supra* note [538].
540. P. Yeoh. 2015. "CG failures and the road to financial crime". *Journal of Financial Crime*, Vol. 23 (1): 216-230.
541. K. Philipps. 2008. *Bad money: Reckless finance, failed politics, and the global crisis of American capitalism*. New York: Viking.
542. Levine 2013, *supra* note [538].
543. Heremans 2006, *supra* note [537].
544. J.L.F. Sanchez, M.D.O. Zamanillo & M. Luna. 2020. "How CG mechanisms of banks have changed after the 2007-08 financial crisis". *Global Policy* Vol. 11 (2020): 1-10.

the transforming of some practices in their governance mechanisms with improvements in the structure and functioning of directors' boards, improvements in the compensation policy for banks' executives, together with the implementation of CSR committees. These changes taken together give support for the governance convergence paradigm.[545]

These findings imply that effective bank systems need strong governance practices to achieve and maintain a higher level of public confidence; that the GFC has meant a convergence of governance practices between the common and civil law systems of governance; that the convergence between both systems could be attributed to the improvement in the governance mechanisms of continental European banks thereby increasing their levels of governance effectiveness; that the implementation of CSR or sustainability committees in the banking sector has improved banks' accountability and transparency; and that changes in the compensation policy for banks' executives subsequent to the crisis have improved the banks' governance effectiveness, irrespective of the governance system.[546]

How board characteristics influence governance compliance in the banking industry has also been undertaken in another empirical study. Governance compliance levels illustrate a company's actions in fulfilling regulatory obligations that seeks to protect investors from potential losses in the sector. The study's findings demonstrate that the size of the board commissioners, the proportion of independent commissioners, the experience of commissioners, and the size of the audit committee are factors motivating management in the banking industry to improve their bank's governance compliance.[547] This further suggests that board monitoring serves as an effective mechanism for reducing information asymmetry, while open innovation following regulatory reforms could also increase compliance with laws.[548]

In the final analysis, banks are special, and so is the governance of banks and other financial institutions in comparison with the governance process of nonbanks.[549] Empirical evidence illustrated above mostly confirms this. Banks practicing good governance in the conventional shareholder primacy approach performed less well than banks having less shareholder-prone boards and less shareholder influence. The special governance of banks and other financial institutions is firmly embedded in bank supervisory law and regulation.[550] Shareholder governance and stakeholder governance have been, and still are, the two dominant prevailing regimes in the US and in Europe. This difference though for banks has given way to stakeholder, and especially creditor or debtholder governance, certainly in bank supervision and regulation.

The regulatory core issues for the governance of banks are manifold. A major problem is the composition and qualification of the one-tier or two-tier board. The

545. Sanchez, Zamanillo & Luna 2020, *supra* note [544].
546. Sanchez, Zamanillo & Luna 2020, *supra* note [544].
547. R. Zulfikar, et al. 2020. "CG compliance in banking industry: The role of the board". *Journal of Open Innovative Technology, Market, and Complexity*, Vol. 6 (2020): 137-174.
548. Zulfikar et al. 2020, *supra* note [547].
549. K.J. Hopt. 2020. "CG for banks and financial institutions: Economic theory, supervisory practice, evidence and policy". *ECGI Law Working Paper No. 507/2020 March 2020: 1-36.*
550. Hopt 2020, *supra* note [549].

legislative challenge is to enhance independent as well as qualified control.[551] But the proposal of providing creditors with a special seat on the board disregards the reality of board codetermination. Providing bank supervisors with a permanent seat in the board could generate serious conflicts of interest, as they would need to controversially supervise and enforce themselves in a multitude of bank governance issues.[552] These extend from the duties and liabilities of bank directors, especially where risk and compliance are concerned; remunerations paid to bank directors, and key function holders; and clawback provisions either imposed by law as in the DFA 2010 or introduced by banks themselves, as in the US and the UK.

The heavy focus on the governance lessons from flawed corporate management practices especially in financial services does not necessarily imply that there have been no environmental or social challenges confronting corporate UK, especially in supply chains. The UK Modern Slavery Act 2015 (MSA 2015) has, for example, been widely seen as a landmark piece of legislation, targeted at encouraging businesses to act on the eradication of modern slavery from its operations and supply chains. The Transparency in Supply Chain (TSC) provisions in section 54 of the legislation require companies to publish a statement of the steps they have taken during the reporting year to ensure that slavery and human trafficking do not occur in the running of their supply chains. The aim of the TSC provision is to promote a race to the top by motivating businesses to address modern slavery risks, thereby enhancing competition to help raise such standards as the appropriate and effective response to the problem.

The Business & Human Rights Resources Centre (BHRRC), the only public repository of such statements in the UK, has evaluated the compliance of more than sixteen thousand of these statements issued by the largest UK companies over the past six years, and has concluded in its February 2021 report "Modern Slavery Act: Five Years of Reporting" that this legislation has fared poorly in it stated intentions. Owing to the lack of monitoring and enforcement, these submitted statements have failed to drive systemic corporate actions to eliminate forced labor, even in high-risk sectors. Ironically, the legislation explicitly states that an in-scope company may state that it has taken no action to address modern slavery risks during the reporting years and still be compliant with the law.

While awareness of modern slavery has in part been raised with the help of the media, the evaluation has indicated no material improvements in many companies' policies, practices, or performances. This is largely because the legislation does not impose any legally binding standards on in-scope companies to take steps to effectively resolve labor exploitation risks in their business operations. The narrow focus of this Act in placing modern slavery as distinct from other species of labor abuse and disclosure requirements have excluded the spectrum of labor abuse risks that could lead to or are clear evidence of modern slavery. Labor abuse takes place on a continuum where all kinds of exploitation intermingle with social-economic factors, including modern slavery. Hence, despite six years of persistent noncompliance by

551. Hopt 2020, *supra* note [549].
552. Hopt 2020, *supra* note [549].

some 40% of in-scope companies, there was zero injunctions/penalties applied to companies when failing to report over the past six years.

This is in sharp contrast to section 307 of the Tariff Act in the US where goods suspected of being manufactured with force labor have been banned from entry to the country leading to multi-million-dollar repayment of recruitment fees by supplier to this lucrative market. In fact, in much of 2020 and 2021, the US has taken such tough actions on various leading global gloves manufacturing companies in Asia in the midst of the COVID-19 pandemic. The absence of enforcement of the reporting requirement itself and the absence of mandatory reporting criteria have resulted in only some 60% of in-scope companies reporting under the law, with the bulk of them publishing only general statements that failed to comply with the law's intention. The Corporate Justice Coalition in its October 2017 report "Risk Averse: Company Reporting on Raw Material and Sector-Specific Risks under The Transparency in Supply Chains Clause in the UK Modern Slavery Act 2015" suggested that MNCs associated with high risk sectors or materials and commodities have not been sufficiently transparent in their disclosures.

The COVID-19 pandemic showed clearly the deficiencies of this legislation in helping to protect the economic and health welfares of some 25 million victims of forced labor across the world, and ergo, the urgent need for legally binding obligations on in-scope companies that are adequately and forcefully implemented and going beyond mere shallow reporting requirements. The BHRRC report demonstrated that the "nudge" strategy advocated by a Nobel Laurette to encourage voluntary corporate transparency toward systemic change in business operations and supply chains could not work this time. Thus, transparency is necessary, but relying on voluntary disclosure alone is insufficient to deter abusive labor management practices. The BHRRC draws attention to alternative legal frameworks, like mandatory human rights due diligence and import bans linked to trade regulations. More responsible businesses are now seeking harmonization of standards of human rights and legal certainty against others undercutting them with less costly but ruthless labor management practices.

Additionally, it recommended new legislation to impose legal liability on all companies in all sectors for failures to prevent human rights abuses in their turfs; the introduction of import bans for goods suspected of being produced with forced labor; and the application of these laws to public procurements. This stern action at discouraging the use of forced labor is now pursued equally in earnest by the EC, when its President Ursula von der Leyen on September 15, 2021, announced plans to ban products made by forced labor, adding that human dignity and freedom were more important than making profits. The UK government has responded on June 15, 2021, with the Modern Slavery (Amendment) Bill with the following amendments:

(1) Making it a criminal offense to supply a false modern slavery and human trafficking statement.
(2) Making it a criminal offense for companies to continue to use supply chains that fail to show minimum standards of transparency.
(3) To improve standards of TSCs pertaining to modern slavery and human trafficking.

The above aside, the UK has in August 2020 also published a consultation on a new supply chain due diligence law targeted at protecting global rainforest and other sensitive habitats. The Environment Bill 2021 according to the Environment Secretary (ES) sets the gold standard for improving air quality, protecting nature, increasing recycling, and cutting down plastic waste. This together with the Agricultural Bill and Fisheries Bill are expected to provide a legal framework for the environment for the UK external to the EU. The Environmental Bill among others would require the ES to review and report every two years on developments in international environmental protection laws which appear to the ES to be of significance. The legislation also provides for a new watchdog, namely the Office for Environmental Protection (OEP) to oversee the implementation of environmental law by government and public agencies. The bill further requires the ES to set at least one long-term legally binding environmental target, including requiring the minister to have due regard to policy statements on environmental principles when making decisions, as well as a requirement for fifteen-year Environmental Improvement Plans. Importantly, the Bill incorporates restrictions on illegal deforestation by mandating large designated businesses to evaluate their supply chains pertaining to forest risk commodities to ensure that local laws are complied with.

The UK has also announced that the country would make climate-related financial disclosures fully mandatory by 2025 via TCFD. This TCFD regime would then be applicable to all UK-registered companies, pension schemes, financial advisers, insurers and other entities. Such and more rules to come reflect UK's initiatives toward requiring specific accountability from companies. David Dinsdale's June 2021 article "How the UK Is Promoting "Social Value" Through Its Public-Sector Procurement Process" in Sustainable Brands highlighted UK's Procurement Policy Note (PPN) 06/20. This ensures that social value is explicitly assessed, meaning that under the new model, at least 10% of every public procurement decision is based on the scoring of a social value proposal attached to the procurement bid. Recognizing that social value could assume different forms, the UK provided a Green Book policy document offering guidance on activities that improve economic, social, and environmental well-being of the relevant area. The new regime would favor suppliers committed to reducing carbon footprint and encouraging their polluting peers, such as those selling software and services, to reduce reliance on consultants who have to be flown in accompanied by large carbon footprints. The PPN recognizes five areas under the social value umbrella. These include COVID-19 recovery plans, addressing economic inequality, fighting climate change, inclusion, fighting modern slavery, and improving health, well-being and community integration within the workforce.

Many of these social and environmental issues hitherto have not led to regulatory reforms until in more recent years. For example, lawmakers have been relatively slow when responding to public expectations and wills for actions against climate change that is still being awaited, but as alluded to above, changes appear to be on the horizon. The BOE, for instance, published its climate-related financial disclosure in June 2021 setting out its approach for managing the risks from climate change across its entire operations. The BoE report stressed that the bank would continue to hold firms it regulates to high standards by assessing their progress against the bank's climate-related supervisory expectations and their resiliency to different climate scenarios. The FCA Policy Statement PS20/17 confirms that it is introducing a new rule requiring commercial entities with a UK premium listing, including sovereign-controlled commercial enterprises to incorporate a statement in their annual financial reports spelling out whether they have made disclosures consistent with the TCFD recommendations, giving reasons where they have not made disclosures consistent with TCFD's recommendations and remedial actions with timelines. The statement would have to include where they may have included disclosures in documents other than their annual reports, and where in their annual financial reports the various disclosures could be found. The FCA has also on September 6, 2021, announced the application window for its second Green FinTech Challenge, having successfully conducted the first in 2018. This initiative has been launched to support the development and live market testing on new products and services that would aid UK's transition to a net-zero economy.

The PwC July 2021 ESG report "Embracing ESG Transformation" cited its recent survey insights that ESG is viewed as a central priority across the UK asset management space. This is increasingly seen as being propelled by a challenging regulatory environment, rising investor demand for ESG investing, and the appetite for a more purposeful culture. The majority of survey responding firms see their ESG initiatives as more than compliance routine, and indeed a value creation exercise and a commercial necessity in the markets. PwC suggests that for those others yet to respond strategically, they should commence their transformation journeys now by embedding ESG factors across the full spectrum of their business and operating models. This should extend from their risk management frameworks and investment approach to corporate matters, like diversity and inclusion, as well as the managing of their carbon footprints. Such initiatives would help them to fulfill their mission in establishing a more purposeful culture, in playing a more active role in addressing vital societal challenges, and in driving sustainable value creation across their businesses.

Thus, all said, the UK demonstrates its commitment to ESG factors from climate to forced labor through the rollout of mandatory climate disclosure; BOE's PRA Supervisory Statement SS3/19 outlining its expectations beyond current material risk disclosures obligation for financial services pertaining to their assessment of climate risk in the contexts of governance arrangements, risk management, stress testing and scenario analysis and disclosures; and FRC's recommendations for UK public interest entities to report voluntarily on climate change risk responses to meet expectations of stakeholders, including investors, and in line with TCFD and SASB metrics. These and other initiatives show the UK's resolve to deal with ESG factors in the economy, and in particular the business sector through both voluntary and mandatory reporting on ESG and related matters. The UK has also on November 18, 2020, released a policy paper "The Ten Point Plan for a Green Industrial Revolution" with details of GBP 12 billion state investment with sector-specific targets for carbon capture storage and utilization, electric vehicles, nuclear, hydrogen, and offshore wind. This was followed through with a six-month progress report on May 18, 2021, that provided further details on the various milestones achieved to date. Also, the UK would cohost with Italy the COP26 conference in November 2021 with the agenda of accelerating action toward addressing the missions of the Paris Agreement and the UN Framework Convention on Climate Change.

The EU since the 1990s has engaged with ESG and in particular climate-linked disclosures obligations since the 1990s, but has accelerated various other initiatives subsequent to the release of the 2015 UN 2030 Sustainable Developments agenda, and the Paris Agreement inked by 190 economies with the aims of mitigating the impacts of climate change, reducing global GHG emissions, and strengthening the resilience and capacities to withstand the effects of climate change. These are reflected in the EC's Financing Sustainable Goal Action Plan announced in March 2018. The said plan has the aims of promoting transparency and long-termism in financial and economic activities, mainstreaming sustainability in risk management, and resurging capital flows to sustainable investments for sustainable and inclusive agenda. This mission statement is supported by legislative proposals for reforms to promote sustainability priorities among capital market investment enterprises and insurance distributors, designing of new benchmarks for the carbon effects on investments, regulating disclosures pertaining to sustainable investment and risks, and the developing of a Taxonomy, or a unified classification system for identifying and defining ESG factors. The March 2018 Action Plan in conjunction with these has initiated various EU-wide directives targeting the strengthening of climate-linked corporate disclosures and governance.

Thus far, significant progress has been achieved for the EU Taxonomy, the NFRD, and the integration of the task force on climate-related financial disclosure. The EU Taxonomy Regulation released in June 2020 mandates NFRD requiring in-scope companies to disclose designated metrics on the degree their activities are environmentally sustainable to at least one of the environmentally sustainable economic activity listed in the EU Taxonomy. Such activities must also do no significant harm to any of the other environmental aims, adhere to minimum social safeguards, and conform to the technical screening criteria. The NFRD requires companies to align with the double materiality approach when they report on how sustainability impacts their performance, status, and progress, or the outside-in perspective; and on their effects on people and the planet, or the inside-out perspective. EC's nonbinding guidelines for this released in June 2019 explained that the double materiality standard takes cognizance of the matter that as markets and public policies evolved in response to climate change, the plus and minus outcomes of corporate activities on the climate would in turn generate challenges and opportunities that are likely to be financially material.

Noting later that the NFRD on its own is generally viewed as not fit for purpose in terms of meeting the needs of users, the EC on April 21, 2021, adopted a proposal for CSRD that would amend the current NFRD requirements. The major amendments would include ensuring that all information is incorporated as part of companies' management report, disclosed in digital machine-readable format; specifying in details the information companies should report to fall in line with mandatory EU sustainability reporting standards; requiring assurance of sustainability data; and extending the scope of these reporting requirements to more enterprises, including all listed and large enterprises other than listed microenterprises. Thus, the CSRD when adopted would require NFRD conformance by all large enterprises, meaning those with more than 250 employees and balance sheet exceeding GBP 20 million, or more than GBP 40 million in net sales turnover, all public-listed enterprises other than listed microenterprises. The CSRD also requires in-scope entities to conform to the double materiality standard, the reporting standards of the European Financial Reporting Advisory Group (EFRAG) when released, and getting limited assurance from third parties, like auditors, that there are no material deficiencies or flaws in the companies' disclosures. Further, nonfinancial disclosure would have to incorporate key performance metrics showing the degree to which their activities are sustainable under the EU Taxonomy; major risk pertaining to sustainability matters and how they are being addressed; due diligence process pertaining to sustainability issues, potential adverse effects on the business and steps taken to prevent and minimize these; roles of respective organs within the enterprise with respects to these disclosure obligations; targets linked to sustainability issues; and reviews of the impact of sustainability matters on the enterprise's overall business model and strategy with a view of ensuring that the enterprise's approach is compatible with a transition to a sustainable economy and the aims and objectives of the 2015 Paris Agreement. These disclosures are to be made in the annual reports of companies. Importantly, the CSRD when adopted would require EU Member States to implement its provisions by December 1, 2022.

To minimize disruptions to entities already reporting such data, the EC clarified on April 21, 2021, when adopting the proposal for a CSRD that sustainability reporting standards would likely take into account current standards and frameworks for sustainability reporting and accounting where suitable, inclusive of those from the TCFD. The TCFD was set up by the FSB in December 2015. It is an independent global entity, with the aims of developing recommendations for more effective climate-linked disclosures for boosting more informed investment, credit and insurance underwriting decisions, and for facilitating stakeholders' understanding of financial services' exposures to climate-linked risks. The TCFD published its recommendations for a framework of climate-linked financial disclosures accordingly on June 15, 2017. These have been widely embraced, including by the Group of Seven that subsequently on June 5, 2021, released a statement advocating for compulsory disclosures of climate-linked financial risks as per its framework. The TCFD structured its financial framework within four designated niches. These cover the metrics and targets employed to evaluate and manage climate-related risks and opportunities where such information is material; how the enterprise evaluates and manages climate-linked risks; the actual and potential effects of climate-linked challenges and opportunities on the enterprise's business, strategy and financial strategy where the data is material; and the enterprise's governance with regards to climate-linked challenges and opportunities.

As the TCFD heads toward its final guidance in the later part of 2021, it issued in June 2021 its proposed guidance on climate-related metrics, targets, and transition plans. The proposed guidance provided useful definitions for key terminologies. These include climate-related metrics, defined as a quantity indicative of the level of historical, current, and forward-looking climate-related risks and opportunities for a given enterprise. These indicators are used to monitor climate-related risks and opportunities and can also be employed to measure progress against climate-related targets over the duration of the period for which a target is set. Definitions are also provided for climate-related financial impact, climate-related target, and transition plans.

The TCFD adds that enterprises should disclose climate-related metrics, climate-related financial impacts, climate-related targets, and key activities and milestones of its transition plan. While some data might be more applicable for internal decision-making, in-scope reporting enterprises should not take too tight restrictions for market access to data. An enterprise when differentiating between more access to data and avoidance of disclosure should endeavor to disclose more instead of less to facilitate clearer appreciation and understanding of disclosures by users. Major information, like climate-linked metrics and targets that are highly pertinent to calibrating and reporting material financial risk, should be located in corporate annual report or in publicly accessible investor gatherings. Enterprises are also advised to apply quantitative and qualitative scenario evaluation in the designing and testing of metrics, targets, and transition plans developed. TCFD's final guidance would, among others, include standardized climate-related metrics, calibrations pertaining to climate-linked financial impacts, as well as transition planning measurements, like decarbonization routes.

EFRAG, a nonprofit entity, advises the EC on matters relating to IFRS, and in particular, the development of the proposed CSRD. It released its recommendations to the EU for the development of sustainability reporting standards on March 31, 2021, after having completed its due process endorsement advise pertaining to IFRS 17. These cover proposals for a coherent and comprehensive set of reporting standards incorporating all sustainability factors with a double materiality perspective; detailed directions and milestones for developing these standards; as well as proposals for mutually reinforcing cooperation standard-setting and global setting initiatives of the EU. Its guidelines are premised on the operationalization of the key ideas of double materiality through defining and implementing this in each of its two elements. As such, it advocates EU's future standard-setters to provide the standards for impact materiality, via the inside-out perspective of the double materiality standard.

This would then call for identification of sustainability material issues in the context of the in-scope reporting company's own operations and its impact materiality, or value chain. This is to be further premised on the urgency derived from social and environmental public policy agendas and boundaries; the scale, scope and probability of actual positive impacts on people and planet linked to the enterprise's operations and value chain, and the severity and where suitable, the probability of actual and potential negative impacts on planet and people. EFRAG stressed further that financial materiality for sustainability reporting cannot be merely extrapolated from financial materiality for financial reporting, and as such, it instead recommends that the ascertainment of financial materiality relies on qualitative, nonmonetary quantitative data while taking cognizance of the dynamic relationships between them. Pre-financial impacts could evolve to become material for financial reporting gradually over time.

The 2018 Action Plan generated too the EU SFDR. This complements the other disclosure initiatives with a disclosure framework for entities operating, selling products, or managing funds in the EU. These cover financial services and asset manage ment enterprises, including financial advisers, investment firms, pension funds, insurance entities, and banks. The SFDR has the primary goal of preventing greenwashing of investment activities through the imposition of sustainability disclosures requirements, such as exemplified by the joint investigations of Deutsche Bank AG's asset management company, the DWS Group, by the US Department of Justice (DOJ), the SEC and German regulators subsequent to the allegations of the former sustainability head of the DWS that the DWS had overstated the amounts it invested in assets based on ESG factors. The SFDR framework requires financial market participants to disclose sustainability risks in their investment decisions and through this seeks to deal with greenwashing threats. A sustainability risk under the SFDR is deemed as an environmental event, or situation, such that when it happens could exert an actual or potential material negative effect on an investment value.

Hence, financial institutions are required to disclose how sustainability risks are included in their decision-making process, the main negative effect of investment decisions on sustainability matters; and where the enterprise markets products with sustainability features, it is required to disclose the premise for their accuracies, but where it treats the sustainability risks as nonrelevant, it is required to equally disclose the basis for this. Where in-scope reporting entities market products with environmental or social features, they need to provide product-level disclosures, but they also need to provide disclosures even when the marketed products do not have such features. Indeed, ETFs or bonds claiming to exert positive effects on the planet have to invest mainly in sustainable enterprises, or enterprises showing designated positive outcomes, like progress toward low carbon. Those enterprises offering sustainability-featured products, following the SFDR, would have to disclose the sustainability indicators applied to assess the success of the sustainable investment objective, the approach employed for screening the investments, the governance practices at the investee enterprise, whether they incorporate carbon emission reduction, benchmarks, and so on.

The 2018 Action Plan beyond the above also promotes sustainable governance, by taking the long-term perspective for capital markets. As such, the EC has been directed to deliberate on the need to require corporate boards to frame and disclose sustainable strategies reinforced by suitable due diligence processes across the supply chain against measurable sustainability targets, including identification of directors' roles and responsibilities pertaining to this. EU's posture to make use of TCFD and other third-party standards have started to motivate other jurisdictions to do the same, or equivalent pathways, such as witnessed in the UK, and in various US MNCs, despite slowness in the US regulatory process because of the lack of enthusiasms for these kinds of developments under the previous Trump administration. However, going by the stance of the Biden administration, since late 2020, there are early signs for formal regulatory guidance, but less clear signs on the form this would take because of the pushback from significant partisan politics.

The EU is therefore generally relatively ahead of the US and UK when it comes to the advocation of ESG regulatory initiatives and ESG-integrated reporting agenda in their respective economies. The EU's sustainable finance regulatory framework comprises the SFDRs (SFDR (Regulation (EU) 2019/2088)), the NFRD (NFRD (Directive

2014/95/EU), and the EU Taxonomy (Regulation (EU) 2020/852)). The SFRD incorporates a regime of disclosure requirements for financial market participants, as well as financial advisers to deter greenwashing and enhance market transparency. The NFRD mandates large enterprises to disclose nonfinancial, inclusion and diversity data in their annual reports and on their websites. With EC's adoption of the Proposal for a CSRD on April 21, 2021, amendments to the existing NFRD reporting requirements of the NFRD would include extending the scope to all large companies and all companies listed on regulated markets, other than listed microenterprises. The CSRD is expected to in-scope 49,000 companies compared to 11,000 under the previous NFRD, applies double materiality (or corporate disclosure on how sustainability matters impact it, as well as society and the environment), as well as mandating the use of the EU sustainability standards set by EFRAG. It will also require limited assurance of the sustainability data, digitalizing sustainability information, and start reporting to the new reporting standards in 2024, using the fiscal year 2023 information. The EU Taxonomy through its classification system seeks to help companies to define whether their economic activities are environmentally sustainable with the overall underlying objective of promoting and facilitating sustainable investments.

Stuart, Revis, Bentes, Macleod & Haque in their August 23, 2021 article "EU: European Commission Adopts Proposal for New Carbon Border Adjustment Mechanism" in Global Compliance News from Baker McKenzie highlighted that the EU would require importers to report the embedded emission in particular carbon-intensive products, initially limited to aluminum, cement, iron and steel, electricity and fertilizer, and thus to account for these emissions. This is scheduled to take effect in a transitional form from January 1, 2023, and fully operational from January 1, 2026. The Carbon Border Adjustment Mechanism (CBAM) seeks to complement the EU Emissions Trading System (EU ETS) to level the playing field between EU and non-EU businesses. This is to ensure that the production of carbon-intensive goods does not migrate from within the EU to third economies to leverage on less stringent climate policies. This EU initiative represents part of the EU's "Fit for 55" policy package to cut down on GHG emissions by at least 55% compared to 1990 levels by 2030 and eventually achieve climate neutrality in the EU by 2050. This "Green Deal" Fit for 55 initiative is a menu of linked policy proposals to strengthen eight existing regimes of legislation, including the Energy Tax Directive and the EU ETs for launching various new initiatives, of which, the CBAM is one.

US ESG disclosure requirements are also not found in an overarching framework, and rely similarly on a patchwork of ESG-related or climate-related disclosure regime flowing from the guidance of various US federal agencies. This includes the Corporate Governance Improvement and Investor Protection Act that has gone through Congress, but is unlikely to get support from the Senate because of the heavy pushback from the partisanship lawmaking process. In any case, this said bill requires listed enterprises to make material disclosures pertaining to ESG matters, and to empower the SEC to specify the boundaries of these disclosures. The US Chamber of Commerce (USCC) is also against the bill, arguing that the US Supreme Court decision in *TSC Industries, Inc. v. Northway, Inc., 426 U.S. 438 (1976)*, articulating the requirement of materiality in securities fraud cases, already provides adequate ESG-linked guidance to investors.

There is, on the other hand, powerful support from the US largest public defined benefit pension fund, namely the California State Teachers' Retirement System (CalSTRS) with some USD 465 billion AUM and representing some 2 million members. CalSTRS asserts that it has been restricted from sufficiently executing its fiduciary duty in the absence of high-quality, consistent, and comparable disclosures by public issuers. It claims that these disclosures could assist investors allocate capital and manage stewardship in companies to achieve long-term sustainable enterprise value creation, as well as motivate business enterprises to be more alert to ESG risk considerations.

Various other US federal agencies have recently in varying ways explored or addressed climate-linked implications and how these are affecting their strategies, policies and actions. Though most, like the SEC, have yet to issue formal financial disclosure guidance, they are likely to address these climate change risks to the US financial system.

The Commodity Futures Trading Commission (CFTC) in its September 9, 2020 Report "Managing Climate Risk in the U.S. Financial System" announced that climate change constitutes a materially significant risk to the stability of the US financial system and to the sustainability of the national economy. The Report highlighted the systemic risks posed by climate change; financial regulators being empowered by flexible and wide-ranging authority for dealing with these threats; regulators' constant struggles with inadequate data and analytical tools for measuring and managing such risks, including the balancing of transparency and privacy concerns; the absence of common definitions and standards for climate-linked data and financial products; the failures of current corporate disclosures on these risks; the growing appetite for ESG information; and the need for undertaking more robust US international engagements.

The CFTC accordingly recommends all federal agencies, like the FSOC, to include climate-linked risks into their mandates and consider formulating strategies to integrate these risks into their oversight role; and to collaborate with international forums, like the G7 and G20, the Central Banks and Supervisors Network for Greening the Financial System (NGFS), the Sustainable Insurance Forum, and the Coalition of Finance Ministers for Climate Actions to ensure the positioning of climate change risk as a priority agenda. Its other recommendations include requiring the integration of climate risk monitoring into the governance frameworks of business enterprise; reviewing pertinent laws and regulations to confirm or support the suitability of making investment decisions using ESG factors in retirement and pension plans under the ERISA and non-ERISA managed situations with fiduciary duty obligations; clarifying the materiality definition using qualitative and quantitative analysis when making medium and long-term disclosures on climate risks; collaborating with private sector initiatives to support the advancement of US-appropriate standardized and consistent classification systems; collaborating with private sector initiatives to support the availability of consistent, comparable, and reliable climate risk data; and exploring the option of integrating climate risk into corporate balance sheet and asset purchasing processes.

The Acting Chairman of the CFTC Rostin Behnam recently announced on March 17, 2021, that the CFTC has set up the Climate Risk Unit (CRU) to support the agency's mission by concentrating on the role of derivatives in understanding, pricing and addressing climate-linked risk and transitioning to a low-carbon economy. This unit is further envisaged to accelerate early CFTC's engagements in support of industry-led and market-driven processes for dealing with climate change, as well as the larger ESG space critical for ensuring that new products and markets fairly facilitate hedging, price discovery, market transparency, and capital allocation.

The Federal Reserve (Fed) on March 19, 2021, announced first that its financial monitoring framework is sufficiently flexible to broadly include many key elements of climate-linked risks. Second, while acknowledging the financial stability threats of these risks, the Fed stresses the need for more research and analysis when incorporating these into financial stability monitoring, including the need for major improvements in data and models. The Fed advocates third that domestic and global transparency initiatives surrounding climate-linked financial exposures could help to clarify the nature and scope of financial stability risks linked to climate change. To address these and other matters, the Fed set up the Supervision Climate Committee (SCC) to help identify climate-related risks and design initiative to ensure the resilience of enterprises under its purview; and the Financial Stability Climate Committee (FSCC) entrusted with identifying, evaluating, and resolving climate-related risks to financial stability and exploring the potential for complex interactions across the financial system, as well as enhancing the Fed's international engagements and influence on these and related matters.

Detterman, Hopkins, Stern, Gage & Tipple in their August 2021 article "Environmental Marketing Claims: Regulation and Litigation Outlook" in *The National Law Review* reported that the Fair Trade Commission (FTC) would be revising its earlier 1992 and 2012 "Green Guides" on environmental marketing claims. While not independently enforceable, those practices inconsistent with the "Green Guides" could give rise to a breach of section 5 of the FTC Act, or some state consumer protection legislations. It is envisaged that the revisions would explore the incorporation of investor preferences, as well as regulatory guidance from the EU. The FTC on December 22, 2020, announced its commitment to reducing carbon emissions and to the promoting of environmentally friendly innovation. It further clarified that besides collaborating with the Department of Energy on higher standards and labeling of energy efficiency, the FTC would also take various steps to protect consumers, including protecting energy consumers from abusive energy suppliers applying deceptive marketing practices, deterring greenwashing and other deceptive environmental claims, and discouraging anticompetitive mergers and conduct in the energy sector.

The SEC on March 4, 2021, announced the formation of a Climate and ESG Task Force in its Enforcement Division. Celita Soehner & Jeffrey Boujoukos in their June 2021 article "ESG Disclosures and Traps for the Unwary—What's Workable?" in *Reuters* cautioned issuer companies and others to be mindful of disclosure risks where applicable. Earlier, Tomasi, Kirwan & Vedvig in their September 2021 article "SEC Movement on ESG Disclosures: SEC and Investors Enhance Focus on Climate Change and Other ESG Disclosures" in *The National Law Review* suggests that the actions the SEC would take under its new Task Force and "enhanced focus" on climate change and ESG disclosures would be more aggressive compared to SEC's earlier 2010 climate change guidance. The authors cautioned issuers that new rules could likely be more prescriptive and extensive than the principles-based 2010 guidance. As such, they advocated that public companies should consider a more thorough review of their ESG-linked disclosures that have been filed with the SEC to date so as to identify gaps and to confirm and verify information provided in such disclosures. This kind of gap analysis would help issuers toward a robust and rigorous review of ESG and climate change disclosures going forward. The authors further advised issuers of the need to ensure that statements made are supportable and not perceived as an effort at greenwashing, as courts may find that unsupportable statements on environmental initiatives are not mere puffery but actionable causes of action under anti-fraud laws.

Mayer Brown's March 2021 article "SEC's Division of Examinations 2021 Exam Priorities-Investment Advisers and Investment Companies" drew attention to the February 25, 2021 announcement by the SEC Acting Chair that the agency would focus on climate-related disclosures. The SEC on March 23, 2021, stated that it would enhance its focus on climate and ESG-linked risks by monitoring proxy voting policies and practices to ensure voting aligns with investors' best interests and expectations, including the business continuity plans of business enterprises in the context of intensifying physical risks linked to climate change. Pertaining to in-scope investment advisors, the SEC cautioned that it would focus on products and services publicized as sustainable, socially responsible, and ESG-conscious. The SEC would also review the consistency and adequacy of those disclosures, and the review of fund advertising for false and misleading statements. Pertaining to Fintech and financial services in general, the SEC stated that its audits would focus on whether companies operate consistently in alignments with their representations to customers and investors via whatever media. The SEC has to date taken more than fifty enforcement actions, with many against broker-dealers on fraud allegations, like individuals running Ponzi scheme, illegal securities offerings and undisclosed payments, but not showing signs of shifting trends, as yet.

The SEC's Division of Examinations issued on April 9, 2021 a Risk Alert, with reference to investment advisers, registered investment companies and private funds offering ESG products and services. It contains observations from recent examinations of these in-scope businesses, giving illustrations of both best practices and problematic behaviors pertaining to ESG matters. Coming at a time of its intended focus on ESG issues, this suggests the potential intention to use the existing disclosure and fiduciary framework for ESG matters in the asset management space, instead of designing for a new procedural approach. The SEC found some companies greenwashing by issuing potentially misleading statements pertaining to their ESG investments through claims that they had designated formal systems in place for investing, but in reality, those systems were never implemented, not developed to deter illegal activities, or not constructed to prevent inaccurate or misleading ESG-linked disclosures. Best practices detected include the integrating of compliance personnel familiar with the companies' identified ESG-linked practices for avoiding materially misleading claims in their ESG-linked marketing materials; the preparation of detailed ESG investment policies and procedures together with research, selection, due diligence and monitoring; disclosing how investments were made under ESG frameworks; providing explicit and simple disclosures pertaining to the companies' approaches to ESG investing, like the highlighting of a company's reliance on third-party advisers to undertake its underlying ESG analysis and managing of ESG-linked funds, inclusive of disclosures in marketing materials offering options on ESG matters.

The Office of Information and Regulatory Affairs on June 11, 2021, issued its Spring 2021 Unified Agenda of Regulatory and Deregulatory Actions report that included short- and long-term regulatory actions that administrative agencies plan to take. These included notable proposed and final SEC rulemaking areas, like disclosure pertaining to climate risk, human capital, together with workforce diversity and corporate board diversity, and cybersecurity risk; investment fund rules, including money market funds, private funds, and ESG funds; and others. The SEC's AMAC on July 7, 2021, approved recommendations by its Subcommittee to implement diversity and inclusion disclosures by registered investment advisers and funds, as well as the strengthening of ESG disclosures for public enterprises and investment products. In support of its recommendations, the committee cited research demonstrating USD 70 trillion of funds under management globally, where less than 1% are managed by minority or female-owned companies. The SEC has also been urged to promote meaningful, consistent and comparable disclosures of material ESG matters by stock issuers, suggest best practices for ESG investment product disclosures, together with explicit descriptions of the product's strategy and investment priorities, as well as product disclosures aligning with a taxonomy developed by the ICI. The Board of Governors of ICI has previously on July 23, 2020, unanimously endorsed the White Paper "Funds' Use of ESG Integration and Sustainable Investing Strategies" authored by ICI ESG Working Group that included encouraging the use of consistent terminology when describing ESG integration and sustainable investing strategies.

Finally, Maria Teresa Cometto in her September 2021 article "Letter from US: SEC Looks Towards Mandatory SEC Disclosure by Companies" in *IPE* that October could be the month when the SEC will propose new rules on climate change and other ESG matters. Feedbacks from consultations that closed on mid-June 2021 ranged from calls for mandatory, annual ESG disclosures in annual reports, to claims that climate-linked disclosures are politically charged, and as such outside the SEC's mission. Cometto further clarified that Gary Gensler, the new SEC chair, had in his end of July 2021 speech at a webinar organized by the UN-backed PRI stated that today's investors are asking for the ability to compare companies with each other. He believed that in general, it is with mandatory disclosures that investors can benefit from that comparability and consistency, whereas with voluntary disclosures, this can lead to a wide range of inconsistent disclosures. She additionally mentioned that CalSTRS, the New York State Common Retirement Fund, and most large public pension funds are in support of this approach. They, together with 180 investors with AUMs reaching USD 2.7 trillion, signed a June 2021 letter coordinated by the sustainability nonprofit Ceres, calling upon the SEC to require all companies to disclose climate risk on an annual basis at the minimum. Cometto clarified that existing SEC guidelines for climate change reporting do not spell out specific required disclosures, with companies having the discretions on what to report. Among those opposing enhanced mandatory ESG disclosures, Cometto cited the US Oil and Gas Association. The Western Energy Alliance claimed in a letter to the SEC that the decision when taken would see the SEC redefining its mission without Congressional authority, thereby expanding its regulatory authority beyond investor protection and capital formation. The National Mining Association argues that the SEC should not create a one-size-fits-all prescriptive, rules-based mandatory disclosure regime given the breadth and scope of information already provided on a voluntary basis.

She also drew attention to remarks from SEC Commissioners opposing enhanced ESG disclosures. This includes SEC commissioner Hester Peirce who in July 2021 had urged the IFRS Foundation not to wade into sustainability standard-setting, as this would improperly equate sustainability standards with financial reporting standards and generate the risk of misleading investors because sustainability standard-setting is an inherently more subjective, less precise, less-focused, more open-ended activity than financial accounting standard-setting. SEC Commissioner Elad Roisman drew attention to SEC's challenges of keeping focused on materiality in ESG rulemaking, and acquiring and maintaining the competency to develop and oversee a disclosure framework that incorporates particularly "E" and "S" information. Commissioner Allison Herren Lee in her June 2021 keynote address at the 2021 Society for Corporate Governance National Conference welcomed 2021's annual proxy season with its unprecedented support for climate-linked proposals, including for racial equity, political spending, and other ESG shareholder initiatives. Lee viewed this as a trend placing greater responsibility on corporate boards to integrate climate and ESG into their decision-making, risk management, compensation, and corporate transparency initiatives.

Then there are the Executive Orders (EO) from the Office of the US President. Sharece Thrower in her January 2021 article "What Is an Executive Order, and Why Don't Presidents Yes Them All the Time" in The Conversation explained that the courts view EO as legally valid, unless they violate the Constitution or existing statutes. EO are unilateral actions giving presidents several advantages, enabling them to move first and act alone in policymaking. Presidents frequently employ them to advance their biggest agenda items through creating task forces or policy initiatives and directing rulemaking. However, EO could be constrained by Congress in various ways, and also could be revoked, and as such are not as durable as laws and regulations. Incoming presidents frequently reverse previous orders, especially those of political opponents.

President Biden, barely hours after taking the oath of office, executed nine EO. Executive actions from President Biden included ordering the Director of the Office of Management Budget (OMB) in conjunction with the Chair of the Council of Economic Adviser, the Director of the National Economic Council, the National Climate Advisor, and the Secretary of the Treasury to publish annually the federal government's climate risk exposure, and improve the accounting of climate-linked expenditures and where suitable curb the federal government's long-term fiscal exposures to climate-related financial risks. The Director of the National Economic Council and OMB's Director have also been instructed by an executive order to develop recommendations for the National Climate Task Force on approaches to integrate climate-linked risk into federal financial management and financial reporting. The Secretary of Labor has been instructed by executive action to explore ways to protect the life savings and pensions of US workers from climate-linked financial risk threats. EO have also been made for the development of climate-linked government-wide financial risk strategy to cover financial needs linked with achieving net-zero GHG emissions for the US economy no later than 2050, and seeking niches where public and private partnerships could help the country in addressing those financing needs. The executive actions also included measurement, evaluation, mitigation and disclosure of climate-linked financial risk to enhance the long-term stability of federal operations.

All in all, the Biden administration has provided clear signals on his big climate change agenda. Taken together with the US currently falling relatively behind the EU and the UK in the framing of various ESG disclosure frameworks, as well as the aggressive postures of international forums on ESG-related matters, it is likely that the US would head toward the issuance of formal ESG guidance, as a matter of time or when, what form, and not so much on the question of if.

ESG reporting in the US, UK, and the EU has a mix of mandatory and voluntary elements, including flexibility, largely because of the complexity and evolving nature of ESG reporting. As such, reporting companies in most jurisdictions, including those in these jurisdictions, have the choice of disclosing ESG information in their annual reports, as stand-alone sustainability reports, or as integrated reports where financial and sustainability information is integrated into one document.

Earlier, the investing community latched on to the ESG terminology and ideas pushed by the UN PRI in 2004-2005, especially institutional investors enthusiastically seeking to integrate ESG when making transaction decisions based on ESG factors or portfolio integration, and in interacting and engaging with issuer companies and voting their shares in particular ways. This is though not altogether novel, as FTSE4Good Index Series were launched in 2001, well before the onset of PRI. The FTSE4Good and the FTSE Russell have had almost two decades of index level return, and over that time, the ESG evaluation process and inclusion criteria have evolved to keep them aligned with industry trends and investor needs. In general, these indices claimed to align with the UN SDGs, have precise rules and focus on data, use transparent methodology, and strong governance process and structures overseen by independent external committees comprising experts within the academia, unions, civil society organizations (CSOs), the investment community, and businesses in general.

FTSE Russell's ESG Ratings, for example, measure the overall quality of a company's management against the tripartite ESG pillars within the context of fourteen designated themes. The "E" factor includes biodiversity, climate change, pollution and resources, supply chain and water security; the "S" factor includes customer responsibility, health and safety, human rights and community, labor standards, and supply chain, while the "G" factor includes anti-corruption, CG, risk management, and tax transparency.

Florian Berg, Kronelia Fabisik & Zacharias Sautner in their ESGI August 2021 empirical-based article "Is History Repeating Itself? The (Un)predictable Past of ESG Ratings" highlighted the following:

(1) AUM from 2010 to 2020 using ESG investing strategies by US-domiciled institutions expanded from USD 3 trillion to more than USD 17 trillion, with one in three US dollars invested now being managed according to ESG

principles. The key challenge in quantifying how well an enterprise performs with respect to ESG factors has been addressed through the use of ESG ratings or scores designed by ESG data providers, led by MSCI's Refinitiv ESG; and Sustainalytics provided by S&P Global and Vigeo-Eiris. ESG ratings matter for investors because fund flows react strongly to the ESG ratings. Questions and doubts are nevertheless raised over their reliability, constancy, and overall quality.

(2) Research insights suggest large disagreements across major ESG rating providers in their evaluations of companies' ESG quality. The MSCI appears to give higher ESG scores to companies linked to it via institutional ownership than to other companies. Some 26% of investment professionals surveyed expressed their concerns with ESG rating reliability, despite some 82% using ESG data in the investment process. Members of the SEC's AMSC have also stated that ESG scores do not go back far in history and are often backfilled.

(3) The empirical analysis undertaken suggests that the score changes have in part been data-mined, such that companies that did better in a particular year experienced *ex post* upgrades in the scores for that year. Data rewriting, as such, alters the outcomes of predictive regressions relating ESG ratings to future stock returns; that is to say, there is outperformance of shares with high-ESG scores in the rewritten data, but not in the initial data. The researchers argue that the outcome of their study reflect the incentive of the data provider to introduce a positive relationship between ESG scores and returns in the data so as to show that their ESG scores are useful for data users developing ESG-linked investing strategies. Accordingly, the researchers claimed that the big differences in outcomes that they documented have implications for empirical test strategies using the provider's ESG data. Going forward, the researchers advocated that investment professionals have to verify whether the original or rewritten ESG scores are required to undertake their tests.

Other empirical studies, such as seen in Ilze Zumente and Natalja Lace in their 2021 article "ESG Rating-Necessity for the Investor or the Company?" in *Sustainability* suggests substantial divergence in the ratings given to European companies. Arising from this empirical and related insights, the researchers suggest that companies should pay attention to the methodologies and practices applied by different agencies to ensure that their initiatives are suitably evaluated, whereas investors should be mindful of the correlation coefficient of only 0.58 between the two most popular ESG ratings. Their analysis on Central and Eastern Europe (CEE) companies further shows significant differences in the trading volume between companies that have been awarded an ESG score and those that have not. This thereby implies the importance of the ESG ratings not only for the investors but also for the issuing companies. In another 2021 article in *Sustainability* "ESG Ratings and Stock Performance During the COVID-19 Crisis," Nils Engelhardt, Jens Ekkenga and Peter Posch find high-ESG-rated European companies to be linked with higher abnormal returns and lower stock volatility, that the social score to be the predominant drivers of their analysis, and that

ESG is value-enhancing in low-trust economies, and in countries with inferior regulations and where lower disclosure standards prevail.

Diving into the digital era, Arthus Hughes, Michael Urban and Dariousz Wojcik in their 2021 *Sustainability* article "Alternative ESG Ratings: How Technological Innovation Is Reshaping Sustainable Investment" suggest that differences in traditional ESG ratings and alternative AI-based ESG ratings are driven by differences in ESG paradigms premised on key issues selection, differences in data sources analyzed, differences in weighting structures for rating aggregation, and differences in controversy analysis. Overall, their analysis shows that the benefits of alternative ESG ratings provided by the AI-based approach included higher levels of standardization, a transparent outside-in perspective on ratings, a more democratic aggregation process, and rigorous real-time analytics. They additionally contended that these characteristics reflect a geographic reconfiguration of ESG rating construction, extending from financial agglomerations to technological and digital spaces of innovation. They further asserted that while alternative AI-based ESG ratings make major promises on how technology could reform sustainable investing, risks remain.

The above concerns on the quality of ESG ratings as provided led to the need for the ratings of raters, something seen earlier in credit ratings provided by the world's four leading CRAs. Sustainability began its Rate the ESG Raters series in 2010. Its "Rate the Raters 2019: Expert Survey Results" report released in 2020 generated the following findings:

(1) Investors and asset managers approach ESG differently.
(2) ESG ratings are employed on a regular basis by many investors, but evaluated differently by each.
(3) ESG ratings are not the only inputs.
(4) Business models matter.
(5) Ratings challenge and occasionally frustrate investors.
(6) ESG ratings have assisted mainstream sustainable investing.
(7) There is no single go-to rating for all investors.
(8) Investors want ESG raters to provide real-time data in shorter reports, and that ESG would potentially become better integrated into traditional financial reporting and research.
(9) Investors want companies to provide better ESG data disclosure, focus on what is most material to the business and to more fully integrate ESG information into financial statements. Other than data, investors want ESG information in one place, commentaries on how corporate leadership thinks about ESG factors and how they fit corporate strategy, as well as information on climate exposure in alignment with TCFD guidelines.
(10) The top sources of ESG information for the investing community are ESG ratings, direct engagements, company reports and in-house research.

Arising from the above and other insights, *Sustainability* recommended the following to issuer companies:

(1) Own your data and your story.
(2) Make your data investor-ready.
(3) Identify priority ESG approaches and proactively engage.
(4) Prioritize among ESG ratings.
(5) Monitor and manage priority ESG ratings.
(6) Know your benchmarks and be alert to red lists.
(7) Ensure ESG drives performance, not just reporting.

The 2020 OECD report "ESG Investing: Practices, Progress and Challenges" coauthored by Boffo and Patalano highlighted the wide categories of metrics, methodologies and approaches that, while valid, contributed to varying outcomes, adding to a menu of ESG investment practices that in sum arrive at an industry consensus on the profile of high-ESG portfolios that may remain open to interpretations. The key findings of their study suggest that ESG ratings differ considerably, depending on the providers selected. This can happen for various reasons, like differences in frameworks, measures, key indicators and metrics, data use, qualitative judgment, and weighting of subcategories. The mixed results over more than ten years raised questions as to the true extent to which ESG drives performance. The researchers argued that the lack of comparability of ESG metrics, ratings, and investing approaches make it difficult for investors to differentiate between managing material ESG risks within their investment mandates, and pursuing ESG outcomes that may need a trade-off in financial performance.

The researchers nevertheless contended that despite these limitations, ESG reporting and scoring have the potential of unlocking significant reams of information on the management and resilience of companies when seeking long-term value creation. ESG ratings as such could be an important market-based mechanism to help investors better align their portfolios with environment and social criteria that align with sustainable development. The meaningfulness of ESG investing needs more initiatives toward consistency of metrics, comparability of ratings methodologies, transparency, and alignment with financial materiality. The researchers advocated that global guidance may be required, despite initiatives by standard-setting entities, regulators, and private sector participants in different jurisdictions, so as to ensure market efficiency, resilience and integrity. In the context of these plethoras of concerns, that are by no means trivial, or easy to solve by market mechanisms, it might be feasible to consider the setting up of independent rate the raters' supervisory bodies along the lines of that created and now successfully relied upon in general in the credit ratings industry worldwide.

6.04 ESG SCANDALS PERSISTENCE

Most major corporate scandals appearing thus far other than those from oil-spilling disasters flow from flaws in the governance or "G" part of the ESG paradigm. This section explores why this appears to be the case, despite the designing and redesigning of both soft and hard laws claiming not to let these recur. Governance scandals in the banking industry keep recurring, and the equivalent seems to be the case too for the nonbanking corporate sectors. Insights from seminal cases in the digital era in the US, the UK, Australia, and elsewhere suggest the persistence of this flaw, despite the implementation of various hard and soft laws to deal with them. These would now be discussed.

The first has to do with widespread financial reporting irregularities and the incentives, opportunities and rationalization in the corporate fraud triangle that arose in the US in the 1930s.[553] Notorious cases exemplified by Insull Utility Investments Company and Ivar Kreuger using complex pyramidal schemes corporate structures, together with inflated assets accounting, and the failure of a big auditing firm to uncover fictitious asset accounting at McKesson & Robins, contributed to the acceleration of the enactment of the SA 1933 and the SEA 1934.[554] At the time, the attention was on corporate frauds and controversies over auditor responsibility and accountability, while the governance lexicon was not yet brought into use. Corporate hierarchies and tight financial regulations curbed frauds subsequent to 1934, but these also brought entrepreneurship advocates like Schumpeter to lament the demise of the entrepreneurs, compounded as it was by the rise of the technocrats of Galbraith's new industrial state.[555]

The maiden reference to governance process flaws was brought up in the *Maxwell*[556] case in the 1970s, *Polly Peck*[557]case in the late 1980s, and the *BCCI*[558] case in 1991 in the UK. These cases showed remarkable resemblance of being led and managed by domineering CEOs sidelining the board, especially independent directors, abusive diversion of corporate assets, excessive risk-taking through overabundant use of debts, financial reporting irregularities, and weaknesses of external auditing. Corporate scandals, such as these, that unfolded at the time, were one of the reasons for the setting up of the CC to study governance issues. This ultimately led to the release of the 1992 Cadbury Report that recommended the use of best CG Code practices.[559] The Code, among others, recommends board independence with sufficient numbers of NEDs of calibers, such that no one individual has unfettered decision-making powers. However, the CC has been careful in stressing the need for a balance to be struck, as no system of control, or level of governance, could eliminate the risk of fraud without shackling business innovations. Still, the late 1980s and early 1990s were rocked by various notorious corporate scandals suggesting that corporate activities have been plagued by frauds and poor internal and external controls.[560] These continued to recur,

553. H. van Driel. 2019. "Financial fraud, scandals and regulation: A conceptual framework and literature review". *Business History,* Vol. 61 (8): 1259-1299.
554. B. Eichengreen. 2014. *Hall of mirrors: The great depression, the Great Recession, and the uses and misuses of history.* New York: Oxford University.
555. S. Toms. 2019. "Financial scandals: A historical overview". *Accounting and Business Research,* Vol. 49 (5): 477-499.
556. *Maxwell v. Department of Trade and Industry (CA 1974) [1974] QB 523, [1974] 2 WLR 338.*
557. Polly Peck International, re (No2) (ChD 1993) [1994] 1 BCLC 574.
558. Bank of Credit and Commerce International SA, re (no. 3) (CA 1992) [1993] BCLC 1490.
559. Cadbury Report. 1992. *Report of the Committee on the Financial Aspects of CG.* London: Gee.
560. S. Toms. 2019. "Financial scandals: A historical overview". *Accounting and Business Research,* Vol. 49 (5): 477-499.

despite fresh attempts in making financial reporting and accounting standards up to the mark, or fit for purpose.

The late 1990s saw extensive financial reporting irregularities of another variant in corporate America. Here, many so-called Dotcom pretenders engaged in fraudulent claims of high corporate profitability made through deceptive and abusive use of off-balance sheet mechanisms, like opaque complex structured financial products and opaque special purpose acquisition companies (SPACs).[561] The fall of Enron and WorldCom in 2001 drew out unprecedented series of corporate and accounting malfeasance that had fraudulently masked and fueled the market boom. It started with the revelations brokered by a whistleblowing corporate insider[562] that the then widely admired Enron[563] had manipulated its profitability by masking its debts in off-book partnerships while simultaneously manipulating also the California and Texas energy markets. This was followed almost a year later by the collapse of WorldCom,[564] that was bigger in terms of bankruptcy size, but less complicated in terms of corporate and financial complexities, but still equally damning.

Toward the end of 2002, more than two dozen large public corporations conceded inflating their revenues through various accounting gimmicks that initially escaped the scrutiny of their statutory auditors. It had become increasingly apparent that as these shenanigans came to light that these were somehow condoned by captive board of directors, and abetted by the deregulations of telecommunications[565] and financial services[566] that had spiked the market. Matters came to a head subsequent to the resignation of NYSE Chairman Richard Grasso. The reinforced outrage pertains to very loose oversights, including the revelations that the Big Board's directors had only a vague understanding of how the overgenerous compensation package given to Grasso might have compromised the CEO entrusted with the overseeing of their industry's practices.[567]Even more disturbing were the revelations that ten of Wall Street's largest investment banking firms agreed to pay USD 1.4 billion in penalties to settle charges of fraudulent practices they had partake in during the heady days of the capital market in the late 1990s. These fraudulent activities were unmasked by the then New York Attorney General Eliot Spitzer who found market analysts had distorted their

---

561. D.J. Morrisey. 2005. "After the ball is over: Investor remedies in the wake of the Dot-Com crash and recent corporate scandals". *Nebraska Law Review*, Vol. 83 (3): 732-765; B. Taylor. 2006. "CG: The crisis, investors' losses and the decline in public trust". In D. Hahn & B. Taylor (eds.). *Strategische Unterhmungsplanung- Strategische Unternehmungsfuhrung*. Berlin: Springer.
562. S. Watkins, 2003. "Former Enron Vice-President Sherron Watkins on the Enron Collapse". *Academy of Management Executive*, Vol. 17 (4):119-125.
563. *Skilling v. United States (No. 08-1394) 2010*; B. McLean & P. Elkind. 2004. *The smartest guys in the room: The amazing rise and scandalous fall of Enron*. London: Portfolio Trade.
564. *SEC v. WorldCom, Inc., 273 F. Supp. 2d 431 (S.D.N.Y. 2003).*
565. S. Cork. 2002. "From boom to bust". *Insolvency Law and Practice*, Vol. 18 (6): 197-199.
566. S. Kornrich & A. Hicks. "The rise of finance: Causes and consequences of financialization". *Socio-Economic Review*, Vol. 13 (3); 411-415; D. Silvers & H. Slavkin. 2008. "The legacy of deregulation and the financial crisis". *Journal of Business & technology Law*, Vol. 4 (2): 304-347; J. Crotty. 2009. "Structural causes of the global financial crisis: A critical assessment of the new financial architecture". *Cambridge Journal of Economics*, Vol. 33 (2009): 563-580.
567. K. Eichenwald. 2003. "In a string of corporate troubles, critics focus on board's failings". *New York Times 21/09/03*, section 1, p. 1.

research report or stock ratings to gain investment banking business for their clients, and were rewarded for their deceptions by huge payouts.[568]

It is helpful to note that Rule 10b-5 of the SEA 1934 is a criminal prohibition prohibiting all deceitful practices and schemes to defraud pertaining to securities transactions. In the six decades that followed this legislation, the court had implied a private right of action from that rule, thereby enabling defrauded investors to use it to recover damages.[569] In turn, brokers' practices have been highly regulated by the SEC and by self-regulatory agencies, such as the NYSE and the National Association of Securities Dealers.[570] However, between the mid-1970s and the mid-1990s, federal securities laws had become progressively less hospitable to the claims of investors, mainly arising from the flow of new legislations and judicial interpretation of existing legislations.[571]

Foremost in the 1970s, the Supreme Court imposed new restrictions on private claims pursued under Rule 10b-5. These cases require the plaintiff to allege that an actual securities transaction had happened,[572] that the defendant acted with scienter,[573] and that deception had been involved through misrepresentation or a nondisclosure of material fact.[574] The first case decision ruled out 10b-5 claims arising from a fraud that caused an investor to refrain from transacting in particular securities;[575] the second implied that mere misrepresentation was no longer actionable under that provision of the federal securities laws,[576] while the third decision demanding actual deception appeared to preclude claims not having to do with actual misstatement or concealment of material fact.[577] Subsequent rulings from the High Court and lower federal appellate courts extended additional barrier to investor suits. A ruling from the Supreme Court, for example, shortened statutes of limitations in securities fraud cases,[578] a Second Circuit Court decision condoned deceptive exaggerations by a broker on the basis that it was not material, or that the investor's reliance on such statements was unjustified,[579] and a Second Circuit opinion[580] that appeared to apply a very narrow interpretation of the parole evidence rule to disregard blatantly false oral statements by a broker that were denied by boilerplate disclosures in written documents extended to the investor. These inhospitable rulings were reinforced by two

568. New York Times. 2003. "Finding fraud on Wall Street", *New York Times Editorial 29/04/03, A28; In re Merrill Lynch & Co., 273 F. Supp. 2d 351 (S.D.N.Y. 2003).*
569. *Kardon v. National Gypsum Co., 69F. Supp. 512 (E.D. Pa. 1946); Herman & MacLean v. Huddleston, 459 U.S. 375 (1983).*
570. T.L. Hazen. 2009. *The law of securities regulation, 6th edition.* Eagan: West Academic Publishing.
571. M.L. Steinberg. 1996. "Securities arbitration: Better for investors than the courts?". *Brooklyn Law Review*, Vol. 62 (4): 1503-1532.
572. *Blue Chip Stamps v. Manor Drug Stores, 421 U.S. 723 (1975).*
573. *Ernst & Ernst v. Hochfelder, 425 U.S. 185 (1976).*
574. *Santa Fe Indus v. Green, 430 U.S. 462 (1977).*
575. *Blue Chip Stamps, 421 U.S. at 755.*
576. *Hochfelder, 425 U.S. at 194.*
577. *Santa Fe Indus. 430 U.S. at 475-476.*
578. *Lampf, Pleva, Lipkind, Prupis & Petigrew v. Gilbertson*, 501 U.S. 350 (1991).
579. *Zerman v. Ball*, 735 F. 2d 15, 21 (2d Cir. 1984).
580. *Acme Propane, Inc. v. Tenexco, Inc. 844 F. 2d 1317, 1325 (7th Cir. 1988); Zubrist v. Coal-X Inc., 708 F. 2d 1511 (10th Cir. 1983).*

Supreme Court decisions in the mid-1990s that closed the courthouse entrance on meaningful investor claims.

In the first, the Court provided an overly restrictive interpretation to an express cause of action that could have provided liability for fraud in securities sales upon a lesser demonstration of intent than the scienter requirement of Rule 10b-5.[581] while the second[582] interpreted Rule 10b-5 as precluding a remedy against those who were secondarily responsible for a securities fraud, directly ruling out assisting and abetting liability, and likely respondent superior claims,[583]too. On top of this, the Litigation Reform Act 1995 (PSLRA) ushered in a host of restrictions on claims under the federal securities laws, in particular, a more stringent legislative reinforcement of the requirement in Federal Rule of Civil Procedure 9(b) that fraud be pled with particularity.[584] These restrictive developments placed various difficult barriers for investors who had sought relief for the deceptive frauds perpetrated during the 2000 Dotcom bubble, but preliminary results in one suit arising from the Enron debacle[585] showed some juridical sympathy for shareholder rights.

The class action suit targeted Enron's former lead officers and directors, lawyers and auditors, and banks providing various financial services that included the underwriting of its securities and loans offered to various SPACs that enjoyed important but undisclosed relationships with it. The company's operations have been described as an enormous Ponzi scheme.[586] It purported to be generating income from arm's-length transactions with SPACs that it in reality controlled, and where the resulting false revenues propped the corporation's share price artificially high to enable it to continuously raise fresh capital from public securities offerings. Corporate insiders have been enriched through these, while the sham dealings carved up huge fees for the corporation's lawyers, outside accountants, and bankers. These people were allegedly complicit in the fraudulent activity.[587] The court found that, for the most part, the plaintiffs had met their pleading standards by alleging, with the requisite particularity, that each defendant was potentially culpable for primary involvements in the fraud.[588]

A different series of court actions fanning out of such corporate scandals targeted Merrill Lynch, one of the major securities firms that sponsored and allegedly profited from fraudulent research report by its analysts, did not fare so well for the plaintiffs. The court regarded their claims with scant sympathy.[589] On the other hand, investors found more promise of relief in a major consolidated action challenging the practices of a number of investment banks that drove up the price of IPOs that they underwrote,

581. *Gustafson v. Alloyd Co., 513 U.S. 561 (1995).*
582. *Cent. Bank of Denver, N.A. v. First Interstate Bank of Denver, N.A., 511 U.S. 164 (1994).*
583. E. Mason. 2003. "Brokers face rash of angry investors". *Boston Business Journal 06/06/03,* https://www.bizjournals.com/boston/stories/2003/06/09/story2.html?page=1, accessed November 10, 2020.
584. *FED. R. Civ. P. 9(b).* The PSLRA inserted that provision to the SEA as new section 21D(b).
585. *In re Enron Corp. Sec., Derivative & ERISA Litig., 235 F. Supp 2d 549 (S.D. Tex. 2002).*
586. J. Toobin. 2002. "The man changing Enron". *New Yorker 09/09/02,* p. 86.
587. *Re Enron, 235 F. Supp 2d* at 614.
588. *In re Enron, 235 F. Supp. 2d* at 636-656.
589. *In re Merrill Lynch, 273 F. Supp. 2d* at 358-377.

some over three hundred high-tech and Internet companies.[590] The court in a similar vein also upheld claims under section 10(b) for material misstatements and market manipulation.

The enactment of SOX, together with bold supportive monetary policy actions of the Fed under the baton of Alan Greenspan, helped to provide good foundation for the next subsequent half decade of good economic growth, that in reality were fanned again by artificial financial props, this time in even more complicated structured products dressed as tantalizing high-profit generating schemes. The 2000 Dotcom bubble saw corporations in high street making massive abusive use of off-balance sheet devices, but this time around in 2007, banks and financial services providers were the ones using these devices massively in a manipulative fashion that they once condemned. Owing to the nature of banking and financial services, the impact on the economy was massive and could not be curbed in the same manner as what happened in the Dotcom bubble because this had vast contagion effect,[591] that later radiated out of the US into other linked economies, like the UK,[592] the EU, and other major economies.

Various US mega global banks were seriously implicated with contributions to the contagion. The whole shameful saga began with the sale of Bear Sterns to JP Morgan Chase to avoid bankruptcy, as engineered by the Federal Reserve in March 2008. Escalation of unemployment from 5% to 10% toward the final quarter of 2009 was accentuated by more mortgage foreclosures and more steep falls in property prices. The US government took over or bailed out Fannie and Freddie Mac to avoid their potential collapse at about the same time. Merrill Lynch, the then world's biggest brokerage firm, was sold to Bank of America, after being inflicted by massive losses arising from derivatives trading. The bailout was overseen by the US Treasury as a TBTF enterprise[593] with heavy contagion implications in mid-September 2008. Also substantially harmed by derivatives trading, Lehman Brothers (LB) was declared bankrupt in mid-September 2008, when the Federal Reserve failed to locate suitable purchaser for the firm. AIG, a leading global insurance firm which was steeply involved in complex structured products, like collateralized debt obligations (CDOs), was declared a TBTF, and too had to be saved by emergency lending from the Federal Reserve in mid-September 2008. The US Treasury noting the potential heavy and possibly fatal blows to the US economy launched a USD 700 billion Troubled Asset Relief Program (TARP) in mid-October that became effective in December 2008.

Sensing the contagion risk of the crisis, the Federal Reserve launched a multitrillion initiative injecting liquidity into financial services firms through purchase of bad diminished assets to help sustain global liquidity via arrangements with other central

590. *In re Initial Pub. Offering Sec. Litig., 241 F. Supp. 2d 281 (S.D.N.Y. 2003).*
591. M. Jickling. 2010. "Causes of the financial crisis". *Congressional Research Service (CRS) Report 7-5700 09/04/10*, https://fas.org/sgp/crs/misc/R40173.pdf, accessed November 10, 2020.
592. L.S. Talani. 2011. "The impact of the global financial crisis on the City of London: Towards the end of hegemony?." *Competition and Change*, Vol. 15 (91): 11-30.
593. R. Pozen. 2010. *Too big to save? How to fix the U.S. financial system.* New Jersey: John Wiley & Sons Inc.

banks. Iceland's banking system collapsed, and had to be nationalized by its government in October 2008, while the UK launched a GBP 500 support initiative for seriously impacted UK banks. The following month, China announced a CNY 586 billion injection to stimulate its economy and indirectly contributed to the global rescue efforts. This was followed by numerous Summit Meetings of G20 Finance Ministers and Central Bank Governors from November 2008 to November 2012 and beyond. The US went further with a USD 787 billion stimulus plan in mid-February 2009. By December 2009, the Eurozone mired with high debts, and large budget deficits in Italy, Spain, Portugal and Greece became plagued by risks of bank insolvencies on massive scales from December 2009 to December 2012. These necessitated bailouts in various Member States, including Greece and the UK. The US responded further with enactment of DFA 2010 and its implementation from August 2010 to December 2012. The world economy gradually recovered, with big contributions to the turnaround by many large Asian economies that had deployed their surplus savings well when compared to the earlier 1997 AFC.

The above macroeconomic insights served to show the big risks flowing from the greater financialization of the global economy, and in particular in big advanced economies of the US, UK, and the EU. Importantly, it showed how and why big economies could contain the crisis when working together decisively and quickly. These macro aspects aside, the micro aspects, and in particular the conduct and behaviors of the implicated banks and the failures of various financial gatekeepers in doing the right things merit good attention too.

Bear Stearns threw a shine on the then brewing crisis when it got acquired by JP Morgan Chase in March 2008. The Financial Crisis Inquiry Commission (FCIC) report[594] concluded that the failure of Bear Stearns and its resulting government-assisted rescue were caused by its excessive exposures to risky mortgage assets, its reliance on short-term funding, and high debt levels. In turn, these deficiencies flowed from flawed governance and risk management, exemplified by its executive and employee compensation system that was based primarily on return on equity metrics, thereby creating incentive to apply excessive debt levels and with focus on short-term quarterly or annual profits that provided the tripartite links between compensation, profits, and share prices. Bear's governance culture was described as being straight out of the 1920s, with the board meeting just six times annually, and leaving the primary oversight of the firm to its all-insider executive committee.[595] It only had a finance and risk committee barely a year before its downfall, while two members of its audit committee appeared overloaded with duties in six other enterprises. There was pushback against this contention, with the observation that there were no Enron-style frauds. There have been also little criticisms of the governance of companies that were not under severe financial stress, directors of troubled firms orchestrating CEO turnover at rates exceeding the norm in public enterprises, and governance processes

594. FCIC. 2011. *Final report of the National Commission on the causes of the financial and economic crisis in the United States*, Washington, DC: FCIC.
595. J.R. Finlay. 2008. "Outrage of the week: Leadership fiddles while Bear Stearns burns", http://finlayongovernance.com/?p=423, accessed November 10, 2020.

operating well in corporations removed from the S&P 500. This evidence implies that there were no good justifications for fundamental reforms of the then state of governance arrangements.[596] Still, Bears had to be rescued through a government-assisted purchase led by JP Morgan, as the government considered it too interconnected to fail. The failures in Bears in part have been attributed to inadequate supervision by the SEC, in particular for its failure to restrict the highly risky postures in Bears that facilitated undue leverage, but insufficient liquidity.[597]

The FCIC unsurprisingly report concluded that the business approach of government-sponsored enterprises (GSEs) of Fannie Mae and Freddie Mac as private sector, publicly traded, profit-making enterprises with implicit government backing and a public mission has been fundamentally flawed. The FCIC was of the view that Fannie Mae had engaged in extremely risky practices. These were shown in actions taken to meet Wall Street expectations for growth and artificially increasing market shares to ensure generous compensation for employees, while balancing this with the realization of affordable housing goals imposed by the Department of Housing and Urban Development, especially from 2005 on, led to its fall. The GSEs justify their activities in part on the broad and sustained public policy support for homeownership. Risky lending and securitization led to significant losses at Fannie Mae, which, together with its excessive leverage permitted by law, contributed to its failure.

The FCIC also observed that governance, including risk management, faltered at the GSEs, in part, because of skewed compensation methodologies.[598] The Office of Federal Housing Enterprise Oversight lacked the authority and capacity to sufficiently regulate the GSEs, as the GSEs exercised considerable political power and have been successfully able to resist legislation and regulatory action that would have strengthened oversight of them and restricted their risk-taking activities. Further, the government's decision in early 2008 in supporting the increase in GSEs' mortgage activities and risk to support the collapsing mortgage market, despite unsound financial health of the enterprises, is also flawed. These led to enhanced losses at the GSEs, but their actions though gave support to the mortgage market. The losses were ultimately borne by taxpayers, and clearly reflected the conflicted nature of the GSEs' dual mandates. However, GSE mortgage securities essentially maintained their value throughout the crisis and did not contribute to the significant financial harm that was central to the crisis. The public actions taken to support Fannie Mae and Freddie Mac have been effective in their short-term goal of supporting the housing market. These also helped to remove the two enterprises as sources of systemic risks to the financial system.[599] Nevertheless, these policy actions have yet to achieve the goal of reforming the system of residential mortgage finance.

596. B.R. Cheffins. 2009. "Did CG "fail" during the 2008 stock market meltdown? The case of the S&P meltdown". *ECGI Working Paper Series in Law No. 124/2009 July 2009*, https://ecgi.global/sites/default/files/working_papers/documents/SSRN-id1396126.pdf, accessed November 10, 2020.
597. FCIC 2011, *supra* note [594].
598. FCIC 2011, *supra* note [594].
599. W.S. Frame, et al. 2015. "The rescue of Fannie Mae and Freddie Mac". *FRBNY Staff Report No. 719 March 2015.*

Merrill Lynch, one of the three major investment banks in the US, had to merge with the Bank of America, but was caught in the tectonic seismic shift from market disruption to market failure because of the bankruptcy of LB. Merrill Lynch disclosed in November 2008 a third-quarter loss of some USD 8.25 billion and a further estimated fourth-quarter loss of some USD 12 billion that eventually turned out to be worse, at USD 15 billion. A day later, it issued a warning alert that its ability to mitigate its risk by selling or hedging its exposures had been weakened by the market environment, with future results continuing to be materially impacted by valuation adjustments applied to these positions because of the extreme volatility of the financial markets. Bank of America's consummation of Merrill Lynch ultimately was rescued by funding from TARP and insurance protection for a market exposure of USD 118 billion in assets. Merrill's acquisition under the direction of the Treasury and the Federal Reserve has been deemed to be in the best interests of the financial systems, the economy and the country as its collapse on the heels of Lehman's failure would have induced systemic havoc or required AIG-style government bailout.[600]

Publicly available facts suggest that Bank of America's board has been grossly negligent in the process used to approve the Merrill acquisition, and accordingly interpreted as being worse than simple negligence.[601] The quality of due diligence was questionable, given that it was achieved in a matter of hours for a big and complex bank that Merrill had been. Indeed, only a deal team with proper skills and sufficient time doing a bottom-up analysis of the internal books could likely have been the only way to achieve reasonable due diligence, especially when the target had been a heavily distressed sizeable ailing financial institution. The merger execution was thus allegedly flawed, while the decision to close the flawed deal had also been equally problematic.

As it is, the Bank of America made the important decisions of not exercising the materially adverse clause, not to renegotiate the purchase price, and not to inform shareholders of accelerating losses at Merrill, before closing the deal. Bank of America when relying on the informed decision process was argued to be entitled to the protection of the BJR, absent disloyalty or bad faith.[602] Though the board's decision could be deemed informed, the board was conflicted, or not independent based on the facts at the time. However, given the absence of a viable legal option, neither the shareholders nor the board could have taken any action to avoid the losses, and therefore the board had no fiduciary duty under state law to disclose the Merrill losses, however material.[603] At the time, market volatility impacted the values of assets and liabilities on a day-to-day, market-to-market basis. On this ground, voluntary disclosure of bad news in an unstable market could have resulted in greater harm to both banks and to a financial market already in peril.[604]

600. R.J. Rhee. 2010. "Case study of the Bank of America and Merrill Lynch merger", *University of Maryland Legal Studies Research Paper No. 2010-21.*
601. W.T. Allen et al. 2001. "Function over form: A reassessment of standards of review on Delaware corporation law". *Business Law,* Vol. 50 (2001): 1287-1300; *Van Gorkom. 488 A. 2d at 873.*
602. *Gantler v. Stephens,* 965 A. 2d 695, 706 (Del. 2009).
603. Rhee 2010, *supra* note [600].
604. Rhee 2010, *supra* note [600].

Insights from the case suggest that more broadly, there was a real possibility, though unlikely, given the facts, that shareholders have been financially harmed in terms of assumption of large short-term losses to avoid the injection of more systemic risk into a crippled financial system. Bank of America's management and its board prompted by government entreaties have been motivated in part at least to advance the public's interest in stabilizing a financial crisis over the shareholders' immediate pecuniary interest. An important aspect of governance revealed by the case has been that governance is not always a purely private matter, but instead can be a public-private coordinated decision in unprecedented times of national crisis or systemic risk.[605] Also, there simply was no injury to shareholders under the assumption that their votes for the merger were not tainted by faulty disclosure.[606] However, board efficacy at Merrill itself could have been compromised by some board members without meaningful accounting or financial expertise, almost the equivalent of Citigroup's board that had a dearth of independent directors with financial expertise at the time.

Also, Merrill's board lacked knowledge about the strategic direction of the firm so as to be able to provide proper oversight of executive decisions. The board, as such, had been compositionally and functionally ill-equipped to effectively perform their governance functions.[607] Also, the part-time nature of boards distorted incentives driven by the short-term outlook many companies felt compelled to adopt due to pressure to continually meet the market's periodic return on investment expectations.[608] This pressure left board members in positions where their duties to monitor managers and to maximize shareholder value were in conflict.[609] To be able to move beyond specific solutions to systemic remedies, there is a need to focus on how to change the functional relationship between the relevant parties to better achieve the desired results. Organizational strategy provides a framework for proposing functional changes at corporate boards.[610] On this perspective, financial failures based on faulty strategy should not be surprising to a board and the shareholders they represent, and instead should have been subject to rigorous review and close scrutiny from a board that functioning in manners more consistent with a skilled system of checks on executive management, as opposed to rubberstamping, that uncritically accepted management's recommendations.[611]

Subsequent to the collapse of the US subprime mortgage market in February 2007, the downturn in the global financial markets accelerated. LB substantially exposed to the US subprime and commercial real estate markets faced enhanced levels of distress. Dick Fuld, LB's CEO, upon failures to secure merger deals with Bank of America and Barclays Bank, was sidelined by US federal officials who began directly

605. Rhee 2010, *supra* note [600].
606. Rhee 2010, *supra* note [600].
607. N.F. Sharpe. 2010. "Rethinking board function in the wake of the 2008 financial crisis". *Journal of Business & Technology Law*, Vol. 5 (1): 99-111.
608. C.A. Williams. 2006. "A Tale of two trajectories". *Fordham Law Review*, Vol. 75 (3): 1629-1660.
609. Williams 2006, *supra* note [608].
610. M.C. Jensen. 2001. *Foundations of organizational strategy*. Boston: Harvard University Press.
611. Jensen 2001, *supra* note [610].

managing the negotiations pertaining to LB's fate. LB's Board ultimately acquiesced to the government's stand in September 2008 that the investment bank's bankruptcy was in the best interest of the national economy. LB's problem had a lot to do with the shifting of its strategy from making money for clients to proprietary trading itself that led to a permissive management culture favoring short-term investment gains and unrealized profits via mark-to-market accounting over financial sustainability.[612]

This was exemplified by the change in lexicon for LB's investments from securities, as typically done by brokerage firms in 2003, to financial instruments in 2007. This reflected its change to a trading firm with primary interest for its own shareholders and management, rather than for its customers, as was the case in 2003. Thus, securities rightfully treated as short-term assets in 2003 became tagged as long-term assets in 2007 because of this dramatic shift in investment approach that had serious cash flow management implications. LB was extremely leveraged, with about 3%-4% of assets from shareholders equity, while the leftover assets were financed by debts.[613] Also, while 48% of LB's long-term assets were financed by short-term debt in 2003, some 91% of its long-term and highly toxic assets were funded by 79% short-term debts. LB was also undercapitalized in 2007 at some 4%,[614] while the stipulated capital requirement was at 10% under the Glass Segal Act, or 7% under Basel III recommendations. This meant that for LB, a mere 3.6% write-down of mortgage-backed or other toxic investments would have eliminated all its capital buffer. The leading causes for LB's eventual bankruptcy were the bazaar for credit default swaps, falsification of financial statement where the Repo 105 procedure played a key role in presenting a healthier financial picture of the bank than it actually was in, as well as alleged unethical behaviors of top executives.[615]

Other than the excessively risky approach taken by LB and others, the governance process for risk management and corporate oversight had been dismal.[616] The CEO at LB was also the Chairperson for its board for well over sixteen years. Other board members also enjoyed their entrenched positions over long periods as most were reelected annually, with the bulk of board members at a very senior age, and were mostly retirees, or from the academia. There were poor visible signs of board independence, while the risk management committee comprising senior retirees with little finance or accounting experiences had only two meetings in 2006 and 2007 before its collapse. There was a heavy reliance on short-term compensation mix, with priority on short-term cash bonus and stock options, while information for these and other vital financial information were masked in opaque reporting disclosures. In short, the board failed poorly at its oversight role, while the CEO cum board Chairman dominated board proceedings to hamper the flow of conventional good governance practices.

612. H. Grove & L. Patelli. 2013. "Lehman Brothers and Bear Stearns: Risk assessment and CG differences?." *Corporate Ownership and Control*, Vol. 11 (1): 611-620.
613. P. Chadha. 2016. "What caused the failure of Lehman Brothers? Could it have been prevented? How? Recommendations for going forward". *International Journal of Accounting Research S1:002*. https://www.doi:10.4172/2472-114X.S1-002, accessed November 10, 2020.
614. Grove & Patelli 2013, *supra* note [612].
615. Chadha 2016, *supra* note [613].
616. Grove & Patelli 2013, *supra* note [612].

In the end, the failure at LB pointed to various interrelated and mutual causes. These included irresponsible lending practices, excessive reliance on credit ratings by investors, extensive view of markets marked by weaker principles and regulatory breach, vicious incentives and asymmetric return arrangements encouraging unwarranted risk-taking, deficient management, weak oversight of entities involved in the marketing and purchasing of complex financial products, and the lack of an effective monitoring and financial regulatory framework.[617]

Other big global banks caught by the crisis included Citigroup (CGR) and GS. CGR has been held up as the poster child for the elusive promises and manifold pitfalls of universal banking. It claimed to be the financial conglomerate of the future with the superior ability to withstand shocks flowing from wide diversified services, and the capacity to provide unparalleled convenience to customers via one-stop shopping for a wide range of banking, securities and insurance services. Toward 2009, such bold claims turned to ashes, as the bank's high-risk, high-growth strategy turned fatal. The dismal outcome of this strategy resulted in the bank having to write down USD 130 billion of its loans and investments from the second half of 2007 through to the end of 2009. The government had to bail out the bank with injection of USD 45 billion fresh capital and a further infusion of USD 500 billion in the form of asset guarantees, debt guarantees and liquidity assistance. All these in short provided more financial assistance to CGR than any other bank during the financial crisis.[618]

CGR's litany of repeated scandals and bailout became serious setbacks for advocates of universal banking. They had earlier claimed that financial conglomerates could withstand the crisis relatively better than stand-alone investment banks, like Bear Stearns, Lehman and Merrill. In reality, the survival of CGR, Bank of America and others depended on the government's preparedness to provide them with enormous bailout packages. This also reflected a wider policy decision that no financial supermarket could possibly be allowed to fail, in other words falling under the TBTF argument.[619]

Management missteps at CGR inflicted heavy losses for shareholders. Its share prices fell by 17% under Chuck Prince, 89% under Vikram Pandit, and subsequent successors had to issue the dismal statement that the bank's shares were trading at only 67% of its book value in January 2013.[620] Toward the end of 2008, the bank became not only TBTF but also too wieldy to manage or regulate, with regulators having to pressure its management to reduce the bank size by divesting noncore assets.[621] CGR then adopted a plan to reduce its assets from USD 2.36 trillion in September 2007 to

617. Chada 2016, *supra* note [613].
618. Y. Onaran. 2011. *Zombie banks: How broken banks and debtor nations are crippling the global economy*. New Jersey: John Wiley.
619. J. Authers. 2012. "Markets make best case for Glass-Stegall". *Financial Times 14/07/12*, http://www.ft.com/cms/s/0/14e08822-eb04-11e2-9fcc-00144feabdc0, accessed November 10, 2020; D. Leonard. 2011. "Company on fire? Light a cigar: Why troubled companies like Citigroup keep hiring Dick Parsons". *Bloomberg Business March 28 – April 3 2011*, pp. 85-90.
620. D. Griffin. 2013. "Citigroup goal is to stop shareholder capital destruction". *Bloomberg 17/01/13*, http://www.bloomberg.com/news/2013-01-17/citi-ceo-says-goal-is-to-stop, accessed November 10, 2020.
621. A. Shin. 2008. "Citi's relentless quest for growth". *Washington Post 25/11/08*.

USD 1.94 trillion in September 2012.[622] Despite this, the bank retained a core group of universal banking operations, including trading in equity and debt securities, trading in foreign exchange, securities underwriting, and other investment banking activities. Hence, despite the bank's unprofitable experiences with capital market activities, it appeared unlikely that it would opt voluntarily to divest those activities and return to its commercial banking root. The bank's cofounders conceded that the universal banking model failed to achieve the bullish projections of success when CGR was created in 1998. Former co-CEO John Reed had to apologize in 2009 for his role in creating CGR and added further that Congress made a mistake when it repealed the Glass-Steagall Act in 1999.[623]

His observation was that the greatest problem the bank encountered was that of clashing cultures between traders and commercial bankers, with the trading culture eventually gaining more prominence and dominance.[624] This enhanced focus on trading ultimately undermined the effectiveness of the bank's risk management system.[625] This has been attributed to the reluctance of risk executives to challenge high-risk capital market transactions, as the completion of those transactions had become the leading metric for determining compensation. Universal banking moreover did not produce the hoped-for savings for CGR because the bank needed to hire highly paid investments bankers to sell sophisticated products. CGR's management changed its initial 2010 assumption that the bank was impregnable to the view of urging policymakers to split up investment banking so that taxpayers and depositors would never be at risk. This option would keep financial leverage of commercial banks at reasonable levels, and with stand-alone investment banks being able to absorb some mistakes without threatening systemic crisis.[626] These conceding statements from the bank's management were largely consistent with the bank's lamentable record of managerial and regulatory failures. The bank's checkered history suggests that the universal banking approach that it adopted has been deeply flawed by its excessive organizational complexity, its vulnerability to culture clashes and conflicts of interest, and its tendency to permit excessive risk-taking within far-flung, semiautonomous units lacking sufficient oversight from either senior management or regulatory agencies.[627]

CGR's other senior board members, like Robert Rubin in the reaffirmation of their faiths in universal banking attributed the bank's problems not on organizational or

622. E. Dash. 2009. "Citigroup plans to split itself up by taking apart the financial supermarket". *New York Times 14/01/09, B1.*
623. B. Ivry. 2009. "Reed says 'I'm sorry' for role in creating Citigroup". *Bloomberg 06/11/09,* http://www.bloomberg.com/apps/news?pid=newsarchive&sid, accessed November 10, 2020.
624. J. Authers. 2013. "Culture clash means banks must split. Says former Citi chief". *Financial Times 08/09/13,* http://www.ft.com/intl/cms/s/0/2cfa6f18-1575-11e3-950a-00144feabdc0, accessed November 10, 2020.
625. Authers 2013, *supra* note [624].
626. K. Wack. 2012. "Weill puts Glass-Steagall back on Washington's agenda". *American Banker 26/07/12.*
627. A.E. Wilmarth Jr. 2014. "Citigroup: A case study in managerial and regulatory failures". *Indiana Law Review,* Vol. 47 (2014): 69-137.

managerial limitations, but rather on a rare confluence of economic events that created a perfect storm that nobody could have foreseen.[628] For him and others, the US needed megabanks like CGR so as to serve global business corporations and to compete with foreign universal banks.[629] Most big banks did not share the view that the TBTF policy has to be the price that must be paid for the continuing existence of global mega banks. This price is seen as simply too big to accept in consideration of the massive governmental bailouts that were needed to rescue CGR, Bank of America and others during the 2007-2009 GFC,[630] besides the enormous economic costs inflicted by the crisis. Also, it could be highly doubtful whether the US, UK, and the EU would have the required fiscal and monetary resources to finance similar bailouts of megabanks should another financial crisis in future decades arise.[631] Instead, others advocate legal reforms that would remove government subsidies currently exploited by financial conglomerates. The removal of such subsidies would subject universal banks to market forces equivalent to those that forced the breakup of many commercial and industrial conglomerates during the 1980s and 1990s.[632] Far-reaching measures, including maximum size caps on financial institutions and a Glass-Steagall type of bank separations, and other capital market activities have also been advocated.[633]

Away from banking, mega insurance entity, AIG had more than USD 1 trillion in assets at the time of the crisis. However, most of its liquid assets, including cash, were held by regulated insurance subsidiaries whose regulators did not allow the cash to flow freely up to the holding company, much less to ailing subsidiaries, like AIG Financial products. Moreover, AIG's liabilities especially those due in the near term were much bigger than the USD 9 billion on hand. The FCIC eventually concluded that AIG failed and has to be bail out by the government. AIG's failure has been attributed primarily to its enormous sales of credit default swaps without providing initial collateral, without setting aside reasonable levels of capital reserves, without sufficient hedging of its exposures, as well as the profound failure in its entire governance process, especially its risk management practices.[634]

Overwhelming deregulation of state and federal regulation over OTC derivatives, credit default swaps, including capital and margin requirements, had rendered the risk of AIG failing becoming more probable. The OTC derivatives market's lack of transparency and of effective price discovery exacerbated the collateral disputes of AIG and GS and similar disputes between other derivatives counterparties. AIG engaged in regulatory arbitrage by setting up a major business in this unregulated product, locating much of the business in London, and selecting a weak federal regulator, the Office of Thrift Supervision (OTS). The OTS failed to effectively supervise AIG and its

628. N.D. Schwartz & E. Dash. 2008. "Where was he wise man?" *New York Times 27/04/08.*
629. R. Nichols. 2013. "U.S. can't afford to break up big banks". *Dallas Morning News 28/01/13.*
630. Wilmarth Jr. 2014, *supra* note [627].
631. Onaran 2011, *supra* note [618].
632. Wilmarth Jr. 2014, *supra* note [627].
633. Insurance Journal (IJ). 2013. "Bipartisan Senate megabank bill would split banking from insurance, other risks". *Insurance Journal 11/07/13*, https://www.insurancejournal.com/news/national/2013, accessed November 10, 2020.
634. FCIC. 2011. *Final report of the National Commission on the causes of the financial economic crisis in the United States.* Washington, DC: FCIC.

affiliates. It did not have the capability to supervise an institution of the size and complexity of AIG. It failed to recognize the risks inherent in AIG's sales of CDSs, and failed to understand its responsibility to oversee the entire company, including AIG Financial Products.[635]

Also, owing to the deregulation of OTC derivatives, state insurance supervisors have been barred from regulating AIG's sale of credit default swaps even though they were similar in effect to insurance contracts. Had they been regulated as insurance contracts, AIG would have been required to maintain sufficient capital reserves, would not have been able to enter into contracts needing the posting of collateral, and would not have been able to provide default protection to speculators. Taken together, this could have prevented AIG from engaging in these highly risky activities. AIG being interlinked with many large commercial banks, investment banks, and other financial institutions via counterparty credit relationships on credit default swaps and securities lending, such that its potential failure would have generated systemic risk. Concluding that AIG was a TBTF enterprise, the government provided more than USD 180 billion for its bailout. In the absence of this, AIG's default and collapse could have brought down counterparties, causing cascading losses and collapses throughout the entire system.[636]

Gatekeepers, like credit ratings agencies (CRAs) and the SEC, have also been criticized for their respective weaknesses. Gatekeepers, other than the SEC, are financial intermediaries providing verification and certification services to investors, and in this sense would include auditors, financial analysts, capital market solicitors, and CRAs.[637] The importance of CRAs grew largely because they could provide the solution to reducing costs linked to financial regulations the moment the SEC and other agencies incorporated the ratings of CRAs into various financial regulations. CRAs were widely criticized for their alleged faulty Triple-A ratings that artificially boosted the market values of these items that attracted investors' interests, but which subsequently fell apart as the markets for these started to tank.[638] The hitherto self-regulatory credit ratings industry because of these issues attracted regulatory attention subsequent to the 2000 Dotcom debacle and more so in the aftermath of the 2007-2008 GFC.

US and UK CRA regulatory reforms, while overlapping in many areas, have been driven by the overriding objective to ensure the quality and integrity of the rating process to achieve investors' protection and financial stability. US instinctively migrated from self-regulation for the industry to CRA supervision by the Credit Rating Agency Reform Act 2006 (CRARA 2006).[639] Section 2(4)-(6) of CRARA 2006 provides for enhancing competition between more than two CRAs. To ensure investor protection, the SEC is empowered to oversee the industry with rulemaking, supervisory, and

635. FCIC 2011, *supra* note [634].
636. FCIC 2011, *supra* note [634].
637. J. Coffee Jr. 2004. "What caused Enron? A capsule social and economic history of the 1990s." In T. Clarke (ed.). *Theories of CG*. New York: Routledge.
638. P. Yeoh. 2012. "External credit assessment institutions: Clash of expectations and accountability issues', *Journal of Corporate Law Studies*, Vol 12 (2): 393-427.
639. P. Yeoh. 2012. "The global financial meltdown: What happened to the gatekeepers in the US and the EU and what to do about them". *Journal of Transatlantic Studies*, Vol. 10 (3): 271-293.

enforcement authority. Section 6(3) of CRARA 2006 requires the SEC to submit an annual report to Congress on transparency, conflicts of interest between and within nationally recognized statistical rating organizations (NRSROs), including the state of competition in the industry. The legislation imposed a disclosure-based registration process for those seeking designation as an NRSRO, with the SEC as the overseeing body, but it or other regulatory agencies were forbidden from regulating the substance of credit ratings or the methodologies CRS employ to make ratings. CRARA 2006 importantly did not provide for private right of action.

The US enacted CRARA 2006, largely because of the limitations of self-regulation, through the use of the best practice code provided by the International Organization of Securities Commission (IOSCO). Before CRARA 2006, the US chose to rely on the IOSCO Code, while the EU relied similarly on this until regulatory interventions in 2009, when equivalent problems cropped up on the EU, and in particular in the UK. Comparatively, the US generally prefers enhanced competition for the ratings industry, scaling back on its applications in the capital markets, use of new provisions for expert liability, and the granting of private rights of actions against CRAs, whereas the EU generally prefers a more aggressive procedure-based compliance approach incorporating detailed registration requirements, and close supervision. Neither explores the use of incentives-based initiatives that provide for credible threats of external disciplinary measures through litigation and competition from alternatives to credit ratings, as encouragements to CRAs in providing consistent quality ratings.[640]

Other gatekeepers have also been heavily criticized for not carrying out the functions expected of them, notably the statutory or external auditors of big businesses. The role and value of external audits have been called into question during the 2007 GFC, as markets did not appear to be assured by unqualified opinions, where many financial institutions either collapsed or had to be bailed out within short periods subsequent to the receiving of such unqualified opinions. These events accelerated suspicions that auditors lacked the claimed expertise to provide an independent and objective evaluation of the financial health of these enterprises. They also led to serious reflections on the role, value, and independence of auditors.[641]

Policymakers have accused professional accounting firms of delivering dodgy auditing, and have even called for full-scale inquiries into the conduct of audit work that signed off the accounts involved.[642] The auditing industry mediated previous financial reporting scandals by revising auditing standards and codes of ethics, with early indications that the same strategy would be applied again.[643] The US PCAOB has been criticized for issuing at the time seven new draft auditing standards without

640. Yeoh 2012, *supra* note [638].
641. P. Sikka. 2009. "Financial crisis and the silence of the auditors". *Accounting, Organizations and Society*, Vol. 34 (6-7): 868-873.
642. Accountancy Age. 2008. https://www.accontancyage.com/accountancyage/analysis/222883 4/0verhaul.auditingbanks-4299027, accessed November 10, 2020.
643. P. Sikka & H. Willmott. 1995. "The power of "independence": Defending and extending the jurisdiction of accounting in the UK". *Accounting, Organizations and Society*, Vol. 20 (6): 547-581.

examining the processes linked to the production of audits, changes in capitalism, or limits of auditing.[644]

It was thus of no great surprise that throughout 2010 and 2011 the role of audit became a number of high-level inquiries in the US, EU, and UK.[645] Indeed, historical analysis of economic and financial crisis, among their causes, has mentioned cases related to managers' irresponsible actions, managers who, together with accounting professionals, opted to alter accounting data so as to create a more appealing image on the market of the company's financial health and prospects.[646] Accounting and auditing professionals instead should have adopted a more responsible attitude, given that their services have a decisive impact on communication. Instead, weaknesses in auditing needed to be attended to, as recommended by an independent review.[647] The sudden and critical failures of large UK corporations like BHS in 2016[648] and Carillon in 2018[649] fueled audit reform discussions. Proposed reformed measures include the following:[650]

(1) Considerations for enhanced directors' accountability for internal controls and dividend modeled after SOX.
(2) Annual resilience statement setting out how directors are assessing their corporations' prospects and evaluations of challenges to their business models over the short, medium and long term, including risks posed by climate change.
(3) Disclosures of directors' audit and assurance policy approach.
(4) Empowering the Audit Reporting and Governance Authority (ARGA) in place of the FRC with civil enforcement action powers against any public interest enterprise (PIE) directors pertaining to corporate reporting and audit-related responsibilities.

644. This was in response to provisions in SOX 2002.
645. Association of Chartered Certified Accountants (ACCA). 2011. "Audit under fire: A review of the post-financial crisis inquiries". https://www.pol-af-auf.pdf, accessed November 10, 2020.
646. M.V. Achim, N.S. Borlea & L. Breban. 2010. "Financial crisis and accounting information: The need for corporate social responsibility in accounting profession". *European Research Studies*, Vol. XIII (3): 39-62.
647. D. Brydon. 2019. "Assess, assure and inform: Improving audit quality and effectiveness: Report of the independent review into quality effectiveness". *Brydon Report December 2019.* https://assets.publishing.service.gov.uk/government/uploads/system/uploads/, accessed November 10, 2020.
648. P. Sweet. 2018. "PwC fined GBP10m over BHS audit failures". *Accountancy Daily 13/06/18*, https://www.accountancydaily.co/pwc-fined-ps10m-over-bhs, accessed November 10, 2020; P. Sikka. 2016. "BHS and the silence of auditors". *The Accountant 15/06/16.*
649. House of Commons. 2018. Carillon. *12th Report of the Work and Pensions Committee of Session 2017-19/10th Report of the Business, Energy and Industrial Strategy Committee of Session 2017-19*, https://publications.parliament.uk/pa/cm201719/cmselect/cmworpen/769/769, accessed November 10, 2020.
650. E. Shimmin & K. Jardaneh. 2021. "UK's audit and CG reform: Changes afoot for UK directors". *Jenner & Block Paper 29/03/21*, https://jenner.com/system/assets/publications/20842/original/UK_Audit_and%20_Corporate_Governance_Reform.pdf?1617033506, accesses March 30, 2021.

(5) Sanctions comprising reprimand, fines, and orders to take action to mitigate effect of a breach, noncompliance declarations, or in serious cases temporary prohibitions on acting as a director of a PIE.

(6) A renewed focus on contractual provisions which allow for clawbacks or the withholding of pending awards to ensure that remuneration could be withheld or recovered in the event of serious director failings so as to strengthen current requirements in the UK's CG code. PIEs consist of corporations with shares traded on regulated markets, credit institutions, and insurance undertakings. This is envisaged to be extended to include other large entities whose audit arrangements are considered a matter of public interest, like private companies with over five hundred employees, a sales turnover of more than GBP 200 million, or a balance sheet of over GBP 2 billion, as well as AIM-listed companies with market capitalizations beyond GBP 200 million.

Events and episodes of corporate failures, subsequent to regulatory responses in the US, UK, and the EU, suggest that while there have been no strong signs of risks of another bout of financial catastrophe of the magnitude and reach of the 2007-2008 GFC, governance flaws observed to be a major contributor of the onset of the crisis have not been comprehensively curbed, judging especially by the persisting scandals in both nonfinancial and financial services corporations. Some of these have been discussed here. These observations give good support to the main findings and conclusions of the 2011 FCIC report. These included the observations that the crisis is the outcome of human action and inaction, not due to flow of natural events. The CEOs of finance services and the public stewards of the financial system have been found ignoring warnings and failing to question, understand, and manage evolving risks within a system essential to the economic welfare of the public.

Quoting from Shakespeare, the FCIC concludes that the fault laid not in the stars, but in people, or rather people's missteps and follies. Indeed, the FCIC further argues that the dramatic failures of governance and risk management at many systematically important financial institutions (SIFIs) have been a key contributor of the crisis, including a mix of excessive borrowing, risky investments, and lack of transparency that puts the financial system on a collision course with the crisis. The FCIC also further argues that the government at the time was ill-prepared for the crisis, and its inconsistent response added to the uncertainty and panic in the financial markets. There had been, in effect, a systemic breakdown in accountability and ethics. Importantly, the claim that no one could have foreseen the crisis coming and thus nothing concrete could have been done is seen as being unhelpful as it could lead to the recurrence of this kind of crisis, and that what is likely needed is the will to investigate and to fix the problems identified.

Guided by the above insights, the US, the EU, and the UK have been proactive in tuning up their regulatory readiness to cope with the kind of risks and unfair competitive practices observed in the previous decade as these respective economies enter the digital era. The UK is likely to implement its current intentions to strengthen ESG practices in the country through updating both the soft and hard law sides. The US is also expected to rein in the market dominating inclinations of its trillion-dollar global double-sided digital platforms. The courts though might take a different view, as seen in the dismissal of antitrust complaints against Facebook recently.[651] The US Congress on the other hand has just passed a legislation that would make it harder for those big platform corporations viewed by many social activists and many lawmakers to pursue without constraints their antitrust business practices.[652] The Congress has on June 16, 2021, also passed legislation that would eventually impose new ESG due diligence and disclosure requirements on listed corporations and others,[653]but though only when confirmed by the Senate. This might appear unlikely, given the highly partisan sentiments in the US now. These various developments are, however, not sending sufficiently clear signals pertaining to the particular direction ESG practices and reporting requirements would apply in the future. EU company law rules also address governance issues, focusing on relationships between the company's management, board, shareholders and other stakeholders, and ergo on the manners the company is managed and controlled. Directive 2007/36/EC sets out shareholders' rights in listed companies; Directive (EU) 2017/828 promotes more long-term engagements of shareholders; Directive 2019/878/EU and Regulation No. 2019/876 setting forth amendments to the respective capital requirements, CG and remunerations in each; the 2018 Commission Implementing Regulation (EU) 2018/1212 facilitates the exercising of shareholder rights; Directive 2004/25/EC sets out minimum standards for takeover bids; the EC's Action Plan on Financing Sustainable Growth; as well as other climate and ESG-related disclosure requirements, as alluded to earlier.

Drawing on insights into analysis thus far, the next chapter would explore in depth on how and why self-regulatory approaches like CG Codes deemed initially as a good foil for corporate excesses somehow also miss the mark. This would be discussed in the context of best ESG practices at the national and global levels.

651. C. Kang. 2021. "Judge throws out 2 antitrust cases against Facebook: The decisions were a major blow to attempts to rein Big Tech. The judge said one of the complaints, from the Federal Trade Commission, lacked facts and gave the agency 30 days to refile it". *The New York Times 28 June 2021.* https://www.nytimes.com/2021/06/28/technology/facebook-ftc-lawsuit.html, accessed June 29, 2021.
652. M. Gordon. 2021. "Big tech breakup on the way? 5 changes Congress wants to see among tech giants". *USA Today 26 June 2021.* https://www.usatoday.com/story/tech/news/2021/06/26/how-congress-trying-rein-in-amazon-google-facebook-apple/5357023001/, accessed June 29, 2021.
653. I. Mirza. 2021. "Congress a step closer to making corporate ESG disclosure mandatory". *JD Supra 24 June 2021.* https://www.jdsupra.com/legalnews/congress-a-step-closer-to-making-8725752/, accessed June 29, 2021.

CHAPTER 7
Global and National ESG Best Practices

Hard laws, such as found in SOX 2002, Banking Laws 2009, DFA 2010, and so on require monitoring, supervision and enforcement by the competent agencies to keep businesses within the boundaries of the laws. In contrast, soft laws, such as found in governance codes and best practices, are generally voluntary in nature on the part of businesses. Most businesses though are expected to follow these, as adherence to best governance practices is generally rewarded with positive market and investors' support. Governance codes though are not as simple as they had been made out to be, and their impacts on the quality of ESG practices have been called into question from time to time, but in particular when big corporate or financial scandals blow up in the media, or when activists or whistleblowers bring them to the attention of the public in general, and to policymakers and regulators in particular. This chapter will cover global best practices advocated by various international forums, as well as those in the US, EU, and the UK.

7.01 GLOBAL ESG BEST PRACTICES

7.01a G20/OECD ESG Principles

As the world awaits the framing of best ESG practices, currently in play now are best governance or "G" practices at both the international and national levels. The G20/OECD Principles of CG and the IOSCO CG Code are good examples of global governance best practices, while national governance best practices codes are exemplified in the UK and many Commonwealth economies that had opted to align with the UK model. The G20/OECD Principles of CG[654] are meant to assist policymakers evaluate and improve the legal, regulatory and institutional framework for CG, with the aim of supporting economic efficiency, sustainable growth and financial stability. They could also provide guidance for stock exchanges, investors, corporations, and others that have roles in the process of developing good CG. The principles focus on listed

654. OECD. 2015. *G20/OECD principles of CG*. Paris: OECD.

corporations, financial and nonfinancial. Where applicable, they could be useful tools for improving governance in non-listed entities, and where adapted could be equally applicable to other private big and small companies. The OECD/G20 Principles of CG first emerged in 1999 as response to the 1997 AFC and other crises that followed subsequently. These have been updated in 2015 as response to the 2007-2009 GFC and the 2012 European banking crises that followed. G20/OECD CG principles have been adopted as one of the FSB's key standards for sound financial systems and the basis for the World Bank reports on the observance of standards and codes in the governance domain.

The G20/OECD view governance as a set of relationship between a company's management, its board, its shareholders, and other stakeholders. The governance process effectively provides the structure through which the objectives of the company are formulated, the means for accomplishing these objectives, and by which its performance is assessed. The "Principles" acknowledge interests of employees and other stakeholders and their contributions to the long-term success and performance of a corporation. ESG factors are taken into account by these Principles. They are though treated more explicitly in various OECD and International Labor Organization (ILO) guidelines.[655] The Principles acknowledged that governance policies play an important role in the achieving of wide economic objectives pertaining to investors' confidence, capital formation, and allocation.

The governance process quality impacts the financial cost for businesses as they access capital for growth. They also provide confidence to those providing capital directly and indirectly, such that these market participants could participate and share in the enterprise's value creation, on fair and equitable terms. Consequently, good governance would reassure shareholders and other stakeholders that their rights are safeguarded, making it possible for corporations to lower their capital cost and facilitate their access to the capital market. For economies and corporations to extract the full benefits of the global capital markets and to sustain the interests of long-term patient capital, governance arrangements need to be credible, well understood across borders, and comply with internationally accepted principles. Even in the unlikelihood of not needing foreign capital sources, a credible governance framework reinforced by effective supervision and enforcement mechanisms would help improve domestic investors' confidence, reduce capital cost, underpin the good running of financial markets, and eventually induce more stable sources of funding.[656]

The "Principles" draw and develop common elements underlying good governance practices found in different approaches using, for example, unitary or two-tier board systems. The "Principles" are nonbinding and without detailed prescriptions for national laws, but have instead sought to identify objectives and recommend various means for achieving them. The idea is to offer a robust, but flexible reference for

655. OECD. 2015. *Annual report on the OECD Guidelines for Multinational Enterprises*. Paris: OECD; OECD. 2021 forthcoming. *A review of the 2009 OECD anti-bribery recommendation*. Paris: OECD; UN Human Rights Office of the High Commissioner. 2011. *Guiding Principles on Business and Human Rights*. New York: UN; ILO 2010. *Declaration on Fundamental Principles and Rights at Work and Its Follow-Up*. Geneva: ILO.

656. OECD 2015, *supra* note [654].

policymakers and market participants to develop their own frameworks for the governance process, while corporations too need to adapt their governance practices so as to align with new demands and ride on new opportunities. Governments take into account the costs and benefits of regulation, as they shape workable regulatory framework with flexibility, to enable markets to operate effectively, and to respond to new expectations of shareholders and stakeholders.[657]

Key G20/OECD ESG Principles are as follows:[658]

(1) Ensuring the Foundation for an Effective ESG Framework
The governance framework should promote transparent and fair markets, and the efficient allocation of resources. It should be consistent with the rule of law and support effective supervision and enforcement. Typically, it comprises elements of legislation, regulation, self-regulatory arrangement, voluntary commitments and business practices that are the outcome of an economy's particular circumstances, history, and tradition. Their ultimate mix between legislation, regulation, self-regulation, co-regulation, voluntary standards and so on would vary from economy to economy. Legislative and regulatory rules could be usefully complemented by soft laws based on the comply and explain principle found in many governance codes, so as to enable flexible approaches. Consultative approaches would help to avoid overregulation, support the entrepreneurial process and limit the risks of damaging conflicts of interest in the private sector and in public institutions. Governance frameworks should be flexible enough to meet the requirements of corporations functioning in widely different circumstances, facilitating the development of new opportunities to create value and to determine the most efficient deployment of resources. These frameworks should allow for proportionality, flexibility, and the varying phases of corporate developments. Where new laws and regulations are required, such as for addressing clear cases of market failures, they should be designed in ways that render them possible for implementation and enforcement, and efficiently and fairly. Relevant competent authorities should have effective enforcement and sanctioning powers to deter dishonest behaviors and provide for sound governance practices. Enforcement could also be further pursued via private actions. The effective balance between public and private enforcements varies, depending upon the particular features of different jurisdictions. While voluntary codes and standards could play important roles in governance arrangements, they could leave shareholders and stakeholders with uncertainty pertaining to their status and implementation, and as such, their status in terms of coverage, implementation, compliance, and sanctions would require clear specifications.
Governance principles are influenced by corporate law, securities regulation, accounting and auditing standards, insolvency law, contract law, labor law,

657. OECD 2015, *supra* note [654].
658. OECD 2015, *supra* note [654].

tax law, and human rights and environmental law. These varieties of legal influences pose the risk of unintentional overlaps and conflicts that might frustrate the ability to pursue key governance objectives. Policymakers and regulators should take cognizance of such risks and take measures to limit them. Share market regulations should be supportive of the governance process. Most large stock exchanges are now profit maximizing and themselves publicly trade corporations operating in competition with other profit maximizing stock exchanges and trading venues. However, irrespective of the particular structure of the stock market, policymakers and regulators should assess its proper role in terms of standard-setting, supervision, and enforcement of governance rules.

Supervisory, regulatory and enforcement responsibilities should be placed with entities that are operationally independent and accountable in the exercise of their functions and powers, have sufficient powers, proper resources and the capacity to perform their functions and exercise their powers, including with respect to the governance domain. High levels of cross-border ownership and trading require robust international cooperation among regulators, including via bilateral and multilateral arrangements for exchange of information. International cooperation is helpful for the governance process, especially where companies are active in many jurisdictions via both quoted and unquoted corporations, and as such might see multiple share market listings on exchanges in different jurisdictions, as many Asian corporations have done in recent years.

(2) The Rights and Equitable Treatment of Shareholders and Key Ownership Functions

The governance framework should protect and facilitate the exercise of shareholders' rights and ensure the equitable treatment of all shareholders, including minority and foreign shareholders. All shareholders should have the opportunity to obtain effective redress for violation of their rights.

(3) Institutional Investors, Stock Markets, and Other Intermediaries

The governance framework should provide sound incentives throughout the investment chain and provide for stock markets to function in a way that contributes to good governance. Institutional shareholders should disclose their policies pertaining to governance, whether with regards to voting at shareholders meetings, direct contacts and dialogues with the board and management, or the use of voluntary stewardship codes.

(4) The Role of Stakeholders in the Governance Process

The governance framework should recognize the rights of stakeholders established by law or through mutual arrangement and encourage active cooperation between corporations and stakeholders in creating wealth, jobs and the sustainability of financially sound corporations. Business enterprises should recognize that the contributions of stakeholders represent a valuable resource for building competitive and profitable companies. Thus, it is the long-term interest of corporations to foster wealth-creating cooperation among stakeholders.

(5) Disclosure and Transparency
The governance framework should ensure that timely and accurate disclosure is made on all material matters pertaining to the corporation, including the financial health, performance, ownership, and the governance structure and process of the corporation

(6) Board Responsibilities
The governance framework should ensure the strategic guidance of the company, the effective monitoring of management by the board, and the board's accountability to the company and the shareholders.
The 2020 OECD Report "ESG Investing: Practices, Progress and Challenges" suggest that further initiatives are needed to strengthen ESG practices to enable their consistency and comparability at the global level involving policymakers, the financial industry, end-investors and other stakeholders that are assisting in shaping ESG practice to improve investors' confidence in the instrument and curb the risk of market fragmentation. The OECD claims it has a role to play in facilitating discussion of challenges and solutions pertaining to ESG investing, including the need for guidance on improving consistency and transparency, alignment with materiality, frameworks, and best practices of benchmark and fund reporting. As a preliminary step toward this agenda, the OECD suggests five high-level considerations. These include ensuring consistency, comparability and quality of core metrics in reporting frameworks for ESG disclosures; ensuring relevance of reporting through financial materiality over the medium and long-term; leveling the playing field between large and small issuers pertaining to ESG disclosure and ratings; and promoting the transparency and comparability of scoring and weighting methodologies of established ESG ratings providers and indices.

7.01b International Organization of Securities Commission (IOSCO) ESG Principles

Membership of the IOSCO comprises mainly capital markets regulators and various central banks' representatives, with the notable presence of those from the US, UK, EU, and big emerging economies' representatives from Brazil, Russia, India, China, South Africa (BRICS). The IOSCO is the global standard setter for the securities sector, as it develops, implements and promotes adherence to internationally recognized standards for securities regulation.[659] The IOSCO collaborates intensively with the G20 and the FSB on the global regulatory agenda to monitor and address emerging financial vulnerabilities that could impact global financial stability.

IOSCO CG Guidelines/Principles focus rightly so on the three long-known challenging areas of BC, remuneration and incentive structures, and risk management

659. IOSCO. 2021. "International Organization of Securities Commissions". *IOSCO March 2021*, https://www.iosco.org/about/pdf/IOSCO-Fact-Sheet.pdf, accessed April 2, 2021.

and internal controls.[660] Where BC is concerned, the IOSCO highlights the need to ensure independent diverse board members via full disclosure of potential conflicts of interests, a critical mass of independent directors, and the appropriate mix and balance of skills, background, and expertise representing a wider range of perspectives.[661] The IOSCO guidance stresses the critical importance for corporations to ensure that board members discharge their responsibilities with the requisite diligence, seek effective board performance through the applications of performance indicators' quantitative data, board evaluation, and suitable nomination and selection processes. Pertaining to remuneration and incentive structures, IOSCO guidance draw attention as to how individual components of existing remuneration plans and variable criteria are linked to a company's short, mid, and long-term goals.

The IOSCO further highlights the board's responsibility for assuring the alignment of key executive remuneration with the company's long-term performance and business community while ensuring that the company is not exposed to unwanted risks disproportionately justified by the need for immediate returns.[662] With regards to risk management and internal controls, IOSCO guidance draws attention as to the criticality of reliable disclosure by companies of pertinent information concerning risk factors arising from the risk identification methodology employed and how they could impact the business; the quality reporting of sustainability, social and cyber risks; as well as periodical assessment of the efficiency and suitability of the companies' systems and control, including identifying deficiencies and the appropriate corrective actions to be taken.[663]

Importantly, the IOSCO guidance stresses that governance is a work in progress.[664] As markets continuously evolve, regulatory frameworks must be regularly reviewed and enhanced to meet the needs of companies and investors, keeping pace with best practices, while acknowledging that good governance could be a major competitive advantage for businesses seeking to access less costly sources of funding. The IOSCO guidance goes further in suggesting that the work in progress would need ongoing interactions among jurisdictions and dialogues with key national stakeholders. This would enable reconciliation between the desire to set agreed and accepted international, benchmarked standards and best practices, and the need to recognize the particular needs of individual jurisdictions. It would further ensure that the commonalities underlying the development of a coherent global governance framework are not overwhelmed by the differences found in particular jurisdictions and would in consequence curb the risk of regulatory arbitrage and the consequential race to the bottom temptation. The IOSCO guidance finally stresses that its guidance should be viewed as the starting phase of an ongoing process to find ways to continue

660. IOSCO. 2016. "Report on CG: Final Report". *IOSCO FR10/16 October 2016.* https://www.iosco.org/library/pubdocs/pdf/IOSCOPD544.pdf, accessed 10/22/20.
661. IOSCO 2016, *supra* note [660].
662. IOSCO 2016, *supra* note [660].
663. IOSCO 2016, *supra* note [660].
664. IOSCO 2016, *supra* note [660].

strengthening especially emerging capital markets via improved CG standards that underpin the parameters of market efficiency, safety, and sustainability.

IOSCO's July 2021 Report "Environmental, Social and Governance (ESG) Ratings and Data Products Providers" observes the lack of standardization of corporate disclosures that impacts the quality and availability of information that could be applied by ESG ratings and data products providers. These observations are consistent with IOSCO's observation from the investor's standpoint, namely that sustainability-linked information needs are currently not being satisfied, and ergo the priority for improving the consistency, comparability, and reliability of sustainability reporting. The IOSCO suggests that ESG ratings and data products providers could request or procure ESG information from entities that are the subject of these ratings or data products on a bilateral basis, and this could help minimize the impact of these various issues. Nevertheless, where such is the case, there might be risks around transparency, verifiability, and the ensuring of a level playing field for both providers and entities that are the subject of these ratings or data products. Standardization of sustainability-related disclosures across jurisdictions could provide the basis for the development of an audit and assurance framework. The IOSCO is collaborating with the IFRS Foundation toward this end. This kind of standardization over time would likely mitigate the issues identified. The IOSCO further finds ESG rating and data products at an early phase of adoption by financial market participants. The market, as such, remains mainly unregulated, with some isolated initiatives at self-regulation via codes of conduct. Various national regulators, industry associations, including providers themselves have advocated for a regulation of the market.

7.02 NATIONAL CG BEST PRACTICES

7.02a UK CG Code

The UK is generally perceived as a world leader mainly in the "G" of ESG initiative. This arises mainly from the outcome of increasing interest in governance matters internal and external to the board room, but in particular as a reaction to scandals, and reflections by shareholders and boards subsequent to serious economic challenges in the 1990s.[665] The 1992 Cadbury Report formalizes and renders explicit CG best practices, hitherto implicit in many UK businesses. This by then widely recognized report sets the agenda for CG reform in the UK, and importantly the forerunner of various policy documents, principles, guidelines and codes of practice in the UK, and admirably across the world. The agency perspective that underpins UK's hitherto shareholder primacy model of governance focuses on aligning managers' interests with those of their shareholders.

The shareholder or principal monitors and controls corporate management or the agent through shareholder meetings at AGMs, direct meetings between a fund manager

665. J. Solomon & A. Solomon. 2004. *CG and accountability*. Chichester: John Wiley & Sons Ltd.

and an investee company director, shareholder resolutions, and the market for corporate control or the takeover mechanism.[666] Institutional shareholders now holding up to 70% stakes in UK listed companies are also now relatively more involved in engaging with ESG matters in these companies than in the past. These aside, fiduciary responsibility is imposed on board members through CA 2006 and other relevant business laws, external financial gatekeepers like the FCA, capital market regulator, like the LSE and AIM, City Code on Takeovers, and the now widely known UK CG Code.

The UK CG Code first emerging in 1992 does not stipulate a rigid set of rules, but instead offers flexibility through the application of Principles and via the "comply or explain" approach. It leaves it to corporate boards to apply the Code Principles wisely and to investors and advisors to evaluate differentiated corporate approaches thoughtfully. The Code lists Principles that draw attention to the value of good governance to long-term, sustainable success. It also includes Provisions giving details on what these would entail, and Guidance on how businesses can show through their disclosures as to how governance of their companies contributes to their long-term sustainable success. The updated 2018 UK CG Code implemented in 2019 is applicable to all companies with a premium listing, whether incorporated in the UK or elsewhere. It comprises five sections.[667]

A. Board leadership and company purpose. The principles are as follows:

(1) A successful company is led by an effective and entrepreneurial board, whose role is to promote the long-term sustainable success of the enterprise, generating value for shareholders and contributing to the wider society.
(2) The board should set the company's purpose, values and strategy, and satisfy itself that these and its culture are aligned. All directors must act with integrity, led by example, and promote the desired culture.
(3) The board should ensure that the necessary resources are in place for the enterprise to meet its objectives and to measure performance against them. The board should further set a framework of prudent and effective controls to enable risk to be evaluated and managed.
(4) To enable the enterprise to meet its responsibilities to shareholders and stakeholders, the board should ensure effective engagement with and encourage participation from these parties.
(5) The board should ensure that workplace policies and practices are consistent with the company's values and support its long-term sustainable success. The worksites itself should be able to raise any matters of concern.

666. Solomon & Solomon, *supra* note [665].
667. Financial Reporting Council (FRC). 2018. "The UK CG Code". *FRC July 2018.* https://www.frc.org.uk/getattachment/88bd8c45-50ea-4841-95b0-d2f4f48069a2/2018-UK-Corporate-Governance-Code-FINAL.PDF, accessed November 10, 2020.

B. Division of board responsibilities. The principles are as follows:

(1) The chair leads the board and is responsible for its overall effectiveness in directing the enterprise. They should demonstrate objective judgment throughout their tenure and promote a culture of openness and debate. Additionally, the chair facilitates constructive board relations and the effective contribution of all NEDs, and ensures that directors receive accurate, timely and clear information.
(2) The board should include an appropriate mix of executives and nonexecutives and in particular, independent NEDs, such that no one individual or small group of individuals dominates the board's decision-making. There should be a clear division of responsibilities between the leadership of the board and the executive leadership of the enterprise's business.
(3) NEDs should have sufficient time to meet their board responsibilities. They should promote constructive challenge, strategic guidance, offer specialist advice and hold management to account.
(4) The board supported by the company secretary should ensure that it has the policies, processes, information, time and resources it needs in order to operate effectively and efficiently.

C. BC, succession and performance evaluation. The principles are as follows:

(1) Appointments to the board should be subject to a formal, rigorous and transparent procedure, and an effective succession plan should be maintained for board and senior management. Appointments and succession plans should be guided by merit and objective criteria, and within this context, should promote diversity of gender, social and ethnic backgrounds, cognitive and personal strengths.
(2) The board and its committee should have a mix of skills, experience and knowledge. Considerations should be given to the length of service of the board as a whole and membership regularly refreshed.
(3) Annual evaluation of the board should consider its composition, diversity and how effectively members work together to achieve objectives. Individual evaluation should demonstrate whether each director continues to contribute effectively.

D. Audit, risk and internal control. The principles are as follows:

(1) The board should establish formal and transparent policies and procedures to ensure the independence and effectiveness of internal and external audit functions and satisfy itself on the integrity of financial and narrative statements.
(2) The board should present a fair, balanced and comprehensible evaluation of the enterprise's position and prospects.

(3) The board should set procedures to manage risk, oversee the internal control framework, and determine the nature and extent of the primary risks the enterprise is willing to take so as to achieve its long-term strategic objectives.

E. Remuneration. The principles are as follows:

(1) Remuneration policies and practices should be designed to support strategy and promote long-term sustainable success. Executive remuneration should be aligned to enterprise purpose and values, and be clearly linked to the successful delivery of the enterprise's long-term strategy.
(2) A formal and transparent procedure for developing policy on executive remuneration and determining director and senior management remuneration should be set up. No director should be involved in deciding their own remuneration outcome; and
(3) Directors should exercise independent judgment and discretion when authorizing remuneration outcomes, taking into account enterprise and individual performance, and wider circumstances.

The FRC which authors and reports on the implementation of the UK CG Code principles and practices has been repeatedly advising reporting companies to avoid the boilerplate approach, provide analysis of principles implementation against the anticipated outcomes for their own future guidance. The advice was given on the basis of the FRC's annual reports on these matters. For much of the time, the UK CG Code has been praised as exemplary and copied and adapted in other advanced and emerging economies.[668] The updated FRC UK CG Code 2018 reminds directors of their duties under S172 of the CA 2006 to promote the success of the company and give due considerations for ESG matters. The FRC in August 2021 released three research reports exploring the Code's provisions on remuneration, workforce engagement and board diversity and effectiveness. The FRC indicated that it would consider these research findings and will take them into account in any future reviews of the UK CG Code.

On the other hand, in the face of recurrences of various corporate scandals, the risk of over-relying on the present Code to monitor corporate and directors' actions has also been raised.[669] Various recent corporate excesses, intensified calls for even more reforms in particular aspects of governance through the deployments of both soft and hard laws have been advanced, with the government responding positively.[670] Subsequent to the Kingman and Brydon reviews and the CMA's market study of statutory

668. OECD. 2021. "OECD CG factbook 2021". https://www.oecd.org/corporate/corporate-governance-factbook.htm, accessed June 11, 2021.
669. P. Yeoh. 2019. "CG codes in the UK: The risk of over-reliance". *Business Law Review*, Vol. 40 (1): 19-27.
670. Business, Energy & Industrial Strategy (BEIS). 2021. "Restoring trust in audit and CG: Consultation on the government's proposals". *BEIS March 2021*. https://assets.publishing.

audit services, the UK government released its March 2021 White Paper "Restoring Trust in Audit and Corporate Governance" with reform proposals that would impact UK listed companies, as well as the largest private companies under the umbrella of public interest entities (PIEs).

Under these reform measures, directors' accountability for their company's internal controls, dividends and capital maintenance would be enhanced, while the new audit regulator's powers would be broadened to strengthen its investigative and enforcement powers pertaining to any wrongdoing by a director. Also, in July 2021, the "FRC Statement of Intent on Environmental, Social and Governance Challenges" was published setting out the challenges flowing from production of ESG data, their audit and assurance, their distribution, their consumption, their supervision, and their regulation. To address these various challenges, the FRC plans to develop Codes, standards, guidance, and collaborate with and influence standard-setters, market participants, regulators and other stakeholders, so as to develop a forward-looking and fit for purpose system. The FRC aims to develop suitable standards and controls, develop strategic robust internal information for high-quality disclosures in a useful format that can contribute to a more effective stakeholder and investment decision-making.

In conjunction with this, the FRC would support appropriate account of ESG issues in the UK CG Code, the UKSC, including making relevant future amendments, the supporting of global standards for nonfinancial reporting, as well as announcing the "FRC Statement on Non-financial Reporting Framework" in November 2020 pertaining to climate-related considerations in corporate reporting and auditing. The FRC review found that boards and companies, auditors, professional associations, regulators and standard-setters need to do more for these ESG considerations. The FRC in particular expects PIEs to report observing guidance from the Task Force on Climate-Related Financial Frameworks and the SASB. The FRC's preliminary review of UK SASB reporting practice found an increase in participation, but that more and better reporting is needed. Subsequent to the Department for Business, Energy & Industrial Strategy's March 2019 "Audit Regime in the UK to Be Transformed with New Regulator" press release, it has been confirmed that a new statutory-based ARGA with enhanced enforcement powers would replace the FRC.

7.02b WP of CG

An industry-led governance best practices initiative led in December 2018 to a CG Code targeted at large private companies in the UK. These standards seek to facilitate compliance with the mandatory obligations for large enterprises, both private and public, to publicly disclose their governance arrangements. The initiative had been primarily prompted by the corporate failure of BHS in 2016.

---

service.gov.uk/government/uploads/system/uploads/attachment_data/file/970676/restoring-trust-in-audit-and-corporate-governance-command-paper.pdf, accessed April 19, 2021.

The unraveling of significant governance failures in both small, large and very large business enterprises in the UK for several decades had on previous occasions given rise to various business and ESG concerns, but the UK appears consistently to view the use CG code as a proportionate remedy. Governance policies and reforms over time have also consistently reflected wider government and business collaborations, a convention now seen again in the WPs for Large Private Enterprises. These have mostly drawn public attention to the need for improved transparency and accountability, and also the risks to wider stakeholders, such as seen in the ongoing COVID-19 pandemic crisis.

Like many governance codes elsewhere, the WPs is a soft law instrument. Corporations opting to use the WPs are asked to apply and explain. The WPs are the UK government's response to its earlier Green Paper on governance reform that had stated that the case for strengthening the governance framework for UK's largest private enterprises is justified, as they have sizeable impacts on the welfare of employee, suppliers, customers and others. James Wates was entrusted as the head of a coalition comprising the British Private Equity and Venture Capital Association, the Confederation of British Industry, the Climate Disclosures Standards Board, the Institute of British Ethics, the Governance Institute, the Institute for Family Business, the Institute of Directors, the Investment Association, Mark Goyder, and the Trades Union Congress. This was set up in January 2018 with the FRC function as its secretariat. The WPs have been formulated following extensive consultations and analysis of existing national and international governance codes, series of roundtable discussions with stakeholders, including inputs from an Executive Sounding Board comprising senior executives from large private enterprises.

The UK in June 2018 introduced the Companies (Miscellaneous Reporting) Regulations 2018 requiring all companies of more than two thousand employees, or a sales turnover of more than GBP 200 million, and balance sheet exceeding GBP 2 billion, that are currently not required to provide a governance statement, to disclose their governance arrangements. The WPs' approach offers sufficient flexibility for a diverse range of companies to explain the application and relevance of their governance practices without being unduly prescriptive. Nothing in the WPs overrides or is intended as an interpretation of directors' duties as found in sections 170-177, in particular section 172 of the CA 2006. Section 172 states that the duty of a director is to promote the success of the company for the benefit of the company as a whole, and that this duty applies to all directors, irrespective of whether the company is public or private, a parent or subsidiary, large or small. The WPs seek to support directors of companies with the greatest interaction with those factors to disclose how the directors have fulfilled adherence to section 172(1)(a)-(f).[671] The WPs, among others, state the following:[672]

671. *The Companies (Miscellaneous Reporting) Regulations 2018.*

672. Financial Reporting Council (FRC). 2018. "The Wates CG Principles for large private companies". *FRC December 2018.* https://www.frc.org.uk/getattachment/31dfb844-6d4b-4093-9bfe-19cee2c29cda/Wates-Corporate-Governance-Principles-for-LPC-Dec-2018.pdf, accessed November 10, 2020.

(1) A director's report has to include a statement of governance arrangements stating which governance code the company has applied in the financial year, how the company applied that code, and whether the company departed from any governance code for the financial year, including the reasons for the departure.
(2) Where the company has not applied any governance code for the financial year, the statement of governance arrangements must provide reasons for that decision and explain what arrangements for governance have been applied for that year.
(3) Companies producing a Strategic Report are now required to provide a section 172(1) statement on their website describing how the directors have had regard to the matters set out in section 172(1)(a)-(f) of CA 2006.
(4) The Directors' Report has also been amended requiring companies to explain how they have engaged with employees, and how directors have regard to employee interests, and the effect of that regard. Large private corporations are also required to explain how they have engaged with suppliers, customers and others in a business relationship with the company.
(5) The new CG reporting requirements are applicable to company reporting for financial years on or after January 1, 2019.
(6) Taking into account various management ownership structures, the "one-size-fits-all" approach to governance in large companies is not deemed appropriate. As such, boards should apply each Principle by considering them individually within the context of the company's particular circumstances. This is not something new, as UK premium listed companies are similarly subject to FCA's Listing Rules requiring a statement as to how the Principles in the UK CG Code had been applied in a manner that stakeholders can evaluate.
(7) In contrast to the UK CG Code, the WPs do not set out detailed provisions, but instead offer guidance under each Principle, and as such, the guidance does not need to be reported on in the same way as premium listed companies need to as provided in the "comply or explain" provisions in the UK CG Code. This is because the WPs' intention is to move beyond a "tick-box approach" to describing and explaining how the implemented practices achieve the code principles to demonstrate those outcomes. This thereby provides enhanced transparency to stakeholders and links to other reporting requirements.
(8) Companies are expected to provide a statement demonstrating how their governance policies and processes operate to achieve the desired outcome for each Principle.
(9) The importance of stakeholder engagement is shown throughout the WPs and corporations should outline methods of engagements with both the workforce and other stakeholders and demonstrate how boards have considered the issues raised.

(10) Subsidiary companies meeting the tests set out in the Regulations are required to make a governance statement.

The six WPs are enumerated as follows:[673]

1 Principle One: Purpose and Leadership

An effective board develops and promotes the purpose of a company and ensures that its values, strategy and culture align with that purpose. A well-developed and defined purpose would help corporations of all sizes and structures frame their business model and develop their strategy, operating practices, workforce management, and approach to risk. All directors have to promote the success of the company. Board members should have a clear appreciation of the shareholders' views, including those with minority interest. To promote a clear sense of purpose and collective visions, directors should appreciate the importance of dialogue with the workforce and wider stakeholders around the company's stated purpose and be proactive in ensuring that it takes place. A company's purpose and values should inform expected behaviors and practices throughout the organization. A healthy culture, defined as a combination of values, attitudes and behaviors manifested by a company in its operations, and relationships with its stakeholders, is pivotal to the company's competitive advantage, and vital to the creation and protection of long-term value. Effective ways for monitoring culture include employee surveys, engagements with trade unions, absentee rates, exit interviews and board feedback sessions. The board is responsible for ensuring that its strategy is clearly communicated and implemented throughout the corporations, and that this together with the company values supports appropriate behaviors and practices. Directors should lead on the setting up of transparent policies pertaining to raising concerns about misconduct and unethical practices, and including effective review processes, as well as managing conflicts of interest, while a balance should be struck between short-term targets or needs, and long-term aspirations.

2 Principle Two: BC

Effective BC needs an effective chairperson and a balance of skills, backgrounds, experience and knowledge, with individual directors having sufficient capacity to make a valuable contribution. The numbers of board members should be guided by the scale and complexity of the enterprise. There should be a serious consideration for separating the chair and CEO to ensure a balance of power and effective decision-making. A balance board promotes effective decision-making and supports delivery of a company's strategy. Board appointments should promote diversity in alignment with the protected characteristics within the Equalities Act 2010. There should be considerations for the value of appointing independent NEDs subject to transparent procedures, in order to offer constructive challenge. This further includes the delegation of some functions to committees that can evaluate designated matters, like risk or remuneration. Directors in enterprise with concentrated share ownerships are often

673. FRC 2018, *supra* note [672].

required to maintain objectivity in complex situations, especially in the presence of an influential shareholder. Regular evaluation of the board could constitute part of board refreshment and succession plans.

3 Principle Three: Director Responsibilities

The board and individual board members should have a clear knowledge of their accountability and responsibilities. Board policies and procedures should support effective decision-making and independent challenges. Clear governance policies, practices and company leadership with clear lines of accountability and responsibility all coming together would promote effective stewardship to deliver long-term value. Policies and procedures governing the internal affairs of the company, including matter pertaining to the authority, accountability, role and conduct of directors, designated information, like shareholders agreement and protection of minority shareholders. The board should agree and set out procedures on how conflicts of interest should be identified and managed. The governance processes should be periodically reviewed by the chairperson and company secretary to confirm they remain fit for purpose, or consider initiatives that could strengthen the governance of the company. Transparent governance policies and practices could clarify the relationships between owners and the company, parent company, or associate company, so as to deliver long-term sustainable success.

Committees can be deployed to assist in the evaluation of issues like financial reporting, risk, succession and remuneration, including authorities delegated to them, with the board retaining responsibility for all final decisions. The risk of individuals enjoying unfettered powers should be mitigated with the provision of independent challenge in board and committee decision-making. Formal and robust internal processes should be established by the board to ensure systems and controls operating effectively, and that the quality and integrity of the information provided to it is reliable, thereby enabling directors to monitor and challenge the performance of the company to make informed decisions. Directors can rely on a wide range of information sources, including financial reporting, key performance indicators, workforce data, environmental data, stakeholder engagement feedback, or consumer data; while board papers and supporting information should be accurate, clear and comprehensive, up-to-date, contain summary contents, inform directors what is expected of them on each matter, and importantly be issued in good time.

4 Principle Four: Opportunity and Risk

A board should promote the long-term sustainable success of the enterprise through identifying opportunities for creating and preserving value, and establishing oversight for the identification and mitigation of risks. Boards are required to evaluate tangible and intangible sources of value and the stakeholders that contribute to it, including the processes for the identification of future opportunities for innovation and entrepreneurship. These opportunities might often be reliant on an agreed risk appetite and the company's long-term strategy and prospects, including the processes for ensuring that emerging new business opportunities of certain values are evaluated and approved at board levels. These include effective management of financial, nonfinancial and reputational risks, and appropriately accounting for them to stakeholders.

The internal control systems that are installed for managing emerging and principal risks should be guided by the size and nature of the business, of which some companies may decide to delegate to committees to oversee. Internal control frameworks should state clearly defined roles and responsibilities for those involved, approach to reporting, and including frequency of reporting and the points at which decisions are made and escalated. These responsibilities could incorporate the developing of appropriate risk management systems identifying emerging and established risks, including ESG challenges impacting the company and its stakeholders. They should also provide agreements on how the principal risks should be managed or mitigated and over what timeframe so as to lower the probability of their occurrence or the scale of their impacts, as well as agreements on the monitoring and review processes.

5 Principle Five: Remuneration

A board should promote executive remuneration structures aligned to the long-term success of an enterprise, taking into consideration pay and conditions elsewhere in the enterprise. Remunerations for directors and senior personnel should be aligned with performance, behaviors, and the achievement of CP, values, and strategy, so as to reinforce a sense of shared purpose. Directors should set up clear policies on remuneration structures and practices which should enable effective accountability to shareholders, and the company's response to issues, like pay ratio and gender pay gap. Policies could include robust consideration of the reputational and behavioral risks to the company that could result from inappropriate incentives and excessive rewards. The benefits of greater transparency of remuneration structures and policies could build trust from wider stakeholders. Enhanced transparency with commentaries on how executive remunerations reflect general practices within the sector are recommended. Remuneration policies and structures for directors and senior personnel could be delegated to a committee which could benefit from the contributions of independent NEDs.

6 Principle Six: Stakeholder Relationships and Engagement

The board should promote effective stakeholder relationships aligned to the enterprise's purpose. The board is responsible for overseeing meaningful engagements with stakeholders, including the workforce, and having due regard for their views when taking decisions. Large enterprises bear responsibility to create and sustain long-term value for their shareholders and stakeholders. As such, boards should consider how a company's activities may impact both current and future stakeholders, like impacts on the environment. A company should identify and prioritize stakeholder relationships for those impacted by company operations and that are integral to its ability to generate and preserve value. Thus, dialogues with both primary and secondary stakeholders would help directors to appreciate the impacts of company policies and practices predict future developments and trends, and reorient strategy. Directors should present to stakeholders a fair, balanced and comprehensible evaluation of the company's status and prospects, and ensure its availability on an annual basis. These evaluations could include guidance from recognized international standards or frameworks that it follows.

For most large enterprises, the workforce would be its largest material stakeholder. Companies should accordingly develop a range of formal and informal channels that would enable them to engage in meaningful two-way dialogues, thereby enabling the workforce to share ideas and concerns with senior personnel. These could include engagements with trade unions, focus or consultative groups. Personnel welfare, policies, and practices should be aligned with the company's purpose and value. These should incorporate clear procedures for raising concerns in the future, like whistleblowing policies. These should be reviewed regularly to ensure their effectiveness. Directors should show how the company has engaged with material stakeholders, and how such dialogues have been taken into account in their decision-making, and where helpful commentaries on any good practice that might have emerged and contributed to the company's success.

It has been contended that the governance answer to the problems generated by large enterprise with significant ESG agendas puts the WPs at the interstices of public-private and the economic versus ethical framing of the enterprise.[674] However, this governance answer cannot be understood or framed merely in the traditional thesis of a private and economic nature. This suggests the need to locate and analyze the WPs within the alternative theoretical paradigm of social contract. Benchmark norms derived from this approach, when used to evaluate the WPs, demonstrate that these fall short of the social expectations for the governance of large private enterprises.[675] The WPs address aspects of procedural benchmark norms like scrutinizing controlling interests, and the avenues available for stakeholder engagements. These, however, did not go far enough to connect governance to business-society relations, as highlighted in the demise of BHS.[676] Nevertheless, the WPs are welcomed as a starting point for large private enterprises to adopt good practices and be accountable for their CG.[677]

Early indications of corporate applications of WPs in corporate UK suggest the following:[678]

(1) Many reporting companies have evidently sought to grasp the spirit of the WPs and have provided good explanations of how their governance arrangements work. Reports seen from companies like Allianz Holdings

674. R.M. Barker & I. H-Y. Chiu. 2019. "Examining the Wates Principles for large private companies as social contract for business-society relations". *ECGI Working Paper Series No. 453/2019 May 2019.*
675. Barker & Chiu. 2019, *supra* note [674].
676. Work and Pensions (WP)/Business, innovations and Skills (BIS) Committees. 2016. "BIIS". *First Report of the WP Committee and Fourth Report of the BIS of Session 2016-17 HC54 20/07/16.* https://publications.parliament.uk/pa/cm201617/cmselect/cmworpen/54/54.pdf, accessed November 10, 2020.
677. Barker & Chiu. 2019, *supra* note [674].
678. J. Wates. 2021. "Early indications of Wates Principles reporting". *FRC February 2021.* https://www.frc.org.uk/getattachment/353e087a-21c2-4d2f-9486-35dcca97ebe0/Wates, accessed March 3, 2021.

(UK), Heathrow, Jaguar Land Rovers and Tata Steel demonstrate rigorous analyses of how the WPs are applied.

(2) Companies faced significant challenges in deciding the right quantity of material to report, as was previously encountered by companies obliged to report against the UK CG Code. There have been tensions between the need to provide sufficient evidence to assure their commitments to governance while needing to keep the report short and easy to read to align with the spirit of the WPs. Feasible resolutions for these include placing some of these materials elsewhere in the Director's Report, such as exemplified by evergreen materials and keeping the focus on governance on what changed year to year. Challenges remained though, especially with regards to the use of box-ticking by some companies, such as shown by a one-sentence response to risk and opportunity.

(3) Some companies did not appear to fully embed "Purpose" in their organization. Companies do state their Purpose, but appeared to lack a sense of authenticity, when relying on the use of marketing materials, rather than relating to this from a governance perspective. There are also failures to provide particular examples of how the purpose has actually guided board-level discussions and decisions. Many failed to make the governance report easily accessible on their websites.

(4) Going forward, the FRC and the Coalition Group highlighted the need for reporting companies to use the WPs not only at year end but throughout all board meetings, and in this regard, fresh thinking on governance could be consulted from FRC contributions, as found in "A Matter of Principles: The Future of Corporate Reporting."

7.02c US Business Roundtable (BRT) ESG Principles

The BRT formed in 1972 is a nonprofit association based in Washington, DC. It represents leading US companies engaged in financial and nonfinancial businesses, and where the deliberations and membership in the BRT involve exclusively the CEOs of these companies. The BRT exerts considerable influence on the direction of rules governing business corporations in the US. The BRT generally adheres to the shareholder primacy model of CG. The BRT published its maiden Commonsense CG Principles (CCGP) in 2016 that have been subsequently updated with Version 2.0 in 2018.[679]

Both versions of the CCGP seek to understand where there has been a broad consensus to enable the establishment of a baseline for ongoing discussions among stakeholders with differing points of view. The conversations, as such, have been

679. H. Grove, et al. 2020. "Analyzing the Business Roundtable statement on the purpose of a corporation and linking it to corporate governance". *Corporate Board: Role, Duties & Composition*, Vol. 16 (1): 19-27.

reframed from advancing individual perspectives to collectively advancing the interests of all stakeholders over the long term, and that is also the primary objective of the BRT Statement on the purpose of a corporation. Key points found in both versions are the following:[680]

(1) Truly independent board of directors are pivotal to effective governance, such that no board should be subservient to the CEO or management. Every board should meet regularly without the CEO present, and every board should have active and direct engagement with executives below the CEO level.
(2) Board diversity is encouraged. Diverse boards make better decisions, so every board should have members with complementary and diverse skills, backgrounds, and experiences. It is also helpful to balance the wisdom and judgment that accompany experience and tenure with the need for fresh thinking and perspectives of new board members.
(3) Every board member needs a strong leader who is independent of management. The board's independent directors are usually in a better position to evaluate whether the roles of chairman and CEO should be separate or combined. Where the board decides on a combined role, it is crucial that the board has a strong independent director with clearly defined authority and responsibility.
(4) The US financial markets have become too obsessed with quarterly earnings forecasts. Enterprises should not be obligated to provide earnings guidance, and should do so only where they believe that doing so would be beneficial to shareholders. Making short-term decisions to beat earnings guidance or other performance yardsticks are likely to be value destructive in the longer term.
(5) A common accounting standard is pivotal for corporate transparency. Thus, while enterprises may employ non-Generally Accepted Accounting Principles (GAAP) to explain and clarify their financial performance, they should not do so in manners that obscure GAAP-reported outcomes. This is of particular relevance since stocks or options-based compensations are clearly a cost of doing business. As such, equity compensation should always be reflected in non-GAAP measurement of earnings.
(6) Effective governance requires constructive engagements between an enterprise and its shareholders. Institutional shareholders who are making decisions on proxy issues vital to long-term value creation should have access to the enterprise, its management, and in some cases, the board. Equally, an enterprise, its management, and board should have access to institutional investors' ultimate decision-makers on those issues.

680. Grove et al. 2020, *supra* note [679]; K. Bresnahan. 2019. "Applying Commonsense Principles 2.0". *The Millstein Center 29 May 2019*. https://millstein.law.columbia.edu/, accessed November 10, 2020.

(7) Dual-class share structures, often seen in founder-led enterprises that give select stockholder outsize voting power, are not deemed as a best practice.
(8) Director compensation should be made up of a substantial portion of equity-based compensation, like company stock/stock options, like some 50% or more. This is to keep the goals of directors in sync with those of investors.
(9) Business enterprises should maintain clawback provisions that enable them to recoup compensation given to executives in the event of earnings restatements.

Commonsense Principles Version 2.0 is built on the strong foundation provided by the 2016 Principles, but seeks to drive forward a more developed appreciation of, and agreement on, the key tenets of governance that support long-term value creation for all stakeholders. These also advocate for enhanced transparency on the part of the enterprise and asset managers to ensure greater understanding between shareholders and the enterprises where they have invested. Key additions to Version 2.0 are as follows:[681]

(1) Board members should be prepared to serve a minimum of three years.
(2) Where board elections are not annual, a business enterprise should offer explanations.
(3) Shareholders and the enterprise are encouraged to engage early on important proxy proposals.
(4) An enterprise should allow some form of proxy access.
(5) Poison pills and other anti-takeover defenses should be subject to a shareholder vote and reassessed by the board on a periodic basis.
(6) Asset managers should disclose whether they rely on proxy advisors to assist their decision-making.
(7) Asset managers should disclose any material conflicts of interest policies in their proxy voting and shareholder engagement activities.
(8) Portfolio managers should be compensated based on performance over a suitable term, given the strategy and investment time horizon for the portfolio.
(9) Asset owners should promote sound, long-term-oriented governance in their direct interactions with both the enterprise and the asset managers.
(10) Asset owners should use yardsticks and performance reports consistent with their investment time horizon to affect governance outcomes with asset managers and assess the asset managers' performances in terms of reruns and governance.

The Commonsense Principles 2.0, while reflecting the status quo of late 2018, would continue to stimulate discussions on how to best serve the long-term interests of

681. Grove et al. 2020, *supra* note [679]; Bresnahan 2019, *supra* note [680].

public enterprises, shareholders and other stakeholders. Owing to the complex nature of the global governance landscape, Version 2.0 focuses on US enterprises. Nevertheless, its ideas and policies could be applicable around the world. Cross-border businesses could benefit from international insights, such as employees and other stakeholders serving on international boards of directors, and minimum board quotas for women representation.

The BRT on August 19, 2019, issued a new "Statement on the Purpose of Corporations" signed by some two hundred CEOs. Representations came from giant global corporations CEOs, like Oracle's Safra Catz, Amazon's Jeff Bezos, Apple's Tim Cook, General Motor's Mary Barra, and Jamie Dimond of JP Morgan Chase. The statement seeks to move beyond its 1997 shareholder primacy commitment to now include commitment to all stakeholders. The signatories commit to deliver value to all of their stakeholders for the future success of their corporations, their communities, and the US. It was, however, unclear as to whether how many of those CEOs who signed up, acted on their own volitions, or had the blessings of either their boards or companies. Importantly, adhering to the governance guidance and recommendations from the Commonsense Principles will not necessarily guarantee that an enterprise will meet the commitments in the BRT Statement. On the other hand, an enterprise could meet the commitments without implementing these principles. Still, it is strongly believed that businesses adopting these principles could likely create governance and strategic management environments that would create long-term value for all stakeholders.[682]

Concerns have been articulated that the BRT Statements have been a public relations gameplay that would unlike change much the manner US corporations are being led and managed. This is shown by Amazon's subsidiary Whole Foods announcing its plans to terminate medical benefits for its entire part-me personnel; GM rejecting workers' pleas for higher wages and stopping the outsourcing of their jobs, despite GM's hefty profits and large tax breaks; and CEO Muilenburg walking away from Boeing with a USD 60 million severance pay notwithstanding the 737 Max scandal.[683]It has though been counterargued that its significance is not so much about transforming corporate behavior, but rather that it confirms a shift in attitude that has already begun. In disavowing shareholder primacy and adopting a wider vision of CP, the BRT Statement has now strengthened the political legitimacy of such initiatives.[684]

To reinforce the newly minted BRT Statement, it has been proposed that every enterprise should devise a set of binding ethical rules approved by shareholders to be part of their bylaws, an initiative that would potentially open them up to shareholder

682. Grove at al. 2020, *supra* note [679].
683. R. Reich. 2019. "The biggest business con of 2019: Fleecing workers while bosses get rich". *The Guardian 29 December 2019.* https://www.theguardian.com/commentisfree/2019/dec/29/boeing-amazon-business-ethics-robert-reich, accessed December 30, 2019.
684. S. Pearlstein. 2019. "Top CEOs are reclaiming legitimacy by advancing a vision of what's good for America". *The Washington Post 19 August 2019.* https://www.washingtonpost.com/business/2019/08/19/top-ceos-are-reclaiming-legitimacy-by-advancing-vision-whats-good-america/, accessed December 30, 2019.

lawsuits should they fail to adhere to those rules.[685] Such binding set of ethical rules could incorporate key ethical dimensions of corporate activities, like relationships with employees; relationships with the communities in which the enterprise transacts its business; relationships with customers; impacts on the environment; and impacts on future generations. These kinds of ethical rules therefore stress the stakeholder-orientation of the BRT Statement. Thus, the future implementation and application of the BRT Statement would be facilitated, when an enterprise is able to design and follow a governance friendly environment generated via the implementation of the guidelines and recommendations from the Commonsense governance Principles.

7.02d US ESG Reporting Best Practice Guide

The better-known ones are from the NYSE and the USCC. Foremost, the NYSE identified the following different kinds of sustainable investing:

(1) Corporate engagement and shareholder action. Here, investing is undertaken to facilitate engagement with company management on ESG issues, and involves voting on or proposing ESG-linked shareholder resolutions.
(2) Impact investing. This involves the desire to achieve positive environmental and social impact beyond financial returns.
(3) Sustainability-theme investing. This involves investing with a particular emphasis on one or more sustainable development themes, like employee diversity or climate change.
(4) ESG integration. This involves the explicit incorporation of ESG risks and opportunities into traditional financial analysis and investment decisions.
(5) Norms-based screening. This involves the screening of investments according to their compliance with international standards and norms, like UN Global Compact.
(6) Positive/best-in-class screening. This involves choosing companies from defined investment universes based on their relative ESG performance.
(7) Negative/exclusionary screening. This involves excluding companies, sectors or countries from the permissible investment universes where these involved have to do with designated activities, like controversial weapons, human rights abuse, and so on.

The NYSE stressed that ESG disclosure or sustainability reporting has to be understood as a way of communicating how the company is managing ESG issues. Disclosures are viewed as outputs targeted at addressing stakeholder demands for transparency and accountability. The reporting process involved could contribute to

685. A.R. Sorkin. 2019. "Ex-corporate lawyer's idea: Rein in sociopaths in the boardroom". *The New York Times 29 July 2019.* https://www.nytimes.com/2019/07/29/business/dealbook/corporate-governance-reform-ethics.html, accessed December 30, 2019. Sorkin citing the suggestions by Jamie Gamble, a partner at a corporate law firm that advises many major US corporations.

improving a company's own understanding of its own ESG risks and opportunities, thereby sustaining a virtuous circle of improvements. Though best practices are targeted at the disclosure/reporting part of the ESG value chain, it impacts other aspects that are relevant for high-quality reporting.

The eight recommended steps are as follows:

1 Identifying the appropriate approach for the company.

ESG benefits, together with increased regulatory focus on ESG issues and the increase in investors incorporating ESG factors into their investment decisions, imply that management of and reporting on ESG matters that are linked to the company's ability to generate value is likely to grow in importance. Prior to a company's thinking about reporting on its ESG performance, it needs to determine which ESG factors are relevant to it, and how these matters fit into its overall business strategy. Some undertake formal evaluation of these matters through external discussions with shareholders and other stakeholders, while others internally examined ESG issues already on the board's agenda, or included in the company's business plan or risk management procedures. Companies need to be able to answer how specific ESG issues selected for focusing on can contribute to its short-term financial performance and/or long-term value creation. Those new to ESG reporting may start by studying what matters their peers are focused on, through reviewing reporting and disclosures from both peers and upstream and downstream companies in the supply chain.

Environmental issues that can contribute to enterprise value creation, or destruction, include those to do with waste, energy, emissions, biodiversity or water. Social issues include those to do with privacy, data security, forced labor, human rights, community relations, occupational health and safety, diversity and inclusion, or employee relations and development. Governance issues include those to do with tax strategy, executive pay, political lobbying, anti-corruption, shareholder rights, risk management, board diversity, and board oversight. Many companies do great things with their ESG initiatives but did not get full recognitions for them because of weak or ineffective communications to stakeholders. This means that a good reporting strategy would ensure that the company's stakeholders acknowledge the company's ESG initiatives.

2 Identifying stakeholders and assessing the state of engagement.

The GRI Standards identify stakeholders as entities or individuals that can reasonably be expected to be significantly impacted by the reporting company's activities, products, or services; or whose actions can reasonably be envisaged to impact the ability of the company to implement its strategies or achieve its objectives. Stakeholders may include communities where the company operates; CSOs; industry regulators; direct suppliers and those further up the supply chain, like customers, and employees. Following their identification, the company puts in place mechanisms for stakeholder engagements with the aim of identifying how stakeholders think about the company, and its conduct, as it relates to their interests. These engagements could help the company to identify key issues that are likely to affect the company's performance directly or indirectly, so as to have ready-to-use plans to deal with their expectations and concerns, and in the process build trusts over time with them. Tools of engagement could include use of town hall meetings, focus-group discussions, media and social media monitoring, interviews, surveys, or regular investors outreach. These engagement processes enable the company to make informed decision about what to report and where to report it, thereby allowing the company to present information in a way that is most relevant to each set of audience. Other users of ESG reporting are interested to know who the company think its key stakeholders are and how it is managing those stakeholder relationships. Further, there are benefits in disclosing how the company performs with metrics relevant to these stakeholders that can help build trust.

3 Evaluating materiality.

This is usually applied in an SEC reporting context to identify what information companies should disclose. Traditional materiality tends to focus on investors as the primary users of reported information. Materiality is essentially a filter that allows the company to ascertain the ESG factors on which the company's stakeholders focused on. The Corporate Reporting Dialogue (CRD) suggests that material information is that which is reasonably capable of making a difference to the proper assessment of the issue under the radar. This inevitably involves a range of stakeholders and in line with the notion of broad stakeholder accountability. Some materiality definitions focused on matters that are financially material or of impact on the company's financial performance, whereas others consider the impacts that the company's activities have on society and the environment, and yet others suggest this distinction is a moot argument because enterprise value creation can only be understood in the context of its operating environment and the impact it has. It is also important to bear in mind that the process of evaluating the company's key ESG and stakeholder issues is an ongoing one, because what is material would change over time owing to changes in the company itself, policy/regulatory changes, and changes in stakeholder expectations.

4 Establishing governance.

Governance is viewed as the system by which companies are directed and controlled. These include oversight structure and processes that formulate company objectives, measure progress and assess outcomes. Strong governance of ESG issues and ESG reporting is the product of ESG initiatives and credible ESG reporting practices. Good governance of ESG reporting requires that ESG statements have clearly defined owners to provide accountability and allocate clear responsibility for various aspects of the strategy. Good practices in ESG governance include clear board oversight of relevant ESG issues in the company's ESG reporting; allocating responsibility to one or more committees of the board; having robust process in place for identifying key ESG risks; knowing how the company will measure success internally before disclosing externally; ensuring that ESG disclosures are accurate; having in place internal controls to measure, monitor, and internally verify ESG-linked performance, including disclosure controls; and building a data gathering process of sufficient quality for external review assurance. Vey importantly, a clear line of board oversight should be evident to any external reviewer, especially on whether the entire board or dedicated committee have that set of responsibilities should be clearly revealed. Also, the board may include key performance indicators connected to the achievement of ESG targets in evaluating management performance.

5 Integrating ESG into business strategy.

Depending on the nature of the strategy and the identified ESG focus areas, responsibility may be distributed across various divisions in the company, with, for example, human resource in charge of diversity, compliance in charge of whistleblowing and anti-corruptions, and so on. On the other hand, dedicated multidisciplinary sustainability teams could be responsible for coordinating across divisions/departments/teams to ensure that agreed ESG focus areas are being implemented and monitored; ongoing reviews of wider sustainability developments are carried out; the company's ESG reporting process is managed; working with investors relations team to engage with institutional investors and to answering investor inquiries pertaining to ESG matters; responding to ESG-specific queries; and responding to ratings agency and ESG index surveys and questionnaires.

6 Telling the company's story.

Effectively telling the company's story would involve setting out the core issues that the company is focused on; narrating how and why the company has opted for particular issues; disclosing the measurements and key performance indicators (KPIs) that the company is using to monitor progress on these issues; and having the company's targets in place with regard to those issues and what processes are also in place to monitor and ascertain progress against those targets, including what governance structures and processes are in place to ensure oversight of ESG matters. Companies providing such disclosures are likely to be more convincing than those merely providing a long list of ESG metrics that appear unlinked to the company and how it is run. In opting for a more focused approach, the company is able to show that it has a strong handle on ESG matters, and is committed to managing them effectively. Companies are advised to formally refresh the materiality process and the messaging for two-way stakeholder engagements, as their stories evolve. The company's stakeholders may encounter their own changing demands for information, such as exemplified in 2021 where European asset managers face new regulations pertaining to reporting on the ESG characteristics of their portfolio companies.

7 Reporting frameworks and standards followed, or in alignment with.

High-quality reporting relies on the disclosures of accurate, balanced, and comparable information that provides genuine insights. Also, most ESG data needs to be contextualized to be understood. Context may be derived from relative performance of the company with reference to its peers or to historical performance; or derived from the company's operating locations. The wide availability of ESG frameworks requires the company to figure out what would yield meaningful and useful disclosures for the company and its key stakeholders. Such analysis requires understanding of the nuances between different disclosure frameworks/standards, which frameworks/standards work best for telling the company's story to its different stakeholders, and which rankings and ratings matter to the people that matters to the company. While a framework is a set of principles and guidance for how a report is structured, standards provide specific replicable and detailed requirements for what should be reported for each relevant topic or theme. Some of the most widely used references reporting frameworks, as well as some more recent standards, include those from the GRI, the SASB, the TCFD, and the World Economic Forum-International Business Council (WEF-IBC). It needs to be noted here that each of these standards reference the stakeholder groups they have been designed to be relevant to.

8 ESG research and ratings.

Beyond the reporting frameworks and standards, there are also third-party research firms that gather ESG information on companies for the aim of scoring ESG performance. Such information is used by investors to inform their investment decision-making. Different firms use different data and methodologies, making it challenging from a resource and cost perspective to address all of these. The company would have to decide which ESG data providers/rankers/raters are most relevant for them and their key stakeholders, and allocate their initiatives accordingly. Several ratings are administered by or connected to companies that construct indices for investment purposes. For instance, the MSCI ESG Research is premised entirely on publicly available information gathered from academic and CSO datasets, company disclosures from MSCI indices, and various media sources. Sustainalytics owned by investment research firm Monringstar sourced their data from companies and civil societies too, but forward drafts of their reports to companies for feedback before publication. S&P ESG/Corporate Sustainability Assessment involves companies' participations by invitation and is able to compare their ESG performance with other companies being rated, while Moody's/Virgeo Eiris covers evaluation of a company's ESG practices, including a view of their alignments with the UN SDGs and the UN Global Compact. Finally, ESG disclosure is most compelling when the company explains why it focuses on the issues that it has, what the company is doing about those issues, and what oversight the company has in place to ensure it stays on track.

Aside from the above guidance provided by the NYSE, the Center for Capital Market Competitiveness of the USCC also provides its version of best practices around stand-alone ESG reports. The aim of this is to help the development of a widely followed approach to voluntary ESG reporting, without the force of statutory requirement. As such, this version allows some disclosure variability, as it acknowledges that the relevance of particular ESG factors differs from industry to industry and enterprise to enterprise, and based on business models, geography, clientele-based and other factors. Contextualizing for these, the guidance below provides best ESG reporting practice, as enterprise continues to enhance their ESG disclosures. Beyond this, the USCC on August 4, 2021, ran an ESG guidance session on "How to Set Standards for ESG Policy," simultaneously releasing its survey on ESG and climate change results showing that most companies have increased their amounts of climate change disclosures. The USCC ESG Reporting Best Practices guide released in November 2019 includes the following:

(1) Calling for a focus on the company's ESG risks and opportunities that have sufficient effects on its long-term operational and financial performance. These should include the company's approach to risk management and making the link between the reported ESG practices and the company's long-term value creation.
(2) Identifying the report's target audience and tailoring the tone and content of its report accordingly, particularly in regard to the usefulness of the information to investors and other stakeholders.
(3) ESG report preparers need to liaise with other operating departments/ functions to ensure all relevant information is gathered and addressed, including different perspectives accounted for, but leaving the determination of the legality of materiality to the legal department.
(4) ESG technical terms without universally accepted definitions have to be written in plain English.
(5) Each company should have the discretion to maintain flexibility, when determining which ESG factors and related metrics to apply, and what are meaningful to their stakeholders, and not necessarily what is identified in other third-party frameworks and standards.
(6) ESG preparers need to explain the basis for their choice of ESG topics and tell why their management believe why those topic and metrics are relevant or important to the company.
(7) ESG information should be easy for users to retrieve, such as through dedicated ESG web pages and links. This need not be achieved via SEC filings, nor should ESG information be required as part of an ESG filing, especially where this is not material under the Supreme Court's well-settled definition of materiality for federal securities laws purposes.
(8) Companies should explore in their voluntary ESG reports descriptions of their internal review and audit processes, or any external verification of the information the company received.

7.02e UK ESG Reporting Best Practice Guide

The London Stock Exchange Group (LSEG) in 2020 released "Your Guide to ESG Reporting: Guidance for Issuers on the Integration of ESG into Investor Reporting and Communication." The LSEG stressed that given the frequent use of ESG data alongside other financial and strategic information in investment analysis and decision-making, there is a compelling case for companies to strengthen their reporting and communication by incorporating ESG matters. This is largely because investors are keen to understand how well companies are managing the risks linked to ESG factors, noting this as a key test of management quality. They are also keen to know the opportunities presented in the green economy, as notably they would continue to allocate capital to companies well placed to benefit from these. As such, issuers should provide investment-grade data and information. In particular, the LSEG stressed the following:

(1) Disclosing the relevance of particular ESG factors to the company's business model and strategy. This should be an integrated component of the company's business drivers, and not merely latched on.
(2) Disclosing how ESG matters may impact the company's business through matters, like new laws and regulation, reputational damage, employee turnover, operating license, litigations, or stakeholder relationships, and how these impacts could affect business strategy and operational and financial performances.
(3) Disclose how the company intends to access the new opportunities and revenue streams generated by green and socially beneficial products and services. In relation to this, the company should disclose how their investments in R&D and innovation would power future growth for the company's business.
(4) Crucially, the company should identify the parts of the business that manufacture or provide goods, products and services delivering environmental solutions and supporting the transition to green economy, including the breakdown and quantity of the associated revenues.
(5) Disclose data that is accurate, timely, aligning with the fiscal year and business ownership model, and premised on consistent global standards to facilitate comparability.
(6) Given that ESG reporting is just one avenue for engagements with investors, regardless of the format used, this should provide a basis for dialogue with investors, but not a substitute for it.

Helen Hopper in her August 2021 article "ESG Regulations: What UK Organisations Must Know to Comply" in *Diligence* highlighted the UK government's aim of developing ESG policy and regulatory landscape that works for the UK market, tailoring many niches of law to UK priorities (like net-zero legislation), and through these, strengthen the UK economy to generate post-COVID growth. Given that investors and consumers are also focusing on ESG performance indicators, it is prudent for UK enterprises to be mindful of the impacts of more intensive ESG regulations. ESG factors are known to be highly interdependent and covering a wide menu of themes that have also grown and transformed in importance and focus over time, such that ESG regulation has been struggling to keep pace. Though there is no one overarching ESG piece of UK legislation, there are various regulations covering aspects of ESG that business enterprises need to comply with in varying manners, depending on their size, sector, or scope. These flow from a range of legislative sources and official guidance, including the MSA 2015, Bribery Act 2010, Disclosure Guidance and Transparency Rules (DTRs), UKSC 2020, Climate Change Act 2008 (CCA), CA 2006, and UK CG Code 2018 (UK CGC). The main ESG disclosure requirements though emanate from the DTRs, CA 2006 and UK CG Code that are frequently principles-based, rather than prescriptive. This could be beneficial in the context of wider coverage, but could leave business enterprises short of guidance about precisely which elements of their operations to track and report on, and which target audiences to address.

Though the bulk of ESG reporting is presently not mandatory in the country, some particular metrics that come under ESG regulation reporting umbrella are mandatory. These include GHG reporting for listed companies since 2013; energy use as required by the Companies (Directors' Report) and Limited Liability Partnerships (Energy and Carbon Report) Regulations 2018; and Gender Pay Gap disclosure for employers with more than 250 personnel. Given the likelihood that ESG regulations with mandatory reporting are likely to grow in scope in the foreseeable future, many forward-looking business enterprises (like the Lloyds Banking Group) are voluntarily adopting frameworks and implementing processes that would enable them to report from a mature position across a wider range of metrics. These initiatives would help keep them in readiness for mandatory ESG reporting. In any case, Chancellor Rishi Sunak has already signaled that mandatory reporting of climate-linked financial information following TCFD guidelines will be implemented across the UK by 2025. Prime Minister Johnson would also be hosting the UN climate change summit, known as COP26 in New York between November 1 and 12, 2021. This was previously scheduled for November 2020 in Glasgow.

Hopper has also provided suggestions for good ESG reporting practice. These involve the following:

(1) High-profiling ESG in the company's board agenda, as well as ensuring that the board has access to expertise and comprehensive ESG data for adequate support of the company's business.
(2) Undertake a materiality evaluation to identify and prioritize ESG niches applicable to the company's business, especially existing ESG-related regulatory requirements.
(3) Map out the targeted audiences for the company's ESG reporting.
(4) Plan and budget for the infrastructure, technology, and resource investments required to support identification of material ESG factors, regulatory compliance, and the tracking of ESG performance.
(5) Getting familiarized with the better-known ESG frameworks and standards and assessing their appropriateness to the company's business.

7.02f EU ESG Reporting Best Practice Guide

The regulation on sustainability-related disclosures in financial services (SFDR) was adopted by the European Parliament and European Council on November 2019, and is applicable to in-scope financial services enterprises from June 2021. This requires asset managers, financial advisers, and other market participants to take into account sustainability and ESG matters in their decision-making around investments, and in providing information about how they account for sustainability risks in their investment advice or decision-making. The idea is to enhance investors' ability to investigate financial enterprises' approach to ESG. These obligations are fixed for enterprises with more than five hundred employees, whereas smaller ones are obliged to either explain how they take these into account, or if not, why they do not. Further obligations apply where products are marketed as ESG or sustainable products, with the legislation SFDR classifying these into mainstream products, products promoting environmental or social characteristics, and those promoting sustainable investments. Though various sustainable investments and funds could be already providing these kinds of information, the standardized-feature of the SFDR would probably facilitate the comparability of products, and for consumers to hold them to higher standards.

Equivalent regulations are being explored in the US, where the SEC has articulated regulations considerations around climate disclosures, especially in more effective enforcements against misleading information provided about ESG investments and disclosures. The UK has also signaled that it would follow TCFD's recommendations and to make climate-related financial disclosures mandatory for in-scope enterprises by 2025. The FCA already has in place a new listing rule on climate-related disclosure for premium listed companies in the capital markets that requires the provision of information on the company's exposure to climate change risks and opportunities.

The European Parliament has already also proposed an obligation to conduct due diligence and a liability provision with respect essentially of ESG concerns for enterprises failing to do so. These would likely be applicable to all large enterprises operating in the EU, as well as listed or high-risk SMEs. This is in conjunction with the UN Guiding Principles on Business and Human Rights, wherein human rights diligence is taken to refer to a process of evaluating the actual and potential human rights effects of an enterprise's operations and following through with communications of how these effects are being addressed. Such obligations extend to those risks directly linked to the enterprise's operations by business relationships, and the wider supply chains. While mindful of commercial confidentiality, these may include providing information on locations, name, products/services supplied, and information pertaining to subsidiaries, suppliers and business partners in the supply value chain, both up and down streams. It is also expected to include obligations to incorporate human rights standards and policies in place, including mechanisms providing remedies for harms flowing from human rights and environmental and governance failures. The mechanisms for distinguishing, causing, contributing and being directly linked to ESG harms adapted from the UN Guiding Principles are though not so easy to follow.

One thing is clear though. European sentiments are heading toward relatively rigid due diligence law, essentially dissimilar to UK's MSA 2015 or California's Transparency in Supply Chains Act of 2010 where both focused on disclosure obligations. EU's equivalent version is likely to require both extensive reporting and designated actions to addressing risks within companies. Hence, instead of requiring companies to alter the way they operate, the aim here is for transparency obligations to promote change in business practices and to promote accountability. Such mandatory ESG disclosures rules, when put into effect, are likely to enhance examination of company decision-making around ESG factors, bringing with them serious implications for legal and reputational risks. A prudent way for responding to these risks is to prepare for alignment to these obligations by closely following available best practice guidance. Alexis See Tho's August 2021 article "5 Steps to Successful ESG Reporting" in *Financial Management* highlighted Siemens Energy's approach in its ESG reporting journey that took several years in the making. This includes the five steps of establishing, assessing, designing, implementing, and assuring in its ESG reporting journey. Anna Maleva-Otto and Joshua Wright in their March 2020 article "New ESG Disclosure Obligations" in the Harvard Law School Forum on CG highlighted the following key steps that asset managers and investment advisers could take to comply with the forthcoming regulations:

(1) In-scope companies would need to evaluate and document the relevance of ESG factors to their investment policies.
(2) They also need to publish on their website information pertaining to their policies on integration of sustainability risks in their investment decision-making processes.
(3) Disclosures on the manner by which sustainability risks are integrated into their investment decisions and advice and the outcomes of the manager's evaluation of the probable effects of sustainability risks on the returns must also be incorporated in the pre-contractual disclosures, as exemplified by the investment management agreement pertaining to a separately managed account, or the private placement memorandum, or prospectus of a fund.
(4) Additional detailed disclosure obligations would apply to investments that are marketed as sustainable investments to align with the requirements of the Taxonomy Regulation, or other products promoting particular ESG characteristics.

Pitted against the context of increased investor demand for ESG-linked focus, regulators in the EU, UK, and the US are getting more concerned with the accuracy, adequacy, and reliability of ESG disclosures and the risk of greenwashing of financial products and services. It would be prudent for companies, especially those in financial services, to adjust their companies' processes and reporting practices to align closely with the applicable ESG laws and regulations.

7.03 REVIEW OF NATIONAL AND GLOBAL ESG REPORTING BEST PRACTICES

The way the G20/OECD and IOSCO CG Principles have been compiled and narrated are encouraging, as they provide sound guidance for the design of effective governance practices, effective monitoring, and effective internal control systems. These range from basic to advanced levels of governance principles and practices. The guidance and recommendations provided put a lot of stress on ESG issues that directors report has to take into due consideration.

Analysis of past and current seminal cases of flawed governance practices at both the financial services and nonfinancial services sectors in both advanced and developing economies demonstrates clearly that major weaknesses in governance practices did not flow from ignorance of viable governance practices. Rather, much of these arose from likely intentional high risk-taking for very high profits ambitions and with actions linked to conflicts of interest of senior management and/or board members that somehow escaped the attention of both internal and external auditing.

These suggest the failures of both internal and external control systems in these seminal cases. When happening on a widespread scale, as in the 2000 Dotcom bubble, the 2007-2009 GFC, and the continuing bad management practices in some big financial services and nonfinancial services corporations, they could inflict very serious financial harms to those directly involved, as well as those indirectly involved. The fact that these have been more highlighted in scandalous cases in the US, UK, and the EU would not necessarily imply that governance practices are undertaken in better ways in developing and emerging economies, as clearly demonstrated in the 1997 AFC. In the 1997 AFC, almost all economies in the region saw the collapse of their economies because of the contagion effects of the then financial crisis occurring there. With the help of guidance from international development agencies like the IMF, the World Bank, the ADB, and others, most of the impacted economies not only recovered within two years but also benefited from vastly improved macroeconomic management, and vast improvements in the governance of their business enterprises. When the 2007-2008 GFC radiated from the advanced economies, they were impacted relatively less, and with some large economies, like China becoming able to contribute from the strength of their savings reserves.

As led by the UK, and for many other economies, governance standards ended up mostly in voluntary codes that helped to promote sustainable ESG practices. Driven by reasons of efficiency and legitimacy, model governance codes mushroomed across the world owing to their practicality and the psychological element attached to them. These developments remain private proclamations of best practice, and lack legal backing. This extralegal characteristic is beneficial as it bypassed national legal and political processes, thereby offering the possibility for companies to directly address their needs in the most flexible and adaptive way and ergo creating the conditions for an accelerated normative convergence. Flexible voluntary codes indeed respond to economic needs and demand. They respond to a microeconomic demand from investors, seemingly willing to pay a governance premium for well-governed companies' shares on the reasoning that a well-governed company is likely to behave more efficiently, in a less risky way, and eventually more profitable. These benefits aside, governance codes also satisfy macroeconomic imperative; as per the World Bank,[686] sound governance practices could increase access to competitive cost external financing leading to larger investments, higher growth, more jobs, and lowered financial crisis risk; and per the OECD,[687] one of the keys to healthy financial markets.

As the abovementioned needs and demands are global in nature and target similar issues, governance codes tend to contain equivalent provisions. The extent of equivalency among governance codes is generally much higher than among company laws and regulations.[688] This codification therefore corresponds to governance codes'

686. S. Claessens. 2006. *CG and development*. Washington, DC: World Bank.
687. OECD. 2008. *CG in Asia*. Paris: OECD.
688. European Commission (EC). 2003. *Modernising company law and enhancing CG in the EU- A plan to move forward*. Brussels: EC.

fundamental standardization function.[689] The conventional governance landscape is, however, transforming. Rooted and evolving without legal constraints, governance is appearing to be a victim of its own success. A series of scandals and failures since the 1970s propelled governance to the forefront of the political and media agenda. Trust and confidence in business morals and self-regulation have plummeted severely, prompting public calls for more intrusive regulations. These have been accompanied by accelerating concerns that governance norms are becoming too serious a matter to be left entirely to the business people. Though these public responses have generally been varied, they however showed a general trend toward legalization or publicization of the governance process, whether via input of public authorities on the elaboration of governance codes; the incorporation of CG requirements into laws, regulations, codifications; or a requirement to publicly declare adherence to a code.[690]

Though governance practices could no longer be viewed as governance without government, there appears to be the absence of legal certainty pertaining to the enforcement of governance provisions owing to the lack of any specific legislative measures. This is disturbing, as when law matters, it is not only the text of the law but also its enforcement that matters. As such, the level of enforcement of soft governance rules would play a more important role, than the quality of law in the books.[691] Empirical evidence suggests a wide consensus that poor enforcement governance codes had an indirect negative impact, as the application of governance rules could not be relied on in the protection of shareholders' rights. This led to the development of substitutes that were relatively less efficient, like the concentration of ownership, that in turn influenced the content and enforcement of governance rules in a self-perpetuating process, besides undermining other governance mechanisms, like board activisms, proxy fights, and hostile takeovers.[692]

Stringent enforcement, on the other hand, would increase the ability of enterprises to attract external financing, and ultimately the extent of general financial development. This contributes to the lower cost of equity capital, especially in the US, EU, and the UK. It helps to explain in part the valuation premium that foreign corporations could benefit from, when cross-listing in these respective jurisdictions.[693] The US experience also demonstrates that where stringent enforcement has been a positive development, excessive enforcement could be counterproductive. In the face of financial crisis and corporate scandals, draconian enforcements linked to overregulation could seriously hike the cost of capital and threaten the market competitiveness

689. D. Seidl. 2007. "Standard setting and following in CG: An observation". *Theoretical Study of the Effectiveness of Governance Code*, Vol. 14 (5): 705-727.
690. V.G. Bruno & S. Claessens. 2007. "CG and regulation: Can there be too much of a good thing?" *ESGI Finance Working Paper No. 142/2007.*
691. E. Berglof & S. Claessens. 2004. "CG and enforcement". *World Bank Policy Research Working Paper 3409.*
692. M.I. Defond &M. Hung. 2003. "Investor protection and CG: Evidence from worldwide CEO turnover". *University of Southern California Leventhal School of Accounting Mimeo 2003.*
693. C. Doidge, A. Karolyi & R. Stulz. 2004. "Why are foreign firms listed in the US worth more?". *Journal of Financial Economics*, Vol. 71 (2004): 205.

of a national economy. This has been observed some two decades subsequent to the enactment of SOX 2002.[694]

Individual enforcement mechanisms extend from private ordering to private law enforcement or public enforcement. Broad consensus has also evolved on the need to strengthen private law enforcement via litigation and arbitration. These are presented as potentially effective tools in the context of investor protection and capital market development.[695] The growing importance of public enforcement via securities commissions, and correspondingly the focus on the capabilities of national securities commissions across the world to fulfill this agenda within the limitations of financial and personnel resources,[696] is gradually though becoming more challenging. It is, however, vitally important to note that enforcement mechanisms are nonexclusive and should be treated as complementing, rather than substituting for one another.[697]

The effectiveness of private ordering, for example, primarily depends on the broader institutional environment where activist movements like shareholder lobbying group would require some legal support. Still, public authorities dealing with governance codes appear to have neglected the matter of governance enforcement, culminating in a deficit of its enforcement.[698] The primary reason for this deficit is that corporations are usually not legally, or practically required, or incentivized to adhere to governance of soft rules, and when required to, corporations generally feel free to show little respect for their actual implications and limit themselves to a box-ticking response.

The enforcement deficit phenomenon helps to explain why although governance models appear to be substantively similar, corporate practices continued to differ vastly among corporations, even more so between economies, and why seeming compliance with these codes has been proven inadequate to deter major governance flaws.[699] There also appears to be a positive correlation between enforcement mechanisms and the legal status of the relevant rules, such that the stronger the legal basis for a rule, the stronger the legal instrument for enforcement. Thus, as in most controversial governance cases, rules have not been directly enshrined in law, but contained in codes that have not been legally binding, but had been referred to by public authorities, regulators, and lawmakers in various innovative manners.[700]

Governance codes have evolved in the first phase without recognition, but as mere recommendations drawn up by professional associations without explicit support

694. I. Zingales. 2007. "Is the US capital market losing its competitive edge?". *ECGI Finance Series No: 192/2007.*
695. J. Armour, et al. 2009. "Private enforcement of corporate law: An empirical comparison of the UK and the US". *ECGI Law Working Paper No. 120/2009.*
696. J.C. Coffee Jr. 2007. "Law and the market: The impact of enforcement". *University of Pennsylvania Law Review,* Vol. 156 (2007): 229-311.
697. V.G. Bruno & S. Claessens. 2006. "CG and regulation: Can there be too much of a good thing?". *ECGI Finance Working Paper No. 142/2007 October 2006.*
698. K. Palepu, T. Khanna & J. Kogan. 2003. "Globalization and similarities in CG: A cross-country analysis". *Harvard University Working Paper May 2003.*
699. A. Pietrancosta. 2011. "Enforcement of CG codes: A legal perspective". *Doctrine,* Vol. RTDF No. ½ (2011): 27-39.
700. Pietrancosta 2011, *supra* note [699].

of public authorities or regulators. The codes have been essentially self-regulatory, its implementation voluntary, and based on self-proclamation, while its enforcements rely on evaluations of market forces, seen not only in price formation but also in decisions made by business associations, CRAs, investment banks, proxy advisors, public opinions, the media, and so forth. This then evolves into the second phase, with some official recognitions that vary, such as found in the NYSE, Nasdaq, Euronext, and LSE; in ad hoc commissions, such as the Belgian Governance Institute; in national securities commissions, like the SEC and FSA; and in federal and state legislatures. Public recognition could come in the form of factual recognition of compliance, as in Germany and Turkey; in contributions by public authorities or private regulators; from the elaborations of governance codes, as in Belgium, Spain, or Luxembourg; through monitoring of companies' compliance with a code, as in the Netherlands or France; via recommendations on code compliance from market operators or securities commission, as in France; and tax breaks extended to corporations applying good and sound governance standards.[701]

The abovementioned two phases of governance regulation development did not involve direct legal requirements, but this did not suggest that they exist totally outside the legal space. These codes of conduct though self-regulatory did interact with the legal system via the judicial channels, contractual channels, incorporations of governance rules in companies' articles of association, and regulatory channels.[702] It has been further envisaged that improved monitoring and enforcement of the codes would have repercussions on the recommendations they contained, in terms of the quality and content of the recommendations, and especially their adaptations to the local context. The third phase would involve the imposition of legal requirements, with the current trends pushing the public recognition process much further through deployments of legal mechanisms that would unlikely abate in a context of reregulation. In this respect, two kinds of legal requirements have been applied in this process by market operators, securities commissions, or legislators.

First, the legal requirements could take the form of the introduction minimally or extensively of governance provisions in legislations.[703] SOX 2002 offers a typical example of extensive legislation of governance provisions pertaining to loans to executive, BC and functioning, auditors' independence, and so on. There has been as yet no jurisdiction making an entire governance code mandatory by law, as governance codes are viewed as a process targeted at facilitating the discovery of optimal solutions, or at best, as mere default rules. Second, these refer to legal disclosure requirements in securities law and regulation of corporate law of compliance with a governance code.[704] Such a kind of requirement is obviously less intrusive, but because of this, potentially more extensive. However, a legal requirement for companies to disclose the extent of their compliance with an entire governance code is gaining more traction. This legal nature of listing conditions was initially required by the LSE, as the listing

701. Pietrancosta 2011, *supra* note [699].
702. Pietrancosta 2011, *supra* note [699].
703. Pietrancosta 2011, *supra* note [699].
704. Pietrancosta 2011, *supra* note [699].

authority in the UK. This has been subsequently taken over by the FSA (and much later by the FCA), thereby changing the legal nature of the listing conditions from private to public.

At the worldwide level, the OECD Principles of CG endorsed by OECD Ministers in 1999 have been progressively updated. Though influential in practice, the OECD Principles could only offer nonbinding standards and good practices owing to the limited legal powers held by their promoters. The OECD Principles do not evoke governance codes that do not have the status of law or regulation. Nevertheless, they do recommend that, when such codes are used as national standards, or as an explicit substitute for legal or regulatory provisions, a clear specification of their status in terms of coverage, implementation, compliance, and sanctions should be provided. Up to now, the OECD evaluates the level of compliance with its Principles of CG via pilot studies in member countries. The EC's initial approach in 2004 created a European CG Forum so as to encourage the coordination and convergence of national codes and the manner they are enforced and monitored. This soft approach eventually gave way to a relatively tougher stance using legally binding provisions, such as found in Directive (2006/43/EC) of May 17, 2006. This requires Member States to require audit committees in public interest entities.

More importantly, Directive (2006/46/EC) of June 14, 2006, amends the 4th and 7th company law directives, whereby companies whose securities are admitted to trading on a regulated market have to include in their documents:

(1) A governance statement containing its main features of internal control and risk management systems.
(2) Information on their anti-takeover protections.
(3) The manners shareholders could exercise their voting rights.
(4) References to the governance code the company is subject to.
(5) The governance code the company opts to voluntarily apply.
(6) All pertinent information related to governance practices adopted in addition to national legal requirements.

Where a company opts not to apply a governance code, or departs from certain provisions of CG code, it should explain its reasons for doing so. Thus, the EU began adopting a disclosure-based approach combining soft law and hard law, whereby all EU companies listed on an EU regulated market would be legally required via hard law to disclose their level of compliance or their level of noncompliance through a legally nonbinding soft law code.[705] The EU engages with the soft law processes as these would enable flexibility, adaptability, besides enabling experimentation, innovation and emulation among companies. It also reflects a bottom-up approach that would help markets to evolve toward convergence. In particular, the comply or explain principles would reflect the consensus among market participants that a one-size-fits-all approach to governance would be inappropriate.

705. P. Zurnbansen 2008. "New governance in European corporate law regulation as transnational legal pluralism". *CLPE Research Paper No. 15/2008.*

As time marches on, answers given across various countries to the simple question of what could be the actions to be taken in cases of noncompliance, incomplete or misleading compliance by reporting companies, have been far from being clear and uniform.[706] This significant problem aside, there are also the practical concerns over whether companies would comply with governance codes, even when not legally bound to do so, thereby leaving the reliance on market pressures for compliance and enforcement. The seeming co-regulation approach assumes that the punishment for breach of governance codes should be more financial, than legal in nature, but empirical evidence appears ambiguous.[707] The level of compliance in the UK appears to be substantive, as reflected by enhanced firm values for those in this category, but evidence from Germany, the Netherlands, Spain, Portugal and Japan showed that voluntary governance initiatives relying on co-regulation did not have impacts on firm values or share prices.[708] These outcomes could be polluted by corporate tendencies to overestimate their own levels of compliance, as they would be able to enjoy the advantage of being exempted from being required to furnish further public explanations; or their fears of market participants not fully understanding their reasons for noncomplying would compel them to apply the whole code without much discernment, and at times with certain degrees of hypocrisy.[709]

The disciplining impact of the comply or explain principle is dependent on the ability of market participants to effectively monitor a company's compliance with governance codes, including evaluation of the reliability or credibility of a company's compliance statement. Even where there appears to be a correlation between a corporation's governance practice and its performance, the message sent to the market in its compliance statement has to be credible. Apart from the concerns raised earlier about the accuracy of the nature of compliance reporting, gatekeepers like auditors, securities commissions and independent regulators only play limited roles in this area. Securities commissions often lacked the power, the will, or the capabilities to do more than a formal compliance check. It appears that public enforcement of governance rules could play an important role, via more informal channels, like persuasion, and not through sanctions or legal actions. Independent regulators, like the FRC, have not been performing up to expectations, and ergo its eventual replacement by a statutory-based entity with wider and stronger enforcement powers.

In this regard, private actors like institutional shareholders and the financial media have been playing crucial roles, as seen in the UK and the US. The intensity of market pressures exemplifies such a role. This intensity would depend on the agendas, intensity, and commitments of institutional shareholders and social activists. A breakthrough example is demonstrated recently with the success of social-good activists led by a small hedge fund with the support of big institutional shareholders in

706. Pientrancosta 2011, *supra* note [699].
707. Pientrancosta 2011, *supra* note [699].
708. Pientrancosta 2011, *supra* note [699].
709. P. Coombes & S. C-Y, Wong. 2006. "Why codes of governance work?" *McKinsey Quarterly* Vol. 2 (2000): 2.

installing three directors on the board of ExxonMobil with the goal of pushing the energy giant to reduce its carbon footprints.[710]

Doubts still linger as to whether, or to what extent, the regulatory approach promoted by the EU has been able to resolve the issues raised by the governance process,[711]in comparison to the prescriptive US approach.[712] Initially, SOX's enormous administrative and transactional costs help to push promoted migrations of US corporations to jurisdictions elsewhere with less onerous governance structures requirements. That triggered calls in the US for revamping of governance rules to resemble the less burdensome and principles-based soft law structures used in the UK and elsewhere. However, eventual evaluation of this option concludes that, given the long-standing and singularity of American predilection for rules-based regulation and litigation, any large-scale transplant of soft law principles into the US governance process is likely to be a practical impossibility.[713] Regardless, effective enforcement has been suggested to be the more effective answer for the success of a disclosure regulation as the new comply or explain procedure,[714] as well as a prerequisite, if this principle is ever to be seen as a credible component, or even a credible alternative basis for public company regulation.[715] This is because the condition for self-enforcement did not appear to be present in all economies, and effective compliance seems to be higher within a legal environment that is unafraid to enforce. Positive incentives though could be considered so as to promote self-enforcement, for instance, via the creation of special categories of stock markets of indices[716] or tax breaks for companies which apply sound governance practices.

As a conventional characteristic of the common law, rather than civil law, more intensive enforcement initiatives are a necessary corollary of the greater flexibility they allow to market participants.[717] Insights from national experience in Germany shows that an insufficient level of compliance with a voluntary code would frequently serve as a justification for its replacement by standard law.[718] Also, the general distrust of self-regulation and self-enforcement arising from the loss of confidence in the financial markets is shining the way for re-legitimization of legal intervention, and particularly

710. M. Phillips. 2021. "Exxon's board defeat signals the rise of social-good activists". *The New York Times 9 June 2021*. https://www.nytimes.com/2021/06/09/business/exxon-mobil-engine-no 1-activist.html, accessed June 15, 2021.
711. European CG Forum (ECGF). 2006. "Statement on the comply-or explain principle". *ECGF 06/03/06.*
712. J.V. Anderson. 2008. "Regulating corporations the American way: Why exhaustive rules and just deserts are the mainstay of U.S. CG". *Duke Law Journal*, Vol. 57 (2008): 1081-1112.
713. Anderson 2008, *supra* note [712].
714. N.O'Shae. 2005. "Governance how we've got where we are and what's next". *Accountancy Ireland.*
715. V.G. Bruno & S. Claessens. 2007. "CG and regulation: Can there be too much of a good thing?". https://www2.nber.org/conferences/2007/si2007/CG/bruno.pdf, accessed November 10, 2020.
716. L.A. Bebchuk & A. Hamdani. 2009. "The elusive quest for global governance standards". *University of Pennsylvania Law Review*, Vol. 157 (5): 1263.
717. J.C. Coffee. 2007. "Law and the market: The impact of enforcement". *University of Pennsylvania Law Review*, Vol. 156 (2007): 229.
718. C. Andres & E. Theissen. 2008. "Setting a fox to keep the geese—Does the comply-or-explain principle work?" *Journal of Corporate Finance*, Vol. 14 (2008): 289.

in the concerning area of governance.[719] As the effective level of enforcement is still being sought, there have been further criticisms on self and soft regulation and advocations for tougher approaches to governance, as demonstrated by the increased political pressures for stronger controls over executive compensations in listed corporations.[720]

Thus, an innovative legislative process could be established, whereby national legislators explicitly set goals for private standards-setter. This would implicitly set the level of required compliance that forewarns intervention in the event of underachievement. It would also be a good counter to self-regulatory approaches that seek primarily to preempt government intervention.[721] Above all, this could even transform into a government-controlled laboratory for hard legislation.[722] Hence, where nonbinding codes are not a source of law in the formal process, they would increasingly be treated as a source of legislative inspiration. In this governance with government tie-in, comply or explain would be more likely reduced to comply or complain.[723] There is though the risk of general pressures for intrusive regulation, and the argument that hard law is the optimal way for addressing GFC and preventing further scandals. This is likely to be the outcome of confirmation bias, rather than rational legal and economic analysis that would have given the comply or explain regulatory approach a chance, as long as it is not empirically proven to be less efficient than substantive regulation.

Overall, despite some years of experience in the use of governance codes, there is still considerable scope for making further improvements in governance reporting. One particular area that could make enterprises take even more serious view of governance practices and the impacts these have on the company and stakeholders is the implications flowing from the perspective of private law, as to whether governance codes could be interpreted as valid enforceable obligations, and if so, toward whom should such an obligation arise.[724]

Corporate codes as declarations to the public are located in a peculiar manner between wrongful behavior and the formal contract, thereby calling for a third source of private law obligations between contract and tort.[725] It has been contended that private law enforcement of corporate codes is in major parts not a matter of far-reaching reforms. It merely instead requires an internal development within the legal system that could be initiated by the courts. Corporate codes could first be interpreted as evidence that is consulted by the courts to determine the enforceable terms in

719. S. Ashby. 2009. "The Turner Review on the global banking crisis: A response from the financial Services Research Forum". https://www.nottingham.ac.uk/business/businesscentres/gcbfi/documents, accessed November 10, 2020.
720. Andres & Theissen 2008, *supra* note [718].
721. A. Indira Anand. 2006. "An analysis of enabling vs. Mandatory CG: Structure pots-SOX". *Delaware Journal of Corporate Law*, Vol. 31 (2006): 229.
722. P. Coombes & S. Y-W. Wong. 2000. "Why codes of governance work". *McKinsey Quarterly*, Vol. 2 (2000): 43.
723. D.M. Trubeck, P. Cottrell & M. Stance. 2005. "Soft law, hard law and European integration: Towards a theory of hybridity". https://media.law.wisc.edu/s/c_8/zy5nj/hybriditypaperapril2005.pdf, accessed November 10, 2020.
724. Bruno & S. Claessens 2007, *supra* note [715].
725. A. Beckers. 2015. *Enforcing corporate social responsibility codes*. Oxford: Hart Publishing.

subsequently concluded contracts, and second, being open to enforcement as relied-upon promises.[726]

However, pertaining to beneficiaries that act to their detriment in relying on corporate codes, and therefore the companies' performance of its promised regulatory role, a reliance-based form of noncontractual liability is still considered a complementary pillar that needs to be taken further. The precise legal basis for this specific reliance-based tort liability depends primarily on whether the corporate code becomes enforceable by contract, or as a public declaration.[727] To the extent that corporate code is viewed as a contractual obligation, the specific rules in tort or quasi-contractual liability pertaining to the negligent performance seem especially suitable.[728] The detrimentally impacted beneficiaries could be qualified incidentally as beneficiaries that are impacted by the performance of the contractual regulatory duties. Relating to the issue of whether establishing such a duty of care of the contracting parties toward the beneficiaries would be fair, just and reasonable, the courts could refer to the need to preserve the evolving regulatory role of companies to pursue political objectives as a normative justification. But from a practical perspective, this suggestion has to remain supplementary and would only be brought into play to the extent that this construction of corporate codes as third-party rights is not feasible.

Pertaining to liability for publicly declared codes, the proposed reliance-based species of legal liability is suggested as a development that needs to be related to the tort law general rules.[729] The suggestion treats reliance-based liability instead as a specific form wherein the public declaration is legally viewed as the basis for establishing reliance-based liability in principle, and accords noncomplying behavior as the wrongful act that gives rise to liability.

The future direction of enforcement mechanisms could be observed from developments in the UK, where the very idea of governance codes really began. The FRC review of governance reporting in the UK for 2020 reveals the following:[730]

(1) Reporting companies appear to be more focused on governance processes, than on meaningful reporting.
(2) The FRC reminds reporting companies to rely less on the tick-box approach, and instead to embrace the aims of the governance principles.
(3) There are encouraging signs of companies going beyond the initiatives introduced. These have been reflected by processes that were followed in discussing outcomes and what impacts they had on the reporting businesses. Measuring and reporting on impact would mean moving away from boilerplate statements toward meaningful reporting. Focusing on impact, while not ignoring the processes involved, would also help companies

726. Beckers 2015, *supra* note [725].
727. Beckers 2015, *supra* note [725].
728. Beckers 2015, *supra* note [725].
729. Beckers 2015, *supra* note [725].
730. FRC. 2020. "Review of CG reporting". *FRC November 2020.* https://www.frc.org.uk/getattachment/c22f7296-0839-420e-ae03-bdce3e157702/Governance-Report-2020-2611.pdf, accessed December 12, 2020.

better assess the effectiveness of their governance and generate better corporate performance and outcomes for shareholders and stakeholders.

(4) With a wide range of ESG issues growing in prominence and attracting greater government and public attention, ignoring best practice guidance generates greater risk. The FRC would be taking steps to engage with companies struggling with the application of the Code, including those that claimed compliance without fully doing so.

(5) Companies better aligned with expectations of the Code and section 172 of CA 2006 have been more equipped to face these said challenges. Those showing healthier corporate cultures and better stakeholder engagements also showed better resilience.

Boards are now expected to raise and answer some of the hardest questions. This is to ensure that the varied risks linked to Brexit, COVID-19 and Climate Change would be effectively addressed and mitigated in corporate operations and strategy. The FRC would be monitoring how companies are reporting on the impact of risks which have manifested, and how boards would be responding in terms of improving their governance, especially on how directors would be discharging their section 172 duty pertaining to social issues. There will be particular focus on the quality of stakeholder engagements, the extent to which they have informed board decisions, and how effectively companies had been responding to issues raised in red alerts.[731]

The governance of the FRC itself is expected to be streamlined via a two-tier system to replace the existing three-tier system. Most of the decision-making effective from January 2021 would be led by the Executive leading a smaller number of board members to achieve leaner decision-making and oversight arrangements.[732]The FRC would also be enhancing its complaints handling processes and its economics and analytics department to further develop its market intelligence, besides updating its budget and strategy processes. To achieve progress in advance of legislation for the audit industry, the FRC would be developing thinking on mandatory share audits to enable challenger firms to participate in the audit of larger corporations.

The FRC's Audit Firm Monitoring and Supervision team would be developing principles for the operational separation of the Big 4 firms' audit practices to ensure those in audit practices are focused on the delivery of high-quality audit.[733] It would also continue developing ideas on the legislation that might be needed for this measure to support BEIS' audit reform agenda. The FRC in this connection would be publishing individual Audit Quality Review reports with the consent of the audit firm in line with the recommendations of John Kingman's report on improving transparency to the market concerning auditing qualities. Where companies or their auditors do not give consent for FRC to publish the reports, the FRC would be proposing to publish an

731. FRC. 2020, "Update on the FRC transformation programme". *FRC 01/05/20*. https://www.frc.org.uk/news/may/update-on-frc-s-transformation-programme, accessed May 1, 2021.
732. FRC 2020, *supra* note [731].
733. FRC 2020, *supra* note [731].

anonymized summary of the report, as an alternative to bring transparency in advance of legislation.

The FRC's revised UKSC took effect at the beginning of 2020 setting substantially higher expectations for how investors manage money on behalf of their clientele and beneficiaries. The revised Code in line with Kingman's recommendations would henceforth focus on the activities and outcomes of effective stewardship, extend to all asset classes, incorporate ESG matters, and the setting of commencement of reporting in 2012.[734] Specific recommendations for enforcement have also been implemented. This includes collaborating with BEIS to strengthen the ARGA agency with new enforcement powers to hold non-accountant directors accountable for their financial reporting duties. Continuing FRC's initiatives, until its replacement by ARGA, would include:[735]

(1) Discussions with key stakeholders and BEIS on the priorities for ARGA.
(2) Plans for future consultation and legislation; reforms that could be prioritized without BEIS consultation or legislation, including careful attention on the impact of COVID-19 on the audit market, stakeholders, and the broader economy.
(3) Ensuring that reforms would be delivered in a proportionate manner.
(4) Providing evidence to the BEIS inquiry on Delivering Audit Reform.
(5) Enhancing the corporate reporting review processes.

The UK's Audit White Paper maps out proposals to strengthen the country's framework for major corporations and the way they would be audited.[736] This was in response to the erosion of stakeholder and wider public trust following a succession of sudden and major corporate collapses that had contributed to serious economic and social harms, including the insolvencies of BHS in 2016 and Carillion in 2018.

The FRC has also revealed that up to a third of audits undertaken by the seven largest audit firms would require improvements or significant improvements.[737] There are also more long-standing concerns about a lack of competition and resilience in the statutory audit market involving UK's largest companies, as well as a perceived failure of the audit product to address growing expectations of users. The Independent Review of the FRC found that the existing regulator lacked the necessary powers and clarity of purpose to hold auditors and directors sufficiently to account and recommended that it be replaced. The Brydon Review had concluded that statutory audits need to become more informative, and that higher expectation should be imposed on directors and auditors to deliver more useful information to users of reports. The Competition and Market Authority (CMA's) Statutory Audit Services Market Study revealed the unhealthy dominance of the statutory audit market for larger companies by a small

734. FRC 2020, *supra* note [731].
735. FRC 2020, *supra* note [731].
736. Department for Business, Energy & Industrial Strategy (BEIS). 2021. "Restoring trust in audit and CG: Consultation on the government's proposals". *BEIS CP 382 March 2021.* https://assets.publishing.service.gov.uk/government/uploads/system/uploads, accessed April 25, 2021.
737. BEIS 2021, *supra* note [736].

concentration of audit firms. It has thus recommended new measures to increase quality, competition and resilience in the delivery of audit. The problems raised by these reports are also found in other jurisdictions, as exemplified by a major fraud at Wirecard, a German payments processor. As the UK seeks to maintain and sustain its reputation as the international business and investment of choice, actions would be needed to address the weaknesses and lack of accountability that the said three reviews had red-flagged. The UK adopts a holistic approach to achieve meaningful and lasting change where directors, auditors, and shareholders all need to come together to play meaningful roles.[738]

All these proposals are thus underpinned by the findings and recommendations from the CMA, and the Brydon and Kingman reports. The proposals focus on reforms for the auditing sector, as audit is seen as key to assuring investors and other stakeholders that corporate reports are both accurate and meaningful. Key proposals include increasing the choice and quality in the audit market, establishing clearer responsibilities for the detection and prevention of fraud, and ensuring that the audit product and audit profession are fit for future needs. Other proposals include plans to empower shareholders and the improving of corporate reporting on key issues in risks, assurance and internal controls, particularly in the largest privately owned companies in meeting the highest standards of reporting, as listed companies already do. UK's high standards are expected to be supported by a strong and independent authority for audit, corporate reporting and governance. The ARGA, as successor to the FRC, would thus be tasked with protecting users of financial reporting by ensuring that those preparing and assuring reports would be held to the highest standards, including the directors who sign off the reports of the largest companies.

The government has accordingly sought public consultations to its following key proposals:[739]

(1) Directors. Proposals for new reporting and attestation requirements covering internal controls, dividend and capital maintenance decisions, and resilience planning designed to sharpen directors' accountability in these key management areas within the largest companies. In this regard, the ARGA will be empowered with effective investigation and civil enforcement powers to hold to account directors of large businesses that are of public importance for violations of their duties pertaining to corporate reporting and audit.

(2) The lack of evolution of the audit product together with the failure of the UK audit market to deliver increased competition, where 97% of FTSE 350 audits are undertaken by just four audit firms, and by extension, points to the need for increased resilience in the supply of audit services to public interest entities (PIEs). The concentration of audit services is weakened further by these firms competing to provide a wide range of services to PIEs and others. To strengthen the resiliency and integrity of the audit markets,

738. BEIS 2021, *supra* note [736].
739. BEIS 2021, *supra* note [736].

the government has proposed the creation of a new stand-alone audit profession underpinned by a common purpose and principles, including a clear public interest focus, reaching across all forms of corporate reporting. Accordingly, new regulatory measures are proposed to increase competition and to reduce the potentials for conflicts of interest, by providing new opportunities for challenger audit firms and new requirements for audit firms to separate their audit and non-audit practices. This is something already provided under SOX and DFA 2010 in the US.

(3) Concerns have arisen that asset managers and asset owners do not sufficiently prioritize audit as a stewardship matter of importance, while institutional shareholders have also been criticized for poor stewardship in the time before the collapse of various prominent entities. Proposals to address these matters include the requirements for companies to set out their approach to audit via publication of an audit and assurance policy on which there would be an advisory shareholder vote, including providing a formal opportunity for shareholders to propose to the audit committee areas of emphasis to be considered within the auditor's annual audit plan.

(4) Following a review of the FRC's role and function, the government has proposed legislation in various key areas to complete the task of remodeling the regulator's function by recommending ARGA as the successor to the FRC. The proposals would include:
   (a) New statutory objectives and functions along with a new statutory levy to replace the existing voluntary levy.
   (b) Empowering the ARGA with competition powers and new powers to strengthen its corporate reporting review function, its oversight audit committees and enforcement powers for the corporate reporting duties of directors, including further powers for deciding which individuals and firms should be approved to audit PIEs.

Though there is general consensus on the benefit of maintaining high audit standards, questions have been raised as to whether giving ARGA greater powers than what the FRC currently enjoy would necessarily lead to more trustworthy and informative corporate reporting and audits.[740] While shareholders and investors are likely to welcome the opportunity to engage with companies over their Audit and Assurance Policy and audit plan, it remains to be seen as to the extent of their involvements, given that many smaller listed companies have not always found it easy to get their shareholders to engage with them. The government proposals have not gone as far as SOX requirements pertaining to the assessment of the company's internal control systems, but these would still include imposing a number of additional reporting requirements on directors, including a new Resilience Statement and Audit and Assurance Policy. It further includes a statement concerning the legality of any

740. J. Perry, et al. 2021. "Restoring trust I audit and CG: A look at the government's White Paper proposals". *Norton Rose Fulbright March 2021,* https://www.nortonrosefulbright.com/-/media/files/nrf/nrfweb/knowledge-pdfs, accessed April 25, 2021.

interim or final dividend the directors proposed to pay that needs to be supported by a confirmation that this would not threaten the company's insolvency over the next two years. It remains to be seen whether such measures would dissuade some good talents from becoming directors of PIEs. There are further concerns that company reporting and audits would entail higher costs owing to the assurance process for a wider range of information going forward, but this along with other concerns mentioned would need to be read again when further details pertaining to them become available.

Directors in the US are now said to be reflecting actively on CP and related matters, especially in the wake of rising concerns over various ESG issues in the midst of the COVID-19 pandemic crisis, and for bigger global MNCs on the implications of the new global tax regime of a minimum 15%, where some 130 nations have agreed to abide by.[741] Directors in the UK on the other hand are contemplating the forthcoming changes in audit and CG reforms highlighted above, and the potential launching of new business rules to enable British business enterprise to compete for better post-Brexit. Potentially, all these and more will involve the making of various serious decisions by business enterprises with long-term impacts for most US and UK firms. In the context of these developments, the next chapter will address the important process of decision-making in companies, and the likely tussles between CEOs, board members, senior management, and shareholders.

Of late, the COVID-19 pandemic brings worksite health safety concerns, together with the simultaneous worries over the humongous effects of climate change on the physical environment. These big matters have accelerated worldwide attention to the "E" and "S" of the ESG paradigm previously dominated by the "G" element. The "E" and the "S" elements have been gaining more attention from policymakers and companies. The UN-led Principles for Responsible Investing (UN PRI) released in 2015 by the then UN Secretary-General drew global attention, and was latched upon by the investment community for application in their industry within the broad umbrella of sustainability or SC operationalized as environment, social, and governance (ESG). There has been general support for this by many big companies and international forums, especially those involved in standards-setting and integrated financial reporting, as led by the SASB, IIRC, GRI, and so on.

The highly respected Chartered Financial Analysts (CFA) Institute in its June 10, 2020 letter to Accountancy Europe drew attention to the vital importance of a common language to enable investors to differentiate between financial value-relevant and values-relevant disclosures to serve the requirements of investors. The Trustees of the IFRS Foundation are now assessing demand for global sustainability standards and determining in what ways the Foundation could contribute to the development of such standards. The varying definitions and reporting approaches and standards of ESG from international entities and from the business space have complicated the largely

741. R. Partington. 2021. "Global tax reform: 130 countries commit to minimum corporate rate: Landmark moment for world economy with OECD plan that also covers prevention of profit-shifting". *The Guardian 1 July 2021*. https://www.theguardian.com/business/2021/jul/01/global-tax-reform-130-countries-commit-to-minimum-corporate-rate, accessed July 2, 2021.

voluntary ESG reporting now being used by businesses in the US, EU, and the UK, and elsewhere. Research on integrated ESG reporting drew attention to the various flaws in voluntary reporting by issuers. These have led to initiatives for mandatory ESG disclosures in the EU, UK, and more recently the US. As the momentum for mandatory ESG reporting accelerates, it would be useful to understand whether the shareholders, the directors or both enjoy the powers to drive ESG reporting in companies. This largely governance (G) issue will be explored in the next chapter.

CHAPTER 8
Delineation of Powers in Corporations

The dawning of the separation between ownership and control in theory and in practice has transformed power structures in companies. With this, the main statutory role of the general meeting is the appointment and removal of board members, and that for the board is to manage and supervise management. The Berle and Means thesis had contended that the structure of corporate law in the US in the 1930s enforced the separation of ownership and control. They have attributed this to the evolution of dispersed ownership, when the appetite for capital grew substantially for business corporations. The resulting ownership structure thus created a control gap that had to be quickly filled by corporate managers.

The concentration of powers in the hands of board members has led to calls for laws and regulations to control the exercise of directors' powers to ensure that these powers would be primarily applied to advance the interests of shareholders in the shareholder primacy model, or in the interests of stakeholders in the stakeholder model. This eventually led to the company as a separate legal entity from its shareholders, the owners of the corporate shares, and the corporate managers. This chapter focuses on discussions on the decision-making process in business corporations. This would be followed by discussions on the powers for shareholders in the corporation, board powers, corporate managerial powers and leadership, and the governance role of takeovers and suppliers of finance. It would then engage in detailed discussions on directors' duties under current and proposed law reforms, board pay, and shareholder remedies when facing powers abuse by board and corporate managers.

8.01 DECISION-MAKING IN CORPORATIONS

As companies evolve in tandem with transformations in the business landscape, changes in the way they plan or do things might change. Indeed, they often do as exemplified in corporate directions and management during the current ongoing COVID-19 pandemic, best seen in the use of virtual AGMs, reliance on work-from-home (WFH) practices, and related developments. The important hallmarks of company law and governance practices are such that they generally accommodate or allow such changes. Companies may change their names, their objects, their articles of association to bigger matters, like dismissals or replacements of directors, or alterations of capital structures.

Flexibilities in corporate procedures allowed the use of written resolutions, meetings, or unanimous approvals, depending on the kind of circumstances in questions. CA 2006 and the IA 1986 in the UK, for example, provide as a general rule that the assent of majority members is valid in making decisions binding all members of the company, irrespective of whether they participated in the decision-making process or not. Rules governing decision-making may require only simple or superma-jorities by special resolutions depending on the matters being put up for voting. The steps to be followed and complied are normally well spelled out in most companies. Also, the articles would give powers to the company to manage the affairs and assets of the company, as the shareholders cannot interfere with the exercise of these powers.[742]

The incorporated enterprise becomes the legal form through which investors could inject capital into the enterprise without being responsible for managing it. Instead, management would be undertaken by directors who would also represent the enterprise or the company in its business engagements with others. Section 154 of CA 2006 actually requires every private company to have at least one director, and every public company to have at least two directors empowered to deal with other persons, and further requiring pertinent information about directors to be furnished to Compa-nies House. Members through their articles of associations determine the matters of management, but the model articles of association[743] require company directors to manage its business. This puts directors at the epicenter of governance process, or the system through which companies are directed and controlled. Those directly involved with the affairs of the company desire it to be managed effectively for their benefits. The directors are uniquely placed in a position to accomplish this, and the only constituent with powers to control them are the members.

The shareholder-primacy approach is anchored on the assumption or belief that members are entitled to profits made by the company, while directors act as stewards for its members. However, companies with large numbers of diverse shareholders or high concentration of shareholders have contributed to tensions on the sharing of powers between these different organs that could give rise to various implications. These would be addressed further in the context of further discussions on the functions or duties of directors, and the powers shareholders effectively hold.

8.02 POWERS AND DUTIES OF DIRECTORS

The powers and duties of directors have been called into question, when corporate scandals unfolded in Dotcom 2000 in the US, the 2007-2008 GFC in the US and UK, the 2012 European Financial Crisis, particular banking scandals moving beyond 2010, and

742. *Automatic Self-Cleansing Filter Syndicate Co v. Cunningham [1906] 2 Ch 34 (CA).*
743. *SI 2008/3229.*

the more recent scandals in big private enterprises in the US, UK, EU and elsewhere. Questions have been raised as to why directors, and in particular CEOs, have been found leading their companies or banks into serious financial harms through what turned out to be allegedly reckless corporate decisions of varying kinds, from corporations taking on excessive unsustainable debt burdens hidden by opaque off-balance sheet mechanisms, as in the extensive Dotcom corporate disasters, and from banks doing the same in the GFC, and so on. There have also been related questions, as to how and why directors are rewarded with very high compensations, despite making these allegedly reckless decisions. A lookback into the nature of the powers and duties of directors, as found in corporate statutes and the common law, would be helpful in discussions of this nature.

The CA 2006 in the UK codified and transformed a company law regime that hitherto relied mostly on common law. The UK government's objective when codifying directors' duties in statutory form has been for the purpose of clarifying the law, apart from making it more accessible. The UK statute draws out eight duties. These comprise a duty to promote the success of the enterprise, a duty to exercise reasonable care, skill and diligence, a duty to exercise independent judgment, a duty to act within powers provided, a duty to avoid conflicts of interest, a duty to declare interests in company business undertakings or ventures, a duty to disclose interests in ongoing company activities, and a duty not to accept benefits from third parties. These appear simple to understand on their own, but could become more difficult to understand and apply in actual business scenarios.

The current ongoing COVID-19 pandemic, corporate and banking scandals, and so on, tell a tale that is not easy to decipher when it comes to the requirement for a director to promote the success of the company, as the director has to be mindful of six criteria when dealing with this undertaking; or when it comes to avoiding conflicts of interests, as a director is allowed to engage in such transactions with approval from shareholders or in particular situations with board approval. The duty to promote the success of a company but taking into account the six listed factors does not necessarily preclude a director from taking actions that could risk harming its social obligations provided the director has considered the action's impact on the matter, has taken into account the other listed factors and other pertinent issues, has conducted in good faith that the action would probably promote the company's success, has complied with the other statutory duties, and that the action would not breach any relevant social obligation laws. In contrast, company directors in the US are guided by the BJR consistently sustained by the US judiciary. The BJR essentially says that boards are presumed to act in good faith, meaning within the fiduciary standards of loyalty, prudence, and care, that directors owe to stakeholders. In the absence of evidence that the board has seriously breached some rule of conduct, the courts will not review or question its decisions.[744] Duty of care is the obligation to act on an informed basis,

744. C. Gerner-Beuerle. 2021. "The duty of care and the business judgment rule: A case study in legal transplants and local narratives" in A. Afsharipout & M. Gelter (eds.). *Comparative CG: Research Handbooks in Comparative Law Series.* Cheltanham: Edward Elgar Publishing.

while the duty of loyalty needs directors to have the interests of the corporations above their own self-interest, or the interests of others.

Where a director breaches his duties, it is for the enterprise, as the aggrieved party, to decide whether to take action against the director or not. However, as the company is in the end controlled by the shareholders, it is ultimately for the shareholders to decide whether the company should initiate action against the director. Where shareholders do not oppose the apparent infringement of duty, the director might not have to be too concerned. Directors' duties should not be read in isolation, as a particular decision or action might involve a breach of more than one duty. This is because compliance with one duty does not necessarily imply compliance with another. Importantly, the UK CG code requires a balanced mix of executive and NEDs. Though the two groups likely perform different functions, English law does not differentiate between them, and as such, all directors under UK laws are subject to the same statutory obligations under CA 2006. Directors of all kinds of UK companies, irrespective of capitalization, private, public, quoted or unquoted have to be mindful of all these duties, and also importantly various designated duties under general company law and regulatory rules to do with corporate insolvencies, antitrust, health and safety, and the environment. Also, directors of listed entities have to bear in mind their responsibilities pertaining to prospectus rules, AIM rules for corporation, disclosure and transparency rules, as well as listing rules in general.[745]

UK listed companies with listed premium shares are further required to state how they have applied the main principles of the UK CG Code, followed by a statement of whether or not the company has complied with the principles throughout the applicable accounting period, and providing explanation for any deviations under the comply or explain approach. The current version would be the UK CG Code 2018 applicable on or after January 1, 2019. This version focused on relationships between companies, shareholders, and stakeholders, besides promoting the importance of setting up a corporate culture aligning with CP, business strategy, integrity promotion, and values diversity. The Code further stresses the application of its principles and reporting on outcomes achieved. Companies should also disclose how they have complied with the Code's Provisions, or provide appropriate explanations as to their individual circumstances.

To improve trust for corporate UK, carefully considered governance policies and practices would be helpful, as these would enable investors to do a more considered view of the governance of the enterprises, especially where explanations have been provided. The FRC's Review of Governance Reporting in November 2020 found that tick-box compliance continues to dominate over high-quality reporting of good governance practices. The FRC criticizes the formulaic approach, as it would lead to boilerplate language, and ineffective reporting, lacking in substance and information about governance outcomes. To improve the quality of "comply and explain" reporting

745. M, Bruce. 2011. *Rights and duties of directors*. 11th edition. West Success: Bloomsbury Professional.

from reporting companies in the UK, the FRC in February 2021 has provided the following guidance:[746]

(1) Companies should offer clarity about the Provisions of the Code that they have departed from by making it easy for readers to find them in their annual report.
(2) Companies should report any departure from any provisions of the Code; and that
(3) Clear and meaningful explanations for departures from the Code should also be provided.

To deliver an honest evaluation of their governance process, companies are advised to provide transparency in terms of both their application of the principles and reporting against the Provisions.[747] This could only be effective if the reports do away with boilerplate language, as they apply the Code to their individual circumstance. This would further require companies to provide full and honest explanations, that in turn would be welcomed by investors, service providers, regulators, and the wider stakeholders. Where companies deviate from any Provisions in the Code, the annual report should clearly show the action taken by the company over what Provisions it had departed from, and what alternative route it has taken; and how this alternative approach would be more efficient and appropriate than that prescribed by the Code, as well as how it would be helping the company to achieve good performance. Feedback and guidance reports, such as these, are signals for directors with such reporting obligations to be delivered better.

Though the Code promotes compliance with best governance practices, independent empirical studies suggest some companies tend to comply with the "letter" of the law, rather than the "spirit," as departures from Code provisions have been accompanied by explanations that have been totally uninformative, or predictable standard statements.[748] In the absence of a formal authority monitoring both the veracity of the statements and the quality of the explanations provided, enforcement and monitoring have been left informally to market participants. The subjectivity of the compliance lexicon has enabled companies to apply the Code flexibly. As such, critics have advanced the idea of replacing the Comply or Explain principles, with Apply or Explain, as this is what companies are actually asked to do. This would signal to investors and shareholders that greater attention would be paid to explanation. This would then enable the identification of non-compliers as those companies that do neither. Worth noting has been the matter of lower compliance for the appropriate balance of NEDs and independent NEDs principle. This has raised some doubts on the effective independence and nonexecutive role of directors.

746. FRC. 2021. "Improving the quality of 'comply or explain' reporting". *FRC February 2021.* https://www.frc.org.uk/getattachment/6a4c93cf-cf93-4b33-89e9-4c42ae36b594, accessed April 11, 2021.
747. FRC 2021, *supra* note [746].
748. S. Arcot, V. Bruno & A. Faure-Grimaud. 2010. "CG in the UK: Is the comply or explain approach working?". *International Review of Law and Economics*, Vol. 30 (2010): 193-201.

As monitoring and analysis of truthfulness of statements are usually costly, dispersed shareholders prefer a formal tick in the Comply or Explain box. This also generally tells why shareholder intervention had not been generally preventive, but typically happens subsequent to periods of bad performance, or revelations by whistleblowers.[749] While board changes and policies changes in US corporations in the early 1990s in the US have been brought about by the lobbying of large shareholders, than by takeovers,[750] UK institutional shareholders have on the whole had shown preference of exit over voicing for change.[751] Firms with concentrated shareholders acting as insiders though in general disclose little information, as they entrench themselves at the expense of minority shareholders.[752] Thus, the effectiveness of the Comply or Explain approach under the shareholder primacy model lays stress on the role of shareholder monitoring. The absence of a formal authority monitoring the Comply or Explain statements, and of better disclosures from companies, turned out to have been very much the general practice. This monitoring limitation has led to current UK reforms requiring the replacing of the FRC with a statutory-empowered monitoring and compliance agency soon.

The stunning failures of US and UK banks following the 2007-2008 GFC, and the apparent lack of attention or lapse of attention from both the US SEC[753] and the then UK FSA[754] have raised public angers, as these were generally not followed by enforcement actions against directors and senior management. Comparative case insights suggest that a few major banks and isolated numbers of bankers at the lower echelons have been held accountable in the US, but to a lesser degree in the UK. These contrast sharply with the earlier Enron-kind corporate financial reporting scandals, or the much earlier Savings and Loans entities,[755] where enforcement actions had been generally taken. However, recent criminal charges against mega banks in the US suggest a policy shift,[756] but this still left complaints about global banks defying US crackdowns by serving affluent criminals and others,[757] despite good guidance from the Bank for

749. P. Yeoh. 2014. "Whistleblowing: Motivations, corporate self-regulation, and the law". *International Journal of Law and Management*, Vol. 56 (6): 459-474.
750. J. Pound. 1993. "The rise of the political model of CG and corporate control". *New York University Law Review*, Vol. 68 (1993): 1003.
751. S. Sappideen. 1997. "Ownership of the large corporation: Why clothe the emperor?". *King's College Law Journal*, Vol. 7 (1997): 27.
752. B.S. Black. 1990. "Shareholder passivity reexamined". *Michigan Law Review*, Vol. 89 (1990): 520.
753. P. Yeoh. 2016. "CG failures and the road to crime". *Journal of Financial Crime*, Vol. 23 (1): 216-230.
754. N. Clayton. 2020. "Stopping bank failures in the UK: A simple proposal for reform". *Journal of International Banking law and Regulation*, Vol. 35 (4): 127-134.
755. P. Yeoh. 2020. "Banks' vulnerabilities to money laundering activities". *Journal of Money Laundering Control*, Vol. 23 (1): 122-135; Yeoh 2016, *supra* note [753].
756. Yeoh 2020, *supra* note [755]; 2016.
757. International Consortium of Investigative Journalists (ICIJ). 2020. "Global banks defy U.S. crackdowns by serving oligarchs, criminals and terrorists: The FinCEN Files show trillion in tainted dollars flow freely through major banks, swamping a broke enforcement system". *ICIJ 20/09/20*. https://www.icij.org/investigations/, accessed January 10, 2021.

International Settlements (BIS).[758] This leaves further the big questions of director's accountability being open to subjective interpretation until regulators begin to work fast in answering these.[759] This includes, especially those with serious involvements in extremely risky financing of financial intermediaries with disproportionately low collateral coverage that quickly collapsed, leaving the impacted banks with serious financial losses exceeding USD 10 billion.[760]

Arguments have now been advanced that ad hoc blend of banking regulation and governance is not the way forward and that attention needs to be provided to formulating clearer statutory governance for systematically important banks (SIBs). Calls, as such, are made for greater enforcements of serious breaches of the governance process by the regulator. UK regulators have been proactive in approving the appointment of bank directors, showing a major deviation from standard governance practices. The fit and proper test currently includes procedural aspects. The rule book has been adjusted by the FSA/FCA/PRA, such that the time a person has to be able to devote in carrying out his/her required duty has to be adequate; otherwise, he/she will not be deemed fit and proper.

These regulators have moved beyond banking collapses to look at the competence and financial expertise of proposed bank directors, but this still occurred at the Co-op Bank where the regulator had been criticized for not objecting to the appointment of a director lacking in experience and essential skills. Strong justifications have now been advanced that all SIBs to provide for a director appointed by the PRA paid by the bank but who owes duties solely to the regulator, and who is appointed to monitor inside going-on in the SIBs. In the event of observations of excessive risk-takings, or engagements in large transactions that could jeopardize the safety of the bank, then these have to be notified by the regulator director to the PRA or FCA. This kind of intrusive approach has been suggested on the grounds that governance flaws of the scale seen in various mega banks could be stopped at the early stages, where remedial measures could still work, rather than at the late stages, where rescue options become more constrained. The FCA and PRA would therefore rely on this approach to ensure that good governance practices take place, and take place across a large number of banks.[761]

Bank directors have been busy beefing up their governance procedures in the midst of ongoing scandals, but nonbank enterprises directors have also been kept busy by challenges thrown up by the impacts of the COVID-19 pandemic on turnarounds and survivals at these corporations, as well as by the increasing reliance on the services

758. BIS. 2015. "Guidelines: CG principles for banks". *BIS July 2015.* https://www.bis.org/bcbs/publ/d328.pdf, accessed November 10, 2020.
759. M. Marcinkowska. 2012. "CG in banks: Problems and remedies". *Financial Assets and Investing*, Vol. 3 (2): 47-67.
760. M. Halftermeyer. 2021. "Nomura, UBS take global banks' Archegos hit to over US$10B". *BNN Bloomberg 27/04/21.* https://ampvideo.bnnbloomberg.ca/nomura-ubs-take-global-banks-archegos, accessed April 28, 2021; L. De Paoli. 2021. "Greensill collapse exposes gap at heart of its technology claims: Company's technology capabilities were limited". *Bloomberg 20/03/21.* https://www.bloomberg.com/news/articles/2021-03-20/greensill-s-collapse-shows-company-had-a-big-technology-gap, accessed April 28, 2021.
761. Clayton 2020, *supra* note [754].

of tech platforms that of late have come under the spotlights over various ESG issues that directors might need to pay greater attention to, going forward.

Policymakers and regulators in the UK have come out with proposals on why governance practices in tech platforms need to improve, while those in the US, albeit a little later, is now also working on prescribing measures to ensure that these platforms do not pose harms to the wider public. The UK focused on online harms to consumer welfare and related matters,[762] while the US is preoccupied with antitrust[763] and disinformation[764] matters. Policymaking responses accelerated, when the COVID-19 pandemic spotlighted the risks posed by harmful activities and content online where opportunists took advantage of the unsettled conditions to spike disinformation and misinformation with serious harms to unsuspecting consumers, children, and Western-style democracy. Both the US and the UK have for long been unashamedly pro-tech in promoting innovations and economic growths, but are keenly aware also of the need to ensure trust in the use of technology that their economies have come to rely on, more and more.

UK's Online Safety Bill would introduce a new duty of care to make companies take responsibility for the welfare and safety of their many users. It would introduce legislation defining what harmful content would be in scope, so as to tackle illegal activity occurring online, and to prevent, in particular, children from being exposed to inappropriate materials. The proposed statute would also address other kinds of harms from dangerous misinformation spreading lies online about vaccine to destructive pro-anorexia contents.[765] The UK is also looking into reforming its criminal law system to ensure that this would be fit for the digital era in providing the protections that victims deserve, especially for dealing with emerging issues, like cyber-flashing and pile-on harassment. In this regard, UK's Office of Communications (Ofcom) being the proposed independent regulator is expected to issue codes of practice outlining the systems and processes that companies need to adopt to fulfill their duty of care.

Ofcom accordingly would be empowered with robust enforcement tools to tackle noncompliance, including the power to issue fines of up to GBP 18 million or 10% of global annual turnover, whichever is higher; and including other business disruption measures against any in-scope company worldwide providing services to UK users.[766] Companies in-scope are also expected to provide mechanisms to allow users to report harmful content of its activity and to appeal the takedown of such contents. Companies providing designated services under Category 1 would be required to publish transparency reports containing information about the initiatives they would be taking to address online harms on those services. While the UK expects to take a proportionate

762. HM Government. 2020. "Online harms white paper: Full government response to the consultation". *HM Government December 2020 CP 354.* https://assets.publishing.service.gov.uk/government, accessed March 2, 2021.
763. N. Pettitt. 2020. *How to evaluate alleged monopolies*. Oxford: OUP; House Judiciary Committee. 2020. "Investigation of competition in digital markets". https://judiciary.house.gov/uploadedfiles/competition_in_digital_markets, accessed January 10, 2021.
764. M. Fuller. 2019. "Big data and the Facebook scandal: Issues and responses". *Theology*, Vol. 122 (1): 14-21.
765. HM Government 2020, *supra* note [762].
766. HM Government 2020, *supra* note [762].

approach to its enforcement activity, it would reserve the right to introduce criminal sanctions for senior managers where they fail to comply with the regulator's information requests.

The COVID-19 pandemic has given rise to questions pertaining to CP for the board, that was hitherto thought to be generally settled, albeit not, convincingly for some. Such dissents have been coming out more forcefully in the US, where ESG matters have become topical themes, in particular the challenges surrounding diversity or inclusiveness, social equity, environmental impacts, apart from governance when applied to the digital economy. Initially, the gathering of top US CEOs in the Business Roundtable (BRT) in 2019 issued a statement defining the purpose of the corporation in stakeholder terms, a direct and intended reversal from earlier statements that defined the duty of directors as serving the interests of shareholders, and along a short-term orientation with eyes on quarterly and annual earnings reports.[767] Shareholder primacy became identified as the major contributor to a wide range of crippling issues from rising income inequality and economic insecurity brought upon by stagnant wages and globalization, to growing environmental harm and climate change.

It has been argued that by focusing on maximizing shareholders profits, other stakeholders, like employees, suppliers, creditors, communities, and the environment got squeezed. Leaders in the 1981 BRT already knew this, when they issued the then statement that the corporation is a force for good, and that a corporation has to consider its impact on all, from shareholders to the society at large, and where its business activities must make social sense, just as its social activities must make business sense.[768] Increased public confidence in business as a positive force in society would nevertheless depend on the way corporations respond to the public's new and expanded expectations pertaining to business.

Despite the release of the 2019 BRT statement on CP, debates over this persisted suggesting that the matter has yet to reach consensus among the CEOs, their boards, and the corporations they lead. Shortly after the release of the BRT's statement, many in the business community, notably the Council of Institutional Investors, forcefully rejected the notion of accountability to a spectrum of stakeholders, declaring that accountability to everyone means accountability to no one. For them, CEOs are employees who work for their shareholders and ergo should focus on creating value for the shareholders, and with concerns that the corporation's primary purpose is slipping away from its shareholder value moorings, thereby enabling the loudest and most passionate activists to set the agenda for asset allocation.[769]

It is, though, not by coincidence, that many of the more urgent problems faced in the US and the UK today have worsened since the time corporations have viewed

767. J.S. Harrison, R.A. Phillips & R.E. Freeman. 2019. "On the 2019 Business Roundtable "Statement on the purpose of a corporation". *Journal of Management*, Vol. 46 (7): 1-15.
768. K. Bresnahan. 2021. "The purpose debate back to the '80s: Business Roundtable's 'Purpose' statement redux'". *Directors & Boards 2021*. https://www.directorsandboards.com/articles/singlepurpose-debate-back-%E2%80%9880s-business-roundtable%, accessed April 29, 2021.
769. R. Rock. 2021. "The purpose debate: Where corporate America has been and where it needs to go". *Directors & Boards 2021*. https://www.directorsandboards.com/articles/singlepurpose-debate-introduction, accessed April 29, 2021.

themselves as only responsible to their shareholders. Turning away from that framework back to the more meaningful stakeholder model where business leaders could be held accountable to primary stakeholders would need changes in the regulation of the equity and debt markets. Insights from the past suggest that statements of good intentions would not necessarily take corporations to where they are hoping to go. Business leaders need to look around and consider what impacts their actions are having on their employees, customers and communities, as this is the only way corporations would prosper, and that business, commerce and the free market would not necessarily fade way, when they embark on this route.[770]

The rule of law though is related to the purpose of the modern corporation. In particular, the rule of law is necessary for a citizen's belief in secure private property rights that provides citizenry confidence to invest in physical capital, human capital, and innovation, the three catalysts of economic growth.[771] The rule of law further allows for an effective judiciary that could enforce legal contracts. Shareholder's reliance on limited liability and debtholder rights originate from legal contracts among shareholders, debtholders and other stakeholders. These spotlight the importance of the rule of law in enabling companies to raise equity and debt financing to culminate in financial development. Thus, the current debate on BRT's 2019 Statement on Corporate Purpose needs to be discussed against this contextual background on the role of the rule of law in the issuance of equity capital to supply financial resources to corporations. Taking this approach, it has been argued that the modern corporation should maximize long-term shareholder value while conforming to the law of the land.

Thus, at the international level, policymakers should focus on improving rule of law to enhance economic prosperity and diminish income inequality; at the individual country level, initiatives should be taken to align shareholder wealth maximization with stakeholder interests.[772] This means the following:

(1) Antitrust policy measures should be vigorously enforced to maintain and enhance competition in product and labor markets.
(2) Management and board compensation should be reformed to focus on creating and sustaining long-term shareholder value.
(3) For many of society's more serious problems, like climate change, corporations would not represent the appropriate level of action, as significant change to address climate change would require public policy changes in a nation and abroad. This would imply joint public-business initiatives.

The above aside, directors would need to examine, whether and to what extent the governance process needs to be adjusted when operating their businesses in an increasingly digital economy. Increasingly many of the largest and most successful

770. Bresnahan 2021, *supra* note [768].
771. S. Bhagat & G. Hubbard, 2021. "Rule of law, and purpose of the corporation". *Corporate Governance International Review (CGIR) 11/03/21.* https://doi:10.1111/corg.12374, accessed April 29, 2021.
772. Bresnahan 2021, *supra* note [768].

businesses now operate and run as open and inclusive platforms.[773] The enterprises like[774] Amazon, Apple, Facebook, Alphabet, and Netflix leverage networked technologies to facilitate economic exchange, transfer information, connect people, and make predictions.[775] All these enterprises facilitate interactions between creators and extractors of value, and by doing this, grow wealth for the platform owner-controllers,[776] culminating in the platform deriving value from its role as an intermediary.[777]

These platform enterprises have already disrupted multiple industries, including those in retail, hotels, taxis, and aggressively into financial services, and others. No doubt, more are expected to emerge over the coming years, doing the same, or even more, using even more powerful technologies with enhanced disruption capabilities. These platform corporations go beyond the deployment of new technologies to facilitate economic and social interactions between interested third parties, as they also organize their internal operations in flatter and more inclusive manners to facilitate collaborations between and among multiple stakeholders, and through this, they have been able to tap opportunities to deliver regular innovations in platform services and functionality.[778]

The merging of these transaction facilitators and organizers-for-innovation in these platforms differentiates them from the more conventional pre-Industry 4.0 businesses that are generally more centralized, and more hierarchical organizational forms.[779] Indeed, some have advocated that all business enterprises, and not just technology firms, should consider operating and organizing as platforms,[780] for failure to do so would invite disruptions by existing platforms that are still aggressively expanding rapidly into new sectors and markets,[781] as exemplified by the likes of Uber[782] and Grab.[783] Both and others have gone from ride-hailing to food deliveries and

773. G.G. Parker & M.W. Van Alstyne. 2018. "Innovation openness and platform control". *Management Science*, Vol. 64 (7): 3015-3032.
774. A. Hagiu. 2014. "Strategic decisions for multisided platforms". *MIT Sloan Management Review Winter 2014,* https://sloanreview.mit.edu/article/strategic-decisions-for-multisided-platforms/, accessed November 10, 2020.
775. G.G. Parker, M.W. Van Alstyne & S.P. Choudary. 2016. *Platform revolution: How networked markets are transforming the economy and how to make them work for you.* New York: Norton.
776. D.S. Evans, A. Hagiu & R. Schmalensee. 2006. *Invisible engines: How software platforms drive innovation and transform industries.* Cambridge: The MIT Press.
777. A. Hagiu & J. Wright. 2015. "Multi-sided platforms". *Harvard Business School Working Paper 15-037.* https://www.hbs.edu/faculty/Pages/item.aspx?num=48249, accessed November 10, 2020.
778. D. Kiron & G. Unruh. 2018. "Corporate 'purpose' is no substitute for good governance". *MIT Sloan Management Review April 2018.* https://sloanreview.mit.edu/article/corporate-purpose-is-no-substitute, accessed November 10, 2020.
779. D. Evans & R. Schmalensee. 2016. *Matchmakers: The new economics of platform businesses.* Cambridge: Harvard University Press.
780. EJ Altman & M. Tushman. 2017. "Platforms, open/user innovation and ecosystems: A strategic leadership perspective". *Harvard Business School Organizational Behavior Unit Working Paper No. 17-076.* https://papers.ssrn.com/sol3/papers.cfm%3fabstract_id%3d2915213, accessed November 10, 2020.
781. Parker, Van Alstyne & Choudary 2016, *supra* note [775].
782. C. Tang & J. Wirtz (forthcoming). "Case study: Uber's unintended burdens" In J. Wirtz & C. Lovelock (eds.). *Services marketing: People, technology, strategy.* New Jersey: World Scientific.

financial services. Thus, these new business models with their distinctive features have notable implications for regulators and the governance process.

Hitherto, governance under the Anglo-Saxon approach has been relying on the primacy of shareholders or the economic-legal-moral owners of a company. Policymakers gradually imposed measures on enterprises to compel directors, executives and managers to perform in the best interests of the shareholder-owners. As discussed earlier, governance procedures had been designed to protect the interests and control of those at the top of the hierarchy, meaning the shareholders, putting other matters to secondary positions. In time, the conversation and practice of governance have become an adaptation to a world of centralized hierarchical organizations, essentially large mega corporations, with governance practices humming best, when large enterprises are the main engines of economic growth. This gradually made less sense in the era of the FIR, where tech companies with flatter innovation-driven platforms rule.[784]

However, the shareholder primacy model did not consistently operate as desired, resulting in various well-documented negative side effects, like a myopic focus on shareholder value and highly bureaucratic organizations. Often, the unintended impact of governance practices has been the entrenchment of inefficient hierarchies, together with the creation of a short-term and overly cautious corporate culture. As enterprises struggle to innovate, they can in the medium to long term become corporations facing extinction. When reviewing this traditional approach to governance, the unintended problems that it has generated, together with recent policies targeted at promoting a longer-term, and more socially and environmentally responsible perspective of governance, there appears to be a tension between the regulatory incentives generated by governance, and the business needs of many digital platform corporations these days.

It has been observed that as enterprises grow, they come to depend on hierarchical organizational structures that is rationalized as a strategy for managing the complexities of scale. But the problem is, such hierarchical organizations could lead to the bureaucratization of enterprise culture. This kind of organization and culture would be feasible in the era of mass production, but could be inappropriate for today's dynamic business realities, as a tension could easily emerge between the structure and culture of an enterprise and what is needed to succeed in digital economies dominated by global digitalized platforms. The impact of this tension would render established enterprises incapable of reacting effectively or fast enough to the challenges of rapid-changes in markets, consumers and technologies, where speed and innovation would count most.

As such, policymakers when seeking to help enterprises in organizing effectively as platforms would need to review their approach to business regulation, especially

783. Grab. 2021. "Grab, the leading superapp for deliveries, mobility and financial services in Southeast Asia, plans to go public in partnership with Altimeter". *Grab 13/04/21*. https://www.grab.com/sg/press/others/grab-go-public-in-partnership-with-altimeter/, accessed April 15, 2021.
784. A. Felsberger, et al. 2020. "The impact of Industry 4.0 on the reconciliation of dynamic capabilities: Evidence from the European manufacturing industries". *Production Planning & Control*. https://doi.org/10.1080/09537287.2020.1810765, accessed November 10, 2020.

with regards to governance practices. There now appears to be a disconnect between the regulatory pressures generated by governance, or in maintaining centralized authorities, hierarchy, and control; and the needs of enterprises when seeking to establish themselves as successful digital platforms, or in connecting and facilitating collaborations among multiple stakeholders in such types of business structures and business models.

The existing regulatory framework therefore appears to promote a negative corporate attitude that is failing platforms that disrupt and decentralize existing business models by eliminating and replacing conventional intermediaries, and by facilitating more direct peer-to-peer (P2P) transactions between services providers/creators/producers on the one hand, and the consumers on the other.[785] This suggests the urgent need for a new regulatory direction or platform governance to address this disconnect involving the participating roles of social media, flatter and open organizations, and directors as feedback providers.

Hitherto, the governance process would refer to an organization's structures and procedures seeking to ensure that authority, responsibility, and control flow downwards from the investors through a board of directors to management and finally to the employees, while accountability would flow upwards. Here, the main goal of governance is to protect the interests of the investor/owner/shareholder. This view of governance is built on the notion of a closed, centralized authority and of a clearly defined hierarchy, meaning the investor-shareholder. This makes sense, when large enterprises are the primary engines of growth. The shareholder primacy model needs enterprises to adopt approaches that ensure that all of the other actors within the enterprise act as if they are investors-shareholders. Thus, by aligning the incentives of the various actors in this manner, enterprise performance as measured by the share price is improved, benefiting most stakeholders in an enterprise, as well as members of the public benefiting from the goods and services that a successful enterprise provides.

This type of framework provides the context for conversations around governance practices in identifying regulations that could compel or nudge agents within the enterprise to act as if they are owners-principals. Through this kind of alignment, governance practices grew to be underpinned by the rise of shareholder primacy, but which also becomes now increasingly linked to corporate scandals. Regulatory responses over the last decade have been driven mostly by the aim of minimizing the risk of corporate scandals. Good governance practices are accordingly associated with the mission of reducing the risk of managerial misbehavior, and when this is successfully achieved, maximization of shareholder value tends to be the outcome. Identifying the structures, processes and mechanisms for achieving these dual goals provide the momentum for much of the regulatory reforms over the last decade, as discussed earlier.

The aims of much of contemporary governance reforms had been to limit the opportunities for managerial deviations, or misbehavior. By this is meant the taking of

785. Z. Wei & M. Lin. 2016. "Market mechanisms in online peer-to-peer lending". *Management Science*, Vol. 63 (12): 4236-4257.

managerial actions that have the high risks of becoming harmful to the shareholder-owners' best interests. A corporate culture that eliminates opportunities for all kinds of misbehaviors had been argued to be the best mechanisms to maximize shareholder value, and hence would be deemed as optimal. This perspective means that executives, managers and other employees are deemed to be motivated by self-interest and to possess a selfish disregard for the negative impacts of their actions on investors. This would call for increasing shareholder control over other actors within the enterprise making it the main goal of governance rules, where many requirements are imposed on enterprises to mitigate this agency risk. Investor confidence in turn would depend substantially on the existence of an accurate and useful governance framework focusing on an accountable board of directors supervising executives; a range of internal control and monitoring processes; transparent information disclosures about the financial affairs of the enterprise; measures formulated to protect the interests of minority shareholders; and with the overall objective of maximizing shareholder value.

Concomitant to the above developments has been the global rise of independent director rules, and notion of an independent board. The latter is viewed as a corporate board with a majority or significant presence of outside directors with no affiliations with the enterprise's top executives, and with no business dealings with the enterprise, so as to minimize the risk of potential conflicts of interest. The argument is that an independent board would provide effective oversight over inside board members and senior corporate managers, and thereby reducing managerial opportunism-illegality. Independent boards are beneficial in that they strengthen control to ensure the enhancement of shareholder value, besides minimizing the risk of destructive managerial behavior with potentially catastrophic outcomes for shareholders while resulting in a healthier investment landscape. Shareholder value advocates have contended that the 2007-2008 GFC was an outcome, rather than a strategy. This implies that increased shareholder value would be a predictable by-product of aligning the interests of executives and management with the interests of shareholders, meaning where management acts opportunistically at the expense of shareholder value, the entire economy would suffer the negative impacts of enterprise's underperformance.[786]

A counterpoint has emerged over the last ten years arguing that a focus on maximizing shareholder value generates a corporate environment where short-term profit and formalistic compliance are prioritized that harm the enterprise and its longer-term prospects of advancing relevancy and being successful.[787] This view contends that increasing corporate managers' accountability to shareholders and shareholder control over managers would not resolve the business needs of most enterprises. It might well generate the counterproductive impact of incentivizing a harmful focus on quarterly financial reporting, thereby producing an unhealthy short-term focus on enterprise share price and market valuation, thereby sidestepping

786. S. Denning. 2017. "Why maximizing shareholder value is a threat to U.S. business". *Strategy & Leadership*, Vol. 45 (6): 3-10.
787. S.M. Bainbridge. 2015. "Preserving director primacy by managing shareholder interventions". In J.G. Hill & S.T. Randall (eds.). *Research Handbook on Shareholder Power and Activism 231*. Cheltenham: Edward Elgar.

the important goals of innovations. This is because shareholder value maximization leads to the preference of focusing on the implementation of business approaches built around existing and successful products/services, where executives with insights and focus on innovation and consumer experience and best positioned to deliver relevancy are sidelined or marginalized from core decision-making processes.[788] It has been further argued that the stress on quarterly earnings metrics and short-term share price performance could easily distract an enterprise from the important business agenda of identifying strategies that could help maintain the enterprise's relevancy over the longer term. From the shareholder primacy perspective, employees are subsets of marginalized stakeholders, and this is problematic, as enterprises need to take care of employees who unlike senior management are directly responsible for the customer.

A shareholder primacy prism could lead to practices running counter to the interests of employees. This is best exemplified by massive layoffs so as to spruce up an enterprise's balance sheet to boost share prices as executive performance is almost evaluated entirely on share price, that is to say, stronger balance sheet and brighter earnings reports equal better share prices equal loftier executive bonus.[789] This could be counterproductive, as instead of maximizing opportunities for employee job satisfaction, it could more probably breed a culture of mistrust between employees, executives, and managers. Also, a model built entirely around financial metrics for measuring business efficiency makes it harder for an enterprise to retain the kind of consumer-oriented focus that is important for maintaining relevancy over the longer term, as consumers are increasingly insisting on constant innovation, quick product evolution, and highly disruptive technologies.[790]

It has been strongly argued that the shareholder prism sets a process of likely inevitable long-term decline into motion, but a customer-first focus is the answer for creating a corporate environment that ensures relevancy for the longer term.[791] Indeed, sustainable enterprise success would reflect this relevancy that contributes to the creation of a stimulating and exciting firm environment that in turn attracts and retains talents.

Given mounting criticisms over the harms posed by shareholder primacy orientation, recent governance practices trends, like stewardship codes and corporate sustainability, have emerged encouraging stakeholders to adopt a more responsible longer-term orientation. The distinctiveness of stewardship codes lies in their efforts to create more engaged and responsible shareholders, especially institutional investors who are increasingly viewed as stewards of an enterprise that take a longer-term

788. T. Ladika & Z. Sautner. 2020. "Managerial short-termism and investment: Evidence from accelerated option investing". *Review of Finance*. https://www.Doi:10.1093/rof/rfz012, accessed January 5, 2021.
789. R. Tortoriello. 2018. "In the money: What really motivates executive performance". *S&P Global Market Intelligence March 2018*. https://www.spglobal.com/marketintelligence/en/documents/sp-global-market-intelligence-executive-compensation-march-2018.pdf, accessed November 10, 2020.
790. S. Blank. 2013. "Why the lean start-up changes everything". *Harvard Business Review May 2013*. https://hbr.org/2013/05/why-the-lean-start-up-changes-everything, accessed November 10, 2020.
791. Blank 2013, *supra* note [790].

perspective of the enterprise, and ergo more likely to adopt a more active role in the supervision of management matters, and importantly contributing to a more balanced corporate culture.[792] Though some institutions spend time and resources on active ownership, significant numbers of institutional investors have not actively engaged with the governance practices of their portfolio companies.[793] The value of shareholder engagement appears to reflect the view that the GFC has been in part contributed by the lack of shareholder interventions.[794]

Stewardship codes then came into play to motivate meaningful and constructive engagements. These promote the point that institutional investors need to be treated as stewards of enterprises, instead of more narrowly, as investors. UK's FRC published the first country-based stewardship code in 2010, setting forth good practices for institutional investors looking to engage with the board and management of quoted enterprises via the comply or explain approach. UK's stewardship code is principles-based, instead of rules-based, putting forth recommendations, instead of rules. Its key principles state that institutional shareholders:[795]

(1) should publicly disclose their policy on how they will discharge their stewardship responsibilities;
(2) should have a robust policy for handling conflicts of interests pertaining to stewardship that should be publicly disclosed;
(3) should monitor their investee companies;
(4) should set explicit guidelines on when and how they will step up their stewardship activities;
(5) should be willing to collaborate with other investors, where needed;
(6) should have explicit policies for voting, including disclosures of voting activity; and
(7) should report regularly on their stewardship and voting routines.

The UKSC 2020 substantially strengthen expectations for how money is invested on behalf of savers and pensioners, while aiming to stimulate enhanced demand for an engaged approach to stewardship and investment decision-making aligned to the investment span of beneficiaries, that are usually long-term. The new code's structure is similar to the UK CG Code, with numbered sections, principles and reporting expectations and reinforced by guidance.[796]

792. J. Harford, A. Kecskes & S. Mansi. 2014. "Do long-term investors improve corporate decision-making?". *Journal of Corporate Finance*, Vol. 50 (2018): 424-452.
793. JE. Fisch, A. Hamdani & S. Solomon. 2018. "Passive investors". *ECGI Law Working Paper No. 414/208*.
794. J. Plender. 2015. *Capitalism: Money, morals and markets*. London: Biteback Publishing.
795. FRC. 2020. "The UK Stewardship Code 2020". https://www.frc.org.uk/getattachment/5aae591d-d9d3-4cf4-814a-d14e156a1d87/Stewardship-Code_Final2.pdf, accessed January 3, 2021.
796. KPMG. 2020. "The UK Stewardship Code 2020". https://assets.kpmg/content/dam/kpmg/uk/pdf/2019/11/uk-stewardship-code-2020.pdf, accessed January 3, 2021.

Another recent reform pertains to the encouragement of corporations to adopt a more responsible and sustainable approach in their business activities.[797] For much of the time, the primary focus is on disclosures and transparency or corporate dissemination of filtered information to investors. The growing discomfort over some current corporate activities reflecting their narrow focus on extracting value generated mistrust and antibusiness sentiments that has since been spiraling in the midst of the ongoing COVID-19 pandemic. Issues range from growing wage disparity between those at the top and the average worker, harmful environmental impacts, abuse of access to state aid, and so on.[798]

Corporations sensing these have restated their corporate mission as discussed earlier in the most recent Business Roundtable initiative. Developments subsequent to this appear to suggest that the corporate response toward the stakeholder-orientation with long-term focus has not been uniform within the business community. There are now concerns that these kinds of initiatives, though relevant and helpful to the practice of good governance, might not operate in the manner policymakers aimed for, or intended. It has been further contended that these measures instead of incentivizing a focus on innovation and relevancy could merely serve to reinforce the shareholder primacy orientation, where stewardship pressures could expose corporations to the unhealthy focus on short-term dividends and share buybacks to placate the market, as exemplified by corporate actions in the US after significantly benefiting from tax cuts, instead of investing for future growth, and paying workers better wages.[799]

The foci on dividends and share buybacks present difficulties for companies to invest in innovations that are essential for maintaining relevancy over the long term. For the digital and networked era in particular, the pertinent question before management is what they need to do to make their enterprises more relevant in grappling with existing and future business opportunities and challenges; and that for regulators is what kind of governance model is best suited to deliver the most innovative businesses for the 21st century. The two approaches highlighted earlier might succeed in promoting long-term shareholder engagement, or more so, sustainable behaviors. However, but they do not do much to promote the kind of constant innovations that are deemed necessary in the digital era. Rather, such codes appear to be more of corrective measures designed to resolve problems created by earlier governance measures or prescriptions, like short-termism and bureaucratization of the corporate culture. These codes might lead to more dynamic and innovative behaviors, but this is not the primary aim of these measures, and doubts are raised as to whether these more recent developments in governance practices actually assist enterprises stay relevant in

797. UBS. 2020. "Sustainable finance: Top trends for 2021". https://c2e2.unepdtu.org/wp-content/uploads/sites/3/2021/02/ubs-sustainable-finance-ten-trends-2021.pdf, accessed January 3, 2021.

798. M. Butterick & A. Charlwood. 2021. "HRM and the COVID-19 pandemic: How can we stop making a bad situation worse?". *Human Resource Management Journal 11/03/21*. https://onlinelibrary.wiley.com/doi/10.1111/1748-8583.12344, accessed March 12, 2021.

799. W. Lazonick, M.E. Sakinc & M. Hopkins. 2020. "Why stock buybacks are dangerous for the economy". *Harvard Business Review 07/01/20*. https://hbr.org/2020/01/why-stock-buybacks, accessed November 10, 2020.

today's highly competitive digital markets. Also, the speed of regulatory change happens so fast that this merely creates a culture of formalistic compliance; such that new governance rules, guidelines, principles or codes are increasingly met with indifference, skepticisms, or even hostility, and with some corporations even experiencing compliance fatigues. This raises the further question as to whether such initiatives even when advanced in board agenda would lead to genuine transformation in the governance and culture of the enterprise, especially with regard to its capacity to innovate.[800]

Accordingly, the digital transformation and the rise of platforms persists as the forgotten agenda in current conversations and practice of governance, until the emergence of a series of high-profile controversies and scandals. These include the use of disinformation and misinformation of line contents found in multisided digital platform companies like Facebook, WhatsApp and YouTube with serious social and political impacts. These and other online services are now being questioned and reevaluated by US, EU, and UK policymakers. Regulators too need to respond, and they could begin by evaluating the likely evolution of platforms and the strategies required for building successful platform of tomorrow. Regulatory measures or platform governance that are more closely aligned with the business needs of such firms could be identified.

Via this, the disconnect that is presently existing between regulatory pressures and business needs could then be bridged to some extent. It must be cautioned that there is no one-size-fits-all framework for digital platforms, as they could take multiple forms, from slightly tweaked versions of conventional centralized corporations to blockchain-based decentralized autonomous organizations. These could be exemplified by well-known platforms like Amazon and Netflix to decentralized platforms like *OpenBazaar*, a P2P trading network, using bitcoin. Every enterprise would, as such, need to analyze and use workable strategies to locate the unique recipe for its platform to maximize creativity and opportunities for innovation.[801]

While taking cognizance of the limits of one-size-fits-all solutions, three interconnecting strategies pertinent to any enterprise seeking to operate as a digital platform could be identified. These could involve:[802]

(1) leveraging on current and near-future digital technologies to generate more community-driven kinds of organizations;
(2) building an open and accessible platform culture; and
(3) facilitating the creation, curation and consumption of meaningful content.

800. M. Fenwick, J.A. McCahery & E.P.M. Vermeulen. 2019. "The end of 'corporate' governance: Hello 'platform' governance". *European Business Organization Law Review*, Vol. 20 (2019): 171-199.
801. Fenwick, McCahery & Vermeulen. 2019, *supra* note [800].
802. Fenwick, McCahery & Vermeulen. 2019, *supra* note [800].

Overlapping technological developments in cheaper and more powerful digital hardware, global communication networks and mass connectivity, cloud-based storage of big data, and automated algorithms matching platform users could provide the foundation and infrastructure for platforms. Digital technology driving the platforms offer peer-to-peer (P2P) solutions, where users could share reviews, experiences, and any other information, thereby helping to connect developers and creators on one side and users on the other.[803] Thus, all entities seeking to operate as platforms need to think and act as if they are a technology entity. It has been observed that those platforms that are successful are characterized by underlying technology that is secure, safe, and reliable for all of the platform's users. They are also user-friendly, continually updating and upgrading its interface, as well as offering users and participants connectivity, choice and convenience, besides enabling monetization, and the boosting of analytical, promotional, and creative activities.

Successful platforms are also marked by open and accessible platform cultures in every aspect of their operations and organizations. This means that the platform and all its participants need to understand clearly what and whom they are dealing with. More centralized platforms need to be open about their processes and inner workings of their technology, while for more decentralized platforms, their code and protocol must be open sources to enable constant testing and updating of weaknesses. A platform in general needs to offer an accessible, honest and personal experience to participants. It further needs to enable participants to verify the reputation of and trust of other participants, facilitate connections to a community of users that matters to them, and encourage creativity and engagement via social media, blogs, and reviews.

Communication in an open platform culture is vital, as smart platforms know that communication is not a one-way process of information disclosure from platform operators to platform users, but rather a more engaged, responsive and open process encouraging mutually productive dialogues. Many alternative mechanisms have been used for communicating within a platform's ecosystem, such as the use of annual letters, instead of annual reports.[804] This aside, successful platforms depend on its leadership and on the leader's ability to listen and engage;[805] as well as forward-thinking to culture and values articulated with transparency, as to who gets rewarded, promoted or let go, and which accordingly attracts talented people seeking much higher degrees of freedom and responsibility.

Business leaders in successful platforms therefore need to be visionary, entrepreneurial and innovation-minded.[806] This would include platform directors, as their ability to add value in the digital era is considerably higher when more digital

803. J.M. Sanchez-Cartas & G. Leon. 2021. "Multisided platforms and markets: A survey of theoretical literature". *Journal of Economic Surveys*, Vol. 35 (2): 452-487.
804. J. Bezoz. 2017. "2017 letter to shareholders: Amazon investor relations". http://phx.corporate-ir.net/phoenix.zhtml%3fc%3d97664%26p%3dirol-reportsannual, accessed November 10, 2020.
805. R. Hastings. 2011. "Freedom and responsibility culture slideshare". https://www.slideshare.net/reed2001/culture-2009, accessed November 10, 2020.
806. R. Hoffman, B. Csnocha & C. Yeh. 2014. *The alliance: Managing talent in the network age.* Cambridge: Harvard Business Review Press.

technology people are appointed to the board.[807] This is necessary for dealing with digital challenges and opportunities in the digital economy, as exemplified by the appointments of Facebook's Sheryl Sandberg and Twitter's Jack Dorsey to the board of The Walt Disney Company.[808]

Interrelating and overlapping with the strategies of leveraging technology, and having the right kind of platform culture, is the vital importance of the delivery of strong platform content, be it products, services, or other creative content that for all must be authentic. It has to establish networks and connections that give a sense of community and is pivotal to the success of both the participants and the platform. Community insights are deemed essential for all platform enterprises as they develop. A stronger platform culture enriches user experience and builds brand loyalty, and such consumer commitment to a product or brand has a commercial value which platforms could then leverage to their benefit in various ways. Indeed, the emergence of network technologies has opened up almost limitless opportunities for connected products, meaning products allowing data to be exchanged between the products and its environment, manufacturer, users, and other devices, or systems. Thus, the smart platforms in sync with the 21st century and more would have all these three alluded to strategies working in tandem and in synergy. It makes business sense for all platforms to pursue this objective, and the objective of platform governance needs to be the identification of regulatory mechanisms that could nudge enterprises in this direction.[809]

In this connection, open communication provides the mechanism for coordinating different stakeholders. This involves a different approach of information dissemination and exchange that characterizes relationship between all participants in the enterprise, where open communication is in particular marked by a more personalized style to communication. Open communication is not limited to information sharing from one part of the enterprise to another or from the enterprise to external parties. It promotes the building of an ongoing and constructive dialogue with other participants in the enterprise and the market, and this would have a significant impact on the enterprise's future performance. It is also about building respect, trust, and loyalty, as well as about recognizing the financial benefits that come from sharing.

More inclusive and meaningful relationships among and between stakeholders could thus be forged by adopting open communications. These foster a sense of belonging thereby helping to expand the pool and diversity of participants with concrete involvements in key decision-making processes. The flowing of more open attitudes toward both insiders and outsiders would considerably positively motivate the kind of individuals responsible for driving the direction of the corporation; and in

807. T. Richards & R. Grossman. 2017. "The board of directors you need for a digital transformation". *Harvard Business Review* 13/07/17. https://hbr.org/2017/07/the-board-directors-you-need, accessed November 10, 2020.
808. Walt Disney Company. 2013. "Jack Dorsey elected to The Walt Disney Company board of directors". https://www.thewaltdisneycompany.com/jack-dorsey-elected-to-the-walt-disney, accessed November 10, 2020.
809. Fenwick, McCahery & Vermeulen. 2019, *supra* note [800].

this sense renders the corporate project more meaningful from the perspective of both insiders and outsiders, as well as from the corporations' perspective.

Along with this, platform corporations would benefit by being better placed to make effective decisions, expanding firm know-how, developing more extensive and deeper networks, retaining more performance-related information necessary for planning, besides offering a more collaborative and meaningful environment for all stakeholders. Indeed, where open communication is undertaken effectively, a whole ecosystem could emerge around the enterprise's communication strategy, as exemplified by the excitements surrounding the annual letters from Buffet and Bezos to their respective stakeholders, and which show that information could be a resource that could be leveraged by open communication to the enterprise's commercial advantage.[810] This would further make the enterprise interesting and relevant for potential and talented employees, as well as investors.

A focus on open communication would necessarily involve a shift in how the role of the board of directors in a large enterprise is viewed. The dominant view for now is to treat the board primarily as the supervisors or monitors of senior managers. Consequentially, the board tends to focus on controlling managerial misbehavior and monitoring the company's past performance, compliance and sustainability, then on active contributions to future performance. Many enterprises, now no longer recognized this as adequate, and that the approach of board independence has missed the opportunity of getting tech-savvy directors to help the enterprise to stay relevant as The Walt Disney Company has done. Board diversity from this perspective could contribute to a more collaborative model of the relationship with management in ensuring the incorporation of different perspectives into the decision-making process in manners that generate genuine value.[811] Such directors could function as feedback providers for better engagement with the inherent uncertainty of disruptive technological and market processes and technology to gain beneficial relevant insights. Where independent directors are concerned, questions have been consistently raised as to the extent these directors would be willing or able to question the actions or decisions of those to whom they would in some sense be obligated to. As such, the extent to which these structural biases could be mitigated could be the primary challenge of implementing a corporate culture, wherein open communication is pervasive.[812]

A connected problem pertains to enterprises relying on technology to provide matchmaking services or the bringing together of individuals, such as exemplified by Airbnb and Uber. The fortunes of these platforms hinge on the ability of service providers and consumers to trust the system. This willingness to trust is generally dependent upon the willingness of participants to take part in and trust a system of

810. K. Berman & J. Knight. 2010. "Financial communication: Warren Buffer style". *Harvard Business Review*. https://hbr.org/2010/03/financial-communication-warren, accessed November 10, 2020.
811. Fenwick, McCahery & Vermeulen. 2019, *supra* note [800].
812. J. Veisdal. 2020. "The dynamics of entry for digital platforms in two-sided markets: A multi-case study". *Electronic Markets*. https://doi.org/10.1007/s12525-020-00409-4, accessed January 3, 2021; J.E. Cohen. 2017. "Law for the platform economy". *U.C. Davis Law Review*, Vol. 51 (1): '33-204.

reviews and ratings. Decisions as to whether to partake in transactions are dependent on narrations on the transaction history of the potential partners, as confirmed by the rating system. Extensive failures to participate would lead to system failures. Interestingly, these matchmaking platforms have deployed a two-way rating system, where service providers are rated by customers, and customers by service providers.[813] This kind of check-and-balance system assists in building trust, via a combination of open communication and algorithms put in place by the platforms, where poor providers or bad customers get canceled out. The reliance on these technologies has grown in importance to other enterprises, such as exemplified by online retailers, like Amazon making rating systems pivotal to their online store in allowing potential customers to decide on particular goods and services drawing on the experience of those who have already purchased them.[814]

These governance strategies could benefit both conventional and emerging FIR enterprises that need to adapt to the unique challenges of the tech-driven global digital economy, or in other words, helping these enterprises to promote a high level of cooperation, loyalty and mutual trust. Foremost, a shift to new forms of communications could be particularly significant in building a healthy bond among stakeholders, and in helping to maintain a corporate culture of openness and honesty. There are increasing signs that the unmediated forms of corporate communications deployed to engage with stakeholders, particularly through an annual letter, are becoming more important than the official annual reports and traditional modes of financial communications. Also, the recent rise in the diversity of personalities appointed to corporate boards confirms the importance of their role in identifying issues and opportunities in connection with disruptive innovations.

Policymakers, as such, would need to consider how best to incentivize corporations to adopt these strategies when designing new regulatory initiatives to assist them to remain competitive in the global digital economy. Further, the rise of digital platforms is disrupting both current hierarchical business models, and the conventional governance approaches. In this respect, existing regulatory models would face an uncertain fate. Economies that could be more successful in navigating this predicament would likely emerge as the most successful in designing a new platform governance underpinned by the promotion of these said strategies, and resulting in them becoming the leading beneficiaries of the transformed digital economy. Therefore, the conventional models of governance practices are an adaptation to a world of hierarchical and centralized organizations and frequently appear ill-suited to the organizational and business needs of digital platforms.

Indeed, most current governance practices address a short-term, compliance-oriented and cautious corporate attitude that would be counterproductive in a setting

813. Federal Trade Commission (FTC). 2016. "The sharing economy: Issues facing platforms, participants, and regulators". *FTC Staff Report November 2016*. https://www.ftc.gov/reports/sharing-economy-issues-facing-platforms-participants-regulators-federal-trade-commission, accessed November 10, 2020.

814. M. Ardolina, et al. 2020. "A business model framework to characterize digital multisided platforms". *Journal of Open Innovation: Technology, Market, and Complexity*, Vol. 6 (2020): 10-32.

where corporations need to be dynamic and continuously adapting to transformative technologies, markets, and evolving consumer demands. As such, until regulators developed a better appreciation of their role in the new multisided platform world, they should avoid intervening.[815] Though not necessarily perfect, the process of cultivating such insights has begun through the identification of the distinctive features of such platforms. These insights have demonstrated the disconnect that exists between digital platforms and governance practices, besides identifying the core strategies that the effective platforms of the 21st century need to adopt. The next step would involve the identification and evaluation of specific regulatory mechanisms that could best incentivize corporations to engage with these strategies.[816]

The advocation for new models for digital governance, when it comes to platforms, suggests a more functional approach, instead of the overly detailed regulation common to static markets. This is necessary when moving toward principles-based regulation, as opposed to rules-based regulation.[817] A platform governance approach, as such, should seek to understand the complex governance relationships and public policy challenges in today's platform society, as well as also asking how these relationships could become more beneficial for the multitude, rather than the few.[818] Recent research has begun extending some possible principles, each with their relative merits and challenges. These include rights-based legal approaches, like international human rights laws, that could possibly provide an avenue for platforms to ground policy decisions and build legitimacy more effectively.[819] Alternative frameworks could extend to aspirational computer science principles for algorithmic systems, including fairness, accountability, transparency, ethics and responsibility, as well as the developing area of data justice that seeks to transcend the focus on individual harms wrought by various data-driven systems toward the application of holistic principles of social justice at a wider level.[820] Yet, still others could include political science and governance studies principles of meaningful democratic accountability and transparency, or CSR and other previous efforts to steer business in the direction of human rights.[821]

The challenge is on how to enshrine these various values through sensible legislation and accountability mechanisms.[822] Principles, values, and imaginaries would be pivotal for grounding the future platform governance research agenda, and scholars would need to be assertive with their ideas. Transformations would not come easily, given that platform corporations have become influential political actors with obvious interest in keeping their dominant market positions. Accordingly, powerful creative thinking would be needed to help disrupt the disruptors and introduce fairer,

815. Fenwick, McCahery & Vermeulen. 2019, *supra* note [800].
816. Fenwick, McCahery & Vermeulen. 2019, *supra* note [800].
817. R. Gorwa. 2019. "What is platform governance?". *Information, Communication & Society*, https://www.tandfonline.com/doi/full/10.1080/1369118X.2019.1573914, accessed November 10, 2020.
818. Gorwa 2019, *supra* note [817].
819. Gorwa 2019, *supra* note [817].
820. Gorwa 2019, *supra* note [817].
821. Gorwa 2019, *supra* note [817].
822. Gorwa 2019, *supra* note [817].

more accountable, and more just forms of platform governance.[823] As regulators and boards struggle to address these alluded to challenges facing business corporations in an increasingly digitalized economy, shareholders too might need to reflect on their influence and powers in facing these challenges too.

8.03 SHAREHOLDER POWERS

In general, a shareholder does not owe fiduciary duty to the company or to fellow shareholders. A shareholder's voting power in law represents a right in property.[824] Other than for consideration of a duty for fairness to other shareholders, a shareholder could vote freely. Outside of these contexts, shareholders in general meeting would enjoy residual control to act on the company's behalf within four identifiable situations:[825]

(1) Remedying those circumstances where directors failed to adhere to procedural rules governing corporate action. Decisions made by directors or CEOs at informal or ad hoc meetings, rather than proper board meetings where the collective views or wisdom or board members could be tapped. Shareholders under such a circumstance could exercise their residual powers in formal general meetings that could provide guidance for future purposes.
(2) Where the board of directors are unable to act or function, such as, when there is breakdown in communications or serious breakdown in directors' relationships with regard to providing oversights to managerial actions or inactions. Shareholders under these situations could harness residual powers to overcome the deadlock.[826]
(3) At times, where directors or CEOs might have acted beyond or in excess of their powers in breach of their duties to the company, shareholders in general meetings could claim residual powers to ratify such infringements of duties. Examples could include situations where executive directors borrowed substantial sums from banks beyond their powers as to the amounts involved, or the use of corporate assets as collaterals, or privately tapped on to business opportunities without proper disclosures. The powers to ratify directors' actions must however not compromise the welfare of minority shareholders, as this could galvanize the latter to litigate against the enterprise, the directors, or the majority shareholders, particularly in family-led or state-led corporations.
(4) Routinely, the board of directors are authorized or empowered to act and to litigate on behalf of the enterprise. However, in situations where the board or majority shareholders in concentrated shareholdings enterprise commit

823. Gorwa 2019, *supra* note [817].
824. *Northern Counties Securities v. Jackson & Steeple Ltd.* [1974] 1 WLR 1133.
825. P. Redmond. 2000. *Companies and securities law: Commentary and materials*. Sydney: LBC Information Services.
826. *Foster v. Foster* [1916] 1 Ch 532.

> breaches or wrongs, such as the transfer of corporate assets for use in other corporate destinations without proper disclosures, but with harmful financial impact to minority shareholders' interests, a shareholder could initiate action against the company, given that directors under such situations would be unlikely to initiate actions against themselves. Such corporate abuses or frauds perpetuated against minority shareholders' interests could lead to shareholders claims against the directors.[827]

UK shareholders' rights pertaining to recovery for losses suffered in relation to their shares have historically been limited, but various approaches have been used to overcome these limitations, and to resolve disputes. Disputes arising from shareholders over various differences are usually handled in mechanisms provided by shareholders' agreements.

Disputes between shareholders and so on could also be resolved through other ways. For example, section 994 CA 2006 provides a statutory basis for a claim where one shareholder accuses the other of unfair prejudice. Shareholders may also pursue claims against directors via sections 170-181 CA 2006 by way of derivative actions. Grievances of minority shareholders in particular extend from compulsory acquisitions of shares, exclusion from management, illiquidity, lack of access to corporate affairs information, meagre or absence of participation in profits, corporate mismanagement or mismanagement of corporate assets, self-interests of block or majority shareholders, improper dilution of voting powers, or disregard for rights granted by statute or the company's constitution.[828] The common law also provides rights for shareholder against directors involving allegations of deceit, but in practice, these rights at common law are limited.

The more direct relationship enforceable by directors pertains to those relationships between shareholders and the company itself. Statutory rights and rights at common law are available to support a claim by shareholders against the company.[829] For listed corporations, sections 90A and 150 Financial Services and Markets Act 2000 establish claims pertaining to public statements made to the market and to shareholders.[830] Common law has consistently provided reliefs for shareholders who are financially harmed by wrongdoings by their enterprise, especially for negligent misstatement and misrepresentation, conspiracy, or the standard torts of deceit.[831] The usual avenue for the resolution of disputes, both between shareholders and between shareholders and others, including the company and the directors is the courts. Investors suffering harm arising from the wrongdoing of another providing investment

827. International Organization of Securities Commissions (IOSCO). 2009. "Protection of minority shareholders in listed issuers: Final report June 2009". https://www.iosco.org/library/pubdocs/pdf/IOSCOPD295.pdf, accessed November 10, 2020.
828. J. Kirkbride, L. Steve & C. Smallman. 2009. "Minority shareholders and corporate governance: Reflections on the derivative action in the UK, the USA and in China". *International Journal of Law and Management*, Vol. 51 (4): 206-219; G. Stedman & J. Jones. 1990. *Shareholders' agreements*. London: Longman.
829. D. Greene 2012. *Shareholder claims*. Bristol: Jordan Publishing Limited.
830. *The Financial Services and Markets Act 2000 (Regulated Activities) *Amendment) Order 2021.*
831. Greene 2012, *supra* note [829].

or banking services could tap on the statutory cost-free scheme from the Financial Ombudsman Service. This is though limited to award of damages of up to GBP 100,000.[832]

Different kinds of tensions occur, as business corporations get more involved in corporate controversies with serious consequences for the enterprise and for the shareholders, and for directors where they are alleged to have been acting recklessly. These various kinds of serious corporate flaws or controversies will be discussed more fully in Chapter 9, following this, where selected seminal US and UK contemporary case insights will be highlighted to illustrate various kinds of corporate excesses committed by companies and directors collectively or individually.

832. Financial Ombudsman Service. 2021. "Financial dispute resolution that's fair and impartial". https://www.financial-ombudsman.org.uk/, accessed April 19, 2021.

CHAPTER 9

ESG Controversies: Selected US and UK Cases

There are good numbers of companies where their annual and accompanying directors' reports make claims of their exemplary governance practices, and yet succumbed to bad governance practices, not too long after the release of these reports. These led to doubts of the veracity, reliability, and accuracy of these reports. These happened to Enron[833] and LB[834] in the US, and Northern Rock[835] and Carillon[836] in the UK. Such and more cases of their equivalent nature have been known for their notoriety. Such companies had been held up as role models of excellent governance practitioners in the course of their business histories, prior to their eventual financial downfalls that were attributed to highly faulty business decisions, serious risk management issues, and even downright frauds. It has been estimated that close to two dozen high-profile corporate scandals[837] collectively erased some USD 750 billion of their shareholder's equity, besides damaging the economic welfares of direct stakeholders, like employees, suppliers, and customers. There is this puzzling question as to why governance controversies of this nature persist in the US, EU, UK and elsewhere after years of debate, and in theory learning and correcting such fatal mistakes. Various suggestions for more effective answers for these kinds of challenging problems have been advanced, including relying on the argument that such governance scandals are the direct outcome of a common set of fourteen interrelated factors that needed comprehensive adjustments. These factors include overconcentration of power, ineffective board of

833. A.W. Dnes. 2005. "Enron, corporate governance and deterrence". *Managerial and Decision Economics*, Vol. 26 (7): 421-429.
834. J.K.M. Mawutor. 2014. "The failure of Lehman Brothers: Causes, preventive measures and recommendations". *Research Journal of Finance and Accounting*, Vol. 5 (4): 85-91.
835. F. Bruni & D.T. Llewellyn. 2009. *The failure of Northern Rock: A multi-dimensional study*. Vienna: The European Money and Finance Forum (SUERF).
836. E. Mujih. 2021. "CG reform and CG failure in the UK". *Company Lawyer*, Vol. 42 (4): 109-119.
837. Business Dictionary. 2020. "A corporate scandal is assumed as a set of questionable, unethical, and/or illegal actions that a person or persons within a corporation engage in". *BusinessDictionary.com*. http://en.wikipedia.org/wiki/List_of_corporate_scandals, accessed November 10, 2020.

directors, investors' passivity, gatekeepers' failures, poor regulations, or the absence of appropriate ethical tone at the top hierarchy.

Combined oversights from these factors further suggest that the root of the problem lies in the way the governance notion has been internalized, or essentially grounded. The relied-upon agency theory perspective is mainly concerned with creating ways to motivate one party or the agent to act on behalf of another, or the principal. Consequently, the good governance of a business, a very complex phenomenon, has been reduced to a mere set of incentives and control mechanisms so as to induce agents or corporate managers to make decisions in the best interests of their principals or shareholders. This agency framework suffers from two flaws. Foremost, viewing the governance process as a mere set of rewards and punishment mechanisms for implementation, to induce the desired behaviors, has enabled business leaders free to view the complex and intrinsically human subject as a mere list of recommended practices to be addressed in alignment with the expectations of outside stakeholders.

These have been amply demonstrated in the LB and other equivalent banking cases where there have been discrepancies between the essence of good governance, as shown in entities where decisions are claimed to have been made in their best long-term interest and wherein people complied with the rules, and in the manner, governance practices have been demonstrated externally. Such for show actions does not really solve actual business problems at hand, and are unsustainable, as they merely paper over the cracks or fault lines. Second, the agency paradigm conceived some five decades earlier is based on the *homo economicus* theory. Research study insights from sociology, psychology, neuroscience, behavioral economics, and so on suggest that this theory takes a very narrow view of human nature. These various studies have also consistently demonstrated that people are irrational, exclusively selfish, and depending on relative economic benefits, not interested in breaking rules.[838] In view of the influence of these studies, a review of the conventional governance framework has been advocated.

Thus, given the above limitations, a new behavioral approach to governance focusing on the psychological aspects of human beings inside corporations has been advanced. This, as further argued, should be based on three main premises previously ignored by the agency framework. It involves the systematic focus on the mitigation of cognitive biases in managerial decisions; the continuous fostering of employee and executive awareness toward the promotion of unselfish cooperative behaviors; and the reduction of the likelihood of frauds and other dishonest acts via new corporate strategies developed subsequent to a deeper understanding of their psychological motivations. This new behavioral approach retains the importance of incentive and control mechanisms in the agency framework. These mechanisms remain relevant, but are still considered insufficient for well-governed entities. The extension of the governance framework beyond the agency paradigm toward a behavioral perspective should therefore be seen as something crucial for restraining all forms of harmful corporate excesses in the foreseeable future.[839]

The above-suggested approach also draws on trust literatures in organizations, stewardship theory, and those to do with intrinsic motivation.[840] Trust

838. A.D.M. da Silveira. 2013. "Corporate scandals of the 21st Century: Limitations of mainstream CG literatures and the need for a new behavioral approach". *School of Economics, Management and Accounting, University of Sao Paulo Working Paper 14/01/13.*
839. da Silveira 2013, *supra* note [838].
840. da Silveira 2013, *supra* note [838].

literature faults agency theory's for precluding trust and cooperation that are seen as crucial elements for maximizing the principal's utility toward the goal of achieving organizational success. Literatures on the stewardship paradigm contend that executives, as stewards of the corporation, are motivated to act responsibly based on the trust assumption. It further claims that managers achieve greater utility when applying a collaborative approach, rather than behaving selfishly, particularly when identifying with organizational values and goals. Motivation literatures argue that nonpecuniary motives influence human behavior, inclusive of intrinsic satisfactions arising from work, the need to earn social approval, as well as the sense of reciprocation. These further argue that extrinsic rewards like those stressed by agency theory could risk undermining the role of intrinsic rewards on motivation, thereby enhancing the agent's opportunistic behavior.

Thus, insights from the above different disciplines suggest that the root cause of the governance scandals in the 21st century or earlier appear to lie in the influence of the *homo economicus* thesis behind the mainstream approach to governance practices. These insights suggest that:[841]

1 people do not make rational decisions;
2 people tend to behave cooperatively, rather than acting selfishly, depending on the social context; and
3 they would behave dishonestly when motivated primarily by psychological factors, instead of designated penalties and the probability of being caught.

Therefore, it is argued that the theoretical answer for the limitations of the agency theory lies in the emergence of a behavioral approach to governance focusing on psychological factors associated with people inside corporations, as alluded to earlier. Interestingly, many of the seminal corporate scandals in the US, the UK, the EU and elsewhere were kept unknown, until their unraveling by insider whistleblowers.[842] Empirical insights suggest that active internal whistleblowing has been associated with fewer and lower levels of government fines and material lawsuits.[843]

This chapter aims to provide further insights on the key factors contributing to faulty governance practices, or the "G" in the ESG paradigm. The chapter will commence with discussions on faulty governance practices in nonfinancial corporations in the US and the UK. These will be followed by further analysis of weak governance practices in financial institutions, and those in technology-based corporations driven by FIR enabling technologies. The idea is to draw out similarities and differences observed in corporations in these clusters caught with bad governance practices. These discussions would also draw out the "E" and the "S" issues in the ESG paradigm where these had significant impacts on the selected companies' operational and financial performances.

841. da Silveira 2013, *supra* note [838].
842. S.R. Stubben & K.T. Welch. 2020. "Evidence on the use and efficacy of internal whistleblowing systems". *Journal of Accounting Research*, Vol. 58 (2): 475-518.
843. Stubben & Welch 2020, *supra* note [842].

9.01 ESG CONTROVERSIES IN NONFINANCIAL CORPORATIONS (NFCs)

9.01a US Corporations

Cases selected for discussions here have to do with various flaws in ESG practices and their wide public interests because of their impacts on their respective businesses, as well as their repercussions to the wider economy. Environment, Social and Governance (ESG) factors represent the issues that have become increasingly topical when discussing governance practices these days, in view of the deep and wide COVID-19 and climate change impacts have on these matters. This is not too far off the CSR days some few years ago when CSR was much talked about and which had fallen off the radar of investing community, given the extensive beliefs that many corporations have either been greenwashing their CSR labels, or in practice, not particularly reporting much on these matters these days. Still, some insights on CSR practices among business corporations could generate some pertinent insights as to how when unattended could turn into governance fault lines or even worse serious corporate scandals of some kind. It is appropriate here to differentiate the nuance between the CSR and ESG paradigms. CSR can be said to involve mainly corporate introspection or internal examination of CSR-related activities, whereas ESG involves primarily evaluation of these activities by external independent third parties, and ergo supposedly more robust and less bias in nature. This perhaps explains why CSR disclosure is said to have fallen in disrepute because of the general positive disclosure bias reporting by notable numbers of large enterprises and MNCs. These have been to some extent revealed in Sabine Einwiller's 2020 article "Negative Disclosures in Corporate Social Responsibility Reporting" in *Corporate Communications: An International Journal.*

Apple, Canon, Coca-Cola and Walmart

The analysis begins by looking into the involvements of four US multinationals (MNCs), namely; Apple, Canon, Coca-Cola, and Walmart in social and environmental conflicts and whether these conflicts impact these corporations' CSR policy, the forerunner of the ESG paradigm. These four MNCs have implemented basic CSR policies before encountering various conflicts. Most of the conflicts experienced by them vary in terms of degrees of severity. Apple, Coca-Cola and Walmart found their corporate reputations dented, while Coca-Cola's conflict issues in India involved claims of water pollutions and overextraction of groundwater, as well as allegations that Coca-Cola beverages produced in India contained high levels of pesticide residues. The overall research yielded the following observations:[844]

844. C.A.C. Torres, et al. 2012. "Four case studies on CSR: Do conflicts affect a company's CSR?", *Utrecht Law Review*, Vol. 8 (3): 51-73.

(1) The negative impacts of the media effects on the corporate image of Coca-Cola extended beyond India, but spread back to the US causing plummeting sales and revenue losses.
(2) For Walmart, it has more to do with labor issues. It comprised a class action lawsuit by former female employees,[845] whereby the plaintiffs alleged gender-based discrimination. Though this was not the first such case that Walmart faced, its relevance has more to do with the fact that the plaintiffs were suing on behalf of themselves, and all women employed by Walmart nationwide, since December 1998 of some 1.5 million women. The US Supreme Court ruled that the case could not be in the plaintiff's favor because they did not have enough in common. Walmart also experienced allegations that two of its subcontractors in Bangladesh have been using child labor.
(3) For Apple, its suppliers have been found to be using underage labor. Also, Apple's reputation is tarnished by its linkage to its subcontractor, Foxconn, where allegations have been made that the employees there were toiling up to seventy hours weekly, ten hours above Apple's Supplier Code. Apple has also been linked with allegations of the poisoning of its workers at Wintek by n-hexane.
(4) Cannon encountered non-severe problems pertaining to stress-related illnesses among employees in the company's subsidiary in Denmark, as well as findings that Japanese employees have been forbidden to sit down during working hours. Neither these nor other conflicts that Cannon faced attracted much media attention.
(5) Responses from the four MNCs vary, ranging from denials to providing remedial solutions.
(6) Coca-Cola resorted to the denial approach at first through the making of various statements in its sustainability and other reports that the allegations have been without basis. The strategy sought to reestablish the MNC's integrity by providing evidence to the contrary. These efforts proved to be inadequate for repairing the MNC's tarnished image, or to regain the trust of consumers in India and elsewhere at the time. The MNC subsequently switched to a more proactive approach targeted at preventing damage to Indian water resources.
(7) The initial lawsuit against Walmart did not succeed, but the claimant later mounted another lawsuit based on individual cases per state that demonstrated clear threats. When Apple faced allegations of being linked to the use of child labor by its subcontractors, it responded through its 2005 Report on Ethical Sourcing that these revelations came about because of the implementation of more stringent anti-child labor issues with the suppliers. Apple, eighteen months after media report on the suicides allegations, joined the Fair Labor Association (FLA) that aimed to set a new

845. *Dukes v. Walmart Stores.*

standard in the electronics industry and to have a supply chain that could be seen as a model for the industry.

(8) Although Canon did not have to seriously deal with damages to its reputation owing to the stress-related illness in Denmark, the company has taken a proactive approach in preventing the emergence of future conflicts whereby for its global Canon policies, the MNC included measures to reduce stress in the workplace.

(9) These four cases show that these MNCs made changes to their CSR policies after controversial conflicts with direct or indirect impacts on their reputations. Coca-Cola, Canon and Walmart came up with the establishments of specific goals that they aimed to achieve at company levels. Apple, rather than making various formal commitments, pledged to change its supplier responsibility practice. All four MNCs though presented in their sustainability reports that their CSR policies have been created as long-term commitments, and not just for resolving emerging crises.

(10) By comparison, Coca-Cola seems to have adopted the more ambitious CSR policies after experiencing conflicts in India. It adopted initiatives tailored to remedy water problems it caused in India, and toward improving its image to customers, including partnerships with the local Indian government. This eventually led to the MNC adopting water management as one of the core elements of its global CSR policy with commitments toward meeting quantifiable goals pertaining to water management efficiency. Coca-Cola did not formally admit that the conflict in India contributed to the main motivation behinds its water adoption policy. Nonetheless, the severe damage inflicted on its reputation by this and the serious fall in revenues linked to this were likely behind its corporate policy to implement a CSR policy premised on water management efficiency in its global operations.

(11) Walmart, as an early implementor of CSR regulations, strengthened its policies after the conflicts, with rebooted policies for appointing women to management positions, and the setting up of a board dedicated toward combating gender discrimination, while increasing the number of audits to curb child labor employment.

(12) Subsequent to the FLA negative report on Foxconn, Apple stated its full support for the FLA recommendations.

(13) The case studies on Apple, Walmart, and Coca-Cola showed that these MNCs adopted changes in their CSR and reporting policies, after the highlighted conflicts occurred. They have been relatively transparent about this, via their public statements, and via their annual and sustainability reports. Though Canon has not been confronted with serious labor issues, it has not been totally free from them. These events show the importance of transparency in the upholding of sustainability standards. Responding positively to earlier public scrutiny because of various conflicts, these MNCs have become role models in their respective industries. Coca-Cola initiated innovative measures in dealing with water management issues,

while Apple set a new labor practice standard in the electronic industry, Walmart sought to be the greenest corporation in the world, and Canon became an exemplar of zero waste management at one of its UK plants.

Fast forward to 2021, Coca-Cola claims that its ESG goals are embedded in how they operate as a business as these are part of their very foundation.[846] Its good ESG ranking in various global indices give good support to this claim.[847] Walmart's ESG medium risk rating is encouraging.[848] Apple's low ESG risk rating has been exemplary.[849] Canon's has also a low ESG risk rating.

Boeing

US MNCs caught with fatality of human lives more recently involved Boeing. This pertained to the crashing of two 737 MAX passenger aircraft. One occurred in Indonesia in late 2018, and the other in Ethiopia in early 2019. These resulted in the subsequent grounding of the entire fleet of 737 MAX jets. This turned the global spotlight on Boeing corporate practices and culture. The crashes have been attributed to design flaws within MAX's new flight control software system set for preventing stalls, internal pressures to keep pace with Airbus, Boeing's main competitor, the airline manufacturer's lack of transparency about the new software, as well as the lack of sufficient monitoring of Boeing by the Federal Aviation Administration (FAA), particularly during MAX's certification, and following the first crash that blamed pilot error.[850]

These, and other factors, like the regulatory capture contention[851] have been the themes of various government reports and investigative journalism articles. Insights from these suggest the importance of ethical responsibilities of Boeing's engineers and the FAA involved in the designing and certifying of MAX, and the need to strengthen the voice of engineers within large technology-based enterprises, as well as the need for greater involvements of professional engineering societies in ethics-related activities, including wider focus on moral courage in engineering ethics education.[852] Similarly, governance process flaws, like the lack of transparency in corporate practices, and the sidelining of engineering monitoring in the company's internal control system also

846. Coca-Cola. 2021. "Refresh the world. Make a difference". https://www.coca-colacompany.com/content/dam/journey/us/en/reports/coca-cola-business-environmental, accessed May 28, 2021.
847. Coca-Cola. 2021. "ESG ranking". https://www.coca-colahellenic.com/en/a-more-sustainable-future/esg-ranking, accessed May 28, 2021.
848. Sustainalytics. 2021. "Company ESG risk ratings: Walmart Inc." https://www.sustainalytics.com/esg-rating/walmart-inc/1008191301, accessed May 28, 2021.
849. Sustainalytics. 2021. "Company ESG risk ratings: Apple Inc." https://www.sustainalytics.com/esg-rating/apple-inc/1007903183/, accessed May 28, 2021.
850. J. Herkert, J. Borenstein & K. Miller. 2020. "The Boeing 737 MAX: Lessons for engineering ethics". *Science and Engineering Ethics*, Vol. 26 (2020): 2957-2974.
851. P. Yeoh. 2019. "Capture of regulatory agencies: A time for reflection again". *Business Law Review*, Vol. 40 (4): 134-145.
852. Herkert, Borenstein & Miller. 2020, *supra* note [850].

helped to escalate these flaws into corporate scandals, such as also found at the Volkswagen US subsidiary of a German plant.[853]

9.01b UK Nonfinancial Corporations

Nonfinancial services entities distressed by governance failures in UK are exemplified by two relatively high-profile cases. These are selected for analysis because of their economic impacts, as well as the serious governance issues they come to be associated with. The rate of corporate failures in the UK has increased. This could be shown by the 6.8% increase in company insolvencies in 2019 over that in 2018, the highest level of underlying insolvencies since 2013.[854] The deterioration has been attributed to an increase in underlying creditors' voluntary insolvencies.[855] The past few years have also witnessed several high-profile failures every year. These are now showing signs as a common feature of governance failures in the UK. This is led by the collapse of Carillon in January 2019, the biggest in the country, for a decade. The case transmitted shockwaves in corporate UK that reverberated across many sectors in the UK and also overseas, as the enterprise has operations in many industries in the country, as well as, abroad.

British Steel and British travel firm Thomas Cook succumbed quickly to the same fate, a year later. The ongoing COVID-19 pandemic would likely draw out more corporate failures, but of significant worries are the discerning signs that such failures are preceded by the publication of financial statements giving these entities healthy or even glowing financial health status. This inconsistency between published financials and the financial fates of these cases raised questions on the quality of corporate disclosures practices, and the efficacy of governance reforms that began with the Cadbury governance code initiative in 1992. The Cadbury Code has been regularly updated, and used by more and more UK listed corporations claiming adherence to the Code, or the Wates CG Principles for other large private enterprises. In fact, some 66% of the FTSE 350 are said to comply with the UK Code compared to some 36% in 2002 when the FTSE 350 CG Review was first launched.[856]

Hence, questions have been raised as to the rise in corporate failures, despite UK enterprises claiming adherence to the UK CG code, and despite regular updating of the

853. M.J.B. Kabeyi. 2019. "CG in manufacturing and management with analysis of governance failures at Enron and Volkswagen corporations". *American Journal of Operations Management and Information Systems*, Vol. 4 (4): 109-123.
854. The Insolvency Service. 2020. "Company insolvency statistics, Q4 October to December 2019". Released 30/01/2020. https://assets.publishing.service.gov.uk/government/uploads/system/uploads/attachment_data/file/861187/Commentary_-_Company_Insolvency_Statistics_Q4_2019.pdf, accessed November 10, 2020.
855. The Insolvency Service. 2020. "Company insolvency statistics, Q4 October to December 2019". https://assets.publishing.service.gov.uk/government/uploads/system/uploads/attachment_data/file/861187/Commentary_-_Company_Insolvency_Statistics_Q4_2019.pdf, accessed November 10, 2020.
856. S. Lowe. 2018. "How will the Revised UK CG Code affect you?". *Grant Thornton 25/07/18.* https://www.grantthornton.co.uk/insights/how-will-the-revised-uk-corporate-governance-Code-affect-you/, accessed November 10, 2020.

UK soft law code to deal with issues uncovered in the revelations of these scandals. Commonly cited failures reasons extend from fraud,[857] mismanagement, accounting irregularities, board risk management failures,[858] and excessive remunerations of corporate executives and CEOs.[859] These attributions could be categorized under the five main principles of the existing UK CG Code, with implications of a correlation between breach of these principles and corporate failures, thereby raising further questions as to the level of compliance with the Code. An empirical study examines three of these main causes, namely, board failure, accountability and directors' remuneration in the context of this soft law Code, and Part 15 and Chapter 6 of CA 2006. The empirical study arrived at the following observations:[860]

(1) Company failures cannot be interpreted as signs of governance failures, even though they provoked reforms in both soft and hard laws in the UK, and mainly hard laws in the US.
(2) The government's view that the self-regulated auditing industry has failed. An independent audit regulator is needed. The government has proposed the setting up of the ARGA to replace the FRC. This view is an indictment on auditors for failing to perform their role in the contracts between them and the companies they audited on.
(3) The governance process in view of its interdisciplinary nature intersects various subject areas, including both soft and hard laws, corporate legal theory, as well as business management theories and practices.
(4) The issue posed by directors' remuneration is best explained by the agency theory.
(5) Overall, governance is a nexus of contracts involving an intense interplay between the various stakeholders involved in the invisible amorphous corporate entity. Governance reforms often involved separate regulatory instruments dealing with these separate contractual relationships, whereas an integrated approach is argued to be the more effective system of governance. The latter is exemplified by the Companies (Directors' Remuneration and Directors Remuneration Report) Regulation 2019. It is only occasionally that a single regulatory framework deals with most of the parties in the nexus of contracts and the issues involved. The governance code and the CA 2006 are fair examples of such an overarching framework, but both were relatively ineffective for different reasons. In the case of the governance code, this has to do with the absence of legal force behind the

857. P. Yeoh. 2009. "Causes of the global financial crisis: Learning from competing insights". *International Journal of Disclosure and Governance,* Vol. 7 (2010): 42-69.
858. B. Hannigan. 2011. "Board failure in the Financial Crisis-Tinkering with Codes and the need for wider CG reforms: Part 1". *Company Lawyer,* Vol. 32 (2011): 363-364.
859. P. Yeoh. 2015. "Regulating executive remuneration in Anglo-American economies". *Business Law Review,* Vol. 36 (2015): 169.
860. E. Muih. 2021. "CG reform and corporate failure in the UK". *Company Lawyer,* Vol. 42 (4): 109-119.

voluntary and self-regulatory practice, and in the case of CA 2006, this was more the outcome of the lack of regular enforcement actions.

Carillon

Further case analysis is undertaken for governance failures at Carillon and Thomas Cook to draw out further insights. The directors of Carillon petitioned for the compulsory liquidation of the company on January 15, 2018, rather than through administration, as Carillon had no real assets left to sell, and the contracts it had were either too complex or insufficiently valuable for banks to lend against them. The Special Managers appointed have also stated that there were no prospects of any returns to Carillon shareholders. The Official Receiver fast-tracked the investigation to ascertain whether the conduct of present and previous directors have caused detriment to the company's creditors, including detriment to employees who are owed money, or to the pension schemes.

The July 10, 2017 profit warning from the company of some GBP 845 million marked the beginning of the end of Carillon. It turned out that faulty decisions in the years leading up to this had contributed to the bellying-up of the company.[861] The stated 2017 losses comprised GBP 375 million from three public-private partnership (PPP) projects in the UK, and GBP 470 from existing markets in the Middle East and Canada. Carillon's half-year financial statements announced on September 29, 2017, showed a whopping loss of GBP 1.2 billion that erased accumulated profits amassed over the previous eight years.

In those eight years from 2009 to 2016, the company paid out some GBP 554 million in dividends, or some three-quarters of the cash generated from operations, and in the five-and-half-year period from January 2012 to June 2017, Carillon paid out GBP 333 million more dividends than the cash generated from operations. The aggregate total in loans increased from GBO 242 million to some GBP 1.3 billion from December 2009 to January 2018, or exceeding five times the value at the beginning of the decade. Depending on the metrics used, Carillon's pension deficit has been the 7th or 15th largest among FTSE 350 companies. The Carillon pension scheme had an estimated Pension Protection Fund (PPF) deficit of about GBP 800-GBP 900 million.[862] The Insolvency Service, the FCA, the FRC, and the Pensions Regulator are investigating the collapse of Carillon, aside from three inquiries conducted by the Select Committees of the House of Commons.

Carillon took on inherently risky projects without robust evaluations or due diligence. The risks of these ventures were aggravated by significant cost overruns that

861. F. Mor, et al. 2018. "The collapse of Carillon". *House of Commons (HC) Briefing Paper Number 8206 14/03/18.*
862. Financial Times. 2018. "Letter to Work and Pensions Select Committee". *Financial Times 26/01/18.* http://www.parliament.uk/documents/commons-committees/work-and-pensions/Correspondence/Letter-from-Carillion-(DB)-Pension-Trustee-Limited-to-the-Chair-relating-to-Carillion-pension, accessed November 10, 2020.

wiped out its traditionally low margins. Average margins in the UK construction industry have been falling from 1.7% in 2016-2017 to 1.5% in 2017-2018.[863] Importantly, Carillon had underestimated costs on previous occasions, as exemplified by the Paddington integrated main works that saw actual costs escalating to GBP 98 million, or more than three times the estimated cost of GBP 27.7 million. Considerable delays for the completion of its large projects in the Middle East, together with those UK domestic projects contributed to the huge losses suffered by the company, but the loss-making way of winning contracts persisted, despite the issuing of profit warnings. This has been further aggravated by poor returns from its aggressive M&A strategy. Some 169 directors have been involved in the managing of Carillon's 326 subsidiaries across the world.

The ensuing complexity in management led to the company finding serious difficulties for its senior management to monitor the company's overall risk exposures, with critics arguing that Carillon had grown too big too fast.[864] Critics further argued that Carillon's board, its senior management team, and its auditor individually, and in combination have serious questions to answer about senior-level decision-making leading to the company's collapse. It has been suggested that, while corporate responsibility remained weak, tighter rules, and penalties need to be applied to change the behaviors of those tending to benefit from the upside, but not bearing the costs of the downside of competitive capitalism.[865]

It should also be noted that businesses, such as Carillon, that underpin the economic wealth of the national economy are connected, and strongly codependent with potential contagion risk impacts. Where the government is a major customer, such as for Carillon, it has significant responsibility as a key customer when using public sector funds for public sector projects to monitor the health of such firms and evaluate the risks prior to issuing payment protection insurance (PPI) and other contracts.[866] There have been encouraging signs of progress, two years after the collapse of Carillon, and a year after the government published its *Outsourcing Playbook* containing reforms to the way it outsourced its services. Improvements though in key areas have been patchy, while reforms have yet to be fully implemented.[867]

863. A. Amir & S. Collinson. 2018. "Part A, Carillon's collapse: Cause". *City-REDI Policy Briefing Series March 2018. http://dx.doi.org/10.13140/RG.2.2.23818.16322,* accessed November 10, 2020.
864. Amir & Collinson 2018, *supra* note [863].
865. Amir & Collinson 2018, *supra* note [863].
866. A. Amir & S. Collinson. 2018. "Part B, Carillon's collapse: Consequences". *City-REDI Policy Briefing Series March 2018.* http://dx.doi.org/10.13140/RG.2.2.17107.27687, accessed November 10, 2020.
867. T. Sasse, C. Britchfield & N. Davies. 2020. "Carillon: Two years on". *Institute for Government (IFG) Insight March 2020.* https://www.instituteforgovernment.org.uk/sites/default/files/publications/carillion, accessed November 10, 2020.

Thomas Cook

The study on the reasons behind the market failure of Thomas Cook tells how the 178-year-old company had been trapped by the glories of its past as a leader of package holidays, with worldwide image and financial strengths in establishing relationships with hundreds of small tour operators, hotels and caterers across the world. Yet, all these supply chain alliances have rendered it very linear, allowing travelers no options or versatility. Thomas Cook fell into liquidation in September 2019, when rescue talks to secure GBP 250 million in contingency funds failed, leaving several thousand travelers without a return ticket home. The impact of Brexit, high debts, and the company's inability to adapt to new digital technology to maintain competitiveness have been cited as the main reasons behind the company's demise.[868] Thomas Cook attributed part of the losses arising from Brexit's confusion that led to lower demand for summer holidays across the market.[869] The company's CEO describes the loss of some USD 2.1 billion as being insurmountable. Thomas Cook came under losses, upon merging with MyTravel Group, an entity that had been only profitable once in its six years' operation. When emergency funding for USD 250 million stalled, the company went into bankruptcy.

Also, as travel bookings business moved further and further online, Thomas Cook failed to keep in sync, and depended on telephone and offices sales. The company had relatively lower profit margins relative to the other travel companies. This has been attributed to the company's failure to adopt the new generation type of operations, like more flexible traveling companies. This caused Thomas Cook customers to run multiple searches to view the same kind of options.[870] On the corporate finance front, the company's share prices fluctuated widely throughout the years, prompted by the failure to bring down its debts meaningfully. Its efforts in creating a new Digital Advisory Board in 2013 to assist management in recognizing leading online trends and raising money from shareholders have not been effective. By the end of 2019, the company's share price had plummeted to 3.50 pence because of the high debts, balance sheet deficit of GBP 3.1 billion, and profit warnings not taken seriously by shareholders and management.[871]

It has been argued that it was not boardroom greed, but sheer incompetence and hubris in the boardroom that became the more direct causes.[872] Board members need to explain why they did not focus on fixing its fragile finances when viable financial restructuring options could be formulated to pare down debts, lower interest costs and allow more investments into new company-owned hotels. The board appears to be

868. D. Salman & D. Seiam. 2020. "The lessons learned from Thomas Cook failures. Is it BREXIT?". *Economics & Law*, Vol. II (II): 14-23.
869. Salman & Seiam 2020, *supra* note [868].
870. Salman & Seiam 2020, *supra* note [868].
871. Salman & Seiam 2020, *supra* note [868].
872. The Guardian. 2019. "Thomas Cook was brought down by incompetence, not boardroom greed: Directors of the failed travel company must explain why they didn't make debt reduction priority". *The Guardian 29/09/19.* https://www.theguardian.com/business/2019/sep/29/thomas-cook-failure, accessed November 10, 2020.

conscious of the risky external environment, when stating in its November 2017 annual report that a highly competitive environment had contributed to the collapse of competitors in the previous years. Answers are also needed from the board, as to the manner and choice of use of exceptional items, especially explanations as to why a GBP 1.1 billion goodwill write-down on the purchase of MyTravel appears only in the 2019 interim accounts, when the acquisition itself occurred in 2007.

The above analysis of big US and UK corporations involved with the undertaking of cross-border traditional businesses suggest their strong appetite for growth in overseas market territories in search of higher sales and profitability. US multinationals with longer commercial histories than UK corporations appear to have relatively greater management expertise in handling overseas subsidiaries and therefore more effective mitigations of threats to their corporate reputation. This is rather surprising as it would appear that some of the legacy skills that the East India Companies enjoyed over others in the colonial years of British history might have been somehow lost. Also, the UK CG Code did not appear to help restrain the aggressive risk appetites of top management echelon, as well as board members, with the lack of accountability being the main risk threat. In contrast, the US MNCs appear to be relatively more sensitive to damages to corporate reputation and litigation threats, mainly because of the impact of SOX and some good lessons learned from the 2000 Enron and Enron-type corporate scandals.

9.02 ESG CONTROVERSIES IN FINANCIAL INSTITUTIONS

9.02a US Financial Institutions

Financial shenanigans and high debts brought down nonfinancial listed firms, including some internet-based corporations in the Dotcom bubble, while big banks and financial intermediaries have been brought down almost for the equivalent reasons in the 2007–2009 CFC, except that they generated the greater risks of contagion scale with economy-wide repercussions. Both these categories of large corporate failures have been treated later as being TBTF entities, meaning they need to be bailed out to avoid contagion effects on the entire economy. The banks and financial houses are selected for analysis here because of their massive contagion impact risk, and their massive governance process flaws. WF and GS have been selected for the US representation, while GC and RBS have been selected to represent the UK cohort.

Wells Fargo (WF)

WF has been once credited for its healthy governing structure with significant equity support from Berkshire Hathaway and even singled out as exemplary by Warren

Buffett[873] amidst the 2007-2009 GFC. WF in 2012 was Berkshire's second largest investment valued at USD 13.7 billion, just behind Coca-Cola then valued at USD 15.6 billion, and ahead of IBM then valued at USD 12.6 billion. Berkshire invested initially USD 289 million in the bank in 1990. Since 2005, Berkshire had been upping its stakes in WF. The bank is ranked first in the US banking industry at the time with a total market value of USD 176 billion, even though it had been ranked only fourth largest, by assets. WF has the most extensive branch network in the US, with 6,200 retail branches in 39 states, serving 1 of every 3 US households, and originating 1 in every 4 home mortgages and services home loans than any other US bank.

The bank has been one of relatively few large US banks that has been focusing almost exclusively on its original mission of commercial banking. It had not diversified into the high risks area of investment banking nor expanded aggressively in Europe, as was the case of its main competitors, and consequentially did not suffer losses from such growth strategies. In fact, some 97% of the bank's assets and 98% of its employees are based in the US. Its main business is driven largely by its dominant cross-selling strategy where additional products are sold to its existing customers, and where the average bank customers used six products from the bank, a steep increase from the one or two way back in the 1980s.[874] WF's success is reflected in the rise of its net income to USD 16 billion in 2011, while its net charge-offs have been 1.25% of its total loan versus 1.8% at Bank of America, 2.19% at JP Morgan Chase, and 3.19% at Citigroup.[875] Above all, WF has been enjoying an appealing risk/reward profile, with analysts then projecting it to achieve annual growth in earnings per share exceeding 10% for the subsequent five years, and with shares reasonably valued at ten times earnings.[876]

Warren Buffett spent some three decades in all praising WF. The bank has, however, been plagued by scandals for the last four years, starting with the revelations that it opened millions of fake accounts for customers. Its shares plummeted seriously prompting the departure of long-term serving CEO John Stumpf, only to be succeeded by a successor of one year amidst criticisms that the bank was not addressing lapses fast enough. Buffet then told the *Financial Times*[877] that the bank should avoid taking on someone from Wall Street, like JP Morgan or GS, as this could attract the interest of Congress. The bank eventually hired Charlie Scharf, a JP Morgan pedigree.[878] Scharf's first year at the bank did not help to erase memories that its woes were over. It has remained under Federal Reserve asset cap since 2018. It reported first quarterly loss in

873. D. Krass. 2012. "Why Warren Buffett keeps adding to his Wells Fargo investment". *Business Insider 05/07/12.* https://www.businessinsider.com/why-warren-buffett-keeps-adding-to-his-wells-fargo, accessed November 10, 2020.
874. Krass 2012, *supra* note [873].
875. Krass 2012, *supra* note [873].
876. Krass 2012, *supra* note [873].
877. S. Kimball. 2019. "Warren Buffett says next Wells Fargo CEO shouldn't come from JP Morgan or Goldman Sachs". *CNBC 07/04/19.* https://www.cnbc.com/2019/04/07/warren-buffet-calls-for-wells-fargo-to-look-beyond-wall-street-for-next-ceo.html, accessed October 18, 2020.
878. H. Levitt & K. Chiglinsky. 2020. "Buffett inches toward Wells Fargo exit as Scharf sets course". Bloomberg 16/10/20. https://www.bloomberg.com/news/articles/2020-10-16/buffett-inches-toward-wells, accessed October 18, 2020.

2020 in more than a decade, had its dividend slashed by 80%, while its shares have underperformed every other lender in the KBW Bank Index over the past six months.[879] Berkshire, since October 2020, is appearing to be inching toward exiting WF.[880]

On paper, the bank had an almost ideal board, filled with independent directors, who met regularly. The bank policy also stated that the independent directors should not be in more than three boards other than that of WF.[881] The board demonstrated diversity, with members elected yearly by the shareholders. Board committees covered all areas of operation and risk, and led by experts in many fields. Elain Chao, for example, was once US Secretary of Labor and an MBA from Harvard with in-depth insights into sales and human-resource matters, while Cynthia Milligan was a former bank regulator and lawyer.

Governance practices, election of directors, qualifications and responsibilities have all been laid out in proxy statements and on the bank's official website.[882] Given that the positions of the CEO and Chairman are not being separated in the bank, WF Lead Director Stephen Sanger, also concurrently the head of the Governance and Nominating Committee, has been empowered to call independent directors to meet and act as sounding boards. Executive remuneration has been a mixture of salary and incentives, while shareholders have a say on pay for the executives. The system also allowed anyone to approach the board via email or by post, and these have been also mentioned in proxy statements. Additionally, WF conducted regular internal audits, including the culture audit to identify any integrity matters, while KPMG functions as the external auditor.

It has been puzzling as to how with a textbook board, one of the best bankers at the time as CEO, and elaborate governance structures, the system failed to curb sales integrity issues. WF also had a clear ethics vision. Most of its directors have not only been independent but also experts in their respective fields. The seven board committees and the position of the lead director have been aimed at ensuring full and fair oversight and conduct of fiduciary duties of the board. Despite these strengths, its hitherto highly respected governance process has not been able to help in preventing the scandal that erupted. In hindsight, analysts have attributed the failure to a sales culture that has been ignoring what customers want; the neglect of early warning signs; a decentralized nature of risk oversight, an unquestioning board, CEO's favoritism, territorialism, and so on.[883]

These serious flaws culminated with the bank paying more than USD 1.5 billion in penalties to federal and state authorities and USD 620 million to resolve lawsuits from customers and shareholders.[884] The Consumer Financial Protection Bureau

879. Levitt & Chiglinsky 2020, *supra* note [878].
880. Levitt & Chiglinsky 2020, *supra* note [878].
881. R. Veetikazhi & G. Krishnan. 2019. "Wells Fargo: Fall from great to miserable: A case study on CG failures". *South Asian Journal of Business and Management Cases*, Vol. 8 (1): 88-99.
882. Veetikazhi & Krishnan 2019, *supra* note [881].
883. Veetikazhi & Krishnan 2019, *supra* note [881].
884. G. McFarlane. 2020. "How Wells Fargo became one of America's biggest banks". *Investopedia 22/08/20.* https://www.investopedia.com/articles/markets/093014/how-wells-fargo, accessed November 10, 2020.

(CFPB) and the Office of the Comptroller of the Currency (OCC) fined WF USD 1 billion for misstatements of its auto loans and mortgage consumers. The SEC's June 2018 investigation found the bank supporting active trading by brokerage clients on high-fee debt products that were supposed to be held for maturity. The bank settled with the SEC without admitting or denying guilt by agreeing to repay USD 1.1 million in ill-gotten gains and USD 4 million in penalty. Three months later, it paid a penalty of USD 2 billion for allegedly misrepresenting the quality of residential mortgage loans a decade previously.[885] Given these records, the bank would find it hard then to claim having a highly sound governance system.

WF, before its present challenges, has been highly praised and respected in the industry. It has been known as the big bank least tarnished by scandals and reputational crises;[886] a history of avoiding the rest of the industry's dumbest mistakes;[887] having chairperson John Stumpf named banker of the year in 2013;[888] having head of retail banking division, Carrie Tolstedt, named the most powerful woman in banking;[889] and being named as 7th most respected company in Barron's list.[890] Responding to the cross-selling scandal, an independent investigation report was undertaken by the bank's independent directors assisted by independent counsel Sherman & Sterling LLP. Some hundred interviews were conducted with searches across more than 35 million documents. This report sharply criticized the bank's leadership, sales culture, performance systems, and organizational structure as root causes of this scandal:[891]

(1) The root cause of sales practice failures has been the distortion of the Community Bank's sales culture and performance management system. These, when combined with aggressive sales management tactics, generated pressures on employees to sell unneeded products to customers, and in some instances to open unauthorized accounts. Community banking, along with wealth and investment management, and wholesale banking, make up the bank's three operating divisions. The bank's decentralized corporate structure extended too much power to the Community Bank's senior leadership who were unwilling to change the sales model or even to concede this as the root cause of the problem. This leadership resisted and impeded external scrutiny or oversight, but when compelled to report, minimized the scale and nature of the problem.

(2) Corporate control functions were constrained by the decentralized organizational structure and a culture of substantial deference to the business units. Additionally, a transactional approach to problem-solving obscured their

885. McFarlane 2020, *supra* note [884].
886. M. Aspan. 2013. "Wells Fargo's John Stumpf, the 2013 Banker of the Year". *American Banker* 21/11/13.
887. A. Lashinsky. 2009. "Riders on the Storm". *Fortune 04/05/2004.*
888. Aspan 2013, *supra* note [886].
889. S. Lepro. 2010. "Well's Tolstedt at Top of Power List". *American Banker 27/09/10.*
890. V.J. Racanelli. 2015. "Apple tops Barron's list of respected companies". *Barron's 27/06/15.*
891. Wells Fargo Independent Directors. 2017. "Sales practices investigation report". Wells Fargo Independent *Directors Sales Practices Investigation Report 10/04/17.* https://www08.wellsfargomedia.com/assets/pdf/about/investor-relations, accessed November 10, 2020.

view of the wider context, whereupon, as a consequence, they missed the opportunities to analyze and flag-up the escalating sales practice issues.

(3) Guided by insights into the bank's decade of success with cross-selling and positive customer and employee survey outcomes, the former CEO has been hesitant in investigating or critically challenging sales practices in the Community Bank. He also failed to appreciate the seriousness of the problem and the substantial reputational risk to WF.

(4) Sales practice risk has not been treated as a noteworthy risk, until 2014, but by early 2015 management reported that corrective actions were working, which in effect was not really the case. Though the board has been regularly engaged with this issue, management reports failed to convey the scale of the problem, with the board only learning that some 5,300 employees had been terminated for sales practices breach from the September 2016 settlements with the Los Angeles Attorney General, the OCC and the CFPB.

The board took significant actions subsequent to the above principal findings.[892] The bank replaced and reorganized the leadership of the Community Bank. It eliminated sales goals and reformed incentive compensation. Centralization of control functions was accelerated. The board rebooted with the separation of the role of the Chairperson and the CEO. The bank further strengthened the charters of Board Committees, besides establishing regular reporting to the board by the new Office of Ethics, Oversight and Integrity. The bank also terminated the services of five senior executives of the Community Bank, as well as imposing forfeitures, clawbacks and compensation adjustments on senior leaders totaling more than USD 180 million.

Thus, WF has been seeking to regain trust by relooking hard at all aspects of its business.[893] Specifically, the bank increased its estimates of the number of potentially unauthorized consumer accounts to 3.5 million and issued a further USD 2.8 million in refunds. It announced further that it had identified sales practice breaches in its auto and mortgage lending divisions. The Federal Reserve Board on the basis of widespread consumer abuses at WF initiated in February 2018 the unprecedented step of imposing a strict limit on the bank's asset size forbidding it to grow past the USD 1.95 trillion in assets it had at year end, until the bank proved improvements in corporate controls. Then Chair of the Federal Reserve Board, Janey Yellen and current Treasury Secretary issued the stern warning that the Fed would not tolerate pervasive and persistent misconduct at any bank, that WF's consumers harmed by the bank, expect robust and comprehensive reforms to ensure that such abuses do not recur, and that the enforcement action taken would ensure that WF would not expand until it is able to do so safely and with the safeguards needed to manage all of its risks and protect its customers.[894]

892. McFarlane 2020, *supra* note [884].

893. B. Tayan. 2019. "The Wells Fargo cross-selling scandal". *Stanford University Graduate School of Business Research Paper No. 17-1*. http://www.gsb.stanford.edu/faculty-research/working-papers, accessed November 10, 2020.

894. Federal Reserve. 2018. "Responding to widespread consumer abuses and compliance breakdowns by Wells Fargo, Federal Reserve restricts Wells' growth until firm improves governance

Aside from internal governance reforms at WF and remedial enforcement actions, further insights are needed, not only for the bank but also for the entire industry to help ensure more effective governance practices. Good answers for the following eight highly pertinent questions from the case could be helpful:[895]

(1) Was the bank wrong in using cross-selling as a metric in its incentive systems? Would this work better if structured differently? Is the evaluation of the independent directors' investigation suggesting that employee pressure was a greater contributor to misconduct than financial incentives more correct?
(2) Branch-level personnel were incentivized to increase products per household, whereas the senior-executive bonus system did not incorporate this metric. Did the disconnect contribute to a failure to identify the problem earlier?
(3) By several measures, the bank's vision, values, and culture have been beneficial to its performance. What factors should management consider to ensure that the bank's compensation and performance systems encourage the achievement of corporate objectives without sacrificing culture?
(4) The financial impact of the bank's cross-selling scandal was relatively small, but the reputational damage was massive. How could the bank prepare against problems that do not appear to be material financially, but eventually highly material on the bank's business and reputation?
(5) The investigation report concluded that a strong centralized risk function was most suited for the effective management of risk, but is this assessment correct? What steps could management in a decentralized entity take to minimize gaps in oversight without unnecessary bureaucracy?
(6) The cross-selling scandal case dramatized the challenge of a high-performing executive whose behavior eventually did not align with the bank's values. How much autonomy should high-performing executives be afforded? How could the bank balance autonomy and accountability?
(7) The investigation largely exonerated the bank's board of directors. How much blame should the board deserve? What could have been done differently to prevent the cross-selling risk from snowballing?
(8) WF had a properly functioning governance system, including risk management, audit, legal and human resources, where each of the dedicated units was at least to various degrees aware of sales practice breaches, but yet no one unit recognized the systemic nature of the problem or took the necessary steps to address it. How could an entity evaluate whether its governance system is effective in identifying and managing risk?

Meanwhile, the new measures taken by WF's present leadership suggest that the bank is heading in the right direction, especially benefiting from its costs cutting

and control. Concurrent with Fed action, Wells to replace three directors by April one by year end". *Federal Reserve Press Release 02/02/18*. https://www.federalreserve.gov/newsevents/pressreleases/enforcement, accessed November 10, 2020.

895. Tayan 2019, *supra* note [893].

initiatives, and despite having to spend billions of dollars for litigation and remediation expenses. The bank's second-quarter results showed a profit of USD 6 billion, or USD 1.38 per share, compared to a net loss of USD 3.85 billion or USD 1.01 per share for the corresponding quarter in the previous year. Soft loan demands together with rock-bottom interest rates though lower net interest income by 11%. WF has fewer means to soften declines in revenue from low interest rates as the bank does not have a large capital markets business like its main rivals. The asset cap imposed in 2018 by the Federal Reserve requires the bank to keep its assets below USD 1.95 trillion, until it shows improvements in its governance and risk controls.[896]

Goldman Sachs

Generally venerable global investment bank, GS is not without governance challenges. Unlike other big US mega banks that were disciplined by fines from the government, the bank made conscious initiatives to appear self-reliant, despite having to rely on USD 995 billion of taxpayers' money to help it weather through the 2007-2008 crisis. The bank did not remerge from the crisis relatively unscathed or unchanged, but case analysis did suggest that it had staying power or business resilience, and enjoyed the uncanny ability to adapt to a changing environment, as well as having the capacity to shape it. It became one of the lead firms whose efforts in ensuring its own survival had broader consequences for the survival of other key entities in the financial services, and by extension, the resilience of the sector as a whole.[897]

The theory of adaptive resilience[898] is understood as the ability of complex systems to adapt to various market and environmental shocks while maintaining their core functions. Pointing to various conceptual limits of regional resilience framework, an empirical case study was undertaken to demonstrate the importance of studying sectorial resilience[899] in combination with regional resilience. This involves analyzing the global value chains and the production networks, upon which firms and industrial sectors operate, and come to rely on, more and more. This study argues the importance of power asymmetries, agency and governance to the study of resilience,[900] with emphasis that in economic contexts characterized by high power asymmetries, strong agents such as lead firms might come to shape the threats and opportunities of weak agents through controlling key resources and influencing policy environment. Thus, this said case study on GS would incorporate the bank's interactions with other key stakeholders, including other systemically important financial institutions (SIFIs),

---

896. N.Z. Hussain & M. Scuffham. 2021. "Wells Fargo wary on prospects of asset restriction easing". *Reuters 15 July 2021.* https://www.reuters.com/business/finance/wells-fargo-beats-profit-estimates-reserve-release-boost-2021-07-14/, accessed July 16, 2021.
897. M.A. Urban, et al. 2019. "Lead firms and sectoral resilience: How Goldman Sachs weathered the global financial crisis". *Financial Geography Working Paper #2.*
898. J. Simmie & R. Martin. 2010. "The economic resilience of regions: Towards an evolutionary approach". *Cambridge Journal of Regions, Economy and Society*, Vol. 3 (2010): 27-43.
899. M. Fromhold-Eisebith. 2015. "Sectoral resilience: Conceptualising industry-specific spatial patterns of interactive crisis adjustment". *European Planning Studies*, Vol. 23 (9): 1675-1694.
900. G. Bristow & A. Healey. 2015. "Crisis response, choice and resilience: Insights from complexity thinking". *Cambridge Journal of Regions, Economy and Society*, Vol. 8 (2015): 241-256.

strategic investors, the US Treasury, the Federal Reserve (FED), and the SEC. The study was structured temporally[901] with analysis long three key time periods:

(1) 1999-2006, with focus on positioning GS in the context of developments that led to the accumulation of systemic risk in the financial markets.[902] This is characterized as the first stage of resilience of vulnerability and exposure to shocks.[903]
(2) 2007-2009, with focus on how GS interacted with other actors, including SIFIs, regulators, and strategic investors to not only protect the bank itself but also ensure the survival of other SIFIs, whose failures would have destabilized the financial system to the point of threatening the bank's own survival. This corresponds to the second and third stages of resilience described correspondingly as depth of reaction to shock, and the extent and nature of adjustment to shock.[904]
(3) 2010-2017, with focus on organizational change of the bank in response to the crisis and its heavy-handed approach to resist against regulation. This corresponds to the fourth stage of resilience of recoverability.[905]

Guided by the above framework, and viewing the US financial system as the sectoral and regional context, the case study approach was used to examine the role of GS in shaping the resilience of the US financial sector in the lead up to, during, and out of the 2007-2009 GFC. Foremost, the bank's rise to prominence has been argued to be linked to its strategic move to aggressively securitize and trade the then booming US real estate market. Developing from this, GS contributed significantly to the accumulation of systemic market risk in 2006. This was not properly understood by lawmakers, regulators, and much of the rest of the US securities market participants. The bank showed remarkable foresight in spotting early signs of the imminent collapse of the US real estate market by offloading much of its long exposures to subprime securities in a move that would later ignite controversy on the legality and morality of investment bankers selling securities they themselves deemed worthless.[906]

Though the action by the bank was subsequently proven correct, it underestimated the interconnectedness of the US financial sector. Subsequent to Lehman Brothers' bankruptcy, Goldman's fate, not dissimilar to a number of other SIFIs, had to rely on support from government agencies.[907] It needs bearing in mind that the massive government-sponsored bailouts were mainly motivated by SIFI's interest to preserve the status quo, and therefore probably not the only course of action available. For that

901. R. Martin & P. Sunley. 2015. "On the notion of regional economic resilience: Conceptualization and explanation". *Journal of Economic Geography*, Vol. 15 (2015): 1-42.
902. P. Yeoh. 2010. "Causes of the global financial crisis: Learning from competing insights". *International Journal of Disclosure and Governance*, Vol. 7 (1): 42-69.
903. Martin & Sunley 2015, *supra* note [901].
904. Martin & Sunley 2015, *supra* note [901].
905. Martin & Sunley 2015, *supra* note [901].
906. Urban et al. 2019, *supra* note [897].
907. A.R. Sorkin. 2009. *Too big to fail: Inside the battle to save Wall Street*. London: Allen Lane.

matter, the US Treasury and the FED's response to the GFC were largely borne out of close negotiations with the management of SIFIs, where GS played a pivotal role. The bank worked tirelessly in these negotiations so as to promote its interests in steering regulators and agencies to avoid both failure and reforms. Goldman made good efforts to distance itself from the notion that it was bailed out too, but in reality, the bank has been one of the largest recipients of government aid.[908]

In the immediate years subsequent to the GFC, the bank persisted as one of the leading actors fighting earnestly the reregulation of the US financial sector. Goldman did not come out of the crisis unscathed or unchanged, but case insights demonstrated clearly that the bank's recovery was as much due to its ability to adapt to a changing environment, as well as its ability to shape it. Through a twist that epitomized power dynamics in US capitalism, Goldman not only navigated but also helped to shape the subsequent mainly reactive regulatory response to the 2007-2008 GFC. This is an approach driven by the differences in resources and lobbying capacity that favor those interests bent on resisting further regulation.[909]

Beyond regulatory capture,[910] the bank has indeed demonstrated its capacity to transform its business model to adapt to the changing demands of the market. While already a global and diversified bank for decades, it has arguably become even more global and diversified subsequent to the GFC. Presently, its extensive network of sixty-one offices spans leading financial centers that include New York, London, Frankfurt, Paris, Hong Kong, Tokyo, and Singapore, and with emerging financial centers at Salt Lake City and Bengaluru focusing on mid- and back-office operations, as well as technology. This further shows its contributions to the recent dispersion of employment in the US financial sector.[911] It also shows technology taking on increasing importance in the bank's dealings across all activities, but especially on asset management and retail online banking. In fact, one-quarter of the bank's workforce have backgrounds in science, technology, engineering or mathematics (STEM).[912] Going forward, financial services that previously defied the predictions of widespread automation is finding technology increasingly recasting its geography. Where Goldman is concerned, it has largely readied itself, and nowhere is this seen more clearly than the pending launch of a crypto team within its global currencies and emerging markets trading division.[913]

Critics have voiced ethical concerns over Goldman's questionable operating practices. These included helping Greece in creative accounting for hiding the real debt level via the application of currency swaps; betting against credit default swaps while

908. Urban et al. 2019, *supra* note [897].
909. J.R. Coffee Jr. 2012. "Political economy of Dodd-Frank: Why financial reform tends to be frustrated and systemic risk perpetuated". *Cornell Law Review*, Vol. 97 (2012): 1019-1082.
910. P. Yeoh. "Capture of regulatory agencies: A time for reflection again". *Business Law Review*, Vol. 40 (4):134-145.
911. D. Wojcik & T. Cojoianu. 2018. "Resilience of the US securities industry to the global financial crisis". *Geoforum*, Vol. 91 (2018): 182-194.
912. Urban et al. 2019, *supra* note [897].
913. H. Son & N. Turak. 2021. "Goldman Sachs internal memo unveils new cryptocurrency, trading team". *CNBC 07/05/21*. https://www.cnbc.com/2021/05/07/goldman-sachs-unveils-new-cryptocurrency-trading-team-in-employee-memo.html, accessed May 9, 2021.

selling those instruments to clients through the ABACUS scheme; as well as the instrumental treatment of customers referred to by the banks as Muppets.[914] This evidence and more suggest the bank's divergence from the fundamental ethical values of the prime interest of shareholders and clients. These said, various events suggest conflicts of interest and insufficient disclosures, and thus in the absence of change in the ethical stance of the bank, governance reforms at the bank would unlikely be effective.[915] This and other equivalent cases in the banking sector proved that, despite the vast set of best practice and recommendations, the main failures causing the then credit crunch and leading to the global economic slowdown related mostly to the systemic shortcomings of governance practices, and the unethical and irresponsible behaviors of quoted corporations and financial institutions.[916] The parade of financial institutions heavily mauled by the financial crisis evinced clearly that neither regulations nor governance practice guidelines assured sound ethical management practices, unless these recommendations are put into force under the conditions of high moral and ethical standards of the executives, board directors and other market participants.[917]

A glimpse of Goldman's governance practices shortcomings was seen between 2012 and 2013 when bribes were alleged to have been offered by the bank to and accepted by officials in 1MDB, an Asian-based government-linked conglomerate. The government of the day enabled Goldman to arrange and underwrite bond issues in 2012 and 2013 for very high underwriting fees. Goldman's Chairperson in Southeast Asia, Tim Leissner, subsequently pleaded guilty in a New York court in November 2018 and implicated others.[918] Subsequent bribes were also allegedly offered to 1MDB officials in the management of its accounts to facilitate the embezzlement, and also allegedly to key personalities in the banks in which the embezzled money was deposited, or through which it was transferred, so as to ignore its illicit nature.[919] There have also been the more recent allegations of overworked junior personnel at the bank of some 100-hour workweeks that Goldman responded with Saturdays off against its Saturday rule.[920] These recent revelations suggest the usefulness of relooking into the bank's governance process practices.

While Goldman has been focusing more on investment banking, WF has been very much a community bank. Goldman had to be rescued by government funding leading into the 2007-2008 GFC when it got into big trouble with excessive participation

914. M. Aluchna. 2015. "CG versus ethics: The case of Goldman Sachs". *Journal of Management and Financial Services*, Vol. VIII (21): 107-130.
915. Aluchna 2015, *supra* note [914].
916. T. Clark & J.F. Chanlat. 2009. "Introduction: Anew order? The recurring crisis in Anglo-American governance and the increasing impact on European Economies and Institutions". In T. Clarke, J.F. Chanlat (eds.). *European CG: Readings and perspectives*. London: Routledge.
917. R. Anderson. 2010. *Risk management and CG*. Paris: OECD.
918. D.S. Jones. 2020. "1MDB corruption scandal in Malaysia: A study of failings in control and accountability". *Public Administration and Policy*, Vol. 23 (1): 59-72.
919. Jones 2020, *supra* note [918].
920. J. Kelly. 2021. "After complaints of '100-hour' workweeks, Goldman Sachs is allowing bankers to take off on Saturdays". *Forbes 23/03/21*. https://www.forbes.com/sites/jackkelly/2021/03/23/after-complaints-of-100-hour-workweeks-goldman-sachs-is-allowing-bankers-to-take-off, accessed March 25, 2012.

in complex structured financial products. Subsequent to that, it got into bad publicity when engaging in financing arrangement for a state-owned investment entity of a middle-income economy that had reported linkages to allegations of corrupt practices, while it was also alleged to have advised Greece in hiding its level of debts. It was also embroiled with allegations of overworking practices more recently. Goldman therefore appears to be caught with excessive risk-taking practices in some years, providing controversial advice for masquerading the level of state debts, and allegations of unsatisfactory work practices. The bank appears to be taking steps to move on with more profitable initiatives.

As for WF, the pressure to earn higher compensation levels and incentives gave way to a culture of false financial reporting in a big section of the community bank. Recent changes at the board and top management level for those alleged to be deeply involved in the undertaking of such bad practices are expected to rid and overhaul its hitherto badly structured compensation scheme. Board members and senior management personnel at WF might need to monitor its working practices and rewards systems more closely to avoid the recurrence of the kind of problems it faced earlier. These two cases show different kinds of operational work issues that when not attended to properly could lead to serious governance process issues.

9.02b UK Financial Institutions

Royal Bank of Scotland (RBS)

The key underlying reasons behind the failure of RBS included poor asset quality arising from aggressive growth, large and uncertain losses in trading activities, and the enhanced exposures to trading book assets resulting from the acquisition of ABN AMRO without adequate due diligence.[921] RBS' failure contained common elements as seen too in the failure of HBOS. These included a brash pursuit of rapid expansion, a failure of internal control, and a failure of regulation.[922] RBS has been the archetype for many of the root causes of the crisis of banking standards and culture, and notably incentives to grow that led to the bank becoming unmanageable and the development of an aura of untouchability around those who were leading the bank to the brink of an abyss.[923]

The government intervened with equity injections totaling GBP 45.5 billion, GBP 20 billion in October 2008, and a further GBP 25.5 billion in February 2009.[924] The average share price at which the government invested in RBS was equivalent to 502 pence, but the bank's share prices subsequent to the release of its quarterly results on May 3, 2013, was 295 pence, resulting in an unrealized paper loss of around GBP 18

921. House of Commons (HC) 175-II. 2013. *Changing banking for good First Report of Session 2013-14*. London: The Stationery Office.
922. HC 175-11. 2013, *supra* note [921].
923. HC 175-11. 2013, *supra* note [921].
924. HC 175-11. 2013, *supra* note [921].

billion. Other than equity injection, the government also extended other forms of support to RBS during and following the crisis.[925]

These included the Treasury providing partial guarantee of up to GBP 282 billion of RBS' assets; government guarantee for certain unsecured bank debts under the Credit Guarantee Scheme (CGS); as well as Treasury support for the Special Liquidity Scheme (SLS). The bank borrowed and repaid GBP 75 billion under the CGS and SLS. Owing to the support given by the government, RBS is obliged to accept various restrictions and restructuring measures under EU state aid rules. These included the suspension of discretionary payments on debt instruments, shrinkage of its balance sheet and disposals of designated businesses like Direct Line, and closing some over three hundred retail branches. On all measures of balance sheet strength, the bank achieved good progress. These further included overall total asset reduction (from GBP 1.5 trillion to GBP 900 billion), wholesale funding reliance, liquidity and capital strength.

These developments had the overall impacts of reducing the risks the bank posed to taxpayers, increasing UK retail and business banking at the expense of its UK bits, and continuing upsurge in commercial banking. Despite the commendable work done by the new management team, RBS' well-being risk and its continued ownership by the government at the time created serious problems for the UK economy. This was because the capital position of the bank remained weak, thereby impairing its ability to provide the levels of lending or competition needed for the restoration of vitality to the banking sector and for the UK's full economic recovery. At the time, RBS continued to be weighed down by uncertainty over legacy assets, and by having the government as its primary shareholders. These problems seen in one of UK's biggest banks could weaken confidence and trust in banks and bank lending, and also undermining broader economic confidence and investment activity for firms not encountering immediate credit limitations.[926] Many options were explored to return the bank to its private root at an early schedule.

The turnaround for the bank that almost broke Britain during the 2007-2008 GFC has not been expected to be easy, especially in rebuilding a reputation tarnished from years of greed, arrogance, hubris and light-touch regulation. However, ten years on, the bank has managed not only to recover its financial footing with help from a taxpayer-funded bailout and more prudent risk-taking but also to commence restoring the trust and loyalty of many individual customers who have been harmed by the financial crisis.[927] RBS has reforged the strongest bonds with retail customers of its NatWest subsidiary with further plans to rebrand the entire group as NatWest. The turnaround measures are still work in progress, with further scope for improvements. The bank needs to further improve customers' experiences, continue to simplify and

925. HC 175-11. 2013, *supra* note [921].
926. HC 175-11. 2013, *supra* note [921].
927. H. Spruit & E. Roma. 2020. "Breaking the Bank: RBS remakes retail operation around customer loyalty". *Bain & Company 18/03/20.* https://www.bain.com/insights/breaking-the-bank-rbs-remakes-retail-operations-around-customer-loyalty/, accessed November 10, 2020.

evolve its legacy IT, accelerate growth in difficult economic environment, and deliver more digital innovations to thrive in the increasingly competitive markets.

By many measures, however, the bank has already orchestrated an impressive turnaround by focusing earnestly on customers' priorities, and training its resources on making customers' lives easier.[928] These stood in sharp contrast to its previous culture that prized unbridled sales growth and sprawling M&A that led to a dubious evaluation of risks leading up to the financial crisis. RBS literally went back to basics to stabilize the bank and make it safe again. The narrow focus on commercial growth in a low-risk way reassured regulators and aligned the bank's government commitments to expand lending. Once these were accomplished, the new CEO appointed in 2013 led the development of a strategy to withdraw from twenty countries, radically scaling back the investment bank, to focus on the UK. The reorientation process, led by the CEO of the Personal Banking division, championed a wider brief, where the bank would strive to help meet customers' goals at all the varied phases of life.

This transformation has been backed with significant resources to understand and address customers' needs, so that RBS could successfully meet customers' expectations for a convenient, responsive, digitally enabled experience.[929] The bank's retail group thus came out with a new mission statement, "Effortless every day, brilliant when it matters." This was further backed up by a coherent strategy and an operational plan that have been sustained over many years. This included the bold elimination of "bad profits" generated by hidden fee, fee income from credit card teaser offers, and different prices or rates in different channels. These demonstrated the bank's seriousness about customer service. To reinforce this, incentives for frontline employees, such as the standard bonus at the branch, or regional level for meeting monthly sales quotas were removed. Also eliminated was variable compensation completely for customer-facing employees, while Net Promoter Score feedback for individual performance evaluation that was not linked to compensation was introduced. This transforms the cheering for sales performance to doing heroic things for the bank's customers, and ergo shifting the perspective from product to customer journey.

The transformation entailed a persistent painstaking process of flagging and eliminating small annoyances for customers and creating a series of small things that assist customers. All these were undertaken without tripping up with regulators over issues, like how to accommodate customers in vulnerable situations.[930] Thus, the new perspective has relevance not only for RBS but also for any financial institutions facing new competition from major technology entities and smaller Fintechs offering attractive digital experiences and different business models. This has been no small change, as most banks still organize around distributing products, with even some purporting to organize around customer journeys via a marketing overlay. Thus, at the newly transformed RBS, product experts became part of teams assigned to particular customer journeys, while distribution experts joined service teams that helped customers

928. Spruit & Roma 2020, *supra* note [927].
929. Spruit & Roma 2020, *supra* note [927].
930. Spruit & Roma 2020, *supra* note [927].

use self-service channels or provide staff assistance when customers desire it. This thereby departs from the old mindset of branch staff "owning" their customers.

Tellers and other frontline personnel have also been trained in new tools, such as recorded customer conversations, and script prompts based on the analysis of past successes support the new behaviors. The bank benefited too from the rerouting of resource allocation to customers' journeys. This is because the changes hinged on self-funding by removing bad costs, simplified overly complex processes, and relied more on digital self-services and automation of back-end processes. The bank consequentially witnessed steady improvements in cost-income ratios that improved from 76% in 2015 to 65% in 2019.[931]

Aside from changing incentives and working approaches, the bank revised how it would hold senior executives accountable.[932] Where hitherto accountability has been divided along narrow products and functions, one executive for mortgages, another for distribution, and so on; RBS now defines accountability for an end-to-end customer journey. The adoption of the end-to-end perspective allows the journey team to generate more value for the customer and the bank, thereby breaking silos at scale. This business model incorporates the customer perspective and also integrates technology staff with business personnel, as exemplified by 1,600 technology and business personnel all working on teams dedicated to particular customer journeys. Another instance is seen in the mortgage business, where mortgages are a pivotal part of a retail bank's economics, and a way for deepening relationships with customers.

New tech-savvy competitors have been emerging with relatively convenient mortgage offers. RBS responds with the approach of building business around helping people through all stages of home buying and ownership, rather than its previous marketing approach of focusing on price, promotions and product features.[933] The new approach involves different departments working in concert, not in different silos, but through the setting up of small cross-functional teams that included people from various departments in the business and IT so as to revamp the entire home ownership journey. Human-focused design, informed by regular customer feedback, guides the mortgage application process, whereby a customer could complete the application on smart mobile devices, instead of in person, and with the bank giving decisions within days, rather than weeks as hitherto. The bank's subsidiary launched UK's first paperless mortgage application in 2017, but now some 93% of all its applications are paperless, with average application-to-offer time shrinking from twenty-three to eleven days.[934]

To avoid ceding ground to digital native insurgents, Nat West also responds with an offering that enables customers to tap an ecosystem of partners for online assistance ranging from shopping for a new property, tracking and borrowing against equity planning schemes, to funding renovations.[935] Backed by teams that incorporate skills

931. Spruit & Roma 2020, *supra* note [927].
932. Spruit & Roma 2020, *supra* note [927].
933. Spruit & Roma 2020, *supra* note [927].
934. Spruit & Roma 2020, *supra* note [927].
935. Spruit & Roma 2020, *supra* note [927].

relating to customer insights and software development and third-party partnering, RBS has been able to launch its first version of this offering in four months, in sharp contrast to previous times that would have needed three times more time.

The new CEO joining RBS in late 2019 reaffirms the bank's commitment to putting customers first. The bank's balance sheet is now strong, with a core equity tier one ratio of 16.2%.[936] The bank also returns to profitability in 2017, having racked up losses of up to GBP 60 billion since 2008. RBS has started to deliver dividends in 2018, and also returning GBP 2.7 billion to shareholders in 2019. New accounts opened exceed accounts closed, while new mortgage lending steadily expanded, rising some 8% in 2019. Digital innovations, like allowing customers to open an account by providing selfies and photos of their passport via smartphone, or the launching of biometric credit cards has also gained customer tractions that in turn motivated customers too. The bank's employee engagement score has risen from 78% in early 2015 to 87% by 2019, versus a global average of 82, while the retail bank with the largest number of personnel has been powering the trend with a score of 91% in 2019.[937] The safeguarding of customer goodwill earned thus far would depend on making continued progress in making end-to-end journeys simpler and more digital, delivering more value to customers, moving faster than competitors, and achieving all these without major errors.

Greensill Capital (GC)

Greensill, founded by Australian, Alex Greensill, about a decade ago focuses on supply chain financing and related services. GC in its initial years has been driven by three main businesses. These consist of supply chain financing/reverse factoring, accounts receivables financing/factoring, and future accounts receivables finance.[938] For conventional factoring, an enterprise would sell the invoices it issued to clients to a third party who would then collect the money owed from the clients, but in reverse factoring, the third party in this case, GC would instead settle debts owed by an enterprise to its suppliers at a slight discount, but more quickly than the original enterprise would have, with the third party later receiving payments from the enterprise.[939] Future accounts receivables finance consists in the lending of money to an enterprise, before a sale has occurred, based on the expectation of future sales and

936. Spruit & Roma 2020, *supra* note [927].
937. Spruit & Roma 2020, *supra* note [927].
938. R. Smith. 2021. "Greensill and supply chain finance: How a contentious funding tool works". *Financial Times 02/03/21*. https://www.ft.com/content/1bbbe94c-9c3d-43d1-bcdd-8add6557c5a7, accessed April 18, 2021.
939. P. Kouvelis & F. Xu. 2021. "A supply chain theory of factoring and reverses factoring". Management Science Forthcoming; J. Liebl, E. Hartmann & E. Feisel. 2016. "Reverse factoring in the supply chain: Objectives, antecedents and implementation barriers". *International Journal of Physical Distribution & Logistics Management, Vol. 40 (4)*. https://doi.org/10.1108/IJPDLM-08-2014-0171, accessed April 18, 2021.

future payments. However, as future accounts receivables finance is based on prospective, and ergo uncertain payments, these are viewed to be risky activities.[940]

While banks have traditionally been providing supply chain financing, regulation and capital restrictions targeting them have rendered such loans less profitable. Such a regulatory trend had led to the emergence of smaller firms, like Stenn International and GC, as they did not have to face equivalent level of scrutiny.[941] Suppliers support this model as they get their debts settled more quickly, while others opposed it as it would enable enterprises to conceal debt levels, besides motivating strategic late payments by the stronger parties in a business relation.

GC relied on loans provided by specialized supply chain investment funds managed by Credit Suisse to finance its activities, with GC regularly issuing notes that were acquired by the investment funds, thereby providing GC with cash support. Repayment of loans was secured by GC's claims to the repayment of the funds paid to its clients' suppliers. However, the Credit Suisse investment funds were alleged to have acquired notes linked to GC's future receivables finance activity, and ergo secured by riskier future and uncertain sales.

The related services included the offering of bonds based on debts GC had acquired, traditional banking services via a German subsidiary, and managing funds in partnership with Credit Suisse and others. The media became interested, when UK's Lord Myners, a former Treasury Minister, asked the UK government whether they would be investigating, or intend to investigate the management of investment valuations and relationships between managers and businesses invested in the GAM Greensill Supply Chain Finance Fund. The said Fund is managed by Zurich-based GAM Goldings, with assistance from London-based GC that has been investing in short-term debts linked to companies' expected payments from customers or payments due to suppliers.[942] GAM's share price has halved in 2018 subsequent to the suspension of its star fund manager Tim Haywood, for what is said to be diligence failure, that Haywood though had denied.[943] Haywood's suspension followed complaints from a whistleblower earlier that the purchase of GBP 550 million of bonds issued by Sanjeev Gupta's GFG Alliance are backed by diesel power generators that had largely remained idle in recent years.[944]

Despite these setbacks, GC has still been able to draw investment of USD 0.8 billion from Softbank in early 2019 to enable it to expand its five hundred strong

940. J. Basquill. 2021. "Non-existent customers: How Greensill's future receivables gamble backfired". Global Trade *Review (GTR) 31/03/21.* https://www.gtreview.com/news/global/non-existent-customers-how-greensills, accessed February 2, 2021.
941. L. De Paoli. 2021. "Greensill collapse exposes gap at heart of its technology claims". Bloomberg 20/03/21. https://www.bloomberg.com/news/articles/2021-03-20/greensill-s-collapse-shows, accessed March 22, 2021; C. Bryant. 2019. "Softbank invests in an opaques $100 billion industry". *Bloomberg 15/05/19.* https://www.bloomberg.com/opinion/articles/2019-05-15/a-100-billion-finance, accessed March 22, 2021.
942. T. Bergin & J. Miller. 2019. "Britain's Lord Myners urges UK to investigate GAM-Greensill fund". 2019. *Reuters 19/06/19.* https://www.reuters.com/article/uk-gam-holdg-investigation-idUKKCN1TK1H0, accessed November 10, 2020.
943. Bergin & Miller 2019, *supra* note [942].
944. Bergin & Miller 2019, *supra* not [942].

personnel in that year to well over thousand in sixteen offices across various parts of the world by early 2021. The equity backup from Softbank has enabled GC to delay its earlier planned IPO. Instead, it went on to pursue other investors for USD 600 million, besides making plans for its IPO in 2023, and disposing off its fleet of expensive corporate planes.[945] A striking development occurred in late 2020, when members of the Big Four and top second echelon BDO all declined to take over from its existing lesser-known external auditor.[946] This could have triggered concerns of market participants given that the CEO in particular had paraded himself and the firm as a classy financial services firm well on the way to the big league.

GC had enjoyed an unsustainable artificially created glorified corporate reputation with plans to float at a USD 7 billion (GBP 5 billion) valuation. That did not happen, and instead the financial services firm became engulfed in various serious controversies, before filing for insolvency protection in March 2021. These included dragging a former UK Prime Minister into media spotlight as it crumbled under a weight of heavy debts, and getting several other financial services firms significantly hurt financially.[947] The FCA has informed a UK Parliamentary Select Committee that it would be formally investigating the circumstances leading to the GC's collapse.[948]

The financial debacles that attracted media attention included the following:

(1) GC's risky exposures to GFG Alliance
Both GC and its German subsidiary Greensill Bank had exposures to GFG Alliance to a tune of USD 5 billion, and in particular GFG relied especially on GC's future accounts receivables finance, such that when GFG defaulted, this led to GC's ultimate insolvency.[949] Tycoon Sanjeev Gupta's commodities empire is now being investigated by UK's Serious Fraud Office (SFO) in a probe that encompasses the conglomerate's links to the collapsed GC. The SFO in a statement said it is investigating suspected fraud, fraudulent trading, and money laundering pertaining to the financing and conduct of the business of enterprises within the Gupta Family Group (GFG) Alliance, including its financing arrangements with GC UK Ltd.[950]

945. J. Steinberg & D. Mavin. 2020. "Softbank-backed startup had a fleet of corporate planes. Not for much longer". *Wall Street Journal*. 02/11/20. https://www.wsj.com/articles/softbank-backed-greensill-ditches, November 10, 2020
946. T. Kinder, R. Smith & A. Massoudi. 2020. "Greensill Capital rebuffed in search for new auditor". *The Financial Times 29/10/20*. https://www.ft.com/content/4ad4ae2b-1ba0-4732-9119-576532b297b4, accessed November 10, 2020.
947. R. Neate. 2021. "FCA investigates Greensill as David Cameron's lobbying texts are made public: Regulator announces move as 56 of ex-PM's messages to Rishi Sunak, Michael Gove and others released". *The Guardian 11/05/21*. https://www.theguardian.com/business/2021/may/11/fca-greensill-david, accessed May 12, 2021.
948. M. Rosca. 2021. "FCA outlines Greensill investigation ahead of public hearings: The FCA is working with German, Swiss and Australian regulators on investigating the Greensill scandal". *Politico 11/05/2*. https://www.politico.eu/article/fca-outlines-greensill-investigations-ahead, accessed May 12, 2021.
949. H. Jones & E. Onstad. 2021. "UK Targets Gupta's GFG Alliance in fraud probe linked to Greensill". *Reuters 14/05/21*. https://www.reuters.com/business/finance/uk-fraud-watchdog-investigating-gfg, accessed May 15, 2021.
950. Jones & Onstad 2021, *supra* note [949].

(2) GC's funding of enterprises linked to Softbank
While Softbank has invested more than USD 0.5 billion into Credit Suisse funds that in turn financed GC's activities, GC in turn provided supply chain financing to various Softbank-backed enterprises to as much as 15% of its assets.[951] GC employed Credit Suisse Group AG's supply chain funds to make a USD 350 million loan to one of its biggest outside backers, private equity firm General Atlantic, s second example of GC lending money to one of its part owners that also benefited from Greensill loans. Softbank itself invested close to USD 1.5 billion in the Credit Suisse funds. GC was plunged into crisis when Credit Suisse froze USD 10 billion in investment funds that GC relied upon to do supply chain finance deals. Credit Suisse followed through with an announcement that it would liquidate the funds.[952]

(3) BaFin investigation
German regulator BaFin investigated Greensill Bank's suspected balance sheet manipulation in 2020. This eventually led to it filing a criminal complaint against Greensill Bank in March 2021 that included the banning of various activities at the bank.[953] BaFin received the first set of warnings in the second quarter of 2020 from a GC whistleblower that some GC assets were backed by fake invoices. The German regulator received another warning in the third quarter of 2020 followed by three more submissions that taken together articulated concerns about the financial situation in the GC Group, as well as various allegations of fraud. Particular concerns were raised about loans GC extended to the GFG Alliance. These refer to metal enterprises owned by a UK steel magnate.[954] The magnate's commodities empire is now being investigated by UK's SFO in a probe that encompasses the conglomerate's links to the collapsed GC. The SFO in a statement said it was investigating suspected fraud, fraudulent trading and money laundering pertaining to financing and conduct of the business of enterprises within the Gupta Family Group Alliance (GFG), including its financing arrangements with GC UK Ltd.

(4) Alleged lobbying activities of ex-UK prime minister for emergency-backed COVID-19 loans at the Treasury.[955]

951. J. Steinberg & D. Mavin. 2021. "Greensill used Credit Suisse investment funds to lend to its own backers: Financial startup made $350 million loan in 2019 to General Atlantic, its second-largest outside investor after Softbank's Vision Fund". *The Wall Street Journal 05/03/21*. https://www.wsj.com/articles/greensill-used-credit-suisse-investment-funds-to-lend-to-its-own-backers, accessed March 7, 2021.
952. Steinberg & Mavin 2021, *supra* note [951].
953. D. Mavin & J. Steinberg. 2021. "Greensill whistleblower tips warned German regulator of fraud last year: An internal German government regulator shows the authorities were scrutinizing Greensill for more than a year before it unraveled". *The Wall Street Journal 31/03/21*. https://www.wsj.com/articles/greensill-whistleblower-tips-warned-german-regulator-of-fraud-last-yea, accessed April 5, 2021.
954. Mavin & Steinberg 2021, *supra* note [953].
955. R. Neate. 2021. "Greensill: The scale of David Cameron's lobbying texts revealed". *The Guardian 11/05/21*. https://www.theguardian.com/2021/may/11/greensill-the-scale-of-david-camerons, accessed May 12, 2021.

Even though the lobbying efforts for access to UK's covid corporate financing facility (CCFF) have been unsuccessful, these eventually led to the current prime minister ordering an inquiry into the collapse of GC, as well as the lobbying activities of the ex-prime minister involved.[956]

(5) Notable lawsuits

A US coal-mining company, Bluestone Resources Inc (BRI), owned by West Virginia governor, Jim Justice, on March 15, 2021, filed a suit against GC for fraud. BRI alleged that GC departed from standard supply chain finance to engage in more speculative practice, by offering loans not only based on debts that other enterprises had already incurred but also based on transactions that GC predicted would occur in the future.[957] Jim Justice, the owner of Bluestone Resources, had borrowed USD 850 million from GC between 2018 and 2021, and is now suing GC in the federal court in New York alleging that GC perpetrated a continuous and profitable fraud on the company under the deception of establishing a long-term financing arrangement with Bluestone.

Typically, Greensill made short-term loans to enterprises to help them manage their cash flows. The Bluestone loan was atypical, as it was supposed to run for several years with short-term loans rolling over continuously. To get this loan, Bluestone paid USD 108 million directly back to GC in the form of fees, and with GC also receiving warrants to purchase a stake in Bluestone worth another USD 100 million.[958] This was an example of a client suing GC for its business practices. A UK-based law firm on the other hand would be spearheading efforts to recover losses from investments linked to the collapsed GC. The firm has been building a group of investors across Europe and Asia with investments in Credit Suisse's USD 10 billion Supply Chain Finance Funds that were backed by GC's existing and future trade receivables.[959]

Consequences following GC's bankruptcy filing that involved damages for those linked with exposures to GC and GFG continued to unravel. The latest of which included the collapse of Italian bank, Aigis Banca (AB), a specialist lender to small and medium-sized businesses. The Bank of Italy ordered the liquidation of AB with its assets transferred to its larger peer competitor, Banca Ifis, that purchased AB's assets and liabilities for the symbolic price of EUR 1.[960] AB's problems appear to stem from

956. J. Elgot. 2021. "Greensill scandal: Government orders inquiry into Cameron lobbying: Independent investigation into former PM's lobbying for now-collapsed firm". *The Guardian 12/04/21.* https://www.theguardian.com/politics/2021/apr/12/greensill-scandal-gordon-brown, accessed April 15, 2021.

957. D. Mavin & J. Steinberg. 2021. "Bluestone Resources sues Greensill Capital for fraud: Suit by coal-mining company owned by West Virginia governor is tied to $850 million loan". *The Wall Street Journal 16/03/21.* https://www.wsj.com/articles/bluestone-resources-sues-greensill-capital-for-fraud, accessed May 25, 2021.

958. Mavin & Steinberg 2021, *supra* note [957].

959. R. Walker. 2021. "Boies Schiller to lead investor fight against Credit Suisse for Greensill losses". *Law.com 24/05/21.* https://www.law.com/international-edition/2021/05/24/boies-schiller-to-lead, accessed May 25, 2021.

960. R. Smith & K. Wiggins. 2021. "Italian bank collapses on exposure to Greensill and GFG". *Financial Times 24/05/21.* https://www.ft.com/content/c02a6e97-5505-4d4a-933f-a0e934ca6eda, accessed May 25, 2021.

investment products linked to invoices it had acquired from GC. These are said to have included receivables-backed notes linked to GFG Alliance's Liberty Commodities business. Before collapsing in March 2021, GC had lent money to enterprises, including the GFG Alliance in exchange for cash. The loans were subsequently repackaged into notes and sold to banks and other investors. GFG had drawn heavily on financing from GC, and the collapse of GC has left the sprawling metal conglomerate teetering on the brink. With the pending GFG defaulting on its debt to GC, purchasers of the loans that included Credit Suisse's asset management arm are expected to face huge losses.[961]

The 20 July Treasury Committee Inquiry Report concluded that the failure at GC does not appear to have led to a threat to financial stability, and therefore does not warrant a need to bring supply chain finance within the regulatory perimeter for financial services. Ongoing work on how supply chain finance is being shown in accounts is being awaited, as this has encouraged the use of supply chain by some companies to obscure their level of indebtedness. The Treasury and the FCA have been asked to give serious consideration to revising the definition of securitization within the Securitization Regulation, given that it appears to have been too narrow.

UK financial institutions have not been entirely spared from the ravages of the 2007-2008 GFC. RBS got hit badly, but a lot of it had to do with poor execution of the bank's overly aggressive approach, as exemplified by poor due diligence practices when making acquisitions, especially for those crossing borders, and their subsequent management. The excessive focus for growth was not matched by corresponding appropriate management support practices leading to dismal failures. Board oversight of the bank's growth direction and internal controls were also not effective. The reorientation of the bank's mission and the enhanced attention given to customer priority initiatives are now providing the bank with a more sustainable growth path. Pressing forward with this new but more feasible growth strategy is expected to turn around the bank's fate more quickly in the immediate years ahead. However, board oversight, more than ever, needs to pay closer attention to the impact on operational fortunes when embarking on new initiatives, including the impacts on internal control and risk management procedures. As for GC, its collapse and eventual bankruptcy appeared inevitable, given the level and complexity of risks perpetuated by its ultra-risky business model that did not appear to be supported by a sound internal control system.

9.03 ESG CONTROVERSIES IN DIGITALIZED BUSINESS CORPORATIONS (DBCs)

The more common and more renown species of DBCs, namely multisided or double-side platforms, have been selected for analysis here. Four such cases would be examined, two each from the US and the UK. The two from the US to be studied are Robinhood and Uber, while Deliveroo and FC from the UK would also be analyzed. These digital platforms powered by FIR technologies like blockchain, AI, IoT, and so

961. Smith & Wiggins 2021, *supra* note [960].

on, have of late been receiving a lot of complaints from users and consumers, as well as lawmakers and regulators for ESG factors reasons. Amazon, Facebook, Apple, and Google besides being criticized for business domination tactics and private data breaches of various kinds have also been criticized too for not putting enough attention on employee and management diversity and inequality issues, as well not giving enough attention to the adverse impacts they exert on millennials, while benefiting a lot from their phenomenal market growth prospects, as exemplified in the case of Robinhood and Facebook.

9.03a US DBCs

Robinhood

This Menlo Park California-based financial services enterprise was founded in 2013 by Co-CEOs Vladimir Tenev, the son of a Bulgarian immigrant working at the World bank, and Baiju Bhatt, also the son of an immigrant physics academic from India. Both were Stanford University classmates with previous experiences in building high-frequency trading platforms for New York financial institutions.[962] The idea behind Robinhood is to provide everyone with access to the financial markets, and not just the privilege affluents, and hence an app democratizing finance to bridge the wealth or investing gap between the financially savvy affluents and relatively newcomers exemplified in the Robinhood clientele base. Bridging such kinds of inequality gaps has been highlighted earlier in Thomas Piketty's much-acclaimed *Capital in the Twenty-First Century*.[963] New tech products like iPhone and bitcoin and new tech entities like Airbnb have been making the scene in response to the 2007-2008 GFC, with stocks transactions increasingly becoming more automated. Tenev and Bhatt sought to make the process even faster. They soon succeeded in leading the creation of a software for high-speed trading that has been eventually sold to hedge funds and investment banks. Initially, Tenev and Bhatt formed Robinhood as a financial news platform, drawing inspiration from Gordon Gekko, the imagined successful trader from the *Wall Street* movie, where Gekko is supposed to have said that in the financial world, the most important commodity is information.

To enable trading on Robinhood for free, the duo designed the practice known as "payment for order flow (PFOF)." This involves the taking of customer orders to buy or sell stocks and routing them to high-frequency trading firms (or market makers) that

962. J. Kauflin & A. Gara. 2020. "The inside story of Robinhood's billionaire founders, option kind cowboys and the Wall Street sharks that feed on them". *Forbes 19/08/20.* https://www.forbes.com/sites/jeffkauflin/2020/08/19/the-inside-story-of-robinhoods, accessed November 10, 2020.
963. S. Kolhatkar. 2021. "Robinhood's big gamble: In eliminating barriers to investing in the stock markets, is the app democratizing finance or encouraging risky behavior?". *The New Yorker 10/05/21.* https://www.newyorker.com/magazine/2021/05/17/robinhoods-big-gamble, accessed May 26, 2021.

partake in stocks transactions to facilitate customer orders.[964] These firms accommodated the orders by buying or selling the shares, as the users have requested, while simultaneously drawing on complex computer algorithms to skim a little of the price the customers get, and keeping it as profits for themselves. Predictable, unsophisticated trade orders usually offered the greatest opportunities for the high-frequency trading entities to gain profits. These entities in exchange for access to the orders paid rebates to the brokerage companies that routed the orders to them. The skimming and rebates are largely unbeknown to the customers giving the orders. PFOF is common among brokers. It is controversial, as it appears to generate an incentive for them to send their customers' orders to whichever market makers are willing to pay them the most. Brokers though are required by the SEC to disclose to their customers that they are doing PFOF, besides also ensuring that their customers would be getting the best prices for their trades.

While PFOF advocates like Robinhood have argued that PFOF would result in customers getting better prices and faster executions, other market experts have counterargued that research findings have shown that small investors would be better served without PFOF. This is the reason that countries like the UK, Canada and Australia have restricted the practice.[965] Various members of the investing community felt PFOF to be an ethical issue and that it did not align with Robinhood's mission, while others deemed this to be a public relations issue, as almost all brokers indulged in the practice, though the way this was communicated to customers could be questioned. Yet, others hold that, because of the hesitancies of brokers in giving customers the flexibility they seek, this has given the space for Robinhood to exploit, as a sort of the "Amazon" of financial services.

Robinhood secured its regulatory license in October 2013, besides getting seed funding from Index Ventures, Horowitz, Lindzon, and others. This occurred at the time when Michael Lewis' "Flash Boys" became a bestseller narrating how high-frequency trading firm as insiders used their superior knowledge to rig the market and exploit regular investors. Rather than mentioning on its website that revenue from PFOF is negligible, Robinhood opted not to provide this information. This early glimpse of the company's compliance procedure was defended later, as part of the lessons from a growing enterprise.[966]

The two cofounders found that while executing a trade that cost brokerages fractions of a penny involved fees of USD 5-USD 10 per trade, apart from requiring account minimums of USD 500 to USD 5,000 from their customers. To provide less costly access for the millennials and other disadvantaged groups, Robinhood launched its LA Hacks in March 2015.[967] Being the first company to introduce premier user experience involving the design of a mobile application to finance that dramatically lowered investing cost, provided Robinhood with the first mover advantage. The app's

964. Kolhatkar 2021, *supra* note [963].
965. Kolhatkar 2021, *supra* note [963].
966. Kolhatkar 2021, *supra* note [963].
967. H. Touryalai. 2014. "Forget $10 trades, meet Robinhood: New brokerage targets millennials with little cash". *Forbes 26/02/14*. https://www.forbes.com/sites/halahtouryalai/2014/02/26/forget, accessed November 10, 2020.

influence has been profound. It managed to encourage an entire population who hitherto were not habitually buying stocks to buy stocks. Robinhood's 13 million users comprise unsurprisingly 80% millennials with an average age of 26, where 50% of the users used the app daily and 90% weekly.[968]

Robinhood detractors have contended that Robinhood along with other popular mobile-phone applications are hardly novel, as smart engineers had simply repurposed many of the design features of slot machines. This is mirrored in Robinhood's pursuit of a frictionless user experience, including the ability to trade partial shares that appear to fit into the trend of nano monetization. This included the notion of video slot machines running on pennies, and online poker Web sites offering players the option of betting a dollar or less on multiple tables simultaneously.[969] The idea behind this is to motivate users to transact by lowering the barriers resistant people might have in making investment decisions, such as without thinking too much or dismally of the monetary consequences. Robinhood though denied this suggestion insisting that this was elitist thinking to deprive the disadvantaged of benefiting from the financialization.

The company makes money from Robinhood Gold, a monthly paid subscription; interchange fee from purchases made with Cash Management Debit card, and fee from program banks; rebates from market makers and trading venues; income generated from cash; and stock loan income from counterparties.[970] In effect, the vast portion of the company's revenue flows from trading volume, where the more users trade, the more Robinhood would make. As such, it has been argued that the interests of Robinhood's users frequently conflict with those of the company. This is because the average individual accumulated wealth through long-term investing, instead of rapidly trading in and out of stocks. Critics further claimed that Robinhood is more about financial entertainment than investment management or wealth building. It promotes activities that appear incredibly exciting and fun, but in reality, frenzied day trading, or sort of legal casino wrapped in smart mobile devices.

Unlike traditional brokerage firms, Robinhood's outsourced customer service has not been entirely satisfactory. Still, Robinhood's PFOF's for options trading has become widely popular with users, even though the risks could rack up enormous losses. With retail trading made easier by the Robinhood app, addiction issues have been common. The company eventually expanded into cryptocurrency in January 2018 in five US states where the company received regulatory permission for such transactions. With growing users' trades, Robinhood upgraded this business division into a subsidiary known as Robinhood Securities. This is headed by a former chief-of-staff of Amazon's CFO. The Financial Industry Regulatory Authority (FINRA)-regulated broker-dealer is registered with the SEC, and is also a member of the Securities Investor Protection Corporation.

968. J. Bevan. 2021. "Robinhood revenue and usage statistics (2021)". *Mobile Marketing Reads 24/02/21*. https://www.mobilemarketingreads.com/robinhood-revenue-and-usage, accessed February 26, 2021.
969. Kolhatkar 2021, *supra* note [963].
970. Bevan 2021, *supra* note [968].

Robinhood has some USD 20 billion AUM, employs some 1,281 personnel, and is buoyed by 13 million users. The enterprise raised USD 110 million in April 2017, and USD 363 million Series D in May 2018. In all, Robinhood raised an aggregate of USD 539 million in venture capital funding against a valuation of USD 5.6 billion in 2018. The enterprise expanded to the UK in 2019, as media reports talked of some USD 200 million further funding against a valuation of USD 7-USD 10 billion range. In May 2020, Robinhood raised USD 280 million in venture funding at a pre-money valuation of USD 8.3 billion led by Sequoia Capital, and a further USD 200 million Series G funding round from D1 Capital Partners. Eventually, Robinhood's valuation reached USD 11.2 billion, subsequent to a USD 200 million funding round.[971]

Robinhood is initially involved in commission-free trades of stocks and ETFs. It launched instant deposits in 2016 crediting users instantly for deposits of up to USD 1,000, and six months later Robinhood Gold offering up to USD 50,000 in instant deposits, as well as margin trading and more market analytics.[972] The company temporarily turned off instant buying power for crypto due to extraordinary market conditions on January 29, 2021, apparently following the 800% surge in digital Dogecoin.[973] It executed over USD 30 billion in trades in 2017, and in August 2017, offered free stocks in exchange for referring new users. Users could trade equities and penny stocks listed with NASDAQ and NYSE with no commissions or hidden fees, including trade option contracts without commissions.[974] It would not, however, support OTC securities like those traded on OTC markets, but typically supports trading stocks and ETFs listed on the NYSE and Nasdaq, American depository receipts, and some 250 highly searched international stocks. E-Trade, TD Ameritrade and Charles Schwab and several other major brokerages announced in quick successions the elimination of trading fees in response to competition posed by Robinhood.[975]

Against a waitlist of more than 1,250,000 for commission-free cryptocurrency trading, Robinhood began offering trading of Bitcoin and Ethereum in California, Massachusetts, Missouri and Montana in February 2018, and in May 2018, it expanded its trading platform to Wisconsin and New Mexico.[976] Available cryptocurrencies for trading at Robinhood include Bitcoin, Bitcoin Cash, Bitcoin SV, Dogecoin, Ethereum Classic, and Litecoin. Against talk of getting a banking license from the OCC,

971. R. Henderson & M. Kruppa. 2020. "Retail trading app Robinhood's value tops $11bn on new fundraising: US platform benefits from a surge in new customers during pandemic lockdown". *Financial Times 17/08/20*. https://www.ft.com/content/b208cbbe-579c-4cbf-9358-01ae02b4381b, accessed November 10, 2020.
972. Robinhood. 2020. "Bigger instant deposits". https://robinhood.com/us/en/support/, accessed November 10, 2020.
973. J. Derrick. 2021. "Robinhood shuts off instant deposits feature for cryptocurrency trading". *Yahoo Finance 29/01/21*. https://finance.yahoo.com/news/robinhood-shuts-off-instant, accessed February 16, 2021.
974. Ultimate Stock Alerts. 2021. "Robinhood penny stocks: What you need to know". https://www.ultimatestockalerts.com/robinhood-penny-stocks/, accessed May 26, 2021.
975. K. Rooney. 2019. "Battle for zero trading fees threatens Robinhood's business model and next leg of growth". *CNBC 04/10/19*. https://www.cnbc.com/2019/10/04/battle-for-zero-trading-fees-pressures, accessed November 10, 2020.
976. Robinhood. 2021. "Commission free cryptocurrency investing". https://robinhood.com/us/en/support/articles/commission-free-cryptocurrency, accessed May 26, 2021.

Robinhood announced in December 2018 that checking and savings accounts, together with debit cards issued by Ohio-based Sutton Bank, would be available in 2019. Instead, the waitlist and sign-up page for these services were removed from its app in January 2019. In October 2019, Robinhood announced a new Cash Management feature with FDIC insurance from various partner banks and an annual 2.5% interest rate that was eventually lowered to 1.8% after a federal rate cut.[977] The enterprise therefore generates revenues from interest earned on customer's cash balances, selling order information to high-frequency traders, and margin trading.

Robinhood's corporate problems keep surging. The outage problems in March 2020 were followed by the suicide of Alex Kearns, a victim of reckless options trading; SEC investigation for failures to fully disclose participation in PFOF; request from The Depository Trust & Clearing Corporation (DTCC) to deposit USD 3 billion in additional collateral. This was eventually resolved, when Robinhood restricted purchases of GameStop and other meme stocks.[978]

Tenev and his colleagues have been surprised by the vitriol directed at them and Robinhood, despite explaining that the company has to freeze the buying of these stocks prematurely so as to address its clearinghouse requirements. Many users refused to accept the explanation even after Robinhood began to restore trading in GameStop, the day after, as many users held the belief that Robinhood was doing this to depress the values of these stocks. Importantly, they began realizing that they were not Robinhood's primary customers as they were led to believe, but were in reality, themselves the products being sold to firms like Citadel Securities, Robinhood's most lucrative customers.[979] This led to lawsuits against the company. This got Dan Gallagher, the Chief Legal Officer at Robinhood worried, as the damage to the company's image had been catastrophic, especially with regards to misinformation and disinformation of collusion with hedge funds that were unpredictable and yet were quickly gaining traction.[980] Despite these setbacks, millions of new users opened accounts, and PFOF revenues for the first quarter of 2021 managed to reach USD 331 million, tripling that of the previous corresponding period.[981]

Robinhood has come under reputation threat risks because of several linked controversial business practices. These included the following:

(1) Robinhood restricted the trading of particular stocks subsequent to initiatives by subreddit users and others to propel their prices. WallStreetBets posters were buzzing eight Reddit stocks, namely, Alibaba, Palantir Technologies, Microvision, Rocket Companies, Tesla, Apple, Advanced Micro Devices, and GameStop. Robinhood's action was heavily criticized by subreddit and

977. T. Porter. 2021. "Robinhood cash management account review: Up to $1.25M in FDIC insurance". *My Bank Tracker 10/05/21*. https://www.mybanktracker.com/checking/reviews/robinhood, 26/05/21.
978. Kolhatkar 2021, *supra* note [963].
979. Kolhatkar 2021, *supra* note [963].
980. Kolhatkar 2021, *supra* note [963].
981. Kolhatkar 2021, *supra* note [963].

Twitter users,[982] as well as by a member of Congress calling its action, as a form of market manipulation to protect the interests of big hedge funds and ergo merited a hearing by the House Committee on Financial Services.[983] This controversy led to negative reviews on Robinhood's app, as well as protests outside Robinhood's headquarters, the SEC in Washington, DC, and the NYSE.[984] This was followed in January 28, 2021, by a class action lawsuit against the company for alleged market manipulation in that Robinhood's app allegedly purposefully, willfully and knowingly removed the stock "GME" from its trading platform in the midst of an unprecedented stock ascent thereby depriving retail investors of the ability to invest in the open-market.[985] The company responded the day after announcing that it would reallow limited purchase of these stocks.[986]

(2) The Massachusetts Securities Division submitted administrative complaints against Robinhood alleging the company's breach of state securities laws by marketing itself to investors in the state without due regard for the best interests of its customers, besides failing to maintain the infrastructures and procedures necessary to cater to the demands of the company's rapidly growing customer base.[987] Owing to Robinhood's gamified interface that enables new unsophisticated investors to participate in advanced derivatives, short sales, and call options, the Massachusetts regulator contended that Robinhood exploited novice investors, as these kinds of trades are conventionally treated as out-of-bounds for such investors owing to the high risks involved in them.

(3) Media reports highlighted in September 2, 2020, that Robinhood came under SEC investigation for failing to fully disclose selling clients' orders to high-speed trading firms that could attract a potential fine of more than USD 10

982. S. Smith. 2021. "Update: What 8 Reddit stocks are still on the list?" *Investor Place 01/02/21.* https://investorplace.com/2021/02/robinhood-restrictions-update-reddit-stocks, accessed May 26, 2021.
983. M. Kelly. 2021. "AOC and others call for investigation into Robinhood's GameStop freeze: It's not clear if Congress plans to act". *The Verge 20/01/21.* https://www.theverge.com/2021/1/28/22254584, accessed May 26, 2021.
984. J. Murdock. 2021. "Robinhood app blocks GME stock trading, is flooded with 1-star reviews". *Newsweek 28/01/21.* https://www.newsweek.com/robinhood-app-one-star-reviews-gamestop, accessed May 26, 2021.
985. R. Brandom. 2021. "Robinhood will allow 'limited buys' of stocks like GameStop starting Fridays: Halting purchases was 'a risks management decision', the company said in a blog post". *The Verge 28/01/21.* https://www.theverge.com/2021/1/28/22255031/robinhood-gamestop, accessed May 26, 2021.
986. Reuters. 2021. "Robinhood lifts trading restrictions on all stocks, including GameStop". *Reuters 06/02/21.* https://www.reuters.com/business/retail-consumer/robinhood-lifts-trading-restrictions, accessed May 26, 2021.
987. N. Raymond. 2021. "Massachusetts regulators seek to revoke Robinhood's license; brokerage sues". *Reuters 16/04/21.* https://www.reuters.com/technology/robinhood-sues-invalidate-massachusetts, accessed May 26, 2021.

million. Eventually, the company paid USD 65 million to resolve the said SEC investigation on December 17, 2020.[988]

(4) Alexander Kearns, a University of Nebraska student after viewing a negative cash balance of USD 730,000 in his Robinhood margin trading account, committed suicide in June 2020. Kearns' suicide note accused the company of allowing him to pile on excessive risk, but this turned out in a subsequent discovery to be a temporary negative balance due to unsettled trading activity. As Kearns' family proceeded to file suit against Robinhood, the company promised to consider additional criteria and education for customers seeking level 3 options authorization.[989]

(5) Robinhood suffered a systemwide all-day outage during the largest daily point gain in Dow Jones' history, thereby preventing users from undertaking more actions on Robinhood's platform, including opening and closing positions. The S&P ascended more than 4.6% during this said outage. The platform users alleged that the outage was the outcome of a coding error pertaining to leap year handling for Saturday February 29, 2019. The company though denied this allegation, but offered compensation on a case-by-case basis. Nevertheless, the company faced another major systemwide outage a week later. Three lawsuits have been mounted against Robinhood in March 2020 due to these outages.[990]

(6) WallStreetBets subreddit in November 2019 shared a glitch that enabled Robinhood Gold users to borrow unlimited funds through selling covered calls where the shares had been bought using leverage. The premium from the call is used to access additional leverage to acquire more shares so as be able to sell more calls, and so on. Though the said loophole was terminated shortly thereafter and the accounts exploiting it suspended, some other accounts suffered six-figure losses by using the infinite money cheat code, as labeled by WallStreetBets users.[991]

(7) Though Robinhood did not find any evidence of abuse, it allegedly conceded in emails to impacted customers in July 2019 to storing customer passwords in cleartext and in readable form across their internal systems. Evidence of more widespread attacks came in 2020 when the company admitted that

988. S. Choe & A. Veiga. 2020. "Robinhood agrees to pay $65 million to settle SEC charges that trading app misled investors". *Chicago Tribune 18/12/20*. https://www.chicagotribune.com/business/ct-biz-robinhood, accessed May 26, 2020.

989. M. Fitzgerald. 2021. "Robinhood sued by family of 20-year-old trader who killed himself after believing he racked up huge losses". *CNBC 08/02/21*. https://www.cnbc.com/2021/02/08/robinhood-sued, accessed May 26, 2021.

990. Global Newswire. 13/04/20. "Lawsuit for Robinhood users over trading outage announced by shareholders foundation". *Global Newswire 13/04/20*. https://www.globenewswire.com/news-release/2020/04/13/2015046/0/en/Lawsuit-for-Robinhood-Users-over-Trading-Outage, accessed May 26, 2021.

991. B. Winck. 2019. "Robinhood has a 'free money cheat' that allowed one user to grow $4000 into $1 million through 'infinite leverage'". *Markets Insider 05/11/19*. https://markets.businessinsider.com/news/stocks/robinhood-infinite-leverage-free-money, accessed May 26, 2021.

almost two thousand Robinhood Markets accounts were compromised in hacking sprees with hackers siphoning off customer funds.[992]

(8) Robinhood also allegedly conceded to receiving close to half of its revenue from PFOF, suggesting that it appears to be taking more cash for orders than rivals by up to 60-to-1 ratio, as per its regulatory submissions. The company was fined USD 1.25 million in 2019 for failing to ensure that its customers received the best price for orders.[993] Robinhood's trades between October 2016 and November 2017 were routed to companies that paid for order flow, with Robinhood failing to consider the price improvements that might have been obtained through other market makers. The FINRA accordingly fined Robinhood for best execution violations pertaining to its customers' equity orders and related supervisory failures from October 2016 to November 2017. As part of this settlement, the company further agreed to retain an independent consultant to undertake a comprehensive review of the firm's systems and procedures related to best execution. The company also faced a class action lawsuit in December 2020, for failing to disclose that a large portion of its revenue depended on payments for order flow.[994]

The above litany of corporate missteps provided fodder for Charlie Munger the Vice Chairman of Berkshire Hathaway and others tearing at Robinhood's trading app for encouraging amateur investors to gamble on stocks and dabbling with risky options trading. The Chairman of O'Shares ETF opined that both Munger and others might have failed to consider that Robinhood with its 20-plus million accounts has contributed a great service for people who never invested in a stock before.[995] As Robinhood was planning for public listing in 2021, it came under Congressional scrutiny in the wake of a trading frenzy in February 2021 surrounding meme stocks, GameStop and AMC. It has also been slapped with a class action lawsuit by customers accusing the company of favoring Wall Street professionals, over retail investors, when it placed temporary trading curbs on those stocks generally favored by Reddit-fueled day traders and other retail investors. Gary Gensler, the newly appointed SEC Chairman, in a testimony before the House Financial Service Committee raised concerns about Robinhood and its game-like features, like points, rewards, leaderboards, and competitions to expand user engagements. Research has suggested that more active trading or

992. S. Alexander. 2020. "Almost 2,000 Robinhood accounts infiltrated in recent hacking sprees: Attacks unleashed a torrent of complaints on social media, where investors recounted futile attempt to call the brokerage". *Bloomberg News 15/10/20*. https://www.bloomberg.com/news/articles/2020-10-15/robinhood, accessed May 26, 2020.
993. M. Ong & M. Rote. 2019. "FINRA fines Robinhood Financial, LLC $1.25 million for best execution violations". *FINRA 19/21/19*. https://www.finra.org/media-center/newsreleases/2019/finra, accessed May 26, 2021.
994. C. Rizzi. 2021. "Inexperienced Robinhood traders charged backdoor fees in undisclosed 'payment for order flow' scheme, Class Action says". *Class Action 04/01/21*. https://www.classaction.org/news/inexperienced-robinhood-traders-charged-backdoor-fees-in-undisclosed-payment-for-order-flow, accessed May 26, 2021.
995. A. Christoforous. 2021. "Robinhood is a 'misunderstood platform': Kevin O'Leary". *Finance Yahoo 07/05/21*. https://finance.yahoo.com/news/robinhood-is-a-misunderstood-platform, accessed May 26, 2021.

even day trading would result in lower returns for the average trader. The SEC accordingly initiated public consultations on new rules that could set boundaries on what sort of features online brokers like Robinhood could employ.[996]

Robinhood has made it possible for its users to trade financial products, without having to pay commission or having to deposit a minimum sum. Hence, its mantra "investing for everyone" has undoubtedly become a powerful slogan supporting the democratization of finance. Spiderman's uncle's "with great power, comes great responsibility" is unfortunately demonstrated in Kearns suicide alluded to earlier. Questions now swirled as to whether trading apps exemplified powerfully by Robinhood have been operating responsibly, especially given its continuing popularity, despite setbacks cropping up.

Unlike trading through conventional brokers, Robinhood's platform makes users feel frictionless, fun, and easy, but though with high risks unbeknown or not too dissuasive to its many users.[997] Those signing up are rewarded with a small slice of free stock, and stimulations by the screen turning different colors, depending on the user's performance, green when up, and red when down. Users are also rewarded with digital confetti upon completion of certain successful transactions. This addictiveness has helped to attract many users to Robinhood in droves, rising from about 1 million in 2016, and adding more than 13 million by early 2020. These soon draw in even more users of the younger age group with smart mobile devices but with no investing experience to gain access to a world of risky assets, and therefore with little appreciation of the serious risks in the world of investing. This risks potentially fatal outcomes, as seen in the Kearns' tragedy, especially without some sort of oversight.

The above aside, the US Congress is now having questions over Robinhood's business model expressing serious reservations about the safeguards in place for the mainly amateur investors, pointing again to the examples of how the 20-year-old Kearns, with no income, was approved by Robinhood to trade options using margins, including incidents when users appeared to have been locked out from making trades for up to seventeen hours during a period of historical market volatility.[998] Serious ethical debates on consumer welfare have now surfaced again on the use of such derivative products that were severely maligned subsequent to the 2007-2008 GFC because of alleged recklessness and exclusionary nature of traditional finance.[999] Fintech start-ups rose in response, promising a significantly more inclusive environment by catering to much wider and more economically diverse demographics, implying that anyone and everyone can have access to a wide range of offerings. This led to investing opportunities provided by Robinhood and others, but with no effective oversight[1000] over the set of dangers involved when offered to beginner traders on the platform.

996. Christoforous 2021, *supra* note [995].
997. International Banker (IB). 2020. "Robinhood and the ethical issues facing fintech"". International Banker 02/10/20. https://internationalbanker.com/brokerage/robinhood-and-the-ethical-issues-facing-fintech, accessed November 10, 2020.
998. IB. 2020, *supra* note [997].
999. IB. 2020, *supra* note [997].
1000. IB. 2020, *supra* note [997].

Robinhood's cofounders on their part have responded with improved customer experience, with some attention to risk matters. Foremost, these involve:[1001]

(1) the considering of additional eligibility criteria and education for consumers seeking higher levels of options trading authorization so as to ensure that users understand the risks linked to more sophisticated options trading;
(2) expanding the educational content pertaining to options trading through additional information and options-education specialist guidance in Robinhood's help center;
(3) improving the use interface pertaining to the app messages and emails that the users received about their multi-leg options spreads; and
(4) adding details to the in-app history page to help users to better understand the mechanics of early options assignments.

The company donated USD 250,000 to the American Foundation for Suicide Prevention. It further committed to working with US policymakers to address their questions and concerns over tech-style investing apps, and aspiring to be the best and safest options platform.[1002]Many Robinhood users disagree that they are relatively less-savvy traders, pointing to chat boards, Facebook groups and Reddit threads that are rife with tales of trading prowess, including daring bets on options, exquisitely timed short-termed maneuvers, and so on.[1003] Still, with more than half of the users being first-timers, it would be extraordinary to have significant numbers of them proving to be market-beaters. In the end, Robinhood is still very much a broker-dealer, and not an investment adviser. As such, Robinhood's traders ought to be cautioned that it could be better for them to really appreciate what they are doing, and not lay the blame on Robinhood when they get financially harmed when making risky investment decisions.[1004]

Also, Robinhood users are generally trading in high volumes, not necessarily on blue chips or needing to go for the long haul; but on lower-price meme stocks that could be traded without having to pay commissions. The Robinhood business model does not appear to rely on users making great, or even prudent investment decisions, but on significant chunks of users feeling comfortable enough with the app to buy into other services over time, as exemplified by Robinhood Gold that offers users access to a pool of borrowed capital to trade as users deemed fit.[1005] Such arrangements usually are structured around interest payments, but Robinhood has converted basically the same fee into a monthly subscription model making it easier to grasp, but just as potentially profitable where the company is concerned.[1006] To Robinhood, it is about giving more

1001. IB. 2020, *supra* note [997].
1002. IB. 2020, *supra* note [997].
1003. R. Walker. 2020. "How Robinhood convinced millennials to trade their way through a pandemic". Marker Medium 01/06/20. https://marker.medium.com/how-robinhood-convinced-millennials-to-trade-their, accessed November 10, 2020.
1004. Walker 2020, *supra* note [1003].
1005. Walker 2020, *supra* note [1003].
1006. Walker 2020, *supra* note [1003].

people a feeling of access to the means that might one day rocket Robinhood users into the top 1% of American society. Importantly, it is about bringing more people into the lucrative financial system, rather than leaving them on the sidelines. This would include seeking out also the *high earning not rich yet millennial* subset, or HENRY.[1007]

Robinhood has on March 23, 2021, confidentially filed a draft registration statement on Form (S-1) with the SEC relating to the proposed IPO of its common stock. The number of shares to be offered and the price range for the proposed offering have yet to be determined. This IPO is set to occur after the SEC completes its review process, and subject to market and related conditions. These will be made in line with registration requirements of the SA 1933. The March 23, 2021, announcement does not constitute an offer to sell or the solicitation of an offer to buy any securities, and is being issued in accordance with Rule 135 of the SA 1933. The envisaged IPO could demonstrate Robinhood's popularity, but this comes in the thick of regulatory controversies. The settlement with industry self-regulator FINRA involves a payment of USD 70 million in penalties and compensation to harmed investors because of FINRA's observation that Robinhood's investing app distributed false and misleading information to its customers, allowed too many people to partake in risky trading, and failing to properly oversee the technology that supported its app. The firm will also be facing charges of failing to disclose how it makes money and not getting best price for its customers.

The perception that Robinhood played a key role in the GameStop saga resulted in the public grilling of CEO Vladimir Tenev in congressional testimony. It is unclear though whether Robinhood's stumbles represent the growing pain of a burgeoning behemoth that is shaking up the staid industry, or they imply a painful crack-up down the line.[1008] What is relatively clear though is the company turning profitable in 2020 with a reported net income of USD 7 million compared to a loss of USD 107 million for 2019.[1009] It is also clear that the investing app has crypto assets under custody of about USD 12 billion as of March 31, 2021, showing a twenty-threefold jump from the previous years, as well as having some 9.5 million customers trading about USD 88 billion in crypto assets on its platform for the same period.[1010] In the meantime, Robinhood subsequent to its settlement with FINRA through a USD 70 million fine for systemic supervisory failures and significant harm to millions of its customers and settlement of a wrongful death lawsuit has filed an S-1 with the SEC ahead of its IPO.[1011] The company is seeking a valuation of some USD 35 billion in its IPO, and where realized would record as the fifth-biggest IPO in the capital market for 2021. Robinhood eventually raised approximately USD 2 billion, selling shares in its IPO at

1007. Walker 2020, *supra* note [1003].
1008. T. Tepper & B. Curry. 2021. "Should you invest in the Robinhood IPO?". *Forbes 30/06/21*. https://www.forbes.com/advisor/investing/robinhood-ipo/, accessed July 7, 2021.
1009. A. Sen & N.Z. Hussain. 2021. "Robinhood reveals breakneck growth, legal pitfalls in IPO filling". Reuters 02/07/21. https://www.reuters.com/technology/online-brokerage-robinhood-makes-ipo-filing-public-2021-07-01/, accessed July 7, 2021.
1010. Sen & Hussain 2021, *supra* note [1009].
1011. P. Donachie. 2021. "Advisors question how FINRA settlement will impact Robinhood". *Wealth Management 2 July 2021*. https://www.wealthmanagement.com/print/136878, accessed July 3, 2021.

around USD 38 each on July 29, 2021, that valued the company at about USD 32 billion. Its major competitors, like Charles Schwab and Interactive Brokers, have respective market capitalization of USD 130 billion and USD 26 billion. Robinhood's biggest investors are Ribbit Capital, NEA, Index Ventures and DST Global.

Uber Technologies Inc (Uber)

San Francisco-based multinational Uber was founded in 2009 by Garrett Camp and Travis Kalanick. It started off as a mobile app for vehicle for hire. It later diversified into food delivery, package delivery, courier, and freight transport.[1012] It now has operations in over nine hundred metropolitans globally, and based on these have thus become one of the biggest players in the gig economy. Its market dominance in the sharing economy has been likened to transformation in many industries that have become popularly referred to as "uberization."[1013] This is unsurprising, as Uber enjoys a more than 70% market share for ride-sharing in the US market and over 20% market share for food delivery because of its early mover advantage.[1014]

Like most tech start-ups, Uber has its ups and downs over the last decade of its commercial history. It became a listed corporation in May 2019 through an IPO.[1015] Despite the fanfare surrounding its IPO, Uber's share suffered the biggest IPO first-day loss in US history at the time, when its debut price closed 11% lower than its IPO price. Surprisingly, while enjoying expansive exposures in the US and worldwide, including respectable growth rates for its services despite regulatory and social barriers, the company has yet to make a profit. Uber achieved USD 11.14 billion turnover in 2020, and a net loss of USD 6.77 billion.[1016] The company has total assets of more than USD 33.25 billion, and shareholders' funds of some USD 13.0 billion. Given its loss-making history, this would suggest that the company is well supported by equities and borrowings from the capital and financial markets, implying a lot of market confidence for its potential, despite current setbacks.

The company has a long history of bad publicities and controversies, as illustrated by the following:[1017]

(1) The use of the aggressive principled confrontation strategy, where Uber would commence operations in places without regard for local regulations.

1012. A. Lashinsky. 2017. *Wild ride: Inside Uber's quest for world domination.* London: Portfolio.
1013. G.F. Davis & A. Sinha. 2021. "Varieties of Uberization: How technology and institutions change the organizations(s) of late capitalism". *Organization Theory*, Vol. 2 (2021): 1-17.
1014. H. Feng, Z. Jiang & M. Li. 2020. "First- or second-mover advantage? The case of IT-enabled platform markets". *MIS Quarterly*, Vol. 44 (3): 3-20.
1015. R. Ungarino. 2019. "Uber tanked 11% after logging the biggest first-day dollar loss in US IPO history (UBER)". *Business Insider 13/05/19.* https://markets.businessinsider.com/news/stocks/uber-technologies, accessed November 10, 2020.
1016. Uber Investor. 2020. "Financials". https://investor.uber.com/financials/default.aspx, accessed November 10, 2020.
1017. K. Taylor & B. Goggin. 2019. "49 of the biggest scandals in Uber's history". *Business Insider 11/05/19.* https://www.businessinsider.com/uber-company-scandals-and-controversies, accessed November 10, 2020.

When confronted with regulatory opposition, Uber would drum up public support for its services, mount political campaigns supported by lobbyists so as to alter regulations in its favor.

(2) Alleged unfair competition against main competitors, like Lyft.
(3) Paying USD 20 million to the Federal Trade Commission (FTC) to resolve allegations of the company misleading drivers about potential learnings.
(4) Conceding to underpaying New York City drivers, and agreeing to settle the due amounts owed plus interest.
(5) Operating during a New York City taxi strike in late January 2017.
(6) Conceding in March 2017 that the company had deployed Greyball software to thwart government regulators, and pledging to terminate the use of the software for this purpose.
(7) Employees' sexual harassment allegations against various senior company officials, including further allegations that the CEO was aware of these. Under serious pressure from investors, CEO Kalanick resigned in June 2017, and also resigned from the board in 2019. This was followed by the CEO selling his shares in the company.
(8) Following a series of allegations of making plans to dig up dirt on particular researchers and journalists, senior vice president Emil Michael resigned.
(9) Paying USD 7 million to 480 workers to settle claims of gender discrimination, harassment and hostile working environment.
(10) A US Chairperson of the US Senate Judiciary Subcommittee on Privacy, Technology and the Law expressed privacy concerns over Uber using its technology and platforms to track journalists and politicians.
(11) Delayed disclosures of data breaches of some 50,000 drivers in February 2015, and some 600,000 drivers and 57 million customers in 2016.
(12) Criminal charges have been filed against former Chief Security Officer, Joe Sullivan, for obstruction of justice when paying a ransom for the 2016 data breach as a bug bounty to conceal its true nature, and for the hackers to falsify nondisclosure agreements to say they had not obtained data.
(13) The "Paradise Papers" revealing that the company had used an offshore company to minimize taxes.
(14) An Amsterdam court ruling that Uber has to reinstate six drivers that were allegedly terminated based solely on algorithms and agreeing also to pay a compensation fee. Such robo-firings are being treated as against Article 22 of the GDPR in the EU.

From general observations, Uber encountered resistance in almost all markets it engages with, from private-car operators, established taxis, and to transit authorities and regulators. For instance, when Uber first began in San Francisco, it received a cease-and-desist order from city and state authorities. Uber challenged the then prevailing framework that was designed to regulate private-car operators, rather than third-party services providers that linked passengers with licensed vehicles. Therefore, when challenged, Uber would persist with its services contending that their services should not be restricted by ambiguities and gaps in the regulatory frameworks. The user base of passengers and drivers for Uber would eventually attain such sizes that regulators would become unable to curb the services. Subsequent cases suggest various governance practices weaknesses in the company. Over the years, these led to protests from cab drivers and other impacted by its services in the US and other parts of the world. However, Uber's challenges were not limited to endless squabbles with local authorities and regulators. Over time, competition, operating, and governance problems popped up like a game of whack-a-mole which Uber continuously struggled to knock down, including the problems alluded to earlier.[1018]

Governance problems eventually crept up Uber's boardroom.[1019] This arose from a sexual harassment complaint against a senior corporate official that eventually led to internal investigations on sexual harassments claims, as well as a parallel investigation into the company's culture and practices by two law firms. Perkins Coie reviewed 213 staff complaints pertaining to discrimination, sexual harassments, unprofessional behaviors, and bullying since 2012. The legal firms recommended the company to take disciplinary actions in 58 cases. This represents 27% of those cases. Separately, Covington, another professional firm drawing on insights from two hundred interviews with current and former employees, and database review of over three million internal documents, recommended various workplace changes for leadership and governance, including recommendations to reallocate some of the CEO's responsibilities to other senior executives, increasing the number of independent directors, increasing the authority of the chief diversity officer, offering leadership coaching to senior executives, reformulation of the company's fourteen cultural values, as well as implementing mandatory sensitivity training for employees.

These recommendations have been unanimously adopted by Uber's board, including announcing the CEO's leave of absence, during which time his responsibilities would be shared among a designated committee, as well as the compelled resignation of board member David Bonderman, for making sexist remarks during a company-wide meeting. This was followed by the resignation of another board member, before the appointment of compromise candidate, Dara Khosrowshahi, known for his successful ten-year tenure at Expedia. Upon appointment, he immediately sought to change Uber's culture through the bottom-up approach, rather than Uber's hitherto top-down culture push.

Kalanick responded with fresh proposals, including committing the company to an IPO by 2019, appointments of Kalanick's two nominations, and appointment of a Softbank nominee.[1020] Softbank, a late-stage start-up investor, announced investment of between USD 1 and 1.25 billion, including the purchase of about USD 9 billion in shares through a tender offer to existing shareholders and employees at a discounted valuation of USD 48 billion. When fully accepted, the tender would provide Softbank with an ownership stake of more than 24%. Uber's board further agreed to add as many as six new directors, three independent, one new chairman, and two designated

1018. D.F. Larcker & B. Tayan. 2017. "Governance gone wild: Epic misbehavior at Uber Technologies". *Rock Center for CG Stanford Closer Look Series- CGRP70 11/12/17.*
1019. Larcker & Tayan 2017, *supra* note [1018].
1020. Larcker & Tayan 2017, *supra* note [1018].

to Softbank, thereby expanding the board size from eleven to seventeen. Softbank also would enjoy the right to end the agreement if it did not receive adequate shares through the tender offer at the discounted price.

On January 18, 2018, Softbank announced that its long-pending deal with Uber was closed with a total of USD 9 billion. It was reported that Software and a consortium of other investors, including Dragoneer Investment Group, Sequoia Capital, and former Chinese rival Didi Chuxing had acquired USD 7.7 billion in extant Uber shares.[1021] These changes and impending changes at the boardroom matter because of the following:[1022]

(1) Uber has a long history of sustained market aggressions and challenging regulators so as to achieve its mission and operating goals. Questions are being raised as to whether this kind of ultra-aggressive risk-seeking behavior would cause further problems in the future, or whether the company would be less successful without this strategy.
(2) The founding CEO had set the tone for Uber with a focus on unrelenting growth with his dominant personality and behavior. Questions were raised on whether this leadership style, and accompanying corporate culture had contributed to Uber's growth and its sustainability, or whether the bottom-up approach preferred by the current professional CEO would be the better fit for the company; and if so, whether the business model of Uber could succeed with a distinctly new management and firm culture.
(3) Questions were raised as to whether Uber's implementation of the Covington's report of a series of leadership, board-related and operational changes to fix its culture, including governance changes in conjunction with the investment from Softbank, would help to improve the governance of Uber.
(4) Questions were also raised, as to whether the bottom-up approach of corporate culture preferred by the professional CEO would be better off for Uber, instead of the hitherto top-down approach; and importantly what implications these would have on governance and leadership, including as to whether the company would need a substantial turnover of management and key nonmanagement employees to successfully transform a cultural shift.

There are signs that the company could be nudging toward better governance practices these days. The UK Supreme Court in September 2020 held that despite historic failings, the company is deemed a fit and proper operator subsequent to some improvements in its practices.[1023] By then, Uber has already become a necessity of life for many Londoners, as well as an essential means of income for drivers looking for

1021. J.D. Rowley. 2018. "Uber finally seals $9 billion deal with SoftBank and others". *Crunchbase 18/01/18.* https://news.crunchbase.com/news/uber-finally-seals-9-billion-deal-softbank-others/, accessed November 10, 2020.
1022. Larcker & Tayan 2017, *supra* note [1018].
1023. D. Medland. 2021. "Uber becomes an unlikely icon in the rise of ESG in CG". Ethical Systems 24/02/21. https://www.ethicalsystems.org/uber-becomes-an-unlikely-icon-in-the-rise-of-esg, accessed February 25, 2021.

flexible working. The Supreme Court's ruling that Uber drivers are workers rather than self-employed is expected to cause ripples for all companies with new business models that seemingly provide easy fix for the needs of frenetic modern-day living, but has played havoc with the value that underpins the thinking of standards on better governance practices. The Supreme Court's unanimous judgment stated that drivers should be considered to be working, not only when driving a passenger but also whenever they were logged in to the app. In other words, the court's decisions valued drivers' time equally, whether they were just driving or just on duty. The court further decided that the drivers were in a position of subordination, as they could only increase their earnings by working longer hours.

Uber has also committed to the environment element, or the "E" in ESG. This is reflected in the company's plans to push for greater use of electrical mobile vehicles in its business. Uber announced in September 2020 that though it would not pay drivers to make the switch to 100% electric vehicles by 2030 in the US, Canada, and Europe, and by 2040 for the rest of the world, it would make driving an electric vehicle more lucrative by adding an extra fee on trips completed in an electric vehicle to incentivize drivers to make the switch.[1024] The company launched its "Uber Green" surcharges in fifteen cities in the US and Canada on September 7, 2020. Riders paying an extra dollar in these cities can specifically request a hybrid or electric vehicle. Drivers using hybrid or electric vehicles to service passengers would earn an extra USD 0.5 per ride, while drivers using specifically battery-electric vehicles would earn another dollar on top of that, or a total of USD 1.50 extra per ride. While the E is important in the push for better ESG, the S in ESG is also critical, as not only they are about monitoring faraway supply chains and nodding to initiatives at diversity and inclusion but also that these three letters in ESG are inextricably linked by human values.[1025]

Successful US double or multisided platforms operate more like conventional multinationals even though they are more driven by technology prowess. Robinhood, unlike other more conventional crowdfunding platform, focused more on providing funding to mainly newly exposed investors using its mobile investment platform to engage in various investing activities, from basic to sophisticated financial products. These even included some selective, but complex crypto assets products. Giving investment access convenience to sophisticated investment products to new entrant investors with modest income levels in the absence of reasonable levels of education on such high-risk products could attract relatively high levels of risks both for the investors and for the fund providers. Uber's business model is thus copied or adapted in many other multisided platforms, both in the US and in other economies aspiring to enjoy a slice of the massive business opportunity. What Uber does in terms of governance practices would be watched closely around the world, especially in the many other economies where it operates. Other equivalent platforms are thus likely to follow the MNC's ESG commitments even though it is still embroiled in sorting out

1024. A.J. Hawkins. 2020. "Uber pledges to shift to '100 percent' electric vehicles by 2030". *The Verge 08/09/20.* https://www.theverge.com/2020/9/8/21427196/uber-promise-100-percent-electric, accessed October 22, 2020.
1025. Medland 2021, *supra* note [1023].

various controversial matters with various national regulators across the world. Relative to other multisided platforms elsewhere, US platforms tend to be relatively more successful when scaling across national borders, owing to their relatively greater business aggressiveness, first mover advantage, and lack of concerns over their market dominance strategy. Their strategy in using market dominance to drive their enterprises though have attracted antitrust regulatory scrutiny, especially in Europe, UK, and elsewhere.

9.03b UK DBCs

Funding Circle (FC)

Three associates from the University of Oxford, namely, Samir Desai, James Meekings and Andrew Mullinger, discussed the feasibility of a peer-to-peer lending platform at a pub in 2008 in the midst of the 2007-2008 GFC.[1026] It was a time when banks in the US, UK, and elsewhere in Europe were retreating from the lending space so as to beef up their balance sheets to align with regulatory demands and standards.[1027] This London-based peer-to-peer (P2P) lending platform enables the public to lend and fund small and medium-sized enterprises (SMEs), and for SMEs to access much-needed capital for their operating needs. Through this platform/exchange, SMEs can access funding at lower costs relative to what they would be able to get from the banks, while the public in turn would be able to become lenders/small financiers and in doing so could make relatively good returns from their capital. The UK government in 2012 deployed the platform to lend GBP 20 million to small businesses in the UK.[1028] Accel Partners together with Ribbit Capital, Union Square Venture and Index Ventures provided USD 37 million of further funding to the London-based P2P crowdfunding platform in 2013.[1029]

The three pals quitted their jobs in 2009 to lay the ground for the launching of FC in August 2010. Indeed, it was in the context of the GFC that the P2P lending industry, or crowdfunding as is generally known globally, grew quickly to emerging as a good source of alternative funding for SMEs with minimum hassle or fuss. FC on its part helped to facilitate GBP 160 million lending between the time of launching to the third quarter of 2013. UK businesses under the P2P crowdfunding scheme could borrow up to GBP 1 million, those in the US up to USD 500,000, and in Germany and the

1026. S. Beame. 2018. "The £1.3bn finance firms that was conceived in a pub". *BBC 22/10/18.* https://www.bbc.com/news/business-45900404, accessed November 10, 2020.
1027. Y. Zhao, P. Harris & W. Lam. 2019. "Crowdfunding industry—History, development, policies, and potential issues". Journal of Public Affairs, Vol. 19 (1): 1-19.
1028. Reuters. 2012. "UK government will lend to business through peer-to-peer website". Reuters 12/12/12. https://www.reuters.com/article/britain-lending/uk-government-will-lend-to-business-through-pee, accessed November 10, 2020.
1029. R. Grant. 2013. "UK-based Funding Circle raises $37M to fund American small businesses". *Venture Beat 23/10/13.* https://venturebeat.com/2013/10/23/uk-based-funding-circle-raises-37m-to-fund, accessed November 10, 2020.

Netherlands of up to EUR 250,000 for a tenure of sixty months. In the initial period of operation, the loan rate was decided via an auction process, but following September 2015, the company determined the loan rate offered based on risks category and loan term.

Until 2014, investors in P2P crowdfunding platforms are not covered by the FSCS in the UK, and ergo would not be able to turn to it for relief as a last resort.[1030] The FCA nevertheless announced in December 2012 that commencing from April 1, 2014, it would regulate P2P lenders, including FC.[1031] Following consultation, the FCA has introduced new rules designed to prevent harms to investors, without stifling innovation in the P2P financial services space. The FCA has placed a limit on investments in P2P agreements for retail customers new to the space of 10% of investable assets, so as to ensure that they do not overexpose themselves to risk.[1032] This rule though will not apply to new retail customers who have received regulated financial advice. Other than this, the new rules would also include the following:[1033]

(1) More explicit disclosure will be needed to clarify what governance arrangements and system and control platforms need to have in place to support the outcomes they advertise. There will be special focus on credit assessment, risks management, and fair valuation practices.
(2) The strengthening of rules on plans for the wind-down of P2P platforms where they fail.
(3) Introducing a requirement that platforms evaluate investors' insights and experience of P2P investments where no advice had been extended to them.
(4) Setting out the minimum information that P2P platforms need to provide to investors.
(5) Applying the Mortgage and Home Finance Conduct of Business (MCOB) sourcebook and other Handbook requirements to P2P platforms that offer home finance products, where at least one of the investors is not an authorized home finance provider.

The MCOB will be applied with immediate effect, that is, as per announcement date. P2P platforms were told to implement the above changes by December 9, 2019.[1034]

Funding from the Accel Partners-led consortium helped to fund FC's expansion into the US market in 2013, where FC merged with San Francisco-based Endurance Lending Network. FC's operations in the US, however, are opened only to accredited

1030. Financial Services Compensation Scheme (FSCS).
1031. T. Mistry, G. Miller, J. W-Povey & P. Landers. 2015. "Alternative lending: A regulatory approach to peer-to-peer lending". https://www.grantthornton.co.uk/globalassets/1.-member-firms/united-kingdom, accessed November 10, 2020.
1032. Financial Conduct Authority (FCA). 2019. "FCA confirms new rules for P2P platforms. FCA 04/06/19. https://www.fca.org.uk/news/press-releases/fca-confirms-new-rules-p2p, accessed November 10, 2020.
1033. FCA 2019, *supra* note [1032].
1034. FCA 2019, *supra* note [1032].

and institutional investors to comply with the regulatory requirements of the 2012 Jumpstart Our Business Startup (JOBS) Act.[1035] FC acquired Zencap in 2015 so as to gain access to markets in the Netherlands, Spain and Germany.[1036]

To provide further funding support for its growing operations, FC listed in the LSE in September 2018 against a valuation of GBP 1.5 billion. Some GBP 300 million was raised in its IPO that accounted up to some 29% of the company's shares.[1037] Despite the public flotation being anchored by the Danish billionaire and owner of Bestseller with agreement to acquire a minimum of 10% of FC's shares, its share price descended by some 24% from its float price of 440p on the first day of trading.[1038]

FC reporting as a listed corporation in 2019 showed a 55% increase in turnover over the previous year, but pretax losses increased from GBP 36.3 million to GBP 50.7 for the corresponding period.[1039] The higher-than-expected losses have been attributed to increasing expenditures on marketing and personnel. The FC SME Income Funds then in April 2019 announced that it would be wound up, and its capital return to shareholders, because of the envisaged uncertain economic environment in July 2019 and the halving of revenue growth.[1040] The media attributed this to the impact prompted by Brexit, rather than any serious flaws in FC's business model.[1041]

Flowing from this, the company announced in August 2019 an increase of 15% in its first half-year losses stemming from growing UK bad debts.[1042] The media highlighted lender's concerns in September 2019 over the 100-day wait for selling off unwanted loans to retrieve their investments, compared to just eight days in January

1035. A.R. Stemler. 2013. "The JOBS Act and crowdfunding: Harnessing the power—and money—of the masses". *Business Horizons*, Vol. 56 (3): 271-275.
1036. J. Evans. 2015. "Funding Circle snaps up German marketplace lender: Deal to acquire Zencap is first foray into continental Europe". *Financial Times 21/10/15.* https://www.ft.com/content/74954e66-770b-11e5-a95a, accessed November 10, 2020.
1037. I. Lunden. 2018. "P2P lender Funding Circle closes flat in London after pricing IPO at the lower end of range and raising £300M". *Tech Crunch 28/09/18.* https://techcrunch.com/2018/09/28/funding, accessed November 10, 2020.
1038. R. Neate. 2018. "Peer-to-peer lender Funding Circle's share plummet on float day: Analysts say company was overvalued as City's 'tech hub' aspirations are deal a blow". *The Guardian 03/10/18.* https://www.theguardian.com/business/2018/oct/03/peer-to-peer-lender-funding, accessed November 10, 2020.
1039. *Funding Circle Holdings Plc Annual Report and Accounts 2019.* https://corporate.fundingcircle.com/download_file/force/334/354, accessed November 10, 2020.
1040. M. Vincent "Fintech Funding Circle shows valuations are a binary choice: Warning exposes the persistent bugs in the peer-to-peer lending program". *Financial Times 03/07/19.* https://www.ft.com/content/3947d204-9ccb-11e9-b8ce-8b459ed04726, accessed November 10, 2020.
1041. N. Pratley. Funding Circle bins the boasts as Brexit bites: Lending platforms revenue growth forecasts have halved as demand for small business loans dries up". *The Guardian 02/07/19.* https://www.theguardian.com/business/nils-pratley-on-finance/2019/jul/02/funding-circle, accessed January 10, 2020.
1042. N. Megaw. "Funding Circle losses widen as bad debts in UK worsen: Higher costs offset rise in first-half-revenue, UK-Based lender says". *Financial Times 08/08/19. https://www.ft.com/content/cd13,* accessed November 10, 2020.

2019, thereby signaling a lack of liquidity for FC's product.[1043] FC tried to allay investors' concerns,[1044] but matters grew worse in April 2020, when the company announced the temporary suspension of its secondary market for loans explaining that the decision to pause the secondary market was to focus on evaluating the potential impact of COVID-19 in the general economic environment.[1045]

FC's total income rose from GBP 177.3 million in 2019 to GBP 222 in 2020, while loss before tax rose from GBP 84.2 to GBP 108.1 for the respective years.[1046] The company's adjusted Earnings before Interest, Tax, Depreciation and Amortization (EBITDA) expanded from negative GBP 27.5 million in 2019 to negative GBP 63.8 million in 2020. Loans under management rose from GBP 3.7 billion in 2019 to GBP 4.2 billion in 2020. Importantly, for FC though is the achievement of profitability of GBP 20.3 million in the second half of 2020, and the robust net assets increase of GBP 218 million, since June 2020. FC on May 19, 2021, announced that trading has been stronger than anticipated in 2021, thus far and that total income and core earnings are anticipated to be ahead of previous expectations. The P2P platform further announced that it anticipates total income to be lower than GBP 120 million and adjusted core earnings to be lower also for the first six months of 2021.[1047] The company gained approval for the government-backed coronavirus loan scheme, but under this scheme the company cannot accept money from retail investors. This is a blow for casual P2P lending, as casual investors accounted for up to 23% of its funding in 2019.[1048] It has yet to reopen its resale market. Still, FC sees path to profitability after the tough market debut.[1049]

FC's governance practices, as gleaned from its 2020 Annual Report, appear to be reasonably balanced and comprehensive. Various linked sections provided salient

---

1043. A. Key. "Funding Circle amateur lenders facing longer waits to cash out: The queue for investors trying to re-sell loans has extended in recent months". *Belfast Telegraph 03/09/19.* https://www.belfasttelegraph.co.uk/business/uk-world/funding-circle-amateur-lenders, accessed November 10, 2020.
1044. N. Megaw. 2019. "Funding Circle seeks to ease fears over withdrawal delays: P2P lender sends letter to investors in an effort to allay capitalisation concerns". *Financial Times 11/10/19.* https://www.ft.com/content/21237c1a-ec3e-11e9-a240-3b065ef5fc55, accessed November 10, 2020.
1045. K. Gaw. 2020. "Funding Circle suspends secondary market: Funding Circle has paused its secondary market indefinitely, as the platform reacts to the coronavirus pandemic". *Peer2Peer Finance News 09/04/20.* https://www.p2pfinancenews.co.uk/2020/04/09/funding-circle, accessed November 10, 2020.
1046. *Funding Circle Holdings Plc Annual Reports and Accounts 2020.* https://corporate.fundingcircle.com/investors/results-and-reports, accessed April 10, 2021.
1047. A. Ramnarayan & R. Armstrong. 2021. "Funding Circle says trading to exceed expectations in 2021 so far". *Yahoo Finance 19/05/21.* https://ca.finance.yahoo.com/finance/news/funding-circle-says, accessed November 10, 2020.
1048. G. Nixon. 2021. "Funding Circle opens its doors to 300,000 businesses after joining loan scheme ... but closes them to personal investors who want to help". *This Money 28/04/20.* https://www.thisismoney.co.uk/money/investing/article-8240125/Funding-Circle, accessed November 10, 2020.
1049. N. Megaw. 2021. "Funding Circle eyes path to profitability after tough market debut: Government-backed loan schemes boos UK peer-to-peer lender looking to stage a 'big comeback'". *Financial Times 25/03/21.* https://www.ft.com/content/8d112aa1-919c-4d60-aab7-a7083945b2b3, accessed March 27, 2021.

information. These included those reports from the Chairman; Board of Directors; CG committee; report of the audit committee; report of the nomination committee; report of the risks and compliance committee; directors' remuneration report; annual reports on remuneration; and importantly statement of directors' responsibilities in respect of the financial statement. Also included were the sectional reports covering division of board responsibilities, BC, succession and evaluation, and those from the audit, risk, and internal control. All these reports fall under the umbrella of CG, numbering some fifty-one pages.[1050]

The Institutional Shareholder Services (ISS) have nevertheless assigned the ISS Governance Quality Scores as of May 30, 2021, at 7; where the pillar scores are 1 for audit, 9 for Board, 1 for shareholder rights, and 6 for compensation.[1051] A decile score of 1 indicates lower governance risk, while 10 suggests higher governance risk. This could be positively counterbalanced by FC's inclusion in FTSE4Good Index, especially for its high score for CC.[1052] The FTSE4Good Index filters listed firms that demonstrate the highest standards of CG and sustainability. The FTSE4Good Index Series is managed by the global index and data provider FTSE Russell that was initially set up in 2001 to provide investors with a transparent benchmark to measure ESG practices. The indexes are deployed by investors to create and evaluate responsible investment funds and other products. FC claims it ranks in the top third of all technology businesses in terms of ESG standards, scoring especially high in the area of governance practices.[1053]

Deliveroo

Roofoods Ltd, better known as Deliveroo, is initiated by William Shu and Greg Orlowski in 2013 in London as an online food delivery enterprise. Since then, it is now operating in over two hundred sites across the UK, selected parts of continental Europe, various Asian localities, and in Kuwait and the United Arab Emirates. Deliveroo's subsidiary manages the preparation of delivery-only meals located off-site from restaurants. This food delivery business gets income by levying restaurants a commission fee, and by imposing order fees from customers. This follows adaptions from the by now common double-sided or multisided platforms, like Uber or Airbnb. Thus, customers booked their food choices from Deliveroo's app or website, whereupon self-employed bicycle or motorcycle couriers transport orders from participating restaurants to them.

To commoditize its business model, Deliveroo collaborates with some of the biggest chain restaurants in each of their operating locality, with the majority being

1050. FC Annual Report 2020. https://fch-12917-s3.s3.eu-west-2.amazonaws.com/live/1016/2816/1085/Funding_Circle_Holdings_plc_Annual_Report_and_Accounts_2020.pdf, accessed March 27, 2021.
1051. Yahoo Finance. 2021. "Funding Circle Holdings Plc". *Yahoo Finance 22/02/21.* https://uk.finance.yahoo.com/quote/FDCHF/profile/, accessed April 26, 2021.
1052. D. Lanyon. 2019. "Funding Circle included in ESG index". *Alternative Finance (AltFi) 29/08/19.* https://www.altfi.com/article/5689_funding-circle-included-in-esg-index, accessed November 10, 2020.
1053. Lanyon 2019, *supra* note [1052].

available exclusively on the company's app, together with thousands of independent restaurants, or other food establishments preparing popular meals. Deliveroo since November 2016 also partners with big brewing houses, like Heineken International. Behind these initiatives is the idea of scaling the company's business in the UK, and elsewhere across selected localities in various parts of the world where freshly prepared meals delivery is likely to enjoy great potential.

Success for scaling underpins the digital double-side platform model whether use in services or product businesses. This helps to explain why Deliveroo is into the launching of Deliveroo's Editions kitchens since April 2017. Such delivery-only kitchens, known as ghost restaurants, enable them to reach customers without having to bear the high maintenance costs found in thriving city or city-like locations, and also to reduce setup costs in comparison to full-service restaurants, thereby taking the takeaway model a step further by delivering these prepared meals to the doorsteps of customers' wishes. The company uses data analytics to identify sites where customer demand for particular cuisines is likely to be high. Data analytics predict which kinds of restaurants would likely succeed. To manage the platform to achieve this business scale objectives, Deliveroo employs more than 2,500 mostly tech-proficient personnel at its London head office. William Shu and Greg Orlowski won recognition as the Best Startup Founders in June 2016, dedicated usually for technology-based entities.

Deliveroo's revenue grew 54% from GBP 772 million in 2019 to GBP 1.2 billion in 2020. These resulted in net losses of GBP 317 million and GBP 226 million for the respective years. As a consequence, the company had to lay off a quarter of its employees in April 2020. Observations for these two years in review included the rise on gross margin or rise in gross profit from GBP 189 million in 2019 to GBP 356 million in 2020; and the faster rate rise in revenue of some 65% between 2019 and 2020 for the UK and Ireland relative to revenue growths in other regions.[1054] The UK and Ireland market contributed GBP 599 million in 2020 compared to GBP 592 million from the remaining markets.

The company besides being subject to intense regulatory scrutiny needs to demonstrate that it stands apart from the food delivery business at large that has been notoriously known for its low margins and low entry barriers.[1055] The company is also exposed to markets that have been less favorable to gig-worker entities, relative to the US. Over 51% of its 2020 gross transaction value originated from the UK and Ireland, with the remainder from its operations in Europe, the Middle East and Asia. Deliveroo added grocery delivery to its platform in 2018 in collaborations with large chains like Amazon's Whole Foods, Waitrose, Marks & Spencer, Co-op, Aldi, and 7-Eleven. As many of these grocery partners maintained their own next-day delivery services, Deliveroo focuses on fulfilling smaller orders with faster turnaround. This is exemplified by its riders fulfilling orders on the platform in under thirty minutes on average in 2020.

1054. H. Chitkara. 2021. "Everything you need to know about the Deliveroo IPO". *Protocol 23/03/21.* https://www.protocol.com/deliveroo-ipo?rebelltitem=1#rebelltitem, accessed March 26, 2021.
1055. Chitkara 2021, *supra* note [1054].

The company launched its IPO on March 31, 2021. This was a widely eagerly anticipated market debut for almost a decade since Glencore went public in 2011.[1056] It was supposed to be the most significant float at the LSE, since The Hut Group went public in September 2020. It was also supposed to be UK's answer to US dominance in the global capital market for high-tech firms. Strongly positive remark also came from the Chancellor of the Exchequer that Deliveroo's entry into the LSE signaled UK's attractiveness as the preferred destination for high-growth tech firms to London.[1057] The market debut turned out to be an anticlimax when its share price closed for the day at GBP 2.87, down 44% from its pre-listing valuation of GBP 3.90 per share, or a market cap of some GBP 7.59 billion.[1058] The valuation was already at the lower end of the reduced range of GBP 3.90-GBP 4.10 against its original range of GBP 3.90-GBP 4.60 Deliveroo set earlier in response to the volatile global market conditions for IPOs. The company had then claimed that it opted to price responsibly within the initial range and at an entry point that maximized long-term value for its institutional and retail investors.

Apart from the fanfare behind the IPO, the company has been encountering persistent controversy over how it pays its drivers. It repeatedly claimed though that this matter has not been impacting it in the lead-up to the IPO. This labor issue story has yet to go away, and in fact some institutional investors have refused to participate in the offering because of this concern. The closing price of the shares for the first trading day appears to provide some early evidence of this thinking. Still, Deliveroo's listing on the LSE tantamounted to some kind of good support for London, as the competing leader for the capital market of the world, at a time when a number of scaled-up privately held tech companies have been and are exercising a lot of options, like acquisitions to bigger rivals, listing in the US market, or are pursuing the SPAC option. Tech enterprises have indeed been generating a lot of the action on the LSE at the money, with four out of five of the last IPOs valued at over GBP 1.5 billion in the last five years coming from the sector.

Irrespective of Deliveroo's debut share price situation, the labor controversy facing the company in its main UK market would likely persist in continuing to embarrass it. UK's Bureau of Investigative Journalism revealed that one in three Deliveroo couriers earn less than the country's minimum wage of GBP 8.72 for those over 25.[1059] The disparity of earnings was striking, with a cyclist in Yorkshire working 180 hours being paid GBP 2 per hour, when the company had typically said its couriers are paid more than GBP 10 an hour on the average. This kind of story persists, not merely because of Deliveroo's case, as it is an industry-wide matter. Uber, as a

1056. D. Smyth. 2021. "Deliveroo IPO: What is the company valued at ahead of its flotation?" *IG 23/03/21.* https://www.ig.com/en/news-and-trade-ideas/deliveroo-ipo--what-is-the-company, accessed April 21, 2021.
1057. The Standard. 2021. "UK hails London mega listing of Deliveroo under dual-class structure". *The Standard 04/03/21*. https://www.thestandard.com.hk/breaking-news/section/2/166760/UK, accessed March 6, 2021.
1058. I. Lunden. 2021. "Deliveroo drags on the LSE at 3.31, down 15% on its 3.90 pricing; closes down 44% on debut at 2.87". *Tech Crunch 31/03/21*. https://techcrunch.com/2021/03/31/deliveroo, accessed April 4, 2021.
1059. Lunden 2021, *supra* note [1058].

consequence of the Supreme Court decision, had to reclassify its 70,000 drivers in the UK as workers to provide them with benefits, although Uber Eats, Deliveroo's main rival, was not included in the case.[1060]

Also, it could be public pressure, rather than regulatory pressure that might help to turn the tide for food delivery drivers, as exemplified by Just Eat, another Deliveroo rival that has just switched to an agency worker model giving drivers the option to work instead under an hourly wage, rather than per ride.[1061] Investors might or might not buy in with pressures of social justice for low-paid delivery people under the gathering momentum for ESG, but the risks of legal actions, the increasing competitiveness in the industry market space because of low entry barriers, and the search for the appropriate triple-bottom-line approach would become formidable business sustainability issues going forward for the company.

Investors are though likely to focus on the economic potential for Deliveroo going forward, particularly when its Prospectus has already flashed out three prominent risks:[1062]

(1) Regulator's approach for the gig-worker model could present various challenges. In the US, California's Proposition 22 passed in November 2020 provides a clear path for Deliveroo's competitors, like Grubhub and DoorDash, but Deliveroo is for the most part operating in markets with evolving regulatory landscapes. The company is already facing legal proceedings pertaining to the status of its independent contractors in Italy, the Netherlands, Spain, France, and the UK, while wider government efforts to challenge the gig labor model are initiated in Australia, the Netherlands, Spain and Italy. The EC itself has launched consultation for the gig-economy working conditions. The company has committed toward engaging regulators and others on the way forward for the gig economy, including fighting court battles where needed and even winning in some cases. Deliveroo concedes that it might not be successful in addressing all these challenges that impact its operations all the time.

(2) The food delivery industry has dozens of deep-pocketed competitors like Amazon and relatively low entry barriers. This market dynamics pose serious threats to the company's objective to achieve financial sustainability. Deliveroo is aware that these larger competitors with relatively superior resources and business networks would be capable of undertaking extensive marketing campaigns aimed at offering discounts to consumers, increasing consumer awareness and driving website visits and app downloads and orders placed through these said platforms.

1060. Lunden 2021, *supra* note [1058].
1061. Lunden 2021, *supra* note [1058].
1062. Deliveroo. 2021. "The IPO March 2021". https://lexismarkettracker.lexisnexis.com/documents/0035/35079/167313/MT_Deliveroo, accessed April 5, 2021.

(3) While economic lockdowns and other restrictions flowing from the COVID-19 pandemic have opened up market opportunities for food delivery participants, this kind of market potential would face threats, when these restrictive conditions gradually eased, especially when the rate of vaccination gathers momentum in both advanced and developing economies. Deliveroo has expressed concerns that the company might not be able to retain their customers and other partners who started using their platforms arising from pandemic-related restrictions or increased their usage.
(4) There are further concerns that, unlike the Airbnb platform that has a defensive moat around its market niche, Deliveroo is not and is actually facing intense competition from Delivery Hero, Uber Eats, Just Eat and DoorDash doing almost the same thing, and despite the positive market environment flowing from COVID-19 restrictions all have yet to make profits.

UK's Finance Secretary stated that he was not embarrassed by Deliveroo's poor market debut price as he contended that share prices fluctuate for many reasons. He further pointed to the example of Facebook. When the company's shares started trading in the US capital market, its share price plummeted by almost half over its initial trading months, before picking up hugely thereafter.[1063]

Leaving aside the matters of market sentiments and share prices, Deliveroo going forward might need to review its business model more closely in view of the fast-changing market conditions and different regulatory sentiments emerging across different major economies of the world where the company runs its business. It might look at how other earlier dual platform operators adjust to evolving conditions for the gig economy, like what Uber is trying to do where ESG issues are concerned.

UK multisided platforms generally resemble the more pioneering and innovative US platforms, especially when raising funds from the stock market using US-style valuations, such as that deployed recently by Wise Plc in its direct listing on the London Stock Market on July 7, 2021.[1064] Tech stocks in the UK seek to replicate what had been done before, as reflected by Deliveroo's use of the dual-class structure pioneered by Facebook. Further observations are needed to assess whether this approach would help to strengthen the expected resilience for these entities. The UK platforms together with others elsewhere are now beginning to face growing ESG-related issues or tensions and would soon need to respond appropriately going forward.

1063. Reuters. 2021. " "Gosh, no!" UK's Sunak says not embarrassed by Deliveroo IPO". *Reuters 31/03/21.* https://www.reuters.com/business/finance/gosh-no-uks-sunak-says-not-embarrassed, accessed April 4, 2021.
1064. S. Gopinath. 2021. "Fintech Wise rises in direct listing in major win for London". *Bloomberg 7 July 2021.* https://www.bloomberg.com/news/articles/2021-07-07/payments-firm-wise-s-listing-bolsters-london-tech-hub-ambitions, accessed July 8, 2021.

Cross-Case Analysis

Apart from the brief comparative assessment of the differences in corporate directions of US and UK corporations, this section tries to draw out the more distinctive similarities and differences if any between corporations involved in conventional nonfinancial businesses (CNFBs), financial institutions (FIs), and digitalized business corporations (DBCs). Businesses involved in traditional retailing or manufacturing tend to observe corporate and other hard laws while claiming they adhere to best governance practices. They get into governance issues when led by domineering CEOs or domineering executive boards, as their independent board members have appeared relatively unable to address the business risks flowing from this. As a consequence, these corporations' fates could be potentially impacted by either reckless growth acquisitions without appropriate due diligence or occasions where financial reporting are distorted, as exemplified by financial reporting practices using off-balance sheet mechanisms in the run-up to the Dotcom bubble burst that led to the regulatory SOX response.

SOX did contribute to improvements in the quality of financial reporting by corporations in general. However, when big global financial institutions also used off-balance sheet mechanisms to conceal actual debt levels deployed to finance costly acquisitions without proper due diligence, these have generally led to massive financial harms for both the institutions involved and investors' interests.

The market for corporate control began operating differently, as other financial institutions became easy fodder for quick growth and quick scaling of share prices to directly benefit top echelon management and executive board members having high shareholdings. Both friendly and unfriendly hostile takeovers do not fight shy of using expensive funds and expensive offers to get targets that might not have been guilty of bad performance, or poor governance practices and therefore needing to be market disciplined by takeovers.

Compared to those CNFBs, FIs pose greater contagion risks when they overload debts to grow very fast. This has been strongly demonstrated when many FIs were found to have similarly used off-balance sheet devices that were criticized by FIs themselves in the run-up to the Dotcom bubble burst. They were thus acting against their own professional advice, and this led to the 2010 DFA in response. Banks and financial institutions themselves because of the nature of their services also double up as gatekeepers for their clientele in the sense that they draw on their professional expertise to caution and advise on any financially imprudent corporate activity, especially those linked to illicit financial flows.[1065] This also explains why banks via the Equator Principle commit to the discouraging of funding for environmental-unfriendly

1065. World Economic Forum (WEF). 2021. "The role and responsibilities of gatekeepers in the fight against illicit financial flows: A unifying framework". *WEF June 2021*. https://star.worldbank.org/sites/default/files/2021-06/WEF_Gatekeepers_A_Unifying_Framework_2021.pdf, 10/07/21; J. Payne. 2015. "The role of gatekeepers". In N. Moloney, E. Ferran & J. Payne (eds.). *The Oxford handbook of financial regulation*. Oxford: OUP.

projects.[1066] Beyond this, FIs in the US and UK are required to have a greater capital buffer as they go about their business, and this they have consistently adhered to as revealed by the yearly bank stress tests. These global banks have since been doing well, even in the present pandemic time, with most improving significantly on their profit surge. The US banks in particular are awaiting signals for higher dividend payments and other pay rewards, but they appear to have short memories for the problems they caused to society throughout the 2007-2008 GFC and how they have been bailed out by taxpayers' money then, and what they need to do further in terms of elevated cyber risk and other forms of risk threats.

In the run-up to the 2007-2008 GFC and the immediately following years, DBCs began to emerge with significant presence in the e-commerce space, followed by multisided platforms, and later by those needing to do with the blockchain technology, such as in health and financial services. Many of these have done reasonably well, as exemplified by insights from the review of four such cases. Governance practices in some of these have been though criticized over unsatisfactory disclosure practices. There are calls that governance practices in multisided platforms ought to be reexamined, using different premises, and even perhaps different metrics. This is because such platforms need to undertake their gatekeeping functions on both sides of their platforms, and there are growing concerns as to whether they could undertake both equally well. The overall observation is that, while board and external parties' oversights on the practice of corporate direction and control in theory ought to be no different, there are in practice some pertinent differences, as FIs and DBCs have particular characteristics of their own. At the minimum, FIs make money with money and have higher contagion risks on the wider economy, while DBCs also tend to generate massive and even overwhelming disruptive impacts on markets destroying in many instances less endowed rivals in their paths.

Best governance practices for these different forms of businesses are already subject to different soft laws and regulations. These have not really proven to be entirely effective, as seen in various corporate problems unraveling during the ongoing COVID-19 pandemic, where various forms of bad corporate practices abound. Take the case of global digital platforms. Google, Amazon, Facebook are increasingly exposed to antitrust and personal data breach litigations. For now, these have been hardly of real financial impact as the fines imposed against these trillion-dollar global enterprises have been well within their capacity to handle. This appears to be equivalent to what big banks are doing in terms of recurring fines for recurring money-laundering activities.

Regulatory interventions for digital platforms now in play include antitrust, content regulation, and data rights. These have yet to show the intended outcomes, while EU's GDPR provides some potential to limit the powers of big data vacuums, like

1066. M. Worsdorfer. 2015. "Equator Principles- Now and then". In M. Schwartz, H. Harriș & D. Comer (eds.). *Research in ethical issues in organizations: The ethical contribution of organizations to society*. Bingley: Emerald; P. Yeoh. 2009. "Sustainable banking: The commercial and legal aspects of private self-regulatory initiatives". *European Energy and Environmental law Review*, Vol. 18 (6): 274-288.

Google and Facebook. This should be examined more closely, strengthened, and spread around the world. When policymakers in the US, UK, the EU and elsewhere take citizens' data more seriously than they do content regulation, there is some hope. This is particularly so when more radical regulatory steps are taken to weaken these behemoths' ability to track everything people do and say, and limit the ways these platforms can use consumer data to influence social connections and political activities. It is after all the medium, and not the message that ultimately matters.[1067]

Regulatory attention might be needed for smaller tech platforms, with many understandably now seeking to enter the capital market much quicker through the SPAC route. SPACs are public-quoted enterprises with a two-year lifespan during which they are expected to locate a private entity with which to merge and accordingly bring public. Promoted as the easier, faster and cheaper way to go public than an IPO, this capital market route has grown in relatively greater popularity in 2020 and going into 2021. This is not something novel, as SPACs of many shapes and sizes have been around since the 1970s when banks started using them and by the 1980s surged in popularity. Initially, their purpose involves converting receivables/debtors into cash by converting them into securities. Investors became interested as SPACs provided provide well-designated cash flows for them and are safe when supported by various credit enhancements. Companies are enthusiastic because they could access cheaper cost credit, get effective tax shields, and the prior mistaken notion that they do not need to show these in the balance sheet, thereby helping to masquerade the extent of corporate debt or financial risk.

The problem started when Enron and others made fraudulent use of these in the late 1990s.[1068] Much has since been forgotten. Recent empirical studies suggest that the costs built into the SPAC structure are subtle, opaque, and far greater than previously believed.[1069] Also, for large numbers of SPACs, post-merger share prices fall, to further suggest that SPAC investors are bearing the cost of the dilution built into the SPAC structure, and ergo subsidizing the companies they bring public, and consequently raises the question of whether this is sustainable going forward.

Meanwhile, the impact of geopolitical-tensions that have been causing massive disruptions to world trade the last few years has worsened. These together with the ongoing COVID-19 pandemic marked by off and on-again economic lockdowns across world economies continues to drive global volatility that itself is driven by these factors, resurging debts, technology and business model disruptions, rising cyber risks, and massive climate change impact on the physical environment. Rather than mainly the governance or "G" focus in the emerging ESG paradigm, both the "E" and the "S" factors have ascended in prominence. These have not escaped the attention of the UN

1067. S. Vaidhyanathan. 2021. "What if regulating Facebook fails? It seems increasingly likely that antitrust and content moderation tools aren't up to the task. Here's what we do next". *Wired 2 July 2021*. https://www.wired.com/story/what-if-regulating-facebook-fails/, accessed July 3, 2021.

1068. S.L. Schwartz. 2002. "Enron and the use and abuse of special purpose entities in corporate structures". *University of Cincinnati Law Review*, Vol. 70 (2002): 1309-1318.

1069. M. Klausener, M. Ohlrogge & E. Ryan. 2021. "A sober look at SPACs". *ECGI Working paper No. 746/2021 April 2021*.

that happens also to be pushing the sustainability and climate change agenda in its SDGs. The Paris Agreement on Climate Change accelerated further attention on these matters. In particular, the UN PRI launched in 2015 has been latched on by the investing community in the propagation of ESG indices for use in the capital markets. Further regulatory interventions into corporate activities with regards to the incorporation of the ESG factors in the EU in particular have enhanced business environment challenges for directors who are expected to continue to lead and manage enterprises under their care under the evolving ESG disclosure regime.

The UK is likely to follow through with its own regulatory climate-related practices and ESG disclosure requirements. This is not unexpected, given that the influential BA subsequent to the findings of its four-year research initiative has advocated in September 2021 that the government must reform company law to place "Purpose" at the fulcrum of corporate activities and the fiduciary duties of board directors. The BA Final September 2021 Report drew inspiration from Professor Colin Mayer of Said Business School at Oxford University who on February 21, 2019, at the Harvard Kennedy School Business and Government Series had defined that the purpose of business is to generate profitable solutions to the problems of people and planet, but not profiting from creating problems, for either. Instead, what businesses do is make commitments to a common purpose while committing to those who help to create that purpose. The BA Final Report (BAFR) suggests that a permissive legal, regulatory, governance and reporting framework is needed to enable and motivate purposeful business, and that the UK, while having such a framework, is not having sufficient accountability for, and implementation of purposeful business. The BA report argues that few companies opted for alternatives within the law to adopt purposes promoting beyond shareholder primacy agenda. There is also inadequate appreciation of and enforcement of directors' duties under the law, while international initiatives for ensuring that companies and investors report their environmental and social impacts are very much work in progress, and lacking in sufficient focus on measuring, valuing and incentivizing CP. The BAFR advocated eight Principles for Purposeful Business. These deal with company law, regulation, ownership, CG, measurement, performance, corporate funding, and corporate investment.

The BAFR further contends that with supportive legal, regulatory, governance and reporting in place, accountability and implementation mechanisms taken together are required to deliver coherent reform. The BAFR suggests that the strengthening of accountability requires governments to locate purpose at the center of company law and the fiduciary responsibility of board directors; regulators empowered to hold directors and controlling owners to account for their CP; companies locating purpose at the center of their annual reporting and demonstrating to their stakeholders how their ownership, governance, strategy, values, cultures, engagements, incentives, financing, and resource allocation deliver it; and investors dialoguing with companies about the nature and implementation of their purposes, including evaluating their performance and future prospects against them. To promote more effective implementation of CP, the BAFR recommends companies to identify long-term committed holders of their shares; advise investors to develop the expertise needed to support long-term financing of both large and small enterprises; lobbies regulators to address impediments that might exist to companies having long-term committed shareholders; and further calls upon governments, companies, and CSOs to coinvest in partnerships based on common purpose around addressing issues, like inequality, social exclusion, biodiversity loss, climate change, and the future of work, or rather hybrid work.

Over in the US, the Biden administration has signed up to the ESG agenda, while the Business Roundtable forum comprising CEOs of leading US global corporations too have signed up to transforming their hitherto shareholder primacy model of governance to the stakeholder model in 2019. Various US federal agencies have also been entrusted with the implementation of ESG disclosure practices and with the SEC likely to come our first with its reporting rules pertaining to ESG practices.

UN Secretary-General Antonio Guterres on September 20, 2021, called on world leaders to take decisive action now to avert climate catastrophe at the emergency summit convened by UK Prime Minister Boris Johnson, pressing them for more actions on climate finance and other measures ahead of the watershed UN COP26 climate conference scheduled for October 2021 in Scotland. This comes hot on the heels of the release of the UN Framework Convention on Climate Change Report on the national contributions of all signatories to the Paris Agreement, warning that the world is heading on a disastrous pathway, and that to limit temperatures rise to 1.5 degrees, a 45% cut in emissions is needed by 2030, and carbon-neutrality by mid-century. Earlier in August 2021, the Influence Map (IM) Report "Climate Funds: Are They Paris Aligned? An Analysis of ESG and Climate-Themed Equity Funds" suggests that some 71% of ESG-themed funds, meaning those claiming to adhere to ESG criteria, are negatively aligned with the aims of the Paris climate agreements. Indeed, instead of taking more aggressive physical measures to mitigate the effects of climate change, much of the world appears to be bent on relying on the deployments of market-friendly instruments, like buying offsets against an entity's "brown" holdings, and the growing application of green financial labeling structures, including the design and promotion of hedging strategies, instead of divesting from or staying away from the funding of environmentally unfriendly ventures. This has been mooted in the Equator Principle, as highlighted in this book author's December 2009 article "Sustainable Banking: The Commercial and Legal Impacts of Private Self-regulatory Initiatives" in the *European Energy and Environmental Law Review*. Katharina Pistor argues in her March 16, 2021 article in *Project Syndicate* "Green Markets Won't Save Us" that while markets are uniquely powerful mechanisms for transmitting information and transforming behaviors, they are eventually social systems anchored on incomplete and constantly shifting foundations, thereby rendering them an unreliable guide for navigating problems of humongous proportions, like climate change. Following through with her September 21, 2021, article "The Myth of Green Capitalism" in the same journal, Pistor argues the following:

(1) The capitalism model as it currently exists is unfit to cope with the fallout from climate change. This in no small way is the outcome of capitalism itself, because the entire capitalist system is based on the privatization of gains and the socialization of losses, but ironically with some good support from the law.

(2) Various legal frameworks provide licenses to externalize the costs of environmental degradation to any entity smart enough to set up a trust or corporate entity before generating pollution. They promote the offloading of accrued environmental liabilities via restructuring in bankruptcies, besides holding emerging economies in particular hostage to global rules that privilege the protection of foreign investors' returns over their own citizens' welfare. This is demonstrated by several litigations taken up against them by global companies under the Energy Charter Treaty for attempting to curtail their carbon dioxide emissions.

(3) It has been estimated by Suzanne Goldenberg in her 2014 article that "Just 90 companies caused two-thirds of man-made global warming emissions" in *The Guardian*. Even if these companies work to decarbonize, their shareholders are likely to resist, while many board directors are also unlikely to deviate from the predominant shareholder primacy approach to avoid risking being sued for violating their fiduciary duties.

(4) As large companies and large banks advocate climate or ESG-related disclosure practices suggesting that shareholders, not managers, must induce the required behavioral change and that answers have to be sought from price mechanism, left unattended is the puzzling thought of why investors with easy exit options and lots of hedging opportunities should give attention to the disclosure of potential harm to entities in their portfolios.

(5) Over the years, debts, complex financial products and other assets have been coded to provide financial advantage to their holders, even as they addle others with enormous liabilities.

(6) Green capitalism advocates are feverishly lobbying governments to subsidize asset substitution, such that when the price of brown assets retreats, the price of green ones would ascend to compensate the asset holders.

(7) Thus, instead of addressing the pertinent questions, policymakers and regulators once again signed up to market-friendly mechanisms and instruments, as alluded to above. The fast-emerging consensus concentrates on financial disclosures as this route appears to promise change without really having to deliver it, as well as generation of employment for entire industries of consultants and advisers with powerful lobbying turfs of their own.

(8) Therefore, research findings, as alluded to above, show that a fresh wave of greenwashing is burgeoning. To fulfill the mission of greening the economy effectively on the other hand would need the canceling of all direct subsidies and tax subsidies for brown capitalism, accelerating the call for a fossil fuel nonproliferation treaty, and placing a moratorium on shielding polluters, their owners and investors from liability for environmental damages, and in the process dismantle also the worst market distortions around.

The future for environmental-friendly actions may not be that dismal, as shown by the good efforts from the BA, and more recently from the September 20, 2021 press release of the CMA "Greenwashing: CMA Puts Business on Notice: The CMA has Warned Businesses They Have until the New Year to Make Sure that Their Environ mental Claims Comply with the Law." The CMA has in this connection published its "Green Claims Code" to help businesses comply with the law. It would also be carrying out a full review of misleading green claims in early 2022 and stands ready to take action against errant enterprises. The CMA guidance sets out the following six Principles:

(1) Claims have to be truthful and accurate.
(2) Claims have to be clear and unambiguous.
(3) Claims must not omit or hide important pertinent information.
(4) Comparisons have to be fair and meaningful.
(5) Claims have to consider the full cycle of the product or services.
(6) Claims have to be substantiated.

The above would likely be followed by other initiatives not only from the UK but also from the EU, the US, and elsewhere. This is because this time around the stakes and motivations for advanced economies that drive global agenda such as the ESG are different. Previously, CSR initiatives, the predecessor of the early versions of ESG, were driven by MNCs as they grow their products and services in emerging and developing economies and other big enterprises using these mainly for marketing and public relations purposes. This time around, climate change and highly unsettling social issues, like inequality, diversity, and worksite health risks, are troubling people and livelihoods globally, but also conspicuously in advanced economies because of the fallout from the COVID-19 pandemic. Further examinations of these old and new challenges and their implications for ESG practices will be discussed in Chapter 10.

CHAPTER 10

Current and Emerging ESG Issues

This chapter grapples with the problems posed by the COVID-19 pandemic for the business sector, in particular the contextual background of a daunting and opaque business and risks environment for the immediate years ahead. Aggravating the challenge would be VUCA flowing from the global landscape that is driven by trade and geopolitical-tensions, massive global debts, FIR enabled technology and business model disruptions, enhanced cyber risk, and regulatory probes. These could generate relentless pressures, albeit differently in magnitudes to CEOs, directors, management, employees, and other stakeholders, especially in the digital and ESG era. The chapter identifies six salient CG themes drawn out from insights generated by other earlier chapters that warrant further discussions because of their substantial implications to the direction and control of business corporations. These pertain to the areas of corporate leadership; risk management; ESG challenges; the market for corporate control; workplace and workforce transformations; and the purpose of business.

The 2020 onset of the COVID-19 pandemic across the world has been a black swan kind of event, catching most economies and businesses off-guard. Most economies came under severe pressures, as markets for most products and services collapse, other than those to do with health and health-related products and services, and those driven by online technologies. Those impacted severely, such as those to do with travel and hospitality had to scramble for whatever market opportunities still available or had to redesign their business models almost overnight to ensure survival. These took heavy tolls on both management and the managed. Corporate leaders operating in severely impacted niches had their leadership skills severely tested while their legions of personnel watch anxiously for news of the fates of the businesses they worked for. The role and challenges for corporate leadership will be discussed in the first section of this chapter in the context of ESG practices.

The challenges of climate change and its economic impact, the economic lockdowns and slowdowns forced upon by health considerations during the ongoing global pandemic, the massive disruptions to business systems and prospects brought upon by the greater harness of FIR enabling technologies, together with enhanced levels of geopolitical tensions all across the world have presented daunting levels of challenges that business corporations would need to fix to ensure their own financial feasibility. Businesses now more than ever would need to manage uncertain business landscapes adroitly to sustain their operations.

These are clearly exemplified by the humongous problems posed by supply chain massive disruptions all across the world, the latest of which has to do with the worldwide shortage of microchips increasingly needed by most products and services linked or serviced by the Internet of Things (IoT). These issues and how risk management would be addressed by corporate boards go beyond financial reporting obligations, as they simply have to be executed well for corporations to stay resilient. The second section of this chapter deals with this.

It was during the stressful corona pandemic situations that business corporations were forced to reflect once again on the short versus long-term value of their respective businesses, or in other words the focus on profit maximization versus long-term financial sustainability. As the pandemic worsened, even advanced economies, like the US, the EU and the UK, with their more superior financial and health systems, had to struggle to avoid serious economic calamities. Hitherto, their respective businesses have been driven largely by the focus on the shareholder primacy approach. However, under the COVID-19 pandemic conditions, businesses are increasingly taking more cognizance of the "E" and the "S" elements of the ESG paradigm. Suddenly, the S element of worker health and related worker economic welfare variables now demand more attention as many lost gainful employments, failed to be compensated fairly, treated equitably, or were snared as casualties of the deadly pandemic. The E element too came into stronger attention, more than ever, as bad environmental conditions aggravated the bad effects of the pandemic, while the G element came under closer scrutiny when various businesses engaged in harmful online activities, deceptive practices, or simply taking reckless actions on the back of wanton corporate greed. This ESG section would thus be discussed in the third section of this chapter.

The financial calamities flowing from the earlier 2000 Dotcom bubble and the 2007-2008 GFC are supposed to have provided good lessons to corporations as to why corporate growth needed to be managed well with appropriate attention given to the nature and means of corporate growth, and not just merely quick growth to achieve higher corporate valuation, even if such is the corporate goal for many businesses. As such, the practice of corporate acquisitions and mergers with little concern over costs and suitability have brought the market for corporate control into some levels of disrepute. The usual more rational basis of growth through corporate acquisitions have been put aside by many businesses, and as the cases discussed earlier have shown, these have led to some severe financial bleeding for those doing these without proper due diligence. The theory and practice of the market for corporate control would be revisited in the fourth section to gain insights as to the better way forward for business corporations.

The fatalities, economic and health sufferings of the wider population, but in particular the twin need to maintain the necessary balance of livelihood and health safety considerations have transformed the nature and significance of worksites and workforce forever. These transformations would likely go on, even with greater deployment of vaccinations, as these changes drafted into use have largely turned out to be relevant and beneficial to many businesses. Businesses need to adjust and manage the implications flowing from these. Corporate boards would nevertheless still need to reflect further on these matters as they have serious financial and health safety implications. The fifth section of this chapter deals with these issues.

The purpose of business since the 1970s has been guided by the shareholder primacy paradigm advocated by Friedman arguing that the sole purpose has been profit maximization in the interests of shareholders. The Business Roundtable (BRT) comprising CEOs of most of the larger US corporations in 2019 responded to a series of high-profile corporate scandals by proclaiming the new direction of business as being driven by the SA where considerations go beyond those for shareholders to include other stakeholders like employees, customers, suppliers, the community and the wider society, or simply put, the ESG paradigm. This sixth section of the chapter dives into the ongoing debates between shareholder primacy and the stakeholder stewardship approach in the context of the corona pandemic era and rising climate change impact on the physical environment in terms of phenomenal loss of properties, businesses, and lives. This will be followed by a final section discussing on why and how business corporations need to reflect the implications on what matters as they digitalized more and more aspects of their business processes. More importantly, the chapter will wrap up with an assessment as to what extent these teased out themes going forward when linked or related together could give guidance as to whether laws, best business practices, or both together should lead the way in getting the direction and control of business corporations executed more effectively.

10.01 CORPORATE LEADERSHIP

The 2020 COVID-19 pandemic has spotlighted at least nine very challenging issues facing individuals and companies across the globe that businesses and policymaker would need to pay serious attention to, so as to help guide their future directions and controls of companies. This matter of corporate leadership falls under the governance or "G" of the ESG paradigm. Effective leadership processes and practices include attention on the following:[1070]

(1) Preparing for and adapting to increased turbulence.[1071] Megatrends, like urbanization, aging populations and increased interconnectedness have converged, making clear that relative stability post-World War II has given way to a period of enhanced turbulence. These suggest that corporate leaders would need to recalibrate their assumptions about constancy. They need to build adaptive capacity, robustness, and resilience deep into their businesses, and reevaluate crisis preparedness throughout their extended enterprises. It has also been increasingly clear that corporate leaders would need to see beyond their organizations by taking a true stakeholder perspective to help resolve oft-overlooked economic, healthcare, housing, justice and other inequities underlying the fragility of the existing order. This should not be seen as the last *annus horribilis* or horrible year. The challenge for business leaders is to step up to be ready for the next one.

(2) Reorienting resilience plans with sensemaking.[1072] Sensemaking is about coming up with effective routines to make clearer sense of the complex

1070. A. MacDonald. 2020. "Nine leadership lessons 2020 gave us". *MIT Sloan Management Review (SMR) 28/12/20.* https://sloanreview.mit.edu/article/nine-leadership-lessons-2020-gave-us/, accessed December 31, 2020.

1071. E.J. McNulty. 2020. "Leading through COVID-19". *SMR 06/03/20* https://sloanreview.mit.edu/article/, accessed December 31, 2020.

1072. D. Anchona. 2020. "The overlooked key to leading through chaos". *SMR 08/09/20.* https://sloanreview.mit.edu/article/the-overlooked-key-to-leading, accessed December 31, 2020.

external world. When the pace of change is that robust, business leaders would need to ensure that people update their comprehension of technology shifts, market shifts, customer shifts, and competition shifts. Updated insights into the world would help the designs of effective actions in responses. For example, those involved in the designing of innovative pharmaceutical products need to be conscious of shifts in scientific knowledge; the new ways that pharmaceutical companies are collaborating with each other; regulators and patients; and new forms of sourcing raw materials. In neglecting sense-making, businesses could be left behind.

(3) Putting care at the center of leadership.[1073] It is now becoming increasingly necessary and urgent, not just desirable to humanize leadership. Hitherto decades ways of portraying, promoting, and practicing leadership through a recipe of passion, vision, and skills would make leaders ill-prepared to recognize and alleviate human sufferings, let alone resolving the systemic issues that caused and perpetuated it. It is timely now for business leaders who care for good leadership to locate care at the center of leadership and to focus on healing and renewing relationships between institutions.

(4) Unleashing the collective genius of boards by treating board and other top-level management meetings as sacred space.[1074] No one single person is expected to have all the solutions being only human. Business leaders need therefore to surround themselves with diversity of thought. Board members should spar each other to do best thinking when engaged in strategic thinking, going beyond what the board should be doing to what it could be doing, meaning doing innovative problem-solving. This would not be about individuals having an aha moment, but more about collective genius or the harnessing of slices of genius to fulfill the collective good. This goes beyond not only sharing one's thinking but also how one is feeling and collective trust for each other's emotions to enable leadership to exercise moral imagination and courage.

(5) Fostering a culture that enables employees.[1075] The pandemic has shown that what businesses encounter have been neither fully controllable nor predictable, in part because every corporation operates interdependently with the community, the economy, and the planet. This suggests how critical it is that business leaders enable people to do their best, individually and collectively by tapping into their needs and strengths in flexible ways and actively managing a culture that supports adaptability and learning.

1073. G. Petriglieri. 2020. "Your people need care, not a battle cry". SMR 20/05/20. https://sloanreview.mit.edu/article/your-people-need-care-not-a-battle-cry/, accessed December 31, 2020.

1074. L.A. Hill. 2020. "Being the agile boss". SMR 11/08/20. https://sloanreview.mit.edu/article/being, accessed December 31, 2020.

1075. J. Howard-Grenville. 2020. "How to sustain your organization's culture when everyone is remote". *SMR 24/06/20.* https://sloanreview.mit.edu/article/how-to-sustain-your-organizations-culture, accessed December 31, 2020.

(6) Building shared understanding through dialogue.[1076] The pandemic has shown how people could be overwhelmed by too much uncertainty or social invalidation. The recreation of a shared social understanding, or a shared reality that enables people to more accurately assess data and effectively coordinate would need to be harnessed. Business leaders engaging in dialogue and developing practices to bridge the wide gap between how different people experience the same world could begin to rebuild and heal their sense of self and community.

(7) Emphasizing work-life balance for board and management teams.[1077] The good news here is that productivity is attaining unprecedented levels, prompted by broad-based transition of work from offices to homes, but the bad part is that mental well-being is suffering as a consequence, with some 94% of employees experiencing stress, since the onset of the pandemic. It is timely for business leaders to draw lessons from Microsoft and others to better structure the work-life boundaries of their teams.

(8) Giving special attention and care to work relationships.[1078] It is all about direction and balance. Against a turbulent environment, business leaders might need to keep both direction and balance by focusing on deepening preexisting, and nurturing new high-quality work relationships while pursuing experimentations. This is because high-quality work relationships help individuals feel safe and supported. Further, they could enable workers to be more discerning in their choices, anchor their organizational commitment, and foster their desires to attain high-performance standards. Through experimentation, business leaders could draw lessons on how to address the fluid needs of both their colleagues and customers.

(9) Building restorative habits into work routines.[1079] Against uncertainty and all the stress that comes with it, business leaders would need to help their teams to stay focused and positive, and this starts with holding it together personally. Business leaders could achieve this simply by adding a new routine to their day to partake in restorative activity.

The pandemic has quickened the acceleration of the convergence of the five global forces of wealth asymmetry, disruption, age disparities, polarization and loss of trust, abbreviated as ADAPT. These together have transformed the way millions of people live and work leading to various suggestions, such as alluded to above, for

1076. M. Hernandez. 2020. "What new normal should we create?". *SMR 22/07/20.* https://sloanreview.mit.edu/article/what-new-normal-should-we-create/, accessed December 31, 2020.

1077. B. Larker. 2020. "How leading companies are innovating remotely". *SMR 14/12/20.* https://sloanreview.mit.edu/article/how-leading-companies-are, accessed December 31, 2020.

1078. E. Crosina. 2020. "Disrupted and stronger: Looking in and looking out". *SMR 01/10/20.* https://sloanreview.mit.edu/article/disrupted-and-stronger-looking, accessed December 30, 2020.

1079. H. Gregersen. 2020. "Digital transformation opens new questions- and new problems to solve". *SMR 28/08/20.* https://sloanreview.mit.edu/article/digital-transformation-opens-new-questions, accessed December 30, 2020.

business leaders to reflect upon. The further positive aspects, at a time of despair, include recognizing the challenges confronting society, internalizing the lessons of the pandemic, and applying the tools and technologies at hand, including those evolving. Through this, business leaders could chart a new more adaptive course. But doing so is likely to exert a fresh set of demands and intense pressures on business leaders. Business leaders already stretched in all directions have never encountered so many dilemmas to navigate and contradictions to reconcile. Aside from managing familiar aspects of their business, they now need to cope with the most fundamental of issues: health, well-being, safety, and financial viability, accompanied by excruciating trade-offs. Solutions appear to contradict with each other, leading to the risks of decisions turning wrong. Many business leaders feel like they need to return to business as normal so as to enable their industries, communities and economies to turn around, but the very act of returning to familiar ways of working could inhibit the ability of all these entities to succeed in the future, largely because the speed of decision-making has accelerated.[1080]

Decisive and seemingly prudent actions taken a month or a week ago could quickly turn redundant, or worse, appearing reckless. In an era of endless days, medium and long-term planning feel futile, while the scope of short-term planning could be a matter of hours. Still, it is precisely such times that people look to leaders to provide stability, hope, and the path forward. The pandemic the world is experiencing thus far is the kind of crucible by which true capabilities of leaders would emerge and reputations forged.[1081] Insights drawn from analysis of the various paradoxes of leadership[1082] suggest that successful leaders of today have to embody and negotiate a set of apparent contradictions so as to thrive in the rapidly turbulent world. This further suggests that business leaders:[1083]

(1) must have the confidence to project a clear strategy, and the humility to correct course and recognize the need for change;
(2) must also be skilled at surveying the landscape perching from atop as they are at ensuring operations function well on the ground;
(3) have to remain rooted in the traditions that made their organizations great while continuously embracing innovation.
(4) need to consider what they need their workers and colleagues to achieve, and then effectively use enabling technology to help to do this in a united front.
(5) need to think globally while acting locally; and

1080. B. Sheppard & S. Anfield. 2020. "The urgent need for sophisticated leadership: The pandemic has highlighted a series of paradoxes inherent to the work of leaders. What comes next will depend on how well they face up to them". *Strategy + Business (S&B) 31/07/20*. https://www.strategy-business.com/article/The-urgent-need-for-sophisticated-leadership?gko=57cc5, accessed December 30, 2020.
1081. Sheppard & Anfield 2020, *supra* note [1080].
1082. B. Sheppard, S. Anfield, A. Jenkins & D. Zarubina. 2020. "Six paradoxes of leadership: Addressing the crisis of leadership". https://www.pwc.com/gx/en/issues/succeeding-in-uncertainty/six, accessed December 30, 2020.
1083. Sheppard & Anfield 2020, *supra* note [1080].

(6) have to demonstrate the ability to negotiate differing viewpoints toward a consensus while maintaining their integrity.

Thus, as the world seeks systematically to repair and configure from the collective trauma and damage being endured due to the corona pandemic, as well as in preparing to be resilient in future crises, there is ergo an urgent need for leaders to understand, accept and embrace these paradoxes. The first step toward recovery is to repair what has been broken, implying the need to act quickly and intelligently. Then, as business leaders adjust to new realities, they need to rethink and design the present with the future in mind. They need too to reconfigure by organizing for the future. This means they need to understand global forces, market structures, and societal needs, as well as being capable of articulating care for and understanding of their community.[1084]

The leadership role of CEOs recently came under some questioning because of the controversial actions of some.[1085] Like the late Steve Jobs, Tesla CEO Elon Musk gets controversial with regulators, owing to some of his gimmicky remarks of late. He has been described as more messianic than Adam Neumann, as allergic to rules and governance as Travis Kalanick, and nearly as narcistic as a previous US President; but somehow extraordinarily successful at turning bold visions into successful enterprises.[1086] Consequentially, Tesla stock has risen astronomically 1,000% since the summer of 2019, thereby making Elon Musk, its biggest shareholder with about 20% stake, the second richest man in the world, and still counting.[1087] Musk's accomplishments are no mean feats, as Tesla achieved five straight quarters of profits, while associate SpaceX has skyrocketed besides receiving a USD 46 billion in further funding in August 2020. Like the late Steve Jobs, generally acknowledged as the greatest executive of this era, Musk is not exhibit A for excellent CEO behavior, or exactly a paragon of exemplary CEO behavior.[1088] Conventional training workshops on role CEO modeling typically recommend senior executives model the behaviors they are seeking to encourage in their managers and workers.[1089]

Indeed, the influential role of CEOs as behavioral models also included negative behavioral patterns. Some respectable corporate researchers have alluded to this some two decades earlier when they advised management personnel not to emulate the distasteful behaviors of corporate leaders, no matter their level of success, lest risk

1084. Sheppard & Anfield 2020, *supra* note [1080].
1085. T. Kinni. 2021. "Do you really want a CEO to be a role model?". *Strategy + Business (S&B) 12/01/21.* https://www.strategy-business.com/blog/Do-you-really-want-a-CEO, accessed March 28, 2021.
1086. A. Murray & D. Meyer. 2020. "The Businessperson of the Year is ... ". *Fortune 02/12/20.* https://fortune.com/2020/12/02/businessperson-of-the-year-2020, accessed March 28, 2021.
1087. Murray & Meyer 2020, *supra* note [1086].
1088. Kinni 2021, *supra* note [1085].
1089. J. Katzenbach, C. Oelschlegel & J. Thomas. 2016. "10 principles of organizational culture". *S&B 15/02/16.* https://www.strategy-business.com/feature/10-Principles-of-Organizational-Culture, accessed March 28, 2021.

being contaminated with distasteful or nasty behaviors and passing these on to others.[1090]

Research further suggests that it is probable that the effectiveness of role modeling is anchored in mirror neurons, or specialized cells found in several areas of the human brain, discovered some three decades ago when neuroscientists who implanted electrodes in monkeys to examine how the monkeys' brains generated hand movements suddenly realized that the same neurons were firing when the monkeys ate and when the monkey watched the scientists ate.[1091] Following this, some researchers have come to view mirror neurons as the biological mechanisms by which humans unconsciously imitate the behaviors of others. This scientific-based observation lends credence to earlier thinking on this matter as alluded to earlier.

Sociologists entered the fray when suggesting the distinction between role models and reference individuals.[1092] When individuals emulate a reference individual, they copy both the good and bad behavioral traits and values without discrimination, whereas when they emulate a role model, the focus is confined to a more limited niche of behaviors and values. This would suggest that the appropriate way to learn from role models is to follow their entrepreneurial behaviors, but without following their bungling ways. Humans have been role modeling people around them since their infant days, and hence not something novel, but what could matter more is to make conscious decisions over who to imitate and why, and thus avoiding copying outright. A good start would involve making a general sense of what a potential corporate leader might need to do in fulfilling their potentials.[1093] This means trying to learn behaviors and approaches while staying anchored to their own values and personalities. Hence, the idea is not to simply emulate successful CEOs, but instead understanding how and why they have been able to accomplish certain things, and then transforming and adopting them.

The role modeling approach goes beyond the above, as the aspiring or transformative CEOs need also to think out which of their behaviors and value merit transmitting. This calls for self-awareness requiring understanding of personal strengths, blind spots, values and personality, and how these qualities of CEOs could impact others.[1094] This also involves CEOs advising subordinates to do as they say most of the time, and not what they do some of the time, such as what Musk does now and then with his tweets.

CEOs and board members functioning as corporate leaders in their respective businesses would continue to be observed on a regular basis, and more so than ever, as business corporations navigate the many risks and threats unleashed by the

1090. R.I. Sutton. 2007. "Why I wrote the non asshole rule". *Harvard Business Review 17/03/07*. https://hbr.org/2007/03/why-i-wrote-the-no-asshole-rule, accessed March 28, 2021.
1091. Kinni 2021, *supra* note [1085].
1092. T. Morgenroth, M.K. Ryan & K. Peters. 2015. "The motivational theory of role modelling: How role models influence role aspirants' goals". *Review of General Psychology*, Vol. 19 (4). https://doi.org/10.1037%2Fgpr0000059, accessed March 28, 2021.
1093. F. Murden. 2020. *Mirror thinking: How role models make us human*. London: Bloomsbury Sigma.
1094. Kinni 2021, *supra* note [1085].

COVID-19 pandemic, while indeed for some, the implementation of strong CG arrangements has become a never-ending pursuit. In reality and in practice, an effective board is more than a sum of its individual members.[1095]

In the UK, and elsewhere, CA 2006 has imposed board members with seven general statutory duties. These include acting within powers set in accordance with the company's constitutions to using those powers only for the purposes for which they were conferred; promoting the success of the company for the benefits of its members; exercising independent judgments; exercising reasonable care, skills and diligence; avoiding conflicts of interest; refraining from accepting bribes from third parties; and declaring where applicable their interests in corporate business transactions.[1096] These aside, they also have the more onerous obligations of setting corporate strategies, directing and controlling the activities of the corporations for the benefit of shareholders, including due considerations for interests of other stakeholders. It is unsurprising because of this for boards of highly successful corporations to have strong governance arrangements, especially in demonstrating strong corporate cultures, wherein board accountability is a central feature.[1097]

Board accountability, in general, is about taking responsibility for all of a company's activities and presenting a fair, balanced and understandable evaluation of a corporation's position and prospects to shareholders and other stakeholders. In listed corporations, board accountability is well structured through guidance provided by the UK CG Code.[1098] Despite not being a mandatory hard law feature, the Code together with the WP[1099] for governance in big private corporations should also be a useful resource for SMEs to help manage risk and to change behaviors.

The first step toward accountability involves a full comprehension and determination of the nature and extent of the risks within the corporation, and to setting clear channels for decision-making and communication.[1100] Transparency and disclosure would hold the key to accountability.[1101] This means that open, clear and honest reporting would help a corporation build relationships with shareholders and other stakeholders from customers, employees, to the community. The annual financial statements would enable the board to communicate the company's financial as well as nonfinancial performance appropriately through both quantitative and qualitative metrics. These would include introspections from the board on CG and other relevant

1095. E. Andrews. 2017. "Board accountability is a key element of strong CG". *Grant Thornton 09/05/17.* https://www.grantthorntonni.com/news-centre/board-accountability-is-a-key, accessed March 28, 2021.
1096. Institute of Directors (IOD). 2018. "Factsheets: Directors' duties and responsibilities". *IOD 22/05/18.* https://www.iod.com/news-campaigns/news/articles/directors-duties, accessed March 28, 2021.
1097. Andrews 2017, *supra* note [1095].
1098. Andrews 2017, *supra* note [1095].
1099. FRC. 2018. "The Wates CG principles for large private companies". *FRC December 2018.* https://www.frc.org.uk/getattachment/31dfb844-6d4b-4093-9bfe-19cee2c29cda/Wates, accessed March 28, 2021.
1100. Andrews 2017, *supra* note [1095].
1101. B. Fong. 2014. "The demand and need for transparency and disclosure in CG". *Universal Journal of Management,* Vol. 2 (2): 72-80.

management routines, and future prospects taking into account the parameters set by the unfolding business landscapes.

The FRC in the UK has highlighted some corporations' penchants for providing box-ticking-like approach, with some treating reporting obligations as a necessary task, rather than a desirable one.[1102] With the latter, it would mean providing financial and directors' reports that are comprehensive and clear while striking a balance in protecting corporate information that could be commercially sensitive. Accountability has to be embedded in a corporation's culture and be subject to review as the corporations evolve, as its risk profile metamorphosed, and as key personnel change.[1103] It has been suggested that a strong ethos of accountability, together with the deployment of relevant best practices, could help in ensuring the protection of directors and corporations' reputations. The time and expenses incurred to help improve accountability processes would give greater confidence to board members when facing scrutiny from shareholders and other stakeholders, as well as regulators, and ergo justifiable expenses.

Corporate directors could be held personally liable for financial damages suffered by a corporation that proved to be outcome of board decisions, or failure to act properly. This explains why corporate directors are provided with Directors Liability Insurance. Directors could also be held liable for various other matters, but more importantly directors should be aware of the impact of the Company Directors' Disqualification Act 1986 (CDDA 1986). This statute provides for director's disqualification from functioning as one for a period of between two to fifteen years. The following circumstances are which applications could be made for the disqualification of a director under it:[1104]

(1) The director has been guilty of three or more defaults in complying with company legislation pertaining to the filing of documents during the preceding five years.
(2) A director who has at any time become insolvent and that the director's conduct as a director of that company renders the director unfit to be concerned in the management of a company.
(3) A director is found to be guilty of wrongful trading as defined in the IA 1986.

IA 1986, on the other hand, provides for the possibility of a director being made personally liable for the company's debts under the following circumstances:[1105]

1102. C. Florio, G. Gotti & R. Stacchezzini. 2021. "New challenges in reporting on CG". *Journal of Management and Governance*, Vol. 25 (2021): 1-5.
1103. D.L. Yohn. 2021. "Company culture is everyone's responsibility". *Harvard Business Review 08/02/21*. https://hbr.org/2021/02/company-culture-is-everyones-responsibility, accessed March 28, 2021.
1104. Company Directors Disqualification Act 1986. https://www.legislation.gov.uk/ukpga/1986/46/contents, accessed November 10, 2020.
1105. Insolvency Act 1986. https://www.legislation.gov.uk/ukpga/1986/45/contents, accessed November 10, 2020.

(1) Wrongful trading. Where a company has gone into insolvent liquidation and before that liquidation occurred, a director knew, or ought to have known, that there was no reasonable prospect that the company could avoid the liquidation; then the court may declare that the director makes a personal contribution to the company's assets. A director would nevertheless not be made personally liable in circumstances where the directors could demonstrate that every step was taken prior to the liquidation to minimize the potential loss to the company's creditors.
(2) Fraudulent trading. Here, the court may also require a director to make a contribution to the company's assets where, in the course of the winding-up of a company, a director was knowingly a party to the carrying on of the company's business with the intent to defraud creditors.

Directors should also take note of the implications of the Health and Safety at Work Act 1974, especially in the wake of the COVID-19 pandemic. This statute provides for the following:[1106]

(1) It places duties on organizations and employers, as well as directors to be personally liable where those duties are breached, as directors in particular have both collective and individual responsibility for health and safety matters at the workplace. Larger public and private corporations are required to have formal procedures for auditing and reporting health and safety performance.
(2) Where health and safety offenses are committed with the consent or connivance of, or is attributable to any neglect on the part of, any director, manager, secretary or other similar officer of the organization, then the person, including the corporations, could be prosecuted under section 37 of the statute.
(3) Those found guilty are liable for fines, and in some circumstances, including imprisonment. Additionally, section 2(1) of the CDDA 1986 empowers the court to disqualify an individual convicted of an offense in connection with the management of a corporation. These include health and safety offenses. Here, no additional investigation or evidence is required, as the power for this is exercised at the discretion of the court.
(4) Individual directors could also be also potentially liable for other related offenses, such as the common law offense of gross negligence manslaughter. In such cases, gross negligence manslaughter is proved when individual officers of a company, business owners, or directors by their own grossly negligent behaviors caused deaths. The offense is punishable up to the maximum life imprisonment.

1106. Health and Safety at Work etc Act 1974. https://www.hse.gov.uk/legislation/hswa.htm, accessed November 10, 2020.

The implications of the Corporate Manslaughter and Corporate Homicide Act 2007 are as follows:[1107]

(1) Under this statute, an offense will be committed where failings by a corporation's senior management are a substantial element in any gross breach of the duty of care owed to the organization's employees or members of the public that resulted in deaths.
(2) The maximum penalty is an unlimited fine, while the court could additionally make a public order requiring the corporations to publish details of its convictions and fines.

The UK responding to criticisms from Transparency International has provided strong signals about the country's serious stance on the matter of bribery and corruption when it passed the Bribery Act 2010 (BA 2010). There are at least five key implications flowing from the analysis of BA 2010.[1108] Foremost, contrary to general criticisms, BA 2010 is not without teeth. Second, the UK's position is not particularly unique, as the US and other EU jurisdictions have broadly equivalent provisions. Third, BA 2010 contrary to criticisms does not rely on a one-size-fits all approach, as allowance is provided for the use of common sense and proportionate approaches. Fourth, significant numbers of regulated firms do not appear to implement comprehensive antibribery systems; and fifth, there are some key differences with the better globally known US Foreign Corrupt Practices Act.

To enable the UK to impose sanctions in response to serious corruption around the world, and to offer UK as the foreign investment destination of choice where bribery and corruption risks are taken seriously, the UK on April 26, 2021, implemented the Global Anti-Corruption Sanctions Regulations 2021 (the Regulations). This legislation sets out a new Global Anti-Corruption Sanctions Regime to combat serious corruption pursuant to the sanctions and the Anti-Money Laundering Act 2018 (SAMLA). The regulations would enable the UK to designate as sanctions targets (such as the targets of asset-freeze sanction and travel restrictions) persons who are or who have been involved in serious corruption around the world, defined as "bribery" or as "misappropriation of property." These two terms are defined broadly as follows:[1109]

(1) Bribery. This includes both providing a financial or other advantage to a foreign public official and a foreign public official receiving a financial or other advantage.

1107. Corporate Manslaughter and Corporate Homicide Act. https://www.legislation.gov.uk/ukpga/2007/19/contents, accessed November 10, 2020.
1108. P. Yeoh. 2012. "Bribery Act 2010: Implications for regulated firms". Journal of Financial Regulation and Compliance, Vol. 20 (3): 264-277; Bribery Act 2010. https://www.legislation.gov.uk/ukpga/2010/pdfs/ukpga_2010023_en.pdf, accessed November 10, 2020.
1109. A. Bernitsa, C. Claypoole & R. Price. 2021. "UK introduces new Global Anti-Corruption Sanctions Regime". *JD Supra 30/04/21*. https://www.jd*supra*.com/legalnews/uk-introduces, accessed April 15, 2021.

(2) Misappropriation of property. This includes where a foreign public official improperly diverts or allocates property (anything of value, including contracts, license, or concessions) entrusted to them in their official capacity, regardless of whether the property is intended to benefit them or a third person.
(3) Designated persons. The Regulations enable the UK through the Foreign Secretary to designate persons as asset-freeze targets or to impose restrictions on their entry to the UK, or both. The approach adopted is equivalent to UK asset-freeze sanctions, like the Global Human Rights Sanctions Regulations 2020. Under the asset-freeze sanction, it is prohibited for persons to:
   (a) deal with funds or economic resources owned, held, or controlled by a designated person;
   (b) make funds or economic resources available directly, or indirectly to or for the benefits of designated persons; and
   (c) engage in international activities designed to circumvent or to enable or facilitate contraventions of the assets freeze.
(4) Parallel to its announcements of the Regulations, the UK published a list of twenty-two individuals[1110] designated under the Regulations on the basis that the UK has reasonable grounds to suspect that they have been involved in serious corruption.
(5) Designated persons under the Regulations. These provide various criteria for ascertaining whether a person might be deemed to be involved in serious corruption. This would include whether they are responsible for or engage in serious corruption within the scope of the Regulations. Further, a person could become a designated person under the Regulations, where they:
   (i) facilitate or provide support for serious corruption;
   (ii) profit financially or obtain any other benefit from serious corruption;
   (iii) conceal or disguise, or facilitate the concealment or disguise of serious corruption or any profits or proceeds from such corruption;
   (iv) transfer or convert or facilitate the transfer or conversion of profit or proceeds from serious corruption; fail intentionally, or recklessly to carry out their responsibility to investigate or prosecute serious corruption; use threats, intimidation or physical force to interfere in or otherwise interfere in any law enforcement or judicial process in connection with serious corruption; and contravene or assist with the contravention of the asset-freeze and travel ban restrictions in the Regulations.
(6) The Regulations empower the Foreign Secretary to designate persons where:
   (i) there are reasonable grounds to suspect that the person is or has been involved in serious corruption, not only as alluded to above, but also as to whether they are: (a) owned or controlled directly or indirectly by, (b)

1110. Office of Financial Sanctions Implementation HM Treasury (OFSIT). 2021. "Global Anti-Corruption: Financial Sanctions Notice." *OFSIT 26/02/21.* https://assets.publishing.service.gov.uk/government/uploads/system/uploads/attachment, accessed May 15, 2021.

acting for or on behalf of, or (c) a member of, or associated with, a person involved in serious corruption;
    (ii) it would be appropriate pertaining to the purposes of the Regulations and the probable significant impacts on that person of designating them.
(7) The list on non-exhaustive factors the UK would regard when considering designation would among others, include the following:
    (i) The UK's anti-corruption policy priority.
    (ii) The scale, nature, and the impact of the corruption.
    (iii) The status, connections, and activities of the involved person.
    (iv) Collective international action.
    (v) Interactions with law enforcement activities; and
    (vi) Risks of reprisals.
(8) Implications. The Regulations as read from the explanatory memorandum demonstrate that the UK is committed to upholding good governance and the rule of law and promoting open societies, where all of these are undermined by serious corruption. The UK also showed preparedness to deploy various tools and mechanisms to curb serious corruption, including, in particular, the possibility of a sanction designation and the application of the asset-freeze restrictions under the Regulations, as part of the country's wider anti-corruption strategy, besides also complementing other instruments, like the BA 2010.

Accordingly, business corporations subject to the UK sanctions regime have to continue to take care to comply with the prohibitions on doing business with designated persons, including those newly designated persons targeted by the Regulations. Corporations operating globally that have adopted policies not to engage in activities with persons subject to international and national sanctions frameworks would need to update their policies and procedures to reflect the new UK regime, as failing to do so would likely cause reputational harm, apart from attracting legal consequences.

There have been in recent years increasing attention on whistleblowing, especially when case studies, such as alluded to earlier, showed how these have helped to expose harmful corporate scandals. Both the US and UK have reasonably reliable whistleblowing laws and regulations.[1111] Whistleblowing procedures helping to uncover wrongdoing or detrimental mistakes within corporations have become integral to good governance and risk management. They enabled potentially serious problems to be detected early, apart from providing opportunities to correct weaknesses so as to deter recurrence. In keeping aware of serious business threats and other connected issues, corporations would be able to manage market-notification obligations and more effective public relations, recognize unsatisfactory performance and avoid potentially

1111. P. Yeoh. 2014. "Whistleblowing: Motivations, corporate self-regulation, and the law". *International Journal of Law and Management*, Vol. 56 (6): 459-474.

costly employment suits.[1112] The spotlight on whistleblowing as being fundamental to good performance has been especially observed in financial services, where now the FCA has imposed the Senior Managers and Certification Regime (SMCR) requiring corporations to appoint a whistleblower's champion.[1113] The role of whistleblowing though has also gone beyond financial services. The 2016 report[1114] on whistleblowing in the National Health Service (NHS), for example, stimulated a package of reforms at ensuring that speaking up becomes business as usual within the NHS. A primary purpose of these said reforms is to imitate the open reporting culture in other safety-critical spaces, especially in aviation.

Though there is no general obligation for workers to disclose misdeeds, particular employee groups, especially those in regulated sectors, would have designated reporting obligations to their employers or regulators. As such, the Employment Rights Act 1996 (ERA), as amended by the Public Interest Disclosure Act 1998 (PIDA) in the UK, provides protection to workers making non-vindictive or corporate relevant revelations by protecting them against detrimental treatment, and in the case of employees from being terminated for disclosing particular kinds of qualifying protected disclosure.[1115] To give adequate protection, compensations for successful Employment Tribunal whistleblowing claims are without ceilings. These legal protections though refer only to dismissal or detriment in an employment context, and do not as such provide immunity from criminal prosecutions, where a whistleblower is implicated with criminal conduct. There are, however, no requirements outside financial services in the UK for corporations to have whistleblowing mechanisms.

Nevertheless, the EU Whistleblower Directive on the protection of persons reporting on the violations of EU laws has been adopted in October 2019. Under this, EU Member States would have until October 2021 among others to implement measures requiring entities with fifty or more employees to set up internal reporting channels and to respond to reported concerns within three months.[1116] An All-Party Parliamentary Group (APPG) in the UK in July 2019 recommended the launching of mandatory internal and external reporting mechanisms together with meaningful penalties for those failing to comply with requirements across all economic terrains.[1117]

1112. J. Naylor, A. Wilson, S. Casey & E. Proudlock. 2020. "Whistleblowers: The UK perspective". *Linklaters 06/02/20.* https://www.linklaters.com/en/insights/publications/2020/february/gir-the-, accessed November 10, 2020; T. Stocker, N. McInnes, L. Gillespie, S. Keen, O. Toceswicz, A. Wood & R. Devaney. 2020. "Part II: Global investigations around the world" in The practitioner's guide to global investigation—Fourth edition, London: Global Investigations Review (GIR).

1113. FCA. 2019. "The Senior Managers and Certification Regime: Guide for FCA solo-regulated firms". *FCA July 2019.* https://www.fca.org.uk/publication/policy/guide-for-fca-solo-regulated-firms.pdf, accessed November 10, 2020.

1114. NHS. 2016. "Whistleblowing in the NHS". *NHS 14/06/16.* https://www.birmingham.ac.uk/Documents/college-social-sciences/social-policy/hsmc-library/snappy-searches/Whistleblowing, accessed November 10, 2020.

1115. D. Lewis. 2008. "Ten years of Public Interest Disclosure legislation in the UK: Are whistleblowers adequately protected?" *Journal of Business Ethics,* Vol. 82 (2): 497-507.

1116. J.T. Stappers. 2021. "EU Whistleblower Protection Directive: Europe on whistleblowing". *ERA Forum,* Vol. 22 (2021): 87-100.

1117. C. Cox. 2019. "All Party Parliamentary Group. Whistleblowing: The personal cost of doing the right thing and the cost to society of ignoring it". *Patient Safety Learning (PSL) Hub 07/10/19.*

Further, the APPG has suggested to the UK government to ban the use of nondisclosure agreements (NDAs) highlighted by the #MeToo movement[1118] in recent years in whistleblowing cases.

Another recurring theme often found in conversations on business ethics are insider trading scandals. Celebrities, like talk show hosts, have been sent to prison for this.[1119] A more recent case in the US involves Lordstown Motors, an Ohio-based electric vehicle start-up. The company faces scrutiny over five of its top executives selling chunks of their company's shares a month before it revealed unexpectedly high losses.[1120] Insider trading, hitherto argued to be a victimless crime[1121] by some is where company executives profit from price-sensitive, nonpublic information, have routinely damaged corporate reputations, claimed jobs of CEOs and others, and attracted regulatory fines and jail time.[1122] Owing to this, more companies are paying closer attention to the sensitivity of material, nonpublic information their executives have access to before being publicly available and sufficiently assimilated in the share prices concerned.[1123]

Research suggests that most boards, executives and general counsel find unscrupulous trading behavior to be problematic and go to significant lengths to constrain it. Many companies, as such, are voluntarily imposing restrictions on insider trades beyond what is required by the law.[1124] They are doing this to address and mitigate legal or reputational risks. Gary Gensler, the newly appointed chair of the SEC, has recently announced that the SEC is drafting new rules to restrict the use of loopholes found in Rule 10b5-1[1125] that allows senior company executives to set up plans with a

---

https://www.pslhub.org/learn/culture/whistle-blowing/all-party-parliamentary-group-whistleblowing-the-personal-cost-of-doing-the-right-thing-and-the-cost-to-society-of-ignoring, accessed November 10, 2020.

1118. E. Otte. 2021. "Toxic secrecy: Non-disclosure agreements and #MeToo". *Kansas Law Review*, Vol. 69 (2021): 545-574.

1119. S.S. Cheng. 2011. "A corporate hero with scandal: Lessons learned from Martha Stewart's insider trading crisis". *International Journal of Humanities and Social Science*, Vol. 1 (15): 12-24.

1120. B. Foldy. 2021. "Lordstown Motors executives sold stock ahead of reporting results and before troubles came to light: A board special committee concluded the share sales 'were made for reasons unrelated to the performance of the company'". *The Wall Street Journal 21 June 2021*. https://www.wsj.com/articles/lordstown-motors-executives-sold-stock-ahead-of-reporting-results-and-before-troubles-came-to-light-11624273380, accessed June 22, 2021.

1121. R. Legendre. 2018. "Insider taring: The case against the "victimless crime" hypothesis". *Financial Review*, Vol. 23 (2): 127-142.

1122. M. Rothfeld & D. Strumpf. 2012. "Gupta gets two years for leaking inside tips". *The Wall Street Journal 25 October 2012*. https://www.wsj.com/articles/SB10001424052970203897404578077050403577468, accessed October 26, 2012.

1123. W.R. Guay, S. Kim, & D. Tsui. 2021. "Determinants of insider trading windows". *Harvard Law School Forum on CG 2 June 2021*. https://corpgov.law.harvard.edu/2021/06/02/determinants-of-insider-trading-windows/, accessed June 3, 2021.

1124. Guay, Kim & Tsui 2021, *supra* note [1123].

1125. D.S. Larcker, B. Lynch, P. Quinn, B. Tayan & D.J. Taylor. 2021. "Gaming the system: Three "red flags" or potential 10B5-1 abuse". *Stanford Closer Look Series 19 January 2021*. https://www.gsb.stanford.edu/sites/default/files/publication-pdf/cgri-closer-look-88-gaming-the-system.pdf, accessed January 20, 2021.

preestablished formula to trigger share sales at those times when they do not have access to inside information.[1126]

Companies generally identify their executives and other employees with stock compensation insiders. Other enforcement agencies, like the DOJ and the SEC, apply an expanded definition that covers external parties, including investment advisers, auditors, lawyers, and others with access to material, nonpublic, and price-sensitive information. Company insiders have access to routine information like quarterly earnings releases, and less routine events, like M&A deals or regulatory approvals for new drugs, or unanticipated losses. Board of directors and general counsel generally frame a company's insider trading policies, as senior executives may have conflicts of interest. An empirical study looking into such issues raised the following queries:[1127]

(1) How soon after each quarterly earnings announcements should insiders be allowed to trade?
(2) Upon insider trading being allowed to commence after the earnings announcement, how long should insiders be allowed to trade before the window is again shut?
(3) For what kinds of firm-specific events will an ad hoc blackout window be imposed on sider trading?
(4) Looking at whether an abnormal absence of trading in a given quarter is related to information about material future corporate events that may trigger capital market responses, like changes in share prices or trading volumes.

The study found that companies' information asymmetry concerns and external and internal monitoring mechanisms are the main reasons that go into the design of insider trading policies against the reality of most senior executives receiving the bulk of their compensations in the form of stocks, options, and restricted stocks, companies:[1128] The study's other findings include the following:[1129]

(1) Firms with greater analysts following, institutional ownership, and board independence have trading windows that end earlier in the quarter. This pattern suggests that external monitoring disciplines the strictness of insider trading policy, rather than serving as a substitute mechanism for monitoring insider trading that could allow for less restrictive trading windows.
(2) Mixed evidence of liquidity needs of executives or other employees shaping the design of insider trading windows. For instance, companies whose CEOs hold more equity tend to face stricter insider trading policies, but those companies with higher trading volumes and stock price volatility tend to impose less stringent policies.

1126. Guay, Kim & Tsui 2021, *supra* note [1123].
1127. Guay, Kim & Tsui 2021, *supra* note [1123].
1128. Guay, Kim & Tsui 2021, *supra* note [1123].
1129. Guay, Kim & Tsui 2021, *supra* note [1123].

Given the above insights and more, the researchers for the said study suggest the following going forward:[1130]

(1) Regulators take a more balanced approach. For now, regulators appear to be focused on more constraints, more disclosure and pulling back on insider trading to prevent misbehavior. Companies though have been taking their insider trading policies seriously. They do recognize their informational problems, and the liquidity concerns that their executives have, and are tailoring their insider trading practices, policies, and restrictions as a function of their current situation.
(2) The SEC requires all companies to institute insider trading policies, but their disclosure is voluntary. However, by making these insider trading policies public, all investors will know when a company's insiders are not in the market or in the markets. Corporate executives could be a little apprehensive that other investors could take advantage of that information, but that could be a relatively low cost to greater transparency.
(3) In the face of evidence that investors do not seem to quickly and efficiently impound all the information from the absence of trading during blackout periods, there is an opportunity here to educate investors to be more alert to trading absences.
(4) That even with requisite checks and balances, insider trading abuses will not vanish, but relevant research insights such as offered in the said study could help to catalyze the right approaches among companies. The Lordstown Motors case appears to be an example of seemingly brazen ways to profit from insider trading at the expense of minority shareholders. This appears to be a pretty clear-cut case of executives engaging in behaviors that they should not have, and a case where the corporate controls around insider trading are either lax or flawed or both. Such abhorrent behaviors can never be totally eliminated, but it is helpful for companies to understand the actions that their peers are taking to curb this. Research insights such as this could help triangulate toward the mapping out of best practices.

As for harms flowing from the activities of multisided and other online platforms, directors in the US would be monitoring closely the expected new laws flowing from US legislatures;[1131] while directors in the UK would have to be mindful of the Online Safety Bill released on May 12, 2021.[1132] There has been growing worries about harmful

1130. Knowledge Wharton (KW). 2021. "How companies are working to curb insider trading". *KW 6 June 2021*. https://knowledge.wharton.upenn.edu/article/how-companies-are-working-to-curb-insider-trading/, accessed June 7, 2021.
1131. T. Wheeler. 2021. "Facebook says it supports internet regulation. Here's an ambitious proposal that might actually make a difference". *Time 05/04/21*. https://time.com/5952630/facebook, accessed June 10, 2021.
1132. J. Woodhouse. 2021. "Regulating online harms". *House of Commons Research Briefing Paper 8743 28/05/21*. https://commonslibrary.parliament.uk/research-briefings/cbp-8743/, accessed June 10, 2021.

content and activity online. These included age-inappropriate content, cyberbullying, as well as materials promoting violence and self-harm. The COVID-19 pandemic has witnessed groups deploying social media platforms to spread anti-vaccine misinformation. Children's charities, researchers and policymakers have contended that self-regulation by internet companies would not be sufficient to keep users safe and that statutory regulation should be introduced. The UK government's "Online Harms Paper" released in April 2019 has taken the view that existing regulatory and voluntary initiatives to keep users, particularly children, safe need to be reinforced by a single regulatory framework to address a range of harms. Importantly, it proposed a duty of care for internet entities, including social media platforms, where an independent regulator would oversee and enforce compliance with the duty.

The initial government response to the White Paper consultation in February 2020 announced, among others, that the UK is heading toward making Ofcom, the country's communications regulator, also the regulator for online harms.[1133] The full government response released on December 15, 2020,[1134] confirms that indeed a duty of care would be imposed through the Online Safety Bill and that Ofcom would be the regulator. As expected, reactions have been mixed, with some critics claiming that the framework would threaten freedom of expression and privacy, while others raise concerns about the definition of harm. The Queen's Speech on May 11, 2021, introducing the Online Safety Bill would impose duties of care on providers of online content-sharing platforms and search services. Ofcom has been empowered to enforce compliance, as well as power to fine entities of up to GBP 18 million, or 10% of annual global turnover, whichever is higher, and including the power to block access to sites. The draft bill would also bring user-generated online scams into the scope of the regulatory framework. While the UK government claims that the draft Bill would protect freedom of expression, critics remain unconvinced.[1135]

More difficult for directors to handle though are the hardships posed by cybersecurity breaches. Attacks on major corporations and critical infrastructures have threatened the US and other economies.[1136] Colonial, the oil pipeline involved, paid the hacker, DarkSide, USD 4.4 million in Bitcoin for a key to unlock its files, even though Colonial's CEO admitted not feeling comfortable seeing money going to the hackers.[1137]

1133. Department for Digital, Culture, Media & Sport (DDCMS) & Home Office (HO). "Consultation outcome: Online Harms White Paper-Initial consultation response". *DDCMS & HO. February 20.* https://www.gov.uk/government/consultations/online-harms-white-paper/public, accessed December 18, 2020.

1134. DDCMS & HO. 2020. "Consultation outcome: Online Harms White paper: Full government response to the consultation". *DDCMS & HO 15/12/20.* https://www.gov.uk/government/consultations/online-harms-white-paper/outcome/online-harms-white-paper-full-government-response, accessed December 28, 2020.

1135. N. Lomas. 2021. "UK publishes draft Online Safety Bill". *Tech Crunch 12/05/21.* https://techcrunch.com/2021/05/12/uk-publishes-draft-online-safety-bill, accessed May 19, 2021.

1136. R. Dudley & D. Golden. 2021. "The Colonial pipeline ransomware hackers had a secret weapon: Self-promoting cybersecurity firms. Five months before DarkSide attacked the Colonial pipeline, two researchers discovered a way to rescue its ransomware victims. Then an antivirus company's announcement alerted the hackers". *MIT Technology Review 24/05/21.* https://www.technologyreview.com/2021/05/24/, accessed May 28, 2021.

1137. Dudley & Golden 2021, *supra* note [1136].

Then ransomware thereafter disrupted quickly JBS' beef plants in the US, as well as, many of its poultry farms.[1138] Both these and other attacks have raised new questions about the vulnerability of critical US businesses, with the US government urging companies to act quickly on ransomware defenses.[1139] The onslaught of attacks in recent months seemed new, with hackers holding services hostage and demanding payments that have snowballed into a lucrative business for criminal hackers.[1140]

US cities, hospitals, and even the US military had too been targeted. The crux of the problem is not simply a matter of awareness. The root of the problem though could be said to go back years, or the outcome of years of US inactions, despite the country's overall cybercrime response that involves putting agents on the ground around the world to accomplish tactical victories in jurisdictions that were otherwise uncooperative. In general, defense against such attacks fell down the list of US national priorities, even as ransomware itself boomed or took off some five years ago. The business model for these attacks has in recent times become different and far simpler. Ransomware criminals commenced by indiscriminately infecting vulnerable machines without giving due regard for exactly what they were doing, or who they were targeting. Now, the operations are far more sophisticated and the payouts more bountiful. These ransomware sponsors now reimburse specialist hackers to go big game hunting and to seek out massive targets that could pay out rich bounties.[1141]

All involved gets paid lucratively such that it is becoming increasingly irresistible, especially when the perpetuators suffer no consequences when they shrewdly work in safe harbors or in countries where they could avoid prosecutions. This applies to Russia and elsewhere with high tolerance for cybercriminals. Thus, the safe harbors for cybercriminals, together with the mostly unregulated cryptocurrency used to facilitate the crime have made this very favorable for the hackers. Also, the business ecosystem has become more connected and insecure than ever, culminating with the uncomfortable consequence that weak cybersecurity together with ubiquitous connectivity equals increasingly vulnerable targets. Hence, while everything in the US or the UK, from banks to factories, is linked to the internet, a lot of these are not adequately secured. The free market globally has repeatedly failed to address some of the world's biggest cybersecurity problems. This could well be attributable to the ransomware

1138. J. Creswell, N. Perloth & N. Scheiber. 2021. "Ransomware disrupts meat plants in latest attack on critical U.S. business". *The New York Times 01/06/21.* https://www.times.com/2021/06/01/business/meat, accessed June 2, 2021.

1139. D.E. Sanger & N. Perlroth. 2021. "White House warns companies to act now on ransomware defenses: An open letter urged them to take many of the defensive steps that the federal government requires of its agencies and contractors". *The New York Times 03/06/21.* https://www.nytimes.com/2021/06/03/us/politics/ransomware-cybersecurity-infrastructure.html, accessed June 8, 2021.

1140. P.H. O'Neill. 2017. "Ransomware is now a $2 billion-per-year criminal industry". *Cyber Scoop 21/11/07.* https://www.cyberscoop.com/ransomware-2-billion-bitdefender-gpu-encryption/, accessed June 8, 2021.

1141. S. Frankoff & B. Hartley. 2018. "Big game hunting: The evolution of INDRIK SPIDER from Dridex wire fraud to BitPaymer targeted ransomware". *Crowd Strike 14/11/18.* https://www.crowdstrike.com/blog/big-game-hunting-the-evolution-of-indrik-spider-from-dridex-wire-fraud-to-bitpaymer-targeted, accessed June 8, 2021.

crisis becoming a problem with magnitudes that no private sector could address in isolation.

While ransomware and cybercrime become increasingly national security threats with potential harms to humans, as in the case of attacks against hospitals or pharmaceutical companies, it is also becoming increasingly evident that officials from powerful economies like the US and the UK have mainly succeeded in observing the disasters unfold. But what needs to happen is a global partnership between countries and companies to take ransomware head-on.[1142] Hopefully, the momentum to alter the status quo has begun with the release of the recent major cybersecurity executive order from the office of the US President.[1143] Business corporations are now giving the matter a priority for corporate action, after no less than 290 US companies became impacted by ransomware attacks in 2021.[1144] The UK appears to take a serious view of cybersecurity risks with its national strategy 2016-2021. The UK claims that its sustained strategic investment and whole of society approach delivered thus far via its National Cyber Security Strategy has ensured that the country is well placed to respond to the changing environment and to seizing new opportunities.[1145]

Meanwhile, the US DOJ and its partners have been able to retrieve almost all of the Bitcoin ransom paid to the perpetrators of the cyberattack on Colonial Pipeline. This is a sign that law enforcement is capable of pursuing online criminals even when they operate outside the country's borders through the tracking of cryptocurrency, identifying digital wallets, and seizing funds that represent a potentially powerful tool in curbing ransomware attacks in particular. Law enforcement agencies recovered about 63.7 Bitcoin traced to recipients of a 75-Bitcoin ransom paid by Colonial that had earlier resulted in a shutdown of the country's largest gas pipeline, culminating in fuel shortages across the east coast.[1146] However, because of the declining value of Bitcoin since the ransom was paid, the US seizure amounted to USD 2.3 million, or half of the USD 4.4 million paid in ransom. The seizure further demonstrates that new financial technologies attempting to anonymize payments would not provide a cover from behind to enable criminals to profit from online thefts. Importantly, it also signals the value of early notification to law enforcement when corporations become aware that

1142. Institute for Security + Technology (IST). 2021. "Combating ransomware. A comprehensive framework for action: Key recommendations from the Ransomware Task Force". https://securityandtechnology.org/wp-content/uploads/2021/04/IST-Ransomware-Task-Force_Final_Report.pdf, accessed May 28, 2021.

1143. K. Brueninger & A. Macias. 2021. "Biden signs executive order to strengthen U.S. cybersecurity defense after Colonial Pipeline hack". *CNBC 12/05/21.* https://www.cnbc.com/2021/05/12/biden, accessed May 28, 2021.

1144. A. Din. 2021. "A new report shows that 6 ransomware gangs impacted more than 290 companies in 2021: The attacks we see in the news are only a small piece of the real number of victims, according to the report". Meimdal Security 20/05/21. https://heimdalsecurity.com/blog/6-ransomware-gangs-impacted-more-than-290, accessed June 7, 2021.

1145. Cabinet Office. 2020. "National Cyber Security Strategy 2016-2021". *Cabinet Office Progress Report Autumn 2020.* https://assets.publishing.service.gov.uk/government/uploads/system/, accessed May 28, 2021.

1146. C. Strohm & A. Sebenius. 2021. "Colonial Pipeline's Bitcoin ransom mostly recouped by U.S.". *Bloomberg 08/06/21.* https://www.bloomberg.com/news/articles/2021-06-07/doj-to-discuss-ransomware, accessed June 7, 2021.

they were targeted by criminal hackers.[1147] Still, as shown in ransomware events subsequent to Colonial Pipeline, the problem persists,[1148] especially when the perpetrators could continue to operate from safe harbor jurisdictions, like Russia. The authorities in response have been nudging businesses to take more proactive actions to give cybersecurity risk protection greater attention by fining those failing to respond adequately.[1149]

Corporate leadership actions more recently have come under investors ire over their remuneration policies. Corporate bosses are said to be behaving, as if the COVID-19 never happened. Bonuses secured in 2019, paused in 2020 as businesses sought state help, are returning quick in 2021. Shareholder stance on high executive pay appears to be hardening, with corporations from Morrisons to Cine world in the UK seeing investors' opposition. Major shareholder groups in JD Sports are preparing to vote against the GBP 6 million pay deal for its executive chairman, twelve months to February 2020, in the face of the company's refusal to refund GBP 86 million of government furlough cash being the irritant. Others coming under investors ire include Boohoo, Foxtons, and Savills. Under current UK CG rules though, a shareholder vote on executive pay is advisory, and that only a vote on the overall pay policy that must be held every three years is binding. Most of these said companies have ignored the shareholders. Thus, while shareholders' activisms generate headlines, it achieved little in practice. There is the risk of overstating the extent of shareholder opposition to indulgent top pay awards, as up to July 2021, three advisory votes pay awards have been voted down, with the CEOs still ending up getting their pays.[1150]

This issue has always been consistently challenging, given the mix of NEDs, high representations of consultants from accountancy firms, and significant representation from private equity firms in remuneration committees. Investment advisory services firms have claimed that increasing numbers of companies have sought advice on CG, but in particular, pay matters. They further claimed that through them, investors groups are having impacts, despite the high-profile cases where votes have been ignored. Worker lobby groups have sought to inject a measure of realism into pay awards, by giving workers a voice or better still a place in the company's remuneration committee. Though some progress has been achieved, as noted earlier, with some 37% of FTSE 100 companies trimming executive pay during the corona pandemic shutdown in the UK, only 13% cut their bonuses and long-term facilities that form the bulk of

1147. Strohm & Sebenius 2021, *supra* note [1146].
1148. Associated Press. 2021. "New ransomware attack paralyzes hundreds of U.S. companies". *Associated Press 2 July 2021.* https://www.usnews.com/news/business/articles/2021-07-02/new-ransomware-attack-paralyzes-hundreds-of-us-companies, accessed July 3, 2021. US cybersecurity agency, Huntress Labs, has revealed that two hundred US businesses have been hit after an incident at the Miami-based IT firm Kaseya, potentially making the latest in a line of hacks destabilizing US companies.
1149. A. Schneider. 2021. "Pipeline companies will have to report cyberattacks to the government". *NPR 26 May 2021.* https://www.npr.org/2021/05/26/1000400943/homeland-security-expected-to-issue-1st-cybersecurity-regs-for-pipelines, accessed May 27, 2021.
1150. P. Inman. 2021. "Investors turn ire on firms whose executives are set to cash in". *The Guardian 26 June 2021.* https://www.theguardian.com/business/2021/jun/26/investors-turn-ire-on-firms-whose-executives-are-set-to-cash-in, accessed June 27, 2021.

executive pay awards.[1151] The debate between the need for attractive pay awards to attract and retain talents versus the need to have worker representation on boards and remuneration committees to provide companies with a bit of real-world perspective would thus continue to haunt the boardroom corridors. Businesses could find it helpful to find the acceptable balance between these opposing views.

10.02 RISK MANAGEMENT

Risk management, including cyber security breach risk, might need an overhaul. Calamitous events are likely to take place more frequently in the immediate future, and beyond profound health and economic uncertainties. Geopolitical risks, climate change, digital revolution, and stakeholder expectations are envisaged to become more impactful.[1152] Geopolitical risks provide the backdrop for such threats, with the world becoming more interconnected as observed in supply chains, traveling and information flows, but this connectivity is under severe stress, as many corporations have not designed robust systems within the global system that would enable them to continue functioning smoothly when connections are suddenly turned off, as exemplified by the Colonial Pipeline incident. Climate change suggests massive structural shifts to corporations' risk-return profiles that would accelerate in nonlinear manners. To ensure business resilience, business corporations would accordingly need to navigate these threats, inclusive of pressures from governments and global environmental watchdogs and activists, investors and the community at large. The transformational promise from the ongoing digital revolution is also paralleled by the potential for large-scale failures and security violations with rapid seismic consequences. Increasing and escalating stakeholders' expectations for appropriate corporate behaviors suggest that businesses need to act lawfully coupled with a renewed sense of CSR that now is driven by its new ESG montage. Employees have now joined traditional social activists in raising matters about corporate policies and action.[1153] Sensing the momentum, regulator and government attention is increasingly reflecting social concerns, ranging from data privacy to climate change.

It has been suggested that to respond effectively, corporations would need to adopt dynamic and flexible risk management to navigate in the unpredictable landscape where quick change is the norm. Risk management maturity varies across industries and companies. Generally, banks are observed to have the most mature approach, followed by those engaged in businesses where safety is crucial, including oil and gas, advanced manufacturing, and pharmaceuticals. Given the spates of

1151. Inman 2021, *supra* note [1150].
1152. R. Jain et al. 2020. "Meeting the future: Dynamic risk management for uncertain times". McKinsey & Company 17 November 2020. https://www.mckinsey.com/business-functions/risk/our-insights/meeting-the-future-dynamic-risk, accessed December 28, 2020.
1153. P. Ghosh. 2021. "Activist shareholder wins two seats on ExxonMobil's board amid battle over climate change". *Forbes 26 May 2021*. https://www.forbes.com/sites/palashghosh/2021/05/26/activist-shareholder-group-wins-two-seats-on-exxon-mobils-board-amid-battle-over-climate-change/?sh=1893da2e42b2, accessed May 27, 2021.

disasters from services to manufacturing, most corporations would need to reboot and strengthen their handle on risks management so as to be more ready for the next normal.

Robust dynamic risk management comprised three core component activities. These would involve reflecting on the following:[1154]

(1) Detecting potential new risks and weaknesses in controls. These would involve seeking answers to the following questions:
  (a) How would the risk play out over time?
  (b) Is the company ready to respond to systemic risks?
  (c) What new risks lurk in the future?
(2) Determining the appetite for risk-taking. These would require seeking solutions to the following questions:
  (a) How much risk could the company take?
  (b) Could any risks be avoided entirely?
  (c) Does the company's risk appetite sufficiently reflect the company's control effectiveness?
(3) Making decisions on the appropriate risk management approach. These would require answering the following:
  (a) How should the company mitigate the risks it is taking?
  (b) How would the company respond if a risk event or control breakdown takes place?
  (c) How could the company build and strengthen institutional resilience? In this regard, corporations would need to prepare to balance focus on six dimensions, namely, financial resilience; operational resilience; technological resilience; organizational resilience, reputational resilience; and business model resilience.[1155]
(4) Overall, the following five actions could be taken by corporations to develop dynamic risk management systems:
  (a) Resetting the aspiration for risk management.
  (b) Establishing agile risk management practices.
  (c) Drawing on the power of data and analytics.
  (d) Developing risk talents for the future.
  (e) Fortifying risk culture.

The world continues to face uncertainty; unprecedented changes; rising risk levels; rising expectations of customers, employees, shareholders, governments and the community at large. Against this kind of contextual background, businesses would need to rethink their approach to risk management, so as to turn this into a dynamic

1154. Jain et al. 2020, *supra* note [1152].
1155. F. Nauck, L. Pancaldi, T. Poppensieker & O. White. 2021. "The resilience imperative: Succeeding in uncertain times: Strengthening institutional resilience has never been more important". *McKinsey & Company 17/05/21*. https://www.mckinsey.com/business-functions/risk/our-insights/the-resilience-imperative, accessed May 19, 2021.

source of competitive advantage,[1156] rather than as a malaise that merely needed curing. The UK's White Paper on Restoring Trust in Audit and CG puts a shine on the importance of business resiliencies.[1157] It has introduced an annual resilience statement among its other new reporting requirements setting out how directors are assessing their companies' prospects, including addressing challenges to their business models over the short, medium-, and long-term, and including risks posed by climate change.[1158]

Risk-taking, on the other hand, is fundamental in the generation of economic growth and welfare equity. Yet, managerial risk aversion and career concerns could generate incentives for managers to invest in ventures with less risk and potentially negative net present value. The phenomenon of risk-related agency conflict between managers and shareholders gets particularly acute as shareholder governance weakens and managerial ability to pursue self-interest or entrenchment increases. Little insights are available however on whether CG regulations that increased board independence and realigned managerial incentives to alleviate this conflict have been generally sufficiently effective. In particular, insights are helpful on whether regulatory-imposed improvements in BC and practices could discipline entrenched managers by compelling them to refocus on riskier, but more value-adding ventures. The managerial entrenchment paradigm argues that higher numbers of anti-takeover provisions (ATPs) subject managers to less monitoring and disciplinary power of the market for corporate control, culminating in managerial entrenchment.[1159] This playing it safe managerial behavior tends to be demonstrated in enterprises with poor external shareholder governance as measured by the numbers of ATPs adopted by the enterprise.[1160] To curb this risk-related conflict, the board could be empowered to design appropriate incentives and to discipline management. There is no evidence on the role of internal CG in incentivizing managers to increase investments in calculated risky ventures to benefit shareholders.

In this regard, SOX has mandated the requirement of independence of the majority of board members, and of all members of nominating, compensation and audit committees. This mandatory increase in board and committees' independence significantly reduced managerial discretion and power over previously insider-dominated boards. As such, SOX could be expected to moderate managerial preferences for risk reduction and increase value-adding risk-taking and investment even when external shareholder governance proxied by ATPs remains weak. A recent

1156. Jain et al. 2020, *supra* note [1152].
1157. Department for Business, Energy & Industrial Strategy (DBEIS). 2021. "Open consultation. Restoring trust in audit and corporate governance: Proposals on reforms". *DBEIS 18/03/12.* https://www.gov.uk/government/consultations/restoring-trust-in-audit-and-corporate, accessed March 15, 2021.
1158. E. Shimmin & K. Jardaneh. 2021. "UK's audit and corporate governance reforms: Changes afoot for UK directors". *Jenner & Block 29/03/21.* https://jenner.com/system/assets/publications/20842/original/UK_Audit_and%20, accessed March 30, 2021.
1159. C. Sundaramuthy. 2000. "Antitakeover provisions and shareholder value implications: A review and contingency framework". *Journal of Management*, Vol. 26 (2000): 1005-1030.
1160. T.A. Gomley & D.A. Matsa. 2016. "Playing it safe? Managerial preferences, risk, and agency conflicts". *Journal of Financial Economics*, Vol. 122 (2016): 431-455.

empirical study suggests that entrenched enterprises significantly increase risk-taking in value-adding ventures subsequent to SOX.[1161] The findings suggest that while having a majority independent board and fully independent audit and nominating committees does not appear to rein in CEO's risk aversion, a fully independent compensation committee could provide an effective way for incentivizing CEOs to pursue riskier investments that also add value. This implies that regulators should focus on compelling directors to frame suitable pay packages for CEOs.[1162]

Also, the outcomes of governance regulations have been found to differ across enterprises, thereby confirming the limited usefulness of one-size-fits-all policies. Positive impacts of the compensation committee's full independence are evident only in corporations with entrenched management operating in low-cost information environments, whereas a fully independent but misinformed compensation committee with scant insights into corporations inside issues might be unsuccessful in framing pay packages that could mitigate managerial risk aversion. This implies that other mechanisms need to be considered to enhance risk-taking in entrenched enterprises operating in a high-cost information environment.[1163] Until the insights from these empirical studies, some overly cautious managers tend to avoid profitable ventures with reasonable risk levels to stay within their comfort zones, but in the process deprives their enterprises of growing more profitably.

PwC's December 2020 White Paper "Risk Oversight and the Board of Directors: Navigating a Complex, Evolving Area" best sums this with the following concluding remarks:

(1) Board directors play a pivotal role in overseeing risk and keeping shareholders informed in a business environment that is becoming more complex and linked (such as played out in the convergence of the COVID-19 pandemic, climate change impacts, and various social upheavals).
(2) Board directors collectively and in designated committees should reflect on whether there is diversity of experience, thought, gender and ethnicity to bring different perspectives on risk.
(3) Crucially, board directors need to understand the company's Enterprise Risk Management Initiatives, and how they can contribute.
(4) Board directors could introspect on its own structure for oversight, and deliberate on the necessity of having a separate risk committee. They also need to assess what information has been provided to the enterprise's various stakeholders about the enterprise's risks management initiatives and activities.

1161. O. Pryshchepa. 2021. "Disciplining entrenched managers through corporate governance reform: Implications for risk-taking behaviour". *Corporate Governance: An International Review (CGIR)*, 1-24. https://doi.org/10.1111/corg.12370, accessed May 19, 2021.
1162. Pryshchepa 2021, *supra* note [1161].
1163. Pryshchepa 2021, *supra* note [1161].

(5) Finally, by studying and refining the company's approach to risk oversight, a board can deliver enhanced value to the company's primary and secondary stakeholders.

10.03 THE ENVIRONMENT, SOCIAL, AND GOVERNANCE (ESG) MANTRA

The hitherto CSR penchant has now evolved into ESG. This is now accelerating in momentum in both advanced and developing economies as a consequence of the ongoing COVID-19 pandemic. ESG constitutes a generic term commonly used in capital markets and by investors to evaluate corporate ESG activities and to determine the future financial performance of companies.[1164] ESG factors are in general, a subset of nonfinancial performance metrics used to identify matters pertaining to sustainable, ethical and CG matters like managing a company's carbon footprint to ensuring that systems are in place to ensure accountability. ESG are also factors applied in investment considerations. It is thus used in risk assessment strategies incorporated in both investment decisions and the risk management processes.

A main ESG investment notion is ESG integration. The UN Principles for Responsible Investing define this as the explicit and systematic inclusion of ESG matters in investment analysis and investment decisions.[1165] That is to say, ESG integration is the analysis of all material factors in investment analysis and investment decisions, including ESG factors. It means practitioners would be analyzing financial information and ESG information; identifying material financial factors and ESG factors; evaluating the potential impact of material financial factors on economic, country, sector, and company performance; and making investment decisions that include considerations of all material factors, including ESG factors.[1166] However, it does not mean that certain sectors, countries and companies are prohibited from investing; traditional financial factors, such as interest risk are ignored; every ESG issue for every company/issuer must be assessed and valued; every investment decision is impacted by ESG issues; or that portfolio returns are sacrificed to perform ESG integration techniques.[1167]

A main component of ESG integration is risk reduction and/or returns generation. Many investors have turned to ESG factors as another approach to identify and to avoid risk in an individual corporation or sector. Some practitioners used ESG data to seek investment opportunities. For instance, there are those analyzing automotive counters to assess how they are reacting to trends in car electrification. They factor this

1164. Adec Innovations. 2021. "What is ESG?". https://www.esg.adec-innovations.com/, accessed May 11, 2021.
1165. UN Principles for Responsible Investment (UNPRI). 2018. "What is ESG integration?". *UNPRI 28/04/18.* https://www.unpri.org/investor-tools/what-is-esg-integration/3052.article., accessed May 11, 2021.
1166. UNPRI 2018, *supra* note [1165].
1167. UNPRI 2018, *supra* note [1165].

assessment into their revenue forecasts, while others would invest in corporations with strong ESG management that are likely to outperform in the long run.

The other key ESG integration component is materiality.[1168] This is because ESG integration involves integrating only the material ESG issues that are deemed highly likely to impact corporate performance and investment performance. Where ESG issues are considered material, an evaluation of their impact would be undertaken, and where the ESG issues are analyzed and found not to be material, an assessment would not be undertaken.

ESG factors are therefore three central factors used in measuring the sustainability and ethical impact of a corporation.[1169] Though not generally financial, ESG factors have a material impact on the long-term risk and return of investments, as it is incorporated into risk mitigation, and compliance and investment strategies. Corporations using ESG standards are generally more conscientious, less risky and are more likely to succeed in the long run. Though there has been a lingering misperception that the body of empirical evidence shows that ESG considerations adversely impact financial performance, for many investment professionals, a key idea in the assessment of ESG issues is that systematically considering ESG issues would lead to more complete investment analyses and better-informed investment decisions.[1170] Responsible investors generally used ESG metrics as a framework to screen investments or assess risks in investment decision-making. Environmental factors determine a corporation's stewardship of the environment focusing on waste and pollution, resource depletion, GHG emissions, deforestation, and climate change.[1171] Social factors examine how a corporation treats people focusing on employee relations and diversity, working conditions, local communities, health and safety, and conflict.[1172] Governance factors examine corporate policies and how a corporation is governed, focusing on tax strategy, executive compensation, donations and political lobbying, corruption and bribery, and board diversity and structure.[1173]

Financial analysts have already identified topical areas for the reporting of ESG issues for use in financial analysis of company performance.[1174] These include energy efficiency, GHG emissions, staff turnover, training and qualification, maturity of workforce, absenteeism rate, litigation risks, corruption, and revenues from new products. Corporate environmental activities deemed as ESG factors include managing resources and preventing pollution, reducing emissions and climate impact, and executing environmental reporting or disclosures.[1175] Environmental positive outcomes include avoiding or minimizing environmental liabilities, lowering costs and enhancing profitability via energy and other efficiencies, and reducing regulatory, litigation and reputational risk. Social risks refer to the impact that corporations have

1168. UNPRI 2018, *supra* note [1165].
1169. Adec Innovations 2021, *supra* note [1164].
1170. Adec Innovations 2021, *supra* note [1164].
1171. Adec Innovations 2021, *supra* note [1164].
1172. Adec Innovations 2021, *supra* note [1164].
1173. Adec Innovations 2021, *supra* note [1164].
1174. Adec Innovations 2021, *supra* note [1164].
1175. Adec Innovations 2021, *supra* note [1164].

on the community. These are addressed by corporate social activities like promoting health and safety, encouraging positive labor-management relations, promoting human rights and focusing on product integrity. Social positive consequences include increasing productivity and morale, reducing turnover and absenteeism and improving brand loyalty.[1176] Governance risks pertain to the way corporations are managed. These addressed things like corporate brand, independence and diversity, corporate risks management and excessive executive compensation via CG activities like enhancing diversity and board accountability, protecting shareholders and their rights, and reporting and disclosing information.[1177] Governance positive consequences include aligning interests of shareholders and management, and avoiding harmful financial surprises.

ESG has been argued to be good for business by the financial community for various reasons. These would include the following:[1178]

(1) ESG could be an investment philosophy or it could represent the core values of companies. When businesses seek to act sustainably, they take actions in areas of interest represented by ESG, so as to provide value to their investors. ESG standards, as such, would provide another level of due diligence that would be in the best interests of shareholders. In 2006, when the UN initiated the UNPRI, and watchdogs like MSCI and Bloomberg commenced monitoring ESG, it became overwhelmingly clear that this has not been a fad, as ESG weeds out unsustainable corporations with outdated practices and harmful side impacts while also minimizing risk for investors as they invest in more responsible corporations with greater probability of succeeding in the long run.[1179]

(2) In Bloomberg's The Year Ahead Summit in New York in 2016, the key takeaways pertaining to ESG have been the following:[1180]
   (a) ESG has been a bolt-on to the side of business as usual for some years.
   (b) Businesses have reevaluated their place in ESG spaces for more than five years.
   (c) One of ESG's equivalents is the triple-bottom line of economic, social and environmental sustainability.
   (d) Sustainable enterprises are builders of profit, as well as builders of society. Stakeholders would include primary shareholders, customers, employees, suppliers, and local communities. Profit is seen as a means to develop share value, social sustainability and environmental sustainability, rather than the end-all and be-all for an enterprise.

1176. Adec Innovations 2021, *supra* note [1164].
1177. Adec Innovations 2021, *supra* note [1164].
1178. Adec Innovations 2021, *supra* note [1164].
1179. Trilinc Global. 2016. "ESG & impact investing". *Trilinc Global 21/03/16*. https://www.trilincglobal.com/esg-impact-investing/, accessed November 10, 2020.
1180. Bloomberg. 2016. "Bigger than the bottom line: Why ESG is good for business". *Bloomberg 29/10/16*. https://www.bloomberg.com/news/videos/2016-10-28/bigger-than-the-bottom-line, accessed November 10, 2020.

(e) Sustainability, ESG or responsible growth, is an investment, not a cost. The whole mission of ESG for a company pertains to sustainability and responsibility. This would mean transparency and applying ESG standards and policies to a company's operations. For example, in 2015, the Bank of America reevaluated its practices and established more businesses with renewable energy practices, adjusted its employee contracts, and promoted diversity in the bank and in senior management. These policy measures and more have helped the bank to achieve a profit of USD 16.5 billion in that year.

(f) The financial services industry predicted more than USD 13 trillion in additional growth for the renewable energy sector.

There is thus in both academic and professional environments growing evidence that investors are becoming aware of the ESG and corporate finance relationship. In a recent survey of global asset managers, some 72% of the respondents incorporate ESG principles into their investment approaches and decision-making processes; 90% believe that ESG-integrated portfolios are likely to outperform the markets and non-ESG-integrated portfolios, while some of the institutional respondents believed that there are potential challenges associated with ESG evaluation and disclosure.[1181]

Empirical studies provide support for the positive relationship between ESG and positive investment performance, with one in particular demonstrating that portfolios with a greater eco-efficiency score provide better investment returns.[1182] Some 2,200 individual studies from 1970 to 2015 identified a drastic increase in ESG studies since 2000. Research in this area though extensive and accelerating is still inconclusive depending on data sample, sample period, empirical methods, and different industries or countries.[1183] Within these 2,200 studies, about 90% of them suggest nonnegative relationships between ESG and financial performance variables, while most report the positive impact of ESG factors on corporate financial performance. Importantly, they demonstrate that the positive relationship between ESG and corporate finance is stable over time.[1184]

Drawing on these insights, another more recent empirical study while conceding that it is hard to generalize on the positive impact of ESG factors on corporate financial performance, argues that certain component and aggregate ESG variables positively impact targeted performance indicators.[1185] Also, the split regression analyses using twenty-five subsample dataset shows the positive impact of ESG factors on corporate

1181. RBC Global Asset Management (RGAM). 2018. *Charting a sustainable advantage*. Toronto: RGAM.
1182. J. Derwall, N. Guenster, R. Bauer & K. Koedijk. 2005. "The ecoefficiency premium puzzle". *Financial Analysts Journal*, Vol. 61 (2): 51-63.
1183. G. Friede, T. Busch & A. Bassen. 2015. "ESG and financial performance: Aggregate evidence from more than 2000 empirical studies" *Journal of Sustainable Finance & Investment*, Vol. 5 (4): 210-233.
1184. Friede, Busch & Bassen 2015, *supra* note [1183].
1185. S. Kim & Z. Li. 2021. "Understanding the impact of ESG practices in corporate finance". *Sustainability*, Vol. 13 (2021): 3746-3760.

profitability for enterprises with large total assets values. Within different ESG components, CG was found to be the most significant impact on corporate profitability. The positive relationship between governance and corporate profitability is only seen in enterprises with strong governance. As for the relationship between ESG and credit risks, all the ESG factors have a significant impact on credit rating. Despite social, governance and total ESG score having a significant impact on credit rating, the environmental score has a surprisingly negative effect on the credit rating, and social factor has the most significant impact on credit rating. The overall survey findings suggest that ESG factors matter in terms of corporate financial performance and risk.[1186] Nevertheless, the effects vary across different dimensions, such as ESG categories, strength and weakness, and enterprise size.

There is now a push in the US to bring ESG into the quarterly earnings call. Quarterly results still in general move markets. Questions are increasingly raised as to why quarterly earnings call focus on short-term profit taking over long-term investments in employees, research and development, and sustainability, given that ESG matters have direct, material impacts on how well businesses succeed in the long run. As such, strong arguments are made for corporations to integrate ESG wholly into their business strategies, instead of being relegating these to a sidebar.[1187] There are, however, various challenges when taking this route.

Foremost, corporations are habitually reporting on ESG via other channels, like corporate websites, CDP, annual sustainability reports, and ESG investor calls. These channels though might not require or receive the same level of analysis that earnings call disclosures do, meaning businesses might not be accustomed to reporting with rigor on ESG activities.[1188] Further, corporations generally do not monitor ESG's financial impacts, but instead report on financial and ESG completely separately. This further means that ESG data is becoming seemingly "soft" to some observers. Additionally, on quarterly earnings calls, corporations could be playing to analysts whom they assume do not care about ESG. While CEOs often claim that analysts do not ask for ESG information, analysts on the other hand have claimed that, since CEOs are not providing these, ESG matters could not have been material to their businesses. The reality is probably that there have been limited discussions and disclosures on ESG issues.[1189]

Still, corporations are making modest progress. Between 2018 to 2020, earnings calls transcripts witnessed a 671% rise in references to ESG, and a 751% rise in references to diversity, equity and inclusion (DEI).[1190] Preliminary evidence also suggests that businesses' increased discussions of ESG correlates with enhanced ESG

1186. Kim & Li 2021, *supra* note [1185].
1187. B. Tomlinson, T. Whelan & K. Eckerle. 2021. "How to bring ESG into the quarterly earnings call: Stop treating environmental, social, and governance strategies as a sidebar and integrate them into regular financial reporting". *MIT Sloan Management Review (SMR) 10/05/21.* https://sloanreview.mit.edu/article/how-to-bring-esg-into-the-quarterly-earnings-call/?og=Summer+2021+Issue+Tiled, accessed May 15, 2021.
1188. Tomlinson, Whelan & Eckerle. 2021, *supra* note [1187].
1189. Tomlinson, Whelan & Eckerle. 2021, *supra* note [1187].
1190. Tomlinson, Whelan & Eckerle. 2021, *supra* note [1187].

performance and that earnings calls are featuring more and more designated discussions on human capital, racial equity, and related DEI themes.[1191] Further, the COVID-19 pandemic has accelerated inclusions of ESG-linked disclosures. There are discussions on earnings calls about sick leave, holiday pay, hazard pay, and access to protective equipment. Despite these developments, ESG information is still not fully integrated into the discussions on core business strategy and financials that quarterly earnings calls feature. A five-part framework has been designed to help listed corporations advance these initiatives. These five steps should offer guidance in addressing challenges to better integrating ESG content into quarterly earnings calls:[1192]

(1) Laying the groundwork. Participants in earnings calls are more likely to treat ESG information more positively if they have prior encounters with ESG disclosures. This kind of familiarity could be generated by consistently sharing sustainability data through annual sustainability reports providing key performance indicators (KPIs) on financially relevant matters for the corporations, together with financial data that link its sustainability performance with financial performance. Financially pertinent ESG disclosures in the proxy statement could also be shared to foster deeper, more valuable exchanges with investors. For example, in retail, pay equity, diversity and other work-related matters should be disclosed. The hosting of ESG-specific calls with investors to inform them about how the corporation's ESG strategy delivers short- and long-term value not only deepens their understanding of the issues but also promotes connections with ESG-focused investors, building on year-round bilateral investor-engagement initiatives. Businesses could also integrate ESG content into the investor-day presentations, together with comments from the CEO and CFO on ESG strategy and the financial outcomes achieved.

(2) Adapt the earnings call schedule. To ensure that ESG issues are fully integrated, it would be helpful to provide quarterly updates on key ESG performance and ESG-driven financial measures, like revenues from more sustainable products and services, improved retention rates, as well as operational efficiencies via waste reduction. To provide participants with enhanced insights into the implementation of a company's long-term ESG strategies, the broadening of discussions of performance, and more specific details on how recent ESG performance compares with expectation, it would be helpful also to use one of the four quarterly calls to engage in deeper discussion of ESG. Another tactical way is to focus the CEO segment of the call on a high-level view of CP and how the corporation builds value by engaging stakeholders on the most material ESG matters. Nestle, for instance, features key elements of its shared value and sustainability approach on earnings calls since the first quarter of 2019. How a corporation adapts its earnings call schedule would depend on whether its ESG data is accessible on a quarterly

1191. Tomlinson, Whelan & Eckerle. 2021, *supra* note [1187].
1192. Tomlinson, Whelan & Eckerle. 2021, *supra* note [1187].

basis, and on the extent to which ESG matters are key to the strategies or products being deliberated. When ESG is being presented appropriately together with wider themes, like shared value and CP, management would be clearly signaling that ESG is a core business strategy and that it influences the way a business is being managed.

(3) Reporting on and fully explaining the return on ESG investment. Though interesting in some manner, disclosures on ESG progress in isolation would not be truly of interest to most analysts. It would be better instead to present the longer-term plan at the outset by explaining the substantive ESG matters that the corporation is managing, followed by the reporting of the financial impact of ESG initiatives. For instance, when a business is investing in a more climate-resilient supply chain, disclosing the reduction in supply chain disruptions prompted by climate-related severe weather or drought, and the revenues are retained because the company can maintain continuous supply in the face of such events. No doubt understanding the return on ESG investment would likely need new ways of gathering financial data. This means the top management office would have to collaborate closely with the ESG team and other divisions in developing and using additional financial metrics and reporting systems. There might also be the need to monetize intangibles like risk mitigation that requires creative efforts. A good example for making such calculations is the Stern Center's Return on Sustainability Investment (ROSI) methodology.[1193]

(4) Developing cross-functional collaborations. ESG-related enhanced disclosures frequently compelled functions within a corporation to collaborate closely. Investor relations and corporate sustainability functions, for example, might need to codevelop content, like the summary of a company's materiality assessment and single-slide summaries of how the company is investing to grow value by addressing the most relevant ESG matters. While the sustainability units could convey the technical specifics, the investor relations unit with better understanding of the expectations of the earnings call audience could contribute in conveying the technical content in a clear, concise format that analysts could use. The CFO and the sustainability unit, for example, could jointly identify KPIs that facilitate ROI calculations for individual ESG investments so as to show how those investments generate value for the company. Also, management could implement various steps to promote stable internal processes for collaboration. It could, for instance, convene ESG working groups or task forces that meet regularly throughout the year to sew together pertinent teams and data. Boards of directors additionally could have ESG written directly into the remit of the full board,

1193. New York University Stern Center for Sustainable Business. 2021 "Return on sustainability investment (ROSI) methodology". https://www.stern.nyu.edu/experience-stern/about/departments-centers-initiatives/centers-of-research/center-sustainable-business/research/return-sustainability, accessed May 23, 2021.

besides allocating ESG oversight to the nominating and governance committees to ensure that ESG is not missed at those key levels of strategic oversight.

(5) Treating the earnings call as theatric. Earnings calls are tightly staged, tightly managed spectacles, with the company and the analysts performing as key actors in the drama. As such, when management teams are adding ESG as a strategy element, it is vital to draw the assistance of analysts to shift part of the quarterly conversation toward longer-term ESG themes.

It would be tactical to approach the sell-side analysts, the most vocal participants on the earnings call, in advance. For example, they could be prompted to ask how the company is investing in products and services that reduce customers' GHG emissions, and how the company is forecasting the growth in sales of those offerings. Various companies like Tesla have expanded the scope of investors engaged in earnings call discussions through encouraging their retail investors to submit questions on its earnings calls by giving them a platform to do this easily and thereby widening the discussions. It needs stressing that earnings calls are events involving participants that need attention so as to advance the company's ESG goals. The orchestrating part should not be thought of as being deceptive, but as efforts to ensuring that the ESG narrative is presented in ways that inform and animate everyone present.

Finally, sound performance on material ESG matters and those matters' direct relationship to financial performance could be observed increasingly as pivotal components of the corporate narrative. Management teams, over time, could treat differentiated sustainability strategies as sources of competitive advantage.[1194] No doubt, investors would seek to quantify the value of this advantage, and they would expect management to explain that value and all of the ESG elements that contributed to it on the quarterly earnings call.

Meanwhile, for banks and other financial entities involved in the financial services business, the focus on ESG challenges bank executives to identify how ESG matters will be transmitted through the economy and impact a financier's portfolio of risks. Financial institutions have been for years fine-tuning their risks management approaches. This is because, while ESG matters may constitute macroeconomic concerns, they could have very real microeconomic consequences. ESG risks are likely to impact traditional credit, market, liquidity, operational, legal and reputational risks that financial firms need to manage through systematic and robust systems. This is the lens via which financial regulators and supervisors would evaluate banks' initiatives in this niche. Simply put, ESG is a credit, reputational and supervisory risk issue. When banks lend money and takes on credit risk pertaining to ESG sensitive assets and/or business practices, the underlying assumptions pertaining to creditworthiness and collectability might turn out to be fragile and completely overwhelming with disastrous

1194. Tomlinson, Whelan & Eckerle. 2021, *supra* note [1187].

consequences.[1195] Also, under even the best circumstances, other lender's declining appetites for financing particular kinds of activities could generate meaningful rollover risk.

ESG transition risks could also lead to cash flow disruptions that impede the ability to service debts.[1196] For instance, an accelerated transition to green energy or a significant price change on carbon emissions could lead to cash flow shocks to the oil and gas sectors from the combined impact of greater costs and lower demand. In the case of consumer portfolio, hikes in flood insurance could impact borrowers' ability to service existing mortgage debts. The average cost of insurance policies climbed by 11.03% in 2020, while the Federal Emergency Management Agency's Flood 2.0 changes could further increase this to some 25% annually for certain higher risk properties. Government responses to lobbying, regulatory and public pressures seeking to induce banks to cut their financial services to lower priority but still lawful sectors of the economy by limiting industrial activities that form the basis for loan or investment repayment could have serious ramifications for both borrowers and lenders. These public policies and regulatory risks are formidable challenges for banks and others engaged in financial services, and which are now enhanced by ESG regulating rising to the top of national and international agendas.[1197] While some may pooh-pooh such ESG matters as a mainly public relations matter, recent regulatory statements and actions demonstrate that ESG is not likely to be limited to the turf of public relations.[1198] as is apparently alleged to be the case with CSR, ESG's equivalent predecessor. This suggests that prioritizing on ESG fundamentals from the perspective of credit risk and safety and soundness could be the more effective way to safeguard banks and financial institutions in the turbulent CUVA environment.

Regulators are already seeking to frame risk management with regards to ESG as a core competency for both financial and nonfinancial services businesses. This suggests that ESG impacts on credit and revenue risks need to be handled beyond the confines of top echelons of management, and be embedded in business operations in its entirety. Particularly for banks, there are important functions to manage for the three risk lines of defense, from the business side to the compliance and risk sides to audit.[1199] While it is unclear as to how quick regulators and supervisors would be able to advance the ESG agenda going forward, it is nevertheless quite likely that a clearer set of supervisory expectations for ESG would emerge over the coming years. On a

1195. G. Brasington & B. Dudley. 2021. "ESG isn't just PR- it's the new frontier in risk management". *American Banker 7 July 2021*. https://www.americanbanker.com/opinions/esg-isnt-just-pr-its-the-new-frntier-in-risk-management?position=editorial-18campaignname=V2_AB, accessed July 8, 2021.
1196. Brasington & Dudley 2021, *supra* note [1195].
1197. Brasington & Dudley 2021, *supra* note [1195].
1198. F. Fomasari. 2020. "Knowledge and power in measuring sustainable corporations. Stock exchanges as regulators of esg factors disclosure". *Washington University Global Studies Law Review*, Vol. 19 (2): 167-234.
1199. I. Mirza. 2021. "Congress a step closer to making corporate ESG disclosure mandatory". *JD Supra 28 June 2021*. https://www.jdsupra.com/legalnews/congress-a-step-closer-to-making-9721287/#:~:text=Congress%20A%20Step%20Closer%20to%20Making%20Corporate%20ESG%20Disclosure%20Mandatory,-Isa%20Mirza&text=On%20June%2016%2C%202021%2C%20the,H.R., accessed June 29, 2021.

more positive note, businesses could find it more helpful to go beyond the compliance function for ESG matters, and to treat it more beneficially as value creating so as to use it to achieve enduring business success.[1200] Finally, the "G" or governance reform element in ESG has been found in a recent empirical study across 3,514 companies in 34 countries to boost the CSR performance of a company, or in other words, the study suggests that corporate board reforms implemented primarily to ensure finances returns to shareholders via the improving of board oversight appear to also to have a positive spillover for nonfinancial stakeholders.[1201]

Meanwhile, the EC calls the governance problem as one of harmful short-termism that damages the environment, the climate, and stakeholders. The EC on the basis of this calls for feedback on its analysis and recommendations.[1202] The EC consultation report has been criticized as follows:[1203]

(1) The report mistakenly conflates time-horizon problems with externalities and distributional concerns. This is because cures for one are not cures for the others, while a cure for one may also exacerbate the others.
(2) The report's main ostensible evidence for increase in corporate short-termism is rising gross payouts like dividends and stock repurchases. But the more pertinent measure to identify companies' ability to fund long-term investment is net payouts, or gross payouts minus equity issuances, which is lower and has left much funds available for long-term and short-term investment.
(3) When looking for other evidence for short-termism, the report selectively picks academic studies supporting its views on short-termism, but failed to engage with substantial counterpoint literature. There have been significant studies failing to detect short-termism, and some substantial studies showing excessive long-termism. Some short-termism is conceptually an unfortunate but an inevitable side effect of effective CG, and might not be first order problem needing wholesale reform.
(4) The report highlights remedial solutions that have little evidentiary support and, for some, there is real evidence that the remedial solutions could be counterproductive and expensive.

Drawing on the arguments and insights as alluded to above, suggested reformulations of the EC's recommendations have been made as follows:[1204]

1200. PwC. 2021. "Private equity's ESG journey: From compliance to value creation: Global private equity responsible investment survey 2021". https://www.pwc.com/gx/en/services/sustainability/publications/private-equity-and-the-responsible-investment-survey.html, accessed July 9, 2021.
1201. G. Hinks. 2021. "Good governance boost companies' CSR performance". *Board Agenda 5 July 2021*. https://boardagenda.com/2021/07/05/good-governance-boosts-companies-csr-performance/, accessed July 6, 2021.
1202. EY. 2020. "Study on directors' duties and sustainable CG: Final report". *EY Report Prepared for the EC B-1049 July 2020.*
1203. M.J. Roe et al. 2021. "The European Commission's sustainable governance report: A critiques". *ESGI Working Paper No. 553/2020 April 2021.*
1204. Roe et al. 2021, *supra* note [1203].

(1) The EC notes the narrow interpretation of directors' duties and company's interest that tend to favor short-term maximization of shareholders' value. The EC recommends an EU-wide formulation requiring directors to properly balance alongside interests of shareholders, long-term interests of the company of five to ten years; interests of employees, interests of customers, interests of the local communities; and importantly to identify and mitigate sustainability risks and impacts. Most parties are aware that balancing of interests has been decades-long struggle in the Europe, US and elsewhere. European and US economies, for instance, are still divided on the justifications of carbon taxes. Making directors mostly elected by shareholders and highly unrepresentative of the citizenry to resolve such problems by making complicated trade-offs might not be feasible. A relatively more effective approach could be for policymakers to decide on these issues directly, such as by incentivizing carbon avoidance by rules and a carbon tax or by promoting carbon capture via rules and rewards for burying environmental carbon, instead of expecting business corporations to faithfully implement any new rules.

(2) The report blames investors pressures for short-termism, in particular, the board's focus on short-term financial returns to shareholders at the expense of long-term value creation, shorter tenure of shares and increased frequency of portfolio turnovers, as well as the combined roles of activist investors and quarterly returns disclosures and earnings guidance. The report did consider but ultimately rejects the ideas of incentivizing longer shareholder periods and prohibitions of quarterly earnings reporting and earnings guidance for listed companies. Critics argue that the main premise behind short-termism could be faulty:
   (a) This is because holdings of long-term investors like index funds have in reality increased over the last couple of decades, even while the remaining short-term investors with little impact on CG trade increasingly frequently thereby driving up the average turnover rate.
   (b) Mainstream research has demonstrated hedge fund activisms have been increasing productivity, innovations, and key investments at targeted companies, without any signs of long-run reversals.
   (c) The impacts of earnings guidance and quarterly reporting disclosure and the consequential recommendations to extend this to every six months are doubtful and unlikely to foster longer-term planning.

(3) The allegation of corporate failures to identify and manage relevant sustainability risks and impacts and the consequential recommendation for boards to integrate sustainability aspects of risk, opportunities, and impacts into business strategy and to disclose appropriately has been questioned, given that the report's own survey findings show 85.7% of respondents declaring to having a sustainability strategy already. Though there is no harm for this, it is doubtful doing so would have more than a minor impact on global warming, unless corporate incentives are better aligned with climate sustainability.

(4) The report recommends aligning executive remuneration policy with long-term and sustainability goals by the following:
  (a) Regulating executives' ability to sell shares they receive as pay. This is already firmly established in the CG codes and national statutes of many economies as standard practice with minimum holding periods of three to five years.
  (b) Making compulsory the inclusion of nonfinancial, ESG metrics linked to a company's sustainability targets in executive pay schemes. This deserves support, but to make it work, there have to be relevant outcomes that are both measurable and meaningful. However, to be meaningful, a metric has to be one that directors can directly influence and that is already not captured by other regulations.
  (c) There is though the further question as to why society should depend on companies' executive packages instead of regulating the issues directly. Indeed, where there is a public benefit on fining errant directors and executives, then there is good justification for regulators to consider fines that are imposed directly on the miscreants, instead of depending on companies to in practice fine executives and directors who diminish the public good.

(5) The idea of including a sustainability criterion in the board nomination process, while unlikely major potential risk is questioned over the expectations it raised unnecessarily as to its effectiveness.

(6) The report recommends requiring the board to establish mechanisms for engaging with and involving internal and external stakeholders in identifying, preventing and mitigating sustainability risks and impacts as part of their business strategy. Different stakeholders would have different, often conflicting interests. This means the need to prioritize on which matters more to the company's business and so on. There is clearly the need to think through the implications.

(7) The report alleges that directors' duty to act in the long-term interest of the company is limited, and as a solution it suggests allowing stakeholders other than shareholders to bring suits in courts for alleged breach by directors of the duty of care and loyalty. This recommendation ignores the BJR in play in the US and other economies, and elsewhere implicitly recognized[1205] via various procedural hurdles to claims against directors. Different doctrinal constructions across different jurisdictions broadly yield equivalent outcomes. Comparative law experts argue that judges are ill-equipped to assess highly concentrated business decisions given the hazy standards and hindsight bias; the risk of legal error linked to aggressively enforcing the duty of care might

1205. M. Gelter. 2012. "Why do shareholder derivative suits remain rare in continental Europe". *Brooklyn Journal of International Law*, Vol. 37 (3): 843-892.

lead to corporate decision-makers to prioritize safe ventures with lower returns over calculated risky ventures with higher expected returns.[1206]

10.04 MARKET FOR CORPORATE CONTROL

The market for corporate control pertains to a takeover market where undervalued or underperforming enterprises become attractive takeover targets by potential acquirers.[1207]It only emerged as a meaningful phenomenon in 1965 when Manne coined the term.[1208] Market discipline producers reward them with profits when they generate value for consumers and punish them with losses when failing to generate sufficient value for consumers. The disciplinarians are ergo, the consumers. The market for corporate control is no different in principle, but here shareholders discipline the managers of corporations with listed shares to act in the best interests of shareholders. Where share prices of enterprises are lower than they could be if managed more effectively, they risk becoming attractive takeover targets. Bidders could vote in a new board of directors when buying up enough shares to replace the supposedly inept management team. When the new corporate leadership achieves positive results in terms of improved corporate performance and higher profits leading to higher share prices, the bidders would make profits. However, takeovers are not the only source of market discipline for enterprises, as robust competition exists in product markets, labor markets, and capital markets for equity and debt. The competition landscapes in these other markets too discipline management and corporate owners of most enterprises, whether closely held or privately held, but the market for corporate control nevertheless provides a further source of market disciplines for quoted corporations' managers.

Generally, the performance of free enterprise economies with public companies, such as those in the US and the UK, is underpinned by a robust, properly functioning market for corporate control. Listed companies are generally acknowledged as highly efficient and socially desirable, but they are said to be unlikely to perform, as well as, anticipated in the absence of an effective market for corporate control. Research insights show shareholders in companies that are targets of takeovers averaged 40%-50% above the prices at which their shares trade immediately prior to the takeover, but the empirical evidence on returns to bidders appear inconclusive.[1209] This is attributed to measurement difficulties, inherent in the latter, and the effects of regulation.

1206. R. Kraakman, J. Armour, P. Davies, L. Enriques, H. Gamsmann, G. Hertig, K. Hopt, H. Kanda, M. Pargendler, W-G Ringe & E. Rock. 2017. *The anatomy of corporate law: A comparative and functional approach*. Oxford: OUP.
1207. J. Pound. 1993. "The rise of the political model of corporate governance and corporate control". *New York University Law Review*, Vol. 69 (1993): 1003-1017.
1208. H.G. Manne. 1965. "Mergers and the market for corporate control". *Journal of Political Economics*, Vol. 73 (1965): 110-112.
1209. J.R. Macey. 2008. "Market for corporate control". In D.R. Henderson (ed.). *Concise Encyclopaedia of Economics*. Indianapolis: Library of Economics and Liberty.

The significance of the market for capital control is linked to the economics of public enterprises. These listed corporations can be more efficient at deploying capital compared to private entities.[1210] This is because public corporations enable accumulations of large levels of capital without state interference, as those companies needing vast capital to grow big and fast can sell shares to the public, as this is relatively the most efficient way to raise big capital. Second, public enterprises enable the separate roles for investors and management; and third, public enterprises enable more efficient risk-taking in the economy. However, agency costs arise when the investment and management functions are separated, especially when shareholders are dispersed. Shareholders faced an array of collective-action problems preventing them from coalescing to counter inept management, as exemplified by the rational ignorance phenomenon where the cost to an individual shareholder to ferret out corporate wrongdoing is formidably high, as well as the free rider problem plaguing shareholders. This overwhelmingly suggests that the market for corporate control is the only known remedy for all of these collective-action problems.

The market for corporate control need not always be associated with hostile takeovers, especially in market situations where combinations for scale efficiencies are the main objective. But it comes with significant financing and transaction costs. Where the motives and evidence for takeovers are in questions or in doubts, shareholders can mount the poison pill defense. These are rights freely distributed to target company shareholders that provide the shareholders with the rights to purchase shares in the target company, or the bidding company in the case of a merger, at significant discounts in price when a triggering event occurs, such as the accumulation of voting shares in the target above a designated threshold without the approval of the target company's board of directors.[1211] Such rights imposed burdensome financial penalties on the hostile acquirers, besides also diluting the voting power of the acquirer's existing holdings in the company.

As such, poison pills are effective at deterring hostile bidders because when the target company shareholders exercise their rights, they could severely dilute the bidder's stake in the targets. Poison pills are popular anti-takeover instruments, but the courts police their abuse by target-corporation board of directors. Bidders in turn could counter the impacts of poison pills through making their tender offer contingent on the target company board nullifying the pill.[1212] They could also launch a proxy contest by soliciting target shareholders' votes to remove the incumbent directors of the target company, or get institutional investors to voice disapprovals for the use of poison pills. The bigger problem though for the takeover market is not the poison pill, but anti-takeover laws and regulations. Delaware laws, for example, prohibit a hostile acquirer from completing a takeover by merging with the target for at least three years subsequent to buying a controlling interest, unless the bidder either obtains the

1210. Macey 2008, *supra* note [1209].
1211. Macey 2008, *supra* note [1209].
1212. Macey 2008, *supra* note [1209].

approval of the target company's board of directors or acquires more than 85% of the target's shares.[1213]

The main criticism against the market for capital control is its overconcentration on shareholders and not enough attention on other stakeholders, like workers and the local communities. This though is counterargued by the claims that anti-takeover laws tend to create large inefficiencies by reducing the quantity and quality of the monitoring of public companies' management, and those anti-takeover laws do not help the other stakeholders, but simply entrench target company management. Empirical insights suggest that takeovers improve efficiency, promote employment, and enhance societal wealth, and that no contractual agreement provides these other stakeholders with any say in the takeover decisions.[1214]

The other main criticism is that the market for corporate control pressures managers and executive directors to focus on short-term share price performance, rather than on long-term sustainability. This is countered by the claims that share prices reflect the present value of future returns to shareholders and are ergo a measure of the long term.[1215] Significantly, this is reflected in high share prices for tech companies without current profit metrics, but with high market potential over the long run. Further, the market for corporate control is critical to the free market, with takeovers vastly improving the efficiency of listed companies by providing monitoring and disciplines for management and by aligning managers' incentives with those of outside investors. Regulations against this often implemented at the behest of entrenched managers seeking to be insulated from this market offer no benefits for shareholders who could easily protect themselves via contract, but importantly regulations against the market for corporate control deprive shareholders of wealth and reduce the efficiency of companies.[1216]

Corporate legal theory raises the difficult question as to whether large companies should be viewed as hierarchical enclaves operating apart from markets, or as enterprises that operate within markets and ergo under market control. Mainstream views favor market control underpinned by two basic assumptions; first, shareholders possess the right incentives to mitigate the management agency problem, and second, competitive markets are intrinsically superior to institutions as coordinators of production.[1217] Recent developments on the other hand seem to support this majority position, turning shareholder empowerment from a normative aspiration to a positive reality.[1218] The rise of activist investors and hedge funds ushered in the unprecedented shift in power from managers to shareholders who become empowered to determine business decisions, especially in listed corporations.

1213. Macey 2008, *supra* note [1209].
1214. Macey 2008, *supra* note [1209].
1215. Macey 2008, *supra* note [1209].
1216. Macey 2008, *supra* note [1209].
1217. W.W. Bratton & S.M. Sepe. 2020. "Corporate law and the myth of efficient market control". Cornell Law Review, Vol. 105 (3): 675-740.
1218. M. Kahan & E.B. Rock. 2007. "Hedge funds in corporate governance and corporate control". *Corporate Governance Law Review*, Vol. 3 (2): 134-205.

The efficient market control claim examined under the lens of general equilibrium (GE) theory suggests first the pitfalls and risk of ever-increasing shareholder powers. Economic theory does not favor market control of the corporation, but rather poses a fundamental trade-off between agency cost reduction and market inefficiency. This economic insight when applied to legal theory suggests that private bargaining emerges as the better alternative to address this trade-off than would be through corporate law reforms. This further insight supports Delaware's equitable adjudication system and its flexible case-by-case approach as particularly suited to the mediation of the bargaining process between managers and empowered shareholders.

This approach argues that the market control paradigm underpinned by the principal-agent narrow partial equilibrium framework deals with one market at a time, thereby taking the market in isolation when determining the equilibrium outcome,[1219] but more importantly these unimaginative theories are advanced on the *ceterus paribus* assumption, where all things are treated as being equal.[1220] The principal-agent approach accordingly assumes that management moral hazard is the enterprise's only unresolved problem, and as such applies market control to minimize the agency cost's outcome. It follows from this that agency cost reduction and therefore greater shareholder influence always enhance efficiency, as all other things are assumed to be not only equal but also efficient. Further, under the premise that management moral hazard is the enterprise's sole problem, the principal-agency approach implies market shareholders as having better aligned incentives than managers and accordingly attach efficient outcomes to shareholder governance. However, another line of partial equilibrium analysis, namely models of management myopia,[1221] shifts the locus of imperfection from management moral hazard to the asymmetric information problem on the premise that market shareholders know less about the business of the enterprise than its managers. These models on the basis of this different assumption formally demonstrate that inefficiencies would result under greater shareholder voice.

Things, in general, have been different, during the time of separated ownership and control, when unrestrained management power was emphatically the most important governance problem. The economics of agency in that sense sufficiently addressed the emerging policy issues. Presently though, there is a different more complex practice situation to deal with, but to deal with this adequately, the corporate legal theory has to be reframed taking into account the GE's more in-depth theory of markets and prices. This would throw up three pivotal insights. First, the GE paradigm suggests that the assumption that consumer surplus would be maximized when competitive markets guide production is false, unless this also includes the complete markets assumption where everything could be transacted and parties involved

1219. M.C. Jensen & W.H. Meckling. 1976. "Theory of the firm: Managerial behavior, agency costs and ownership structure. *Journal of Financial Economics*, Vol. 3 (1976): 305.
1220. R.M. Starr. 2011. *General equilibrium theory: A introduction*. New York: Cambridge University Press.
1221. J.C. Stein. 1989. "Efficient capital markets. Inefficient firms: A model of myopic corporate behavior". *Quarterly Journal of Economics November 1989: 655-669.*

addressed uncertainty by insuring their preferences in advance.[1222] But, fast reasonable observations would conclude that markets are in fact not complete, and the moment this is factored in, GE would demonstrate that market control produces inefficient outcomes.[1223]

Second, when the GE models of business decision-making by shareholders are imposed on corporate legal theory, these models generate insights into distorted incentives arising from market incompleteness, with the shareholders making production decisions premised on idiosyncratic consumption preferences, rather than fundamental value. Also, the GE models further show uncertainty undermining market pricing accuracy, which is replicated by contemporary asset pricing theory. These together completely undercut corporate law's prevailing market control paradigm.[1224] It is though unsafe to take the premise that agency cost reduction stemming from the shareholder power shift maximizes value. Instead, this leads to a two-sided incentive problem, with one pertaining to managers that are already well covered in corporate legal theory and the other pertaining to the less examined shareholders.

GE, on the other hand, does not show how to optimally address the two-sided problem of agency costs and market inefficiency. It would appear that the shift of decision-making power to shareholders transforms the corporation into a hybrid form straddling the markets and the enterprise. There is thus far no available GE theory showing the best way of handling this hybrid corporate form. Moreover, while partial equilibrium examples show that agency cost reduction enhances enterprise value, simultaneously GE models might appear to support a policy presumption against shareholder empowerment. A closer observation suggests that management moral hazard remains in the GE framework as a source of market incompleteness, thereby impeding any anti-shareholder or pro-management presumptions.[1225]

Insights from the above analysis provide the following two recommendations:[1226]

(1) The first suggests a moratorium on policy proposals favoring either market control or management insulation. While GE's eventual normative teaching is negative, it is not necessarily irrelevant as it implies a presumption that proposals either for market control or for management insulation lack support in economic theory and have distortionary impacts in practices.
(2) Economic theory advises that in an imperfect world, off-market contracting that directs incentives in the apt direction provides a more promising road to productive efficiency than does market control. The more promising bargaining but not necessarily efficient bargaining theory has it that the party with bargaining power controls the outcome whether or not the outcome is optimal. This implies that the possibility of contracting does not preclude

1222. G. Debreu. 1959. *Theory of value: An axiomatic analysis of economic equilibrium*. New Haven: Yale University Press.
1223. Y. Lengwiler. 2006. *Microfoundations of financial economics: An introduction to general equilibrium asset pricing*. New Jersey: Princeton University Press.
1224. Bratton & Sepe 2020, *supra* note [1217].
1225. Bratton & Sepe 2020, *supra* note [1217].
1226. Bratton & Sepe 2020, *supra* note [1217].

> suboptimal results, as it cannot exclude the opportunistic abuse of bargaining powers by either empowered shareholders or managers. The challenge today for corporate law is ergo to avoid distortionary dominance for the bargaining process by either contracting party.

Extending from the above recommendations, it has been predicted that corporate law as interpreted and enforced in Delaware, the most popular home for many US enterprises, is well placed to face the challenges posed by the hybrid corporation. Rather than imposing maximizing directives premised on economic theory, that have instead left the basic alignment of the parties' entitlements to the parties' own bargaining process, resolving problems emerging via a pragmatic process of equitable adjudication merits attention. Delaware chancellors, as equity adjudicators, enjoy wide latitude to shape ever-changing economic scenarios and legal relationships. In view of the insights alluded to above, this flexible approach could be justified as economically astute.[1227]

In the current context, economic theory poses a fundamental trade-off between market inefficiency and agency costs; and presently under this, there is no template for efficient corporate law reforms. Given this, there is good argument for a fresh start for the theory of the firm.[1228] While the agency theory's moral hazard account is no longer adequate to depict the more important problems in CG, there could be no reversion to the earlier notion of corporations as hierarchies operating outside of markets, as market forces now direct business decisions at the highest hierarchy. The future appears to lie with the economics of mechanisms design that could help in answering several questions to do with the efficient structuring of the corporate bargaining process. These questions include matters of optimal board decision-making, shareholder biases, conditions that could catalyze such biases, manner of internalizing externalities that incomplete markets cannot internalize, and on how to generate managerial incentives that are compatible with shareholder interest as well as with interest of the community as a whole.[1229]

As the world struggles to find answers for the dilemma that corporations faced, it is helpful also to understand why financialization and financiers blew up the postwar industrial corporation to considerably reduce the role of the postwar managerial class. That could begin with an understanding of the character of the post-1982 business expansion at investment bank Drexel Burnham Lambert. At the time, the new preaching of shareholder value has insisted that managers act in the pecuniary interests of shareholders, frequently meaning cutting wages, foregoing long-term investments, or disposing of assets, all to be undertaken so as to achieve enormous profits. There were no hard laws saying that US enterprises must be motivated to maximize short-term profit before this with most postwar industrial enterprises focusing on

1227. Bratton & Sepe 2020, *supra* note [1217].
1228. P. Walker. 2021. *Foundations of organisational economics: Histories of the predictions of the firm and production. Abingdon: Routledge*; Bratton & Sepe 2020, *supra* note [1217].
1229. Bratton & Sepe 2020, *supra* note [1217].

long-term growth metrics, but the shareholder value revolution in the 1980s transformed prevailing corporate share market prices as the metric of corporate success.[1230]

It was a series of at times hostile corporate takeovers that gave prominence and merits for the shareholder value paradigm that commenced in the late 1970s when the oil wealth-minted class with surpluses from the high prices of the then oil shock embraced the notion that the shares of large diversified energy entities were trading below the value of their physical assets.[1231] For instance, Texas oilman Boone Pickens tried convincing the majority of the Gulf Oil shareholders the idea of enhancing shareholder value, by stripping off assets unrelated to the oil business while returning cash to the shareholders, and following up with offering the stripped-down oil entity back to the public, with the goal of fetching a higher value. In the end, Pickens never acquired majority control, and instead management bought back the shares that Pickens and his merry allies accumulated at prices above the going market rate, way above what this group had originally paid.

Subsequently, Pickens, Houston oilman Oscar Wyatt and New Yorker Carl Icahn among other corporate raiders applied this strategy successfully. They were largely able to succeed because institutional investors, especially public and private pension funds, joined their quests. This saw the critical economic sites shifting from income to property, where the working class used debts to compensate for flagging pay and to sustain consumption, while these said leveraged buyouts demonstrated how property owners could employ debt to leverage up their profits from their investments. All in, relative income growth shifted away from labor to capital. Shareholder value became the mantra for a wave of leveraged corporate buyouts and associated M&A.

Merger guidelines changed in 1982, where the DOJ changed the standard for evaluating merger from the goal of preserving and promoting market structures conducive to competition to only whether its outcome would or would not maintain prices above competitive levels. This signaled the growing influence of the University of Chicago Law and Economics movement, arguing that the only relevant standard for antitrust enforcement was consumer welfare or lower prices, not market structure or barriers to entry. The courts began stripping antitrust prescriptions against vertical and horizontal mergers out of the law, and as such between 1985 and 1989, there were many leveraged buyouts in excess of USD 250 billion.[1232] What made the buyout leveraged was the newly burgeoning debt market in junk bonds driven by investment bankers, like Drexel Burnham Lambert.[1233] After the investor groups accumulated large enough stock position, they offered corporate boards a bid to buy out the company and take possession and ownership of it.

Thence, publicly traded corporations became privately owned. This entailed the impacted corporations raising cash to meet the debt obligations. This meant selling physical assets and aggressive slimming of operating costs. It eventually led to vertical and horizontal disintegration of the postwar industrial corporation, more purging of

1230. J. Levy. 2021. *Ages of American Capitalism*. New York: Random House.
1231. Levy 2021, *supra* note [1230].
1232. Levy 2021, *supra* note [1230].
1233. Levy 2021, *supra* note [1230].

fixed capital and more hemorrhaging of blue-collar jobs, before being sold back to public capital markets, in anticipation that the new rising share price had justified the original acquisitions. Rightful questions like whether even if the share price rose this could be taken to necessarily mean that the underlying company was more valuable than it had been before the leveraged buyout was seldom if ever raised at the time.[1234]

The shareholder value mantra surged in the 1990s, in the 2000s and even into the FIR era, where early digitalized platform companies became endeared species in the capital markets, followed not too far off by so-called tech start-ups where corporate valuation need not necessarily have to be based on past profit track records, but high market growth potential would do, with the banking and capital market communities giving strong support. This of late extended into the use of special purpose acquisition companies (SPACs), enabling yet to be profitable entities becoming listed vehicles compared to the conventional IPO routes that would likely require more public and regulatory scrutiny. This penchant for relentless enhancement of shareholder value benefited financially both the principal and agent, thereby giving support to the thesis of alignment of shareholder and management interest, and importantly for the good of the entire corporation.

As a series of high-profile corporate scandals broke out in recent years in both the US and the UK, corporate leaders under the banner of the respectable Business Roundtable in late 2019 voiced out for businesses to transform more into ESG-led corporations, or led by the stakeholder paradigm. The breaking out of the COVID-19 pandemic in early 2020 buttressed this newfound aspiration, as many businesses, other than the tech platforms and those involved in personal protection equipment (PPE), sought to stay afloat and to take greater care of employee welfare.

In this kind of scenario, the market for corporate control thesis became increasingly controversial. Takeovers that were supposed to discipline corporate ineptitude are guided by takeover codes, such as found in the UK. On October 27, 2020, the UKTP published consultation on various significant changes to the treatment of condition and preconditions to offers and the timetable that has to be adhered to under the UK Takeover Code.[1235] The Panel following consultation closure on January 15, 2021, would issue a RS in the Spring of 2021. When revised, "The Code is designed to ensure that the shareholders in an offeree company are treated fairly and are not denied an opportunity to decide on the merits of a takeover and that shareholders in the offeree company of the same class are afforded equivalent treatment by the offeror. The Code also provides an orderly framework within which takeovers are conducted. In addition, it is designed to promote in conjunction with other regulatory regimes, the integrity of the financial markets."[1236]

The Code is further designed to strike an appropriate balance between the interests of the offeror, or offerors in a competitive context, the offeree, the company,

1234. Levy 2021, *supra* note [1230].
1235. Takeover Panel. 2020. "The Takeover Panel: Public Consultation by the Code Committee". *The Takeover Panel PCP 2020/1, 27 October 2020.* https://www.thetakeoverpanel.org.uk/wp-content/uploads/, accessed November 10, 2020.
1236. Section 2(a) of the Takeover Code.

and the shareholders in the offeree company. This means taking into account the requirement of General Principle 2 that "The holders of the securities of an offeree company must have sufficient time and information to enable them to reach properly informed decision on the bid"; and General Principle 8 that "An offeree company must not be hindered in the conduct of the affairs for longer than is reasonable by a bid for the securities." Changes to the Code would entail the following:[1237]

(1) The renaming of key events under and reordering of the Code timetable for contractual offers, including a new procedure for suspending the timetable to address delays in getting official authorizations or regulatory clearances.
(2) The removing of the special treatment that the Code has historically provided for the impact on offers of Phase 2 references and decisions by the UK CMA, or the EC, both with regards to timetable suspension and the inclusion and invoking of conditions and preconditions.
(3) The launching of a major extension in the availability of withdrawal rights for target shareholders having already accepted an offer prior to it becoming unconditional, in that they will be exercisable from the outset of the offer.

The Takeover Panel has published final text changes to the Takeover Code and confirmed that they would take effect on July 5, 2021. The key changes entail the following:[1238]

(1) A single date for satisfaction of all conditions.
(2) Acceptance condition last to be satisfied.
(3) Long-stop dates for contractual offers.
(4) Acceleration statements through which a bidder would be able to bring forward the unconditional date and set a shorter timescale in which all conditions must be satisfied or waived.
(5) Acceptance condition invocation notices that provide more certainty for target shareholders, thereby replacing the current system of closing dates that cause the offer to lapse without having to forewarn shareholders.
(6) New prescribed dates by which a bidder will be required to announce levels of acceptance via a regulatory information service.
(7) Target company shareholders accepting an offer will be able to withdraw their acceptance from the outset of the offer until such time as the acceptance condition is satisfied, the offer lapses, or is withdrawn.
(8) A new regime is set out for addressing any competition and other regulatory authorizations and clearances that cannot be obtained within the standard sixty-day Code timetable.

1237. L. Levy, et al. 2020. "Overhaul proposed to UK Takeover Code: Offer timetable and offer conditions". *Shearman & Stirling 27 November 2020.* https://www.shearman.com/perspectives/2020/11/overhaul-proposed-to, accessed November 29, 2020.
1238. D. Acres, et al. 2021. "Significant changes to the UK takeover Code confirmed". Dentons 23 April 2021. https://www.jdsupra.com/legalnews/significant-changes-to-the-uk-takeover-1517620/, accessed April 25, 2021.

(9) Clarificatory changes to promote market integrity, including the following:
    (i) In line with current practice, the consent of the Panel is required to enable a bidder to invoke a condition or precondition to which the material significance test applies.
    (ii) The Panel will judge whether circumstances are of material significance to the bidder in the context of the offer by reference to facts of each case at the time the relevant circumstances arise, and will not be drawn on whether a condition or precondition can be invoked until this time.
    (iii) A list of those conditions and preconditions to which the material significance tests does not apply. In view of the conditions alluded to above, conditions pertaining to UK and EC competition clearances no longer fall into the category of conditions which are excluded from the material significance test.

The changes introduced recognized the cross-border element of takeovers as by harmonizing the treatment of clearances; this would introduce a consistent treatment across all clearances to which a takeover offer is subject to thereby eliminating the separate way with which the Code currently deals with UK and EC competition conditions.[1239] This would imply in practice removing the automatic lapse referred to earlier, with the outcome that where a bidder wishes to invoke unilaterally a bid condition pertaining to the clearance from the UK or EU agencies, it would have to show to the Panel that the circumstances are of material significance to the bidder in the context of the offer, as is already the situation for non-UK or EU clearances. The change is applicable regardless of whether the bid is made by way of contractual offer or scheme of arrangement. The threshold as to whether the circumstances are of material significance is high. A bid would continue where the material significance threshold is unable to be satisfied, notwithstanding any ongoing clearance processes and any conditions to clearances imposed by the competent authorities.

Further, the consequence of canceling the distinction between the deadline for satisfying the acceptance condition and the compliance to other conditions is that an offer will no longer have interim closing dates. Presently, interim closing date enables the bidder either to lapse or to extend the offer; it has not become unconditional as to acceptances on those dates. The revised Code stipulates that where the acceptance condition is not satisfied, and a bidder seeks to lapse its offer by invoking the acceptance condition prior to the deadline for all conditions to be met, it has to extend an acceptance condition invocation notice on target shareholders of at least fourteen days' notice. This revision helps to provide enhanced certainty to target shareholders as a bidder is not presently required to provide a notice ahead of any given interim closing date confirming that it would lapse, or would extend its offer, if the acceptance conditions are not satisfied.[1240] The published changes would likely also impact bid

1239. C. Chapman & A. Stanfield. 2021. "Impact of changes to the Takeover Code on bid financing". https://lpscdn.linklaters.com/knowledge/-/media/digital-marketing-image, accessed May 15, 2021.
1240. Chapman & Stanfield 2021, *supra* note [1239].

financing documentation, especially in relation to particular funds provisions and acquisition undertakings.[1241]

While 2020 precipitated extraordinary state intervention in UK and elsewhere, 2021 looks set to be the year that regulatory interventions in M&A precipitate changes to the way dealmakers approach transactions. Market sentiment for 2021 is generally positive, given the absence of unanticipated shocks, the resolution of Brexit, a new US administration, and the extensive rollout of COVID-19 vaccines. Still, state intervention would be felt even for businesses not conventionally viewed as regulated, as regulators pushed to introduce a wide range of rules impacting investments in multiple sectors. Successful execution for acquisition in 2021 and beyond would require navigation of a complex and evolving legal and regulatory landscape. The CMA, for example, appears to be taking an expansive approach to jurisdiction. As reflected by developments in cases like Sabre/Farelogix and Roche/Spark, the CMA is making dynamic forward-looking evaluation of parties' overlaps, even in cases in which the target has no revenues directly attributable to the UK.[1242]

In summary, it is worth mentioning that corporate takeovers in the US and the UK could be friendly or hostile depending on how the target company's management team receives the bidder's initial acquisition offer. Most, however, are friendly in nature,[1243] but takeovers can be hostile.[1244] Signs in the market heading into the second half of 2021 and beyond point to disruptive forces itching to acquire coveted assets. The abundance of capital and number of prospective buyers seeking deals makes hostile bids more likely by aggressors. Activist investors in some cases are partnering aggressors in lieu of taking their issues directly to the shareholders of the target, where proxy fights seek to install dissident directors who are more friendly to a deal than incumbents.

Shoring this present trend are many public corporations that are ripe for picking. Record highs in major market indices hide the fact that companies have not participated in recent expansion in private equity multiples.[1245] Such stragglers are not endeared, and frequently undervalued, especially when measured from the highs prior to the onset of the COVID-19 pandemic in early 2020. This, together with good access to capital, and the challenges in some industries to locate meaningful levels of organic growth, at least during the ongoing pandemic conditions, are favorable for hostile takeover activity.[1246] Regardless of the motivation, the present climate means that boards and management teams need to watch their backs and be ready for the

1241. Chapman & Stanfield 2021, *supra* note [1239].
1242. C. Campbell, D. Abernethy, N. Cline & R. McLaren. 2021. "M&A report 2021: Rising regulation requires agility from M&A deal teams". *Latham Watkins 16 March 2021*. https://www.iflr.com/article/b1qxj8rpnlfsd6/mampa-report-2021-rising-regulation-requires-agility-from-mampa-deal-teams, accessed March 21, 2021.
1243. T. Adkins. 2021. "How can a company resist a hostile takeover?". *Investopedia 29 May 2021*. https://www.investopedia.com/ask/answers/042315/how-can, accessed May 30, 2021.
1244. D. Farkas, J. Frankl & R. Kueppers. 2021. "Hostile takeover bids on the rise in 2021-Will you be ready?". *JD Supra 31 March 2021*. https://www.jdsupra.com/legalnews/hostile-takeover, accessed April 19, 2021.
1245. Farkas Frankl & Kueppers. 2021, *supra* note [1244].
1246. Farkas Frankl & Kueppers. 2021, *supra* note [1244].

challenge of an unsolicited takeover bid or other seemingly milder tactic, like proxy contests.

While a good range of takeover defense strategies exist across the board for corporate managers and directors to oppose hostile takeover attempts, the larger question remains pertaining to a manager's fiduciary duty to his/her shareholders. Unsurprisingly, shareholders and managers frequently do not share the same sentiments toward the market for corporate control. In general, shareholders are supportive of ensuring the company is susceptible to a takeover as such a potentiality keeps the managers on their toes, and where a takeover does happen, the shareholders usually stand to benefit from the hefty premium on their investment, while managers have almost diametrically opposite incentives as they would prefer that their actions be wholly unconstrained.[1247] This aside, most managers of listed corporations could risk losing their jobs where a takeover happens. Where a management team opts to resist a hostile takeover bid, they need to reflect on the options available.

Foremost, any defense enabling incumbent managers to hold a veto to hostile offers would be alarming to shareholders.[1248] Differential voting rights or dual-class shares and poison pills though effective for warding off hostile bidders prevent the market for corporate control from functioning efficiently. Of late, high-profile battles over the reallocation of control rights are emerging. For example, Google sought to entrench its founders' control by recapitalizing from a dual-class into a triple-class structure, whereas in contrast the CBS board attempted to dilute its controlling shareholders by distributing a voting stocks dividend empowering minority shareholders to block a merger it viewed to be harmful.[1249] These cases raised a fundamental question in corporate law, as to the proper judicial response to self-dealing claims regarding reallocations of corporate control rights. Research suggests that the reallocation of control rights raises an inevitable trade-off between investors' protection from agency costs and the controller's ability to pursue its idiosyncratic mission, thereby making the value of different allocations of control rights both company specific and individual specific. The policy implications of insights on this suggest courts treat reallocations of control rights as issues of charter interpretation as to who has the power to decide such reallocations and avoid reviewing the discretion to use that power.[1250] Where the charter is silent, it is further suggested that courts should enforce the decision of the parties as to reallocations of control rights and apply the BJR.[1251]

Second, defenses that intentionally maimed a corporation's balance sheet are dangerous.[1252]While asset and liability restructuring could be effective in certain situations, shareholders though could suffer significant losses once key assets are

1247. B.A. Korman. 2017. "The corporate game of thrones and the market for corporate control". *Journal of Business and Technology Law*, Vol. 12 (2): 165-192.
1248. R.S. Ruback. 1987. "An overview of takeover defenses". In A.J. Auerbach (ed.). *Mergers and acquisitions*. University of Chicago: Cago Press.
1249. Z. Goshen & A. Hamdani. 2020. "Corporate control, dual class, and the limits of judicial review". *Columbia Law Review*, Vol. 120 (4): 941-994.
1250. Goshen & Hamdani 2020, *supra* note [1249].
1251. Goshen & Hamdani 2020, *supra* note [1249].
1252. Ruback 1987, *supra* note [1248].

disposed or needless debts are incurred.[1253] Third, defenses inhibiting managers from holding takeover veto rights and do not maim a company's balance sheet, like staggered boards, ESOPs, supermajority voting provisions and other shark repellant type amendments mechanisms would unlikely maim the shareholders' investment positions, and are as such reliable defenses to deploy.[1254] Still, any takeover defense could detract the market's efficiency. The efficiency metrics though fail to account for human emotions that are pivotal to those in charge of corporations when such critical decisions have to be made. With free market capitalism and all of its greed, the market for corporate control could be a perilous place to be, as just like when playing the game of thrones, there are unlikely to be middle paths, the choice is between success and failure.[1255]

More recently, the US is initiating studies on the ease with which many M&As have been successfully undertaken. The new Biden administration seeks a review of current rules to assess whether they have proven to be overly permissive, thereby enabling already-dominant businesses to become even more dominant in their respective sectors.[1256] Over 75% of US industries, smaller numbers of large entities, are said to be controlling more of the business than they did two decades ago, such as witnessed in financial services, healthcare, agriculture and so on. The consequential lack of competition has driven up prices for consumers. Markups have tripled for many consumer items, including necessities, but the barriers to competition have also been driving down wages for workers, or by as much as 17% of advertised wages, while noncompete agreements in jobs have also made it harder for workers to switch to better-paying options. Taken together, inadequate competition has held back new business formation by as much as 50% since the 1970s, providing fewer opportunities for small businesses to access markets to earn decent returns, culminating in productivity growth decline, business innovation and investment decline, and above all, income, wealth, and inequality.

A historic Executive Order (EO) has been made to promote competition in the US economy. This covers seventy-two initiatives by more than a dozen federal agencies to quickly resolve some of the most pressing competition problems across the US economy. The EO further encourages the leading antitrust agencies to focus enforcement efforts on problems in key markets and coordinates other agencies' ongoing response to corporate consolidation:[1257]

1253. Korman 2017, *supra* note [1247].
1254. Korman 2017, *supra* note [1247].
1255. Korman 2017, *supra* note [1247].
1256. J. Fineman. 2021. "DOJ, FTC heads says current merger guidelines deserve 'hard look'". *Seeking Alpha 9 July 2021.* https://seekingalpha.com/news/3714085-doj-ftc-heads-says-current-merger-guidelines-deserve-hard-look, accessed July 10, 2021.
1257. Whitehouse. 2021. "Fact Sheet: Executive Order on promoting competition in the American economy". *Whitehouse 9 July 2021.* https://www.whitehouse.gov/briefing-room/statements-releases/2021/07/09/fact-sheet-executive-order-on-promoting-competition-in-the-american-economy/, accessed July 10, 2021.

(1) Leading competition regulatory agencies, like the DOJ and FTC, are being called upon to enforce the antitrust laws vigorously and recognize that the law allows them to challenge prior bad mergers.
(2) Consolidating enforcement focus on labor markets, agricultural markets, healthcare markets, and the tech sector.
(3) Setting up of a White House Competition Council led by the Director of the National Economic Council to monitor progress on finalizing the initiatives in the Order and to coordinate the federal government's responses to the rising power of large corporations in the economy.

Overall, the EO takes aim at big tech, targets monopoly risks in noncompete clauses, and businesses involved in drugs and pharmaceuticals, ocean shipping and railways, and in in-flight baggage fees, bank-switching costs, meat-labeling practices, and many more. Early signs of antitrust agencies moving in this direction included DOJ's suit to block the merger of insurance giants Aon and Willis Towers Watson, and FTC challenging the vertical merger of the biotech companies Illumina and Grail.

The US Senate has also just approved the US Innovation and Competition Act[1258] targeting China and other economies. The bill commits USD 250 billion in funding for scientific research, subsidies for chipmakers and robot makers, and an overhaul of the National Science Foundation.[1259] US businesses, especially those involved in technology, will therefore need to navigate across a regulatory landscape that provides not only new opportunities but also new challenges for many big tech businesses.

10.05 WORKPLACE AND WORKFORCE TRANSFORMATIONS

The COVID-19 pandemic is likely to have transformed the structure and other dynamics of workplaces and workforce skills and expectations. This is largely because ESG has because of the pandemic been brought to the fore to grip the attention of directors, management, regulators and employees. It is about both safety at work places and diversity and inclusiveness issues. For a start, post-pandemic working is likely to be hybrid,[1260] meaning the combination of remote and on-site working in a general sense, but gets hazy when getting into details. In spite of the adoption of the hybrid model, most businesses have nevertheless only started to think through and articulate the specifics of how to implement a more permanent mix of remote and

1258. *S.1260-US Innovation and Competition Act of 2021, 117th Congress (2021-2022).* https://www.congress.gov/bill/117th-congress/senate-bill/1260/text, accessed June 9, 2021.
1259. T. Franck. 2021. "Senate passes $250 billion bipartisan tech and manufacturing bill aimed at countering China". *CNBC 8 June 2021.* https://www.cnbc.com/2021/06/08/senate-passes-bipartisan-tech-and-manufacturing-bill-aimed-at-china.html, accessed June 9, 2021.
1260. A. Alexander, et al. 2021. "What executives are saying about the future hybrid of work". *McKinsey 17 May 2021.* https://www.mckinsey.com/business-functions/organization/our-insights/what-, accessed May 20, 2021 Between December 2020 and January 2021, McKinsey surveyed and analyzed responses from a hundred respondents at the C-suite, vice president and director level from different industries across the US, Asia, Europe and Latin America. Survey findings confirmed that productivity and customer satisfaction have increased during the pandemic.

on-site working for all roles that are not essential to perform on-site. Consequentially, many personnel are anxious about this. Still, the sustainability of pandemic-style productivity gains could well depend on how corporate leaders and directors address the anxiety their employees feel, and including the associated levels of burnout. A notable observation is that businesses with the biggest productivity increases during the pandemic have supported and encouraged small moments of engagement among their employees, moments in which coaching, mentorship, idea sharing, and coworking take place. Such businesses are now preparing for hybrid working by training managers for remote leadership, by reimagining processes, and by rethinking how to help employees grow in their roles.

An empirical study recently examined what is currently happening at work sites with regards to the five key concepts of diversity, inclusion, belonging, equity, and respects.[1261] These concepts all surfaced at various intervals in recent years, including the onset of the corona pandemic. The research outcomes demonstrate that the new concepts in the US often emerge in tandem with social movements and highly publicized workplace challenges. The study further demonstrates a high correlation between managerial involvements and better work engagement, job satisfaction, sense of belonging and reduced turnover intent. Respondents to the study confirmed that access to education and training and internal diversity partners are the most effective mechanisms for empowering them to give feedback at work, and that mentorship and sponsorship opportunities are essential for developing an inclusive climate. The research additionally demonstrates that while diverse workforces and inclusive culture and policies are essential, measuring the impact is critical to the health and success of a business. Also, managerial involvements, workforce policies and mentoring and sponsorship initiatives were the most common factors shaping inclusivity in the workplace.

Using the corporate law perspective, another related research demonstrates that corporate fiduciaries are bound by their duties of loyalty to implement affirmative steps to ensure that corporations comply with important civil rights and antidiscrimination laws and norms designed to ensure fair access to economic opportunity.[1262] The study further suggests how corporate law principles like the BJR do not just authorize, but indeed encourage US corporations to implement effective action to help reduce racial and gender inequality, and increase inclusion, tolerance and diversity given the rational premise that exists linking DEI practices, corporate reputation, and sustainable enterprise value. Through incorporating requirements to comply with key antidiscrimination laws mandatorily, and enabling corporate DEI policies that go further than the legal minimum, corporate law offers critical tools with which businesses may achieve DEI goals that other reforms do not. This can embed a commitment to DEI in all aspects of corporate interactions with customers, communities, employees, and society in

1261. S.J. Creary, N. Rothbard & J. Scruggs. 2021. "Improving workplace culture through evidence-based diversity, equity and inclusion practices". *Wharton Working Paper May 2021*. Applied-Insights-Lab-Report.pdf (upenn.edu), accessed June 11, 2021.
1262. C. Brummer & L.E. Strine Jr. 2021. "Duty and diversity". *Harvard Law School Discussion Paper No. 2021-2.*

general. The challenge therefore for corporate boards involves taking effective actions to help reduce racial and gender inequality in economies with plural communities.

The clarifications that the above study provide would not by itself resolve the lack of representativeness of US boards and management teams. It would also not provide simple solutions to the wider equity challenges that have to be addressed if corporate boards are to answer the growing expectation that they treat all their stakeholders with equal respect. Internal corporate actions would be able to deal with critical matters that current external reforms either overlook or are unable to solve without contributing in conjunction with internal corporate actions. The emerging external law initiatives to boost DEI in the behavior of US businesses, while making some contributions, have important limitations in terms of their applications only to public enterprises, their inability to resolve the full extent of issues where sensitivity to DEI issues is important to corporate treatment of stakeholders, and the difficulty any external regulation has in embedding values and norms in a complex enterprise, unless the leaders of that enterprise support those themselves.[1263] The fuller delivery of DEI in creating a fairer society, as well as a stronger, more resilient and sustainably profitable US business could only be achieved where businesses themselves embrace these values in all the important ways wherein they impact their stakeholders and society. Thus, corporate law itself has a positive role to play in supporting businesses to take ambitious actions to boost DEI, thereby contributing to a more inclusive and fair economy and nation.

For some time, corporate law has been misunderstood where social issues are concerned, but which happens to make business sense. Diversity is one niche now where corrective measures are needed, and this is gradually recognized by US businesses themselves. But their ability to stay focused on this has been erratic, with still substantial resistance to DEI in US society. The study demonstrates that corporate law fiduciary duty does not deter directors and managers from boosting DEI, but instead pushes corporate managers legally, financially, and reputationally to focus on these important matters as part of their duty to promote the best interests of the company, increase its sustainable profitability for the benefits of its shareholders, as well as ensure that the company respects the laws of the society that chartered it.[1264] In short, corporate law enables and in fact motivates corporate leaders to do the appropriate thing. It is up to them and the institutional investors to which they owe their positions, as fiduciary duty law is clear on this. The eventual question is not whether business leaders are able to implement DEI, but their willingness to do so.[1265]

The 2021 UK leadership diversity survey report was undertaken between November and December 2020 through an in-depth questionnaire sent to Board and C-suite members across a varied range of organizations. The survey focusing on inclusion and diversity (I&D) yielded the following findings:[1266]

1263. Brummer & Strine Jr. 2021, *supra* note [1262].
1264. Brummer & Strine Jr. 2021, *supra* note [1262].
1265. Brummer & Strine Jr. 2021, *supra* note [1262].
1266. Board Agenda. 2021. "UK leadership diversity report 2021". https://boardagenda.com/resource/uk-leadership-diversity-report-2021/, accessed June 11, 2021.

(1) The overwhelming majority of respondents who say there is no diversity on their board also state that their organizations do not partner with I&D membership organizations or associations.
(2) Respondents who work for a company with diversity on their board are twice as likely to also be working for an organization that has set targets for diversity for both the board and the leadership team.
(3) Organizations with diversity on their board are far more likely to reduce bias in recruiting for the leadership team, and also when recurring for board positions.
(4) Overall, the desire for greater diversity is growing.

The above findings and more taken together suggest that the more diverse UK companies are doing the following to successfully achieve higher inclusiveness and diversity (I&D) at the leadership level within their own organizations:

(1) Understanding the diversity ratios of their board and leadership team, including those of their competitors.
(2) Partnering with diverse organizations to connect with and stay connected to diverse talent.
(3) Ensuring all employees know about their I&D initiatives and measures for reducing bias.
(4) Setting targets, but ensuring that these are properly applied and managed.
(5) Developing with a focus on gender and ethnicity and proceeding further to include other more challenging attributes.

In general, businesses need to integrate awareness and commitment to I&D into the culture and business practices across the organization and measure the impacts on an ongoing basis. To become truly diverse, businesses need to have genuine appetites within their organizations to locate candidates with diverse experiences. Each of the ESG elements should not be treated in isolation, but to be managed together. The legal community has cautioned that increased attention on ESG challenges has now come from employee, consumers, shareholders, stakeholders and governments across the world.

Observation of litigation risks in MNCs and other large enterprises suggests that only the energy and mining sectors have been highly attuned to ESG matters, and this is surprising given that ESG issues are a growing litigation risk. Insurers too are also treating ESG as one of the major risk trends to financial services. Also, to maintain their competitive edge in the tech sector, both the US and the UK prioritize I&D across the workforce as a must to ensure varied ways of thinking out new ideas. Despite this, many members of certain people group still find it difficult to enter and progress in the technology space. There is the further matter of ensuring that new tech products are as inclusive as possible. Given these trends, those corporations involved in the sector could benefit from establishing I&D goals, tackling bias, investing in diverse talent, and creating an equity culture.[1267]

At this juncture, it is worth recalling that the UK government proposed in August 2017 eight reforms across the three areas of pay, employee and stakeholder voice, and the governance of large companies. These have all been incorporated in The Companies (Miscellaneous Reporting) Regulations 2018 that came into effect in 2019. In particular, the government requires public enterprise with more than 250,000 UK employees to report annually the ratio of CEO pay to the median pay, 25th percentile, and 75th percentile pay of their UK workforce, together with a narrative explaining changes from the ratio from year to year. This has become effective from 2020 onward. Paralleling this requirement is the 2018 CG Code that specifically refers to the role of the workforce and promotes their involvements in CG. Principle D of the Code stipulates that in order for the enterprise to discharge its responsibilities to shareholders and stakeholders, the board should ensure effective engagement with and encourage participation from these parties. The FRC commissioned a report to provide deeper insights into the current intersection of CG with employee voice in the light of requirements in the 2018 CG Code for boards to ensure effective workforce engagement.

The study examined the approaches businesses have taken to provide a workforce voice in the boardroom, why different approaches have been taken, what these changes have meant in practice, and how effective they have been from both a management and workforce perspective. The study yielded the following insights:[1268]

(1) Analysis of the three core options for workforce engagement of a worker director, designated NED and advisory panel revealed that 68% of respondents have adopted one or more of these as a direct consequence of the Code, with 40% having appointed a designated NED, 12% having established an advisory panel, and 16% having combined an advisory panel with a designated NED.
(2) Advisory panels, many of which are newly created bodies, provide examples of innovation. These bodies operate in a range of forms, have a variety of names, are sometimes elected by workers, but are more often appointed by managers. For enterprises without panels and relying solely on designated NEDs, there is often some ambiguity regarding the role of these NEDs and how they should interface with existing engagement structures. The few examples of worker directors suggest that this approach is not incompatible with the UK CG framework. Worker directors play a valuable role when engaging fully in board deliberations and discharging their legal duties

1267. A. Hurst. 2021. "The biggest diversity, equity and inclusion trends in tech". *Information Age 4 June 2021.* https://www.information-age.com/biggest-diversity-equity-inclusion-trends-tech, accessed June 16, 2021.
1268. C. Rees & P. Brione. 2021. "Workforce engagement and the UK CG Code: A review of company reporting and practice". *FRC May 2021.* https://www.frc.org.uk/getattachment/56bdd5ed-3b2d-4a6f-a62b-979910a90a10/FRC-Workforce-Engagement-Report_May-2021.pdf, accessed June 9, 2021.

without issue, as well as honoring the trust placed in them with confidential information. There are though differences of experience between worker directors seeking to bring the views of the whole workforce to the board and those seen as only providing only an individual worker view.

(3) The current position on workforce engagements for most companies represent more of an evolution of existing practices than a revolution in approach. Others appear to have adopted the path of least resistance and did little to develop even rudimentary workforce engagement mechanisms beyond the annual staff survey.

(4) For the vast majority of cases, decisions on approaches to workforce engagements were made by the board without consultation with the workforce. There were significant gaps in reporting around what the outcomes or impact of workforce engagement had been for most companies. Many of these arrangements though are still in their infancy. Companies with more mature, long-standing practices have been able to embed these into their culture and processes, while new arrangements set up in response to the Code could still be encountering teething problems. The more pragmatic companies are reflecting and learning lessons after the first year or two of practice and adjusting to the way their voice mechanisms operate. There is therefore a lot more companies could learn from one another in terms of best practice.

Given the above insights, the study recommended the following for improvements in future years:[1269]

(1) Representativeness and breath of coverage to ensure that the employee voice reflects the geography and demography of the workforce.
(2) Depth of coverage is crucial to properly integrate different engagement and voice channels, including collective terms of employee representation.
(3) Providing for regular and structured input from the workforce, particularly during periods of accelerated change.
(4) Workforce representative, whether sitting on a panel or as workforce director should be chosen with some input from the workforce.
(5) Energies should be focused mainly on the substance of workforce engagement, rather than the process.
(6) Agenda setting works best when there is a balance between topics of management interest and topics of workforce interest.
(7) Meaningful dialogues with the workforce also requires an effective feedback loop, based on informed employee voice.
(8) To make workforce engagement effective, boards need to properly reflect on the purpose they want that engagement to serve. In other words, whether they are looking for a sounding board for proposals, a greater diversity of

1269. Rees & Brione 2021, *supra* note [1268].

perspectives, a channel to raise workforce concerns, or to shift the purpose and values of the company in new directions.

The principled and practical case for a greater workforce voice in the governance process has grown stronger than ever. There are growing signs that the calls for a shift away from shareholder primacy and toward more responsible long-term and stakeholder-oriented business models have entered mainstream. The COVID-19 pandemic has intensified these concerns, with many companies arguing that any long-term recovery strategy needs to be underpinned upon working toward a more inclusive and sustainable economy with greater resilience for the future. Despite this development, many FTSE 350 annual reports still appear to downplay the importance of workforce engagement, with still significant numbers relegating it to boilerplate language in a formulaic table of stakeholders.[1270] There is though some refreshing evidence of a great deal of innovation and fresh thinking in this niche as exemplified by the pockets of good practice found in the study.

A larger international ESG study comprising respondents from the US, Brazil, the UK, Germany and India from March 29 to April 23, 2021, generated the following findings:[1271]

(1) Some 83% of consumers think companies should be actively shaping ESG best practices.
(2) Some 91% of business leaders take the view that their company has a responsibility to act on ESG matters.
(3) Some 86% of employees prefer to work for companies that care about the same issues as they do.
(4) Overwhelming majority of both consumers and employees said they are more likely to buy from or work for companies that share their values across the elements of ESG. In view of the corona pandemic, a larger pool of conscientious consumers is more willing to pay more for healthier, safer, more environmentally and socially conscious products and brands.
(5) Interestingly, consumers are not convinced that businesses are making adequate investments in ESG matters.
(6) Executives concede that pursuing growth and ESG remains a balancing act, even as they see long-term ESG advantages.
(7) Growth targets and regulatory complexity are the top barriers to ESG progress.

Arising from the above findings and more, consumers opine that companies could make progress on ESG issues by creating new financial incentives linked to social good. Employees say companies should embed ESG directly into corporate strategy,

1270. Rees & Brione 2021, *supra* note [1268].
1271. PwC. 2021. "Beyond compliance: Consumers and employees want business to do more on ESG: How business can close the expectations gap". *PwC 2 June 2021*. https://www.pwc.com/us/en/services/consulting/library/consumer-intelligence, accessed June 10, 2021.

while business leaders say businesses should have social responsibility roles report directly to the CEO. Guided by these feedbacks, businesses can advance their ESG agenda by telling a cohesive and balanced narrative. This could be achieved by proactively communicating the complexity of ESG issues, for instance, how jobs and skills could be impacted by plant closures required to speed the transition to a low-carbon economy or to ensure health and safety conditions impacted by the pandemic. Such issues could be more effectively communicated through social media sources. Corporations thus would be eventually rewarded for enhanced commitments to proper management of ESG concerns, besides eventually benefiting from likely fewer regulatory investigations, lawsuits, and other disruptions. However, it pays to take a more cautionary stance with regards to ESG, as while securities laws in the US require companies disclose material information to investors, companies have not revealed about ESG. This has prompted the SEC to look further as to how to turn this gap into a more robust ESG disclosure obligation.

The harder issues involving laws and regulations impacting worker welfare and worker safety have been revisited or reviewed in some cases in both the US and the UK amidst the COVID-19 pandemic, but there are emerging signs of bottlenecks with regards to the flow of direct labor arising from worker hesitancy because of various social and economic reasons.[1272] Those business corporations facing relatively more difficulties in this area would have to look for ways to quell the problem and get the labor they need. Individual businesses could offer higher wages to access labor from rivals, but this is not an economy-wide solution without significant inflation of prices that customers pay. This suggests appropriate monetary policy response from the Federal Reserve too. To resolve the labor shortage difficulties, policymakers, regulators, and businesses would need to work together in a united front.

As for businesses, they need to quickly work on their return-to-work plans. For many businesses in the early months of the pandemic and the transition to remote work led to a rise in productivity. Despite the uncertainty and volatility of the global crisis, many work teams are enabled by a strong foundation of social capital that has been forged by previous long-term collaboration and in-person interactions. Established social capital makes it relatively easy to shift to remote work without losing a sense of the larger organizational context. However, over time, organizations shift in the way they operate, including for those where many employees are working remotely, as the economic situation evolves and teams are disbanded and reformed to face the tough competitive landscapes. An unintended side effect of persistent remote work during the pandemic has been that social capital networks within organizations have weakened, making it more difficult for workers to maintain the same high level of productivity. Microsoft CEO Satya Nadella has confirmed this phenomenon of depletion of social capital in May 2020.[1273] When deliberating on the matter of returning to

1272. B. Conerly. 2021. "The labor shortage is why supply chains are disrupted". *Forbes 7 July 2021.* https://www.forbes.com/sites/billconerly/2021/07/07/the-labor-shortage-is-why-supply-chains-are-disrupted/?sh=1c83b64301d5, accessed July 8, 2021.

1273. New York Times. 2020. "What Satya Nadella thinks". *The New York Times 14 May 2020.* https://www.nytimes.com/2020/05/14/business/dealbook/satya-nadella-microsoft.html, accessed November 10, 2020.

work, whether in person, full time, or in hybrid situations, corporate leaders have been urged to think strategically about how their plans could address the following three critical areas:[1274]

(1) Thinking and reflecting on the opportunities to develop weak ties. This means when planning how and when to have people in the office, leaders need to include times that both allows groups who work together to interact face-to-face effectively to get work done and facilitates interactions among those who do not necessarily depend on one another for work. Growing the opportunity for the development of weak ties to improve the social capital of the network of the company is important for employees working in place before the pandemic and for new employees as well.
(2) Making online team formation a standard. It is important to have ideas on how team forms, and preparing for a future optimized for flexibility and hybrid work environments. Instead of returning to the status quo, it is likely to be more beneficial to form through face-to-face kickoff events with new teams wholly online at the beginning. This means thinking about how the contributions of all team members could be maximized, regardless of where they are.
(3) Supporting younger employees in the company. In a time of hybrid work, there is the further need of ensuring the prioritizing and onboarding of the younger employees in the company's return-to-work plans. Younger employees have unique needs to in a remote environment and would need proactive support so as to gain their footing in the company when daily observation, apprenticeship, and face-to-face interaction may no longer be the norm. Opportunities have to be provided for young employees to interact both with one another and with older, more experienced mentors.

Overall, corporate leaders need to continue to balance managing the many ongoing impacts of the pandemic while simultaneously transitioning to a work pattern that includes more in-person contacts. Research insights have generally suggested that companies and employees would likely be most productive where they could leverage all that has been learned in the past year about effective remote work and focus on in-person work solutions in the niches that require the most support.[1275]

Worksites, working conditions, and workers welfare because of the dominant impact of the corona pandemic and its seismic disruptions to markets and supply chains for many businesses have been transformed quickly even as more insights are being sought for the best way forward. Providing safe, secure and healthy work environments together with DEI have become best practices backed by various

1274. J.J. Deal & A. Levenson. 2021. "Figuring out social capital is critical for the future of hybrid work: The networks of employee relationships have been depleted during the pandemic, but companies can address this by focusing on three key areas in their return-to-work plans". *MIT Sloan Management Review 1 July 2021*. https://sloanreview.mit.edu/article/figuring-out-social-capital-is-critical-for-the-future-of-hybrid-work/, accessed July 2, 2021.
1275. Deal & Levenson 2021, *supra* note [1274].

regulatory support measures. Businesses are still walking the fine line where these matters are concerned, while policymakers and regulators are monitoring and even intervening more and more because of growing public attention on these matters, given the lessons from the ongoing corona pandemic. As such, it is important for directors and senior management to plan well for these challenges so as not to be caught napping should things go wrong badly, but importantly leveraging on these to enhance the competitiveness of their industries.

10.06 PURPOSE OF BUSINESS

It has been a good two turbulent years since the Business Roundtable representing the CEOs of America's largest corporations issued a formal statement calling for businesses to serve all stakeholders.[1276]Since then, ExxonMobil has announced a five-year plan to reduce GHG emissions and churn out ads stating its commitment to a green future.[1277] Cigarette MNC, Philip Morris, is flashing its intentions to assist smokers to quit,[1278] while Facebook[1279] initiated calls along with other digital platforms for fresh internet regulations. This raises questions as to whether today's corporate executives are ushering a new era of corporate responsibility, or merely protecting their own powers.[1280]

Back then in the early 1970s, business leaders and prominent academicians hold the view that the enterprise's sole commitment was to their shareholder. This perspective entered mainstream through the works of Milton Friedman,[1281] with subsequent theoretical and empirical inputs from Michael Jensen.[1282] CEOs like General Electric's Jack Welch[1283] and the merry hordes of management consultants had by the 1980s began normalizing the preoccupation with shareholder value, no doubt

1276. Business Roundtable (BRT). 2019. "Business Roundtable redefines the purpose of a corporation to promote 'An economy that serves all Americans'". *BRT 19 August 2019*. https://www.businessroundtable.org/business-roundtable-redefines-the-purpose-of-a-corporation-to, accessed December 15, 2020.
1277. E. Rosenbaum. 2020. "Oil giant Exxon Mobil pushes new climate change plan as activist investors circle". *CNBC 14 December 2020*. https://www.cnbc.com/2020/12/14/exxon-mobil-begins-to-mount, accessed December 15, 2020.
1278. Philip Morris. 2021. "See why facts matter: Better decisions start with better information". https://www.pmi.com/better, accessed May 19, 2021.
1279. Facebook. 2021. "It's time for updated internet regulations". https://about.fb.com/regulations/, accessed May 19, 2021.
1280. D. Acemoglu. 2021. "CEOS are the problem". *Project Syndicate 2 June 2021*. https://www.project-syndicate.org/commentary/rein-in-ceos-to-stop-anti-social-corporate, accessed June 5, 2021.
1281. M. Friedman. 1970. "A Friedman doctrine—The social responsibility of business is to increase its profits". The *New York Times 13 September 1970*. https://www.nytimes.com/1970/09/13/archives/a-friedman-doctrine-the-social-responsibility-of-business-is-to.html, accessed December 15, 2020.
1282. M.C. Jensen & K.J. Murphy. "Performance pay and top-management incentives". *Journal of Political Economy*, Vol. 98 (2): 225-264.
1283. R. Slater. 1998. *Jack Welsch & the G.E. way: Management insights and leadership secrets of the legendary CEO.* New York McGraw-Hill.

with further support from the then influential Du Pont[1284] financial model. Under cover of delivering better value to shareholders, businesses started downsizing their workforces, limiting wage growth, and offshoring tasks.

While shareholder primacy advocates would not have entertained the frauds linked to Enron and Enron-type corporate scandals, it was not difficult to understand how obsessions with increasing share price might entice some executives to go a step too far. A 2020 survey of the two hundred highest paid CEOs at public companies showed that even in a gilded age of executive pay, 2020 was a blowout year despite the impact of the corona pandemic.[1285] The staggering spike in pay is attributed in large part to linking CEOs' pay to stock prices. This pay-for-performance structure is intended to align managers' incentives with those of shareholders.

Given the startling revelations, it also raises questions about how much credit executives deserve for rising share prices, and whether the performance conditions attached to stock awards are adequately tough. CEO pay rose 14.1% in 2020, while the median worker got a 1.9% raise. CEOs in the survey received 274 times the pay of the median employee, some 245 times more than the previous year, while two-thirds of companies with the largest pay packages had wider gaps between executive and employee after the pandemic. Equally stunning is the revelation that only some 2% of shareholders' nonbinding votes on say on pay have historically gone against management, with recent high-profile condemnations coming at GE[1286] and Starbucks.[1287] Though votes against pay packages are on the rise in 2021, these tend to come in well below 50% disapproval. Also stunning that in a year of vast difficulties, eight CEOs received pay packages exceeding USD 100 million, whereas the year before, only one CEO breached that threshold.[1288]

Also striking has been the revelation in another survey that almost all UK and EU companies surveyed included ESG metrics in their incentive compensation plans, compared to less than one-fourth of US companies surveyed.[1289] Additionally, UK and EU companies had a much higher rate of ESG inclusion in long-term incentive plans. These revelations confirm that UK and EU companies are well ahead of the US in the inclusion of ESG metrics in incentive plans, and their approach to measuring and rewarding ESG achievements could be a harbinger of strategies for applications by US

1284. P. Courtis. 2003. "DU PONT Ration: A comprehensive measure of business performance". *European Research Studies*, Vol. VI (1-2): 1-30.
1285. The New York Times. 2021. "Meagre rewards for workers exceptionally rich pay for CEOs". The New York *Times 11 June 2021*. https://www.nytimes.com/2021/06/11/business/ceo-pay-compensation-stock.html, accessed June 12, 2021.
1286. J. Dinapoli & R. Singh. 2021. "GE shareholders reject CEO Culp's $230 mln pay in rare rebuke". *Reuters 4 May 2021*. https://www.reuters.com/business/general-electric-shareholders, accessed May 6, 2021.
1287. A. Lucas. 2021. "Starbucks shareholders vote against executive pay plan". *CNBC 18 March 2021*. https://www.cnbc.com/2021/03/18/starbucks-shareholders-vote, March 21, 2021.
1288. The New York Times 2021, *supra* note [1285].
1289. Business Wire. 2021. "Pay governance survey indicates UK and EU companies overwhelmingly lead US companies in ESG inclusion in incentive compensation plans". Business Wire 7 June 2021. https://www.businesswire.com/news/home/20210607005154/en/, accessed June 9, 2021.

companies over the next few years.[1290] There are though growing views that US companies would use 2021 as a launching pad for finalizing and rolling out ESG metrics in 2022 incentive plans.[1291]

The corona pandemic has inflicted enormous disruptions on the business landscape. There are the shocking evaporations of hitherto stable consumer markets, massive disruptions to the global supply chain, and the evidential impacts of climate change. These have led to the convergence of a growing consensus that maximizing shareholder value should not be the sole mission for a business enterprise. Less obvious though is what alternative model to follow. The Business Roundtable appears to argue for a new charter for executives to empower them to take into consideration a wider set of interests. This would likely give even more powers to executives, given that the existing model of shareholder primacy has already handed them massive powers. Many executive chairmen and CEOs regardless of ownership status presently lead corporations with their own personal vision, with little social oversight, as executive compensation escalated to dizzy heights. As highlighted earlier, businesses hit hard by the pandemic still extended handsome pay packages to CEO and other senior board members, while workers and other stakeholders suffered vastly in terms of health and finance.[1292]

Given early signs of the above, when far more than expected empowered CEOs are provided with vague mandates to pursue stakeholder interests as they see fit, it is contended that abuses would not be far behind. These could extend from CEOs' favored projects, like the Metropolitan Museum of Art,[1293] charter school initiatives,[1294] or veiled forms of influence peddling cloaked astutely under philanthropic causes.[1295] Going by the existing incentive structure, there are not much restraints on companies gathering massive amounts of consumer data, disempowering workers and citizens, and erecting of tyrannical new kinds of surveillance, even while advertising and proclaiming philanthropy and ethical standards. Nothing also stands in the way of companies from undertaking excessive automation to trim labor costs or destroying jobs to squeeze more money for the benefits of shareholders and themselves. What the

1290. Business Wire 2021, *supra* note [1289].

1291. L. Delevingne, A. Grundler & S. Keane. 2020. "The ESG premium: New perspectives on value: In a new survey, executives and investment professionals largely agree that environmental, social and governance programs create short- and long-term value-though perceptions of how have changed over the past decade". *McKinsey February 2020.* https://www.mckinsey.com/~/media/McKinsey/Business%20Functions/Sustainability, accessed March 19, 2020.

1292. The New York Times. 2021. "CEO pay remains stratospheric even at companies batter by pandemic: While millions of people struggled to make ends meet, many of the companies hit hardest in 2020 showered their executives with riches". *The New York Times 24 April 2021.* https://www.nytimes.com/2021/04/24/business/ceos-pandemic-compensation.html, accessed April 29, 2021.

1293. The Metropolitan Museum of Art (The Met). 2021. "Corporate patrons". *The Met June 2021.* https://www.metmuseum.org/-/media/files/join-and-give/corporate-, accessed June 17, 2021.

1294. S. Tan. 2016. "Facebook charter school collaboration draws fans and sceptics". *KQED* 27 December 2016. https://www.kqed.org/news/11233119/facebook-charter-school-collaboratio, accessed June 17, 2021.

1295. M. Bertrand, et al. 2020. "Tax-exempt lobbying: corporate philanthropy as a tool of political influence". *American Economic Review*, Vol. 110 (7): 2065-2102.

Business Roundtable appears to prefer from businesses as solution for today's problems is unlikely to reverse these highlighted ongoing antisocial trends, short of a two-thronged approach.

Foremost, the legal and institutional constraints on business leaders require strengthening. Recall how during the 2007-2008 GFC, various CEOs of banks and financial institutions exited their turfs with lucrative payouts, despite recklessly contributing massively to the financial malaise of these financial institutions without disciplinary sanctions or criminal prosecutions taken against them. These were discussed extensively earlier, but such repugnant behaviors have not gone totally away, as banks continue to be disciplined by regulators for engaging in all forms of abuses.[1296] Questions have been consistently raised as to why hardly any bankers went to serve jail time subsequent to the 2007-2008 GFC, or properly sanctioned, when obviously committing misdeeds with impunity. While some businesses are good examples of the TBTF, many more are not TBTF cases that do not merit financial help from state coffers, but instead to be appropriately disciplined for displaying reckless behaviors. This has been attributed to prosecutorial fiascos, corporate lobbying, trial losses, rotating door career syndrome, and culture shifts that appeared to have sapped the will and ability to prosecute top corporate leaders.[1297]

As such, regulations and laws are required to mark out clearer red lines. Corporate leaders should not be given the discretionary powers to decide whether to partake in aggressive tax avoidance schemes and paying themselves with the tax savings gained;[1298] to engage in carbon trading or reduction of carbon footprints schemes;[1299] or to pursue incessant automation at the expense of the welfare of low-educated workers without adequate provision of safety nets.[1300] The UK's Law Commission present consultation for corporate criminal liability is a step in the right direction.[1301] All these said issues impact the prospects for sustaining a functioning society. As such, they should not be left to the goodwill of self-interested CEOs.[1302]

Second, it is further contended that corporations, such as those cited earlier, are virtue signaling, as they have come under increasing pressures from civil societies, but

---

1296. P. Yeoh. 2015. "Corporate governance failures and the road to crime". *Journal of Financial Crime*, Vol. 23 (1): 216-230.
1297. J. Eisinger. 2017. *The chickenshit club: Why the justice department fails to prosecute executives*. New York: Simon & Schuster.
1298. P. Yeoh. 2018. "Tax efficient and tax secrecy destinations: Legal, okay, or not?". Business Law Review, Vol. 39 (2): 34-43.
1299. P. Yeoh. 2009. "Sustainable banking: The commercial and legal impacts of private-self regulatory initiatives". *European Energy and Environmental Law Review*, Vol. 18 (6): 274-288; P. Yeoh. 2008. "Is carbon finance the answer to climate control?". *International Journal of Law and Management*, Vol. 50 (4): 189-206.
1300. S. Scarpetta & M. Pearson. 2021. "What happened to jobs at high risk of automation?". *OECD Policy Brief on the Future of Work January 2021*. https://www.oecd.org/future-of-work/reports-and-data/what-happened-to-jobs-at-high-risk-of-automation-2021.pdf, accessed March 19, 2021.
1301. Law Commission. 2021. "Corporate criminal liability: A discussion paper". *Law Commission 9 June 2021*. https://s3-eu-west-2.amazonaws.com/lawcom-prod-storage-11jsxou24uy7q/uploads/2021/06/Corporate-Criminal-Liability-Discussion-Paper.pdf, accessed June 10, 2021.
1302. Acemoglu 2021, *supra* note [1280].

not because their corporate leaders have suddenly become more public-spirited. These kinds of pressures from civic activists work better when regulations and laws are clear as to which counts as miscreant corporate behaviors, be it aggressive tax evasion, accounting falsifications, reckless risk-taking, unfair/unexplained enrichment, or simple cases of environmental pollution.[1303] There is hardly a good reason to believe that those earlier mentioned companies, or others, are committed to overhauling their socially destructive business models. These could turn out to be their public relations initiatives equivalent perhaps to the earlier condemned greenwashing stance.[1304] Recall that many members of the Business Roundtable did not proclaim their redirection to the stakeholder model with official backings of their boards, and have yet to do so, two years after the event. These cited earlier examples, though few in numbers, suggest that civic activism is starting to bite, but this could be made more effective in conjunction with relevant regulations and laws. This two-throng approach might be the better answer toward the enhancement of corporate responsibility, instead of mostly whitewashing or greenwashing campaigns designed to defuse criticisms and demobilizing critics.

10.07 DIRECTION AND CONTROL OF COMPANIES IN THE DIGITAL ERA

The impacts of digitalization on business direction and control of companies are still unraveling. For now, the little that is known has been linked to businesses successfully digitalizing their business system and processes to have the perceived edge over their competitors.[1305] The larger reality though has been the phenomenal difficulties faced by businesses on how they could do this to capture value.[1306] A McKinsey survey prior to the onset of COVID-19 reveals some 92 % of businesses surveyed believing that their business models would have to change, given the rate of digitalization at the time.[1307] Survey results suggest that having the technologies on hand is insufficient, as businesses need to make the technology-supported changes that differentiate successful

1303. Acemoglu 2021, *supra* note [1280].
1304. E. Gil-Cordero, et al. 2021. "Measuring behavioral intention through the use of greenwashing: A study of the mediating effects and variables involved". *Sustainability*, Vol. 13 (2021): 6720-6731.
1305. B. Nikmehr, et al. 2021. "Digitalization as a strategic means of achieving sustainable efficiencies in construction management: A critical review". *Sustainability*, Vol. 13 (2021): 5040-5051; OECD. 2021 *The digital transformation of SMEs*. Paris: OECD.
1306. P.C. Verhoef, et al. 2021. "Digital transformation: A multidisciplinary reflection and research agenda". *Journal of Business Research*, Vol. 122 (2021): 889-901.
1307. H. De La Boutetiere, A. Montager & A. Reich. 2018. "Unlocking success in digital transformations: Digital transformations are even more difficult than traditional change efforts to pull off. But the results from the most effective transformations point to five factors for success". *McKinsey October 2018*. https://www.mckinsey.com/~/media/mckinsey/business%20functions/organization/our%20insights/unlocking%20success%20in%20digital%20transformations/unlocking-success-in-digital-transformations.pdf?shouldIndex=false, accessed November 10, 2020; M.A. Ilcus. 2018. "Impact of digitalization in business world". *Review of International Comparative Management*, Vol. 19 (4): 350-358.

transformations from the rest. Research further suggests that the route to success involves twenty-one ways falling under the following five umbrella categories:[1308]

(1) Having the right, digital-savvy leaders in place.
(2) Building capabilities for the workforce of the future.
(3) Empowering people to work in new ways.
(4) Giving day-to-day tools a digital upgrade.
(5) Communicating frequently via traditional and digital methods.

The pandemic has accelerated this timeline, with estimates suggesting that the business landscape has moved three to four years forward in a matter of months.[1309] The idea of a tipping point for technology absorption or digital disruption is not altogether novel, but the above said survey data suggest that the COVID-19 crisis is a tipping point of historic proportions, where more changes would be needed as the economic and human situations evolve. The findings also suggest that some significant lessons could be drawn from the initiatives companies have already embarked upon. These include the importance of learning, both tactically, in the process of making particular changes to businesses, like which technologies to execute and how; and corporate wise regarding how to manage change at a pace that exceeds that of previous experiences. As the pace of change is unlikely to slow down, both kinds of learning would be critical going forward.[1310]

Digital transformation is now becoming pivotal for sustaining business resilience. Digitalization has become essential for keeping current business models viable while helping to generate new income streams. But, in this FIR era, the enabling technologies while likely to be superior, are not only complex but also move extremely fast, such that it has not been easy for corporate leaders to play the needed technology catching-up game just to stay resilient. Digital transformation is expanding the scope of board's mandates, and flashing up new frontiers in risk and competition. Responding to these challenges would not necessarily imply completely overhauling the board model, but does need a thoughtful reflection on where to focus directors' attentions and actions. Boards addressing the following five strategic and operational questions are said to be likely to lead their companies to digital transformations that provides today's competitive advantage:[1311]

1308. De La Boutetiere, Montager & Reich 2018, *supra* note [1307].
1309. L. LaBerga, et al. 2020. "How COVID-19 has pushed companies over the technology tipping point-and transformed business forever: A new survey finds that responses to COVID-19 have speeded the adoption of digital technologies by several years-and that many of these changes could be here for the long haul". *McKinsey October 2020.* https://www.mckinsey.com/~/media/mckinsey/business%20functions/strategy%20and%20corporate%20finance/our%20insights/how%20covid%2019%20has%20pushed%20companies%20over%20the%20technology%20tipping%20point%20and%20transformed%20business%20forever/how-covid-19-has-pushed-companies-over-the%20technology%20tipping-point-final.pdf?shouldIndex=false, accessed November 10, 2020.
1310. LeBerga, O'Toole & Smaie 2020, *supra* note [1309].
1311. C. Huber, A. Sukharrevsky & R. Zemmel. 2021. "5 questions boards should be asking about digital transformation". *Harvard Business Review 21 June 2021.*

(1) Does the board understand the implications of digital and technology adequately to lead with valuable guidance? Bringing in tech experts, setting up of advisory units, or educational tours of successful tech entities might not be sufficient. To be more effective, boards could:
   (a) take a more strategic view when bringing in new directors, especially as to their actual experience in digital transformation, and whether these would fit with the company's digital strategy; and
   (b) put board members through intensive training workouts led by external experts or top technologists from the company itself and focus on the business implications of key technologies and methodologies. The idea is not so much about digital skills, but the shifting of mindsets especially for CEOs who need to take charge rather than letting the company be led by chief information/technology officers.

(2) Does the board fully understand whether the digital transformation has altered how the business and sector generate value? Boards generally have been entrusted to push company leadership on business models, and value creation and capture. From the digital transformation perspective, the following three vectors of value have been identified:
   (i) Whether the scale would be financially attractive enough. Business aspirations generally tend to be particular increments over previous years, and mainly conservative in nature. The pandemic has taught many companies that they could take huge leaps when under pressure. As a rule of thumb, digital initiatives are expected to drive more than 20% of operating profits, even as revenues and profits continue to surge. Board thinking needs therefore to find ways where digital would help to achieve this through the maneuvering of the company's technology model, operating model, or business model, or even that for the industry.
   (ii) The source of value creation is not necessarily confined to efficiency and cost cutting. Board leaders could drive management to develop a better understanding of the company's real sources of competitive advantage, especially as to how the transformation could leverage these advantages to deliver significant new sources of revenues.
   (iii) While many companies focus their investment horizons over the short term, Amazon, in contrast, has a seven-year horizon for its investments. Digital transformation could cost and takes a longer gestation period, such as to require a longer-term horizon. This kind of longer-term horizon could be hard for companies focusing on the short term, particularly in the capital markets. A clear view of long-term value involving the use of multiyear operating expenditures and so on would be helpful here. A long-term perspective of where value is heading in an industry is key to making the right assumptions about the benefits of digital transformation.

(3) Why do boards need to monitor and have regular feedbacks as to whether their digital transformation process is on the right track? This will require honest objective evaluation of the implemented strategy and the various

milestones in the company's digitalization roadmap. At times, this may require the vetting to be done by independent sources. Also, instead of spreading its resources across many initiatives as typically encountered in business digitalization, a company would do better by focusing on the two or three domains that could create the most value for the company. Further, when monitoring progress, boards are advised to focus on two sets of metrics:

(i) The first tracks outcomes and important leading indicators linked to value, like customer fulfilment in e-commerce. The idea of measuring ROI is to set up baselines as starting points against which to track progress.

(ii) The second addresses changes in behaviors and processes deep in the company. A key metric of this kind is the speed with which new ideas are being translated into frontline tools, while another involves gauging the percentage of talent that is actually working in agile teams where true changes take place.

(4) Why do boards need to have a sufficiently expansive view of talents?

(5) Why do boards need to have a clear view of emerging threats? These could extend from cybersecurity to competitive threats. Enhanced insights could be tapped by taking the outsider view as some hedge funds have now done via AI.

Finally, digital transformation involves businesses extracting data from consumers for monetization. This has driven controversies as to the extent to which this has been ethically undertaken. Regulators these days, whether in the US and the UK, and even more so in the EU, are demanding good answers for this from those businesses making good income out of this. All kinds of policy responses have been made, but a suggestion has been made about the simplicity of the matter by changing the way businesses, consumers and regulators think about this exchange between businesses and consumers in "barter" term. It has been argued that doing this will clarify the minds of regulators and investors to focus on the scale and nature of long-concealed exchanges that now lie at the center of the tech world, and how to create a more acceptable framework that protects consumers.[1312]

10.08 THE ESSENCE OF ESG

Businesses in most sectors and in most economies are now operating in the digital era, or at a time where incredible speed, complexity, and scale decide the outcomes and sustainability of business performance. It is in this context that the direction and control of companies or CG are being played out. Here, it is board leadership that decides on the business mission, be it through shareholder primacy or that of stakeholders, that also takes into account ESG considerations and cybersecurity risk

1312. G. Tett. 2021. "The data economy is a barter economy". *Harvard Business Review 6 July 2021.* https://hbr.org/2021/07/the-data-economy-is-a-barter-economy, accessed July 7, 2021.

that arises from operating in the digital era. The "E" element focuses on the impact of climate change on corporate performance, while the "S" focuses on the hybrid models of worksites and worker welfare. The "G" element focuses on board oversight of the direction and control of companies subject to the market for corporate control and the limits imposed by relevant aspects of hard corporate laws, as well as best practices in the form of soft law codes. These then are argued to be the essentials of the governance process in the digital era.

As mentioned earlier, Professor Colin Mayer of Oxford University has said that CP concerns companies finding solutions to the problems of people and planet, but not profiting from creating problems of either. This sounds a bit like the idea behind social entrepreneurship. In any case, there is greater consensus on this matter of business purpose than in finding how best to operationalize this notion, without the taking of untended, or unnecessary reputational and litigation risks for companies and board directors, especially with regards to increasing the disclosures of ESG and diversity data.[1313]

1313. M. Callahan, D.F. Larcker & B. Tayan. "The general counsel view of ESG risk". Rock Center for Corporate *Governance at Stanford University Working Paper 15 September 2021*.

CHAPTER 11

Concluding Note

Governance, or the board direction and control of company performance, has consistently struggled with the questions as to whether the quality of the governance process is mainly driven by the internal or external governance process, or both. It has been accepted in mainstream research that the quality of the governance process tends to be linked to success in enterprise performance or company resilience. It is also a general consensus that the quality or standard of the governance process is the outcome of the combined impacts of the internal and external governance processes. The internal governance process has to do with board oversight of the direction and control of the enterprise covering such areas as the leadership and management roles of directors pertaining to business purpose or mission, strategy formulation and execution, internal controls, and all things to do within an enterprise. It includes the management of relationships between shareholders and directors, or the principal-agency paradigm. This says that shareholders in advanced Western capitalist economies like the US, EU, and the UK entrust the management of the enterprise to directors, while directors owed fiduciary duties to shareholders. The book though does not deal with the governance system involving concentrated shareholdings typically found in family-run enterprises and government-linked companies (GLCs) commonly found in some European continental economies or various emerging economies. The external governance process involves gatekeeping function roles of policymakers; public regulators; and private regulators, like the capital markets, CRAs, external or statutory auditors, banks and financial institutions; and best practices guidance from industries, national, and international forums.

The book argues that the quality or standard of the governance process in the US, EU, and the UK economies are driven by processes of both internal and external governance mechanisms. Noting the expansiveness of these respective processes, the book focuses on the more major issues flashed out, as the governance process evolves over the last four-five decades. As much of the issues and challenges deal with human behaviors, the insights drawn from the in-depth examinations of this phenomenon need to be continually reviewed. As it is, the book looks at the ESG phenomenon, or the wider view of the governance process in the contexts of the COVID-19 pandemic, climate change risks, and the digitized economy, with focus on the US, UK, and the EU. In particular, the book examines the probable impacts of the ESG factors on the operational and financial performance of companies, and why integrated ESG reporting disclosure is likely to become mandatory in these respective jurisdictions.

11.01 INTERNAL ESG PROCESS

The recognition of the governance paradigm in the modern era began in 1999 in the UK through the work of the CC that was set up to probe into bad business practices with consequential financial harm to both investors and the company itself because of errant behaviors of corporate leaders. This explains why the work of the CC focuses on the financial aspects. The CC eventually came out with a CG Code providing guidance to companies as to how best to ensure that board oversight of the direction and control of a company falls in line with the interests of primary shareholders. The US has its equivalent best practice version, first introduced by the Business Roundtable, a formal gathering of CEOs of America's leading business corporations sometime in the 1970s. In the US case, the CG term at the time was not used, but instead the equivalent idea was spelled out in its best practice guidance, though much earlier in the 1930s, hints of the usual CG matters have been provided by the Berle and Means thesis. These renown business researchers called for the aligning of board and shareholder interests because of the problems created by dispersed share ownership.

Theoreticians introduced the agency paradigm, where the shareholders or principals entrusted the work of business management to the directors, or the board, as agents. This implies directors run the company for the primary interest of shareholders. In practice, the synchronization of interests between directors and the shareholders has frequently encountered various forms of difficulties, despite having help and guidance from both hard and soft laws governing business practices.

Activists have argued for the expansion of fiduciary duties of directors to primary shareholders to include other stakeholders, like employees, suppliers and the local communities. Stakeholders impacted in varying degrees by irresponsible actions of corporate leaders are increasingly showing interests in seeing the lessening of seismic corporate failures brought about by reckless risk-taking, or sheer dishonesty buttressed by wanton greed of directors. These stakeholders are therefore earnestly seeking to identify what could be further done to improve matters. Again, they found almost the same causes of irresponsible corporate failures perpetuated by bad directors aided by other interested stakeholders, and gaps in enforcement actions. Again, a litany of cases showed almost the equivalent actions of errant directors and others without commensurate repercussions to them, despite the overhauling of corporate legislations, and other soft laws reforms.

The claims in the preamble of legislations or CG codes echoing the repeated mantra of never letting such big corporate scandals recur are beginning to ring hollow. While enforcing agencies have been successful in sending some miscreant directors linked to the 2000 Dotcom scandals in the US to jail time, there have been hardly similar actions taken in the aftermath of the 2007-2008 GFC against bank directors widely called out for having engaged in reckless actions leading to the potential downfall of the banks they lead, if not for bailout support provided by state agencies in the US and the UK. Financial restructuring initiatives together with bank reform measures provided avenues for these large global US and UK banks to turn around. However, these banks in subsequent years have been linked to money-laundering and related activities.[1314] The impacted banks paid fines without admitting guilt, and agreed to be monitored for good behavior for a year, or in other cases, agreed to abide by deferred prosecution agreements. In other words, the directors have not been sanctioned personally, leaving the banks or rather the shareholders of the bank to pick up the tab, when these activities have been allegedly undertaken by the directors.

The above developments brought a lot of public angst and unease against not only bank directors but also other business directors. Many of these directors are found to be linked to faulty decision-making in big matters, without proper due diligence. The US with plenty of prosecutor options at its disposal did not look to lawmaking in response, but the UK has responded with fresh measures lately[1315] so as to keep big companies, and errant directors in line, and in the process give board oversight of the direction and control of companies the due regulatory attention it needed. Law reform advocates in the UK have cited recent failures of the UK SFO to prosecute large companies and senior individuals as evidence of the need for reform on corporate criminal liability. In general, it is relatively easier to apply the identification principles in small, rather than big companies. This is because the governance structures of large entities often suggest that the autonomy required to be treated as the directing mind and will for designated transactions or series of events is not an individual, as authority is often retained by the board or delegated to groups of individuals in designated committees. There are though exceptions to the identification principle, including the failure to prevent facilitation of tax evasion and failure to prevent bribery offenses principle, as well as strict liability criminal offenses in environmental, health and safety and consumer protection laws. The UK government in 2020 in response to its 2017 consultation on economic crime concluded that there has been no clear view on what corporate liability offenses could be drafted to replace the identification principle, and hence no significant evidence was submitted supporting the case for a change in the law. There have been also questions raised as to whether there is a need for criminal sanctions in the already heavily regulated financial services sector. However, it has been observed that these various leading global banks continue to offend and pay the due fines as if to indicate a gaming process in motion, without little signs of remorse from the banks involved. The same too can be said of global digital platform companies that continually test the resolve of regulators with their market-dominating and private data infringing actions.

The SFO repeated calls for reforms, particularly after the recent collapse at trial of its prosecution on an entity where the court held that the identification principle has not been fulfilled by the prosecution simply relying on the alleged involvement of very

1314. P. Yeoh. 2016. "CG failures and the road to crime". *Journal of Financial Crime*, Vol. 23 (1): 216-230.
1315. J. O'Brien & O. Dixon. 2014. "Deferred prosecutions in the corporate sector". *Seattle University Law Review*, Vol. 37 (2014): 475-509.

senior individuals in the alleged wrongdoing. The court ruled that the entity's governance structures meant that these senior figures did not have the requisite authority to complete the transactions involved.[1316] The UK government in response in November 2020 directed the Law Commission to outline an assessment of different options for reform. Responses to the June 9, 2021, Law Commission is due by the end of August 2021.[1317] Law reformists point to recently failed prosecutions that corporate wrongdoing at senior levels has gone unpunished, expect tough measures to follow. Directors individually or collectively as a board might find it useful to monitor the outcome of the process.

As businesses and policymakers struggle to find the appropriate solutions, COVID-19 and its pandemic impacts on the business front have accelerated and magnified the usual problems linked to bad business practices. In the midst of all these, the ESG mantra has also accelerated. The pandemic and increasing digitalization of the economy have upgraded the ESG cause in business practices. Hitherto, governance principles since the 1990s have guided business practices in companies with dispersed ownership, as well as those with concentrated ownership. The reason is simple. Countries in advanced and emerging economies with heavy capitalism or even social capitalism orientations are aware of the importance of this when they compete for capital or funding to finance their economies or businesses. Most are aware that commonly held governance practices, such as the role of board oversight, role of independent board members, reliable internal controls, protections for minority shareholders, and so on, attract equity investors and debt financiers. They claim in general to adhere to best business practices, inclusive of ESG factors. They also claimed to frown upon bad corporate practices. They point to the use of both soft and hard laws in their respective countries serving to keep companies and directors from becoming errant. The "E" and the "S" elements of the ESG paradigm have over the past three decades or so exist as subsets of the greater governance process, and at best in the form of CSR practices that eventually degenerated into mere marketing and public relations gimmicks. It was the impacts of the UN PRI and private initiative of the investing community in 2015 that raised the profiles of the "E" and "S" elements into the same level as the governance or "G" part of the ESG thesis.

Very importantly, where the "E" of ESG is concerned, the Conference of the Parties (COP) refers to the 197 jurisdictions that agreed to the UN Framework Convention on Climate Change at a meeting in 1994. This ratified the treaty seeking to address dangerous human activities on the climate system through stabilizing the levels of greenhouse gas emissions under the convention. COP's 26th meeting recently completed on November 12, 2021, in Glasgow is suitably abbreviated as COP26. This

1316. P. Rappo & A. Al-Zarrad. 2021 "The Serco episode concludes: Where to next for the SFO?" *DLA Piper Paper 10 May 2021*. https://www.dlapiper.com/en/us/insights/publications/2021/05/the-serco-episode-concludes/, accessed May 11, 2021.

1317. Law Commission. 2021. "Corporate criminal liability: A discussion paper". Law Commission 9 June 2021. https://s3-eu-west-2.amazonaws.com/lawcom-prod-storage-11jsxou24uy7q/uploads/2021/06/Corporate-Criminal-Liability-Discussion-Paper.pdf, accessed June 10, 2021.

UN-sponsored seminal conference on climate change mitigation ended positively for some and negatively for others.

Still, the global engagement, deliberations and consensus reached determine the global response to climate change and transform the landscape where businesses operate. Participants generally also agreed that the private domain will provide the only real chance for going round a climate disaster via a comprehensive total economic transformation. As such, businesses would have to come to terms with a world where the environment would materially influence business strategies and actions. The more important lessons or guides from COP26 include the political wills of governments to push through necessary regulatory reforms, the necessity for businesses to sincerely and passionately make the transformative actions required, enough funding support from affluent nations and global financial institutions, the benefit of going forward with the establishment of a global market in carbon offsets and emissions trading, and the need to put greater attention to biodiversity and related issues.

The COVID-19 pandemic in the form of health risks, diversity and inequality challenges at worksites, together with the serious effects of climate change in the form of massive floods and widespread forest fires, have hoisted these two "E" and "S" elements alongside governance in equivalent importance. The popular drive now is for governance practices to incorporate the "E" and the "S" elements in a tripartite form. This appears to be the direction going forward. Now national policymakers, regulators, businesses, and social activists are busy designing the ESG metrics and standards alongside international multilateral institutions to enable ESG goals to be tracked, measured and addressed, and followed across the world. These have earlier been tried before at the height of the CSR days, but without much success as many businesses are alleged to have been engaged with whitewashing or greenwashing practices. Time will tell whether the present ESG drive would succeed, or go the way the CSR years did.

Corporate leaders to whom the shareholders have entrusted the destinies of companies they invested in have become all-powerful, as alleged in several litigations against some corporate leaders. Observations of several high-profile cases have supported this. There have been many good examples of failures, especially by NEDs in curbing the domineering behaviors of CEOS that led to the downfall of both big banks and big corporations. This sets the context of a similar allegation which union pension fund and asset managers have brought against Tesla's CEO Elon Musk over the allegation that the celebrity CEO strong-armed Tesla's board of directors into depleting the company's assets with the USD 2.6 billion all-stock deal for Solar City.[1318] Musk has contended that he holds the same 22 percentage of equity in both companies and there has been no cash involved in the strategic merger deal sought to combine Tesla's battery business with SolarCity's sustainable energy generation. The lawsuit on the other hand has alleged that Musk has pushed the Tesla board into agreeing to pay more for SolarCity and misleading shareholders about the company's deteriorating financial health. Tesla's board has previously settled an equivalent lawsuit last year for USD 60

1318. T. Hals & S. Jackson. 2021. "Musk tells SolarCity trial that Tesla would 'die' if he wasn't CEO". *Reuters* 13 July 2021. https://www.reuters.com/business/musk-testify-defense-teslas-26-bln-deal-solarcity-2021-07-12/, accessed July 13, 2021.

million paid by insurance without admitting guilt. They might soon need to give clearer signs with regards to Musk's behavior as the CEO, now that Tesla's stock price and the Nasdaq 100 index has fallen from 0.83 to 0.14, largely attributed to the company's USD 1.5 billion exposure to Bitcoin.[1319]

This has not been consistently the case though, as small activist shareholders have also been successful in helping to change board orientation in several equally high-profile cases when pushing for greater focus on ESG matters.[1320] Board oversight powers enable directors to lead and manage companies in their own way toward not only corporate success but also downfall, when recklessly done. These have been shown in various cases in the US, the EU, and the UK. These cases and more have also shown that there could be limits to these when shareholders decide to act for their agenda in courts.

Three key lessons flow from the outcomes of these cases.[1321] First, companies are set up with a series of checks and balances, and one of them has been the ability to replace directors where investors are unhappy with the direction of the company. This has proven to be more reflective in theory than in practice. Election of board members has been not particularly democratic, when insiders select the candidate, and no one runs against them. The primary shareholder model has been entirely based on a mechanism for minimizing agency costs. When investors have no recourse, when they are not happy with an investment, other than selling the share when it is undervalued, capital cost would reflect the additional risk, but when this becomes intolerable as demonstrated in recent cases, shareholders would recognize the potential for generating value by leveraging shareholder discontent to support meaningful change. Second, past performance is no guarantee of future performance. Even though a business model has been successful, this does not necessarily mean that it should not be continually reexamined.

The business and scientific case for environmental and social matters has been made decades ago, but the COVID-19 pandemic and the huge benefits of digitalization have now pushed political and consumer consensus to a tipping point where failures to adapt to the changing environment could slide corporate fortunes badly and quickly. Third, index funds, pension funds, and other major institutional investors have majority or near-majority permanent holdings. They might be hesitant in launching dissident campaigns themselves, but they would be happy to support one where they also do not believe that directors have been providing adequate board oversight, and this implies directors needing to make the case to the market on a regular basis. Directors, as such, should avoid responding to criticisms with hostility, but instead

1319. J. Ossinger. 2021. "Tesla correlation to big tech breaks down. Blame bitcoin". *Bloomberg 15 July 2021.* https://www.bloomberg.com/news/articles/2021-07-15/bitcoin-seen-as-reason-for-sliding-tesla-correlation-to-big-tech?utm_source = google&utm_medium = bd&cmpId = google, accessed July 16, 2021.

1320. N. Minow. 2021. "Memo to corporate directors: Three lessons from the Exxon-Mobil activist victory". *Harvard Law School Forum on CG 30/05/21.* https://corpgov.law.harvard.edu/2021/05/30/memo-to-corporate-directors-three-lessons-from-the-exxon-mobil-activist-victory/, accessed June 1, 2021.

1321. Minow 2021, *supra* note [1320].

with constructive engagements. This further means paying more attention to independence that goes beyond resume disclosures, soliciting suggestions from investors and ensuring that all directors know their obligations as fiduciaries is to shareholders, not executives, and that their actions make that message clear to shareholders as well.

Directors of late in some big companies in the US and UK have attracted criticisms over hike in pays and linked financial incentives in the midst of massive economic sufferings. The US has via legislative reforms like SOX 2002 and the 2010 DFA and other regulatory initiatives provided various guard rails against excessive rewards for corporate leaders. However, judging by events in recent years up to now,[1322]some companies and banks are still bent on doing what they did in the past. Against the background of widespread financial hardships, these actions attract considerable criticisms.

According to research from London-based independent High Pay Centre, FTSE 100 chief executives earn a median of GBP 3.6 million (USD 4.9 million) a year, more than hundred times the GBP 31,463 earned by full-time employees.[1323] Tim Steiner, the highest-paid CEO of supermarket Ocado was paid GBP 58.7 million in 2019, or 2,605 times the company's staff on average; in other words, in one day he earned seven times their annual salary. In the US, Washington DC-based think tank Economic Policy Institute showed CEOs of 350 largest US corporations earned an average of USD 21.3 million (GBP 16.9 million) in 2019. This sets the CEO-to-worker pay ratio of 320 to 1, or more than five times the level in 1989. These findings are troubling, given that the COVID-19 pandemic has worsened inequality across the world, exposing low-income wage earners to greater health risks, job losses, and dramatic fall in well-being. These stark divisions have grown into sharper focus, as awareness grows of the value of essential workers, often with few employment rights and little pay. There is growing confusion and disappointments over these extraordinary high salaries that top corporate leaders persist in earning. Equally, questions persist as to how these big pay packages come about, by whom, how they get through, and whether they should continue to have a place in post-pandemic society.

It has been pointed out that executive pay gap began sometime in the 1980s in the Reagan and Thatcher years. Their political philosophies drove deregulation, privatization and free market capitalism, but taking a dim view on labor. There are pros and cons on the impact of such policy measures. However, FTSE 100 data since 2000 demonstrated that all-employee pay increased around 3% annually on overage, whereas CEO pay increased by about 10% annually after executive pay became linked to share prices and asset-based rewards. The *raison d'etre* for this is the notion and practice of paying a CEO according to a company's financial performance, they being the most important factor of success. CEOs are paid basic salaries and performance-linked bonuses and stock options that enable them to acquire company shares at

1322. P. Yeung. 2021. "Why CEOs make so much money: It seems like the salaries of big-time CEOs just keep getting bigger. But why do they make so much, and has it always been this way?". *BBC 27 January 2021*. https://www.bbc.com/worklife/article/20210125-why-ceos-make-so-much-money, accessed January 28, 2021.
1323. Yeung 2021, *supra* note [1322].

predetermined prices, and hence Ocado CEO Steiner's 2019 pay package included a bonus of GBP 54 million for achieving a five-year growth incentive plan that measures the company's share price growth relative to the FTSE 100.[1324]

When powers of shareholders, and in particular institutional shareholders, grow, they pressure for booming share prices that lead to booming pay packages for CEOs, duly approved by fellow directors eager to please their investors with continuing cycles of price-driven salaries. Compensation committees generally rely on conventional measures of past experience and performance as well as benchmarking[1325] as part of the pay determination process. Research suggests[1326]that it is this that has been accelerating pay inflation as such peer companies enable justification of the high level of CEO pay. This is viewed as problematic, as in general, compensation committees often report directly to the CEO, lack impartiality. It is further observed empirically that the strongest correlation between pay and company financial measures is not financial performance, but rather corporate size, as in practice, bigger enterprises have more funds to pay.[1327]This also suggests why companies seek to grow big and fast, as seen in many bank mergers and other corporate fiascos[1328] not undertaken with proper due diligence.

Supporters of current CEO pay systems justify this by pointing to the exceptional talents of Jobs at Apple, Bezos at Amazon, and Musk at Tesla. This has been the case for many founder-CEOs, but the role of the average CEO, who is not a founder, nor a successful visionary, according to one research, has been overstated, and that enterprises can do well not because of this factor alone, but due to booming economic conditions, oligopolistic practices, or even highly positive worker contributions.[1329] The 2000 Dotcom fiasco and the 2007-2008 GFC showed good examples as to how performance and pay do not always align. Controversial high pays of CEOs continue to haunt corporate corridors, when executives are seen to still get handsome pay rewards even though the companies they lead have not been performing because of the impact of the pandemic.[1330] This came to a head at British Gas with a five-day strike, as response plans to reduce workforce and shifting of employees to new contracts with

1324. P. Willman & A. Pepper. 2020. "The role played by large firms in generating income inequality: UK FTSE 100 pay practices in the late twentieth and early twenty-first centuries". *Economy and Society*, Vol. 49 (4): 516-539.
1325. S. Clifford. 2017. *The CEO pay machine: How it trashes America and how to stop it*. New York: Blue Rider Press; L. Bebchuk & J. Fried. 2006. *Pay without performance: The unfulfilled promise of executive compensation*. Cambridge: Harvard University Press.
1326. M. Faulkender & J. Yang. 2010. "Inside the black box: The role and compositions of compensation peer groups". *Journal of Financial Economics*, Vol. 96 (2): 257-270.
1327. Willman & Pepper 2017, *supra* note [1324].
1328. Treasury. 2013. "RBS and the case of a bad bank: The government's review". *Treasury Report November 2013*. https://assets.publishing.service.gov.uk/government/uploads/system/uploads/attachment_data/file/254540/PU1581_RBS_bad_bank_Govt_review.pdf, accessed November 10, 2020.
1329. D. Bolchover. 2012. *Pay check: Are top earners really worth it?*. London: Coptic.
1330. D. Gelles. 2021. "C.E.O. pay remains stratospheric, even at companies battered by pandemic". *New York Times 24 April 2021*. https://www.nytimes.com/2021/04/24/business/ceos-pandemic-compensation.html, accessed April 25, 2021.

fewer rights became hugely resisted.[1331] This comes after the CEO of Centrica, the parent company, received a 44% pay rise to GBP 2.4 million. Such case examples reflect a vortex of self-interest between shareholders, board members and executives and help to explain why CEO pay continues to hike in this manner.[1332]

With enhanced disclosure obligations on executive pays in both the UK and the US, there have been some improvements. There are signs that the rise of CEO pay is at least slowing, and has in fact said to have plateaued in recent years at around GBP 4-5 million. This has been attributed to the changing mindsets of institutional investors and sovereign wealth funds funded by the general public via pension and investment funds. Such institutions are becoming more sensitive to the growing unease over this phenomenon.[1333] There is also the growing pressure of accountability pushed in policymaking corridors proposing time limits on company stock sales to shift the focus from short-term shareholder returns to the longer-term goals of stakeholders,[1334]and from private sector initiatives[1335]such as seen in San Francisco and Portland in the US where businesses are taxed if their pay ratio is too high thereby creating an explicit economic incentive for greater equality. There have also been nice gestures exemplified by executives at Boeing, Marriott and PwC voluntarily sacrificing some of their pay to save staff jobs in 2020, but commentators argue that enterprises could take more substantial meaningful steps to reduce pay gaps. These could include having worker voice in boardrooms, as well as better reporting of company pay data to increase accountability.[1336] With global slowdowns on the horizon, as the pandemic rages on, the scrutiny of inequality would likely heighten, especially when, for example, gender pay gap data in British investment banking showed UK investment banks pay women 56% of what their male colleagues make, according to a Bloomberg September 28, 2021 article authored by Wilson, Dakers & Greenfield.

On a more positive note, even as shareholder litigation fears over excessive director pay have subsided in the past few years, the numbers of companies applying a ceiling to directors' compensations continued to grow.[1337] A review of proxy statements in the disclosures of the percentage of companies reporting some kind of

1331. BBC. 2021. "British gas staff start five-day strike in 'fire and rehire' row". *BBC 7 January 2021*. https://www.bbc.com/news/business-55562904, accessed January 8, 2021.
1332. Bolchover 2012, *supra* note [1329].
1333. Willman & Pepper 2020, *supra* note [1324].
1334. E. Warren. 2019. "Accountable Capitalism Act". https://www.warren.senate.gov/imo/media/doc/Accountable%20Capitalism%20Act%20One-Pager.pdf, accessed November 10, 2020.
1335. P. Michalowski. 2019. "San Francisco proposes tax on businesses with high executive pay". *PwC June 2019*. https://www.pwc.com/us/en/services/tax/state-local-tax/library/newsletters/salt-insights/san-francisco-proposes-tax-on-businesses-with-high-executive-pay.html#:~:text=This%20tax%20would%20be%20imposed,(San%20Francisco%20Initiative%20Ordinance.), accessed November 10, 2020.
1336. P. Eavis. 2020. "As the pandemic forced layoffs, CEOs give up little". *The New York Times 29 July 2020*. https://www.pwc.com/us/en/services/tax/state-local-tax/library/newsletters/salt-insights/san-francisco-proposes-tax-on-businesses-with-high-executive-pay.html#:~:text=This%20tax%20would%20be%20imposed,(San%20Francisco%20Initiative%20Ordinance.), accessed November 10, 2022.
1337. M. Tonello, et al. 2021. "Director compensation practices in the Russell 3000 and S&P 500". *Harvard Law School Forum on CG 16 June 2021*. https://corpgov.law.harvard.edu/2021/06/16/director-compensation-practices-in-the-russell-3000-and-sp-500, accessed June 17, 2021.

director pay ceiling has grown from 48.7% to 61.5% in Russell 3000, and from 53% to 66.9% in the S&P 500. Specifically, the share of companies imposing limits on total director compensation whether in cash only or in cash and equity has risen to 26.9% in the Russell 3000 and 28.9% in the S&P 500. Also, around 30% of S&P companies have dollar-denominated equity limits, and 16.3% of Russell 3000 companies disclose share-denominated equity limits.

The launching of compensation limits for directors could help mitigate the risks of litigation, including heading off objections from proxy advisers. The Institutional Shareholders Services (ISS) consider, in particular, the adoption of pay limits when evaluating NED compensation policies, for which management seeks shareholder ratification.[1338] It also advises a vote against directors responsible for framing board compensation at a company that demonstrates excessive director pay for two successive years, unless it discloses a compelling reason, or other mitigating factors for being that different. Another large proxy advisory service[1339]in the US also cautions about the risks of excessive pay, as this could compromise the objectivity and independence of NEDs. Its guidelines though are not clear on what should be treated as excessive, and also fail to equally stress the importance of benchmarking by company size and industry. It has been contended that over time, and for reasons mentioned earlier, a ceiling for director equity pay might become a standard part of all or most director equity plans.[1340] To set a ceiling on cash payments, management could submit a proposal on the specific issues of director compensation limit for a vote at the next annual meeting. Such an action would provide equivalent legal protection as equity pay ceilings in equity plans. As an alternative, a change in the board or committee charter that applies an overall ceiling to total director compensation amounts could be sought, but this would not grant legal protection, unless ratified by shareholders.

Given the growing emerging threats from geopolitical tensions in global trade trends, the resurgences of narrow isolationist national trade practices threatening basic global trade rules governed and enforced by the World Trade Organization (WTO), cybersecurity risk, and the ongoing virus pandemic, many businesses have to adjust or even overhaul their business risk management practices. Geopolitical and related risk management is one critical business area that directors need to roll up their sleeves, but even more so in the cybersecurity risk domain. Critical business risks include those to do with massive disruptions in supply chains, market space collapse, financial structures falling apart, dramatic shifts in worker working habits, and cybersecurity threats.

While the forces impacting a company's risk profile could emanate from external and internal sources, and directors could respond with risk management systems

1338. Institutional Shareholders Services (ISS). 2020. "US proxy voting guidelines: Benchmark policy recommendations". *ISS 9 November 2020*. https://www.issgovernance.com/file/policy/active/americas/US-Voting-Guidelines.pdf, accessed November 10, 2020.
1339. Glass Lewis. 2021. "2021 proxy paper: Guidelines: An overview of the Glass Lewis approach to proxy advice: US". *Glass Lewis November 2020*. https://www.glasslewis.com/wp-content/uploads/2020/11/US-Voting-Guidelines-GL.pdf?hsCtaTracking=7c712e31-24fb-4a3a-b396-9e8568fa0685%7C86255695-f1f4-47cb-8dc0-e919a9a5cf5b, accessed December 12, 2020.
1340. Tonello et al. 2021, *supra* note [1337].

supported by third-party help, the directors are unlikely to be able to delegate off their responsibility. Depending on the situation, corporate leaders might have to evaluate the impact that political and media scrutiny on the company's operations in one area has on its holdings in other locales. Hence, they might have to balance given the risks, near and long-term market priorities, and deal with a global workforce holding divergent views on data privacy and human rights. These risks could be addressed through a five-throng framework:[1341]

(1) Board actions in examining the wider strategic landscape, full range of risk scenarios and consequences, or key decision points.
(2) Crafting short-term, medium and long-term strategies to ensure the company's ability to grapple with fast-changing or emergency situations, and making the necessary investments needed to seize opportunities and become more resilient.
(3) Think critically about the corporate narrative. It should consider the trade-offs of framing how the company talks about itself if that narrative could generate conflicts with stakeholders, and what the potential remedies could be.
(4) Apply refreshed risk frameworks and guidelines. To deal with high-risk markets because of political instability, or the threats of international sanctions, the board could develop market-specific evaluations or compacts that fuse corporate strategy and risk management.
(5) Secure stakeholders' hearts and minds. The board can cultivate cohesiveness by bringing key stakeholders together to share views and collaborate.

With accelerating turbulence swirling within economies and globally, the board have to be on guard. The board needs to regularly look up from tending to the immediate needs, like cybersecurity threats of their operating environments, to learn, adapt, and prepare for external and internal shocks and pressures.[1342]

A further pivotal agenda for board attention and action concerns digital transformations. Many digital trends that began or accelerated during the COVID-19 pandemic, from self-installation of internet services to mobile banking and virtual medical visit would likely stay. The challenge for the board is how to link with their customers in a highly accelerated digital world.[1343] Hitherto, reputation-dented mega banks like the RBS and WF have shown how and why digital transformations are not about being

1341. A. Grant, Z. Haider & A. Levy. 2021. "How global companies can manage geopolitical risk: Global enterprises can proactively manage the threats that escalating international and international political tensions posed to their operations, performance and culture". *McKinsey July 2021*. https://www.mckinsey.com/business-functions/risk/our-insights/how-global-companies-can-manage-geopolitical-risk, accessed July 16, 2021.
1342. Grant, Haider & Levy 2021, *supra* note [1341].
1343. A. Sraders. 2021. "What will 'chapter 2 of the digital economy' look like? Here's what these finance execs think". *Fortune 22 April 2021*. https://fortune.com/2021/04/21/financial-industry-digital-transformation-paypal-dan-schulman-ibm-wells-fargo-prudential-bitcoin-banking-apps/, accessed April 23, 2021.

digital, but about creating value. Boards could look to five specific areas where they could have the most impact:[1344]

(1) The board's goal is not merely about understanding the technology, but to understand its implications, meaning how its digital transformation can unlock new sources of revenue and to help strengthen the company gain competitive advantage.
(2) The creation of value aligns with the board's most important mandate. Boards could examine value across scale, source, and scope.
(3) Monitor whether the digital transformation is delivering. While board members may have some type of dashboard to review, the metrics do not show whether digital is happening. This could involve looking into the pace with which new ideas are transformed into frontline tools, the percentage of talents actually working in agile teams where true change occurs, or the tracking of the return on investment of digital and technical investments.
(4) Get expansive about talent. Boards would need to engage with senior leadership on progress made in developing their in-house digital talent. It is not so much about hiring the company's way to victory, but the upgrading of talent as a core corporate initiative to move past outdated training approaches toward targeted learning journeys that map to the capability needs of the company for the next six to twelve months.
(5) Responding to where nontraditional emerging risks are. Thus, though cybersecurity is now a top board agenda item, local compliance or national security laws, for instance, have generated risks when companies have their servers located in these corresponding locations. This means the board would need to expand their views of where threats exist, as digital businesses expand into new domains. E-commerce businesses getting into data management, tech companies getting into banking, or retailing getting into logistics are good examples.

Prior to the onset of COVID-19, boards have already been having concerns about the impact of digitalization on their business models. They now need to be proactive in leading their companies' response and to accelerate their digital transformation initiatives. A further example, on what boards might need to pay some attention to, pertains to whistleblowing in the digital era. Whistleblowing has helped to uncover the misdeeds found in many corporate scandals,[1345] but reviews of existing practices in various businesses have put a shine on virtual whistleblowing and that it has become increasingly common, given the associated benefits of speed, anonymity, and impact. Virtual forms of whistleblowing have procedural and substantive implications on

1344. C. Huber, A. Sukharevsky & R. Zemmel. 2021. "How boards can help digital transformations: Board can add value to their business's digital transformation in five specific areas". *McKinsey June 2021.* https://www.mckinsey.com/business-functions/mckinsey-digital/our-insights/how-boards-can-help-digital-transformations, accessed July 16, 2021.
1345. P. Yeoh. 2014. "Whistleblowing: Motivations, corporate self-regulation, and the law". *International Journal of Law and Management*, Vol. 56 (6): 459-474.

matters like privacy and anonymity, rewards and reprisals, as well as legal protections. The following measures have been suggested to advance the positive outcomes of whistleblowing in the digital era while ameliorating those that are negative.[1346]

(1) To deter unjustifiable whistleblowing, a culture of ethics, accountability and transparency should be fostered, where employees are able to raise criticisms without fear. These avenues include multiple channels for employee involvement and empowerment via joint labor-management committees, suggestions schemes, or gainsharing and similar incentives for work improvements. All these could help to prevent problems that could prompt external whistleblowing, especially in its virtual form.

(2) Boards could devise a social media policy, a confidentiality policy, and an information systems policy. These should all be appropriately communicated to employees so that they become fully aware of their responsibilities in posting, or discussing organizational data online, whether using their personal devices, or the company's. To forestall potential legal scrutiny, such policies have to be clear, reasonable, well communicated, consistently enforced, and comply with any applicable collective agreement and the law. The company should also provide due process for anyone accused of wrongdoing. This means adequate notice, a fair hearing, and judgment based on evidence.

(3) Good public relations, treating business partners and customers fairly and establishing an effective one-point whistleblowing contact line are likely to help in deterring external whistleblowing.

(4) Boards should prepare how to respond when faced with virtual whistleblowing crisis. Although the nature and cause of whistleblowing could vary, a company needs to have a preestablished process that lays out various kinds of scenario, which organ to make decisions and take actions, what actions to be taken, timing for responses, channels of communications, rationale for the decision, and the process of evaluating effectiveness and remedies. These preparations should be informed by key corporate principles and priorities, instead of short-term, self-interested attempts to defend the company's image at all costs. For example, the company should be ready, depending on the situation, to admit mistakes, deny an accusation of wrongdoing, correct a wrongdoing, negotiate a compromise, or initiate action against a whistleblower. Legal experts should be on hand to deal with potential defamation case where a whistleblower has provided data online, untruthfully or maliciously.

1346. H. Lam & M. Harcourt. 2019. "Whistle-blowing in the digital era: Motives, issues and recommendations". *New Technology, Work and Employment,* Vol. 34 (2): 174-190.

11.02 EXTERNAL GOVERNANCE PROCESS

Seismic corporate scandals that broke out in the 1990s in the UK, and in late 1990s in the US, brought responses from policymakers and regulators in both the UK and the US. The UK responded with soft law CG code that listed companies have to abide by, along with other relevant provisions in company law. The US responded with SOX that adds more layers of directors' accountability, and including some provisions for other financial gatekeepers. Both policy measures in the UK and the US essentially sought to deter companies and their boards from improper obligatory financial disclosures. The UK at the time opts to rely more on soft law codes, whereas the US in line with its rules-based business law approach chooses to rely more on hard laws, rather than merely on best practices offered by the Business Roundtable. The UK though in the face of the unfolding of more serious corporate scandals in the early 2000 adapted its usual approach by a comprehensive redesigning of its company law into the massive CA 2006. This new statute for the first time in UK corporate history codified directors' duties hitherto driven mainly by common law principles.

This legislation makes a not so clear glimpse of the direction of business purpose, whether through the shareholder primacy approach or the SA. This is because the enlightened shareholder approach that the statute introduces is not exactly clear-cut. This said guidance for company directors tells them to manage their enterprises successfully through entrepreneurial insights and effective direction and control, but with due regards for interests of employees, customers, suppliers and the local communities to ensure the long-term sustainability of their respective enterprises. This approach appears to be a hybrid between the shareholder primacy and stakeholder-oriented approach. The hard law implications for "due regards" seems to be equivocal, as to whether it is more aspirational or a must in law. The ambiguous corporate law landscape and the general enforcement weakness taken together have not been particularly helpful in curbing corporate excesses in terms of reckless risk-taking, perverse incentive pay limitations, general ineffective contributions from independent board members, general shareholder apathy, general failures of gatekeeping functions from state to private actors, and so on.

These seem to repeat the weaknesses found in prior-SOX and prior CA 2006 years. Both relevant soft and hard laws have been in play, but yet seismic corporate failures occur, while repercussions on directors and others involved have not commensurate with their severities. The public in general, and consumers, employees, and investors in particular have become angry and disillusioned with these financially harmful events. Again, the state responded with so-called tougher measures, like enhancing accountability measures for directors and others. In the US, this came in the form of the 2010 DFA, while the UK reformed or rather updated its CG code, together with piecemeal legislative measures targeted at board pay and so on, but no singular framework to address the governance flaws.

Policymakers and others in the US believe that reforms via the comprehensive 2010 DFA framework would do the trick this time around, while the UK seems to think that its updated CG Code and the newly minted Wates CG framework for large private enterprises together with reforms in banking laws would be enough to forestall potential risks flowing from bad behaviors of corporate leaders and gaps in monitoring and enforcement. As it turns out, in both the US and the UK, these measures did not deter corporate adventurers from gaming the system again. Case studies of failed big and smaller corporations provide good evidence of this. The EU instituting equivalent measures has also faced such recurring problems.

Various experts have cautioned that governance practices in the digital era would necessitate adaptation or reforming of current governance process best practices, together with adaptations, or even the overhaul of existing company laws so as to fit businesses practices in the digital economy. In one situation, experts have been able to illustrate the crucial role law could play in resolving digitalization development in the financial sector by offering a framework of legally enforceable principles and values in which such innovations could occur without threatening the general basis of financial markets law, and more generally the rule of law and basic human rights.[1347] Others argue that a tension exists between the incentive created by modern governance and the business needs of today's digital platforms. This needs a new regulatory direction that draws on three interconnected strategies. It would involve the creation of more community-driven forms of organization, the design of open and accessible platform culture, and facilitating the creation, curation and consumption of meaningful content.[1348] Thus, the features of digital platforms are consistent with network theory applications where stakeholders are the nodes rotating around the platform.

Digital platforms in this sense are a new virtual stakeholder that links shareholders, managers, employees, customers, suppliers and so on. When traditional stakeholders become digitally linked via bridging platforms, they help to improve their risk-adjusted return proceeds arising partly from better and more timely flow of digitized information. Conflicts of interest arising from interactions among composite stakeholders are reshaped by interfacing digital platforms through the sharing of data. The goal here is the design of better ecosystems that could converge interests and make the digital supply and value chain more resilient, and even more eco-friendly.[1349] Yet, still others point to weaponries available from FIR enabling technologies for the pursuance of competitive dominance strategy in the marketplace. These are already successfully deployed by Facebook, Google, Amazon, newly emerging Fintech like Revolut and Robinhood. However, this kind of market dominance strategy risks generating further anti-competition risks that are already attracting regulators' attention and responses, and in some situations leading to enforcement actions and fines. These developments suggest that digital transformation of businesses could generate technological and market competitive advantages. These benefits though need to be

1347. I. HY. Chiu & G. Deipenbrock (eds.). 2021. *Routledge handbook of financial technology and law*. Abingdon: Routledge.
1348. M. Fenwick, J.A. McCahery & E.P.M. Vermeulen. 2019. "The end of 'corporate' governance: Hello 'platform' governance". *European Business Organization Law Review*, Vol. 20 (2019): 171-199.
1349. R. Moro-Visconti. 2020. "Corporate governance, digital platforms and network theory: Information and risk-return of connected stakeholders". *Managing Control*, Vol. 2 (2020): 179-204; R. Moro-Visconti. 2021. "Networking digital platforms and healthcare project finance bankability". *Sustainability*, Vol. 13 (9): 5061-5078.

managed without getting into trouble with anti-competition laws as the company grows bigger and stronger in the market place.

Time will tell whether this will lead to the escalation of anti-competition practices or breach of data privacy laws and regulations, or whether with the easier access to such powerful technologies it would become harder for companies to lean on the business dominance strategy, given the equalization effect provided by more widely available technology. In the meantime, available business laws in the land would tell which would be the more likely direction, as far as allegations of anti-competition business practices in the digital business world are concerned. Facebook, for example, has been sued for various anti-competition practices in the US, but the courts have ruled in its favor citing the absence of convincing data showing its dominance in the marketplace.[1350] Still, Facebook, Google and Amazon are being continuously sued in the US and elsewhere for anti-competition practices, or breach of data privacy.[1351] For example, regulators in the US are reported to be appealing their allegations against Facebook soon. These suggest the law is still hard at work, and that technology power does not have all its way.

When it comes to the domain of external governance, there is the need for companies not only to comply with all kinds of corporate and business laws that each particular business has to adhere to. Working and collaborating alongside with other companies in business networks and so on, a company can do its part in providing feedbacks to the policymakers and regulatory agencies, whether particular laws or particular aspects of the law are accomplishing their intended goals, whether there have been unintended side effects that have become harmful to the prospects of businesses going forward. Apart from giving feedbacks to the government's consultation papers, such as those to do with corporate criminal liability or business online harms, companies can play more proactive roles by lobbying for government policies and measures that could strengthen business resilience in economic crisis situations, such as when the economy has to lock down for health protection and safety.

These are matters company directors would have to give some attention to, as shareholders are more likely to just draw attention to them, but only galvanized the board to take actions when they feel that the company is not heading in the right direction, such as the recent moves by some to successfully pressure even very big companies to pay fair attention to surging ESG matters. Another good example comes from a recent US Supreme Court decision that the US Alien Tort Statute cannot be applied extraterritorially as this would tantamount to an extension of US laws beyond US borders.[1352] The irony is that the US operates extraterritorially most of the time, trying telling those foreign companies fined for violating its sanctions against Iran and

1350. S. Rodriguez. 2021. "Judge dismisses FTC and state antitrust complaints Facebook". *CNBC 28 June 2021.* https://www.cnbc.com/2021/06/28/judge-dismisses-ftc-antitrust-complaint-against-facebook.html, accessed June 29, 2021.

1351. K. Ridley. 2021. "Google battles landmark UK class action over alleged iPhone tracking". *Reuters 28 April 2021.* https://www.reuters.com/technology/google-battles-landmark-uk-class-action-over-alleged-iphone-tracking-2021-04-28/, accessed April 29, 2021.

1352. *Nestle USA, Inc. v. John Doe I, et al./Cargill, Inc. v. John Doe I, et al. (2020).* https://www.supremecourt.gov/opinions/20pdf/19-416_i4dj.pdf, accessed July 13, 2021.

other designated countries. Here, because the MNC involved has its headquarters in the US, it successfully argued that it could not be held accountable for childhood slavery misdeed committed in faraway Africa. Given this, it would be impossible for US companies engaging in unlawful behavior abroad to be made accountable going by the US Supreme Court decision. This decision means that US companies would have little incentive to change their business behaviors while doing business overseas. Extraterritorially is, however, not necessarily the issue. What really matters is for US and other advanced economies when doing business in emerging economies with very limited legal frameworks to stand up for ESG matters without compromise or double standards. Or else, such companies might end up with more pervasive or larger problems in the court of public opinion, particularly from the increasingly conscious younger generations of consumers and employees who are more sensitive to such matters.[1353]

Apart from public sector or state-run regulators that put law or rules and enforcing them against errant companies, external governance is also shaped by the actions of private national and international standards-setters with statutory powers, or with various forms of market disciplining powers. These would include capital market regulators, banks and challenger banks, CRAs, best practice coordinators, and statutory auditors. These so-called corporate gatekeepers[1354] have not always been attentive or alert or meeting up to their tasks. These are shown in many clear instances in the 2000 Dotcom debacle and the 2007-2008 GFC. It has been more than a good decade following these crises, and although there have been significant improvements in corporate behaviors with far fewer corporate misdeeds, governance flaws as understood in its modern ESG parlance have not really gone away. There are still flaws, harmful corporate misdeeds that the media have been happy and eager to report on. The recent revelations from empirical studies that various businesses have allegedly made false claims as to their ESG credentials and so on should alert board directors to be more careful in their ESG disclosures, whether made voluntarily or with obligations.

Again, companies would need to do their part in keeping within the rules in the business world, and not just be complacent with ticking the box where compliance is concerned.[1355] For example, they need to show they walk the talk on ESG matters, and so on. They also need to work and share with these various gatekeepers on getting the laws right in terms of balance or fairness to business, investors, and consumers, and other stakeholders. Current ESG ratings provided by supposedly independent private sector raters are troubled by various flaws extending from the use of faulty calibrations, inconsistencies, and so on. Just like the early years of the CRAs, and just like them before regulatory interventions, ESG rating providers are not being overseen by any particular entity. International standards-setters and others are striving to improve the process, but while this is progressing, it might be useful to look into the benefits of

1353. J.E. Stiglitz & G. Heal. 2021. "Are US corporations above the law?". *Project Syndicate 12 July 2021*. https://www.project-syndicate.org/commentary/nestle-cargill-chocolate-child-slavery-case-by-joseph-e-stiglitz-and-geoffrey-heal-2021-07, accessed July 13, 2021.

1354. P. Yeoh. 2012. "External credit assessment institutions: Clash of expectations and accountability issues". *Journal of Corporate Law Studies*, Vol. 12 (2): 393-427.

1355. E. Mujih. 2021. "Do not simply tick the box: The effectiveness of the CG Code 2018 in the absence of an implementation mechanism", *Company Lawyer*, Vol. 42 (2): 43-50.

having an independent entity to oversee the quality of ESG ratings along the line of those now provided for the credit rating industry. Walking this fine line is not going to be easy, but still needs to be done. The CRAs have improved their functions considerably, after law reforms in the US and in Europe.

Statutory auditing gatekeepers are not attracting that much regulatory attention in the US now, since SOX and DFA. In the UK, however, law reforms are in motion to blunt the dominance of the Big Four in the business and to isolate their auditing activities from their consultancy activities, something already addressed in both SOX and DFA. There could be future challenges as the Big Four operate cross-borders in the US, EU and the UK. Banks and other financial intermediaries are known for their services from the consumption front, but there is not so much widespread awareness of their gatekeeping functions. They have front row seats when it comes to reckless risks-taking, excessive pay packages, excessive borrowings, or erratic inorganic business growths. Importantly, they have the capacity to influence those companies involved, given the level of service they provide to these companies. There are procedures and rules governing the gatekeeping functions of these gatekeepers. For example, the professional communities providing support services to businesses have to abide by anti-money laundering procedures and rules in onshore and offshore financial centers. The Equator Principles that some 116 financial institutions in more than 37 jurisdictions have signed up to cover attention to ESG considerations when looking at project financing.

Observations of ongoing practices and seminal cases have shown harmful outcomes when these gatekeepers fail to do their part properly. What these cases often illustrate is the failure to enforce on the part of some of these gatekeepers, or gaps and loopholes in applicable laws, or in many instances arising from both. Then, there are unwitting interferences from powerful policymakers. Take the case of harmful online content that US and UK governments are heaping on online platforms like Facebook. They attribute the harms flowing from irresponsible messaging passing through Facebook. The UK and Australia are reportedly already making laws to hold messaging platforms more accountable for contents passing through their platforms, with the EU and US also getting ready. Digital platform companies argue against putting them in policing roles. So, the tug-up wars between policymakers and regulators and business corporations continue, with both sides not so keen on taking up the gatekeeping role. Still, businesses in general go by existing rules and procedures. This for the most part keeps more actors in than out of line.

The book drawing on insights from contemporary literature and business law cases suggests that the direction and control of business are shaped by board oversight of both internal control systems and external laws and regulations, as well as by best business practices. In other words, corporation behaviors and actions are policed by hard and soft laws. The in-depth probing of contemporary cases and business practices in the US and the UK, together with insights from other large economies, like the EU, suggests that in the pursuit of business success, company directors would need to lead with an entrepreneurial outlook, apart from having to abide by the rules and procedures set out in their company charter and in the governing company law statute. Successful companies have shown that while compliance to rules matter, equally, but perhaps even more importantly, having the right strategy and having the right execution strategies matter even more. Even unsuccessful companies show why they could fail even when fully abiding by the rules. Thus, setting the right business purpose, the right business strategy, and the right balance of law and strategy considerations could matter even more. This was advocated by the author of this book in a 2007 article "The Direction and Control of Corporations: Law or Strategy?" in the *Managerial Law* journal.

This is another way of saying that the hitherto governance lexicon has proven to be not particularly helpful, as it tends to get companies into the corporate law compliance mode. This is generally reflected in the corporate box-ticking mentality, when it comes to rules and regulations. It would be far more helpful for both companies and regulators to focus on board oversight on the direction and control of companies. This way, they get to put positive entrepreneurial outcomes at the top of the company's agenda. This way also implies that the board need not spend time trying to fit into the shareholder primacy or stakeholder governing model. They could opt for the workable model for their particular circumstances, as long as this does not breach the law. This has been the thinking of Friedman when mooting the purpose of business is to achieve profitability, but always doing this within the law. This is clear-cut, unambiguous and easy to follow by all primary shareholders and stakeholders.

A final lesson drawn is that policymakers and regulators should avoid the usual rhetoric when making law reforms in response to financial crisis with the "never letting this happen again" mantra, as often events happening after putting the law in action show almost immediate recurrences. Repetition of these strong emotive words is beginning to ring hollow, besides giving the implications that the drafted laws have been badly designed or were knee-jerk responses, when in reality, the new crises might have been boosted by other factors or bad intentions on the part of some market participants by gaming the system through abusive means. This again suggests the importance of quick enforcement actions, drawing on the hot-stove rule where punishments when done quick remind people that misdeeds lead to quick disciplinary remedial actions and hence not worth the risk. There is no way to achieve a zero level of misdeeds, as events in the current COVID-19 pandemic show clearly show.

11.03 FINAL WORDS

It is argued here that instead of getting overenthusiastic about the misdeeds of business practices and risking the continuous over-layering of more procedures and laws, it might be relatively easier to focus on the disclosure obligations of company directors and others and their personal accountabilities. This means quickly disciplining them when they run clear foul of the law, and when the governing laws are not so clear, let the market decide through the market for corporate control, and so on. This approach could also be considerably made more effective when corporate gatekeepers also keep to their part of the bargain and avoid risking foul of the laws governing their activities. This book differentiates from the usual company law books on the same theme as it gives good attention to efficacious business theories and practices which directors may consider relevant and beneficial. It also differentiates from business books on the same topic, in that it draws attention to applicable laws and regulations with strong implications for business management. Hopefully, as somebody once said, companies and individuals should be served with the justice they deserve as they navigate the business terrain.

Finally, it has to be said that current and emerging ESG practices and ESG disclosures in corporate reports are not entirely novel, as governance practices and disclosures obligations imposed before these have engaged with the "E" and "S" elements, though not in current more emphatic manners. It took the combined effects of the COVID-19 pandemic, the calamitous effects of climate change, and various notable social upheavals to raise heightened attention for environmental and social issues. The book has also demonstrated the unfortunate durability of faulty governance practices, despite the claims by lawmakers that laws and law reforms would never let these recur. Maybe, it is time to prioritize on the enforcements of ESG rules, something that has not been done so well previously under its narrower traditional version. This means beefing up the needed resources of enforcement agencies and backing them with the needed political resolve to enable them to carry out their tasks effectively. It also means providing business corporations with market-based incentives when they walk on the right side of rules and regulations. It takes the length of a book to say all these mainly because of the need to support the calls with evidential-based arguments, even as it might appear obvious, something which most researchers learn the hard way to do.

www.ingramcontent.com/pod-product-compliance
Lightning Source LLC
LaVergne TN
LVHW020645300926
849161LV00004B/826